Course	Survey of Accounting
Course Number	**ACCT 203**
	GEORGE MASON UNIVERSITY
	ACCOUNTING AREA

D1377254

http://create.mcgraw-hill.com

ISBN-10: 1308222149   ISBN-13: 9781308222141

Contents

Credits

Introducing Accounting in Business

Learning Objectives are classified as conceptual, analytical, or procedural.

A Look at This Chapter

Accounting is crucial in our information age. In this chapter, we discuss the importance of accounting to different types of organizations and describe its many users and uses. We explain that ethics are essential to accounting. We also explain business transactions and how they are reflected in financial statements.

A Look Ahead

Chapter 2 describes and analyzes business transactions. We explain the analysis and recording of transactions, the ledger and trial balance, and the double-entry system. More generally, Chapters 2 and 3 use the accounting cycle to show how financial statements reflect business activities.

Learning Objectives

CONCEPTUAL

C1 Explain the purpose and importance of accounting. (p. 4)

C2 Identify users and uses of, and opportunities in, accounting. (p. 5)

C3 Explain why ethics are crucial to accounting. (p. 7)

C4 Explain generally accepted accounting principles and define and apply several accounting principles. (p. 9)

C5 *Appendix 1B*—Identify and describe the three major activities of organizations. (p. 27)

ANALYTICAL

A1 Define and interpret the accounting equation and each of its components. (p. 15)

A2 Compute and interpret return on assets. (p. 23)

A3 *Appendix 1A*—Explain the relation between return and risk. (p. 27)

PROCEDURAL

P1 Analyze business transactions using the accounting equation. (p. 16)

P2 Identify and prepare basic financial statements and explain how they interrelate. (p. 20)

Decision Insight

A **Decision Feature** launches each chapter showing the relevance of accounting for a real entrepreneur. An **Entrepreneurial Decision** problem at the end of the assignments returns to this feature with a mini-case.

Accounting for Twitter

"There is so much going on here . . ."
—**BIZ STONE** (CENTER)

SAN FRANCISCO—"We came across the word 'twitter,' and it was just perfect," recalls Jack Dorsey (right of photo). "The definition was 'a short burst of inconsequential information,' and 'chirps from birds,' and that's exactly what the product was." Today, Twitter boasts over 200 million users. Founded by Jack, along with Biz Stone and Evan Williams (left), Twitter (**Twitter.com**) is "facilitating connections between businesses and individuals in meaningful and relevant ways," says Jack. Along the way, the young entrepreneurs had to learn accounting and the details of preparing and interpreting financial statements.

"There is so much going on here," explains Biz when describing Twitter's business model. However, admits Evan, "We did a poor job of communicating." Important questions involving business formation, transaction analysis, and financial reporting arose. The entrepreneurs eventually met those challenges and, in the process, set Twitter apart. "If you stand pat," says Evan, "you risk being stagnant."

Information is the focus within Twitter's accounting records and systems. Jack recalls that when they launched Twitter, there were all these reasons why they would not succeed. He applied their similar "can-do" approach to accounting information. "My whole philosophy is making tech [and accounting] more accessible and human," says Jack. This includes using accounting information to make key business decisions.

Twitter is the language of micro-blogging, and accounting is the language of business. "Twitter is so many things: a messaging service, a customer-service tool, a real-time search," explains Biz, and the accounting system had to capture those things. Biz adds that Twitter is exploring additional "interesting ways to generate revenue." That revenue-stream is reflected in its financial statements, which are based on transaction analysis and accounting concepts.

Twitter's revenues exhibit growth and reflect what experts call the *monetizing* of its business. A recent study by the marketing firm SocialTwist found that the click-through rate was 19 for Twitter, which is the number of clicks on an embedded link. This compares with 3 clicks for Facebook links. Twitter's revenues in the recent year were estimated at $45 million, which are projected to exceed $100 million next year. Twitter also tracks its expenses and asset purchases. Twitter owners have an estimated valuation of between $5 and $10 billion!

The three entrepreneurs emphasize that accounting records must be in order for Twitter to realize its full potential. Many experts predict a public offering of its stock within the next two years, which could generate untold wealth. Still, Evan recognizes that "so many people here [at Twitter] contribute to that success." He also emphasizes that learning is a key to their business success. "I realized," insists Evan, "I could buy accounting books and learn something that people spent years learning."

[Sources: Twitter Website, January 2013; *Entrepreneur*, December 2010; *USA Today*, May 2009; Smedio.com, June 2011; *San Francisco Chronicle*, March 2011; SocialTwist.com, October 2010; *The Wall Street Journal*, February 2011]

Chapter Preview

*A **Preview** opens each chapter with a summary of topics covered.*

Today's world is one of information—its preparation, communication, analysis, and use. Accounting is at the core of this information age. Knowledge of accounting gives us career opportunities and the insight to take advantage of them. This book introduces concepts, procedures, and analyses that help us make better decisions, including career choices. In this chapter we describe accounting, the users and uses of accounting information, the forms and activities of organizations, and several accounting principles. We also introduce transaction analysis and financial statements.

Introducing Accounting in Business

Importance of Accounting
- Accounting information users
- Opportunities in accounting

Fundamentals of Accounting
- Ethics—key concept
- Generally accepted accounting principles
- International standards

Transaction Analysis
- Accounting equation
- Transaction analysis—illustrated

Financial Statements
- Income statement
- Statement of retained earnings
- Balance sheet
- Statement of cash flows

IMPORTANCE OF ACCOUNTING

C1   Explain the purpose and importance of accounting.

Why is accounting so popular on campus? Why are there so many openings for accounting jobs? Why is accounting so important to companies? Why do politicians and business leaders focus on accounting regulations? The answer is that we live in an information age, where that information, and its reliability, impacts us all.

Accounting is an information and measurement system that identifies, records, and communicates relevant, reliable, and comparable information about an organization's business activities. *Identifying* business activities requires that we select relevant transactions and events. Examples are the sale of iPhones by **Apple** and the receipt of ticket money by **TicketMaster**. *Recording* business activities requires that we keep a chronological log of transactions and events measured in dollars. *Communicating* business activities requires that we prepare accounting reports such as financial statements, which we analyze and interpret. (The financial statements and notes of **Polaris** are shown in Appendix A near the end of this book. This appendix also shows the financial statements of **Arctic Cat**, **KTM**, and **Piaggio**.) Exhibit 1.1 summarizes accounting activities.

Real company names are printed in bold magenta.

Accounting is part of our everyday lives. Our most common contact with accounting is through credit approvals, checking accounts, tax forms, and payroll. These experiences tend to focus on the recordkeeping parts of accounting. **Recordkeeping,** or **bookkeeping,** is the recording of transactions and events, either manually or electronically. This is just one part of accounting. Accounting also identifies and communicates information on transactions and events, and it includes the crucial processes of analysis and interpretation.

Technology is a key part of modern business and plays a major role in accounting. Technology reduces the time, effort, and cost of recordkeeping while improving clerical accuracy. Some small organizations continue to perform various accounting tasks manually, but even they are impacted

EXHIBIT 1.1

Accounting Activities

Identifying	Recording	Communicating
Select transactions and events	Input, measure, and log	Prepare, analyze, and interpret

by technology. As technology makes more information available, the demand for accounting increases and so too the skills for applying that information. Consulting, planning, and other financial services are now closely linked to accounting. These services require sorting through data, interpreting their meaning, identifying key factors, and analyzing their implications.

Users of Accounting Information

Accounting is called the *language of business* because all organizations set up an accounting information system to communicate data to help people make better decisions. Exhibit 1.2 shows that accounting serves many users (this is a partial listing) who can be divided into two groups: external users and internal users.

External users

Internal users

EXHIBIT 1.2

Users of Accounting Information

- Lenders   • Consumer groups
- Shareholders   • External auditors
- Governments   • Customers

- Officers   • Sales staff
- Managers   • Budget officers
- Internal auditors • Controllers

External Information Users   **External users** of accounting information are *not* directly involved in running the organization. They include shareholders (investors), lenders, directors, customers, suppliers, regulators, lawyers, brokers, and the press. External users have limited access to an organization's information. Yet their business decisions depend on information that is reliable, relevant, and comparable. **Financial accounting** is the area of accounting aimed at serving external users by providing them with *general-purpose financial statements*. The term *general-purpose* refers to the broad range of purposes for which external users rely on these statements. Following is a partial list of external users and some decisions they make with accounting information.

 C2 Identify users and uses of, and opportunities in, accounting.

- *Lenders* (creditors) loan money or other resources to an organization. Banks, savings and loans, co-ops, and mortgage and finance companies are lenders. Lenders look for information to help them assess whether an organization is likely to repay its loans with interest.

- *Shareholders* (*investors*) are the owners of a corporation. They use accounting reports in deciding whether to buy, hold, or sell stock.

- *Directors* are typically elected to a *board of directors* to oversee their interests in an organization. Since directors are responsible to shareholders, their information needs are similar.

- *External* (independent) *auditors* examine financial statements to verify that they are prepared according to generally accepted accounting principles.

- *Nonexecutive employees* and *labor unions* use financial statements to judge the fairness of wages, assess job prospects, and bargain for better wages.

- *Regulators* often have legal authority over certain activities of organizations. For example, the Internal Revenue Service (IRS) and other tax authorities require organizations to file accounting reports in computing taxes. Other regulators include utility boards that use accounting information to set utility rates and securities regulators that require reports for companies that sell their stock to the public.

- *Voters, legislators,* and *government officials* use accounting information to monitor and evaluate government receipts and expenses.

- *Contributors* to nonprofit organizations use accounting information to evaluate the use and impact of their donations.

- *Suppliers* use accounting information to judge the soundness of a customer before making sales on credit.
- *Customers* use financial reports to assess the staying power of potential suppliers.

Internal Information Users **Internal users** of accounting information are those directly involved in managing and operating an organization. They use the information to help improve the efficiency and effectiveness of an organization. **Managerial accounting** is the area of accounting that serves the decision-making needs of internal users. Internal reports are not subject to the same rules as external reports and instead are designed with the special needs of internal users in mind. Following is a partial list of internal users and some decisions they make with accounting information.

- *Research and development managers* need information about projected costs and revenues of any proposed changes in products and services.
- *Purchasing managers* need to know what, when, and how much to purchase.
- *Human resource managers* need information about employees' payroll, benefits, performance, and compensation.
- *Production managers* depend on information to monitor costs and ensure quality.
- *Distribution managers* need reports for timely, accurate, and efficient delivery of products and services.
- *Marketing managers* use reports about sales and costs to target consumers, set prices, and monitor consumer needs, tastes, and price concerns.
- *Service managers* require information on the costs and benefits of looking after products and services.

Opportunities in Accounting

Accounting information is in all aspects of our lives. When we earn money, pay taxes, invest savings, budget earnings, and plan for the future, we use accounting. Accounting has four broad areas of opportunities: financial, managerial, taxation, and accounting-related. Exhibit 1.3 lists selected opportunities in each area.

EXHIBIT 1.3

Accounting Opportunities

Opportunities in Accounting

Financial	Managerial	Taxation	Accounting-related	
• Preparation	• General accounting	• Preparation	• Lenders	• FBI investigators
• Analysis	• Cost accounting	• Planning	• Consultants	• Market researchers
• Auditing	• Budgeting	• Regulatory	• Analysts	• Systems designers
• Regulatory	• Internal auditing	• Investigations	• Traders	• Merger services
• Consulting	• Consulting	• Consulting	• Directors	• Business valuation
• Planning	• Controller	• Enforcement	• Underwriters	• Forensic accounting
• Criminal investigation	• Treasurer	• Legal services	• Planners	• Litigation support
	• Strategy	• Estate plans	• Appraisers	• Entrepreneurs

EXHIBIT 1.4

Accounting Jobs by Area

Private accounting 58%

Government, not-for-profit and education 19%

Public accounting 23%

Exhibit 1.4 shows that the majority of opportunities are in *private accounting,* which are employees working for businesses. *Public accounting* offers the next largest number of opportunities, which involve services such as auditing and tax advice. Still other opportunities exist in government and not-for-profit agencies, including business regulation and investigation of law violations.

Accounting specialists are highly regarded and their professional standing is often denoted by a certificate. Certified public accountants (CPAs) must meet education and experience requirements, pass an examination, and exhibit ethical character. Many accounting specialists hold certificates in addition to or instead of the CPA. Two of the most common are the certificate in management accounting (CMA) and the certified internal auditor (CIA). Employers also look for specialists with designations such as certified bookkeeper (CB), certified payroll professional (CPP), personal financial specialist (PFS), certified fraud examiner (CFE), and certified forensic accountant (CrFA).

Demand for accounting specialists is strong. Exhibit 1.5 reports average annual salaries for several accounting positions. Salary variation depends on location, company size, professional designation, experience, and other factors. For example, salaries for chief financial officers (CFO) range from under $100,000 to more than $1 million per year. Likewise, salaries for bookkeepers range from under $30,000 to more than $80,000.

Point: The largest accounting firms are Deloitte, Ernst & Young, KPMG, and PricewaterhouseCoopers.

Point: Census Bureau (2011) reports that for workers 25 and over, higher education yields higher average pay:
Advanced degree $81,568
Bachelor's degree 57,326
High school degree 36,876
No high school degree. 26,124

Field	Title (experience)	2011 Salary	2016 Estimate*
Public Accounting	Partner	$202,000	$223,000
	Manager (6–8 years)	97,500	107,500
	Senior (3–5 years)	75,000	83,000
	Junior (0–2 years)	57,500	63,500
Private Accounting	CFO	242,000	267,000
	Controller/Treasurer	157,500	174,000
	Manager (6–8 years)	91,500	101,000
	Senior (3–5 years)	74,500	82,000
	Junior (0–2 years)	53,000	58,500
Recordkeeping	Full-charge bookkeeper	59,500	65,500
	Accounts manager	52,000	57,500
	Payroll manager	55,500	61,000
	Accounting clerk (0–2 years)	38,500	42,500

EXHIBIT 1.5

Accounting Salaries for Selected Fields

Point: For updated salary information:
Abbott-Langer.com
www.AICPA.org
Kforce.com

* Estimates assume a 2% compounded annual increase over current levels (rounded to nearest $500).

Quick Check   Answers — p. 29

Answers — p. 29

1. What is the purpose of accounting?
2. What is the relation between accounting and recordkeeping?
3. Identify some advantages of technology for accounting.
4. Who are the internal and external users of accounting information?
5. Identify at least five types of managers who are internal users of accounting information.

Quick Check is a chance to stop and reflect on key points.

Point: U.S. Bureau of Labor (June 2011) reports higher education is associated with a lower unemployment rate:
Bachelor's degree or more 4.4%
High school degree 10.0%
No high school degree. 14.3%

FUNDAMENTALS OF ACCOUNTING

Accounting is guided by principles, standards, concepts, and assumptions. This section describes several of these key fundamentals of accounting.

Ethics—A Key Concept

The goal of accounting is to provide useful information for decisions. For information to be useful, it must be trusted. This demands ethics in accounting. **Ethics** are beliefs that distinguish right from wrong. They are accepted standards of good and bad behavior.

Identifying the ethical path is sometimes difficult. The preferred path is a course of action that avoids casting doubt on one's decisions. For example, accounting users are less likely to trust an auditor's report if the auditor's pay depends on the client's success . To avoid such concerns, ethics rules are often set. For example, auditors are banned from direct investment in their

 C3 Explain why ethics are crucial to accounting.

Point: Sarbanes-Oxley Act requires each issuer of securities to disclose whether it has adopted a code of ethics for its senior officers and the contents of that code.

EXHIBIT 1.6

Guidelines for Ethical
Decision Making

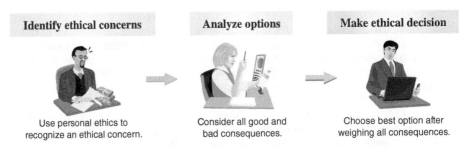

Identify ethical concerns	Analyze options	Make ethical decision
Use personal ethics to recognize an ethical concern.	Consider all good and bad consequences.	Choose best option after weighing all consequences.

client and cannot accept pay that depends on figures in the client's reports. Exhibit 1.6 gives guidelines for making ethical decisions.

Accountants face many ethical choices as they prepare financial reports. These choices can affect the price a buyer pays and the wages paid to workers. They can even affect the success of products and services. Misleading information can lead to a wrongful closing of a division that harms workers, customers, and suppliers. There is an old saying: *Good ethics are good business.*

Some people extend ethics to *social responsibility,* which refers to a concern for the impact of actions on society. An organization's social responsibility can include donations to hospitals, colleges, community programs, and law enforcement. It also can include programs to reduce pollution, increase product safety, improve worker conditions, and support continuing education. These programs are not limited to large companies. For example, many small businesses offer discounts to students and senior citizens. Still others help sponsor events such as the Special Olympics and summer reading programs.

Point: The American Institute of Certified Public Accountants' *Code of Professional Conduct* is available at **www.AICPA.org**.

Decision Insight boxes highlight relevant items from practice.

Decision Insight

Virtuous Returns Virtue is not always its own reward. Compare the S&P 500 with the Domini Social Index (DSI), which covers 400 companies that have especially good records of social responsibility. We see that returns for companies with socially responsible behavior are roughly on par with those of the S&P 500 for the past 10-year period (Domini.com, 2011 Annual Report). Copyright © 2005 by KLD Research & Analytics, Inc. The "Domini 400 Social Index" is a service mark of KLD Research & Analytics. ■

Fraud Triangle

The fraud triangle is a model created by a criminologist that asserts the following *three* factors must exist for a person to commit fraud: opportunity, pressure, and rationalization.

Opportunity is one side of the fraud triangle. A person must envision a way to commit fraud with a low perceived risk of getting caught. Employers can directly reduce this risk. An example of some control on opportunity is a pre-employment background check. *Pressure,* or incentive, is another side of the fraud triangle. A person must have some pressure to commit fraud. Examples are unpaid bills and addictions. *Rationalization,* or attitude, is the third side of the fraud triangle. A person who rationalizes fails to see the criminal nature of the fraud or justifies the action.

It is important to recognize that all three factors of the fraud triangle must usually exist for fraud to occur. The absence of one or more factors suggests fraud is unlikely.

The key to dealing with fraud is to focus on prevention. It is less expensive and more effective to prevent fraud from happening than it is to try to detect the crime. By the time the fraud is discovered, the money is gone and chances are slim that it will be recovered. Additionally, it is costly and time-consuming to investigate a fraud.

Both internal and external users rely on internal controls to reduce the likelihood of fraud. *Internal controls* are procedures set up to protect company property and equipment, ensure reliable accounting reports, promote efficiency, and encourage adherence to company policies. Examples are good records, physical controls (locks, passwords, guards), and independent reviews.

▨ Decision Insight

They Fought the Law Our economic and social welfare depends on reliable accounting. Some individuals forgot that and are now paying their dues. They include Raj Rajaratnam (in photo), an investor, convicted of trading stocks using inside information; Bernard Madoff of Madoff Investment Securities, convicted of falsifying securities records; Bernard Ebbers of WorldCom, convicted of an $11 billion accounting scandal; Andrew Fastow of Enron, guilty of hiding debt and inflating income; and Ramalinga Raju of Satyam Computers, accused of overstating assets by $1.5 billion. ∎

Generally Accepted Accounting Principles

Financial accounting is governed by concepts and rules known as **generally accepted accounting principles (GAAP).** We must understand these principles to best use accounting data. GAAP aims to make information *relevant, reliable,* and *comparable.* Relevant information affects decisions of users. Reliable information is trusted by users. Comparable information is helpful in contrasting organizations.

In the United States, the **Securities and Exchange Commission (SEC),** a government agency, has the legal authority to set GAAP. The SEC also oversees proper use of GAAP by companies that raise money from the public through issuances of their stock and debt. Those companies that issue their stock on U.S. exchanges include both *U.S. SEC registrants* (companies incorporated in the United States) and *non-U.S. SEC registrants* (companies incorporated under non-U.S. laws). The SEC has largely delegated the task of setting U.S. GAAP to the **Financial Accounting Standards Board (FASB),** which is a private-sector group that sets both broad and specific principles.

| **C4** | Explain generally accepted accounting principles and define and apply several accounting principles. |

Point: State ethics codes require CPAs who audit financial statements to disclose areas where those statements fail to comply with GAAP. If CPAs fail to report noncompliance, they can lose their licenses and be subject to criminal and civil actions and fines.

International Standards

In today's global economy, there is increased demand by external users for comparability in accounting reports. This demand often arises when companies wish to raise money from lenders and investors in different countries. To that end, the **International Accounting Standards Board (IASB),** an independent group (consisting of individuals from many countries), issues **International Financial Reporting Standards (IFRS)** that identify preferred accounting practices.

If standards are harmonized, one company can potentially use a single set of financial statements in all financial markets. Differences between U.S. GAAP and IFRS are decreasing as the FASB and IASB pursue a *convergence* process aimed to achieve a single set of accounting standards for global use. More than 115 countries now require or permit companies to prepare financial reports following IFRS. Further, non-U.S. SEC registrants can use IFRS in financial reports filed with the SEC (with no reconciliation to U.S. GAAP). This means there are *two* sets of accepted accounting principles in the United States: (1) U.S. GAAP for U.S. SEC registrants and (2) either IFRS or U.S. GAAP for non-U.S. SEC registrants.

The SEC is encouraging the FASB to change U.S. GAAP over a period of several years by endorsing, and thereby incorporating, individual IFRS standards into U.S. GAAP. This endorsement process would still allow the FASB to modify IFRS when necessary. The SEC would:

- Maintain its statutory oversight of the FASB, including authority to prescribe accounting principles and standards for U.S. issuers.
- Contribute to oversight and governance of the IASB through its involvement on the IFRS Foundation Monitoring Board.

The FASB would continue, but its role would be to provide input and support to the IASB in crafting high-quality, global standards. The FASB is to develop a transition plan to effect these changes over the next five years or so. For updates on this roadmap, we can check with the AICPA (IFRS.com), FASB (FASB.org), and IASB (ifrs.org).

IFRS

Like the FASB, the IASB uses a conceptual framework to aid in revising or drafting new standards. However, unlike the FASB, the IASB's conceptual framework is used as a reference when specific guidance is lacking. The IASB also requires that transactions be accounted for according to their substance (not only their legal form), and that financial statements give a fair presentation, whereas the FASB narrows that scope to fair presentation *in accordance with U.S. GAAP.* ∎

Conceptual Framework and Convergence

The FASB and IASB are attempting to converge and enhance the **conceptual framework** that guides standard setting. The FASB framework consists broadly of the following:

- **Objectives**—to provide information useful to investors, creditors, and others.
- **Qualitative Characteristics**—to require information that is *relevant, reliable,* and *comparable.*
- **Elements**—to define items that financial statements can contain.
- **Recognition and Measurement**—to set criteria that an item must meet for it to be recognized as an element; and how to measure that element.

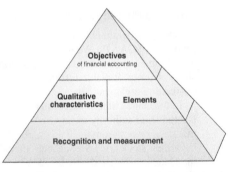

For updates on this joint FASB and IASB conceptual framework convergence we can check with FASB.org or ifrs.org Websites. We must remember that U.S. GAAP and IFRS are two similar, but not identical, systems. However, their similarities greatly outweigh any differences. The remainder of this section describes key principles and assumptions of accounting.

Decision Insight

Principles and Scruples Auditors, directors, and lawyers are using principles to improve accounting reports. Examples include accounting restatements at Navistar, financial restatements at Nortel, accounting reviews at Echostar, and expense adjustments at Electronic Data Systems. Principles-based accounting has led accounting firms to drop clients deemed too risky. Examples include Grant Thornton's resignation as auditor of Fremont General due to alleged failures in providing information when promised, and Ernst and Young's resignation as auditor of Catalina Marketing due to alleged accounting errors. ∎

Principles and Assumptions of Accounting   Accounting principles (and assumptions) are of two types. *General principles* are the basic assumptions, concepts, and guidelines for preparing financial statements. *Specific principles* are detailed rules used in reporting business transactions and events. General principles stem from long-used accounting practices. Specific principles arise more often from the rulings of authoritative groups.

We need to understand both general and specific principles to effectively use accounting information. Several general principles are described in this section that are relied on in later chapters. General principles (in purple font with white shading) and assumptions (in red font with white shading) are portrayed

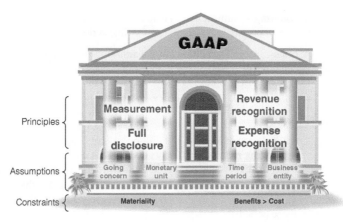

EXHIBIT 1.7

Building Blocks for GAAP

as building blocks of GAAP in Exhibit 1.7. The specific principles are described as we encounter them in the book.

Accounting Principles   General principles consist of at least four basic principles, four assumptions, and two constraints.

- *Measurement* The **measurement principle,** also called the **cost principle,** usually prescribes that accounting information is based on actual cost (with a potential for subsequent adjustments to market). Cost is measured on a cash or equal-to-cash basis. This means if cash is given for a service, its cost is measured as the amount of cash paid. If something besides cash is exchanged (such as a car traded for a truck), cost is measured as the cash value of what is given up or received. The cost principle emphasizes reliability and verifiability, and information based on cost is considered objective. *Objectivity* means that information is supported by independent, unbiased evidence; it demands more than a person's opinion. To illustrate, suppose a company pays $5,000 for equipment. The cost principle requires that this purchase be recorded at $5,000. It makes no difference if the owner thinks this equipment is worth $7,000. Later in the book we introduce *fair value* measures.

  Point: The cost principle is also called the *historical cost principle.*

- *Revenue recognition* Revenue (sales) is the amount received from selling products and services. The **revenue recognition principle** provides guidance on when a company must recognize revenue. To *recognize* means to record it. If revenue is recognized too early, a company would look more profitable than it is. If revenue is recognized too late, a company would look less profitable than it is. Three concepts are important to revenue recognition. (1) *Revenue is recognized when earned.* The earnings process is normally complete when services are performed or a seller transfers ownership of products to the buyer. (2) *Proceeds from selling products and services need not be in cash.* A common noncash proceed received by a seller is a customer's promise to pay at a future date, called *credit sales.* (3) *Revenue is measured by the cash received plus the cash value of any other items received.*

  Example: When a bookstore sells a textbook on credit is its earnings process complete? *Answer:* A bookstore can record sales for these books minus an amount expected for returns.

- *Expense recognition* The **expense recognition principle,** also called the **matching principle,** prescribes that a company record the expenses it incurred to generate the revenue reported. The principles of matching and revenue recognition are key to modern accounting.

- *Full disclosure* The **full disclosure principle** prescribes that a company report the details behind financial statements that would impact users' decisions. Those disclosures are often in footnotes to the statements.

Decision Insight

Revenues for the Green Bay Packers, New England Patriots, New York Giants, and other professional football teams include ticket sales, television and cable broadcasts, radio rights, concessions, and advertising. Revenues from ticket sales are earned when the NFL team plays each game. Advance ticket sales are not revenues; instead, they represent a liability until the NFL team plays the game for which the ticket was sold. At that point, the liability is removed and revenues are reported. ▪

Accounting Assumptions   There are four accounting assumptions: the going-concern assumption, the monetary unit assumption, the time period assumption, and the business entity assumption.

- *Going concern* The **going-concern assumption** means that accounting information reflects a presumption that the business will continue operating instead of being closed or sold. This implies, for example, that property is reported at cost instead of, say, liquidation values that assume closure.

Point: For currency conversion: xe.com

- *Monetary unit* The **monetary unit assumption** means that we can express transactions and events in monetary, or money, units. Money is the common denominator in business. Examples of monetary units are the dollar in the United States, Canada, Australia, and Singapore; and the peso in Mexico, the Philippines, and Chile. The monetary unit a company uses in its accounting reports usually depends on the country where it operates, but many companies today are expressing reports in more than one monetary unit.

- *Time period* The **time period assumption** presumes that the life of a company can be divided into time periods, such as months and years, and that useful reports can be prepared for those periods.

Point: Abuse of the entity assumption was a main culprit in **Enron**'s collapse.

- *Business entity* The **business entity assumption** means that a business is accounted for separately from other business entities, including its owner. The reason for this assumption is that separate information about each business is necessary for good decisions. A business entity can take one of three legal forms: *proprietorship, partnership,* or *corporation.*

1. A **sole proprietorship,** or simply **proprietorship,** is a business owned by one person in which that person and the company are viewed as one entity for tax and liability purposes. No special legal requirements must be met to start a proprietorship. It is a separate entity for accounting purposes, but it is *not* a separate legal entity from its owner. This means, for example, that a court can order an owner to sell personal belongings to pay a proprietorship's debt. This *unlimited liability* of a proprietorship is a disadvantage. However, an advantage is that a proprietorship's income is not subject to a business income tax but is instead reported and taxed on the owner's personal income tax return. Proprietorship attributes are summarized in Exhibit 1.8, including those for partnerships and corporations.

EXHIBIT 1.8

Attributes of Businesses

Attribute Present	Proprietorship	Partnership	Corporation
One owner allowed............	yes	no	yes
Business taxed	no	no	yes
Limited liability................	no*	no*	yes
Business entity	yes	yes	yes
Legal entity..................	no	no	yes
Unlimited life	no	no	yes

* Proprietorships and partnerships that are set up as LLCs provide limited liability.

2. A **partnership** is a business owned by two or more people, called *partners,* which are jointly liable for tax and other obligations. Like a proprietorship, no special legal requirements must be met in starting a partnership. The only requirement is an agreement between partners to run a business together. The agreement can be either oral or written and usually indicates how income and losses are to be shared. A partnership, like a proprietorship, is *not* legally separate from its owners. This means that each partner's share of profits is reported and taxed on that partner's tax return. It also means *unlimited liability* for its partners. However, at least three types of partnerships limit liability. A *limited partnership* (*LP*) includes a general partner(s) with unlimited liability and a limited partner(s) with liability restricted to the amount invested. A *limited liability partnership* (*LLP*) restricts partners' liabilities to their own acts and the acts of individuals under their control. This protects an innocent partner from the negligence of another partner, yet all partners remain responsible for partnership debts. A *limited liability company* (*LLC*) offers the limited liability of a corporation and the tax treatment of a partnership (and proprietorship). Most proprietorships and partnerships are now organized as LLCs.

Point: Proprietorships and partnerships are usually managed by their owners. In a corporation, the owners (shareholders) elect a board of directors who appoint managers to run the business.

3. A **corporation,** also called *C corporation,* is a business legally separate from its owner or owners, meaning it is responsible for its own acts and its own debts. Separate legal status

means that a corporation can conduct business with the rights, duties, and responsibilities of a person. A corporation acts through its managers, who are its legal agents. Separate legal status also means that its owners, who are called **shareholders** (or **stockholders**), are not personally liable for corporate acts and debts. This limited liability is its main advantage. A main disadvantage is what's called *double taxation*—meaning that (1) the corporation income is taxed and (2) any distribution of income to its owners through dividends is taxed as part of the owners' personal income, usually at the 15% rate. (For lower income taxpayers, the dividend tax is less than 15%, and in some cases zero.) An *S corporation,* a corporation with special attributes, does not owe corporate income tax. Owners of S corporations report their share of corporate income with their personal income. Ownership of all corporations is divided into units called **shares** or **stock.** When a corporation issues only one class of stock, we call it **common stock** (or *capital stock*).

Decision Ethics boxes are role-playing exercises that stress ethics in accounting and business.

Decision Ethics

Entrepreneur   You and a friend develop a new design for in-line skates that improves speed by 25% to 30%. You plan to form a business to manufacture and market those skates. You and your friend want to minimize taxes, but your prime concern is potential lawsuits from individuals who might be injured on these skates. What form of organization do you set up? ■ [Answer—p. 28]

Accounting Constraints   There are two basic constraints on financial reporting.

- *Materiality*   The **materiality constraint** prescribes that only information that would influence the decisions of a reasonable person need be disclosed. This constraint looks at both the importance and relative size of an amount.
- *Benefit exceeds cost*   The **cost-benefit constraint** prescribes that only information with benefits of disclosure greater than the costs of providing it need be disclosed.

Conservatism and *industry practices* are also sometimes referred to as accounting constraints.

Sarbanes–Oxley (SOX)

Congress passed the **Sarbanes–Oxley Act,** also called *SOX,* to help curb financial abuses at companies that issue their stock to the public. SOX requires that these public companies apply both accounting oversight and stringent internal controls. The desired results include more transparency, accountability, and truthfulness in reporting transactions.

Point: An audit examines whether financial statements are prepared using GAAP. It does *not* attest to absolute accuracy of the statements.

Compliance with SOX requires documentation and verification of internal controls and increased emphasis on internal control effectiveness. Failure to comply can yield financial penalties, stock market delisting, and criminal prosecution of executives. Management must issue a report stating that internal controls are effective. CEOs and CFOs who knowingly sign off on bogus accounting reports risk millions of dollars in fines and years in prison. **Auditors** also must verify the effectiveness of internal controls.

Point: *BusinessWeek* reports that external audit costs run about $35,000 for start-ups, up from $15,000 pre-SOX.

A listing of some of the more publicized accounting scandals in recent years follows.

Company	Alleged Accounting Abuses
Enron	Inflated income, hid debt, and bribed officials
WorldCom	Understated expenses to inflate income and hid debt
Fannie Mae	Inflated income
Adelphia Communications	Understated expenses to inflate income and hid debt
AOL Time Warner	Inflated revenues and income
Xerox	Inflated income
Bristol-Myers Squibb	Inflated revenues and income
Nortel Networks	Understated expenses to inflate income
Global Crossing	Inflated revenues and income
Tyco	Hid debt, and CEO evaded taxes
Halliburton	Inflated revenues and income
Qwest Communications	Inflated revenues and income

To reduce the risk of accounting fraud, companies set up *governance systems*. A company's governance system includes its owners, managers, employees, board of directors, and other important stakeholders, who work together to reduce the risk of accounting fraud and increase confidence in accounting reports.

The impact of SOX regulations for accounting and business is discussed throughout this book. Ethics and investor confidence are key to company success. Lack of confidence in accounting numbers impacts company value as evidenced by huge stock price declines for Enron, WorldCom, Tyco, and ImClone after accounting misconduct was uncovered.

Decision Insight

Economic Downturn, Fraud Upturn? Executives polled show that 80% believe that the economic downturn has or will have a significant impact on fraud control in their companies (Deloitte 2010). The top three responses to the question "What activity would best counter this increased fraud risk?" are tallied in the graphic to the right. ■

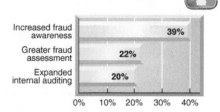

Dodd-Frank

Congress passed the **Dodd-Frank Wall Street Reform and Consumer Protection Act**, or *Dodd-Frank*, in a desire to (1) promote accountability and transparency in the financial system, (2) put an end to the notion of "too big to fail," (3) protect the taxpayer by ending bailouts, and (4) protect consumers from abusive financial services. It includes provisions whose impacts are unknown until regulators set detailed rules. However, a few proposals are notable and include the following:

- Exemption from Section 404(b) of SOX for smaller public entities (whose public value is less than $75 million) from the requirement to obtain an external audit on the effectiveness of internal control over financial reporting.
- Independence for all members of the compensation committee (including additional disclosures); in the event of an accounting restatement, an entity must set policies mandating recovery ("clawback") of excess incentive compensation.
- Requires the SEC, when sanctions exceed $1 million, to pay whistle-blowers between 10% and 30% of the sanction.

Quick Check   Answers — p. 29

6. What are internal controls and why are they important?
7. What three-step guidelines can help people make ethical decisions?
8. Why are ethics and social responsibility valuable to organizations?
9. Why are ethics crucial in accounting?
10. Who sets U.S. accounting rules?
11. How are U.S. companies affected by international accounting standards?
12. How are the objectivity concept and cost principle related?
13. Why is the business entity assumption important?
14. Why is the revenue recognition principle important?
15. What are the three basic forms of business organization?
16. Identify the owners of corporations and the terminology for ownership units.

TRANSACTION ANALYSIS AND THE ACCOUNTING EQUATION

To understand accounting information, we need to know how an accounting system captures relevant data about transactions, and then classifies, records, and reports data.

Accounting Equation

The accounting system reflects two basic aspects of a company: what it owns and what it owes. *Assets* are resources a company owns or controls. Examples are cash, supplies, equipment, and land, where each carries expected benefits. The claims on a company's assets—what it owes—are separated into owner and nonowner claims. *Liabilities* are what a company owes its nonowners (creditors) in future payments, products, or services. *Equity* (also called owner's equity or capital) refers to the claims of its owner(s). Together, liabilities and equity are the source of funds to acquire assets. The relation of assets, liabilities, and equity is reflected in the following **accounting equation:**

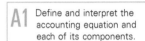

A1 Define and interpret the accounting equation and each of its components.

$$\text{Assets} = \text{Liabilities} + \text{Equity}$$

Liabilities are usually shown before equity in this equation because creditors' claims must be paid before the claims of owners. (The terms in this equation can be rearranged; for example, Assets − Liabilities = Equity.) The accounting equation applies to all transactions and events, to all companies and forms of organization, and to all points in time. For example, Apple's assets equal $116,371, its liabilities equal $39,756, and its equity equals $76,615 ($ in millions). Let's now look at the accounting equation in more detail.

Assets   Assets are resources a company owns or controls. These resources are expected to yield future benefits. Examples are Web servers for an online services company, musical instruments for a rock band, and land for a vegetable grower. The term *receivable* is used to refer to an asset that promises a future inflow of resources. A company that provides a service or product on credit is said to have an account receivable from that customer.

Point: The phrases "on credit" and "on account" imply that cash payment will occur at a future date.

Liabilities   Liabilities are creditors' claims on assets. These claims reflect company obligations to provide assets, products or services to others. The term *payable* refers to a liability that promises a future outflow of resources. Examples are wages payable to workers, accounts payable to suppliers, notes payable to banks, and taxes payable to the government.

Equity   Equity is the owner's claim on assets, and is equal to assets minus liabilities. This is the reason equity is also called *net assets* or *residual equity.*

A corporation's equity—often called stockholders' or shareholders' equity—has two parts: contributed capital and retained earnings. **Contributed capital** refers to the amount that stockholders invest in the company—included under the title **common stock. Retained earnings** refer to **income** (revenues less expenses) that has *not* been distributed to its stockholders. The distribution of assets to stockholders is called **dividends,** which reduce retained earnings. **Revenues** increase retained earnings (via net income) and are resources generated from a company's earnings activities. Examples are consulting services provided, sales of products, facilities rented to others, and commissions from services. **Expenses** decrease retained earnings and are the cost of assets or services used to earn revenues. Examples are costs of employee time, use of supplies, and advertising, utilities, and insurance services from others. In sum, retained earnings is the accumulated revenues less the accumulated expenses and dividends since the company began.

*Key **terms** are printed in bold and defined again in the end-of-book glossary.*

This breakdown of equity yields the following **expanded accounting equation:**

Equity

$$\text{Assets} = \text{Liabilities} + \text{Contributed Capital} + \text{Retained Earnings}$$
$$= \text{Liabilities} + \text{Common Stock} - \text{Dividends} + \text{Revenues} - \text{Expenses}$$

Net income occurs when revenues exceed expenses. Net income increases equity. A **net loss** occurs when expenses exceed revenues, which decreases equity.

Decision Insight

Web Info Most organizations maintain Websites that include accounting data—see Polaris Industries (Polaris.com) as an example. Polaris makes off-road vehicles such as all-terrain vehicles (ATV) and snowmobiles; it also makes on-road vehicles such as motorcycles and small electric vehicles. The SEC keeps an online database called EDGAR (www.sec.gov/edgar.shtml), which has accounting information for thousands of companies that issue stock to the public. The annual report filing for most publicly traded U.S. companies is known as Form 10-K, and the quarterly filing is Form 10-Q. Information services such as Finance.Google.com and Finance.Yahoo.com offer online data and analysis. ■

Transaction Analysis

P1 Analyze business transactions using the accounting equation.

Business activities can be described in terms of transactions and events. **External transactions** are exchanges of value between two entities, which yield changes in the accounting equation. An example is the sale of ad space by Twitter. **Internal transactions** are exchanges within an entity, which may or may not affect the accounting equation. An example is Twitter's use of its supplies, which are reported as expenses when used. **Events** refer to happenings that affect the accounting equation *and* are reliably measured. They include business events such as changes in the market value of certain assets and liabilities and natural events such as floods and fires that destroy assets and create losses. They do not include, for example, the signing of service or product contracts, which by themselves do not impact the accounting equation.

This section uses the accounting equation to analyze 11 selected transactions and events of FastForward, a start-up consulting (service) business, in its first month of operations. Remember that each transaction and event leaves the equation in balance and that assets *always* equal the sum of liabilities and equity.

Point: There are 3 basic types of company operations: (1) **Services**—providing customer services for profit, (2) **Merchandisers**—buying products and re-selling them for profit, and (3) **Manufacturers**—creating products and selling them for profit.

Transaction 1: Investment by Owner On December 1, Chas Taylor forms a consulting business, named FastForward and set up as a corporation, that focuses on assessing the performance of footwear and accessories. Taylor owns and manages the business. The marketing plan for the business is to focus primarily on publishing online reviews and consulting with clubs, athletes, and others who place orders for footwear and accessories with manufacturers. Taylor personally invests $30,000 cash in the new company and deposits the cash in a bank account opened under the name of FastForward. After this transaction, the cash (an asset) and the stockholders' equity each equal $30,000. The source of increase in equity is the owner's investment (stock issuance), which is included in the column titled Common Stock. The effect of this transaction on FastForward is reflected in the accounting equation as follows (we label the equity entries):

	Assets	=	Liabilities	+	Equity
	Cash	=			**Common Stock**
(1)	+$30,000	=			+$30,000 owner investment

Transaction 2: Purchase Supplies for Cash FastForward uses $2,500 of its cash to buy supplies of brand name footwear for performance testing over the next few months. This transaction is an exchange of cash, an asset, for another kind of asset, supplies. It merely changes the form of assets from cash to supplies. The decrease in cash is exactly equal to the increase in supplies. The supplies of footwear are assets because of the expected future benefits from the test results of their performance. This transaction is reflected in the accounting equation as follows:

	Assets			=	Liabilities	+	Equity
	Cash	+	**Supplies**	=			**Common Stock**
Old Bal.	$30,000			=			$30,000
(2)	−2,500	+	$2,500				
New Bal.	$27,500	+	$ 2,500	=			$30,000
		$30,000				$30,000	

Transaction 3: Purchase Equipment for Cash   FastForward spends $26,000 to acquire equipment for testing footwear. Like transaction 2, transaction 3 is an exchange of one asset, cash, for another asset, equipment. The equipment is an asset because of its expected future benefits from testing footwear. This purchase changes the makeup of assets but does not change the asset total. The accounting equation remains in balance.

	Assets			=	Liabilities	+	Equity
	Cash	+	**Supplies**	+	**Equipment**	=	**Common Stock**
Old Bal.	$27,500	+	$2,500			=	$30,000
(3)	−26,000			+	$26,000		
New Bal.	$ 1,500	+	$2,500	+	$ 26,000	=	$30,000
		$30,000				$30,000	

Transaction 4: Purchase Supplies on Credit   Taylor decides more supplies of footwear and accessories are needed. These additional supplies total $7,100, but as we see from the accounting equation in transaction 3, FastForward has only $1,500 in cash. Taylor arranges to purchase them on credit from CalTech Supply Company. Thus, FastForward acquires supplies in exchange for a promise to pay for them later. This purchase increases assets by $7,100 in supplies, and liabilities (called *accounts payable* to CalTech Supply) increase by the same amount. The effects of this purchase follow:

Example: If FastForward pays $500 cash in transaction 4, how does this partial payment affect the liability to CalTech? What would be FastForward's cash balance? *Answers:* The liability to CalTech would be reduced to $6,600 and the cash balance would be reduced to $1,000.

	Assets			=	Liabilities	+	Equity
	Cash	+	**Supplies**	+	**Equipment**	=	**Accounts Payable**	+	**Common Stock**
Old Bal.	$1,500	+	$2,500	+	$26,000	=			$30,000
(4)		+	7,100				+$7,100		
New Bal.	$1,500	+	$9,600	+	$26,000	=	$ 7,100	+	$30,000
		$37,100					$37,100	

Transaction 5: Provide Services for Cash   FastForward earns revenues by selling online ad space to manufacturers and by consulting with clients about test results on footwear and accessories. It earns net income only if its revenues are greater than its expenses incurred in earning them. In one of its first jobs, FastForward provides consulting services to a power-walking club and immediately collects $4,200 cash. The accounting equation reflects this increase in cash of $4,200 and in equity of $4,200. This increase in equity is identified in the far right column under Revenues because the cash received is earned by providing consulting services.

	Assets					=	Liabilities	+		Equity	
	Cash	+	**Supplies**	+	**Equipment**	=	**Accounts Payable**	+	**Common Stock**	+	**Revenues**
Old Bal.	$1,500	+	$9,600	+	$26,000	=	$7,100	+	$30,000		
(5)	+4,200									+	$4,200 consulting
New Bal.	$5,700	+	$9,600	+	$26,000	=	$7,100	+	$30,000	+	$ 4,200
		$41,300							$41,300		

Transactions 6 and 7: Payment of Expenses in Cash   FastForward pays $1,000 rent to the landlord of the building where its facilities are located. Paying this amount allows FastForward to occupy the space for the month of December. The rental payment is reflected in the following accounting equation as transaction 6. FastForward also pays the biweekly $700 salary of the company's only employee. This is reflected in the accounting equation as transaction 7. Both transactions 6 and 7 are December expenses for FastForward. The costs of both rent and salary are expenses, as opposed to assets, because their benefits are used in December (they

By definition, increases in expenses yield decreases in equity.

have no future benefits after December). These transactions also use up an asset (cash) in carrying out FastForward's operations. The accounting equation shows that both transactions reduce cash and equity. The far right column identifies these decreases as Expenses.

	Assets					=	Liabilities	+			Equity			
	Cash	+	**Supplies**	+	**Equipment**	=	**Accounts Payable**	+	**Common Stock**	+	**Revenues**	−	**Expenses**	
Old Bal.	$5,700	+	$9,600	+	$26,000	=	$7,100	+	$30,000	+	$4,200			
(6)	−1,000											−	$1,000	rent
Bal.	4,700	+	9,600	+	26,000	=	7,100	+	30,000	+	4,200	−	1,000	
(7)	− 700											−	700	salaries
New Bal.	$4,000	+	$9,600	+	$26,000	=	$7,100	+	$30,000	+	$4,200	−	$ 1,700	

$$\$39,600 \qquad\qquad \$39,600$$

Transaction 8: Provide Services and Facilities for Credit

FastForward provides consulting services of $1,600 and rents its test facilities for $300 to a podiatric services center. The rental involves allowing members to try recommended footwear and accessories at FastForward's testing area. The center is billed for the $1,900 total. This transaction results in a new asset, called *accounts receivable,* from this client. It also yields an increase in equity from the two revenue components reflected in the Revenues column of the accounting equation:

	Assets							=	Liabilities	+			Equity			
	Cash	+	**Accounts Receivable**	+	**Supplies**	+	**Equipment**	=	**Accounts Payable**	+	**Common Stock**	+	**Revenues**	−	**Expenses**
Old Bal.	$4,000	+		+	$9,600	+	$26,000	=	$7,100	+	$30,000	+	$4,200	−	$1,700
(8)		+	$1,900									+	1,600 consulting		
												+	300 rental		
New Bal.	$4,000	+	$ 1,900	+	$9,600	+	$26,000	=	$7,100	+	$30,000	+	$6,100	−	$1,700

$$\$41,500 \qquad\qquad \$41,500$$

Transaction 9: Receipt of Cash from Accounts Receivable

The client in transaction 8 (the podiatric center) pays $1,900 to FastForward 10 days after it is billed for consulting services. This transaction 9 does not change the total amount of assets and does not affect liabilities or equity. It converts the receivable (an asset) to cash (another asset). It does not create new revenue. Revenue was recognized when FastForward rendered the services in transaction 8, not when the cash is now collected. This emphasis on the earnings process instead of cash flows is a goal of the revenue recognition principle and yields useful information to users. The new balances follow:

Point: Receipt of cash is not always a revenue.

	Assets							=	Liabilities	+			Equity			
	Cash	+	**Accounts Receivable**	+	**Supplies**	+	**Equipment**	=	**Accounts Payable**	+	**Common Stock**	+	**Revenues**	−	**Expenses**
Old Bal.	$4,000	+	$1,900	+	$9,600	+	$26,000	=	$7,100	+	$30,000	+	$6,100	−	$1,700
(9)	+1,900	−	1,900												
New Bal.	$5,900	+	$ 0	+	$9,600	+	$26,000	=	$7,100	+	$30,000	+	$6,100	−	$1,700

$$\$41,500 \qquad\qquad \$41,500$$

Transaction 10: Payment of Accounts Payable

FastForward pays CalTech Supply $900 cash as partial payment for its earlier $7,100 purchase of supplies (transaction 4), leaving $6,200 unpaid. The accounting equation shows that this transaction decreases FastForward's cash by $900 and decreases its liability to CalTech Supply by $900. Equity does not change. This event does not create an expense even though cash flows out of FastForward (instead the expense is recorded when FastForward derives the benefits from these supplies).

	Assets				=	Liabilities	+		Equity		
	Cash	+ **Accounts Receivable**	+ **Supplies**	+ **Equipment**	=	**Accounts Payable**	+ **Common Stock**	+ **Revenues**	− **Expenses**		
Old Bal.	$5,900	+ $ 0	+ $9,600	+ $26,000	=	$7,100	+ $30,000	+ $6,100	− $1,700		
(10)	− 900					− 900					
New Bal.	$5,000	+ $ 0	+ $9,600	+ $26,000	=	$6,200	+ $30,000	+ $6,100	− $1,700		
		$40,600						$40,600			

Transaction 11: Payment of Cash Dividend   FastForward declares and pays a $200 cash dividend to its owner (the sole shareholder). Dividends (decreases in equity) are not reported as expenses because they are not part of the company's earnings process. Since dividends are not company expenses, they are not used in computing net income.

By definition, increases in dividends yield decreases in equity.

	Assets				=	Liabilities	+			Equity	
	Cash	+ **Accounts Receivable**	+ **Supplies**	+ **Equipment**	=	**Accounts Payable**	+ **Common Stock**	− **Dividends**	+ **Revenues**	− **Expenses**	
Old Bal.	$5,000	+ $ 0	+ $9,600	+ $26,000	=	$6,200	+ $30,000		+ $6,100	− $1,700	
(11)	− 200							− $200 dividend			
New Bal.	$4,800	+ $ 0	+ $9,600	+ $26,000	=	$6,200	+ $30,000	− $200	+ $6,100	− $1,700	
		$40,400						$40,400			

Summary of Transactions

We summarize in Exhibit 1.9 the effects of these 11 transactions of FastForward using the accounting equation. First, we see that the accounting equation remains in balance after each transaction. Second, transactions can be analyzed by their effects on components of the

EXHIBIT 1.9

Summary of Transactions Using the Accounting Equation

	Assets				=	Liabilities	+		Equity		
	Cash	+ **Accounts Receivable**	+ **Supplies**	+ **Equipment**	=	**Accounts Payable**	+ **Common Stock**	− **Dividends**	+ **Revenues**	− **Expenses**	
(1)	$30,000				=		$30,000				
(2)	− 2,500		+ $2,500								
Bal.	27,500		+ 2,500		=		30,000				
(3)	−26,000			+ $26,000							
Bal.	1,500		+ 2,500	+ 26,000	=		30,000				
(4)			+ 7,100			+$7,100					
Bal.	1,500		+ 9,600	+ 26,000	=	7,100	+ 30,000				
(5)	+ 4,200								+ $4,200		
Bal.	5,700		+ 9,600	+ 26,000	=	7,100	+ 30,000		+ 4,200		
(6)	− 1,000									− $1,000	
Bal.	4,700		+ 9,600	+ 26,000	=	7,100	+ 30,000		+ 4,200	− 1,000	
(7)	− 700									− 700	
Bal.	4,000		+ 9,600	+ 26,000	=	7,100	+ 30,000		+ 4,200	− 1,700	
(8)		+ $1,900							+ 1,600		
									+ 300		
Bal.	4,000	+ 1,900	+ 9,600	+ 26,000	=	7,100	+ 30,000		+ 6,100	− 1,700	
(9)	+ 1,900	− 1,900									
Bal.	5,900	+ 0	+ 9,600	+ 26,000	=	7,100	+ 30,000		+ 6,100	− 1,700	
(10)	− 900					− 900					
Bal.	5,000	+ 0	+ 9,600	+ 26,000	=	6,200	+ 30,000		+ 6,100	− 1,700	
(11)	− 200							− $200			
Bal.	$ 4,800	+ $ 0	+ $ 9,600	+ $ 26,000	=	$ 6,200	+ $ 30,000	− $ 200	+ $6,100	− $ 1,700	

Point: Knowing how financial statements are prepared improves our analysis of them. We develop the skills for analysis of financial statements throughout the book. Chapter 13 focuses on financial statement analysis.

accounting equation. For example, in transactions 2, 3, and 9, one asset increased while another asset decreased by equal amounts.

Quick Check
Answers — p. 29

17. When is the accounting equation in balance, and what does that mean?

18. How can a transaction not affect any liability and equity accounts?

19. Describe a transaction increasing equity and one decreasing it.

20. Identify a transaction that decreases both assets and liabilities.

FINANCIAL STATEMENTS

P2 Identify and prepare basic financial statements and explain how they interrelate.

This section introduces us to how financial statements are prepared from the analysis of business transactions. The four financial statements and their purposes are:

1. **Income statement**—describes a company's revenues and expenses along with the resulting net income or loss over a period of time due to earnings activities.
2. **Statement of retained earnings**—explains changes in equity from net income (or loss) and from any dividends over a period of time.
3. **Balance sheet**—describes a company's financial position (types and amounts of assets, liabilities, and equity) at a point in time.
4. **Statement of cash flows**—identifies cash inflows (receipts) and cash outflows (payments) over a period of time.

We prepare these financial statements, in this order, using the 11 selected transactions of Fast-Forward. (These statements are technically called *unadjusted*—we explain this in Chapters 2 and 3.)

Income Statement

FastForward's income statement for December is shown at the top of Exhibit 1.10. Information about revenues and expenses is conveniently taken from the Equity columns of Exhibit 1.9. Revenues are reported first on the income statement. They include consulting revenues of $5,800 from transactions 5 and 8 and rental revenue of $300 from transaction 8. Expenses are reported after revenues. (For convenience in this chapter, we list larger amounts first, but we can sort expenses in different ways.) Rent and salary expenses are from transactions 6 and 7. Expenses reflect the costs to generate the revenues reported. Net income (or loss) is reported at the bottom of the statement and is the amount earned in December. Stockholders' investments and dividends are *not* part of income.

Point: Net income is sometimes called *earnings* or *profit.*

Statement of Retained Earnings

Point: The statement of retained earnings is also called the *statement of changes in retained earnings.* Note: Beg. Retained Earnings + Net Income − Dividends = End. Retained Earnings

The statement of retained earnings reports information about how retained earnings changes over the reporting period. This statement shows beginning retained earnings, events that increase it (net income), and events that decrease it (dividends and net loss). Ending retained earnings is computed in this statement and is carried over and reported on the balance sheet. FastForward's statement of retained earnings is the second report in Exhibit 1.10. The beginning balance is measured as of the start of business on December 1. It is zero because FastForward did not exist before then. An existing business reports the beginning balance equal to that as of the end of the prior reporting period (such as from November 30). Fast-Forward's statement shows the $4,400 of net income earned during the period. This links the income statement to the statement of retained earnings (see line ①). The statement also reports the $200 cash dividend and FastForward's end-of-period retained earnings balance.

Balance Sheet

FastForward's balance sheet is the third report in Exhibit 1.10. This statement refers to Fast-Forward's financial condition at the close of business on December 31. The left side of the balance

EXHIBIT 1.10

Financial Statements and Their Links

FASTFORWARD
Income Statement
For Month Ended December 31, 2013

Revenues		
Consulting revenue ($4,200 + $1,600)...............	$ 5,800	
Rental revenue	300	
Total revenues		$ 6,100
Expenses		
Rent expense	1,000	
Salaries expense	700	
Total expenses		1,700
Net income		$ 4,400

Point: A statement's heading identifies the company, the statement title, and the date or time period.

FASTFORWARD
Statement of Retained Earnings
For Month Ended December 31, 2013

Retained earnings, December 1, 2013..........................	$ 0	①
Plus: Net income.......................................	4,400	
	4,400	
Less: Dividends	200	
Retained earnings, December 31, 2013..........................	$ 4,200	

Point: Arrow lines show how the statements are linked. ① Net income is used to compute equity. ② Retained earnings is used to prepare the balance sheet. ③ Cash from the balance sheet is used to reconcile the statement of cash flows.

FASTFORWARD
Balance Sheet
December 31, 2013

Assets		Liabilities	
Cash	$ 4,800	Accounts payable.............	$ 6,200
Supplies	9,600	Total liabilities	6,200
Equipment........	26,000	**Equity**	
		Common stock	30,000
		Retained earnings	4,200
		Total equity	34,200
Total assets	$ 40,400	Total liabilities and equity	$ 40,400

②

Point: The income statement, the statement of retained earnings, and the statement of cash flows are prepared for a *period* of time. The balance sheet is prepared as of a *point* in time.

FASTFORWARD
Statement of Cash Flows
For Month Ended December 31, 2013

Cash flows from operating activities		
Cash received from clients ($4,200 + $1,900)..........	$ 6,100	
Cash paid for supplies ($2,500 + $900)...............	(3,400)	
Cash paid for rent	(1,000)	
Cash paid to employee	(700)	
Net cash provided by operating activities		$ 1,000
Cash flows from investing activities		
Purchase of equipment	(26,000)	
Net cash used by investing activities		(26,000)
Cash flows from financing activities		
Investments by stockholder......................	30,000	
Dividends to stockholder	(200)	
Net cash provided by financing activities		29,800
Net increase in cash		$ 4,800
Cash balance, December 1, 2013		0
Cash balance, December 31, 2013		$ 4,800

③

Point: A single ruled line denotes an addition or subtraction. Final totals are double underlined. Negative amounts are often in parentheses.

sheet lists FastForward's assets: cash, supplies, and equipment. The upper right side of the balance sheet shows that FastForward owes $6,200 to creditors. Any other liabilities (such as a bank loan) would be listed here. The equity balance is $34,200. Line ② shows the link between the ending balance of the statement of retained earnings and the retained earnings balance on the balance sheet. (This presentation of the balance sheet is called the *account form:* assets on the left and liabilities and equity on the right. Another presentation is the *report form:* assets on top, followed by liabilities and then equity at the bottom. Either presentation is acceptable.) As always, we see the accounting equation applies: Assets of $40,400 = Liabilities of $6,200 + Equity of $34,200.

Statement of Cash Flows

Point: Statement of cash flows has three main sections: operating, investing, and financing.

Point: Payment for supplies is an operating activity because supplies are expected to be used up in short-term operations (typically less than one year).

Point: Investing activities refer to long-term asset investments by the company, *not* to owner investments.

FastForward's statement of cash flows is the final report in Exhibit 1.10. The first section reports cash flows from *operating activities.* It shows the $6,100 cash received from clients and the $5,100 cash paid for supplies, rent, and employee salaries. Outflows are in parentheses to denote subtraction. Net cash provided by operating activities for December is $1,000. If cash paid exceeded the $5,100 cash received, we would call it "cash used by operating activities." The second section reports *investing activities,* which involve buying and selling assets such as land and equipment that are held for *long-term use* (typically more than one year). The only investing activity is the $26,000 purchase of equipment. The third section shows cash flows from *financing activities,* which include the *long-term* borrowing and repaying of cash from lenders and the cash investments from, and dividends to, stockholders. FastForward reports $30,000 from the owner's initial investment and the $200 cash dividend. The net cash effect of all financing transactions is a $29,800 cash inflow. The final part of the statement shows FastForward increased its cash balance by $4,800 in December. Since it started with no cash, the ending balance is also $4,800—see line ③. We see that cash flow numbers are different from income statement (*accrual*) numbers, which is common.

Quick Check   Answers — p. 29

21. Explain the link between the income statement and the statement of retained earnings.
22. Describe the link between the balance sheet and the statement of retained earnings.
23. Discuss the three major sections of the statement of cash flows.

GLOBAL VIEW

Accounting according to U.S. GAAP is similar, but not identical, to IFRS. Throughout the book we use this last section to identify major similarities and differences between IFRS and U.S. GAAP for the materials in each chapter.

Basic Principles   Both U.S. GAAP and IFRS include broad and similar guidance for accounting. However, neither system specifies particular account names nor the detail required. (A typical *chart of accounts* is shown near the end of this book.) IFRS does require certain minimum line items be reported in the balance sheet along with other minimum disclosures that U.S. GAAP does not. On the other hand, U.S. GAAP requires disclosures for the current and prior two years for the income statement, statement of cash flows, and statement of retained earnings (equity), while IFRS requires disclosures for the current and prior year. Still, the basic principles behind these two systems are similar.

Transaction Analysis   Both U.S. GAAP and IFRS apply transaction analysis identically as shown in this chapter. Although some variations exist in revenue and expense recognition and other principles, all of the transactions in this chapter are accounted for identically under these two systems. It is often said that U.S. GAAP is more *rules-based* whereas IFRS is more *principles-based.* The main difference on the rules versus principles focus is with the approach in deciding how to account for certain transactions. Under U.S. GAAP, the approach is more focused on strictly following the accounting rules; under IFRS, the approach is more focused on a review of the situation and how accounting can best reflect it. This difference typically impacts advanced topics beyond the introductory course.

PIAGGIO   **Financial Statements**   Both U.S. GAAP and IFRS prepare the same four basic financial statements. To illustrate, a condensed version of Piaggio's income statement follows (numbers are in Euros thousands).

Piaggio manufactures two-, three- and four-wheel vehicles, and is Europe's leading manufacturer of motorcycles and scooters. Similar condensed versions can be prepared for the other three statements (see Appendix A).

PIAGGIO Income Statement (in € thousands) For Year Ended December 31, 2011	
Net revenues	1,516,463
Cost for materials	904,060
Cost for services, leases, employees, depreciation, and other expenses	533,045
Taxes	32,305
Net income (profit)	47,053

Status of IFRS   Accounting impacts companies across the world, which requires us to take a global view. IFRS is now adopted or accepted in over 115 countries, including over 30 member-states of the EU (see gold and light tan shading in the map below). Teal shading in the map reflects a system other than IFRS. The FASB and IASB continue to work on the convergence of IFRS and U.S. GAAP. Further, the SEC has a "roadmap" for ultimate use of IFRS by U.S. companies. Currently, the roadmap extends out over the next several years.

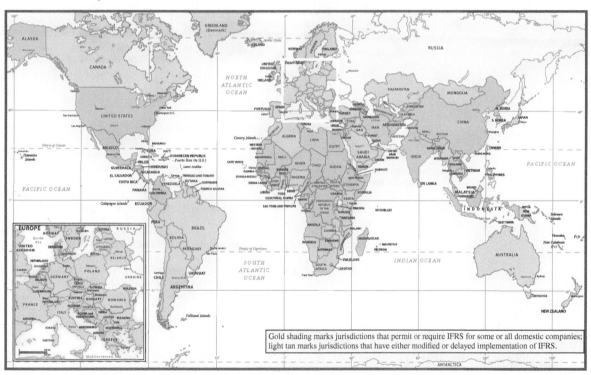

Gold shading marks jurisdictions that permit or require IFRS for some or all domestic companies; light tan marks jurisdictions that have either modified or delayed implementation of IFRS.

Decision Analysis (a section at the end of each chapter) introduces and explains ratios helpful in decision making using real company data. Instructors can skip this section and cover all ratios in Chapter 13.

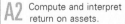

Return on Assets   **Decision Analysis**

A *Decision Analysis* section at the end of each chapter is devoted to financial statement analysis. We organize financial statement analysis into four areas: (1) liquidity and efficiency, (2) solvency, (3) profitability, and (4) market prospects—Chapter 13 has a ratio listing with definitions and groupings by area. When analyzing ratios, we need benchmarks to identify good, bad, or average levels. Common benchmarks include the company's prior levels and those of its competitors.

A2 Compute and interpret return on assets.

24   Chapter 1   Introducing Accounting in Business

This chapter presents a profitability measure: return on assets. Return on assets is useful in evaluating management, analyzing and forecasting profits, and planning activities. Dell has its marketing department compute return on assets for *every* order. **Return on assets (ROA),** also called *return on investment* (*ROI*), is defined in Exhibit 1.11.

EXHIBIT 1.11

Return on Assets

$$\text{Return on assets} = \frac{\text{Net income}}{\text{Average total assets}}$$

Net income is from the annual income statement, and average total assets is computed by adding the beginning and ending amounts for that same period and dividing by 2. To illustrate, Dell reports net income of $3,492 million for fiscal year 2012. At the beginning of fiscal 2012, its total assets are $38,599 million and at the end of fiscal 2012, they total $44,533 million. Dell's return on assets for fiscal 2012 is:

$$\text{Return on assets} = \frac{\$3,492 \text{ million}}{(\$38,599 \text{ million} + \$44,533 \text{ million})/2} = 8.4\%$$

Is an 8.4% return on assets good or bad for Dell? To help answer this question, we compare (benchmark) Dell's return with its prior performance, the returns of competitors (such as Hewlett-Packard, IBM, and Lenovo), and the returns from alternative investments. Dell's return for each of the prior five years is in the second column of Exhibit 1.12, which ranges from 4.8% to 11.1%.

EXHIBIT 1.12

Dell and Industry Returns

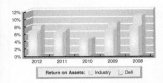

	Return on Assets	
Fiscal Year	**Dell**	**Industry**
2012	8.4%	6.9%
2011	7.3	6.5
2010	4.8	4.7
2009	9.2	7.2
2008	11.1	8.1

Dell shows a fairly stable pattern of good returns that reflect its productive use of assets. There is a decline in its 2009–2010 returns reflecting the recessionary period. We compare Dell's return to the normal return for similar manufacturers of computers (third column). Industry averages are available from services such as Dun & Bradstreet's *Industry Norms and Key Ratios* and The Risk Management Association *Annual Statement Studies*. When compared to the industry, Dell performs slightly above average.

*Each **Decision Analysis** section ends with a role-playing scenario to show the usefulness of ratios.*

■ Decision Maker ◀━━━━━━━━━━━━━━━━━━━━━━━━━━━━━━

Business Owner   You own a small winter ski resort that earns a 21% return on its assets. An opportunity to purchase a winter ski equipment manufacturer is offered to you. This manufacturer earns a 19% return on its assets. The industry return for this manufacturer is 14%. Do you purchase this manufacturer? ■   [Answer—p. 29]

*The **Demonstration Problem** is a review of key chapter content. The Planning the Solution offers strategies in solving the problem.*

DEMONSTRATION PROBLEM

After several months of planning, Jasmine Worthy started a haircutting business called Expressions. The following events occurred during its first month of business.

a. On August 1, Worthy invested $3,000 cash and $15,000 of equipment in Expressions in exchange for its common stock.

b. On August 2, Expressions paid $600 cash for furniture for the shop.

c. On August 3, Expressions paid $500 cash to rent space in a strip mall for August.

d. On August 4, it purchased $1,200 of equipment on credit for the shop (using a long-term note payable).

e. On August 5, Expressions opened for business. Cash received from haircutting services in the first week and a half of business (ended August 15) was $825.

f. On August 15, it provided $100 of haircutting services on account.

g. On August 17, it received a $100 check for services previously rendered on account.

h. On August 17, it paid $125 cash to an assistant for hours worked during the grand opening.

i. Cash received from services provided during the second half of August was $930.

j. On August 31, it paid a $400 installment toward principal on the note payable entered into on August 4.

k. On August 31, it paid $900 cash in dividends to Worthy (sole shareholder).

Required

1. Arrange the following asset, liability, and equity titles in a table similar to the one in Exhibit 1.9: Cash; Accounts Receivable; Furniture; Store Equipment; Note Payable; Common Stock; Dividends; Revenues; and Expenses. Show the effects of each transaction using the accounting equation.

2. Prepare an income statement for August.

3. Prepare a statement of retained earnings for August.

4. Prepare a balance sheet as of August 31.

5. Prepare a statement of cash flows for August.

6. Determine the return on assets ratio for August.

PLANNING THE SOLUTION

- Set up a table like Exhibit 1.9 with the appropriate columns for accounts.
- Analyze each transaction and show its effects as increases or decreases in the appropriate columns. Be sure the accounting equation remains in balance after each transaction.
- Prepare the income statement, and identify revenues and expenses. List those items on the statement, compute the difference, and label the result as *net income* or *net loss*.
- Use information in the Equity columns to prepare the statement of retained earnings.
- Use information in the last row of the transactions table to prepare the balance sheet.
- Prepare the statement of cash flows; include all events listed in the Cash column of the transactions table. Classify each cash flow as operating, investing, or financing.
- Calculate return on assets by dividing net income by average assets.

SOLUTION TO DEMONSTRATION PROBLEM

1.

	Cash	+	Accounts Receivable	+	Furniture	+	Store Equipment	=	Note Payable	+	Common Stock	−	Dividends	+	Revenues	−	Expenses
	Assets							**= Liabilities +**						**Equity**			
a.	$3,000						$15,000				$18,000						
b.	− 600			+	$600												
Bal.	2,400	+		+	600	+	15,000	=			18,000						
c.	− 500															−	$500
Bal.	1,900	+		+	600	+	15,000	=			18,000					−	500
d.						+	1,200		+$1,200								
Bal.	1,900	+		+	600	+	16,200	=	1,200	+	18,000					−	500
e.	+ 825													+	$ 825		
Bal.	2,725	+		+	600	+	16,200	=	1,200	+	18,000			+	825	−	500
f.		+	$100											+	100		
Bal.	2,725	+	100	+	600	+	16,200	=	1,200	+	18,000			+	925	−	500
g.	+ 100	−	100														
Bal.	2,825	+	0	+	600	+	16,200	=	1,200	+	18,000			+	925	−	500
h.	− 125															−	125
Bal.	2,700	+	0	+	600	+	16,200	=	1,200	+	18,000			+	925	−	625
i.	+ 930													+	930		
Bal.	3,630	+	0	+	600	+	16,200	=	1,200	+	18,000			+	1,855	−	625
j.	− 400								− 400								
Bal.	3,230	+	0	+	600	+	16,200	=	800	+	18,000			+	1,855	−	625
k.	− 900											−	$900				
Bal.	$ 2,330	+	0	+	$600	+	$ 16,200	=	$ 800	+	$ 18,000	−	$900	+	$1,855	−	$625

2.

EXPRESSIONS Income Statement For Month Ended August 31		
Revenues		
Haircutting services revenue		$1,855
Expenses		
Rent expense	$500	
Wages expense	125	
Total expenses		625
Net Income		$1,230

3.

EXPRESSIONS Statement of Retained Earnings For Month Ended August 31		
Retained earnings, August 1*		$ 0
Plus: Net income		1,230
		1,230
Less: Dividend to owner		900
Retained earnings, August 31		$ 330

* If Expressions had been an existing business from a prior period, the beginning retained earnings balance would equal the retained earnings balance from the end of the prior period.

4.

EXPRESSIONS Balance Sheet August 31				
Assets		**Liabilities**		
Cash	$ 2,330	Note payable		$ 800
Furniture	600	**Equity**		
Store equipment	16,200	Common stock		18,000
		Retained earnings................		330
		Total equity		18,330
Total assets	$19,130	Total liabilities and equity		$19,130

5.

EXPRESSIONS Statement of Cash Flows For Month Ended August 31		
Cash flows from operating activities		
Cash received from customers	$1,855	
Cash paid for rent	(500)	
Cash paid for wages	(125)	
Net cash provided by operating activities		$1,230
Cash flows from investing activities		
Cash paid for furniture		(600)
Cash flows from financing activities		
Cash investments from stockholders	3,000	
Cash dividends to stockholders	(900)	
Partial repayment of (long-term) note payable	(400)	
Net cash provided by financing activities		1,700
Net increase in cash..................................		$2,330
Cash balance, August 1		0
Cash balance, August 31.............................		$2,330

6. Return on assets $= \dfrac{\text{Net income}}{\text{Average assets}} = \dfrac{\$1,230}{(\$18,000^* + \$19,130)/2} = \dfrac{\$1,230}{\$18,565} = \underline{\underline{6.63\%}}$

* Uses the initial \$18,000 investment as the beginning balance for the *start-up period only*.

Return and Risk Analysis

1A

This appendix explains return and risk analysis and its role in business and accounting.

Net income is often linked to **return.** Return on assets (ROA) is stated in ratio form as income divided by assets invested. For example, banks report return from a savings account in the form of an interest return such as 4%. If we invest in a savings account or in U.S. Treasury bills, we expect a return of around 2% to 7%. We could also invest in a company's stock, or even start our own business. How do we decide among these investment options? The answer depends on our trade-off between return and risk.

Risk is the uncertainty about the return we will earn. All business investments involve risk, but some investments involve more risk than others. The lower the risk of an investment, the lower is our expected return. The reason that savings accounts pay such a low return is the low risk of not being repaid with interest (the government guarantees most savings accounts from default). If we buy a share of eBay or any other company, we might obtain a large return. However, we have no guarantee of any return; there is even the risk of loss.

The bar graph in Exhibit 1A.1 shows recent returns for 10-year bonds with different risks. *Bonds* are written promises by organizations to repay amounts loaned with interest. U.S. Treasury bonds provide a low expected return, but they also offer low risk since they are backed by the U.S. government. High-risk corporate bonds offer a much larger potential return but with much higher risk.

The trade-off between return and risk is a normal part of business. Higher risk implies higher, but riskier, expected returns. To help us make better decisions, we use accounting information to assess both return and risk.

| A3 | Explain the relation between return and risk. |

EXHIBIT 1A.1

Average Returns for Bonds with Different Risks

Business Activities and the Accounting Equation

1B

This appendix explains how the accounting equation is derived from business activities.

There are three major types of business activities: financing, investing, and operating. Each of these requires planning. *Planning* involves defining an organization's ideas, goals, and actions. Most public corporations use the *Management Discussion and Analysis* section in their annual reports to communicate plans. However, planning is not cast in stone. This adds *risk* to both setting plans and analyzing them.

| C5 | Identify and describe the three major activities of organizations. |

Financing   *Financing activities* provide the means organizations use to pay for resources such as land, buildings, and equipment to carry out plans. Organizations are careful in acquiring and managing financing activities because they can determine success or failure. The two sources of financing are owner and nonowner. *Owner financing* refers to resources contributed by the owner along with any income the owner leaves in the organization. *Nonowner* (or *creditor*) *financing* refers to resources contributed by creditors (lenders). *Financial management* is the task of planning how to obtain these resources and to set the right mix between owner and creditor financing.

Investing   *Investing activities* are the acquiring and disposing of resources (assets) that an organization uses to acquire and sell its products or services. Assets are funded by an organization's financing. Organizations differ on the amount and makeup of assets. Some require land and factories to operate. Others need only an office. Determining the amount and type of assets for operations is called *asset management*. Invested

Point: Management must understand accounting data to set financial goals, make financing and investing decisions, and evaluate operating performance.

Point: Investing (assets) and financing (liabilities plus equity) totals are *always* equal.

amounts are referred to as *assets*. Financing is made up of creditor and owner financing, which hold claims on assets. Creditors' claims are called *liabilities*, and the owner's claim is called *equity*. This basic equality is called the *accounting equation* and can be written as: Assets = Liabilities + Equity.

EXHIBIT 1B.1

Activities of Organizations

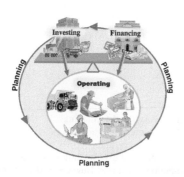

Operating   *Operating activities* involve using resources to research, develop, purchase, produce, distribute, and market products and services. Sales and revenues are the inflow of assets from selling products and services. Costs and expenses are the outflow of assets to support operating activities. *Strategic management* is the process of determining the right mix of operating activities for the type of organization, its plans, and its market.

Exhibit 1B.1 summarizes business activities. Planning is part of each activity and gives them meaning and focus. Investing (assets) and financing (liabilities and equity) are set opposite each other to stress their balance. Operating activities are below investing and financing activities to show that operating activities are the result of investing and financing.

Summary

← *A **Summary** organized by learning objectives concludes each chapter.*

C1   **Explain the purpose and importance of accounting.** Accounting is an information and measurement system that aims to identify, record, and communicate relevant, reliable, and comparable information about business activities. It helps assess opportunities, products, investments, and social and community responsibilities.

C2   **Identify users and uses of, and opportunities in, accounting.** Users of accounting are both internal and external. Some users and uses of accounting include (a) managers in controlling, monitoring, and planning; (b) lenders for measuring the risk and return of loans; (c) shareholders for assessing the return and risk of stock; (d) directors for overseeing management; and (e) employees for judging employment opportunities. Opportunities in accounting include financial, managerial, and tax accounting. They also include accounting-related fields such as lending, consulting, managing, and planning.

C3   **Explain why ethics are crucial to accounting.** The goal of accounting is to provide useful information for decision making. For information to be useful, it must be trusted. This demands ethical behavior in accounting.

C4   **Explain generally accepted accounting principles and define and apply several accounting principles.** Generally accepted accounting principles are a common set of standards applied by accountants. Accounting principles aid in producing relevant, reliable, and comparable information. Four principles underlying financial statements were introduced: cost, revenue recognition, matching, and full disclosure. Financial statements also reflect four assumptions: going-concern, monetary unit, time period, and business entity.

C5ᴮ   **Identify and describe the three major activities of organizations.** Organizations carry out three major activities: financing, investing, and operating. Financing is the means used to pay for resources such as land, buildings, and machines. Investing

refers to the buying and selling of resources used in acquiring and selling products and services. Operating activities are those necessary for carrying out the organization's plans.

A1   **Define and interpret the accounting equation and each of its components.** The accounting equation is: Assets = Liabilities + Equity. Assets are resources owned by a company. Liabilities are creditors' claims on assets. Equity is the owner's claim on assets (*the residual*). The expanded accounting equation is: Assets = Liabilities + [Common Stock − Dividends + Revenues − Expenses].

A2   **Compute and interpret return on assets.** Return on assets is computed as net income divided by average assets. For example, if we have an average balance of $100 in a savings account and it earns $5 interest for the year, the return on assets is $5/$100, or 5%.

A3ᴬ   **Explain the relation between return and risk.** *Return* refers to income, and *risk* is the uncertainty about the return we hope to make. All investments involve risk. The lower the risk of an investment, the lower is its expected return. Higher risk implies higher, but riskier, expected return.

P1   **Analyze business transactions using the accounting equation.** A *transaction* is an exchange of economic consideration between two parties. Examples include exchanges of products, services, money, and rights to collect money. Transactions always have at least two effects on one or more components of the accounting equation. This equation is always in balance.

P2   **Identify and prepare basic financial statements and explain how they interrelate.** Four financial statements report on an organization's activities: balance sheet, income statement, statement of retained earnings, and statement of cash flows.

Guidance Answers to Decision Maker and Decision Ethics

Entrepreneur   (p. 13) You should probably form the business as a corporation if potential lawsuits are of prime concern. The corporate form of organization protects your personal property from lawsuits

directed at the business and places only the corporation's resources at risk. A downside of the corporate form is double taxation: The corporation must pay taxes on its income, and you normally must pay taxes on any money distributed to you from the business (even though the corporation already paid taxes on this money). You should also examine the ethical and socially responsible aspects of starting a business in which you anticipate injuries to others. Formation as an LLC or S corp. should also be explored.

Business Owner   (p. 24) The 19% return on assets for the manufacturer exceeds the 14% industry return (and many others). This is a positive factor for a potential purchase. Also, the purchase of this manufacturer is an opportunity to spread your risk over two businesses as opposed to one. Still, you should hesitate to purchase a business whose return of 19% is lower than your current resort's return of 21%. You are probably better off directing efforts to increase investment in your resort, assuming you can continue to earn a 21% return.

Guidance Answers to Quick Checks

1. Accounting is an information and measurement system that identifies, records, and communicates relevant information to help people make better decisions.

2. Recordkeeping, also called *bookkeeping,* is the recording of financial transactions and events, either manually or electronically. Recordkeeping is essential to data reliability; but accounting is this and much more. Accounting includes identifying, measuring, recording, reporting, and analyzing business events and transactions.

3. Technology offers increased accuracy, speed, efficiency, and convenience in accounting.

4. External users of accounting include lenders, shareholders, directors, customers, suppliers, regulators, lawyers, brokers, and the press. Internal users of accounting include managers, officers, and other internal decision makers involved with strategic and operating decisions.

5. Internal users (managers) include those from research and development, purchasing, human resources, production, distribution, marketing, and servicing.

6. Internal controls are procedures set up to protect assets, ensure reliable accounting reports, promote efficiency, and encourage adherence to company policies. Internal controls are crucial for relevant and reliable information.

7. Ethical guidelines are threefold: (1) identify ethical concerns using personal ethics, (2) analyze options considering all good and bad consequences, and (3) make ethical decisions after weighing all consequences.

8. Ethics and social responsibility yield good behavior, and they often result in higher income and a better working environment.

9. For accounting to provide useful information for decisions, it must be trusted. Trust requires ethics in accounting.

10. Two major participants in setting rules include the SEC and the FASB. (*Note:* Accounting rules reflect society's needs, not those of accountants or any other single constituency.)

11. Most U.S. companies are not directly affected by international accounting standards. International standards are put forth as preferred accounting practices. However, stock exchanges and other parties are increasing the pressure to narrow differences in worldwide accounting practices. International accounting standards are playing an important role in that process.

12. The objectivity concept and cost principle are related in that most users consider information based on cost as objective. Information prepared using both is considered highly reliable and often relevant.

13. Users desire information about the performance of a specific entity. If information is mixed between two or more entities, its usefulness decreases.

14. The revenue recognition principle gives preparers guidelines on when to recognize (record) revenue. This is important; for example, if revenue is recognized too early, the statements report revenue sooner than it should and the business looks more profitable than it is. The reverse is also true.

15. The three basic forms of business organization are sole proprietorships, partnerships, and corporations.

16. Owners of corporations are called *shareholders* (or *stockholders*). Corporate ownership is divided into units called *shares* (or *stock*). The most basic of corporate shares is common stock (or capital stock).

17. The accounting equation is: Assets = Liabilities + Equity. This equation is always in balance, both before and after each transaction.

18. A transaction that changes the makeup of assets would not affect liability and equity accounts. FastForward's transactions 2 and 3 are examples. Each exchanges one asset for another.

19. Earning revenue by performing services, as in FastForward's transaction 5, increases equity (and assets). Incurring expenses while servicing clients, such as in transactions 6 and 7, decreases equity (and assets). Other examples include owner investments (stock issuances) that increase equity and dividends that decrease equity.

20. Paying a liability with an asset reduces both asset and liability totals. One example is FastForward's transaction 10 that reduces a payable by paying cash.

21. An income statement reports a company's revenues and expenses along with the resulting net income or loss. A statement of retained earnings shows changes in retained earnings, including that from net income or loss. Both statements report transactions occurring over a period of time.

22. The balance sheet describes a company's financial position (assets, liabilities, and equity) at a point in time. The retained earnings amount in the balance sheet is obtained from the statement of retained earnings.

23. Cash flows from operating activities report cash receipts and payments from the primary business the company engages in. Cash flows from investing activities involve cash transactions from buying and selling long-term assets. Cash flows from financing activities include long-term cash borrowings and repayments to lenders and the cash investments from, and dividends to, the stockholders.

A list of key terms with page references concludes each chapter (a complete glossary is at the end of the book).

Key Terms

Accounting (p. 4)

Accounting equation (p. 15)

Assets (p. 15)

Audit (p. 13)

Auditors (p. 13)

Balance sheet (p. 20)

Bookkeeping (p. 4)

Business entity assumption (p. 12)

Common stock (p. 13)

Conceptual framework (p. 10)

Contributed capital (p. 15)

Corporation (p. 12)

Cost-benefit constraint (p. 13)

Cost principle (p. 11)

Dividends (p. 15)

Dodd-Frank Wall Street Reform and Consumer Protection Act (p. 14)

Equity (p. 15)

Ethics (p. 7)

Events (p. 16)

Expanded accounting equation (p. 15)

Expense recognition principle (p. 11)

Expenses (p. 15)

External transactions (p. 16)

External users (p. 5)

Financial accounting (p. 5)

Financial Accounting Standards Board (FASB) (p. 9)

Full disclosure principle (p. 11)

Generally accepted accounting principles (GAAP) (p. 9)

Going-concern assumption (p. 12)

Income (p. 15)

Income statement (p. 20)

Internal transactions (p. 16)

Internal users (p. 6)

International Accounting Standards Board (IASB) (p. 9)

International Financial Reporting Standards (IFRS) (p. 9)

Liabilities (p. 15)

Managerial accounting (p. 6)

Matching principle (p. 11)

Materiality constraint (p. 13)

Measurement principle (p. 11)

Monetary unit assumption (p. 12)

Net income (p. 15)

Net loss (p. 15)

Partnership (p. 12)

Proprietorship (p. 12)

Recordkeeping (p. 4)

Retained earnings (p. 15)

Return (p. 27)

Return on assets (p. 24)

Revenue recognition principle (p. 11)

Revenues (p. 15)

Risk (p. 27)

Sarbanes–Oxley Act (p. 13)

Securities and Exchange Commission (SEC) (p. 9)

Shareholders (p. 13)

Shares (p. 13)

Sole proprietorship (p. 12)

Statement of cash flows (p. 20)

Statement of retained earnings (p. 20)

Stock (p. 13)

Stockholders (p. 13)

Time period assumption (p. 12)

Multiple Choice Quiz   Answers on p. 47   mhhe.com/wildFINMAN5e

Additional Quiz Questions are available at the book's Website.

1. A building is offered for sale at $500,000 but is currently assessed at $400,000. The purchaser of the building believes the building is worth $475,000, but ultimately purchases the building for $450,000. The purchaser records the building at:
   a. $50,000
   b. $400,000
   c. $450,000
   d. $475,000
   e. $500,000

2. On December 30, 2012, KPMG signs a $150,000 contract to provide accounting services to one of its clients in 2013. KPMG has a December 31 year-end. Which accounting principle or assumption requires KPMG to record the accounting services revenue from this client in 2013 and not 2012?
   a. Business entity assumption
   b. Revenue recognition principle
   c. Monetary unit assumption
   d. Cost principle
   e. Going-concern assumption

3. If the assets of a company increase by $100,000 during the year and its liabilities increase by $35,000 during the same

year, then the change in equity of the company during the year must have been:
   a. An increase of $135,000.
   b. A decrease of $135,000.
   c. A decrease of $65,000.
   d. An increase of $65,000.
   e. An increase of $100,000.

4. Brunswick borrows $50,000 cash from Third National Bank. How does this transaction affect the accounting equation for Brunswick?
   a. Assets increase by $50,000; liabilities increase by $50,000; no effect on equity.
   b. Assets increase by $50,000; no effect on liabilities; equity increases by $50,000.
   c. Assets increase by $50,000; liabilities decrease by $50,000; no effect on equity.
   d. No effect on assets; liabilities increase by $50,000; equity increases by $50,000.
   e. No effect on assets; liabilities increase by $50,000; equity decreases by $50,000.

5. Geek Squad performs services for a customer and bills the customer for $500. How would Geek Squad record this transaction?

  a. Accounts receivable increase by $500; revenues increase by $500.

  b. Cash increases by $500; revenues increase by $500.

  c. Accounts receivable increase by $500; revenues decrease by $500.

  d. Accounts receivable increase by $500; accounts payable increase by $500.

  e. Accounts payable increase by $500; revenues increase by $500.

A(B) *Superscript letter A (B) denotes assignments based on Appendix 1A (1B).*

🔲 Icon denotes assignments that involve decision making.

Discussion Questions

1. What is the purpose of accounting in society?

2. Technology is increasingly used to process accounting data. Why then must we study and understand accounting?

3. 🔲 Identify four kinds of external users and describe how they use accounting information.

4. 🔲 What are at least three questions business owners and managers might be able to answer by looking at accounting information?

5. Identify three actual businesses that offer services and three actual businesses that offer products.

6. 🔲 Describe the internal role of accounting for organizations.

7. Identify three types of services typically offered by accounting professionals.

8. 🔲 What type of accounting information might be useful to the marketing managers of a business?

9. Why is accounting described as a service activity?

10. What are some accounting-related professions?

11. How do ethics rules affect auditors' choice of clients?

12. What work do tax accounting professionals perform in addition to preparing tax returns?

13. What does the concept of *objectivity* imply for information reported in financial statements? Why?

14. A business reports its own office stationery on the balance sheet at its $400 cost, although it cannot be sold for more than $10 as scrap paper. Which accounting principle and/or assumption justifies this treatment?

15. Why is the revenue recognition principle needed? What does it demand?

16. Describe the three basic forms of business organization and their key attributes.

17. Define (a) *assets*, (b) *liabilities*, (c) *equity*, and (d) *net assets*.

18. What events or transactions change equity?

19. Identify the two main categories of accounting principles.

20. What do accountants mean by the term *revenue?*

21. Define *net income* and explain its computation.

22. Identify the four basic financial statements of a business.

23. 🔲 What information is reported in an income statement?

24. Give two examples of expenses a business might incur.

25. What is the purpose of the statement of retained earnings?

26. 🔲 What information is reported in a balance sheet?

27. The statement of cash flows reports on what major activities?

28. 🔲 Define and explain return on assets.

29.A 🔲 Define return and risk. Discuss the trade-off between them.

30.B Describe the three major business activities in organizations.

31.B Explain why investing (assets) and financing (liabilities and equity) totals are always equal.

32. Refer to the financial statements of Polaris in Appendix A near the end of the book. To what **Polaris** level of significance are dollar amounts rounded? What time period does its income statement cover?

33. Identify the dollar amounts of Arctic Cat's 2011 **Arctic Cat** assets, liabilities, and equity as reported in its statements in Appendix A near the end of the book.

34. Refer to KTM's 2011 balance sheet in Appendix A **KTM** near the end of the book. Confirm that its total assets equal its total liabilities plus total equity.

35. 🔲 Access the SEC EDGAR database (www.SEC. **Polaris** gov) and retrieve Polaris's 2011 10-K (filed February 27, 2012). Identify its auditor. What responsibility does its independent auditor claim regarding Polaris's financial statements?

Connect reproduces assignments online, in static or algorithmic mode, which allows instructors to monitor, promote, and assess student learning. It can be used for practice, homework, or exams.

Quick Study exercises give readers a brief test of key elements.

≣ connect®

Reading and interpreting accounting reports requires some knowledge of accounting terminology. (*a*) Identify the meaning of these accounting-related acronyms: GAAP, SEC, FASB, IASB and IFRS. (*b*) Briefly explain the importance of the knowledge base or organization that is referred to for each of the accounting-related acronyms.

QUICK STUDY

QS 1-1

Identifying accounting terms **C1**

QS 1-2
Identifying accounting users
C2

Identify the following users as either external users (E) or internal users (I).
a. Customers
b. Suppliers
c. Brokers
d. Business press
e. Managers
f. District attorney
g. Shareholders
h. Lenders
i. Controllers
j. FBI and IRS
k. Consumer group
l. Sales staff

QS 1-3
Explaining internal control
C1

An important responsibility of many accounting professionals is to design and implement internal control procedures for organizations. Explain the purpose of internal control procedures. Provide two examples of internal controls applied by companies.

QS 1-4
Accounting opportunities C2

There are many job opportunities for those with accounting knowledge. Identify at least three main areas of opportunities for accounting professionals. For each area, identify at least three job possibilities linked to accounting.

QS 1-5
Identifying ethical concerns C3
This icon highlights assignments that enhance decision-making skills.

Accounting professionals must sometimes choose between two or more acceptable methods of accounting for business transactions and events. Explain why these situations can involve difficult matters of ethical concern.

QS 1-6
Identifying accounting principles
C4

Identify which accounting principle or assumption best describes each of the following practices:
a. In December 2012, Chavez Landscaping received a customer's order and cash prepayment to install sod at a new house that would not be ready for installation until March 2013. Chavez should record the revenue from the customer order in March 2013, not in December 2012.
b. If $51,000 cash is paid to buy land, the land is reported on the buyer's balance sheet at $51,000.
c. Jo Keene owns both Sailing Passions and Dockside Supplies. In preparing financial statements for Dockside Supplies, Keene makes sure that the expense transactions of Sailing Passions are kept separate from Dockside's transactions and financial statements.

QS 1-7
Applying the accounting equation A1

a. Total assets of Charter Company equal $700,000 and its equity is $420,000. What is the amount of its liabilities?
b. Total assets of Martin Marine equal $500,000 and its liabilities and equity amounts are equal to each other. What is the amount of its liabilities? What is the amount of its equity?

QS 1-8
Applying the accounting equation
A1

Use the accounting equation to compute the missing financial statement amounts (*a*), (*b*), and (*c*).

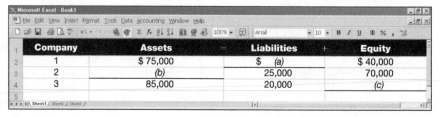

Company	Assets	=	Liabilities	+	Equity
1	$ 75,000		$ *(a)*		$ 40,000
2	*(b)*		25,000		70,000
3	85,000		20,000		*(c)*

QS 1-9
Identifying transactions and events P1

Accounting provides information about an organization's business transactions and events that both affect the accounting equation and can be reliably measured. Identify at least two examples of both (*a*) business transactions and (*b*) business events that meet these requirements.

QS 1-10
Identifying and computing assets, liabilities, and equity P1
Polaris

Use Polaris's December 31, 2011, financial statements, in Appendix A near the end of the book, to answer the following:
a. Identify the dollar amounts of Polaris' 2011 (1) assets, (2) liabilities, and (3) equity.
b. Using Polaris' amounts from part *a*, verify that Assets = Liabilities + Equity.

QS 1-11
Identifying items with financial statements
P2

Indicate in which financial statement each item would most likely appear: income statement (I), balance sheet (B), statement of retained earnings (E), or statement of cash flows (CF).
a. Assets
b. Cash from operating activities
c. Dividends
d. Equipment
e. Expenses
f. Liabilities
g. Net decrease (or increase) in cash
h. Revenues
i. Total liabilities and equity

In a recent year's financial statements, Home Depot reported the following results. Compute and interpret Home Depot's return on assets (assume competitors average a 8.0% return on assets).

Sales	$67,997 million
Net income	3,338 million
Average total assets	40,501 million

QS 1-12
Computing and interpreting return on assets
A2

Answer each of the following questions related to international accounting standards.

a. The International Accounting Standards Board (IASB) issues preferred accounting practices that are referred to as what?

b. The FASB and IASB are working on a convergence process for what purpose?

c. The SEC has proposed a roadmap for use of IFRS by U.S. companies. What is the proposed time period (as suggested by the SEC) for the FASB to endorse IFRS (with necessary exceptions) as U.S. GAAP?

QS 1-13
International accounting standards C4

This icon highlights assignments that focus on IFRS-related content.

connect

Many accounting professionals work in one of the following three areas:

A. Managerial accounting   **B.** Financial accounting   **C.** Tax accounting

Identify the area of accounting that is most involved in each of the following responsibilities:

_____ **1.** Internal auditing.   _____ **5.** Investigating violations of tax laws.

_____ **2.** External auditing.   _____ **6.** Planning transactions to minimize taxes.

_____ **3.** Cost accounting.   _____ **7.** Preparing external financial statements.

_____ **4.** Budgeting.   _____ **8.** Reviewing reports for SEC compliance.

EXERCISES

Exercise 1-1
Describing accounting responsibilities
C2

Accounting is an information and measurement system that identifies, records, and communicates relevant, reliable, and comparable information about an organization's business activities. Classify the following activities as part of the identifying (I), recording (R), or communicating (C) aspects of accounting.

_____ **1.** Analyzing and interpreting reports.   _____ **6.** Establishing revenues generated from a product.

_____ **2.** Presenting financial information.

_____ **3.** Maintaining a log of service costs.   _____ **7.** Determining employee tasks behind a service.

_____ **4.** Measuring the costs of a product.

_____ **5.** Preparing financial statements.

Exercise 1-2
Classifying activities reflected in the accounting system
C1

Part A. Identify the following users of accounting information as either an internal (I) or an external (E) user.

_____ **1.** Research and development director   _____ **5.** Distribution managers

_____ **2.** Human resources director   _____ **6.** Creditors

_____ **3.** Nonexecutive employee   _____ **7.** Production supervisors

_____ **4.** Shareholders   _____ **8.** Purchasing manager

Exercise 1-3
Identifying accounting users and uses
C2

Part B. Identify the following questions as most likely to be asked by an internal (I) or an external (E) user of accounting information.

_____ **1.** What are reasonable payroll benefits and wages?   _____ **5.** Should we spend further research on our product?

_____ **2.** Should we make a five-year loan to that business?   _____ **6.** Which firm reports the highest sales and income?

_____ **3.** What are the costs of our product's ingredients?   _____ **7.** What are the costs of our service to customers?

_____ **4.** Do income levels justify the current stock price?

Assume the following role and describe a situation in which ethical considerations play an important part in guiding your decisions and actions:

a. You are a student in an introductory accounting course.

b. You are a manager with responsibility for several employees.

c. You are an accounting professional preparing tax returns for clients.

d. You are an accounting professional with audit clients that are competitors in business.

Exercise 1-4
Identifying ethical concerns
C3

Exercise 1-5

Identifying accounting principles and assumptions

C4

Match each of the numbered descriptions with the principle or assumption it best reflects. Enter the letter for the appropriate principle or assumption in the blank space next to each description.

A. General accounting principle   **E.** Specific accounting principle
B. Cost principle   **F.** Matching principle
C. Business entity assumption   **G.** Going-concern assumption
D. Revenue recognition principle   **H.** Full disclosure principle

_____ **1.** Usually created by a pronouncement from an authoritative body.
_____ **2.** Financial statements reflect the assumption that the business continues operating.
_____ **3.** Derived from long-used and generally accepted accounting practices.
_____ **4.** Every business is accounted for separately from its owner or owners.
_____ **5.** Revenue is recorded only when the earnings process is complete.
_____ **6.** Information is based on actual costs incurred in transactions.
_____ **7.** A company records the expenses incurred to generate the revenues reported.
_____ **8.** A company reports details behind financial statements that would impact users' decisions.

Exercise 1-6

Learning the language of business

C1–C3

Match each of the numbered descriptions with the term or phrase it best reflects. Indicate your answer by writing the letter for the term or phrase in the blank provided.

A. Audit   **C.** Ethics   **E.** SEC   **G.** Net income
B. GAAP   **D.** Tax accounting   **F.** Public accountants   **H.** IASB

_____ **1.** Principles that determine whether an action is right or wrong.
_____ **2.** Accounting professionals who provide services to many clients.
_____ **3.** An accounting area that includes planning future transactions to minimize taxes paid.
_____ **4.** An examination of an organization's accounting system and records that adds credibility to financial statements.
_____ **5.** Amount a business earns after paying all expenses and costs associated with its sales and revenues.

Exercise 1-7

Distinguishing business organizations

C4

The following describe several different business organizations. Determine whether the description refers to a sole proprietorship, partnership, or corporation.

a. Ownership of Zander Company is divided into 1,000 shares of stock.
b. Wallingford is owned by Trent Malone, who is personally liable for the company's debts.
c. Micah Douglas and Nathan Logan own Financial Services, a financial services provider. Neither Douglas nor Logan has personal responsibility for the debts of Financial Services.
d. Riley and Kay own Speedy Packages, a courier service. Both are personally liable for the debts of the business.
e. IBC Services does not have separate legal existence apart from the one person who owns it.
f. Physio Products does not pay income taxes and has one owner.
g. AJ pays its own income taxes and has two owners.

Exercise 1-8

Using the accounting equation

A1 P1

Check (c) Beg. equity, $60,000

Answer the following questions. (*Hint:* Use the accounting equation.)

a. Office Store has assets equal to $123,000 and liabilities equal to $47,000 at year-end. What is the total equity for Office Store at year-end?
b. At the beginning of the year, Addison Company's assets are $300,000 and its equity is $100,000. During the year, assets increase $80,000 and liabilities increase $50,000. What is the equity at the end of the year?
c. At the beginning of the year, Quaker Company's liabilities equal $70,000. During the year, assets increase by $60,000, and at year-end assets equal $190,000. Liabilities decrease $5,000 during the year. What are the beginning and ending amounts of equity?

Exercise 1-9

Using the accounting equation

A1

Determine the missing amount from each of the separate situations *a*, *b*, and *c* below.

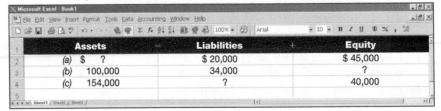

	Assets	=	Liabilities	+	Equity
(a)	$?		$ 20,000		$ 45,000
(b)	100,000		34,000		?
(c)	154,000		?		40,000

Provide an example of a transaction that creates the described effects for the separate cases *a* through *g*.

a. Decreases an asset and decreases equity.

b. Increases an asset and increases a liability.

c. Decreases a liability and increases a liability.

d. Decreases an asset and decreases a liability.

e. Increases an asset and decreases an asset.

f. Increases a liability and decreases equity.

g. Increases an asset and increases equity.

Lena Holden began a professional practice on June 1 and plans to prepare financial statements at the end of each month. During June, Holden (the owner) completed these transactions:

a. Owner invested $60,000 cash in the company along with equipment that had a $15,000 market value in exchange for its common stock.

b. The company paid $1,500 cash for rent of office space for the month.

c. The company purchased $10,000 of additional equipment on credit (payment due within 30 days).

d. The company completed work for a client and immediately collected the $2,500 cash earned.

e. The company completed work for a client and sent a bill for $8,000 to be received within 30 days.

f. The company purchased additional equipment for $6,000 cash.

g. The company paid an assistant $3,000 cash as wages for the month.

h. The company collected $5,000 cash as a partial payment for the amount owed by the client in transaction *e*.

i. The company paid $10,000 cash to settle the liability created in transaction *c*.

j. The company paid $1,000 cash in dividends to the owner (sole shareholder).

Required

Create a table like the one in Exhibit 1.9, using the following headings for columns: Cash; Accounts Receivable; Equipment; Accounts Payable; Common Stock; Dividends; Revenues; and Expenses. Then use additions and subtractions to show the effects of the transactions on individual items of the accounting equation. Show new balances after each transaction.

Zen began a new consulting firm on January 5. The accounting equation showed the following balances after each of the company's first five transactions. Analyze the accounting equation for each transaction and describe each of the five transactions with their amounts.

		Assets				=	Liabilities	+		Equity	
Trans-action	Cash	+	Accounts Receiv-able	+	Office Sup-plies	+ Office Furni-ture =	Accounts Payable	+	Common Stock	+	Revenues	
a.	$40,000	+	$ 0	+	$ 0	+ $ 0 =	$ 0	+	$40,000	+	$ 0	
b.	38,000	+	0	+	3,000	+ 0 =	1,000	+	40,000	+	0	
c.	30,000	+	0	+	3,000	+ 8,000 =	1,000	+	40,000	+	0	
d.	30,000	+	6,000	+	3,000	+ 8,000 =	1,000	+	40,000	+	6,000	
e.	31,000	+	6,000	+	3,000	+ 8,000 =	1,000	+	40,000	+	7,000	

The following table shows the effects of five transactions (*a* through *e*) on the assets, liabilities, and equity of Trista's Boutique. Write short descriptions of the probable nature of each transaction.

	Cash	+	Accounts Receivable	+	Office Supplies	+	Land	=	Accounts Payable	+	Common Stock	+	Revenues
	$ 21,000	+	$ 0	+	$3,000	+	$19,000	=	$ 0	+	$43,000	+	$ 0
a.	− 4,000					+	4,000						
b.				+	1,000				+1,000				
c.		+	1,900									+	1,900
d.	− 1,000								−1,000				
e.	+ 1,900	−	1,900										
	$ 17,900	+	$ 0	+	$4,000	+	$23,000	=	$ 0	+	$43,000	+	$1,900

Exercise 1-14

Preparing an income statement

P2

On October 1, Keisha King organized Real Answers, a new consulting firm; on October 3, the owner contributed $84,000 cash. On October 31, the company's records show the following items and amounts. Use this information to prepare an October income statement for the business.

Cash	$11,360	Cash dividends	$ 2,000
Accounts receivable	14,000	Consulting fees earned	14,000
Office supplies	3,250	Rent expense	3,550
Land	46,000	Salaries expense	7,000
Office equipment	18,000	Telephone expense	760
Accounts payable	8,500	Miscellaneous expenses	580
Common stock	84,000		

Check Net income, $2,110

Exercise 1-15

Preparing a statement of retained earnings P2

Use the information in Exercise 1-14 to prepare an October statement of retained earnings for Real Answers.

Exercise 1-16

Preparing a balance sheet P2

Use the information in Exercise 1-14 (if completed, you can also use your solution to Exercise 1-15) to prepare an October 31 balance sheet for Real Answers.

Exercise 1-17

Preparing a statement of cash flows

P2

Use the information in Exercise 1-14 to prepare an October 31 statement of cash flows for Real Answers. Also assume the following:

a. The owner's initial investment consists of $38,000 cash and $46,000 in land in exchange for its common stock.

b. The company's $18,000 equipment purchase is paid in cash.

c. The accounts payable balance of $8,500 consists of the $3,250 office supplies purchase and $5,250 in employee salaries yet to be paid.

d. The company's rent, telephone, and miscellaneous expenses are paid in cash.

Check Net increase in cash, $11,360

e. No cash has been collected on the $14,000 consulting fees earned.

Exercise 1-18

Analysis of return on assets

A2

Swiss Group reports net income of $40,000 for 2013. At the beginning of 2013, Swiss Group had $200,000 in assets. By the end of 2013, assets had grown to $300,000. What is Swiss Group's 2013 return on assets? How would you assess its performance if competitors average a 10% return on assets?

Exercise 1-19

Identifying sections of the statement of cash flows

P2

Indicate the section where each of the following would appear on the statement of cash flows.

O. Cash flows from operating activity

I. Cash flows from investing activity

F. Cash flows from financing activity

_____ **1.** Cash paid for advertising   _____ **5.** Cash paid for rent

_____ **2.** Cash paid for wages   _____ **6.** Cash paid on an account payable

_____ **3.** Cash paid for dividends   _____ **7.** Cash received from stock issued

_____ **4.** Cash purchase of equipment   _____ **8.** Cash received from clients

---

Exercise 1-20ᴮ

Identifying business activities

C5

Match each transaction or event to one of the following activities of an organization: financing activities (F), investing activities (I), or operating activities (O).

a. _____ An owner contributes resources to the business in exchange for its common stock.

b. _____ An organization sells some of its land.

c. _____ An organization purchases equipment.

d. _____ An organization advertises a new product.

e. _____ The organization borrows money from a bank.

Exercise 1-21

Preparing an income statement a global company

Nintendo Company reports the following income statement accounts for the year ended March 31, 2011. (Japanese yen in millions.)

Net sales	¥1,014,345
Cost of sales	626,379
Selling, general and administrative expenses	216,889
Other expenses	93,456

Use this information to prepare Nintendo's income statement for the year ended March 31, 2011.

Problem Set B located at the end of Problem Set A is provided for <u>each</u> problem to reinforce the learning process.

≣ connect

The following financial statement information is from five separate companies:

PROBLEM SET A

Problem 1-1A
Computing missing information using accounting knowledge

A1 P1

	Company A	Company B	Company C	Company D	Company E
December 31, 2012					
Assets.........................	$55,000	$34,000	$24,000	$60,000	$119,000
Liabilities	24,500	21,500	9,000	40,000	?
December 31, 2013					
Assets.........................	58,000	40,000	?	85,000	113,000
Liabilities	?	26,500	29,000	24,000	70,000
During year 2013					
Stock issuances	6,000	1,400	9,750	?	6,500
Net income (loss)	8,500	?	8,000	14,000	20,000
Cash dividends	3,500	2,000	5,875	0	11,000

Required

1. Answer the following questions about Company A:
   a. What is the amount of equity on December 31, 2012?
   b. What is the amount of equity on December 31, 2013?
   c. What is the amount of liabilities on December 31, 2013?
2. Answer the following questions about Company B:
   a. What is the amount of equity on December 31, 2012?
   b. What is the amount of equity on December 31, 2013?
   c. What is net income for year 2013?
3. Calculate the amount of assets for Company C on December 31, 2013.
4. Calculate the amount of stock issuances for Company D during year 2013.
5. Calculate the amount of liabilities for Company E on December 31, 2012.

Check   (1*b*) $41,500

(2*c*) $1,600
(3) $55,875

Identify how each of the following separate transactions affects financial statements. For the balance sheet, identify how each transaction affects total assets, total liabilities, and total equity. For the income statement, identify how each transaction affects net income. For the statement of cash flows, identify how each transaction affects cash flows from operating activities, cash flows from financing activities, and cash flows from investing activities. For increases, place a "+" in the column or columns. For decreases, place a "−" in the column or columns. If both an increase and a decrease occur, place a "+/−" in the column or columns. The first transaction is completed as an example.

Problem 1-2A
Identifying effects of transactions on financial statements

A1 P1

	Transaction	Balance Sheet			Income Statement	Statement of Cash Flows		
		Total Assets	Total Liab.	Total Equity	Net Income	Operating Activities	Financing Activities	Investing Activities
1	Owner invests cash for its stock	+		+			+	
2	Receives cash for services provided							
3	Pays cash for employee wages							
4	Incurs legal costs on credit							
5	Borrows cash by signing long-term note payable							
6	Pays cash dividend							
7	Buys land by signing note payable							
8	Provides services on credit							
9	Buys office equipment for cash							
10	Collects cash on receivable from (8)							

Problem 1-3A
Preparing an income statement
P2

The following is selected financial information for Elko Energy Company for the year ended December 31, 2013: revenues, $55,000; expenses, $40,000; net income, $15,000.

Required

Prepare the 2013 calendar-year income statement for Elko Energy Company.

Problem 1-4A
Preparing a balance sheet
P2

The following is selected financial information for Amity Company as of December 31, 2013: liabilities, $44,000; equity, $46,000; assets, $90,000.

Required

Prepare the balance sheet for Amity Company as of December 31, 2013.

Problem 1-5A
Preparing a statement of cash flows
P2

Following is selected financial information of ABM Company for the year ended December 31, 2013.

Cash used by investing activities	$(2,000)
Net increase in cash	1,200
Cash used by financing activities	(2,800)
Cash from operating activities	6,000
Cash, December 31, 2012	2,300

Check Cash balance, Dec. 31, 2013, $3,500

Required

Prepare the 2013 statement of cash flows for ABM Company.

Problem 1-6A
Preparing a statement of retained earnings
P2

Following is selected financial information for Kasio Co. for the year ended December 31, 2013.

Retained Earnings, Dec. 31, 2013	$14,000	Cash dividends	$1,000
Net income	8,000	Retained Earnings, Dec. 31, 2012	7,000

Required

Prepare the 2013 statement of retained earnings for Kasio.

Problem 1-7A
Analyzing transactions and preparing financial statements
C4 P1 P2

mhhe.com/wildFINMAN5e

Holden Graham started The Graham Co., a new business that began operations on May 1. The Graham Co. completed the following transactions during its first month of operations.

May 1   H. Graham invested $40,000 cash in the company in exchange for its common stock.
1   The company rented a furnished office and paid $2,200 cash for May's rent.
3   The company purchased $1,890 of office equipment on credit.
5   The company paid $750 cash for this month's cleaning services.
8   The company provided consulting services for a client and immediately collected $5,400 cash.
12   The company provided $2,500 of consulting services for a client on credit.
15   The company paid $750 cash for an assistant's salary for the first half of this month.
20   The company received $2,500 cash payment for the services provided on May 12.
22   The company provided $3,200 of consulting services on credit.
25   The company received $3,200 cash payment for the services provided on May 22.
26   The company paid $1,890 cash for the office equipment purchased on May 3.
27   The company purchased $80 of advertising in this month's (May) local paper on credit; cash payment is due June 1.
28   The company paid $750 cash for an assistant's salary for the second half of this month.
30   The company paid $300 cash for this month's telephone bill.
30   The company paid $280 cash for this month's utilities.
31   The company paid $1,400 cash in dividends to the owner (sole shareholder).

Required

1. Arrange the following asset, liability, and equity titles in a table like Exhibit 1.9: Cash; Accounts Receivable; Office Equipment; Accounts Payable; Common Stock; Dividends; Revenues; and Expenses.

Check (2) Ending balances: Cash, $42,780; Expenses, $5,110

2. Show effects of the transactions on the accounts of the accounting equation by recording increases and decreases in the appropriate columns. Do not determine new account balances after each transaction. Determine the final total for each account and verify that the equation is in balance.

(3) Net income, $5,990; Total assets, $44,670

3. Prepare an income statement for May, a statement of retained earnings for May, a May 31 balance sheet, and a statement of cash flows for May.

Helga Ander started a new business and completed these transactions during December.

Dec. 1   Helga Ander transferred $65,000 cash from a personal savings account to a checking account in the name of Ander Electric in exchange for its common stock.
2   The company rented office space and paid $1,000 cash for the December rent.
3   The company purchased $13,000 of electrical equipment by paying $4,800 cash and agreeing to pay the $8,200 balance in 30 days.
5   The company purchased office supplies by paying $800 cash.
6   The company completed electrical work and immediately collected $1,200 cash for these services.
8   The company purchased $2,530 of office equipment on credit.
15   The company completed electrical work on credit in the amount of $5,000.
18   The company purchased $350 of office supplies on credit.
20   The company paid $2,530 cash for the office equipment purchased on December 8.
24   The company billed a client $900 for electrical work completed; the balance is due in 30 days.
28   The company received $5,000 cash for the work completed on December 15.
29   The company paid the assistant's salary of $1,400 cash for this month.
30   The company paid $540 cash for this month's utility bill.
31   The company paid $950 cash in dividends to the owner (sole shareholder).

Required

1. Arrange the following asset, liability, and equity titles in a table like Exhibit 1.9: Cash; Accounts Receivable; Office Supplies; Office Equipment; Electrical Equipment; Accounts Payable; Common Stock; Dividends; Revenues; and Expenses.

2. Use additions and subtractions to show the effects of each transaction on the accounts in the accounting equation. Show new balances after each transaction.

3. Use the increases and decreases in the columns of the table from part 2 to prepare an income statement, a statement of retained earnings, and a statement of cash flows—each of these for the current month. Also prepare a balance sheet as of the end of the month.

Analysis Component

4. Assume that the owner investment transaction on December 1 was $49,000 cash instead of $65,000 and that Ander Electric obtained another $16,000 in cash by borrowing it from a bank. Explain the effect of this change on total assets, total liabilities, and total equity.

Problem 1-8A
Analyzing transactions and preparing financial statements

C4 P1 P2

mhhe.com/wildFINMAN5e

Check (2) Ending balances: Cash, $59,180, Accounts Payable, $8,550

  (3) Net income, $4,160; Total assets, $76,760

Isabel Lopez started Biz Consulting, a new business, and completed the following transactions during its first year of operations.

a. I. Lopez invests $70,000 cash and office equipment valued at $10,000 in the company in exchange for its common stock.
b. The company purchased a $150,000 building to use as an office. Biz paid $20,000 in cash and signed a note payable promising to pay the $130,000 balance over the next ten years.
c. The company purchased office equipment for $15,000 cash.
d. The company purchased $1,200 of office supplies and $1,700 of office equipment on credit.
e. The company paid a local newspaper $500 cash for printing an announcement of the office's opening.
f. The company completed a financial plan for a client and billed that client $2,800 for the service.
g. The company designed a financial plan for another client and immediately collected an $4,000 cash fee.
h. The company paid $3,275 cash in dividends to the owner (sole shareholder).
i. The company received $1,800 cash as partial payment from the client described in transaction *f*.
j. The company made a partial payment of $700 cash on the equipment purchased in transaction *d*.
k. The company paid $1,800 cash for the office secretary's wages for this period.

Required

1. Create a table like the one in Exhibit 1.9, using the following headings for the columns: Cash; Accounts Receivable; Office Supplies; Office Equipment; Building; Accounts Payable; Notes Payable; Common Stock; Dividends; Revenues; and Expenses.

2. Use additions and subtractions within the table created in part *1* to show the dollar effects of each transaction on individual items of the accounting equation. Show new balances after each transaction.

3. Once you have completed the table, determine the company's net income.

Problem 1-9A
Analyzing effects of transactions

C4 P1 P2 A1

Check (2) Ending balances: Cash, $34,525; Expenses, $2,300; Notes Payable, $130,000

  (3) Net income, $4,500

Problem 1-10A
Computing and interpreting return on assets

A2

Coca-Cola and PepsiCo both produce and market beverages that are direct competitors. Key financial figures (in $ millions) for these businesses over the past year follow.

Key Figures ($ millions)	Coca-Cola	PepsiCo
Sales	$46,542	$66,504
Net income	8,634	6,462
Average assets	76,448	70,518

Required

Check (1a) 11.3%; (1b) 9.2%

1. Compute return on assets for (a) Coca-Cola and (b) PepsiCo.
2. Which company is more successful in its total amount of sales to consumers?
3. Which company is more successful in returning net income from its assets invested?

Analysis Component

4. Write a one-paragraph memorandum explaining which company you would invest your money in and why. (Limit your explanation to the information provided.)

Problem 1-11A
Determining expenses, liabilities, equity, and return on assets

A1 A2

Kyzera manufactures, markets, and sells cellular telephones. The average total assets for Kyzera is $250,000. In its most recent year, Kyzera reported net income of $65,000 on revenues of $475,000.

Required

1. What is Kyzera's return on assets?
2. Does return on assets seem satisfactory for Kyzera given that its competitors average a 12% return on assets?
3. What are total expenses for Kyzera in its most recent year?
4. What is the average total amount of liabilities plus equity for Kyzera?

Check (3) $410,000
(4) $250,000

Problem 1-12A[A]
Identifying risk and return

A3

All business decisions involve aspects of risk and return.

Required

Identify both the risk and the return in each of the following activities:

1. Investing $2,000 in a 5% savings account.
2. Placing a $2,500 bet on your favorite sports team.
3. Investing $10,000 in Yahoo! stock.
4. Taking out a $15,000 college loan toward earning an accounting degree.

Problem 1-13A[B]
Describing organizational activities

C5

A start-up company often engages in the following transactions in its first year of operations. Classify those transactions in one of the three major categories of an organization's business activities.

F. Financing   **I.** Investing   **O.** Operating

_____ **1.** Owner investing land in business.   _____ **5.** Purchasing equipment.
_____ **2.** Purchasing a building.   _____ **6.** Selling and distributing products.
_____ **3.** Purchasing land.   _____ **7.** Paying for advertising.
_____ **4.** Borrowing cash from a bank.   _____ **8.** Paying employee wages.

Problem 1-14A[B]
Describing organizational activities C5

An organization undertakes various activities in pursuit of business success. Identify an organization's three major business activities, and describe each activity.

The following financial statement information is from five separate companies.

Problem 1-1B
Computing missing information
using accounting knowledge

A1 P1

	Company V	Company W	Company X	Company Y	Company Z
December 31, 2012					
Assets	$54,000	$80,000	$141,500	$92,500	$144,000
Liabilities	25,000	60,000	68,500	51,500	?
December 31, 2013					
Assets	59,000	100,000	186,500	?	170,000
Liabilities	36,000	?	65,800	42,000	42,000
During year 2013					
Stock issuances	5,000	20,000	?	48,100	60,000
Net income or (loss)	?	40,000	18,500	24,000	~~32,000~~
Cash dividends	5,500	2,000	0	20,000	8,000

(handwritten: 52,000)

Required

1. Answer the following questions about Company V:
   a. What is the amount of equity on December 31, 2012?
   b. What is the amount of equity on December 31, 2013?
   c. What is the net income or loss for the year 2013?
2. Answer the following questions about Company W:
   a. What is the amount of equity on December 31, 2012?
   b. What is the amount of equity on December 31, 2013?
   c. What is the amount of liabilities on December 31, 2013?
3. Calculate the amount of stock issuances for Company X during 2013.
4. Calculate the amount of assets for Company Y on December 31, 2013.
5. Calculate the amount of liabilities for Company Z on December 31, 2012.

Check (1*b*) $23,000

(2*c*) $22,000

(4) $135,100

Identify how each of the following separate transactions affects financial statements. For the balance sheet, identify how each transaction affects total assets, total liabilities, and total equity. For the income statement, identify how each transaction affects net income. For the statement of cash flows, identify how each transaction affects cash flows from operating activities, cash flows from financing activities, and cash flows from investing activities. For increases, place a "+" in the column or columns. For decreases, place a "−" in the column or columns. If both an increase and a decrease occur, place "+/−" in the column or columns. The first transaction is completed as an example.

Problem 1-2B
Identifying effects of
transactions on financial
statements A1 P1

	Transaction	Balance Sheet			Income Statement	Statement of Cash Flows		
		Total Assets	Total Liab.	Total Equity	Net Income	Operating Activities	Financing Activities	Investing Activities
1	Owner invests cash for its stock	+		+			+	
2	Buys building by signing note payable							
3	Pays cash for salaries incurred							
4	Provides services for cash							
5	Pays cash for rent incurred							
6	Incurs utilities costs on credit							
7	Buys store equipment for cash							
8	Pays cash dividend							
9	Provides services on credit							
10	Collects cash on receivable from (9)							

Problem 1-3B
Preparing an income statement
P2

Selected financial information for Offshore Co. for the year ended December 31, 2013, follows.

Revenues	$68,000	Expenses	$40,000	Net income	$28,000

Required

Prepare the 2013 income statement for Offshore Company.

Problem 1-4B
Preparing a balance sheet
P2

The following is selected financial information for TLC Company as of December 31, 2013.

Liabilities	$64,000	Equity	$50,000	Assets	$114,000

Required

Prepare the balance sheet for TLC Company as of December 31, 2013.

Problem 1-5B
Preparing a statement of cash flows
P2

Selected financial information of HalfLife Company for the year ended December 31, 2013, follows.

Cash from investing activities	$1,600
Net increase in cash	400
Cash from financing activities	1,800
Cash used by operating activities	(3,000)
Cash, December 31, 2012	1,300

Required

Prepare the 2013 statement of cash flows for HalfLife Company.

Problem 1-6B
Preparing a statement of retained earnings
P2

Following is selected financial information of ATV Company for the year ended December 31, 2013.

Retained Earnings, Dec. 31, 2013	$47,000	Cash dividends	$ 7,000
Net income	5,000	Retained Earnings, Dec. 31, 2012	49,000

Required

Prepare the 2013 statement of retained earnings for ATV Company.

Problem 1-7B
Analyzing transactions and preparing financial statements
C4 P1 P2

Holly Nikolas launched a new business, Holly's Maintenance Co., that began operations on June 1. The following transactions were completed by the company during that first month.

June 1 H. Nikolas invested $130,000 cash in the company in exchange for its common stock.
   2 The company rented a furnished office and paid $6,000 cash for June's rent.
   4 The company purchased $2,400 of equipment on credit.
   6 The company paid $1,150 cash for this month's advertising of the opening of the business.
   8 The company completed maintenance services for a customer and immediately collected $850 cash.
   14 The company completed $7,500 of maintenance services for City Center on credit.
   16 The company paid $800 cash for an assistant's salary for the first half of the month.
   20 The company received $7,500 cash payment for services completed for City Center on June 14.
   21 The company completed $7,900 of maintenance services for Paula's Beauty Shop on credit.
   24 The company completed $675 of maintenance services for Build-It Coop on credit.
   25 The company received $7,900 cash payment from Paula's Beauty Shop for the work completed on June 21.
   26 The company made payment of $2,400 cash for equipment purchased on June 4.
   28 The company paid $800 cash for an assistant's salary for the second half of this month.
   29 The company paid $4,000 cash in dividends to the owner (sole shareholder).
   30 The company paid $150 cash for this month's telephone bill.
   30 The company paid $890 cash for this month's utilities.

Required

1. Arrange the following asset, liability, and equity titles in a table like Exhibit 1.9: Cash; Accounts Receivable; Equipment; Accounts Payable; Common Stock; Dividends; Revenues; and Expenses.

2. Show the effects of the transactions on the accounts of the accounting equation by recording increases and decreases in the appropriate columns. Do not determine new account balances after each transaction. Determine the final total for each account and verify that the equation is in balance.

3. Prepare a June income statement, a June statement of retained earnings, a June 30 balance sheet, and a June statement of cash flows.

Check   (2) Ending balances: Cash, $130,060; Expenses, $9,790

(3) Net income, $7,135; Total assets, $133,135

Truro Excavating Co., owned by Raul Truro, began operations in July and completed these transactions during that first month of operations.

Problem 1-8B
Analyzing transactions and preparing financial statements

C4 P1 P2

July	1	R. Truro invested $80,000 cash in the company in exchange for its common stock.
	2	The company rented office space and paid $700 cash for the July rent.
	3	The company purchased excavating equipment for $5,000 by paying $1,000 cash and agreeing to pay the $4,000 balance in 30 days.
	6	The company purchased office supplies for $600 cash.
	8	The company completed work for a customer and immediately collected $7,600 cash for the work.
	10	The company purchased $2,300 of office equipment on credit.
	15	The company completed work for a customer on credit in the amount of $8,200.
	17	The company purchased $3,100 of office supplies on credit.
	23	The company paid $2,300 cash for the office equipment purchased on July 10.
	25	The company billed a customer $5,000 for work completed; the balance is due in 30 days.
	28	The company received $8,200 cash for the work completed on July 15.
	30	The company paid an assistant's salary of $1,560 cash for this month.
	31	The company paid $295 cash for this month's utility bill.
	31	The company paid $1,800 cash in dividends to the owner (sole shareholder).

Required

1. Arrange the following asset, liability, and equity titles in a table like Exhibit 1.9: Cash; Accounts Receivable; Office Supplies; Office Equipment; Excavating Equipment; Accounts Payable; Common Stock; Dividends; Revenues; and Expenses.

2. Use additions and subtractions to show the effects of each transaction on the accounts in the accounting equation. Show new balances after each transaction.

3. Use the increases and decreases in the columns of the table from part 2 to prepare an income statement, a statement of retained earnings, and a statement of cash flows—each of these for the current month. Also prepare a balance sheet as of the end of the month.

Check   (2) Ending balances: Cash, $87,545; Accounts Payable, $7,100

(3) Net income, $18,245; Total assets, $103,545

Analysis Component

4. Assume that the $5,000 purchase of excavating equipment on July 3 was financed from an owner investment of another $5,000 cash in the business in exchange for more common stock (instead of the purchase conditions described in the transaction). Explain the effect of this change on total assets, total liabilities, and total equity.

Nico Mitchell started a new business, Nico's Solutions, and completed the following transactions during its first year of operations.

Problem 1-9B
Analyzing effects of transactions

C4 P1 P2 A1

a. N. Mitchell invests $90,000 cash and office equipment valued at $20,000 in the company in exchange for its common stock.

b. The company purchased a $150,000 building to use as an office. It paid $40,000 in cash and signed a note payable promising to pay the $110,000 balance over the next ten years.

c. The company purchased office equipment for $25,000 cash.

d. The company purchased $1,200 of office supplies and $1,700 of office equipment on credit.

e. The company paid a local newspaper $750 cash for printing an announcement of the office's opening.

f. The company completed a financial plan for a client and billed that client $2,800 for the service.

g. The company designed a financial plan for another client and immediately collected a $4,000 cash fee.

h. The company paid $11,500 cash in dividends to the owner (sole shareholder).

i. The company received $1,800 cash from the client described in transaction *f*.

j. The company made a payment of $700 cash on the equipment purchased in transaction *d*.

k. The company paid $2,500 cash for the office secretary's wages.

Required

1. Create a table like the one in Exhibit 1.9, using the following headings for the columns: Cash; Accounts Receivable; Office Supplies; Office Equipment; Building; Accounts Payable; Notes Payable; Common Stock; Dividends; Revenues; and Expenses.

2. Use additions and subtractions within the table created in part *1* to show the dollar effects of each transaction on individual items of the accounting equation. Show new balances after each transaction.

3. Once you have completed the table, determine the company's net income.

Check   (2) Ending balances: Cash, $15,350; Expenses, $3,250; Notes Payable, $110,000

         (3) Net income, $3,550

Problem 1-10B
Computing and interpreting return on assets

A2

AT&T and Verizon produce and market telecommunications products and are competitors. Key financial figures (in $ millions) for these businesses over the past year follow.

Key Figures ($ millions)	AT&T	Verizon
Sales	$126,723	$110,875
Net income	4,184	10,198
Average assets	269,868	225,233

Required

Check   (1*a*) 1.6%; (1*b*) 4.5%

1. Compute return on assets for (*a*) AT&T and (*b*) Verizon.

2. Which company is more successful in the total amount of sales to consumers?

3. Which company is more successful in returning net income from its assets invested?

Analysis Component

4. Write a one-paragraph memorandum explaining which company you would invest your money in and why. (Limit your explanation to the information provided.)

Problem 1-11B
Determining expenses, liabilities, equity, and return on assets

A1 A2

Carbondale Company manufactures, markets, and sells snowmobile and snowmobile equipment and accessories. The average total assets for Carbondale is $3,000,000. In its most recent year, Carbondale reported net income of $201,000 on revenues of $1,400,000.

Required

1. What is Carbondale Company's return on assets?

2. Does return on assets seem satisfactory for Carbondale given that its competitors average a 9.5% return on assets?

Check   (3) $1,199,000

         (4) $3,000,000

3. What are the total expenses for Carbondale Company in its most recent year?

4. What is the average total amount of liabilities plus equity for Carbondale Company?

All business decisions involve aspects of risk and return.

Required

Identify both the risk and the return in each of the following activities:

1. Stashing $500 cash under your mattress.

2. Placing a $250 bet on a horse running in the Kentucky Derby.

3. Investing $20,000 in Nike stock.

4. Investing $35,000 in U.S. Savings Bonds.

A start-up company often engages in the following activities during its first year of operations. Classify each of the following activities into one of the three major activities of an organization.

F. Financing   **I.** Investing   **O.** Operating

_____ **1.** Providing client services.   _____ **5.** Supervising workers.

_____ **2.** Obtaining a bank loan.   _____ **6.** Owner investing money in business.

_____ **3.** Purchasing machinery.   _____ **7.** Renting office space.

_____ **4.** Research for its products.   _____ **8.** Paying utilities expenses.

Identify in outline format the three major business activities of an organization. For each of these activities, identify at least two specific transactions or events normally undertaken by the business's owners or its managers.

This serial problem starts in this chapter and continues throughout most chapters of the book. It is most readily solved if you use the Working Papers that accompany this book (but working papers are not required).

SP 1 On October 1, 2013, Adria Lopez launched a computer services company, **Success Systems,** that is organized as a corporation and provides consulting services, computer system installations, and custom program development. Lopez adopts the calendar year for reporting purposes and expects to prepare the company's first set of financial statements on December 31, 2013.

Required

Create a table like the one in Exhibit 1.9 using the following headings for columns: Cash; Accounts Receivable; Computer Supplies; Computer System; Office Equipment; Accounts Payable; Common Stock; Dividends; Revenues; and Expenses. Then use additions and subtractions within the table created to show the dollar effects for each of the following October transactions for Success Systems on the individual items of the accounting equation. Show new balances after each transaction.

Oct. 1 A. Lopez invested $55,000 cash, a $20,000 computer system, and $8,000 of office equipment in the company in exchange for its common stock.

      3 The company purchased $1,420 of computer supplies on credit from Harris Office Products.

      6 The company billed Easy Leasing $4,800 for services performed in installing a new Web server.

      8 The company paid $1,420 cash for the computer supplies purchased from Harris Office Products on October 3.

     10 The company hired Lyn Addie as a part-time assistant for $125 per day, as needed.

     12 The company billed Easy Leasing another $1,400 for services performed.

     15 The company received $4,800 cash from Easy Leasing as partial payment toward its account.

     17 The company paid $805 cash to repair computer equipment damaged when moving it.

     20 The company paid $1,940 cash for advertisements published in the local newspaper.

Check Ending balances: Cash,
$52,560; Revenues, $11,408;
Expenses, $3,620

22   The company received $1,400 cash from Easy Leasing toward its account.
28   The company billed IFM Company $5,208 for services performed.
31   The company paid $875 cash for Lyn Addie's wages for seven days of work this month.
31   The company paid $3,600 cash in dividends to the owner (sole shareholder).

Beyond the Numbers (BTN) is a special problem section aimed to refine communication, conceptual, analysis, and
research skills. It includes many activities helpful in developing an active learning environment.

Beyond the Numbers

**REPORTING IN
ACTION**

A1 A2 A3

Polaris

Check (2) 19.9%

BTN 1-1   Key financial figures for Polaris's fiscal year ended December 31, 2011, follow.

Key Figure	In Thousands
Liabilities + Equity.........	$1,228,024
Net income	227,575
Revenues	2,656,949

Required

1. What is the total amount of assets invested in Polaris?
2. What is Polaris's return on assets for 2011? Its assets at December 31, 2010, equal $1,061,647 (in thousands).
3. How much are total expenses for Polaris for the year ended December 31, 2011?
4. Does Polaris's return on assets for 2011 seem satisfactory if competitors average an 18% return?

Fast Forward

5. Access Polaris's financial statements (Form 10-K) for years ending after December 31, 2011, from its Website (Polaris.com) or from the SEC Website (www.SEC.gov) and compute its return on assets for those years. Compare the December 31, 2011, year-end return on assets to any subsequent years' returns you are able to compute, and interpret the results.

**COMPARATIVE
ANALYSIS**

A1 A2 A3

Polaris

Arctic Cat

Check (2b) 5.0%

BTN 1-2   Key comparative figures ($ thousands) for both Polaris and Arctic Cat follow.

Key Figure	Polaris	Arctic Cat
Liabilities + Equity..........	$1,228,024	$272,906
Net income	227,575	13,007
Revenues and sales	2,656,949	464,651

Required

1. What is the total amount of assets invested in (*a*) Polaris and (*b*) Arctic Cat?
2. What is the return on assets for (*a*) Polaris and (*b*) Arctic Cat? Polaris's beginning-year assets equal $1,061,647 (in thousands) and Arctic Cat's beginning-year assets equal $246,084 (in thousands).
3. How much are expenses for (*a*) Polaris and (*b*) Arctic Cat?
4. Is return on assets satisfactory for (*a*) Polaris and (*b*) Arctic Cat? (Assume competitors average an 18% return.)
5. What can you conclude about Polaris and Arctic Cat from these computations?

BTN 1-3 Craig Thorne works in a public accounting firm and hopes to eventually be a partner. The management of Allnet Company invites Thorne to prepare a bid to audit Allnet's financial statements. In discussing the audit fee, Allnet's management suggests a fee range in which the amount depends on the reported profit of Allnet. The higher its profit, the higher will be the audit fee paid to Thorne's firm.

ETHICS CHALLENGE

C3 C4

Required

1. Identify the parties potentially affected by this audit and the fee plan proposed.

2. What are the ethical factors in this situation? Explain.

3. Would you recommend that Thorne accept this audit fee arrangement? Why or why not?

4. Describe some ethical considerations guiding your recommendation.

BTN 1-4 Refer to this chapter's opening feature about Twitter. Assume that the owners desire to expand their online services to meet people's demands regarding online services. They eventually decide to meet with their banker to discuss a loan to allow Twitter to expand.

COMMUNICATING IN PRACTICE

A1 C2

Required

1. Prepare a half-page report outlining the information you would request from the owners if you were the loan officer.

2. Indicate whether the information you request and your loan decision are affected by the form of business organization for Twitter.

BTN 1-5 Visit the EDGAR database at (www.sec.gov). Access the Form 10-K report of Rocky Mountain Chocolate Factory (ticker RMCF) filed on May 24, 2011, covering its 2011 fiscal year.

TAKING IT TO THE NET

A2

Required

1. Item 6 of the 10-K report provides comparative financial highlights of RMCF for the years 2007–2011. How would you describe the revenue trend for RMCF over this five-year period?

2. Has RMCF been profitable (see net income) over this five-year period? Support your answer.

BTN 1-6 Teamwork is important in today's business world. Successful teams schedule convenient meetings, maintain regular communications, and cooperate with and support their members. This assignment aims to establish support/learning teams, initiate discussions, and set meeting times.

TEAMWORK IN ACTION

C1

Required

1. Form teams and open a team discussion to determine a regular time and place for your team to meet between each scheduled class meeting. Notify your instructor via a memorandum or e-mail message as to when and where your team will hold regularly scheduled meetings.

2. Develop a list of telephone numbers and/or e-mail addresses of your teammates.

ENTREPRENEURIAL DECISION

A1 P1

Check (2) 10.7%

BTN 1-7 Refer to this chapter's opening feature about Twitter. Assume that the owners decide to open a new Website devoted to micro-blogging for accountants and those studying accounting. This new company will be called AccounTwit.

Required

1. AccounTwit obtains a $500,000 loan and the three owners contribute $250,000 in total from their own savings in exchange for common stock in the new company.
   a. What is the new company's total amount of liabilities plus equity?
   b. What is the new company's total amount of assets?
2. If the new company earns $80,250 in net income in the first year of operation, compute its return on assets (assume average assets equal $750,000). Assess its performance if competitors average a 10% return.

HITTING THE ROAD

C2

BTN 1-8 You are to interview a local business owner. (This can be a friend or relative.) Opening lines of communication with members of the business community can provide personal benefits of business networking. If you do not know the owner, you should call ahead to introduce yourself and explain your position as a student and your assignment requirements. You should request a 30-minute appointment for a face-to-face or phone interview to discuss the form of organization and operations of the business. Be prepared to make a good impression.

Required

1. Identify and describe the main operating activities and the form of organization for this business.
2. Determine and explain why the owner(s) chose this particular form of organization.
3. Identify any special advantages and/or disadvantages the owner(s) experiences in operating with this form of business organization.

GLOBAL DECISION

A1 A2 A3

KTM
Polaris
Arctic Cat

BTN 1-9 KTM (KTM.com) is a leading manufacturer of offroad and street motorcycles, and it competes to some extent with both Polaris and Arctic Cat. Key financial figures for KTM follow.

Key Figure*	Euro in Thousands
Average assets.................	465,550
Net income...................	20,818
Revenue.......................	526,801
Return on assets...............	4.5%

* Figures prepared in accordance with International Financial Reporting Standards.

Required

1. Identify any concerns you have in comparing KTM's income and revenue figures to those of Polaris and Arctic Cat (in BTN 1-2) for purposes of making business decisions.
2. Identify any concerns you have in comparing KTM's return on assets ratio to those of Polaris and Arctic Cat (computed for BTN 1-2) for purposes of making business decisions.

ANSWERS TO MULTIPLE CHOICE QUIZ

1. c; $450,000 is the actual cost incurred.
2. b; revenue is recorded when earned.
3. d;

Assets	=	Liabilities	+	Equity
+$100,000	=	+35,000	+	?

Change in equity = $100,000 − $35,000 = $65,000

4. a
5. a

Analyzing and Recording Transactions

A Look Back

Chapter 1 defined accounting and introduced financial statements. We described forms of organizations and identified users and uses of accounting. We defined the accounting equation and applied it to transaction analysis.

A Look at This Chapter

This chapter focuses on the accounting process. We describe transactions and source documents, and we explain the analysis and recording of transactions. The accounting equation, T-account, general ledger, trial balance, and debits and credits are key tools in the accounting process.

A Look Ahead

Chapter 3 extends our focus on processing information. We explain the importance of adjusting accounts and the procedures in preparing financial statements.

Learning Objectives

CONCEPTUAL

C1 Explain the steps in processing transactions and the role of source documents. (p. 52)

C2 Describe an account and its use in recording transactions. (p. 53)

C3 Describe a ledger and a chart of accounts. (p. 56)

C4 Define *debits* and *credits* and explain double-entry accounting. (p. 57)

ANALYTICAL

A1 Analyze the impact of transactions on accounts and financial statements. (p. 61)

A2 Compute the debt ratio and describe its use in analyzing financial condition. (p. 71)

PROCEDURAL

P1 Record transactions in a journal and post entries to a ledger. (p. 58)

P2 Prepare and explain the use of a trial balance. (p. 67)

P3 Prepare financial statements from business transactions. (p. 68)

Decision Insight

Some Like It Hot

"You can still excel if you work really hard and follow your dreams!"

—MISA CHIEN (ON LEFT)

LOS ANGELES—"We call our customers Nomsters!" exclaims Misa. "There's an entire Nom Nom movement." **Nom Nom Truck (NomNomTruck.com)** is a mobile food business and the brainchild of Misa Chien and Jennifer Green. (Nom Nom is drawn from the sound "nom nom nom" when eating something "oh so tasty.") Their specialty is the Vietnamese baguette sandwich, called *banh mi*, a sort of Vietnamese subsandwich. "It's portable, it's fast, and has a fresh taste that you can't get from a burrito or hamburger," states Jennifer.

To pursue their business ambitions, Misa and Jennifer took business courses. They learned about recordkeeping processes, transaction analysis, inventory accounting, and financial statement reporting. "We did lose a lot of money initially," explains Misa. "We didn't have the right pricing structure." With careful analysis of their accounting reports, Misa and Jennifer solved the problem. Their business is now profitable and they have a reliable accounting system to help them make good business decisions.

"We had to account for product expenses, trucking expenses, supplier payments, and other expenses such as salaries, rent and insurance," explains Misa. At the same time, the two have grown sales and expanded their food offerings. "Sales have definitely increased," says Misa. "People totally embraced us!"

The two insist that it is crucial to track and account for all revenues and expenses, including what is invested in the business. They maintain that success requires proper accounting for and analysis of the financial side. "There was a point when we couldn't keep up," recounts Misa. Given the importance of accounting, "we [now] have a bookkeeper and an accountant!" The women emphasize the value of a great business model along with a sound accounting system. "It's really easy to balance both now that we've been in the business for awhile," explains Misa.

"The bigger message of our company", says Jennifer, "is that each of us can succeed no matter what our starting point". "You have to be responsible for yourself," adds Misa. "We want to make people happy through our food!"

[Sources: *Nom Nom Truck Website,* January 2013; *Inc.,* June 2011; *Bundle.com,* October 2010; *VirgoBlue.net,* September 2011; *CNNMoney,* October 2011.]

Chapter Preview

Financial statements report on the financial performance and condition of an organization. Knowledge of their preparation, organization, and analysis is important. A main goal of this chapter is to illustrate how transactions are recorded, how they are reflected in financial statements, and how they impact analysis of financial statements. Debits and credits are introduced and identified as a tool in helping analyze and process transactions.

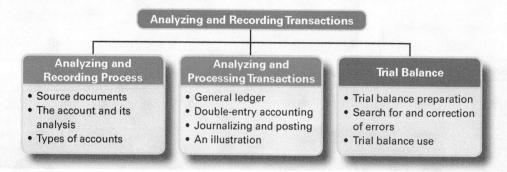

Analyzing and Recording Transactions

Analyzing and Recording Process	Analyzing and Processing Transactions	Trial Balance
• Source documents • The account and its analysis • Types of accounts	• General ledger • Double-entry accounting • Journalizing and posting • An illustration	• Trial balance preparation • Search for and correction of errors • Trial balance use

ANALYZING AND RECORDING PROCESS

EXHIBIT 2.1

The Analyzing and Recording Process

The accounting process identifies business transactions and events, analyzes and records their effects, and summarizes and presents information in reports and financial statements. These reports and statements are used for making investing, lending, and other business decisions. The steps in the accounting process that focus on *analyzing and recording* transactions and events are shown in Exhibit 2.1.

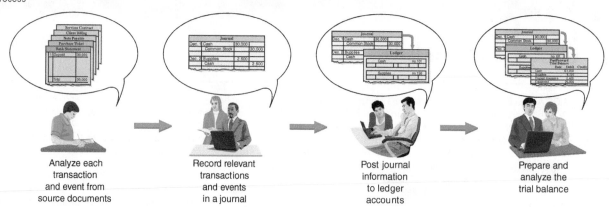

Analyze each transaction and event from source documents

Record relevant transactions and events in a journal

Post journal information to ledger accounts

Prepare and analyze the trial balance

C1 Explain the steps in processing transactions and the role of source documents.

Business transactions and events are the starting points. Relying on source documents, the transactions and events are analyzed using the accounting equation to understand how they affect company performance and financial position. These effects are recorded in accounting records, informally referred to as the *accounting books,* or simply the *books.* Additional steps such as posting and then preparing a trial balance help summarize and classify the effects of transactions and events. Ultimately, the accounting process provides information in useful reports or financial statements to decision makers.

Source Documents

Source documents identify and describe transactions and events entering the accounting process. They are the sources of accounting information and can be in either hard copy or electronic form. Examples are sales tickets, checks, purchase orders, bills from suppliers, employee earnings records, and bank statements. To illustrate, when an item is purchased on credit, the seller usually prepares at least two copies of a sales invoice. One copy is given to the buyer. Another copy, often sent electronically, results in an entry in the seller's information system to record the sale. Sellers use invoices for recording sales and for control; buyers use them for recording purchases and for monitoring purchasing activity. Many cash registers record information for each sale on a tape or electronic file locked inside the register. This record can be used as a source document for recording sales in the accounting records. Source documents, especially if obtained from outside the organization, provide objective and reliable evidence about transactions and events and their amounts.

Point: To ensure that all sales are rung up on the register, most sellers require customers to have their receipts to exchange or return purchased items.

■ Decision Ethics

Cashier   Your manager requires that you, as cashier, immediately enter each sale. Recently, lunch hour traffic has increased and the assistant manager asks you to avoid delays by taking customers' cash and making change without entering sales. The assistant manager says she will add up cash and enter sales after lunch. She says that, in this way, the register will always match the cash amount when the manager arrives at three o'clock. What do you do? ■   [Answer—p. 76]

The Account and Its Analysis

An **account** is a record of increases and decreases in a specific asset, liability, equity, revenue, or expense item. Information from an account is analyzed, summarized, and presented in reports and financial statements. The **general ledger,** or simply **ledger,** is a record containing all accounts used by a company. The ledger is often in electronic form. While most companies' ledgers contain similar accounts, a company often uses one or more unique accounts because of its type of operations. As shown in Exhibit 2.2, accounts are classified into three general categories based on the accounting equation: asset, liability, or equity.

C2 Describe an account and its use in recording transactions.

EXHIBIT 2.2

Accounts Organized by the Accounting Equation

Asset Accounts   Assets are resources owned or controlled by a company, and those resources have expected future benefits. Most accounting systems include (at a minimum) separate accounts for the assets described here.

Cash   A *Cash* account reflects a company's cash balance. All increases and decreases in cash are recorded in the Cash account. It includes money and any medium of exchange that a bank accepts for deposit (coins, checks, money orders, and checking account balances).

Accounts Receivable   *Accounts receivable* are held by a seller and refer to promises of payment from customers to sellers. These transactions are often called *credit sales* or *sales on account* (or *on credit*). Accounts receivable are increased by credit sales and are decreased by customer payments. A company needs a separate record for each customer, but for now, we use the simpler practice of recording all increases and decreases in receivables in a single account called Accounts Receivable.

Point: Customers and others who owe a company are called its **debtors.**

Note Receivable   A *note receivable,* or promissory note, is a written promise of another entity to pay a definite sum of money on a specified future date to the holder of the note. A company holding a promissory note signed by another entity has an asset that is recorded in a Note (or Notes) Receivable account.

Prepaid Accounts   *Prepaid accounts* (also called *prepaid expenses*) are assets that represent prepayments of future expenses (*not* current expenses). When the expenses are later incurred, the amounts in prepaid accounts are transferred to expense accounts. Common examples of prepaid accounts include prepaid insurance, prepaid rent, and prepaid services (such as club memberships). Prepaid accounts expire with the passage of time (such as with rent) or through use (such as with prepaid meal tickets). When financial statements are prepared, prepaid accounts are adjusted so that (1) all expired and used prepaid accounts are recorded as regular expenses and (2) all unexpired and unused prepaid accounts are recorded as assets (reflecting future use in future periods). To illustrate,

Point: A college parking fee is a prepaid account from the student's standpoint. At the beginning of the term, it represents an asset that entitles a student to park on or near campus. The benefits of the parking fee expire as the term progresses. At term-end, prepaid parking (asset) equals zero as it has been entirely recorded as parking expense.

when an insurance fee, called a *premium,* is paid in advance, the cost is typically recorded in the asset account Prepaid Insurance. Over time, the expiring portion of the insurance cost is removed from this asset account and reported in expenses on the income statement. Any unexpired portion remains in Prepaid Insurance and is reported on the balance sheet as an asset. (An exception exists for prepaid accounts that will expire or be used before the end of the current accounting period when financial statements are prepared. In this case, the prepayments *can* be recorded immediately as expenses.)

Supplies Accounts　*Supplies* are assets until they are used. When they are used up, their costs are reported as expenses. The costs of unused supplies are recorded in a Supplies asset account. Supplies are often grouped by purpose—for example, office supplies and store supplies. *Office supplies* include stationery, paper, toner, and pens. *Store supplies* include packaging materials, plastic and paper bags, gift boxes and cartons, and cleaning materials. The costs of these unused supplies can be recorded in an Office Supplies or a Store Supplies asset account. When supplies are used, their costs are transferred from the asset accounts to expense accounts.

Equipment Accounts　*Equipment* is an asset. When equipment is used and gets worn down, its cost is gradually reported as an expense (called depreciation). Equipment is often grouped by its purpose—for example, office equipment and store equipment. *Office equipment* includes computers, printers, desks, chairs, and shelves. Costs incurred for these items are recorded in an Office Equipment asset account. The Store Equipment account includes the costs of assets used in a store, such as counters, showcases, ladders, hoists, and cash registers.

Buildings Accounts　*Buildings* such as stores, offices, warehouses, and factories are assets because they provide expected future benefits to those who control or own them. Their costs are recorded in a Buildings asset account. When several buildings are owned, separate accounts are sometimes kept for each of them.

Land　The cost of *land* owned by a business is recorded in a Land account. The cost of buildings located on the land is separately recorded in one or more building accounts.

Decision Insight

Women Entrepreneurs　The Center for Women's Business Research reports that women-owned businesses, such as **Nom Nom Truck**, are growing and that they:

- Total approximately 11 million and employ nearly 20 million workers.
- Generate $2.5 trillion in annual sales and tend to embrace technology.
- Are philanthropic—70% of owners volunteer at least once per month.
- Are more likely funded by individual investors (73%) than venture firms (15%). ■

Liability Accounts　Liabilities are claims (by creditors) against assets, which means they are obligations to transfer assets or provide products or services to others. **Creditors** are individuals and organizations that have rights to receive payments from a company. If a company fails to pay its obligations, the law gives creditors a right to force the sale of that company's assets to obtain the money to meet creditors' claims. When assets are sold under these conditions, creditors are paid first, but only up to the amount of their claims. Any remaining money, the residual, goes to the owners of the company. Creditors often use a balance sheet to help decide whether to loan money to a company. A loan is less risky if the borrower's liabilities are small in comparison to assets because this means there are more resources than claims on resources. Common liability accounts are described here.

Accounts Payable　*Accounts payable* refer to oral or implied promises to pay later, which usually arise from purchases of merchandise. Payables can also arise from purchases of supplies, equipment, and services. Accounting systems keep separate records about each creditor. We describe these individual records in Chapter 4.

Note Payable　A *note payable* refers to a formal promise, usually denoted by the signing of a promissory note, to pay a future amount. It is recorded in either a short-term Note Payable account or a long-term Note Payable account, depending on when it must be repaid. We explain details of short- and long-term classification in Chapter 3.

Unearned Revenue Accounts   **Unearned revenue** refers to a liability that is settled in the future when a company delivers its products or services. When customers pay in advance for products or services (before revenue is earned), the revenue recognition principle requires that the seller consider this payment as unearned revenue. Examples of unearned revenue include magazine subscriptions collected in advance by a publisher, sales of gift certificates by stores, and season ticket sales by sports teams. The seller would record these in liability accounts such as Unearned Subscriptions, Unearned Store Sales, and Unearned Ticket Revenue. When products and services are later delivered, the earned portion of the unearned revenue is transferred to revenue accounts such as Subscription Fees, Store Sales, and Ticket Sales.[1]

Point: If a subscription is canceled, the publisher is expected to refund the unused portion to the subscriber.

Accrued Liabilities   *Accrued liabilities* are amounts owed that are not yet paid. Examples are wages payable, taxes payable, and interest payable. These are often recorded in separate liability accounts by the same title. If they are not large in amount, one or more ledger accounts can be added and reported as a single amount on the balance sheet. (Financial statements often have amounts reported that are a summation of several ledger accounts.)

Decision Insight

Revenue Spread   The New York Giants have *Unearned Revenues* of about $100 million in advance ticket sales. When the team plays its home games, it settles this liability to its ticket holders and then transfers the amount earned to *Ticket Revenues.* ■

Equity Accounts   The owner's claim on a company's assets is called *equity,* or *stockholders' equity,* or *shareholders' equity.* Equity is the owners' *residual interest* in the assets of a business after deducting liabilities. Equity is impacted by four types of accounts: common stock, dividends, revenues, and expenses. We show this visually in Exhibit 2.3 by expanding the accounting equation. (As Chapter 1 explains, the accounts for dividends, revenues, and expenses are reflected in the retained earnings account, and that account is reported in the balance sheet.)

Point: Equity is also called *net assets.*

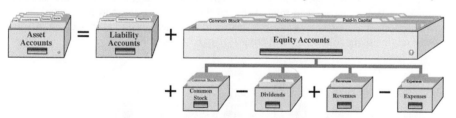

EXHIBIT 2.3

Expanded Accounting Equation

Common Stock   When an owner invests in a company in exchange for common stock, the invested amount is recorded in an account titled **Common Stock.** Any further owner investments are recorded in this account.

Point: The Dividends account is sometimes referred to as a *contra equity* account because it reduces the normal balance of equity.

Dividends   When the company pays any cash dividends, it decreases both the company's assets and its total equity. Dividends are not expenses of the business. They are simply the opposite of owner investments. A **Dividends** account is used in recording asset distributions to stockholders (owners).

Point: The withdrawal of assets by the owners of a corporation is called a *dividend.*

Revenue Accounts   Revenues and expenses also impact equity. Examples of revenue accounts are Sales, Commissions Earned, Professional Fees Earned, Rent Revenue, and Interest Revenue. *Revenues increase equity* and result from products and services provided to customers.

---

[1] In practice, account titles vary. As one example, Subscription Fees is sometimes called Subscription Fees Revenue, Subscription Fees Earned, or Earned Subscription Fees. As another example, Rent Earned is sometimes called Rent Revenue, Rental Revenue, or Earned Rent Revenue. We must use good judgment when reading financial statements because titles can differ even within the same industry. For example, product sales are called *sales* at Polaris, *net sales* at Arctic Cat, and *net revenues* at Piaggio. Generally, the term *revenues* or *fees* is more commonly used with service businesses, and *net sales* or *sales* with product businesses.

Expense Accounts   Examples of expense accounts are Advertising Expense, Store Supplies Expense, Office Salaries Expense, Office Supplies Expense, Rent Expense, Utilities Expense, and Insurance Expense. *Expenses decrease equity* and result from assets and services used in a company's operations. The variety of revenues and expenses can be seen by looking at the *chart of accounts* that follows the index at the back of this book. (Different companies sometimes use different account titles than those in this book's chart of accounts. For example, some might use Interest Revenue instead of Interest Earned, or Rental Expense instead of Rent Expense. It is important only that an account title describe the item it represents.)

Decision Insight

Sporting Accounts   The Miami Heat, Los Angeles Lakers, and the other NBA teams have the following major revenue and expense accounts:

Revenues	Expenses
Basketball ticket sales	Team salaries
TV & radio broadcast fees	Game costs
Advertising revenues	NBA franchise costs
Basketball playoff receipts	Promotional costs ■

ANALYZING AND PROCESSING TRANSACTIONS

This section explains several tools and processes that comprise an accounting system. These include a ledger, T-account, debits and credits, double-entry accounting, journalizing, and posting.

Ledger and Chart of Accounts

C3 Describe a ledger and a chart of accounts.

The collection of all accounts and their balances for an information system is called a *ledger* (or *general ledger*). If accounts are in files on a hard drive, the sum of those files is the ledger. If the accounts are pages in a file, that file is the ledger. A company's size and diversity of operations affect the number of accounts needed. A small company can get by with as few as 20 or 30 accounts; a large company can require several thousand. The **chart of accounts** is a list of all ledger accounts and includes an identification number assigned to each account. A small business might use the following numbering system for its accounts:

Chart of Accounts	
101–199	Asset accounts
201–299	Liability accounts
301–399	Equity accounts
401–499	Revenue accounts
501–699	Expense accounts

These numbers provide a three-digit code that is useful in recordkeeping. In this case, the first digit assigned to asset accounts is a 1, the first digit assigned to liability accounts is a 2, and so on. The second and third digits relate to the accounts' subcategories. Exhibit 2.4 shows a partial

EXHIBIT 2.4

Partial Chart of Accounts for FastForward

Chart of Accounts							
Acct. No.	Account Name	Acct. No.	Account Name	Acct. No.	Account Name
101	Cash	236	Unearned consulting revenue	406	Rental revenue
106	Accounts receivable			622	Salaries expense
126	Supplies	307	Common stock	637	Insurance expense
128	Prepaid insurance	318	Retained earnings	640	Rent expense
167	Equipment	319	Dividends	652	Supplies expense
201	Accounts payable	403	Consulting revenue	690	Utilities expense

chart of accounts for FastForward, the focus company of Chapter 1. (Please review the more complete chart of accounts that follows the index at the back of this book.)

Debits and Credits

A **T-account** represents a ledger account and is a tool used to understand the effects of one or more transactions. Its name comes from its shape like the letter T. The layout of a T-account, shown in Exhibit 2.5, is (1) the account title on top, (2) a left, or debit side, and (3) a right, or credit, side.

The left side of an account is called the **debit** side, often abbreviated *Dr.* The right side is called the **credit** side, abbreviated *Cr.*[2] To enter amounts on the left side of an account is to *debit* the account. To enter amounts on the right side is to *credit* the account. Do not make the error of thinking that the terms *debit* and *credit* mean increase or decrease. Whether a debit or a credit is an increase or decrease depends on the account. For an account where a debit is an increase, the credit is a decrease; for an account where a debit is a decrease, the credit is an increase. The difference between total debits and total credits for an account, including any beginning balance, is the **account balance.** When the sum of debits exceeds the sum of credits, the account has a *debit balance.* It has a *credit balance* when the sum of credits exceeds the sum of debits. When the sum of debits equals the sum of credits, the account has a *zero balance.*

| C4 | Define *debits* and *credits* and explain double-entry accounting. |

EXHIBIT 2.5

The T-Account

Account Title	
(Left side)	(Right side)
Debit	*Credit*

Point: Think of *debit* and *credit* as accounting directions for left and right.

Double-Entry Accounting

Double-entry accounting requires that for each transaction:

- At least two accounts are involved, with at least one debit and one credit.
- The total amount debited must equal the total amount credited.
- The accounting equation must not be violated.

This means the sum of the debits for all entries must equal the sum of the credits for all entries, and the sum of debit account balances in the ledger must equal the sum of credit account balances.

The system for recording debits and credits follows from the usual accounting equation—see Exhibit 2.6. Two points are important here. First, like any simple mathematical relation, net increases or decreases on one side have equal net effects on the other side. For example, a net increase in assets must be accompanied by an identical net increase on the liabilities and equity

"Total debits equal total credits for each entry."

Assets		=	Liabilities		+	Equity	
Debit for increases	**Credit for decreases**		**Debit for decreases**	**Credit for increases**		**Debit for decreases**	**Credit for increases**
+	**−**		**−**	**+**		**−**	**+**
Normal				**Normal**			**Normal**

EXHIBIT 2.6

Debits and Credits in the Accounting Equation

side. Recall that some transactions affect only one side of the equation, meaning that two or more accounts on one side are affected, but their net effect on this one side is zero. Second, the left side is the *normal balance* side for assets, and the right side is the *normal balance* side for liabilities and equity. This matches their layout in the accounting equation where assets are on the left side of this equation, and liabilities and equity are on the right.

Recall that equity increases from revenues and stock issuances, and it decreases from expenses and dividends. These important equity relations are conveyed by expanding the accounting equation to include debits and credits in double-entry form as shown in Exhibit 2.7.

Increases (credits) to common stock and revenues *increase* equity; increases (debits) to dividends and expenses *decrease* equity. The normal balance of each account (asset, liability, common stock, dividends, revenue, or expense) refers to the left or right (debit or credit) side

Point: Debits and credits do not mean favorable or unfavorable. A debit to an asset increases it, as does a debit to an expense. A credit to a liability increases it, as does a credit to a revenue.

---

[2] These abbreviations are remnants of 18th-century English recordkeeping practices where the terms *debitor* and *creditor* were used instead of *debit* and *credit*. The abbreviations use the first and last letters of these terms, just as we still do for Saint (St.) and Doctor (Dr.).

EXHIBIT 2.7

Debit and Credit Effects for
Component Accounts

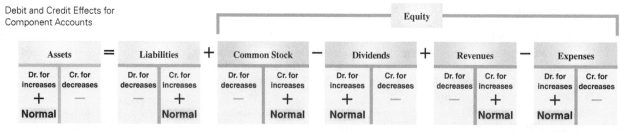

where *increases* are recorded. Understanding these diagrams and rules is required to prepare, analyze, and interpret financial statements.

The T-account for FastForward's Cash account, reflecting its first 11 transactions (from Exhibit 1.9), is shown in Exhibit 2.8. The total increases in its Cash account are $36,100, the total decreases are $31,300, and the account's debit balance is $4,800. (We illustrate use of T-accounts later in this chapter.)

EXHIBIT 2.8

Computing the Balance for
a T-Account

Point: The ending balance is on the side with the larger dollar amount. Also, a plus (+) and minus (−) are not used in a T-account.

Cash			
Receive investment by owner for stock	30,000	Purchase of supplies	2,500
Consulting services revenue earned	4,200	Purchase of equipment	26,000
Collection of account receivable	1,900	Payment of rent	1,000
		Payment of salary	700
		Payment of account payable	900
		Payment of cash dividend	200
Balance	4,800		

Quick Check

Answers — p. 77

1. Identify examples of accounting source documents.
2. Explain the importance of source documents.
3. Identify each of the following as either an asset, a liability, or equity: *(a)* Prepaid Rent, *(b)* Unearned Fees, *(c)* Building, *(d)* Wages Payable, and *(e)* Office Supplies.
4. What is an account? What is a ledger?
5. What determines the number and types of accounts a company uses?
6. Does *debit* always mean increase and *credit* always mean decrease?
7. Describe a chart of accounts.

Journalizing and Posting Transactions

P1 Record transactions in a journal and post entries to a ledger.

Processing transactions is a crucial part of accounting. The four usual steps of this process are depicted in Exhibit 2.9. Steps 1 and 2—involving transaction analysis and the accounting equation—were introduced in prior sections. This section extends that discussion and focuses on steps 3 and 4 of the accounting process. Step 3 is to record each transaction chronologically in a journal. A **journal** gives a complete record of each transaction in one place. It also shows debits and credits for each transaction. The process of recording transactions in a journal is called **journalizing.** Step 4 is to transfer (or *post*) entries from the journal to the ledger. The process of transferring journal entry information to the ledger is called **posting.**

Journalizing Transactions   The process of journalizing transactions requires an understanding of a journal. While companies can use various journals, every company uses a **general journal.** It can be used to record any transaction and includes the following information about each transaction: ⓐ date of transaction, ⓑ titles of affected accounts, ⓒ dollar amount of each

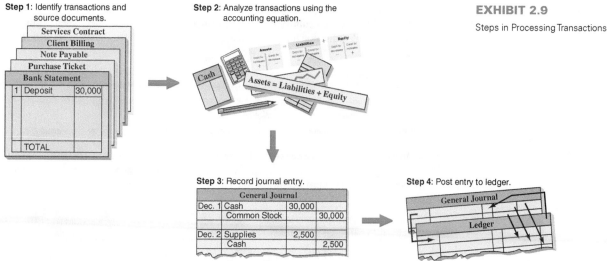

EXHIBIT 2.9

Steps in Processing Transactions

debit and credit, and ⓓ explanation of the transaction. Exhibit 2.10 shows how the first two transactions of FastForward are recorded in a general journal. This process is similar for manual and computerized systems. Computerized journals are often designed to look like a manual journal page, and also include error-checking routines that ensure debits equal credits for each entry. Shortcuts allow recordkeepers to select account names and numbers from pull-down menus.

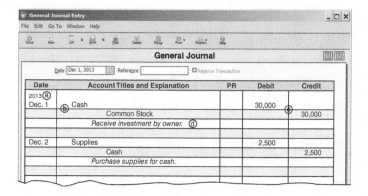

EXHIBIT 2.10

Partial General Journal for FastForward

To record entries in a general journal, apply these steps; refer to the entries in Exhibit 2.10 when reviewing these steps.

a. Date the transaction: Enter the year at the top of the first column and the month and day on the first line of each journal entry.

b. Enter titles of accounts debited and then enter amounts in the Debit column on the same line. Account titles are taken from the chart of accounts and are aligned with the left margin of the Account Titles and Explanation column.

c. Enter titles of accounts credited and then enter amounts in the Credit column on the same line. Account titles are from the chart of accounts and are indented from the left margin of the Account Titles and Explanation column to distinguish them from debited accounts.

d. Enter a brief explanation of the transaction on the line below the entry (it often references a source document). This explanation is indented about half as far as the credited account titles to avoid confusing it with accounts, and it is italicized.

Point: There are no exact rules for writing journal entry explanations. An explanation should be short yet describe why an entry is made.

A blank line is left between each journal entry for clarity. When a transaction is first recorded, the **posting reference (PR) column** is left blank (in a manual system). Later, when posting entries to the ledger, the identification numbers of the individual ledger accounts are entered in the PR column.

 IFRS

IFRS requires that companies report the following four basic financial statements with explanatory notes:

- Balance sheet
- Statement of changes in equity (or statement of recognized revenue and expense)
- Income statement
- Statement of cash flows

IFRS does not prescribe specific formats; and comparative information is required for the preceding period only. ■

Balance Column Account   T-accounts are simple and direct means to show how the accounting process works. However, actual accounting systems need more structure and therefore use **balance column accounts,** such as that in Exhibit 2.11.

EXHIBIT 2.11

Cash Account in Balance Column Format

General Ledger					
Cash					Account No. 101
Date	Explanation	PR	Debit	Credit	Balance
2013 Dec. 1		G1	30,000		30,000
Dec. 2		G1		2,500	27,500
Dec. 3		G1		26,000	1,500
Dec. 10		G1	4,200		5,700

The balance column account format is similar to a T-account in having columns for debits and credits. It is different in including transaction date and explanation columns. It also has a column with the balance of the account after each entry is recorded. To illustrate, FastForward's Cash account in Exhibit 2.11 is debited on December 1 for the $30,000 owner investment, yielding a $30,000 debit balance. The account is credited on December 2 for $2,500, yielding a $27,500 debit balance. On December 3, it is credited again, this time for $26,000, and its debit balance is reduced to $1,500. The Cash account is debited for $4,200 on December 10, and its debit balance increases to $5,700; and so on.

Point: Explanations are typically included in ledger accounts only for unusual transactions or events.

EXHIBIT 2.12

Posting an Entry to the Ledger

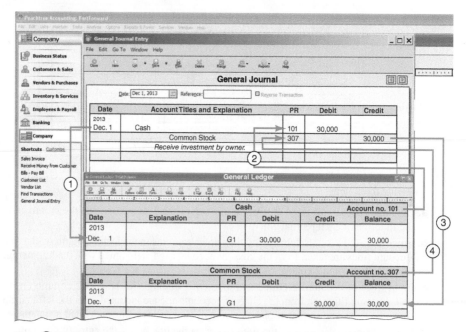

Point: The fundamental concepts of a manual (pencil-and-paper) system are identical to those of a computerized information system.

Key: ① Identify debit account in Ledger: enter date, journal page, amount, and balance.
  ② Enter the debit account number from the Ledger in the PR column of the journal.
  ③ Identify credit account in Ledger: enter date, journal page, amount, and balance.
  ④ Enter the credit account number from the Ledger in the PR column of the journal.

The heading of the Balance column does not show whether it is a debit or credit balance. Instead, an account is assumed to have a *normal balance*. Unusual events can sometimes temporarily give an account an abnormal balance. An *abnormal balance* refers to a balance on the side where decreases are recorded. For example, a customer might mistakenly overpay a bill. This gives that customer's account receivable an abnormal (credit) balance. An abnormal balance is often identified by circling it or by entering it in red or some other unusual color. A zero balance for an account is usually shown by writing zeros or a dash in the Balance column to avoid confusion between a zero balance and one omitted in error.

Posting Journal Entries   Step 4 of processing transactions is to post journal entries to ledger accounts (see Exhibit 2.9). To ensure that the ledger is up-to-date, entries are posted as soon as possible. This might be daily, weekly, or when time permits. All entries must be posted to the ledger before financial statements are prepared to ensure that account balances are up-to-date. When entries are posted to the ledger, the debits in journal entries are transferred into ledger accounts as debits, and credits are transferred into ledger accounts as credits. Exhibit 2.12 shows the *four steps to post a journal entry*. First, identify the ledger account that is debited in the entry; then, in the ledger, enter the entry date, the journal and page in its PR column, the debit amount, and the new balance of the ledger account. (The letter *G* shows it came from the General Journal.) Second, enter the ledger account number in the PR column of the journal. Steps 3 and 4 repeat the first two steps for credit entries and amounts. The posting process creates a link between the ledger and the journal entry. This link is a useful cross-reference for tracing an amount from one record to another.

> **Point:** Computerized systems often provide a code beside a balance such as *dr.* or *cr.* to identify its balance. Posting is automatic and immediate with accounting software.

> **Point:** A journal is often referred to as the *book of original entry.* The ledger is referred to as the *book of final entry* because financial statements are prepared from it.

Analyzing Transactions — An Illustration

We return to the activities of FastForward to show how double-entry accounting is useful in analyzing and processing transactions. Analysis of each transaction follows the four steps of Exhibit 2.9.

|A1| Analyze the impact of transactions on accounts and financial statements.

Step 1 Identify the transaction and any source documents.
Step 2 Analyze the transaction using the accounting equation.
Step 3 Record the transaction in journal entry form applying double-entry accounting.
Step 4 Post the entry (for simplicity, we use T-accounts to represent ledger accounts).

Study each transaction thoroughly before proceeding to the next. The first 11 transactions are from Chapter 1, and we analyze five additional December transactions of FastForward (numbered 12 through 16) that were omitted earlier.

> **Point:** In the Demonstration Problem at the chapter end we show how to use "balance column accounts" for the ledger.

FASTForward

1. Receive investment by Owner

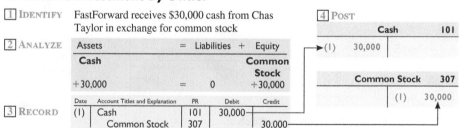

2. Purchase Supplies for Cash

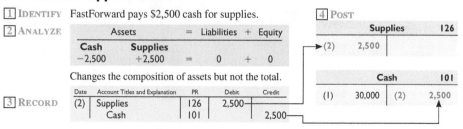

3. Purchase Equipment for Cash

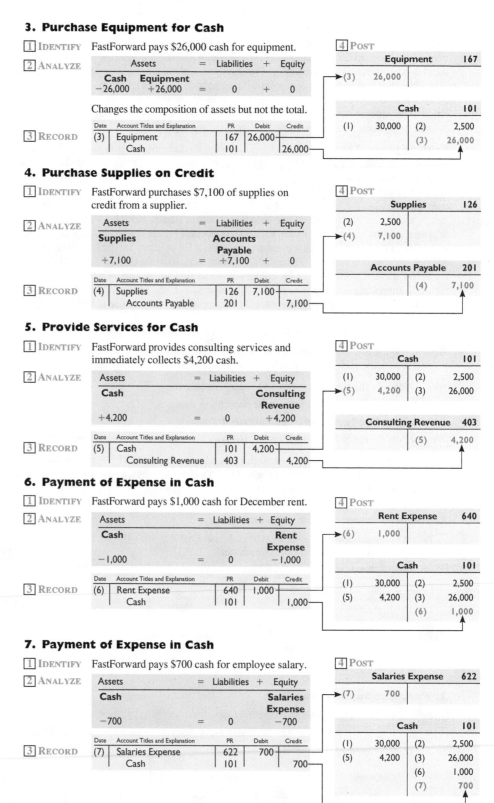

1 IDENTIFY   FastForward pays $26,000 cash for equipment.

2 ANALYZE

Assets	=	Liabilities	+	Equity

Cash	Equipment				
−26,000	+26,000	=	0	+	0

Changes the composition of assets but not the total.

3 RECORD

Date	Account Titles and Explanation	PR	Debit	Credit
(3)	Equipment	167	26,000	
	Cash	101		26,000

4 POST

Equipment		167
(3)	26,000	

Cash		101
(1)	30,000	(2)	2,500
		(3)	26,000

4. Purchase Supplies on Credit

1 IDENTIFY   FastForward purchases $7,100 of supplies on credit from a supplier.

2 ANALYZE

Assets	=	Liabilities	+	Equity

Supplies		Accounts Payable		
+7,100	=	+7,100	+	0

3 RECORD

Date	Account Titles and Explanation	PR	Debit	Credit
(4)	Supplies	126	7,100	
	Accounts Payable	201		7,100

4 POST

Supplies		126
(2)	2,500	
(4)	7,100	

Accounts Payable		201
		(4)	7,100

5. Provide Services for Cash

1 IDENTIFY   FastForward provides consulting services and immediately collects $4,200 cash.

2 ANALYZE

Assets	=	Liabilities	+	Equity

Cash			Consulting Revenue
+4,200	=	0	+4,200

3 RECORD

Date	Account Titles and Explanation	PR	Debit	Credit
(5)	Cash	101	4,200	
	Consulting Revenue	403		4,200

4 POST

Cash		101
(1)	30,000	(2)	2,500
(5)	4,200	(3)	26,000

Consulting Revenue		403
		(5)	4,200

6. Payment of Expense in Cash

1 IDENTIFY   FastForward pays $1,000 cash for December rent.

2 ANALYZE

Assets	=	Liabilities	+	Equity

Cash			Rent Expense
−1,000	=	0	−1,000

3 RECORD

Date	Account Titles and Explanation	PR	Debit	Credit
(6)	Rent Expense	640	1,000	
	Cash	101		1,000

4 POST

Rent Expense		640
(6)	1,000	

Cash		101
(1)	30,000	(2)	2,500
(5)	4,200	(3)	26,000
		(6)	1,000

7. Payment of Expense in Cash

Point: *Salary* usually refers to compensation for an employee who receives a fixed amount for a given time period, whereas *wages* usually refers to compensation based on time worked.

1 IDENTIFY   FastForward pays $700 cash for employee salary.

2 ANALYZE

Assets	=	Liabilities	+	Equity

Cash			Salaries Expense
−700	=	0	−700

3 RECORD

Date	Account Titles and Explanation	PR	Debit	Credit
(7)	Salaries Expense	622	700	
	Cash	101		700

4 POST

Salaries Expense		622
(7)	700	

Cash		101
(1)	30,000	(2)	2,500
(5)	4,200	(3)	26,000
		(6)	1,000
		(7)	700

8. Provide Consulting and Rental Services on Credit

1 IDENTIFY   FastForward provides consulting services of $1,600 and rents its test facilities for $300. The customer is billed $1,900 for these services.

2 ANALYZE

3 RECORD

4 POST

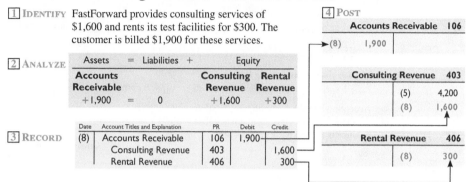

Point: Transaction 8 is a **compound journal entry,** which affects three or more accounts.

9. Receipt of Cash on Account

1 IDENTIFY   FastForward receives $1,900 cash from the client billed in transaction 8.

2 ANALYZE

3 RECORD

4 POST

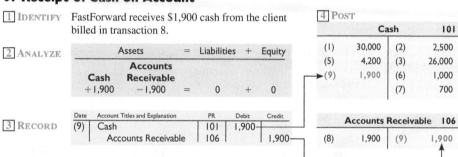

Point: The *revenue recognition principle* requires revenue to be recognized when earned, which is when the company provides products and services to a customer. This is not necessarily the same time that the customer pays. A customer can pay before or after products or services are provided.

10. Partial Payment of Accounts Payable

1 IDENTIFY   FastForward pays CalTech Supply $900 cash toward the payable of transaction 4.

2 ANALYZE

3 RECORD

4 POST

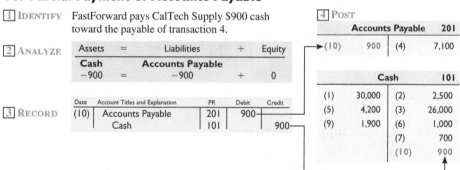

11. Payment of Cash Dividend

1 IDENTIFY   FastForward pays $200 cash for dividends.

2 ANALYZE

3 RECORD

4 POST

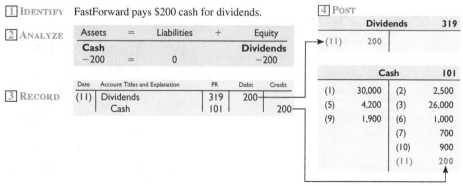

12. Receipt of Cash for Future Services

1 IDENTIFY   FastForward receives $3,000 cash in advance of providing consulting services to a customer.

2 ANALYZE

Assets	=	Liabilities	+	Equity
Cash	=	**Unearned Consulting Revenue**	+	
+3,000	=	+3,000	+	0

Accepting $3,000 cash obligates FastForward to perform future services and is a liability. No revenue is earned until services are provided.

3 RECORD

Date	Account Titles and Explanation	PR	Debit	Credit
(12)	Cash	101	3,000	
	Unearned Consulting Revenue	236		3,000

4 POST

Cash			101
(1)	30,000	(2)	2,500
(5)	4,200	(3)	26,000
(9)	1,900	(6)	1,000
(12)	3,000	(7)	700
		(10)	900
		(11)	200

Unearned Consulting Revenue			236
		(12)	3,000

13. Pay Cash for Future Insurance Coverage

1 IDENTIFY   FastForward pays $2,400 cash (insurance premium) for a 24-month insurance policy. Coverage begins on December 1.

2 ANALYZE

Assets		=	Liabilities	+	Equity
Cash	**Prepaid Insurance**	=		+	
−2,400	+2,400	=	0	+	0

Changes the composition of assets from cash to prepaid insurance. Expense is incurred as insurance coverage expires.

3 RECORD

Date	Account Titles and Explanation	PR	Debit	Credit
(13)	Prepaid Insurance	128	2,400	
	Cash	101		2,400

4 POST

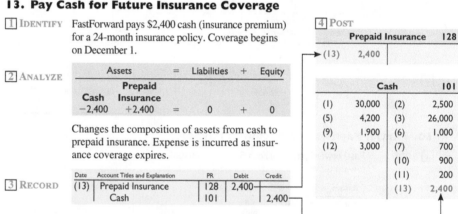

Prepaid Insurance			128
(13)	2,400		

Cash			101
(1)	30,000	(2)	2,500
(5)	4,200	(3)	26,000
(9)	1,900	(6)	1,000
(12)	3,000	(7)	700
		(10)	900
		(11)	200
		(13)	2,400

14. Purchase Supplies for Cash

1 IDENTIFY   FastForward pays $120 cash for supplies.

2 ANALYZE

Assets		=	Liabilities	+	Equity
Cash	**Supplies**	=		+	
−120	+120	=	0	+	0

3 RECORD

Date	Account Titles and Explanation	PR	Debit	Credit
(14)	Supplies	126	120	
	Cash	101		120

4 POST

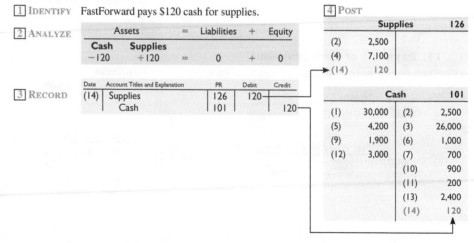

Supplies			126
(2)	2,500		
(4)	7,100		
(14)	120		

Cash			101
(1)	30,000	(2)	2,500
(5)	4,200	(3)	26,000
(9)	1,900	(6)	1,000
(12)	3,000	(7)	700
		(10)	900
		(11)	200
		(13)	2,400
		(14)	120

15. Payment of Expense in Cash

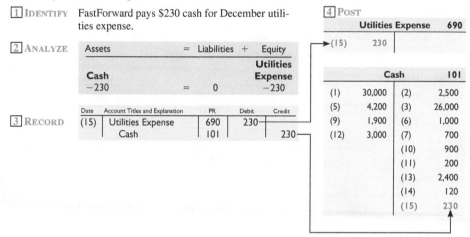

| ① IDENTIFY | FastForward pays $230 cash for December utilities expense. |

② ANALYZE

Assets	=	Liabilities	+	Equity
				Utilities Expense
Cash				
−230	=	0		−230

③ RECORD

Date	Account Titles and Explanation	PR	Debit	Credit
(15)	Utilities Expense	690	230	
	Cash	101		230

④ POST

Utilities Expense   690

| (15) | 230 | |

Cash   101

(1)	30,000	(2)	2,500
(5)	4,200	(3)	26,000
(9)	1,900	(6)	1,000
(12)	3,000	(7)	700
		(10)	900
		(11)	200
		(13)	2,400
		(14)	120
		(15)	230

16. Payment of Expense in Cash

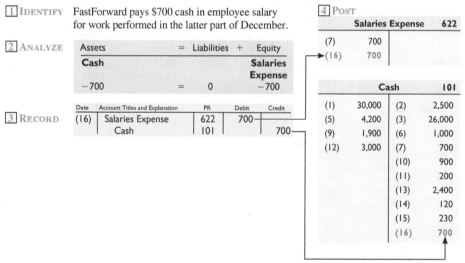

| ① IDENTIFY | FastForward pays $700 cash in employee salary for work performed in the latter part of December. |

② ANALYZE

Assets	=	Liabilities	+	Equity
Cash				**Salaries Expense**
−700	=	0		−700

③ RECORD

Date	Account Titles and Explanation	PR	Debit	Credit
(16)	Salaries Expense	622	700	
	Cash	101		700

④ POST

Salaries Expense   622

| (7) | 700 | |
| (16) | 700 | |

Cash   101

(1)	30,000	(2)	2,500
(5)	4,200	(3)	26,000
(9)	1,900	(6)	1,000
(12)	3,000	(7)	700
		(10)	900
		(11)	200
		(13)	2,400
		(14)	120
		(15)	230
		(16)	700

Point: We could merge transactions 15 and 16 into one *compound entry.*

Accounting Equation Analysis

Exhibit 2.13 shows the ledger accounts (in T-account form) of FastForward after all 16 transactions are recorded and posted and the balances computed. The accounts are grouped into three major columns corresponding to the accounting equation: assets, liabilities, and equity. Note several important points. First, as with each transaction, the totals for the three columns must obey the accounting equation. Specifically, assets equal $42,470 ($4,350 + $0 + $9,720 + $2,400 + $26,000); liabilities equal $9,200 ($6,200 + $3,000); and equity equals $33,270 ($30,000 − $200 + $5,800 + $300 − $1,400 − $1,000 − $230). These numbers prove the accounting equation: Assets of $42,470 = Liabilities of $9,200 + Equity of $33,270. Second, the common stock, dividends, revenue, and expense accounts reflect the transactions that change equity. The latter three account categories underlie the statement of retained earnings. Third, the revenue and expense account balances will be summarized and reported in the income statement. Fourth, increases and decreases in the cash account make up the elements reported in the statement of cash flows.

Debit and Credit Rules

Accounts	Increase (normal bal.)	Decrease
Asset	Debit	Credit
Liability	Credit	Debit
Common Stock	Credit	Debit
Dividends	Debit	Credit
Revenue	Credit	Debit
Expense	Debit	Credit

Point: Technology does not provide the judgment required to analyze most business transactions. Analysis requires the expertise of skilled and ethical professionals.

EXHIBIT 2.13

Ledger for FastForward (in T-Account Form)

General Ledger

Assets		=	Liabilities		+	Equity	

Assets

Cash		101
(1)	30,000	(2)	2,500
(5)	4,200	(3)	26,000
(9)	1,900	(6)	1,000
(12)	3,000	(7)	700
		(10)	900
		(11)	200
		(13)	2,400
		(14)	120
		(15)	230
		(16)	700
Balance	4,350		

Accounts Receivable		106
(8)	1,900	(9)	1,900
Balance	0		

Supplies		126
(2)	2,500		
(4)	7,100		
(14)	120		
Balance	9,720		

Prepaid Insurance		128
(13)	2,400		

Equipment		167
(3)	26,000		

Liabilities

Accounts Payable		201
(10)	900	(4)	7,100
		Balance	6,200

Unearned Consulting Revenue		236
		(12)	3,000

Equity

Common Stock		307
		(1)	30,000

Dividends		319
(11)	200		

Consulting Revenue		403
		(5)	4,200
		(8)	1,600
		Balance	5,800

Rental Revenue		406
		(8)	300

Salaries Expense		622
(7)	700		
(16)	700		
Balance	1,400		

Rent Expense		640
(6)	1,000		

Utilities Expense		690
(15)	230		

Accounts in this white area reflect those reported on the income statement.

$42,470	=	$9,200	+	$33,270

Quick Check

Answers — p. 77

8. What types of transactions increase equity? What types decrease equity?

9. Why are accounting systems called *double-entry?*

10. For each transaction, double-entry accounting requires which of the following? *(a)* Debits to asset accounts must create credits to liability or equity accounts, *(b)* a debit to a liability account must create a credit to an asset account, or *(c)* total debits must equal total credits.

11. An owner invests $15,000 cash along with equipment having a market value of $23,000 in a company in exchange for common stock. Prepare the necessary journal entry.

12. Explain what a compound journal entry is.

13. Why are posting reference numbers entered in the journal when entries are posted to ledger accounts?

TRIAL BALANCE

Double-entry accounting requires the sum of debit account balances to equal the sum of credit account balances. A trial balance is used to confirm this. A **trial balance** is a list of accounts and their balances at a point in time. Account balances are reported in their appropriate debit or credit columns of a trial balance. A trial balance can be used to confirm this and to follow up on any abnormal or unusual balances. Exhibit 2.14 shows the trial balance for FastForward after its 16 entries have been posted to the ledger. (This is an *unadjusted* trial balance—Chapter 3 explains the necessary adjustments.)

FASTFORWARD Trial Balance December 31, 2013	Debit	Credit
Cash	$ 4,350	
Accounts receivable	0	
Supplies	9,720	
Prepaid insurance	2,400	
Equipment	26,000	
Accounts payable		$ 6,200
Unearned consulting revenue		3,000
Common stock		30,000
Dividends	200	
Consulting revenue		5,800
Rental revenue		300
Salaries expense	1,400	
Rent expense	1,000	
Utilities expense	230	
Totals	$ 45,300	$ 45,300

EXHIBIT 2.14

Trial Balance (Unadjusted)

Point: The ordering of accounts in a trial balance typically follows their identification number from the chart of accounts.

Preparing a Trial Balance

Preparing a trial balance involves three steps:

1. List each account title and its amount (from ledger) in the trial balance. If an account has a zero balance, list it with a zero in its normal balance column (or omit it entirely).
2. Compute the total of debit balances and the total of credit balances.
3. Verify (*prove*) total debit balances equal total credit balances.

The total of debit balances equals the total of credit balances for the trial balance in Exhibit 2.14. Equality of these two totals does not guarantee that no errors were made. For example, the column totals still will be equal when a debit or credit of a correct amount is made to a wrong account. Another error that does not cause unequal column totals occurs when equal debits and credits of an incorrect amount are entered.

Searching for and Correcting Errors If the trial balance does not balance (when its columns are not equal), the error (or errors) must be found and corrected. An efficient way to search for an error is to check the journalizing, posting, and trial balance preparation

P2 Prepare and explain the use of a trial balance.

Point: A trial balance is *not* a financial statement but a mechanism for checking equality of debits and credits in the ledger. Financial statements do not have debit and credit columns.

Example: If a credit to Unearned Revenue was incorrectly posted from the journal as a credit to the Revenue ledger account, would the ledger still balance? Would the financial statements be correct? *Answers:* The ledger would balance, but liabilities would be understated, equity would be overstated, and income would be overstated (all because of overstated revenues).

Point: The IRS requires companies to keep records that can be audited.

in *reverse order.* Step 1 is to verify that the trial balance columns are correctly added. If step 1 fails to find the error, step 2 is to verify that account balances are accurately entered from the ledger. Step 3 is to see whether a debit (or credit) balance is mistakenly listed in the trial balance as a credit (or debit). A clue to this error is when the difference between total debits and total credits equals twice the amount of the incorrect account balance. If the error is still undiscovered, Step 4 is to recompute each account balance in the ledger. Step 5 is to verify that each journal entry is properly posted. Step 6 is to verify that the original journal entry has equal debits and credits. At this point, the errors should be uncovered.[3]

If an error in a journal entry is discovered before the error is posted, it can be corrected in a manual system by drawing a line through the incorrect information. The correct information is written above it to create a record of change for the auditor. Many computerized systems allow the operator to replace the incorrect information directly.

If an error in a journal entry is not discovered until after it is posted, we do not strike through both erroneous entries in the journal and ledger. Instead, we correct this error by creating a *correcting entry* that removes the amount from the wrong account and records it to the correct account. As an example, suppose a $100 purchase of supplies is journalized with an incorrect debit to Equipment, and then this incorrect entry is posted to the ledger. The Supplies ledger account balance is understated by $100, and the Equipment ledger account balance is overstated by $100. The correcting entry is: debit Supplies and credit Equipment (both for $100).

Using a Trial Balance to Prepare Financial Statements

P3 Prepare financial statements from business transactions.

This section shows how to prepare *financial statements* from the trial balance in Exhibit 2.14 and from information on the December transactions of FastForward. These statements differ from those in Chapter 1 because of several additional transactions. These statements are also more precisely called *unadjusted statements* because we need to make some further accounting adjustments (described in Chapter 3).

EXHIBIT 2.15

Links between Financial Statements across Time

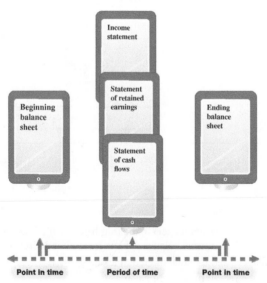

How financial statements are linked in time is illustrated in Exhibit 2.15. A balance sheet reports on an organization's financial position at a *point in time.* The income statement, statement of retained earnings, and statement of cash flows report on financial performance over a *period of time.* The three statements in the middle column of Exhibit 2.15 link balance sheets from the beginning to the end of a reporting period. They explain how financial position changes from one point to another.

Preparers and users (including regulatory agencies) determine the length of the reporting period. A one-year, or annual, reporting period is common, as are semiannual, quarterly, and monthly periods. The one-year reporting period

---

[3] *Transposition* occurs when two digits are switched, or transposed, within a number. If transposition is the only error, it yields a difference between the two trial balance totals that is evenly divisible by 9. For example, assume that a $691 debit in an entry is incorrectly posted to the ledger as $619. Total credits in the trial balance are then larger than total debits by $72 ($691 − $619). The $72 error is *evenly* divisible by 9 (72/9 = 8). The first digit of the quotient (in our example it is 8) equals the difference between the digits of the two transposed numbers (the 9 and the 1). The number of digits in the quotient also tells the location of the transposition, starting from the right. The quotient in our example had only one digit (8), so it tells us the transposition is in the first digit. Consider another example where a transposition error involves posting $961 instead of the correct $691. The difference in these numbers is $270, and its quotient is 30 (270/9). The quotient has two digits, so it tells us to check the second digit from the right for a transposition of two numbers that have a difference of 3.

is known as the *accounting,* or *fiscal, year.* Businesses whose accounting year begins on January 1 and ends on December 31 are known as *calendar-year* companies. Polaris is a calendar-year company. Many companies choose a fiscal year ending on a date other than December 31. Arctic Cat is a *noncalendar-year* company as reflected in the headings of its March 31 year-end financial statements in Appendix A near the end of the book.

Income Statement   An income statement reports the revenues earned less the expenses incurred by a business over a period of time. FastForward's income statement for December is shown at the top of Exhibit 2.16. Information about revenues and expenses is conveniently taken from the trial balance in Exhibit 2.14. Net income of $3,470 is reported at the bottom of the statement. Owner investments and dividends are *not* part of income.

Statement of Retained Earnings   The statement of retained earnings reports information about how retained earnings change over the reporting period. FastForward's statement of retained earnings is the second report in Exhibit 2.16. It shows the $3,470 of net income, the

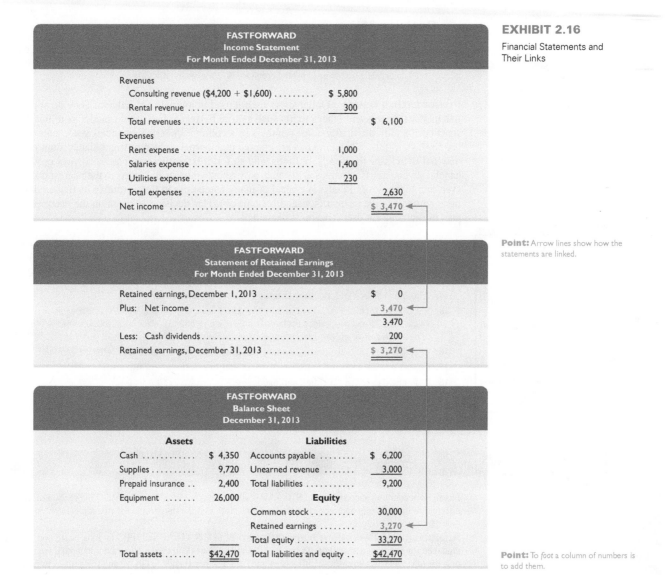

Point: A statement's heading lists the 3 W's: **W**ho—name of organization, **W**hat—name of statement, **W**hen—statement's point in time or period of time.

EXHIBIT 2.16

Financial Statements and Their Links

Point: Arrow lines show how the statements are linked.

Point: To *foot* a column of numbers is to add them.

$200 dividend, and the $3,270 end-of-period balance. (The beginning balance in the statement of retained earnings is rarely zero; an exception is for the first period of operations. The beginning balance in January 2014 is $3,270, which is December's ending balance.)

Balance Sheet   The balance sheet reports the financial position of a company at a point in time, usually at the end of a month, quarter, or year. FastForward's balance sheet is the third report in Exhibit 2.16. This statement refers to financial condition at the close of business on December 31. The left side of the balance sheet lists its assets: cash, supplies, prepaid insurance, and equipment. The upper right side of the balance sheet shows that it owes $6,200 to creditors and $3,000 in services to customers who paid in advance. The equity section shows an ending balance of $33,270. Note the link between the ending balance of the statement of retained earnings and the retained earnings balance. (Recall that this presentation of the balance sheet is called the *account form:* assets on the left and liabilities and equity on the right. Another presentation is the *report form:* assets on top, followed by liabilities and then equity. Either presentation is acceptable.)

Point: An income statement is also called an *earnings statement, a statement of operations,* or a *P&L* (profit and loss) *statement.* A balance sheet is also called a *statement of financial position.*

Point: While revenues increase equity, and expenses decrease equity, the amounts are not reported in detail in the statement of retained earnings. Instead, their effects are reflected through net income.

Point: Knowing how financial statements are prepared improves our analysis of them.

Decision Maker

Entrepreneur   You open a wholesale business selling entertainment equipment to retail outlets. You find that most of your customers demand to buy on credit. How can you use the balance sheets of these customers to decide which ones to extend credit to? ■   [Answer—p. 76]

Presentation Issues   Dollar signs are not used in journals and ledgers. They do appear in financial statements and other reports such as trial balances. The usual practice is to put dollar signs beside only the first and last numbers in a column. **Polaris**'s financial statements in Appendix A show this. When amounts are entered in a journal, ledger, or trial balance, commas are optional to indicate thousands, millions, and so forth. However, commas are always used in financial statements. Companies also commonly round amounts in reports to the nearest dollar, or even to a higher level. Polaris is typical of many companies in that it rounds its financial statement amounts to the nearest thousand (or million). This decision is based on the perceived impact of rounding for users' business decisions.

off the mark .com   by Mark Parisi

HE CONTINUED ACCOUNTING RIGHT THROUGH HIS COFFEE BREAK…THEN HIS LUNCH BREAK. CLEARLY, MYRON WAS "IN THE ZONE."

Quick Check   Answers — p. 77

14. Where are dollar signs typically entered in financial statements?
15. If a $4,000 debit to Equipment in a journal entry is incorrectly posted to the ledger as a $4,000 credit, and the ledger account has a resulting debit balance of $20,000, what is the effect of this error on the Trial Balance column totals?
16. Describe the link between the income statement and the statement of retained earnings.
17. Explain the link between the balance sheet and the statement of retained earnings.
18. Define and describe revenues and expenses.
19. Define and describe assets, liabilities, and equity.

GLOBAL VIEW

Financial accounting according to U.S. GAAP is similar, but not identical, to IFRS. This section discusses differences in analyzing and recording transactions, and with the preparation of financial statements.

Analyzing and Recording Transactions   Both U.S. GAAP and IFRS include broad and similar guidance for financial accounting. As the FASB and IASB work toward a common conceptual framework over the next few years, even those differences will fade. Further, both U.S. GAAP and IFRS apply transaction analysis and recording as shown in this chapter—using the same debit and credit system and accrual account-ing. Although some variations exist in revenue and expense recognition and other accounting principles, all of the transactions in this chapter are accounted for identically under these two systems.

Financial Statements   Both U.S. GAAP and IFRS prepare the same four basic financial state-ments. A few differences within each statement do exist and we will discuss those throughout the book. For example, both U.S. GAAP and IFRS require balance sheets to separate current items from noncurrent items. However, while U.S. GAAP balance sheets report current items first, IFRS balance sheets normally (but are not required to) present noncurrent items first, and equity before liabilities. To illustrate, a con-densed version of Piaggio's balance sheet follows (numbers using Euros in thousands).

PIAGGIO

PIAGGIO			
Balance Sheet (in thousands of Euros)			
December 31, 2011			
Assets		**Equity and Liabilities**	
Noncurrent assets	1,010,476	Total equity	446,218
Current assets	509,708	Noncurrent liabilities	429,689
		Current liabilities	644,277
Total assets	1,520,184	Total equity and liabilities	1,520,184

Accounting Controls and Assurance   Accounting systems depend on control procedures that assure the proper principles were applied in processing accounting information. The passage of SOX leg-islation strengthened U.S. control procedures in recent years. However, global standards for control are diverse and so are enforcement activities. Consequently, while global accounting standards are converg-ing, their application in different countries can yield different outcomes depending on the quality of their auditing standards and enforcement.

Decision Insight

Accounting Control Recording valid transactions, and not recording fraudulent transactions, enhances the quality of financial statements. The graph here shows the percentage of employ-ees in information technology that report observing specific types of misconduct within the past year [Source: KPMG 2009]. ■

Breaching database controls   23%
Mishandling private information   22%
Breaching customer privacy   16%
Falsifying accounting data   9%

0%   10%   20%   30%
Percent Citing Misconduct

 Debt Ratio   **Decision Analysis**

An important business objective is gathering information to help assess a company's risk of failing to pay its debts. Companies finance their assets with either liabilities or equity. A company that finances a rela-tively large portion of its assets with liabilities is said to have a high degree of *financial leverage*. Higher financial leverage involves greater risk because liabilities must be repaid and often require regular interest payments (equity financing does not). The risk that a company might not be able to meet such required payments is higher if it has more liabilities (is more highly leveraged). One way to assess the risk associ-ated with a company's use of liabilities is to compute the **debt ratio** as in Exhibit 2.17.

A2 Compute the debt ratio and describe its use in analyzing financial condition.

$$\text{Debt ratio} = \frac{\text{Total liabilities}}{\text{Total assets}}$$

EXHIBIT 2.17

Debt Ratio

Point: Compare the equity amount to the liability amount to assess the extent of owner versus nonowner financing.

To see how to apply the debt ratio, let's look at Skechers's liabilities and assets. The company designs, markets, and sells footwear for men, women, and children under the Skechers brand. Exhibit 2.18 computes and reports its debt ratio at the end of each year from 2006 to 2011.

EXHIBIT 2.18

Computation and Analysis of Debt Ratio

$ in millions	2011	2010	2009	2008	2007	2006
Total liabilities	$ 389	$ 359	$246	$204	$201	$288
Total assets	$1,282	$1,305	$996	$876	$828	$737
Debt ratio	0.30	0.28	0.25	0.23	0.24	0.39
Industry debt ratio	0.47	0.49	0.51	0.50	0.46	0.48

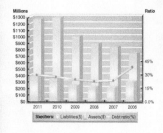

Skechers's debt ratio ranges from a low of 0.23 to a high of 0.39—also, see graph in margin. Its ratio is lower, compared with the industry ratio. This analysis implies a low risk from its financial leverage. Is financial leverage good or bad for Skechers? To answer that question we need to compare the company's return on the borrowed money to the rate it is paying creditors. If the company's return is higher, it is successfully borrowing money to make more money. A company's success with making money from borrowed money can quickly turn unprofitable if its own return drops below the rate it is paying creditors.

■ Decision Maker

Investor   You consider buying stock in Converse. As part of your analysis, you compute its debt ratio for 2011, 2012, and 2013 as: 0.35, 0.74, and 0.94, respectively. Based on the debt ratio, is Converse a low-risk investment? Has the risk of buying Converse stock changed over this period? (The industry debt ratio averages 0.40.) ■   [Answer—p. 76]

DEMONSTRATION PROBLEM

(This problem extends the demonstration problem of Chapter 1.) After several months of planning, Jasmine Worthy started a haircutting business called Expressions. The following events occurred during its first month.

a. On August 1, Worthy invested $3,000 cash and $15,000 of equipment in Expressions in exchange for common stock.

b. On August 2, Expressions paid $600 cash for furniture for the shop.

c. On August 3, Expressions paid $500 cash to rent space in a strip mall for August.

d. On August 4, it purchased $1,200 of equipment on credit for the shop (using a long-term note payable).

e. On August 5, Expressions opened for business. Cash received from haircutting services in the first week and a half of business (ended August 15) was $825.

f. On August 15, it provided $100 of haircutting services on account.

g. On August 17, it received a $100 check for services previously rendered on account.

h. On August 17, it paid $125 to an assistant for hours worked during the grand opening.

i. Cash received from services provided during the second half of August was $930.

j. On August 31, it paid a $400 installment toward principal on the note payable entered into on August 4.

k. On August 31, it paid $900 cash in dividends to Worthy (sole shareholder).

Required

1. Open the following ledger accounts in balance column format (account numbers are in parentheses): Cash (101); Accounts Receivable (102); Furniture (161); Store Equipment (165); Note Payable (240); Common Stock (307); Dividends (319); Haircutting Services Revenue (403); Wages Expense (623); and Rent Expense (640). Prepare general journal entries for the transactions.

2. Post the journal entries from (1) to the ledger accounts.

3. Prepare a trial balance as of August 31.

4. Prepare an income statement for August.

5. Prepare a statement of retained earnings for August.

6. Prepare a balance sheet as of August 31.

7. Determine the debt ratio as of August 31.

Extended Analysis

8. In the coming months, Expressions will experience a greater variety of business transactions. Identify which accounts are debited and which are credited for the following transactions. (*Hint:* We must use some accounts not opened in part 1.)

   a. Purchase supplies with cash.

   b. Pay cash for future insurance coverage.

   c. Receive cash for services to be provided in the future.

   d. Purchase supplies on account.

PLANNING THE SOLUTION

- Analyze each transaction and use the debit and credit rules to prepare a journal entry for each.
- Post each debit and each credit from journal entries to their ledger accounts and cross-reference each amount in the posting reference (PR) columns of the journal and ledger.
- Calculate each account balance and list the accounts with their balances on a trial balance.
- Verify that total debits in the trial balance equal total credits.
- To prepare the income statement, identify revenues and expenses. List those items on the statement, compute the difference, and label the result as *net income* or *net loss*.
- Use information in the ledger to prepare the statement of retained earnings.
- Use information in the ledger to prepare the balance sheet.
- Calculate the debt ratio by dividing total liabilities by total assets.
- Analyze the future transactions to identify the accounts affected and apply debit and credit rules.

SOLUTION TO DEMONSTRATION PROBLEM

1. General journal entries:

General Journal

Page 1

Date	Account Titles and Explanation	PR	Debit	Credit
Aug. 1	Cash	101	3,000	
	Store Equipment	165	15,000	
	Common Stock	307		18,000
	Owner's investment for stock.			
2	Furniture	161	600	
	Cash	101		600
	Purchased furniture for cash.			
3	Rent Expense	640	500	
	Cash	101		500
	Paid rent for August.			
4	Store Equipment	165	1,200	
	Note Payable	240		1,200
	Purchased additional equipment on credit.			
15	Cash	101	825	
	Haircutting Services Revenue	403		825
	Cash receipts from first half of August.			

[continued on next page]

[continued from previous page]

15	Accounts Receivable	102	100	
	Haircutting Services Revenue	403		100
	To record revenue for services provided on account.			
17	Cash	101	100	
	Accounts Receivable	102		100
	To record cash received as payment on account.			
17	Wages Expense....................................	623	125	
	Cash	101		125
	Paid wages to assistant.			
31	Cash	101	930	
	Haircutting Services Revenue	403		930
	Cash receipts from second half of August.			
31	Note Payable	240	400	
	Cash	101		400
	Paid an installment on the note payable.			
31	Dividends	319	900	
	Cash	101		900
	Paid cash dividend.			

2. Post journal entries from part 1 to the ledger accounts:

General Ledger

Cash   **Account No. 101**

Date	PR	Debit	Credit	Balance
Aug. 1	G1	3,000		3,000
2	G1		600	2,400
3	G1		500	1,900
15	G1	825		2,725
17	G1	100		2,825
17	G1		125	2,700
31	G1	930		3,630
31	G1		400	3,230
31	G1		900	2,330

Accounts Receivable   **Account No. 102**

Date	PR	Debit	Credit	Balance
Aug. 15	G1	100		100
17	G1		100	0

Furniture   **Account No. 161**

Date	PR	Debit	Credit	Balance
Aug. 2	G1	600		600

Store Equipment   **Account No. 165**

Date	PR	Debit	Credit	Balance
Aug. 1	G1	15,000		15,000
4	G1	1,200		16,200

Note Payable   **Account No. 240**

Date	PR	Debit	Credit	Balance
Aug. 4	G1		1,200	1,200
31	G1	400		800

Common Stock   **Account No. 307**

Date	PR	Debit	Credit	Balance
Aug. 1	G1		18,000	18,000

Dividends   **Account No. 319**

Date	PR	Debit	Credit	Balance
Aug. 31	G1	900		900

Haircutting Services Revenue Account No. 403

Date	PR	Debit	Credit	Balance
Aug. 15	G1		825	825
15	G1		100	925
31	G1		930	1,855

Wages Expense   **Account No. 623**

Date	PR	Debit	Credit	Balance
Aug. 17	G1	125		125

Rent Expense   **Account No. 640**

Date	PR	Debit	Credit	Balance
Aug. 3	G1	500		500

3. Prepare a trial balance from the ledger:

EXPRESSIONS Trial Balance August 31	Debit	Credit
Cash	$ 2,330	
Accounts receivable	0	
Furniture	600	
Store equipment	16,200	
Note payable		$ 800
Common stock		18,000
Dividends	900	
Haircutting services revenue		1,855
Wages expense	125	
Rent expense	500	
Totals	$20,655	$20,655

4.

EXPRESSIONS Income Statement For Month Ended August 31		
Revenues		
Haircutting services revenue		$1,855
Operating expenses		
Rent expense	$500	
Wages expense	125	
Total operating expenses		625
Net income		$1,230

5.

EXPRESSIONS Statement of Retained Earnings For Month Ended August 31	
Retained earnings, August 1	$ 0
Plus: Net income	1,230
	1,230
Less: Cash dividends	900
Retained earnings, August 31	$ 330

6.

EXPRESSIONS Balance Sheet August 31			
Assets		**Liabilities**	
Cash	$ 2,330	Note payable	$ 800
Furniture	600	**Equity**	
Store equipment	16,200	Common stock	18,000
		Retained earnings	330
		Total equity	18,330
Total assets	$19,130	Total liabilities and equity	$19,130

7. Debt ratio $= \dfrac{\text{Total liabilities}}{\text{Total assets}} = \dfrac{\$800}{\$19,130} = \underline{\underline{\textbf{4.18\%}}}$

8a. Supplies *debited*
          Cash *credited*

8b. Prepaid Insurance *debited*
          Cash *credited*

8c. Cash *debited*
          Unearned Services Revenue *credited*

8d. Supplies *debited*
          Accounts Payable *credited*

Summary

C1 **Explain the steps in processing transactions and the role of source documents.** The accounting process identifies business transactions and events, analyzes and records their effects, and summarizes and prepares information useful in making decisions. Transactions and events are the starting points in the accounting process. Source documents identify and describe transactions and events. Examples are sales tickets, checks, purchase orders, bills, and bank statements. Source documents provide objective and reliable evidence, making information more useful. The effects of transactions and events are recorded in journals. Posting along with a trial balance helps summarize and classify these effects.

C2 **Describe an account and its use in recording transactions.** An account is a detailed record of increases and decreases in a specific asset, liability, equity, revenue, or expense. Information from accounts is analyzed, summarized, and presented in reports and financial statements for decision makers.

C3 **Describe a ledger and a chart of accounts.** The ledger (or general ledger) is a record containing all accounts used by a company and their balances. It is referred to as the *books*. The chart of accounts is a list of all accounts and usually includes an identification number assigned to each account.

C4 **Define *debits* and *credits* and explain double-entry accounting.** *Debit* refers to left, and *credit* refers to right. Debits increase assets, expenses, and dividends while credits decrease them. Credits increase liabilities, common stock, and revenues; debits decrease them. Double-entry accounting means each transaction affects at least two accounts and has at least one debit and one credit. The system for recording debits and credits follows from the accounting equation. The left side of an account is the normal balance for assets, dividends, and expenses, and the right side is the normal balance for liabilities, common stock, and revenues.

A1 **Analyze the impact of transactions on accounts and financial statements.** We analyze transactions using concepts of double-entry accounting. This analysis is performed by determining a transaction's effects on accounts. These effects are recorded in journals and posted to ledgers.

A2 **Compute the debt ratio and describe its use in analyzing financial condition.** A company's debt ratio is computed as total liabilities divided by total assets. It reveals how much of the assets are financed by creditor (nonowner) financing. The higher this ratio, the more risk a company faces because liabilities must be repaid at specific dates.

P1 **Record transactions in a journal and post entries to a ledger.** Transactions are recorded in a journal. Each entry in a journal is posted to the accounts in the ledger. This provides information that is used to produce financial statements. Balance column accounts are widely used and include columns for debits, credits, and the account balance.

P2 **Prepare and explain the use of a trial balance.** A trial balance is a list of accounts from the ledger showing their debit or credit balances in separate columns. The trial balance is a summary of the ledger's contents and is useful in preparing financial statements and in revealing recordkeeping errors.

P3 **Prepare financial statements from business transactions.** The balance sheet, the statement of retained earnings, the income statement, and the statement of cash flows use data from the trial balance (and other financial statements) for their preparation.

Guidance Answers to Decision Maker and Decision Ethics

Cashier The advantages to the process proposed by the assistant manager include improved customer service, fewer delays, and less work for you. However, you should have serious concerns about internal control and the potential for fraud. In particular, the assistant manager could steal cash and simply enter fewer sales to match the remaining cash. You should reject her suggestion without the manager's approval. Moreover, you should have an ethical concern about the assistant manager's suggestion to ignore store policy.

Entrepreneur We can use the accounting equation (Assets = Liabilities + Equity) to help us identify risky customers to whom we

would likely not want to extend credit. A balance sheet provides amounts for each of these key components. The lower a customer's equity is relative to liabilities, the less likely you would extend credit. A low equity means the business has little value that does not already have creditor claims to it.

Investor The debt ratio suggests the stock of Converse is of higher risk than normal and that this risk is rising. The average industry ratio of 0.40 further supports this conclusion. The 2013 debt ratio for Converse is twice the industry norm. Also, a debt ratio approaching 1.0 indicates little to no equity.

Guidance Answers to Quick Checks

1. Examples of source documents are sales tickets, checks, purchase orders, charges to customers, bills from suppliers, employee earnings records, and bank statements.

2. Source documents serve many purposes, including record-keeping and internal control. Source documents, especially if obtained from outside the organization, provide objective and reliable evidence about transactions and their amounts.

3.

Assets	Liabilities	Equity
a,c,e	b,d	—

4. An account is a record in an accounting system that records and stores the increases and decreases in a specific asset, liability, equity, revenue, or expense. The ledger is a collection of all the accounts of a company.

5. A company's size and diversity affect the number of accounts in its accounting system. The types of accounts depend on information the company needs to both effectively operate and report its activities in financial statements.

6. No. Debit and credit both can mean increase or decrease. The particular meaning in a circumstance depends on the *type of account*. For example, a debit increases the balance of asset, dividends, and expense accounts, but it decreases the balance of liability, common stock, and revenue accounts.

7. A chart of accounts is a list of all of a company's accounts and their identification numbers.

8. Equity is increased by revenues and by owner investments. Equity is decreased by expenses and dividends.

9. The name *double-entry* is used because all transactions affect at least two accounts. There must be at least one debit in one account and at least one credit in another account.

10. The answer is (c).

11.

Cash	15,000	
Equipment	23,000	
Common Stock		38,000
Investment by owner of cash and equipment.		

12. A compound journal entry affects three or more accounts.

13. Posting reference numbers are entered in the journal when posting to the ledger as a cross-reference that allows the record-keeper or auditor to trace debits and credits from one record to another.

14. At a minimum, dollar signs are placed beside the first and last numbers in a column. It is also common to place dollar signs beside any amount that appears after a ruled line to indicate that an addition or subtraction has occurred.

15. The Equipment account balance is incorrectly reported at $20,000—it should be $28,000. The effect of this error understates the trial balance's Debit column total by $8,000. This results in an $8,000 difference between the column totals.

16. An income statement reports a company's revenues and expenses along with the resulting net income or loss. A statement of retained earnings reports changes in retained earnings, including that from net income or loss. Both statements report transactions occurring over a period of time.

17. The balance sheet describes a company's financial position (assets, liabilities, and equity) at a point in time. The retained earnings amount in the balance sheet is obtained from the statement of retained earnings.

18. Revenues are inflows of assets in exchange for products or services provided to customers as part of the main operations of a business. Expenses are outflows or the using up of assets that result from providing products or services to customers.

19. Assets are the resources a business owns or controls that carry expected future benefits. Liabilities are the obligations of a business, representing the claims of others against the assets of a business. Equity reflects the owner's claims on the assets of the business after deducting liabilities.

Key Terms

Account (p. 53)

Account balance, or Balance (p. 60)

Balance column account (p. 60)

Chart of accounts (p. 56)

Compound journal entry (p. 63)

Credit (p. 57)

Creditors (p. 54)

Debit (p. 57)

Debt ratio (p. 71)

Dividends (p. 55)

Double-entry accounting (p. 57)

General journal (p. 58)

General ledger (p. 53)

Journal (p. 58)

Journalizing (p. 58)

Posting (p. 58)

Posting reference (PR) column (p. 60)

Source documents (p. 52)

T-accounts (p. 57)

Trial balance (p. 67)

Unearned revenue (p. 55)

Multiple Choice Quiz   Answers on p. 93   mhhe.com/wildFINMAN5e

Additional Quiz Questions are available at the book's Website.

1. Amalia Company received its utility bill for the current period of $700 and immediately paid it. Its journal entry to record this transaction includes a
   a. Credit to Utility Expense for $700.
   b. Debit to Utility Expense for $700.
   c. Debit to Accounts Payable for $700.
   d. Debit to Cash for $700.
   e. Credit to Common Stock for $700.

2. On May 1, Mattingly Lawn Service collected $2,500 cash from a customer in advance of five months of lawn service. Mattingly's journal entry to record this transaction includes a
   a. Credit to Unearned Lawn Service Fees for $2,500.
   b. Debit to Lawn Service Fees Earned for $2,500.
   c. Credit to Cash for $2,500.
   d. Debit to Unearned Lawn Service Fees for $2,500.
   e. Credit to Common Stock for $2,500.

3. Liang Shue contributed $250,000 cash and land worth $500,000 to open his new business, Shue Consulting Corporation. Which of the following journal entries does Shue Consulting make to record this transaction?

   a. Cash Assets 750,000
       Common Stock   750,000

   b. Common Stock 750,000
       Assets   750,000

   c. Cash 250,000
       Land 500,000
       Common Stock   750,000

   d. Common Stock 750,000
       Cash   250,000
       Land   500,000

4. A trial balance prepared at year-end shows total credits exceed total debits by $765. This discrepancy could have been caused by
   a. An error in the general journal where a $765 increase in Accounts Payable was recorded as a $765 decrease in Accounts Payable.
   b. The ledger balance for Accounts Payable of $7,650 being entered in the trial balance as $765.
   c. A general journal error where a $765 increase in Accounts Receivable was recorded as a $765 increase in Cash.
   d. The ledger balance of $850 in Accounts Receivable was entered in the trial balance as $85.
   e. An error in recording a $765 increase in Cash as a credit.

5. Bonaventure Company has total assets of $1,000,000, liabilities of $400,000, and equity of $600,000. What is its debt ratio (rounded to a whole percent)?
   a. 250%
   b. 167%
   c. 67%
   d. 150%
   e. 40%

🔲 Icon denotes assignments that involve decision making.

Discussion Questions

1. Provide the names of two (a) asset accounts, (b) liability accounts, and (c) equity accounts.
2. What is the difference between a note payable and an account payable?
3. 🔲 Discuss the steps in processing business transactions.
4. What kinds of transactions can be recorded in a general journal?
5. Are debits or credits typically listed first in general journal entries? Are the debits or the credits indented?
6. Should a transaction be recorded first in a journal or the ledger? Why?
7. If assets are valuable resources and asset accounts have debit balances, why do expense accounts also have debit balances?
8. 🔲 Why does the recordkeeper prepare a trial balance?
9. If an incorrect amount is journalized and posted to the accounts, how should the error be corrected?
10. Identify the four financial statements of a business.
11. 🔲 What information is reported in a balance sheet?
12. 🔲 What information is reported in an income statement?
13. 🔲 Why does the user of an income statement need to know the time period that it covers?
14. Define (a) assets, (b) liabilities, (c) equity, and (d) net assets.
15. Which financial statement is sometimes called the statement of financial position?
16. 🔲 Review the Polaris balance sheet in Appendix A. Identify three accounts on its balance sheet that carry debit balances and three accounts on its balance sheet that carry credit balances.   **Polaris**
17. Review the Arctic Cat balance sheet in Appendix A. Identify an asset with the word receivable in its account title and a liability with the word payable in its account title.   **Arctic Cat**
18. Locate KTM's income statement in Appendix A. What is the title of its revenue account?   **KTM**
19. Refer to Piaggio's balance sheet in Appendix A. What does Piaggio title its current asset referring to merchandise available for sale?   **PIAGGIO**

connect

Identify the items from the following list that are likely to serve as source documents.

a. Sales ticket
b. Income statement
c. Trial balance
d. Telephone bill
e. Invoice from supplier
f. Company revenue account
g. Balance sheet
h. Prepaid insurance
i. Bank statement

Identify the financial statement(s) where each of the following items appears. Use I for income statement, E for statement of retained earnings, and B for balance sheet.

a. Office equipment
b. Cash dividends
c. Revenue
d. Prepaid insurance
e. Office supplies
f. Rent expense
g. Cash
h. Unearned rent revenue
i. Accounts payable

Identify the normal balance (debit or credit) for each of the following accounts.

a. Office Supplies
b. Dividends
c. Fees Earned
d. Wages Expense
e. Accounts Receivable
f. Prepaid Rent
g. Wages Payable
h. Building
i. Common Stock

Indicate whether a debit or credit *decreases* the normal balance of each of the following accounts.

a. Service Revenue
b. Interest Payable
c. Accounts Receivable
d. Salaries Expense
e. Common Stock
f. Prepaid Insurance
g. Buildings
h. Interest Revenue
i. Dividends
j. Unearned Revenue
k. Accounts Payable
l. Land

Identify whether a debit or credit yields the indicated change for each of the following accounts.

a. To increase Land
b. To decrease Cash
c. To increase Office Expense
d. To increase Fees Earned
e. To decrease Unearned Revenue
f. To decrease Prepaid Rent
g. To increase Notes Payable
h. To decrease Accounts Receivable
i. To increase Common Stock
j. To increase Store Equipment

Prepare journal entries for each of the following selected transactions.

a. On May 15, DeShawn Tyler opens a landscaping company called Elegant Lawns by investing $70,000 cash along with equipment having a $30,000 value in exchange for common stock.
b. On May 21, Elegant Lawns purchases office supplies on credit for $280.
c. On May 25, Elegant Lawns receives $7,800 cash for performing landscaping services.
d. On May 30, Elegant Lawns receives $1,000 cash in advance of providing landscaping services to a customer.

A trial balance has total debits of $20,000 and total credits of $24,500. Which one of the following errors would create this imbalance? Explain.

a. A $2,250 debit to Utilities Expense in a journal entry is incorrectly posted to the ledger as a $2,250 credit, leaving the Utilities Expense account with a $3,000 debit balance.
b. A $4,500 debit to Salaries Expense in a journal entry is incorrectly posted to the ledger as a $4,500 credit, leaving the Salaries Expense account with a $750 debit balance.
c. A $2,250 credit to Consulting Fees Earned in a journal entry is incorrectly posted to the ledger as a $2,250 debit, leaving the Consulting Fees Earned account with a $6,300 credit balance.
d. A $2,250 debit posting to Accounts Receivable was posted mistakenly to Land.
e. A $4,500 debit posting to Equipment was posted mistakenly to Cash.
f. An entry debiting Cash and crediting Accounts Payable for $4,500 was mistakenly not posted.

QS 2-8

Classifying accounts in financial statements

P3

Indicate the financial statement on which each of the following items appears. Use I for income statement, E for statement of retained earnings, and B for balance sheet.

a. Services Revenue	**e.** Equipment	**i.** Dividends
b. Interest Payable	**f.** Prepaid Insurance	**j.** Office Supplies
c. Accounts Receivable	**g.** Buildings	**k.** Interest Expense
d. Salaries Expense	**h.** Rental Revenue	**l.** Insurance Expense

---

QS 2-9

International accounting standards

C4

Answer each of the following questions related to international accounting standards.

a. What type of entry system is applied when accounting follows IFRS?

b. Identify the number and usual titles of the financial statements prepared under IFRS.

c. How do differences in accounting controls and enforcement impact accounting reports prepared across different countries?

EXERCISES

Exercise 2-1

Steps in analyzing and recording transactions   C1

Order the following steps in the accounting process that focus on analyzing and recording transactions.

_____ **a.** Analyze each transaction from source documents.

_____ **b.** Prepare and analyze the trial balance.

_____ **c.** Record relevant transactions in a journal.

_____ **d.** Post journal information to ledger accounts.

Exercise 2-2

Identifying and classifying accounts

C2

Enter the number for the item that best completes each of the descriptions below.

1. Asset	**3.** Account	**5.** Three
2. Equity	**4.** Liability	

a. An _____ is a record of increases and decreases in a specific asset, liability, equity, revenue, or expense item.

b. Accounts payable, unearned revenue, and note payable are examples of _____ accounts.

c. Accounts receivable, prepaid accounts, supplies, and land are examples of _____ accounts.

d. Accounts are arranged into _____ general categories.

e. Common stock and dividends are examples of _____ accounts.

Exercise 2-3

Identifying a ledger and chart of accounts

C3

Enter the number for the item that best completes each of the descriptions below.

1. Chart   **2.** General ledger

a. The _____ is a record containing all accounts used by a company.

b. A _____ of accounts is a list of all accounts a company uses.

Exercise 2-4

Identifying type and normal balances of accounts

C4

For each of the following (1) identify the type of account as an asset, liability, equity, revenue, or expense, (2) identify the normal balance of the account, and (3) enter *debit* (*Dr.*) or *credit* (*Cr.*) to identify the kind of entry that would increase the account balance.

a. Cash	**e.** Accounts Receivable	**i.** Fees Earned
b. Legal Expense	**f.** Dividends	**j.** Equipment
c. Prepaid Insurance	**g.** License Fee Revenue	**k.** Notes Payable
d. Land	**h.** Unearned Revenue	**l.** Common Stock

Exercise 2-5

Analyzing account entries and balances

A1

Use the information in each of the following separate cases to calculate the unknown amount.

a. Corentine Co. had $152,000 of accounts payable on September 30 and $132,500 on October 31. Total purchases on account during October were $281,000. Determine how much cash was paid on accounts payable during October.

b. On September 30, Valerian Co. had a $102,500 balance in Accounts Receivable. During October, the company collected $102,890 from its credit customers. The October 31 balance in Accounts Receivable was $89,000. Determine the amount of sales on account that occurred in October.

c. During October, Alameda Company had $102,500 of cash receipts and $103,150 of cash disbursements. The October 31 Cash balance was $18,600. Determine how much cash the company had at the close of business on September 30.

Groro Co. bills a client $62,000 for services provided and agrees to accept the following three items in full payment: (1) $10,000 cash, (2) computer equipment worth $80,000, and (3) to assume responsibility for a $28,000 note payable related to the computer equipment. The entry Groro makes to record this transaction includes which one or more of the following?

a. $28,000 increase in a liability account

b. $10,000 increase in the Cash account

c. $10,000 increase in a revenue account

d. $62,000 increase in an asset account

e. $62,000 increase in a revenue account

f. $62,000 increase in an equity account

Exercise 2-6

Analyzing effects of transactions on accounts

A1

Prepare general journal entries for the following transactions of a new company called Pose-for-Pics.

Aug.   1   Madison Harris, the owner, invested $6,500 cash and $33,500 of photography equipment in the company in exchange for common stock.

2   The company paid $2,100 cash for an insurance policy covering the next 24 months.

5   The company purchased office supplies for $880 cash.

20   The company received $3,331 cash in photography fees earned.

31   The company paid $675 cash for August utilities.

Exercise 2-7

Preparing general journal entries

P1

Use the information in Exercise 2-7 to prepare an August 31 trial balance for Pose-for-Pics. Begin by opening these T-accounts: Cash; Office Supplies; Prepaid Insurance; Photography Equipment; Common Stock; Photography Fees Earned; and Utilities Expense. Then, post the general journal entries to these T-accounts (which will serve as the ledger), and prepare the trial balance.

Exercise 2-8

Preparing T-accounts (ledger) and a trial balance   P2

Prepare general journal entries to record the transactions below for Spade Company by using the following accounts: Cash; Accounts Receivable; Office Supplies; Office Equipment; Accounts Payable; Common Stock; Dividends; Fees Earned; and Rent Expense. Use the letters beside each transaction to identify entries. After recording the transactions, post them to T-accounts, which serves as the general ledger for this assignment. Determine the ending balance of each T-account.

a. Kacy Spade, owner, invested $100,750 cash in the company in exchange for common stock.

b. The company purchased office supplies for $1,250 cash.

c. The company purchased $10,050 of office equipment on credit.

d. The company received $15,500 cash as fees for services provided to a customer.

e. The company paid $10,050 cash to settle the payable for the office equipment purchased in transaction c.

f. The company billed a customer $2,700 as fees for services provided.

g. The company paid $1,225 cash for the monthly rent.

h. The company collected $1,125 cash as partial payment for the account receivable created in transaction f.

i. The company paid $10,000 cash in dividends to Spade (sole shareholder).

Exercise 2-9

Recording effects of transactions in T-accounts

A1

Check   Cash ending balance, $94,850

After recording the transactions of Exercise 2-9 in T-accounts and calculating the balance of each account, prepare a trial balance. Use May 31, 2013, as its report date.

Exercise 2-10

Preparing a trial balance   P2

Examine the following transactions and identify those that create revenues for Valdez Services, a company owned by Brina Valdez. Prepare general journal entries to record those revenue transactions and explain why the other transactions did not create revenues.

a. Brina Valdez invests $39,350 cash in the company in exchange for common stock.

b. The company provided $2,300 of services on credit.

c. The company provided services to a client and immediately received $875 cash.

d. The company received $10,200 cash from a client in payment for services to be provided next year.

e. The company received $3,500 cash from a client in partial payment of an account receivable.

f. The company borrowed $120,000 cash from the bank by signing a promissory note.

Exercise 2-11

Analyzing and journalizing revenue transactions

A1 P1

Exercise 2-12
Analyzing and journalizing
expense transactions

A1 P1

Examine the following transactions and identify those that create expenses for Valdez Services. Prepare general journal entries to record those expense transactions and explain why the other transactions did not create expenses.

a. The company paid $12,200 cash for payment on a 16-month old liability for office supplies.
b. The company paid $1,233 cash for the just completed two-week salary of the receptionist.
c. The company paid $39,200 cash for equipment purchased.
d. The company paid $870 cash for this month's utilities.
e. The company paid $4,500 cash in dividends.

Exercise 2-13
Preparing an income
statement

C3 P3

Carmen Camry operates a consulting firm called Help Today, which began operations on August 1. On August 31, the company's records show the following accounts and amounts for the month of August. Use this information to prepare an August income statement for the business.

Cash	$ 25,360		Dividends	$ 6,000
Accounts receivable	22,360		Consulting fees earned	27,000
Office supplies	5,250		Rent expense	9,550
Land	44,000		Salaries expense	5,600
Office equipment	20,000		Telephone expense	860
Accounts payable	10,500		Miscellaneous expenses	520
Common stock	102,000			

Check   Net income, $10,470

Exercise 2-14
Preparing a statement
of retained earnings   P3

Use the information in Exercise 2-13 to prepare an August statement of retained earnings for Help Today. (The owner invested a total of $102,000 in the company in exchange for common stock on August 1.)

Exercise 2-15
Preparing a balance sheet   P3

Use the information in Exercise 2-13 (if completed, you can also use your solution to Exercise 2-14) to prepare an August 31 balance sheet for Help Today.

Exercise 2-16
Computing net income

A1

A corporation had the following assets and liabilities at the beginning and end of this year.

	Assets	Liabilities
Beginning of the year	$ 60,000	$20,000
End of the year	105,000	36,000

Determine the net income earned or net loss incurred by the business during the year for each of the following *separate* cases:

a. Owner made no investments in the business and no dividends were paid during the year.
b. Owner made no investments in the business but dividends were $1,250 cash per month.
c. No dividends were paid during the year but the owner did invest an additional $55,000 cash in exchange for common stock.
d. Dividends were $1,250 cash per month and the owner invested an additional $35,000 cash in exchange for common stock.

Exercise 2-17
Analyzing changes in a
company's equity

P3

Compute the missing amount for each of the following separate companies *a* through *d*.

	A	B (a)	C (b)	D (c)	E (d)
1					
2	Equity, December 31, 2012	$ 0	$ 0	$ 0	$ 0
3	Owner investments for stock during the year	110,000	?	87,000	210,000
4	Dividends during the year	?	(47,000)	(10,000)	(55,000)
5	Net income (loss) for the year	22,000	90,000	(4,000)	?
6	Equity, December 31, 2013	104,000	85,000	?	110,000
7					

Assume the following T-accounts reflect Belle Co.'s general ledger and that seven transactions *a* through *g* are posted to them. Provide a short description of each transaction. Include the amounts in your descriptions.

Exercise 2-18
Interpreting and describing transactions from T-accounts

A1

Cash			
(a)	6,000	(b)	4,800
(e)	4,500	(c)	900
		(f)	1,600
		(g)	820

Office Supplies	
(c)	900
(d)	300

Prepaid Insurance	
(b)	4,800

Equipment	
(a)	7,600
(d)	9,700

Automobiles	
(a)	12,000

Accounts Payable			
(f)	1,600	(d)	10,000

Common Stock		
		(a)	25,600

Delivery Services Revenue		
		(e)	4,500

Gas and Oil Expense	
(g)	820

Use information from the T-accounts in Exercise 2-18 to prepare general journal entries for each of the seven transactions *a* through *g*.

Exercise 2-19
Preparing general journal entries

P1

Posting errors are identified in the following table. In column (1), enter the amount of the difference between the two trial balance columns (debit and credit) due to the error. In column (2), identify the trial balance column (debit or credit) with the larger amount if they are not equal. In column (3), identify the account(s) affected by the error. In column (4), indicate the amount by which the account(s) in column (3) is under- or overstated. Item (a) is completed as an example.

Exercise 2-20
Identifying effects of posting errors on the trial balance

A1 P2

	Description of Posting Error	(1) Difference between Debit and Credit Columns	(2) Column with the Larger Total	(3) Identify Account(s) Incorrectly Stated	(4) Amount that Account(s) Is Over- or Understated
a.	$3,600 debit to Rent Expense is posted as a $1,340 debit.	$2,260	Credit	Rent Expense	Rent Expense understated $2,260
b.	$6,500 credit to Cash is posted twice as two credits to Cash.				
c.	$10,900 debit to the Dividends account is debited to Common Stock.				
d.	$2,050 debit to Prepaid Insurance is posted as a debit to Insurance Expense.				
e.	$38,000 debit to Machinery is posted as a debit to Accounts Payable.				
f.	$5,850 credit to Services Revenue is posted as a $585 credit.				
g.	$1,390 debit to Store Supplies is not posted.				

You are told the column totals in a trial balance are not equal. After careful analysis, you discover only one error. Specifically, a correctly journalized credit purchase of an automobile for $18,950 is posted from the journal to the ledger with a $18,950 debit to Automobiles and another $18,950 debit to Accounts Payable. The Automobiles account has a debit balance of $37,100 on the trial balance. Answer each of the following questions and compute the dollar amount of any misstatement.

Exercise 2-21
Analyzing a trial balance error

A1 P2

a. Is the debit column total of the trial balance overstated, understated, or correctly stated?

b. Is the credit column total of the trial balance overstated, understated, or correctly stated?

c. Is the Automobiles account balance overstated, understated, or correctly stated in the trial balance?

d. Is the Accounts Payable account balance overstated, understated, or correctly stated in the trial balance?

e. If the debit column total of the trial balance is $200,000 before correcting the error, what is the total of the credit column before correction?

Exercise 2-22

Interpreting the debt ratio and return on assets

A2

a. Calculate the debt ratio and the return on assets using the year-end information for each of the following six separate companies ($ thousands).

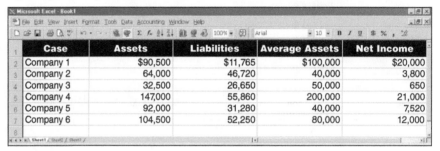

Case	Assets	Liabilities	Average Assets	Net Income
Company 1	$90,500	$11,765	$100,000	$20,000
Company 2	64,000	46,720	40,000	3,800
Company 3	32,500	26,650	50,000	650
Company 4	147,000	55,860	200,000	21,000
Company 5	92,000	31,280	40,000	7,520
Company 6	104,500	52,250	80,000	12,000

b. Of the six companies, which business relies most heavily on creditor financing?

c. Of the six companies, which business relies most heavily on equity financing?

d. Which two companies indicate the greatest risk?

e. Which two companies earn the highest return on assets?

f. Which one company would investors likely prefer based on the risk–return relation?

Exercise 2-23

Preparing a balance sheet following IFRS

P3

BMW reports the following balance sheet accounts for the year ended December 31, 2011 (euro in millions). Prepare the balance sheet for this company as of December 31, 2011, following the usual IFRS formats.

Current liabilities	€11,519	Noncurrent liabilities	€7,767
Current assets	17,682	Noncurrent assets	9,826
Total equity	8,222		

PROBLEM SET A

Problem 2-1A

Preparing and posting journal entries; preparing a trial balance

C3 C4 A1 P1 P2

Aracel Engineering completed the following transactions in the month of June.

a. To launch the company, Jenna Aracel, the owner, invested $100,000 cash, office equipment with a value of $5,000, and $60,000 of drafting equipment in exchange for common stock.

b. The company purchased land worth $49,000 for an office by paying $6,300 cash and signing a long-term note payable for $42,700.

c. The company purchased a portable building with $55,000 cash and moved it onto the land acquired in b.

d. The company paid $3,000 cash for the premium on an 18-month insurance policy.

e. The company completed and delivered a set of plans for a client and collected $6,200 cash.

f. The company purchased $20,000 of additional drafting equipment by paying $9,500 cash and signing a long-term note payable for $10,500.

g. The company completed $14,000 of engineering services for a client. This amount is to be received in 30 days.

h. The company purchased $1,150 of additional office equipment on credit.

i. The company completed engineering services for $22,000 on credit.

j. The company received a bill for rent of equipment that was used on a recently completed job. The $1,333 rent cost must be paid within 30 days.

k. The company collected $7,000 cash in partial payment from the client described in transaction g.

l. The company paid $1,200 cash for wages to a drafting assistant.

m. The company paid $1,150 cash to settle the account payable created in transaction h.

n. The company paid $925 cash for minor maintenance of its drafting equipment.

o. The company paid $9,480 cash in dividends.

p. The company paid $1,200 cash for wages to a drafting assistant.

q. The company paid $2,500 cash for advertisements on the Web during June.

Required

1. Prepare general journal entries to record these transactions (use the account titles listed in part 2).

2. Open the following ledger accounts—their account numbers are in parentheses (use the balance column format): Cash (101); Accounts Receivable (106); Prepaid Insurance (108); Office Equipment (163); Drafting Equipment (164); Building (170); Land (172); Accounts Payable (201); Notes Payable (250); Common Stock (307); Dividends (319); Engineering Fees Earned (402); Wages Expense (601); Equipment Rental Expense (602); Advertising Expense (603); and Repairs Expense (604). Post the journal entries from part 1 to the accounts and enter the balance after each posting.

3. Prepare a trial balance as of the end of June.

Check (2) Ending balances: Cash, $22,945; Accounts Receivable, $29,000; Accounts Payable, $1,333

(3) Trial balance totals, $261,733

Denzel Brooks opens a Web consulting business called Venture Consultants and completes the following transactions in March.

Problem 2-2A

Preparing and posting journal entries; preparing a trial balance

C3 C4 A1 P1 P2

mhhe.com/wildFINMAN5e

Sage 50

March	1	Brooks invested $150,000 cash along with $22,000 in office equipment in the company in exchange for common stock.
	2	The company prepaid $6,000 cash for six months' rent for an office. (*Hint:* Debit Prepaid Rent for $6,000.)
	3	The company made credit purchases of office equipment for $3,000 and office supplies for $1,200. Payment is due within 10 days.
	6	The company completed services for a client and immediately received $4,000 cash.
	9	The company completed a $7,500 project for a client, who must pay within 30 days.
	12	The company paid $4,200 cash to settle the account payable created on March 3.
	19	The company paid $5,000 cash for the premium on a 12-month insurance policy. (*Hint:* Debit Prepaid Insurance for $5,000.)
	22	The company received $3,500 cash as partial payment for the work completed on March 9.
	25	The company completed work for another client for $3,820 on credit.
	29	The company paid $5,100 cash in dividends.
	30	The company purchased $600 of additional office supplies on credit.
	31	The company paid $500 cash for this month's utility bill.

Required

1. Prepare general journal entries to record these transactions (use the account titles listed in part 2).

2. Open the following ledger accounts—their account numbers are in parentheses (use the balance column format): Cash (101); Accounts Receivable (106); Office Supplies (124); Prepaid Insurance (128); Prepaid Rent (131); Office Equipment (163); Accounts Payable (201); Common Stock (307); Dividends (319); Services Revenue (403); and Utilities Expense (690). Post the journal entries from part 1 to the ledger accounts and enter the balance after each posting.

3. Prepare a trial balance as of the end of March.

Check (2) Ending balances: Cash, $136,700; Accounts Receivable, $7,820; Accounts Payable, $600

(3) Total debits, $187,920

Karla Tanner opens a Web consulting business called Linkworks and completes the following transactions in its first month of operations.

Problem 2-3A

Preparing and posting journal entries; preparing a trial balance

C3 C4 A1 P1 P2

Sage 50

April	1	Tanner invests $80,000 cash along with office equipment valued at $26,000 in the company in exchange for common stock.
	2	The company prepaid $9,000 cash for 12 months' rent for office space. (*Hint:* Debit Prepaid Rent for $9,000.)
	3	The company made credit purchases for $8,000 in office equipment and $3,600 in office supplies. Payment is due within 10 days.
	6	The company completed services for a client and immediately received $4,000 cash.
	9	The company completed a $6,000 project for a client, who must pay within 30 days.
	13	The company paid $11,600 cash to settle the account payable created on April 3.
	19	The company paid $2,400 cash for the premium on a 12-month insurance policy. (*Hint:* Debit Prepaid Insurance for $2,400.)
	22	The company received $4,400 cash as partial payment for the work completed on April 9.
	25	The company completed work for another client for $2,890 on credit.
	28	The company paid $5,500 cash in dividends.
	29	The company purchased $600 of additional office supplies on credit.
	30	The company paid $435 cash for this month's utility bill.

86   Chapter 2   Analyzing and Recording Transactions

Required

1. Prepare general journal entries to record these transactions (use account titles listed in part 2).

2. Open the following ledger accounts—their account numbers are in parentheses (use the balance column format): Cash (101); Accounts Receivable (106); Office Supplies (124); Prepaid Insurance (128); Prepaid Rent (131); Office Equipment (163); Accounts Payable (201); Common Stock (307); Dividends (319); Services Revenue (403); and Utilities Expense (690). Post journal entries from part 1 to the ledger accounts and enter the balance after each posting.

3. Prepare a trial balance as of April 30.

Problem 2-4A
Computing net income from equity analysis, preparing a balance sheet, and computing the debt ratio

C2 A1 A2 P3

The accounting records of Nettle Distribution show the following assets and liabilities as of December 31, 2012 and 2013.

December 31	2012	2013
Cash	$ 64,300	$ 15,640
Accounts receivable	26,240	19,390
Office supplies	3,160	1,960
Office equipment	44,000	44,000
Trucks	148,000	157,000
Building	0	80,000
Land	0	60,000
Accounts payable	3,500	33,500
Note payable	0	40,000

Late in December 2013, the business purchased a small office building and land for $140,000. It paid $100,000 cash toward the purchase and a $40,000 note payable was signed for the balance. Mr. Nettle had to invest $35,000 cash in the business (in exchange for common stock) to enable it to pay the $100,000 cash. The business also pays $3,000 cash per month for dividends.

Required

1. Prepare balance sheets for the business as of December 31, 2012 and 2013. (*Hint:* Report only total equity on the balance sheet and remember that total equity equals the difference between assets and liabilities.)

2. By comparing equity amounts from the balance sheets and using the additional information presented in this problem, prepare a calculation to show how much net income was earned by the business during 2013.

3. Compute the 2013 year-end debt ratio (in percent and rounded to one decimal).

Problem 2-5A
Analyzing account balances and reconstructing transactions

C1 C3 A1 P2

Yi Min started an engineering firm called Min Engineering. He began operations and completed seven transactions in May, which included his initial investment of $18,000 cash. After those seven transactions, the ledger included the following accounts with normal balances.

Cash	$37,641
Office supplies	890
Prepaid insurance	4,600
Office equipment	12,900
Accounts payable	12,900
Common stock	18,000
Dividends	3,329
Engineering fees earned	36,000
Rent expense	7,540

Required

1. Prepare a trial balance for this business as of the end of May.

Analysis Components

2. Analyze the accounts and their balances and prepare a list that describes each of the seven most likely transactions and their amounts.

3. Prepare a report of cash received and cash paid showing how the seven transactions in part 2 yield the $37,641 ending Cash balance.

Business transactions completed by Hannah Venedict during the month of September are as follows.

a. Venedict invested $60,000 cash along with office equipment valued at $25,000 in exchange for common stock of a new company named HV Consulting.

b. The company purchased land valued at $40,000 and a building valued at $160,000. The purchase is paid with $30,000 cash and a long-term note payable for $170,000.

c. The company purchased $2,000 of office supplies on credit.

d. Venedict invested her personal automobile in the company in exchange for more common stock. The automobile has a value of $16,500 and is to be used exclusively in the business.

e. The company purchased $5,600 of additional office equipment on credit.

f. The company paid $1,800 cash salary to an assistant.

g. The company provided services to a client and collected $8,000 cash.

h. The company paid $635 cash for this month's utilities.

i. The company paid $2,000 cash to settle the account payable created in transaction *c*.

j. The company purchased $20,300 of new office equipment by paying $20,300 cash.

k. The company completed $6,250 of services for a client, who must pay within 30 days.

l. The company paid $1,800 cash salary to an assistant.

m. The company received $4,000 cash in partial payment on the receivable created in transaction *k*.

n. The company paid $2,800 cash in dividends.

Required

1. Prepare general journal entries to record these transactions (use account titles listed in part 2).

2. Open the following ledger accounts—their account numbers are in parentheses (use the balance column format): Cash (101); Accounts Receivable (106); Office Supplies (108); Office Equipment (163); Automobiles (164); Building (170); Land (172); Accounts Payable (201); Notes Payable (250); Common Stock (307); Dividends (319); Fees Earned (402); Salaries Expense (601); and Utilities Expense (602). Post the journal entries from part 1 to the ledger accounts and enter the balance after each posting.

3. Prepare a trial balance as of the end of September.

Problem 2-6A
Recording transactions; posting to ledger; preparing a trial balance
C3 A1 P1 P2

Check (2) Ending balances: Cash, $12,665; Office Equipment, $50,900

(3) Trial balance totals, $291,350

At the beginning of April, Bernadette Grechus launched a custom computer solutions company called Softworks. The company had the following transactions during April.

a. Bernadette Grechus invested $65,000 cash, office equipment with a value of $5,750, and $30,000 of computer equipment in the company in exchange for common stock.

b. The company purchased land worth $22,000 for an office by paying $5,000 cash and signing a long-term note payable for $17,000.

c. The company purchased a portable building with $34,500 cash and moved it onto the land acquired in *b*.

d. The company paid $5,000 cash for the premium on a two-year insurance policy.

e. The company provided services to a client and immediately collected $4,600 cash.

f. The company purchased $4,500 of additional computer equipment by paying $800 cash and signing a long-term note payable for $3,700.

g. The company completed $4,250 of services for a client. This amount is to be received within 30 days.

h. The company purchased $950 of additional office equipment on credit.

i. The company completed client services for $10,200 on credit.

j. The company received a bill for rent of a computer testing device that was used on a recently completed job. The $580 rent cost must be paid within 30 days.

k. The company collected $5,100 cash in partial payment from the client described in transaction *i*.

l. The company paid $1,800 cash for wages to an assistant.

m. The company paid $950 cash to settle the payable created in transaction *h*.

n. The company paid $608 cash for minor maintenance of the company's computer equipment.

o. The company paid $6,230 cash in dividends.

p. The company paid $1,800 cash for wages to an assistant.

q. The company paid $750 cash for advertisements on the Web during April.

PROBLEM SET B

Problem 2-1B
Preparing and posting journal entries; preparing a trial balance
C3 C4 A1 P1 P2

88

Chapter 2   Analyzing and Recording Transactions

Required

1. Prepare general journal entries to record these transactions (use account titles listed in part 2).

2. Open the following ledger accounts—their account numbers are in parentheses (use the balance column format): Cash (101); Accounts Receivable (106); Prepaid Insurance (108); Office Equipment (163); Computer Equipment (164); Building (170); Land (172); Accounts Payable (201); Notes Payable (250); Common Stock (307); Dividends (319); Fees Earned (402); Wages Expense (601); Computer Rental Expense (602); Advertising Expense (603); and Repairs Expense (604). Post the journal entries from part 1 to the accounts and enter the balance after each posting.

3. Prepare a trial balance as of the end of April.

Problem 2-2B

Preparing and posting journal entries; preparing a trial balance

C3 C4 A1 P1 P2

Zucker Management Services opens for business and completes these transactions in November.

Nov. 1   Matt Zucker, the owner, invested $30,000 cash along with $15,000 of office equipment in the company in exchange for common stock.

   2   The company prepaid $4,500 cash for six months' rent for an office. (*Hint:* Debit Prepaid Rent for $4,500.)

   4   The company made credit purchases of office equipment for $2,500 and of office supplies for $600. Payment is due within 10 days.

   8   The company completed work for a client and immediately received $3,400 cash.

   12   The company completed a $10,200 project for a client, who must pay within 30 days.

   13   The company paid $3,100 cash to settle the payable created on November 4.

   19   The company paid $1,800 cash for the premium on a 24-month insurance policy.

   22   The company received $5,200 cash as partial payment for the work completed on November 12.

   24   The company completed work for another client for $1,750 on credit.

   28   The company paid $5,300 cash in dividends.

   29   The company purchased $249 of additional office supplies on credit.

   30   The company paid $831 cash for this month's utility bill.

Required

1. Prepare general journal entries to record these transactions (use account titles listed in part 2).

2. Open the following ledger accounts—their account numbers are in parentheses (use the balance column format): Cash (101); Accounts Receivable (106); Office Supplies (124); Prepaid Insurance (128); Prepaid Rent (131); Office Equipment (163); Accounts Payable (201); Common Stock (307); Dividends (319); Services Revenue (403); and Utilities Expense (690). Post the journal entries from part 1 to the ledger accounts and enter the balance after each posting.

3. Prepare a trial balance as of the end of November.

Problem 2-3B

Preparing and posting journal entries; preparing a trial balance

C3 C4 A1 P1 P2

Humble Management Services opens for business and completes these transactions in September.

Sept. 1   Henry Humble, the owner, invests $38,000 cash along with office equipment valued at $15,000 in the company in exchange for common stock.

   2   The company prepaid $9,000 cash for 12 months' rent for office space. (*Hint:* Debit Prepaid Rent for $9,000.)

   4   The company made credit purchases for $8,000 in office equipment and $2,400 in office supplies. Payment is due within 10 days.

   8   The company completed work for a client and immediately received $3,280 cash.

   12   The company completed a $15,400 project for a client, who must pay within 30 days.

   13   The company paid $10,400 cash to settle the payable created on September 4.

   19   The company paid $1,900 cash for the premium on an 18-month insurance policy. (*Hint:* Debit Prepaid Insurance for $1,900.)

22   The company received $7,700 cash as partial payment for the work completed on September 12.

24   The company completed work for another client for $2,100 on credit.

28   The company paid $5,300 cash in dividends.

29   The company purchased $550 of additional office supplies on credit.

30   The company paid $860 cash for this month's utility bill.

Required

1. Prepare general journal entries to record these transactions (use account titles listed in part 2).

2. Open the following ledger accounts—their account numbers are in parentheses (use the balance column format): Cash (101); Accounts Receivable (106); Office Supplies (124); Prepaid Insurance (128); Prepaid Rent (131); Office Equipment (163); Accounts Payable (201); Common Stock (307); Dividends (319); Service Fees Earned (401); and Utilities Expense (690). Post journal entries from part 1 to the ledger accounts and enter the balance after each posting.

3. Prepare a trial balance as of the end of September.

Check   (2) Ending balances: Cash, $21,520; Accounts Receivable, $9,800; Accounts Payable, $550

(3) Total debits, $74,330

The accounting records of Tama Co. show the following assets and liabilities as of December 31, 2012 and 2013.

Problem 2-4B
Computing net income from equity analysis, preparing a balance sheet, and computing the debt ratio

C2 A1 A2 P3

December 31	2012	2013
Cash	$20,000	$ 5,000
Accounts receivable	35,000	25,000
Office supplies	8,000	13,500
Office equipment	40,000	40,000
Machinery	28,500	28,500
Building	0	250,000
Land	0	50,000
Accounts payable	4,000	12,000
Note payable	0	250,000

Late in December 2013, the business purchased a small office building and land for $300,000. It paid $50,000 cash toward the purchase and a $250,000 note payable was signed for the balance. Joe Tama, the owner, had to invest an additional $15,000 cash (in exchange for common stock) to enable it to pay the $50,000 cash toward the purchase. The business also pays $250 cash per month for dividends.

Required

1. Prepare balance sheets for the business as of December 31, 2012 and 2013. (*Hint:* Report only total equity on the balance sheet and remember that total equity equals the difference between assets and liabilities.)

2. By comparing equity amounts from the balance sheets and using the additional information presented in the problem, prepare a calculation to show how much net income was earned by the business during 2013.

3. Calculate the December 31, 2013, debt ratio (in percent and rounded to one decimal).

Check   (2) Net income, $10,500

(3) Debt ratio, 63.6%

Roshaun Gould started a Web consulting firm called Gould Solutions. He began operations and completed seven transactions in April that resulted in the following accounts, which all have normal balances.

Problem 2-5B
Analyzing account balances and reconstructing transactions

C1 C3 A1 P2

Cash	$19,982
Office supplies	760
Prepaid rent	1,800
Office equipment	12,250
Accounts payable	12,250
Common stock	15,000
Dividends	5,200
Consulting fees earned	20,400
Operating expenses	7,658

Required

Check   (1) Trial balance total, $47,650

1. Prepare a trial balance for this business as of the end of April.

Analysis Component

2. Analyze the accounts and their balances and prepare a list that describes each of the seven most likely transactions and their amounts.

(3) Cash paid, $15,418

3. Prepare a report of cash received and cash paid showing how the seven transactions in part 2 yield the $19,982 ending Cash balance.

Problem 2-6B

Recording transactions; posting to ledger; preparing a trial balance

C3   A1   P1   P2

Nuncio Consulting completed the following transactions during June.

a. Armand Nuncio, the owner, invested $35,000 cash along with office equipment valued at $11,000 in the new company in exchange for common stock.

b. The company purchased land valued at $7,500 and a building valued at $40,000. The purchase is paid with $15,000 cash and a long-term note payable for $32,500.

c. The company purchased $500 of office supplies on credit.

d. A. Nuncio invested his personal automobile in the company in exchange for more common stock. The automobile has a value of $8,000 and is to be used exclusively in the business.

e. The company purchased $1,200 of additional office equipment on credit.

f. The company paid $1,000 cash salary to an assistant.

g. The company provided services to a client and collected $3,200 cash.

h. The company paid $540 cash for this month's utilities.

i. The company paid $500 cash to settle the payable created in transaction *c.*

j. The company purchased $3,400 of new office equipment by paying $3,400 cash.

k. The company completed $4,200 of services for a client, who must pay within 30 days.

l. The company paid $1,000 cash salary to an assistant.

m. The company received $2,200 cash in partial payment on the receivable created in transaction *k.*

n. The company paid $1,100 cash in dividends.

Required

1. Prepare general journal entries to record these transactions (use account titles listed in part 2).

Check   (2) Ending balances: Cash, $17,860; Office Equipment, $15,600

2. Open the following ledger accounts—their account numbers are in parentheses (use the balance column format): Cash (101); Accounts Receivable (106); Office Supplies (108); Office Equipment (163); Automobiles (164); Building (170); Land (172); Accounts Payable (201); Notes Payable (250); Common Stock (307); Dividends (319); Fees Earned (402); Salaries Expense (601); and Utilities Expense (602). Post the journal entries from part 1 to the ledger accounts and enter the balance after each posting.

(3) Trial balance totals, $95,100

3. Prepare a trial balance as of the end of June.

SERIAL PROBLEM

Success Systems

A1   P1   P2

(This serial problem started in Chapter 1 and continues through most of the chapters. If the Chapter 1 segment was not completed, the problem can begin at this point. It is helpful, but not necessary, to use the Working Papers that accompany this book.)

SP 2 On October 1, 2013, Adria Lopez launched a computer services company called **Success Systems,** which provides consulting services, computer system installations, and custom program development. Adria adopts the calendar year for reporting purposes and expects to prepare the company's first set of financial statements on December 31, 2013. The company's initial chart of accounts follows.

Sage 50

Account	No.	Account	No.
Cash	101	Common Stock	307
Accounts Receivable	106	Dividends	319
Computer Supplies	126	Computer Services Revenue	403
Prepaid Insurance	128	Wages Expense	623
Prepaid Rent	131	Advertising Expense	655
Office Equipment	163	Mileage Expense	676
Computer Equipment	167	Miscellaneous Expenses	677
Accounts Payable	201	Repairs Expense—Computer	684

Required

1. Prepare journal entries to record each of the following transactions for Success Systems.

Oct. 1   Adria Lopez invested $55,000 cash, a $20,000 computer system, and $8,000 of office equipment in the company in exchange for its common stock.

  2   The company paid $3,300 cash for four months' rent. (*Hint:* Debit Prepaid Rent for $3,300.)

  3   The company purchased $1,420 of computer supplies on credit from Harris Office Products.

  5   The company paid $2,220 cash for one year's premium on a property and liability insurance policy. (*Hint:* Debit Prepaid Insurance for $2,220.)

  6   The company billed Easy Leasing $4,800 for services performed in installing a new Web server.

  8   The company paid $1,420 cash for the computer supplies purchased from Harris Office Products on October 3.

  10   The company hired Lyn Addie as a part-time assistant for $125 per day, as needed.

  12   The company billed Easy Leasing another $1,400 for services performed.

  15   The company received $4,800 cash from Easy Leasing as partial payment on its account.

  17   The company paid $805 cash to repair computer equipment that was damaged when moving it.

  20   The company paid $1,940 cash for advertisements published in the local newspaper.

  22   The company received $1,400 cash from Easy Leasing on its account.

  28   The company billed IFM Company $5,208 for services performed.

  31   The company paid $875 cash for Lyn Addie's wages for seven days' work.

  31   The company paid $3,600 cash in dividends.

Nov. 1   The company reimbursed Adria Lopez in cash for business automobile mileage allowance (Lopez logged 1,000 miles at $0.32 per mile).

  2   The company received $4,633 cash from Liu Corporation for computer services performed.

  5   The company purchased computer supplies for $1,125 cash from Harris Office Products.

  8   The company billed Gomez Co. $5,668 for services performed.

  13   The company received notification from Alex's Engineering Co. that Success Systems' bid of $3,950 for an upcoming project is accepted.

  18   The company received $2,208 cash from IFM Company as partial payment of the October 28 bill.

  22   The company donated $250 cash to the United Way in the company's name.

  24   The company completed work for Alex's Engineering Co. and sent it a bill for $3,950.

  25   The company sent another bill to IFM Company for the past-due amount of $3,000.

  28   The company reimbursed Adria Lopez in cash for business automobile mileage (1,200 miles at $0.32 per mile).

  30   The company paid $1,750 cash for Lyn Addie's wages for 14 days' work.

  30   The company paid $2,000 cash in dividends.

2. Open ledger accounts (in balance column format) and post the journal entries from part 1 to them.

3. Prepare a trial balance as of the end of November.

Check   (2) Cash, Nov. 30 bal., $48,052

(3) Trial bal. totals, $108,659

Beyond the Numbers

REPORTING IN ACTION

A1 A2

Polaris

BTN 2-1   Refer to Polaris's financial statements in Appendix A for the following questions.

Required

1. What amount of total liabilities does it report for each of the fiscal years ended December 31, 2011 and 2010?
2. What amount of total assets does it report for each of the fiscal years ended December 31, 2011 and 2010?
3. Compute its debt ratio for each of the fiscal years ended December 31, 2011 and 2010. (Report ratio in percent and round it to one decimal.)
4. In which fiscal year did it employ more financial leverage (December 31, 2011 or 2010)? Explain.

Fast Forward

5. Access its financial statements (10-K report) for a fiscal year ending after December 31, 2011, from its Website (Polaris.com) or the SEC's EDGAR database (www.sec.gov). Recompute its debt ratio for any subsequent year's data and compare it with the debt ratio for 2010 and 2011.

COMPARATIVE ANALYSIS

A1 A2

Polaris

Arctic Cat

BTN 2-2   Key comparative figures for Polaris and Arctic Cat follow.

($ thousands)	Polaris		Arctic Cat	
	Current Year	Prior Year	Current Year	Prior Year
Total liabilities	$ 727,968	$ 690,656	$ 89,870	$ 78,745
Total assets	1,228,024	1,061,647	272,906	246,084

1. What is the debt ratio for Polaris in the current year and for the prior year?
2. What is the debt ratio for Arctic Cat in the current year and for the prior year?
3. Which of the two companies has the higher degree of financial leverage? What does this imply?

ETHICS CHALLENGE

C1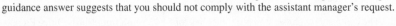

BTN 2-3   Review the *Decision Ethics* case from the first part of this chapter involving the cashier. The guidance answer suggests that you should not comply with the assistant manager's request.

Required

Propose and evaluate two other courses of action you might consider, and explain why.

COMMUNICATING IN PRACTICE

C1 C2 A1 P3

BTN 2-4   Lila Corentine is an aspiring entrepreneur and your friend. She is having difficulty understanding the purposes of financial statements and how they fit together across time.

Required

Write a one-page memorandum to Corentine explaining the purposes of the four financial statements and how they are linked across time.

BTN 2-5   Access EDGAR online (www.SEC.gov) and locate the 2011 year 10-K report of Amazon.com (ticker AMZN) filed on February 1, 2012. Review its financial statements reported for years ended 2011, 2010, and 2009 to answer the following questions.

TAKING IT TO THE NET
A1

Required

1. What are the amounts of its net income or net loss reported for each of these three years?

2. Does Amazon's operating activities provide cash or use cash for each of these three years?

3. If Amazon has a 2011 net income of more than $600 million and 2011 operating cash flows of nearly $4,000 million, how is it possible that its cash balance at December 31, 2011, increases by less than $1,500 million relative to its balance at December 31, 2010?

BTN 2-6   The expanded accounting equation consists of assets, liabilities, common stock, dividends, revenues, and expenses. It can be used to reveal insights into changes in a company's financial position.

TEAMWORK IN ACTION
C1 C2 C4 A1

Required

1. Form *learning teams* of six (or more) members. Each team member must select one of the six components and each team must have at least one expert on each component: (*a*) assets, (*b*) liabilities, (*c*) common stock, (*d*) dividends, (*e*) revenues, and (*f*) expenses.

2. Form *expert teams* of individuals who selected the same component in part 1. Expert teams are to draft a report that each expert will present to his or her learning team addressing the following:

  a. Identify for its component the (i) increase and decrease side of the account and (ii) normal balance side of the account.

  b. Describe a transaction, with amounts, that increases its component.

  c. Using the transaction and amounts in (*b*), verify the equality of the accounting equation and then explain any effects on the income statement and statement of cash flows.

  d. Describe a transaction, with amounts, that decreases its component.

  e. Using the transaction and amounts in (*d*), verify the equality of the accounting equation and then explain any effects on the income statement and statement of cash flows.

3. Each expert should return to his/her learning team. In rotation, each member presents his/her expert team's report to the learning team. Team discussion is encouraged.

BTN 2-7   Assume Misa Chien and Jennifer Green of Nom Nom Truck plan on expanding their business to accommodate more product lines. They are considering financing their expansion in one of two ways: (1) contributing more of their own funds to the business or (2) borrowing the funds from a bank.

ENTREPRENEURIAL DECISION
A1 A2 P3

Required

Identify at least two issues that Misa and Jennifer should consider when trying to decide on the method for financing their expansion.

**ENTREPRENEURIAL
DECISION**

A1 A2 P3

BTN 2-8   Angel Martin is a young entrepreneur who operates Martin Music Services, offering singing lessons and instruction on musical instruments. Martin wishes to expand but needs a $30,000 loan. The bank requests Martin to prepare a balance sheet and key financial ratios. Martin has not kept formal records but is able to provide the following accounts and their amounts as of December 31, 2013.

Cash..............	$ 3,600	Accounts Receivable....	$ 9,600	Prepaid Insurance.....	$ 1,500
Prepaid Rent........	9,400	Store Supplies.........	6,600	Equipment...........	50,000
Accounts Payable....	2,200	Unearned Lesson Fees...	15,600	Total Equity*.........	62,900
Annual net income...	40,000				

* The total equity amount reflects all owner investments, dividends, revenues, and expenses as of December 31, 2013.

Required

1. Prepare a balance sheet as of December 31, 2013, for Martin Music Services. (Report only the total equity amount on the balance sheet.)
2. Compute Martin's debt ratio and its return on assets (the latter ratio is defined in Chapter 1). Assume average assets equal its ending balance.
3. Do you believe the prospects of a $30,000 bank loan are good? Why or why not?

HITTING THE ROAD

C1

BTN 2-9   Obtain a recent copy of the most prominent newspaper distributed in your area. Research the classified section and prepare a report answering the following questions (attach relevant classified clippings to your report). Alternatively, you may want to search the Web for the required information. One suitable Website is CareerOneStop (www.CareerOneStop.org). For documentation, you should print copies of Websites accessed.

1. Identify the number of listings for accounting positions and the various accounting job titles.
2. Identify the number of listings for other job titles, with examples, that require or prefer accounting knowledge/experience but are not specifically accounting positions.
3. Specify the salary range for the accounting and accounting-related positions if provided.
4. Indicate the job that appeals to you, the reason for its appeal, and its requirements.

GLOBAL DECISION

A2

KTM

Polaris

Arctic Cat

BTN 2-10   KTM (www.KTM.com) is a leading manufacturer of offroad and street motorcycles, and it competes to some extent with both **Polaris** and **Arctic Cat**. Key financial ratios for the current fiscal year follow.

Key Figure	KTM	Polaris	Arctic Cat
Return on assets.........	4.3%	18.5%	4.8%
Debt ratio.............	54.8%	59.3%	32.9%

Required

1. Which company is most profitable according to its return on assets?
2. Which company is most risky according to the debt ratio?
3. Which company deserves increased investment based on a joint analysis of return on assets and the debt ratio? Explain.

ANSWERS TO MULTIPLE CHOICE QUIZ

1. b; debit Utility Expense for $700, and credit Cash for $700.

2. a; debit Cash for $2,500, and credit Unearned Lawn Service Fees for $2,500.

3. c; debit Cash for $250,000, debit Land for $500,000, and credit Common Stock for $750,000.

4. d

5. e; Debt ratio = $400,000/$1,000,000 = <u>40%</u>

Adjusting Accounts and Preparing Financial Statements

A Look Back

Chapter 2 explained the analysis and recording of transactions. We showed how to apply and interpret company accounts, T-accounts, double-entry accounting, ledgers, postings, and trial balances.

A Look at This Chapter

This chapter explains the timing of reports and the need to adjust accounts. Adjusting accounts is important for recognizing revenues and expenses in the proper period. We describe how to prepare financial statements from an adjusted trial balance, and how the closing process works.

A Look Ahead

Chapter 4 looks at accounting for merchandising activities. We describe the sale and purchase of merchandise and their implications for preparing and analyzing financial statements.

Learning Objectives

CONCEPTUAL

C1 Explain the importance of periodic reporting and the time period assumption. (p. 98)

C2 Explain accrual accounting and how it improves financial statements. (p. 99)

C3 Identify steps in the accounting cycle. (p. 116)

C4 Explain and prepare a classified balance sheet. (p. 117)

ANALYTICAL

A1 Explain how accounting adjustments link to financial statements. (p. 109)

A2 Compute profit margin and describe its use in analyzing company performance. (p. 121)

A3 Compute the current ratio and describe what it reveals about a company's financial condition. (p. 121)

PROCEDURAL

P1 Prepare and explain adjusting entries. (p. 100)

P2 Explain and prepare an adjusted trial balance. (p. 110)

P3 Prepare financial statements from an adjusted trial balance. (p. 110)

P4 Describe and prepare closing entries. (p. 112)

P5 Explain and prepare a post-closing trial balance. (p. 114)

P6 *Appendix 3A*—Explain the alternatives in accounting for prepaids. (p. 125)

P7 *Appendix 3B*—Prepare a work sheet and explain its usefulness. (p. 127)

P8 *Appendix 3C*—Prepare reversing entries and explain their purpose. (p. 131)

Decision Insight

Dorm Roomies to Fashion Divas

"Do what you love and love what you do."
—**ASHLEY COOK** (ON RIGHT)

NEW YORK—"Never in a million years did I think that just three months after graduation I would already have my own business," recalls Ashley Cook. "It is a lot of work, but a dream come true!" Ashley, along with Danielle Dankner, launched **ash&dans** (**ashanddans.com**), an affordable line of scarves and embellished jersey pieces, including tops and dresses. "We learn something new everyday," explains Ashley. "We enjoy both the business side and the creative side and fill each day with equal amounts of both."

Ashley and Danielle explain how they set up an accounting system early on to account for all business activities, including cash, revenues, receivables, and payables. They also had to learn about the deferral and accrual of revenues and expenses. Setting up an accounting system was an important part of their success, explains Ashley. "The reason we were able to make things work was because we were extremely prudent with our money. We kept our costs down to a minimum . . . [and] because we were so careful with our buying, we were able to cover our costs by selling our product and keeping very little inventory."

"It is amazing how much we have developed our business savvy," says Ashley. This includes monitoring the adjusting of accounts so that revenues and expenses are properly reported

so that good decisions are made. Adds Ashley, "We do everything inhouse . . . from design to marketing to PR to sales to accounting."

Financial statement preparation and analysis are tasks that Ashley and Danielle emphasize. Although they insist on timely and accurate accounting reports, Ashley says "we are very happy with how our business started and how it has grown." To achieve that growth, Ashley and Danielle took time to understand accounting adjustments and their effects. It is part of the larger picture. "People love our story." For that to continue, they insist that a reliable accounting system is necessary . . . otherwise the business side would fail.

"We look forward to growing our brand, continually challenging ourselves and coming up with innovative designs," says Ashley. She also offers a little advice: "Educate yourself and surround yourself with people who know more than you do. Never be afraid to ask questions or take risks." Adds Danielle, "The most difficult part was simply learning to block out the non-believers."

[Sources: *ash&dans Website*, January 2013; *Under30CEO*, March 2010; *ClosetVanity.com*, December 2011; *Washington Magazine*, October 2010; *YHP,* December 2009]

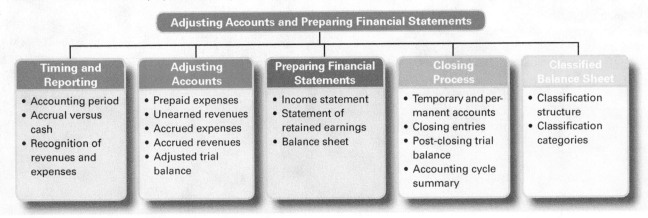

Chapter Preview

Chapters 1 and 2 described how transactions and events are analyzed, journalized, and posted. This chapter describes important adjustments that are often necessary to properly reflect revenues when earned and expenses when incurred. This chapter also describes financial statement preparation. It explains the closing process that readies revenue, expense, and dividend accounts for the next reporting period and updates retained earnings. It also explains how accounts are classified on a balance sheet to increase their usefulness to decision makers.

Adjusting Accounts and Preparing Financial Statements

Timing and Reporting	Adjusting Accounts	Preparing Financial Statements	Closing Process	Classified Balance Sheet
• Accounting period • Accrual versus cash • Recognition of revenues and expenses	• Prepaid expenses • Unearned revenues • Accrued expenses • Accrued revenues • Adjusted trial balance	• Income statement • Statement of retained earnings • Balance sheet	• Temporary and permanent accounts • Closing entries • Post-closing trial balance • Accounting cycle summary	• Classification structure • Classification categories

TIMING AND REPORTING

This section describes the importance of reporting accounting information at regular intervals and its impact for recording revenues and expenses.

The Accounting Period

C1 Explain the importance of periodic reporting and the time period assumption.

The value of information is often linked to its timeliness. Useful information must reach decision makers frequently and promptly. To provide timely information, accounting systems prepare reports at regular intervals. This results in an accounting process impacted by the time period (or periodicity) assumption. The **time period assumption** presumes that an organization's activities can be divided into specific time periods such as a month, a three-month quarter, a six-month interval, or a year. Exhibit 3.1 shows various **accounting,** or *reporting,* **periods.** Most organizations use a year as their primary accounting period. Reports covering a one-year period are known as **annual financial statements.** Many organizations also prepare **interim financial statements** covering one, three, or six months of activity.

"Polaris announces annual income of . . ."

EXHIBIT 3.1

Accounting Periods

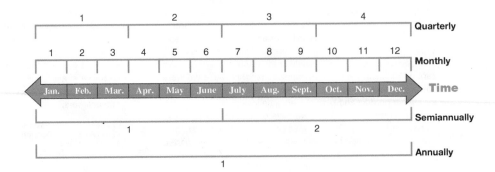

The annual reporting period is not always a calendar year ending on December 31. An organization can adopt a **fiscal year** consisting of any 12 consecutive months. It is also acceptable to adopt an annual reporting period of 52 weeks. For example, Gap's fiscal year consistently ends the final week of January or the first week of February each year.

Companies with little seasonal variation in sales often choose the calendar year as their fiscal year. Facebook, Inc., uses calendar year reporting. However, the financial statements of The Kellogg Company (the company that controls characters such as Tony the Tiger, Snap! Crackle! Pop!, and Keebler Elf) reflect a fiscal year that ends on the Saturday nearest December 31. Companies experiencing seasonal variations in sales often choose a **natural business year** end, which is when sales activities are at their lowest level for the year. The natural business year for retailers such as Walmart, Target, and Macy's usually ends around January 31, after the holiday season.

Accrual Basis versus Cash Basis

After external transactions and events are recorded, several accounts still need adjustments before their balances appear in financial statements. This need arises because internal transactions and events remain unrecorded. **Accrual basis accounting** uses the adjusting process to recognize revenues when earned and expenses when incurred (matched with revenues).

 C2   Explain accrual accounting and how it improves financial statements.

Cash basis accounting recognizes revenues when cash is received and records expenses when cash is paid. This means that cash basis net income for a period is the difference between cash receipts and cash payments. Cash basis accounting is not consistent with generally accepted accounting principles (neither U.S. GAAP nor IFRS).

It is commonly held that accrual accounting better reflects business performance than information about cash receipts and payments. Accrual accounting also increases the *comparability* of financial statements from one period to another. Yet cash basis accounting is useful for several business decisions—which is the reason companies must report a statement of cash flows.

To see the difference between these two accounting systems, let's consider FastForward's Prepaid Insurance account. FastForward paid $2,400 for 24 months of insurance coverage that began on December 1, 2013. Accrual accounting requires that $100 of insurance expense be reported on December 2013's income statement. Another $1,200 of expense is reported in year 2014, and the remaining $1,100 is reported as expense in the first 11 months of 2015. Exhibit 3.2 illustrates this allocation of insurance cost across these three years. Any unexpired premium is reported as a Prepaid Insurance asset on the accrual basis balance sheet.

EXHIBIT 3.2

Accrual Accounting for Allocating Prepaid Insurance to Expense

Alternatively, a cash basis income statement for December 2013 reports insurance expense of $2,400, as shown in Exhibit 3.3. The cash basis income statements for years 2014 and 2015 report no insurance expense. The cash basis balance sheet never reports an insurance asset because it is immediately expensed. This shows that cash basis income for 2013–2015 fails to match the cost of insurance with the insurance benefits received for those years and months.

EXHIBIT 3.3

Cash Accounting for Allocating Prepaid Insurance to Expense

Recognizing Revenues and Expenses

Point: Recording revenue early over-states current-period revenue and income; recording it late understates current-period revenue and income.

Point: Recording expense early over-states current-period expense and understates current-period income; recording it late understates current-period expense and overstates current-period income.

We use the time period assumption to divide a company's activities into specific time periods, but not all activities are complete when financial statements are prepared. Thus, adjustments often are required to get correct account balances.

We rely on two principles in the adjusting process: revenue recognition and expense recognition (the latter is often referred to as matching). Chapter 1 explained that the *revenue recognition principle* requires that revenue be recorded when earned, not before and not after. Most companies earn revenue when they provide services and products to customers. A major goal of the adjusting process is to have revenue recognized (reported) in the time period when it is earned. The **expense recognition** (or **matching**) **principle** aims to record expenses in the same accounting period as the revenues that are earned as a result of those expenses. This matching of expenses with the revenue benefits is a major part of the adjusting process.

Matching expenses with revenues often requires us to predict certain events. When we use financial statements, we must understand that they require estimates and therefore include measures that are not precise. Walt Disney's annual report explains that its production costs from movies, such as its *Pirates of the Caribbean* series, are matched to revenues based on a ratio of current revenues from the movie divided by its predicted total revenues.

Decision Insight

Diamond Foods, Inc., a popular snack maker, was recently investigated for postponing expenses related to payments to its walnut growers. This alleged late expense recognition caused income to be overstated in 2011. Further, this misstatement threatened completion of its recent acquisition of **Pringles** (for more details, see *BusinessWeek,* January 17, 2012). ▨

Quick Check

Answers — p. 132

1. Describe a company's annual reporting period.
2. Why do companies prepare interim financial statements?
3. What two accounting principles most directly drive the adjusting process?
4. Is cash basis accounting consistent with the matching principle? Why or why not?
5. If your company pays a $4,800 premium on April 1, 2013, for two years' insurance coverage, how much insurance expense is reported in 2014 using cash basis accounting?

ADJUSTING ACCOUNTS

Adjusting accounts is a three-step process:

Step 1: Determine what the current account balance *equals*.

Step 2: Determine what the current account balance *should equal*.

Step 3: Record an adjusting entry to get from step *1* to step *2*.

Framework for Adjustments

P1 Prepare and explain adjusting entries.

Adjustments are necessary for transactions and events that extend over more than one period. It is helpful to group adjustments by the timing of cash receipt or cash payment in relation to the recognition of the related revenues or expenses. Exhibit 3.4 identifies four types of adjustments.

The left half of this exhibit shows prepaid expenses (including depreciation) and unearned revenues, which reflect transactions when cash is paid or received *before* a related expense or

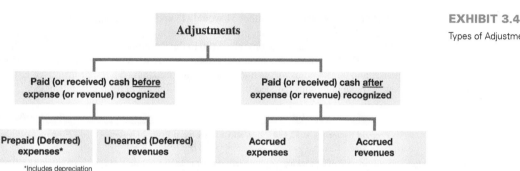

EXHIBIT 3.4

Types of Adjustments

revenue is recognized. They are also called *deferrals* because the recognition of an expense (or revenue) is *deferred* until after the related cash is paid (or received). The right half of this exhibit shows accrued expenses and accrued revenues, which reflect transactions when cash is paid or received *after* a related expense or revenue is recognized. Adjusting entries are necessary for each of these so that revenues, expenses, assets, and liabilities are correctly reported. Specifically, an **adjusting entry** is made at the end of an accounting period to reflect a transaction or event that is not yet recorded. Each adjusting entry affects one or more income statement accounts *and* one or more balance sheet accounts (but never the Cash account).

Point: Source documents provide information for most daily transactions, and in many businesses the recordkeepers record them. Adjustments require more knowledge and are usually handled by senior accounting professionals.

Prepaid (Deferred) Expenses

Prepaid expenses refer to items *paid for* in advance of receiving their benefits. Prepaid expenses are assets. When these assets are used, their costs become expenses. Adjusting entries for prepaids increase expenses and decrease assets as shown in the T-accounts of Exhibit 3.5. Such adjustments reflect transactions and events that use up prepaid expenses (including passage of time). To illustrate the accounting for prepaid expenses, we look at prepaid insurance, supplies, and depreciation.

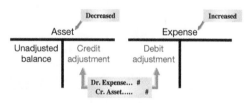

EXHIBIT 3.5

Adjusting for Prepaid Expenses

Prepaid Insurance   We use our 3-step process for this and all accounting adjustments.

Step 1:   We determine that the current balance of FastForward's prepaid insurance is equal to its $2,400 payment for 24 months of insurance benefits that began on December 1, 2013.

Step 2:   With the passage of time, the benefits of the insurance gradually expire and a portion of the Prepaid Insurance asset becomes expense. For instance, one month's insurance coverage expires by December 31, 2013. This expense is $100, or 1/24 of $2,400, which leaves $2,300.

Step 3:   The adjusting entry to record this expense and reduce the asset, along with T-account postings, follows:

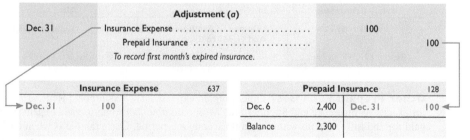

Assets = Liabilities + Equity
−100   −100

Explanation   After adjusting and posting, the $100 balance in Insurance Expense and the $2,300 balance in Prepaid Insurance are ready for reporting in financial statements. *Not* making the adjustment on or before December 31 would (1) understate expenses by $100 and overstate net income by $100 for the December income statement and (2) overstate both prepaid insurance (assets) and equity (because of net income) by $100 in the December 31 balance sheet. (Exhibit 3.2 showed that 2014's adjustments must transfer a total of $1,200 from Prepaid Insurance to Insurance Expense, and 2015's adjustments must transfer the remaining $1,100 to Insurance Expense.) The following table highlights the December 31, 2013, adjustment for prepaid insurance.

Before Adjustment	Adjustment	After Adjustment
Prepaid Insurance = $2,400	**Deduct $100 from Prepaid Insurance Add $100 to Insurance Expense**	**Prepaid Insurance = $2,300**
Reports $2,400 policy for 24-months' coverage.	Record current month's $100 insurance expense and $100 reduction in prepaid amount.	Reports $2,300 in coverage for remaining 23 months.

Supplies   Supplies are a prepaid expense requiring adjustment.

Step 1:   FastForward purchased $9,720 of supplies in December and some of them were used during this month. When financial statements are prepared at December 31, the cost of supplies used during December must be recognized.

Supplies

Dec. 2,6,26 Purchase supplies and record asset

Dec. 31 Supplies used and record expense

Step 2:   When FastForward computes (takes physical count of) its remaining unused supplies at December 31, it finds $8,670 of supplies remaining of the $9,720 total supplies. The $1,050 difference between these two amounts is December's supplies expense.

Step 3:   The adjusting entry to record this expense and reduce the Supplies asset account, along with T-account postings, follows:

Assets = Liabilities + Equity
-1,050   -1,050

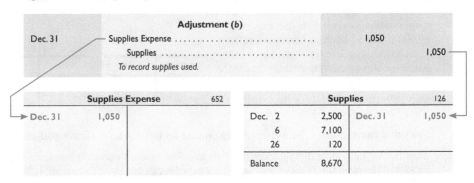

Adjustment (b)

Dec. 31	Supplies Expense	1,050	
	Supplies		1,050
	To record supplies used.		

Supplies Expense		652
Dec. 31	1,050	

Supplies				126
Dec. 2	2,500	Dec. 31	1,050
6	7,100		
26	120		
Balance	8,670		

Explanation   The balance of the Supplies account is $8,670 after posting—equaling the cost of the remaining supplies. *Not* making the adjustment on or before December 31 would (1) understate expenses by $1,050 and overstate net income by $1,050 for the December income statement and (2) overstate both supplies and equity (because of net income) by $1,050 in the December 31 balance sheet. The following table highlights the adjustment for supplies.

Before Adjustment	Adjustment	After Adjustment
Supplies = $9,720	**Deduct $1,050 from Supplies Add $1,050 to Supplies Expense**	**Supplies = $8,670**
Reports $9,720 in supplies.	Record $1,050 in supplies used and $1,050 as supplies expense.	Reports $8,670 in supplies.

Other Prepaid Expenses   Other prepaid expenses, such as Prepaid Rent, are accounted for exactly as Insurance and Supplies are. We should note that some prepaid expenses are both paid for and fully used up within a single accounting period. One example is when a company pays monthly rent on the first day of each month. This payment creates a prepaid expense on the first day of each month that fully expires by the end of the month. In these special cases, we can record the cash paid with a debit to an expense account instead of an asset account. This practice is described more completely later in the chapter.

■ **Decision** Maker

Investor   A small publishing company signs an aspiring Olympic gymnast to write a book. The company pays the gymnast $500,000 to sign plus future book royalties. A note to the company's financial statements says that "prepaid expenses include $500,000 in author signing fees to be matched against future expected sales." Is this accounting for the signing bonus acceptable? How does it affect your analysis? ■   [Answer—p. 132]

Depreciation   A special category of prepaid expenses is **plant assets,** which refers to long-term tangible assets used to produce and sell products and services. Plant assets are expected to provide benefits for more than one period. Examples of plant assets are buildings, machines, vehicles, and fixtures. All plant assets, with a general exception for land, eventually wear out or decline in usefulness. The costs of these assets are deferred but are gradually reported as expenses in the income statement over the assets' useful lives (benefit periods). **Depreciation** is the process of allocating the costs of these assets over their expected useful lives. Depreciation expense is recorded with an adjusting entry similar to that for other prepaid expenses.

Point: Plant assets are also called *Plant & Equipment,* or *Property, Plant & Equipment.*

Point: Depreciation does not necessarily measure decline in market value.

Point: An asset's expected value at the end of its useful life is called *salvage value.*

Step 1:   Recall that FastForward purchased equipment for $26,000 in early December to use in earning revenue. This equipment's cost must be depreciated.

Step 2:   The equipment is expected to have a useful life (benefit period) of four years and to be worth about $8,000 at the end of four years. This means the *net* cost of this equipment over its useful life is $18,000 ($26,000 − $8,000). We can use any of several methods to allocate this $18,000 net cost to expense. FastForward uses a method called **straight-line depreciation,** which allocates equal amounts of the asset's net cost to depreciation during its useful life. Dividing the $18,000 net cost by the 48 months in the asset's useful life gives a monthly cost of $375 ($18,000/48).

Depreciation

Dec. 3   Purchase equipment and record asset

Dec. 31   Allocate asset cost and record depreciation

Step 3:   The adjusting entry to record monthly depreciation expense, along with T-account postings, follows:

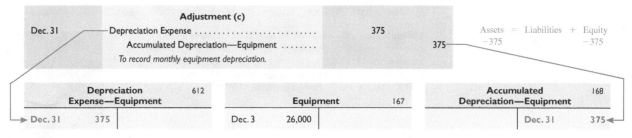

Dec. 31	**Adjustment (c)**			
	Depreciation Expense		375	
	Accumulated Depreciation—Equipment			375
	To record monthly equipment depreciation.			

Assets = Liabilities + Equity
−375   −375

Depreciation Expense—Equipment	612		**Equipment**	167		**Accumulated Depreciation—Equipment**	168
Dec. 31 375			Dec. 3 26,000			Dec. 31 375	

Explanation   After posting the adjustment, the Equipment account ($26,000) less its Accumulated Depreciation ($375) account equals the $25,625 net cost (made up of $17,625 for the 47 remaining months in the benefit period plus the $8,000 value at the end of that time). The $375 balance in the Depreciation Expense account is reported in the December income statement. *Not* making the adjustment at December 31 would (1) understate expenses by $375 and overstate net income by $375 for the December income statement and (2) overstate both assets and equity (because of income) by $375 in the December 31 balance sheet. The following table highlights the adjustment for depreciation.

Before Adjustment	**Adjustment**	**After Adjustment**
Equipment, net = $26,000	Deduct $375 from Equipment, net Add $375 to Depreciation Expense	Equipment, net = $25,625
Reports $26,000 in equipment.	Record $375 in depreciation and $375 as accumulated depreciation, which is deducted from equipment.	Reports $25,625 in equipment, net of accumulated depreciation.

Accumulated depreciation is kept in a separate contra account. A **contra account** is an account linked with another account, it has an opposite normal balance, and it is reported as a subtraction from that other account's balance. For instance, FastForward's contra account of Accumulated Depreciation—Equipment is subtracted from the Equipment account in the balance sheet (see Exhibit 3.7). This contra account allows balance sheet readers to know both the full costs of assets and the total depreciation.

EXHIBIT 3.6

Accounts after Three Months of Depreciation Adjustments

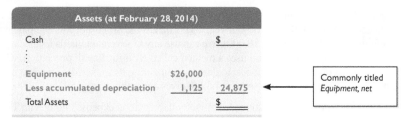

Equipment		167
Dec. 3	26,000	

Accumulated Depreciation—Equipment		168
Dec. 31		375
Jan. 31		375
Feb. 28		375
Balance		1,125

Point: The cost principle requires an asset to be initially recorded at acquisition cost. Depreciation causes the asset's book value (cost less accumulated depreciation) to decline over time.

The title of the contra account, *Accumulated Depreciation,* reveals that this account includes total depreciation expense for all prior periods for which the asset was used. To illustrate, the Equipment and the Accumulated Depreciation accounts appear as in Exhibit 3.6 on February 28, 2014, after three months of adjusting entries. The $1,125 balance in the accumulated depreciation account can be subtracted from its related $26,000 asset cost. The difference ($24,875) between these two balances is the cost of the asset that has not yet been depreciated. This difference is called the **book value,** or the *net amount,* which equals the asset's costs less its accumulated depreciation.

Point: The net cost of equipment is also called the *depreciable basis.*

These account balances are reported in the assets section of the February 28 balance sheet in Exhibit 3.7.

EXHIBIT 3.7

Equipment and Accumulated Depreciation on February 28 Balance Sheet

Assets (at February 28, 2014)		
Cash		$____
⋮		
Equipment	$26,000	
Less accumulated depreciation	1,125	24,875
Total Assets		$____

Commonly titled *Equipment, net*

Decision Maker

Entrepreneur You are preparing an offer to purchase a skate board shop. The depreciation schedule for the shop's building and equipment shows costs of $175,000 and accumulated depreciation of $155,000. This leaves a net for building and equipment of $20,000. Is this information useful in helping you decide on a purchase offer? ■ [Answer—p. 132]

Unearned (Deferred) Revenues

Point: To *defer* is to postpone. We postpone reporting amounts received as revenues until they are earned.

The term **unearned revenues** refers to cash received in advance of providing products and services. Unearned revenues, also called *deferred revenues,* are liabilities. When cash is accepted, an obligation to provide products or services is accepted. As products or services are provided, the unearned revenues become *earned* revenues. Adjusting entries for unearned revenues involve increasing revenues and decreasing unearned revenues, as shown in Exhibit 3.8.

EXHIBIT 3.8

Adjusting for Unearned Revenues

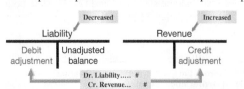

	Decreased			Increased
	Liability			Revenue
Debit adjustment	Unadjusted balance			Credit adjustment
	Dr. Liability..... #			
	Cr. Revenue... #			

An example of unearned revenues is from Gannett Co., Inc., publisher of USA TODAY, which reports unexpired (unearned subscriptions) of $224 million: "Revenue is recognized in the period in which it is earned (as newspapers are delivered)." Unearned revenues are nearly 25% of the current liabilities for Gannett. Another example comes from the Boston Celtics. When the Celtics receive cash from advance ticket sales and broadcast fees, they record it in an unearned revenue account called *Deferred Game Revenues.* The Celtics recognize this unearned revenue with adjusting entries on a game-by-game basis. Since the NBA regular season begins in October and ends in April, revenue recognition is mainly limited to this period. For a recent season, the Celtics' quarterly revenues were $0 million for July–September; $34 million for October–December; $48 million for January–March; and $17 million for April–June.

Unearned Revenues

Dec. 26 Cash received in advance and record liability

Thanks for cash in advance. I'll work now through Feb. 24

Dec. 31 Provided services and record revenue

Returning to FastForward, it also has unearned revenues. It agreed on December 26 to provide consulting services to a client for a fixed fee of $3,000 for 60 days.

Step 1: On December 26, the client paid the 60-day fee in advance, covering the period December 27 to February 24. The entry to record the cash received in advance is

Dec. 26	Cash	3,000	
	Unearned Consulting Revenue		3,000
	Received advance payment for services over the next 60 days.		

Assets = Liabilities + Equity
+3,000   +3,000

This advance payment increases cash and creates an obligation to do consulting work over the next 60 days.

Step 2: As time passes, FastForward earns this payment through consulting. By December 31, it has provided five days' service and earned 5/60 of the $3,000 unearned revenue. This amounts to $250 ($3,000 × 5/60). The *revenue recognition principle* implies that $250 of unearned revenue must be reported as revenue on the December income statement.

Step 3: The adjusting entry to reduce the liability account and recognize earned revenue, along with T-account postings, follows:

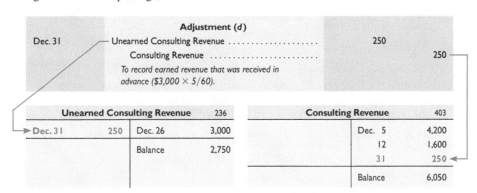

Assets = Liabilities + Equity
             −250   +250

Explanation The adjusting entry transfers $250 from unearned revenue (a liability account) to a revenue account. *Not* making the adjustment (1) understates revenue and net income by $250 in the December income statement and (2) overstates unearned revenue and understates equity by $250 on the December 31 balance sheet. The following highlights the adjustment for unearned revenue.

Before Adjustment	Adjustment	After Adjustment
Unearned Consulting Revenue = $3,000	**Deduct $250 from Unearned Consulting Revenue Add $250 to Consulting Revenue**	**Unearned Consulting Revenue = $2,750**
Reports $3,000 in unearned revenue for consulting services promised for 60 days.	Record 5 days of earned consulting revenue, which is 5/60 of unearned amount.	Reports $2,750 in unearned revenue for consulting services owed over next 55 days.

Accounting for unearned revenues is crucial to many companies. For example, the National Retail Federation reports that gift card sales, which are unearned revenues for sellers, exceed $20 billion annually. Gift cards are now the top selling holiday gift; 57.3% of all gift givers planned to give at least one gift card in 2011 (source: NRF Website).

Accrued Expenses

Accrued expenses refer to costs that are incurred in a period but are both unpaid and unrecorded. Accrued expenses must be reported on the income statement for the period when incurred. Adjusting entries for recording accrued expenses involve increasing expenses and

Point: Accrued expenses are also called accrued liabilities.

EXHIBIT 3.9

Adjusting for Accrued Expenses

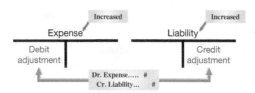

increasing liabilities as shown in Exhibit 3.9. This adjustment recognizes expenses incurred in a period but not yet paid. Common examples of accrued expenses are salaries, interest, rent, and taxes. We use salaries and interest to show how to adjust accounts for accrued expenses.

Accrued Salaries Expense   FastForward's employee earns $70 per day, or $350 for a five-day workweek beginning on Monday and ending on Friday.

Step 1:   Its employee is paid every two weeks on Friday. On December 12 and 26, the wages are paid, recorded in the journal, and posted to the ledger.

Step 2:   The calendar in Exhibit 3.10 shows three working days after the December 26 payday (29, 30, and 31). This means the employee has earned three days' salary by the close of business

EXHIBIT 3.10

Salary Accrual and Paydays

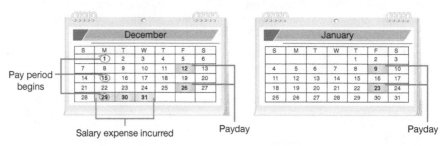

Point: An employer records salaries expense and a vacation pay liability when employees earn vacation pay.

on Wednesday, December 31, yet this salary cost has not been paid or recorded. The financial statements would be incomplete if FastForward failed to report the added expense and liability to the employee for unpaid salary from December 29, 30, and 31.

Step 3:   The adjusting entry to account for accrued salaries, along with T-account postings, follows:

Assets = Liabilities + Equity
        +210   −210

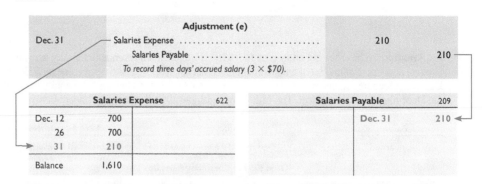

Explanation   Salaries expense of $1,610 is reported on the December income statement and $210 of salaries payable (liability) is reported in the balance sheet. *Not* making the adjustment (1) understates salaries expense and overstates net income by $210 in the December income statement and (2) understates salaries payable (liabilities) and overstates equity by $210 on the December 31 balance sheet. The following highlights the adjustment for salaries incurred.

Before Adjustment	Adjustment	After Adjustment
Salaries Payable = $0	**Add $210 to Salaries Payable** **Add $210 to Salaries Expense**	**Salaries Payable = $210**
Reports $0 from employee salaries incurred but not yet paid in cash.	Record 3 days' salaries owed to employee, but not yet paid, at $70 per day.	Reports $210 salaries payable to employee but not yet paid.

Accrued Interest Expense   Companies commonly have accrued interest expense on notes payable and other long-term liabilities at the end of a period. Interest expense is incurred with the passage of time. Unless interest is paid on the last day of an accounting period, we need to adjust for interest expense incurred but not yet paid. This means we must accrue interest cost from the most recent payment date up to the end of the period. The formula for computing accrued interest is:

Principal amount owed × Annual interest rate × Fraction of year since last payment date.

To illustrate, if a company has a $6,000 loan from a bank at 6% annual interest, then 30 days' accrued interest expense is $30—computed as $6,000 × 0.06 × 30/360. The adjusting entry would be to debit Interest Expense for $30 and credit Interest Payable for $30.

Point: Interest computations assume a 360-day year; known as the *bankers' rule*.

Future Payment of Accrued Expenses   Adjusting entries for accrued expenses foretell cash transactions in future periods. Specifically, accrued expenses at the end of one accounting period result in *cash payment* in a *future period*(s). To illustrate, recall that FastForward recorded accrued salaries of $210. On January 9, the first payday of the next period, the following entry settles the accrued liability (salaries payable) and records salaries expense for seven days of work in January:

Jan. 9	Salaries Payable (3 days at $70 per day)	210	
	Salaries Expense (7 days at $70 per day)	490	
	Cash		700
	Paid two weeks' salary including three days accrued in December.		

Assets = Liabilities + Equity
−700   −210   −490

The $210 debit reflects the payment of the liability for the three days' salary accrued on December 31. The $490 debit records the salary for January's first seven working days (including the New Year's Day holiday) as an expense of the new accounting period. The $700 credit records the total amount of cash paid to the employee.

Accrued Revenues

The term **accrued revenues** refers to revenues earned in a period that are both unrecorded and not yet received in cash (or other assets). An example is a technician who bills customers only when the job is done. If one-third of a job is complete by the end of a period, then the technician must record one-third of the expected billing as revenue in that period—even though there is no billing or collection. The adjusting entries for accrued revenues increase assets and increase revenues as shown in Exhibit 3.11. Accrued revenues commonly arise from services, products, interest, and rent. We use service fees and interest to show how to adjust for accrued revenues.

Point: Accrued revenues are also called *accrued assets.*

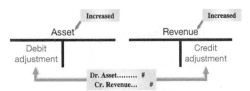

EXHIBIT 3.11

Adjusting for Accrued Revenues

Accrued Services Revenue   Accrued revenues are not recorded until adjusting entries are made at the end of the accounting period. These accrued revenues are earned but unrecorded because either the buyer has not yet paid for them or the seller has not yet billed the buyer. FastForward provides an example.

Step 1:   In the second week of December, it agreed to provide 30 days of consulting services to a local fitness club for a fixed fee of $2,700. The terms of the initial agreement call for FastForward to provide services from December 12, 2013, through January 10, 2014, or 30 days of service. The club agrees to pay FastForward $2,700 on January 10, 2014, when the service period is complete.

Step 2:   At December 31, 2013, 20 days of services have already been provided. Since the contracted services have not yet been entirely provided, FastForward has neither billed the club nor recorded the services already provided. Still, FastForward has earned two-thirds of the 30-day fee, or $1,800 ($2,700 × 20/30). The *revenue recognition principle* implies that it must report the $1,800 on the December income statement. The balance sheet also must report that the club owes FastForward $1,800.

Accrued Revenues

Dec. 31   Record revenue and receivable for services provided but unbilled

Jan. 10   Receive cash and reduce receivable

108 Chapter 3 Adjusting Accounts and Preparing Financial Statements

Step 3: The year-end adjusting entry to account for accrued services revenue is

Assets = Liabilities + Equity
+1,800   +1,800

Dec. 31	**Adjustment (f)**		
	Accounts Receivable	1,800	
	Consulting Revenue		1,800
	To record 20 days' accrued revenue.		

Accounts Receivable			106
Dec. 12	1,900	Dec. 22	1,900
31	1,800		
Balance	1,800		

Consulting Revenue		403
	Dec. 5	4,200
	12	1,600
	31	250
	31	1,800
	Balance	7,850

Example: What is the adjusting entry if the 30-day consulting period began on December 22? *Answer:* One-third of the fee is earned:
Accounts Receivable 900
   Consulting Revenue.... 900

Explanation Accounts receivable are reported on the balance sheet at $1,800, and the $7,850 total of consulting revenue is reported on the income statement. *Not* making the adjustment would understate (1) both consulting revenue and net income by $1,800 in the December income statement and (2) both accounts receivable (assets) and equity by $1,800 on the December 31 balance sheet. The following table highlights the adjustment for accrued revenue.

Before Adjustment	**Adjustment**	**After Adjustment**
Accounts Receivable = $0	**Add $1,800 to Accounts Receivable** **Add $1,800 to Consulting Revenue**	**Accounts Receivable = $1,800**
Reports $0 from revenue earned but not yet received in cash.	Record 20 days of earned consulting revenue, which is 20/30 of total contract amount.	Reports $1,800 in accounts receivable from consulting services provided.

Accrued Interest Revenue In addition to the accrued interest expense we described earlier, interest can yield an accrued revenue when a debtor owes money (or other assets) to a company. If a company is holding notes or accounts receivable that produce interest revenue, we must adjust the accounts to record any earned and yet uncollected interest revenue. The adjusting entry is similar to the one for accruing services revenue. Specifically, we debit Interest Receivable (asset) and credit Interest Revenue.

Future Receipt of Accrued Revenues Accrued revenues at the end of one accounting period result in *cash receipts* in a *future period*(s). To illustrate, recall that FastForward made an adjusting entry for $1,800 to record 20 days' accrued revenue earned from its consulting contract. When FastForward receives $2,700 cash on January 10 for the entire contract amount, it makes the following entry to remove the accrued asset (accounts receivable) and recognize the revenue earned in January. The $2,700 debit reflects the cash received. The $1,800 credit reflects the removal of the receivable, and the $900 credit records the revenue earned in January.

Assets = Liabilities + Equity
+2,700   +900
−1,800

Jan. 10	Cash	2,700	
	Accounts Receivable (20 days at $90 per day)		1,800
	Consulting Revenue (10 days at $90 per day)		900
	Received cash for the accrued asset and recorded		
	earned consulting revenue for January.		

■ **Decision** Maker

Loan Officer The owner of a custom audio, video, and home theater store applies for a business loan. The store's financial statements reveal large increases in current-year revenues and income. Analysis shows that these increases are due to a promotion that let consumers buy now and pay nothing until January 1 of next year. The store recorded these sales as accrued revenue. Does your analysis raise any concerns? ■ [Answer—p. 132]

Links to Financial Statements

The process of adjusting accounts is intended to bring an asset or liability account balance to its correct amount. It also updates a related expense or revenue account. These adjustments are necessary for transactions and events that extend over more than one period. (Adjusting entries are posted like any other entry.)

Exhibit 3.12 summarizes the four types of transactions requiring adjustment. Understanding this exhibit is important to understanding the adjusting process and its importance to financial statements. Remember that each adjusting entry affects one or more income statement accounts *and* one or more balance sheet accounts (but never cash).

A1	Explain how accounting adjustments link to financial statements.

Category	BEFORE Adjusting		Adjusting Entry
	Balance Sheet	Income Statement	
Prepaid expenses†	Asset overstated	Expense understated	Dr. Expense
	Equity overstated		Cr. Asset*
Unearned revenues†	Liability overstated	Revenue understated	Dr. Liability
	Equity understated		Cr. Revenue
Accrued expenses	Liability understated	Expense understated	Dr. Expense
	Equity overstated		Cr. Liability
Accrued revenues	Asset understated	Revenue understated	Dr. Asset
	Equity understated		Cr. Revenue

EXHIBIT 3.12

Summary of Adjustments and Financial Statement Links

* For depreciation, the credit is to Accumulated Depreciation (contra asset).

† Exhibit assumes that prepaid expenses are initially recorded as assets and that unearned revenues are initially recorded as liabilities.

Information about some adjustments is not always available until several days or even weeks after the period-end. This means that some adjusting and closing entries are recorded later than, but dated as of, the last day of the period. One example is a company that receives a utility bill on January 10 for costs incurred for the month of December. When it receives the bill, the company records the expense and the payable as of December 31. Other examples include long-distance phone usage and costs of many Web billings. The December income statement reflects these additional expenses incurred, and the December 31 balance sheet includes these payables, although the amounts were not actually known on December 31.

Point: CFOs often feel pressure to pursue fraudulent accounting due to pressure applied by their superiors, such as overbearing CEOs or aggressive boards.

■ Decision Ethics

Financial Officer At year-end, the president instructs you, the financial officer, not to record accrued expenses until next year because they will not be paid until then. The president also directs you to record in current-year sales a recent purchase order from a customer that requires merchandise to be delivered two weeks after the year-end. Your company would report a net income instead of a net loss if you carry out these instructions. What do you do? ■ [Answer—p. 132]

Quick Check
Answers — p. 132

6. If an adjusting entry for accrued revenues of $200 at year-end is omitted, what is this error's effect on the year-end income statement and balance sheet?
7. What is a contra account? Explain its purpose.
8. What is an accrued expense? Give an example.
9. Describe how an unearned revenue arises. Give an example.

Adjusted Trial Balance

An **unadjusted trial balance** is a list of accounts and balances prepared *before* adjustments are recorded. An **adjusted trial balance** is a list of accounts and balances prepared *after* adjusting entries have been recorded and posted to the ledger.

Exhibit 3.13 shows both the unadjusted and the adjusted trial balances for FastForward at December 31, 2013. The order of accounts in the trial balance is usually set up to match the order in the chart of accounts. Several new accounts arise from the adjusting entries.

EXHIBIT 3.13

Unadjusted and Adjusted Trial Balances

FASTFORWARD
Trial Balances
December 31, 2013

Acct. No.	Account Title	Unadjusted Trial Balance Dr.	Unadjusted Trial Balance Cr.	Adjustments Dr.	Adjustments Cr.	Adjusted Trial Balance Dr.	Adjusted Trial Balance Cr.
101	Cash	$ 4,350				$ 4,350	
106	Accounts receivable	0		(f) $1,800		1,800	
126	Supplies	9,720			(b) $1,050	8,670	
128	Prepaid insurance	2,400			(a) 100	2,300	
167	Equipment	26,000				26,000	
168	Accumulated depreciation—Equip.		$ 0		(c) 375		$ 375
201	Accounts payable		6,200				6,200
209	Salaries payable		0		(e) 210		210
236	Unearned consulting revenue		3,000	(d) 250			2,750
307	Common stock		30,000				30,000
318	Retained earnings		0				0
319	Dividends	200				200	
403	Consulting revenue		5,800		(d) 250		7,850
					(f) 1,800		
406	Rental revenue		300				300
612	Depreciation expense—Equip.	0		(c) 375		375	
622	Salaries expense	1,400		(e) 210		1,610	
637	Insurance expense	0		(a) 100		100	
640	Rent expense	1,000				1,000	
652	Supplies expense	0		(b) 1,050		1,050	
690	Utilities expense	230				230	
	Totals	$45,300	$45,300	$3,785	$3,785	$47,685	$47,685

Each adjustment (see middle columns) is identified by a letter in parentheses that links it to an adjusting entry explained earlier. Each amount in the Adjusted Trial Balance columns is computed by taking that account's amount from the Unadjusted Trial Balance columns and adding or subtracting any adjustment(s). To illustrate, Supplies has a $9,720 Dr. balance in the unadjusted columns. Subtracting the $1,050 Cr. amount shown in the adjustments columns yields an adjusted $8,670 Dr. balance for Supplies. An account can have more than one adjustment, such as for Consulting Revenue. Also, some accounts might not require adjustment for this period, such as Accounts Payable.

PREPARING FINANCIAL STATEMENTS

We can prepare financial statements directly from information in the *adjusted* trial balance. An adjusted trial balance (see the right-most columns in Exhibit 3.13) includes all accounts and balances appearing in financial statements, and is easier to work from than the entire ledger when preparing financial statements.

EXHIBIT 3.14

Preparing Financial Statements (Adjusted Trial Balance from Exhibit 3.13)

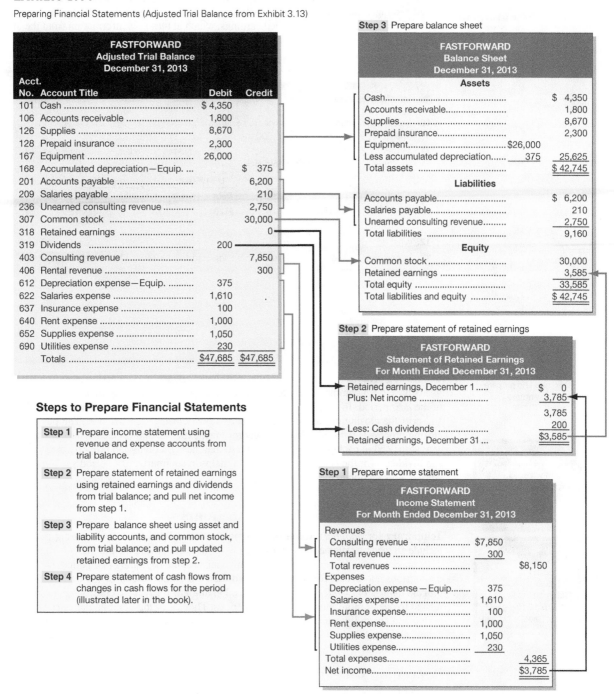

Steps to Prepare Financial Statements

Step 1 Prepare income statement using revenue and expense accounts from trial balance.

Step 2 Prepare statement of retained earnings using retained earnings and dividends from trial balance; and pull net income from step 1.

Step 3 Prepare balance sheet using asset and liability accounts, and common stock, from trial balance; and pull updated retained earnings from step 2.

Step 4 Prepare statement of cash flows from changes in cash flows for the period (illustrated later in the book).

Exhibit 3.14 shows how revenue and expense balances are transferred from the adjusted trial balance to the income statement (red lines). The net income and the dividends amount are then used to prepare the statement of retained earnings (black lines). Asset and liability balances on the adjusted trial balance are then transferred to the balance sheet (blue lines). The ending retained earnings is determined on the statement of retained earnings and transferred to the balance sheet (green lines).

Point: Sarbanes-Oxley Act requires that financial statements filed with the SEC be certified by the CEO and CFO, including a declaration that the statements fairly present the issuer's operations and financial condition. Violators can receive fines and/or prison terms.

Point: Each trial balance amount is used in only *one* financial statement and, when financial statements are completed, each account will have been used once.

We prepare financial statements in the following order: income statement, statement of retained earnings, and balance sheet. This order makes sense because the balance sheet uses information from the statement of retained earnings, which in turn uses information from the income statement. The statement of cash flows is usually the final statement prepared.

Quick Check

Answers — p. 132–133

10. Music-Mart records $1,000 of accrued salaries on December 31. Five days later, on January 5 (the next payday), salaries of $7,000 are paid. What is the January 5 entry?

11. Jordan Air has the following information in its unadjusted and adjusted trial balances. What are the adjusting entries that Jordan Air likely recorded?

	Unadjusted		Adjusted	
	Debit	Credit	Debit	Credit
Prepaid insurance	$6,200		$5,900	
Salaries payable		$ 0		$1,400

12. What accounts are taken from the adjusted trial balance to prepare an income statement?

13. In preparing financial statements from an adjusted trial balance, what statement is usually prepared second?

CLOSING PROCESS

 P4 Describe and prepare closing entries.

The **closing process** is an important step at the end of an accounting period *after* financial statements have been completed. It prepares accounts for recording the transactions and the events of the *next* period. In the closing process we must (1) identify accounts for closing, (2) record and post the closing entries, and (3) prepare a post-closing trial balance. The purpose of the closing process is twofold. First, it resets revenue, expense, and dividends account balances to zero at the end of each period. This is done so that these accounts can properly measure income and dividends for the next period. Second, it helps in summarizing a period's revenues and expenses. This section explains the closing process.

Temporary Accounts
(closed at period-end)

Revenues
Expenses
Dividends
Income Summary

Permanent Accounts
(not closed at period-end)

Assets
Liabilities
Common Stock
Retained Earnings

Temporary and Permanent Accounts

Temporary (or *nominal*) **accounts** accumulate data related to one accounting period. They include all income statement accounts, the dividends account, and the Income Summary account. They are temporary because the accounts are opened at the beginning of a period, used to record transactions and events for that period, and then closed at the end of the period. *The closing process applies only to temporary accounts.* **Permanent** (or *real*) **accounts** report on activities related to one or more future accounting periods. They carry their ending balances into the next period and generally consist of all balance sheet accounts. These asset, liability, and equity accounts are not closed.

Recording Closing Entries

To record and post **closing entries** is to transfer the end-of-period balances in revenue, expense, and dividends accounts to the permanent retained earnings account. Closing entries are necessary at the end of each period after financial statements are prepared because

- Revenue, expense, and dividends accounts must begin each period with zero balances.
- Retained earnings must reflect prior periods' revenues, expenses, and dividends.

An income statement aims to report revenues and expenses for a *specific accounting period*. The statement of retained earnings reports similar information, including dividends. Since revenue, expense, and dividends accounts must accumulate information separately for each period, they must start each period with zero balances. To close these accounts, we transfer their balances first to an account called *Income Summary*. **Income Summary** is a temporary account (only used for the closing process) that contains a credit for the sum of all revenues (and gains) and a debit for the sum of all expenses (and losses). Its balance equals net income or net loss and it is transferred to retained earnings. Next the dividends account balance is transferred to retained earnings. After these closing entries are posted, the revenue, expense, dividends, and Income Summary accounts have zero balances. These accounts are then said to be *closed* or *cleared*.

Exhibit 3.15 uses the adjusted account balances of FastForward (from the left side of Exhibit 3.14) to show the four steps necessary to close its temporary accounts. We explain each step.

Point: To understand the closing process, focus on its *outcomes*—*updating* the retained earnings account balance to its proper ending balance, and getting *temporary accounts* to show *zero balances* for purposes of accumulating data for the next period.

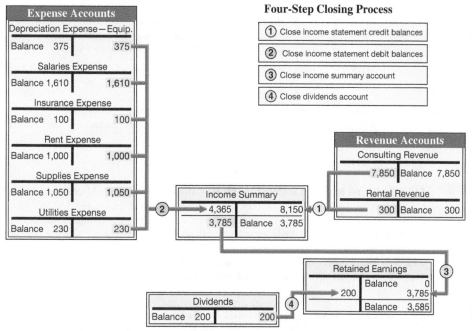

EXHIBIT 3.15

Four-Step Closing Process

Point: Retained Earnings is the only *permanent account* in Exhibit 3.15.

Step 1: Close Credit Balances in Revenue Accounts to Income Summary
The first closing entry transfers credit balances in revenue (and gain) accounts to the Income Summary account. We bring accounts with credit balances to zero by debiting them. For FastForward, this journal entry is step 1 in Exhibit 3.16. This entry closes revenue accounts and leaves them with zero balances. The accounts are now ready to record revenues when they occur in the next period. The $8,150 credit entry to Income Summary equals total revenues for the period.

Step 2: Close Debit Balances in Expense Accounts to Income Summary
The second closing entry transfers debit balances in expense (and loss) accounts to the Income Summary account. We bring expense accounts' debit balances to zero by crediting them. With a balance of zero, these accounts are ready to accumulate a record of expenses for the next period. This second closing entry for FastForward is step 2 in Exhibit 3.16. Exhibit 3.15 shows that posting this entry gives each expense account a zero balance.

Point: It is possible to close revenue and expense accounts directly to retained earnings. Computerized accounting systems do this.

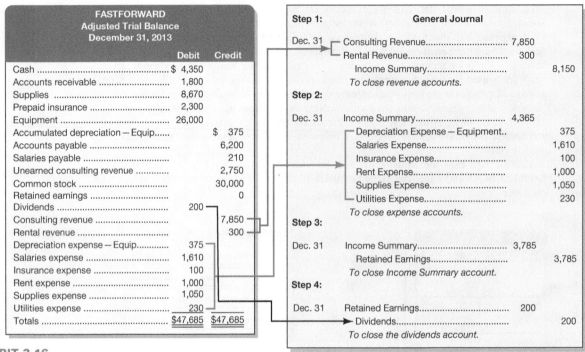

EXHIBIT 3.16

Preparing Closing Entries

Step 3: Close Income Summary to Retained Earnings   After steps 1 and 2, the balance of Income Summary is equal to December's net income of $3,785 ($8,150 credit less $4,365 debit). The third closing entry transfers the balance of the Income Summary account to retained earnings. This entry closes the Income Summary account–see step 3 in Exhibit 3.16. The Income Summary account has a zero balance after posting this entry. It continues to have a zero balance until the closing process again occurs at the end of the next period. (If a net loss occurred because expenses exceeded revenues, the third entry is reversed: debit Retained Earnings and credit Income Summary.)

Step 4: Close Dividends Account to Retained Earnings   The fourth closing entry transfers any debit balance in the dividends account to retained earnings—see step 4 in Exhibit 3.16. This entry gives the dividends account a zero balance, and the account is now ready to accumulate next period's dividends. This entry also reduces the retained earnings balance to the $3,585 amount reported on the balance sheet.

   We could also have selected the accounts and amounts needing to be closed by identifying individual revenue, expense, and dividends accounts in the ledger. This is illustrated in Exhibit 3.16 where we prepare closing entries using the adjusted trial balance. (Information for closing entries is also in the financial statement columns of a work sheet—see Appendix 3B.)

Post-Closing Trial Balance

P5 Explain and prepare a post-closing trial balance.

Exhibit 3.17 shows the entire ledger of FastForward as of December 31 after adjusting and closing entries are posted. (The transaction entries are in Chapter 2.) The temporary accounts (revenues, expenses, and dividends) have ending balances equal to zero.

   A **post-closing trial balance** is a list of permanent accounts and their balances from the ledger after all closing entries have been journalized and posted. It lists the balances for all accounts not closed. These accounts comprise a company's assets, liabilities, and equity, which are identical to those in the balance sheet. The aim of a post-closing trial balance is to verify that

EXHIBIT 3.17

General Ledger after the Closing Process for FastForward

Asset Accounts

Cash — Acct. No. 101

Date	Explan.	PR	Debit	Credit	Balance
2013					
Dec. 1	(1)	G1	30,000		30,000
2	(2)	G1		2,500	27,500
3	(3)	G1		26,000	1,500
5	(5)	G1	4,200		5,700
6	(13)	G1		2,400	3,300
12	(6)	G1		1,000	2,300
12	(7)	G1		700	1,600
22	(9)	G1	1,900		3,500
24	(10)	G1		900	2,600
24	(11)	G1		200	2,400
26	(12)	G1	3,000		5,400
26	(14)	G1		120	5,280
26	(15)	G1		230	5,050
26	(16)	G1		700	**4,350**

Accounts Receivable — Acct. No. 106

Date	Explan.	PR	Debit	Credit	Balance
2013					
Dec. 12	(8)	G1	1,900		1,900
22	(9)	G1		1,900	0
31	Adj.(f)	G1	1,800		**1,800**

Supplies — Acct. No. 126

Date	Explan.	PR	Debit	Credit	Balance
2013					
Dec. 2	(2)	G1	2,500		2,500
6	(4)	G1	7,100		9,600
26	(14)	G1	120		9,720
31	Adj.(b)	G1		1,050	**8,670**

Prepaid Insurance — Acct. No. 128

Date	Explan.	PR	Debit	Credit	Balance
2013					
Dec. 6	(13)	G1	2,400		2,400
31	Adj.(a)	G1		100	**2,300**

Equipment — Acct. No. 167

Date	Explan.	PR	Debit	Credit	Balance
2013					
Dec. 3	(3)	G1	26,000		**26,000**

Accumulated Depreciation—Equipment — Acct. No. 168

Date	Explan.	PR	Debit	Credit	Balance
2013					
Dec. 31	Adj.(c)	G1		375	**375**

Liability and Equity Accounts

Accounts Payable — Acct. No. 201

Date	Explan.	PR	Debit	Credit	Balance
2013					
Dec. 6	(4)	G1		7,100	7,100
24	(10)	G1	900		**6,200**

Salaries Payable — Acct. No. 209

Date	Explan.	PR	Debit	Credit	Balance
2013					
Dec. 31	Adj.(e)	G1		210	**210**

Unearned Consulting Revenue — Acct. No. 236

Date	Explan.	PR	Debit	Credit	Balance
2013					
Dec. 26	(12)	G1		3,000	3,000
31	Adj.(d)	G1	250		**2,750**

Common Stock — Acct. No. 307

Date	Explan.	PR	Debit	Credit	Balance
2013					
Dec. 1	(1)	G1		30,000	30,000

Retained Earnings — Acct. No. 318

Date	Explan.	PR	Debit	Credit	Balance
2013					
Dec. 31	Clos.(3)	G1		3,785	3,785
31	Clos.(4)	G1	200		3,585

Dividends — Acct. No. 319

Date	Explan.	PR	Debit	Credit	Balance
2013					
Dec. 24	(11)	G1	200		200
31	Clos.(4)	G1		200	0

Revenue and Expense Accounts (Including Income Summary)

Consulting Revenue — Acct. No. 403

Date	Explan.	PR	Debit	Credit	Balance
2013					
Dec. 5	(5)	G1		4,200	4,200
12	(8)	G1		1,600	5,800
31	Adj.(d)	G1		250	6,050
31	Adj.(f)	G1		1,800	**7,850**
31	Clos.(1)	G1	7,850		0

Rental Revenue — Acct. No. 406

Date	Explan.	PR	Debit	Credit	Balance
2013					
Dec. 12	(8)	G1		300	**300**
31	Clos.(1)	G1	300		0

Depreciation Expense—Equipment — Acct. No. 612

Date	Explan.	PR	Debit	Credit	Balance
2013					
Dec. 31	Adj.(c)	G1	375		**375**
31	Clos.(2)	G1		375	0

Salaries Expense — Acct. No. 622

Date	Explan.	PR	Debit	Credit	Balance
2013					
Dec. 12	(7)	G1	700		700
26	(16)	G1	700		1,400
31	Adj.(e)	G1	210		**1,610**
31	Clos.(2)	G1		1,610	0

Insurance Expense — Acct. No. 637

Date	Explan.	PR	Debit	Credit	Balance
2013					
Dec. 31	Adj.(a)	G1	100		**100**
31	Clos.(2)	G1		100	0

Rent Expense — Acct. No. 640

Date	Explan.	PR	Debit	Credit	Balance
2013					
Dec. 12	(6)	G1	1,000		**1,000**
31	Clos.(2)	G1		1,000	0

Supplies Expense — Acct. No. 652

Date	Explan.	PR	Debit	Credit	Balance
2013					
Dec. 31	Adj.(b)	G1	1,050		**1,050**
31	Clos.(2)	G1		1,050	0

Utilities Expense — Acct. No. 690

Date	Explan.	PR	Debit	Credit	Balance
2013					
Dec. 26	(15)	G1	230		**230**
31	Clos.(2)	G1		230	0

Income Summary — Acct. No. 901

Date	Explan.	PR	Debit	Credit	Balance
2013					
Dec. 31	Clos.(1)	G1		8,150	8,150
31	Clos.(2)	G1	4,365		3,785
31	Clos.(3)	G1	3,785		0

(1) total debits equal total credits for permanent accounts and (2) all temporary accounts have zero balances. FastForward's post-closing trial balance is shown in Exhibit 3.18. The post-closing trial balance usually is the last step in the accounting process.

EXHIBIT 3.18

Post-Closing Trial Balance

FASTFORWARD Post-Closing Trial Balance December 31, 2013	Debit	Credit
Cash	$ 4,350	
Accounts receivable	1,800	
Supplies	8,670	
Prepaid insurance	2,300	
Equipment	26,000	
Accumulated depreciation—Equipment		$ 375
Accounts payable		6,200
Salaries payable		210
Unearned consulting revenue		2,750
Common stock		30,000
Retained earnings		3,585
Totals	$43,120	$43,120

Accounting Cycle

C3 Identify steps in the accounting cycle.

The term **accounting cycle** refers to the steps in preparing financial statements. It is called a *cycle* because the steps are repeated each reporting period. Exhibit 3.19 shows the 10 steps in the cycle, beginning with analyzing transactions and ending with a post-closing trial balance or

EXHIBIT 3.19

Steps in the Accounting Cycle*

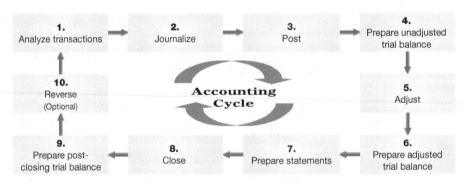

Explanations	
1. Analyze transactions	Analyze transactions to prepare for journalizing.
2. Journalize	Record accounts, including debits and credits, in a journal.
3. Post	Transfer debits and credits from the journal to the ledger.
4. Prepare unadjusted trial balance	Summarize unadjusted ledger accounts and amounts.
5. Adjust	Record adjustments to bring account balances up to date; journalize and post adjustments.
6. Prepare adjusted trial balance	Summarize adjusted ledger accounts and amounts.
7. Prepare statements	Use adjusted trial balance to prepare financial statements.
8. Close	Journalize and post entries to close temporary accounts.
9. Prepare post-closing trial balance	Test clerical accuracy of the closing procedures.
10. Reverse (optional)	Reverse certain adjustments in the next period—optional step; see Appendix 3C.

* Steps 4, 6, and 9 can be done on a work sheet. A work sheet is useful in planning adjustments, but adjustments (step 5) must always be journalized and posted. Steps 3, 4, 6, and 9 are automatic with a computerized system.

reversing entries. Steps 1 through 3 usually occur regularly as a company enters into transactions. Steps 4 through 9 are done at the end of a period. *Reversing entries* in step 10 are optional and are explained in Appendix 3C.

Quick Check   Answers — p. 133

14. What are the major steps in preparing closing entries?

15. Why are revenue and expense accounts called *temporary?* Identify and list the types of temporary accounts.

16. What accounts are listed on the post-closing trial balance?

CLASSIFIED BALANCE SHEET

Our discussion to this point has been limited to unclassified financial statements. This section describes a classified balance sheet. The next chapter describes a classified income statement. An **unclassified balance sheet** is one whose items are broadly grouped into assets, liabilities, and equity. One example is FastForward's balance sheet in Exhibit 3.14. A **classified balance sheet** organizes assets and liabilities into important subgroups that provide more information to decision makers.

C4 Explain and prepare a classified balance sheet.

Classification Structure

A classified balance sheet has no required layout, but it usually contains the categories in Exhibit 3.20. One of the more important classifications is the separation between current and noncurrent items for both assets and liabilities. Current items are those expected to come due (either collected or owed) within one year or the company's operating cycle, whichever is longer. The **operating cycle** is the time span from when *cash is used* to acquire goods and services until *cash is received* from the sale of goods and services. "Operating" refers to company operations and "cycle" refers to the circular flow of cash used for company inputs and then cash received from its outputs. The length of a company's operating cycle depends on its activities. For a service company, the operating cycle is the time span between (1) paying employees who perform the services and (2) receiving cash from customers. For a merchandiser selling products, the operating cycle is the time span between (1) paying suppliers for merchandise and (2) receiving cash from customers.

Point: Current and Noncurrent are also referred to as Short-Term and Long-Term, respectively.

Assets	Liabilities and Equity
Current assets	Current liabilities
Noncurrent assets	Noncurrent liabilities
Long-term investments	Equity
Plant assets	
Intangible assets	

EXHIBIT 3.20

Typical Categories in a Classified Balance Sheet

Most operating cycles are less than one year. This means most companies use a one-year period in deciding which assets and liabilities are current. A few companies have an operating cycle longer than one year. For instance, producers of certain beverages (wine) and products (ginseng) that require aging for several years have operating cycles longer than one year. A balance sheet lists current assets before noncurrent assets and current liabilities before noncurrent liabilities. This consistency in presentation allows users to quickly identify current assets that are most easily converted to cash and current liabilities that are shortly coming due. Items in current assets and current liabilities are listed in the order of how quickly they will be converted to, or paid in, cash.

EXHIBIT 3.21

Example of a Classified
Balance Sheet

SNOWBOARDING COMPONENTS		
Balance Sheet		
January 31, 2013		
Assets		
Current assets		
Cash	$ 6,500	
Short-term investments	2,100	
Accounts receivable, net	4,400	
Merchandise inventory	27,500	
Prepaid expenses	2,400	
Total current assets		$ 42,900
Long-term investments		
Notes receivable	1,500	
Investments in stocks and bonds	18,000	
Land held for future expansion	48,000	
Total long-term investments		67,500
Plant assets		
Equipment and buildings	203,200	
Less accumulated depreciation	53,000	
Equipment and buildings, net		150,200
Land		73,200
Total plant assets		223,400
Intangible assets		10,000
Total assets		$343,800
Liabilities		
Current liabilities		
Accounts payable	$ 15,300	
Wages payable	3,200	
Notes payable	3,000	
Current portion of long-term liabilities	7,500	
Total current liabilities		$ 29,000
Long-term liabilities (net of current portion)		150,000
Total liabilities		179,000
Equity		
Common stock		50,000
Retained earnings		114,800
Total equity		164,800
Total liabilities and equity		$343,800

Classification Categories

This section describes the most common categories in a classified balance sheet. The balance sheet for Snowboarding Components in Exhibit 3.21 shows the typical categories. Its assets are classified as either current or noncurrent. Its noncurrent assets include three main categories: long-term investments, plant assets, and intangible assets. Its liabilities are classified as either current or long-term. Not all companies use the same categories of assets and liabilities for their balance sheets. K2 Sports, a manufacturer of snowboards, reported a balance sheet with only three asset classes: current assets; property, plant and equipment; and other assets.

Current Assets   **Current assets** are cash and other resources that are expected to be sold, collected, or used within one year or the company's operating cycle, whichever is longer. Examples are cash, short-term investments, accounts receivable, short-term notes

receivable, goods for sale (called *merchandise* or *inventory*), and prepaid expenses. The individual prepaid expenses of a company are usually small in amount compared to many other assets and are often combined and shown as a single item. The prepaid expenses likely include items such as prepaid insurance, prepaid rent, office supplies, and store supplies. Prepaid expenses are usually listed last because they will not be converted to cash (instead, they are used).

Long-Term Investments   A second major balance sheet classification is **long-term** (or *noncurrent*) **investments.** Notes receivable and investments in stocks and bonds are long-term assets when they are expected to be held for more than the longer of one year or the operating cycle. Land held for future expansion is a long-term investment because it is *not* used in operations.

Plant Assets   Plant assets are tangible assets that are both *long-lived* and *used to produce* or *sell products and services*. Examples are equipment, machinery, buildings, and land that are used to produce or sell products and services. The order listing for plant assets is usually from most liquid to least liquid such as equipment and machinery to buildings and land.

Point: Plant assets are also called *fixed assets; property, plant and equipment;* or *long-lived assets.*

Intangible Assets   **Intangible assets** are long-term resources that benefit business operations, usually lack physical form, and have uncertain benefits. Examples are patents, trademarks, copyrights, franchises, and goodwill. Their value comes from the privileges or rights granted to or held by the owner. K2 Sports, reported intangible assets of $228 million, which is nearly 20 percent of its total assets. Its intangibles included trademarks, patents, and licensing agreements.

Point: Furniture and fixtures are referred to as F&F, which are classified as noncurrent assets.

Current Liabilities   **Current liabilities** are obligations due to be paid or settled within one year or the operating cycle, whichever is longer. They are usually settled by paying out current assets such as cash. Current liabilities often include accounts payable, notes payable, wages payable, taxes payable, interest payable, and unearned revenues. Also, any portion of a long-term liability due to be paid within one year or the operating cycle, whichever is longer, is a current liability. Unearned revenues are current liabilities when they will be settled by delivering products or services within one year or the operating cycle, whichever is longer. Current liabilities are reported in the order of those to be settled first.

Point: Many financial ratios are distorted if accounts are not classified correctly.

Long-Term Liabilities   **Long-term liabilities** are obligations *not* due within one year or the operating cycle, whichever is longer. Notes payable, mortgages payable, bonds payable, and lease obligations are common long-term liabilities. If a company has both short- and long-term items in each of these categories, they are commonly separated into two accounts in the ledger.

Point: Only assets and liabilities are classified as current or noncurrent.

Equity   Equity is the owner's claim on assets. The equity section for a corporation is divided into two main subsections, common stock and retained earnings.

Quick Check   Answers — p. 133

17. Classify the following assets as (1) current assets, (2) plant assets, or (3) intangible assets: (*a*) land used in operations, (*b*) office supplies, (*c*) receivables from customers due in 10 months, (*d*) insurance protection for the next 9 months, (*e*) trucks used to provide services to customers, (*f*) trademarks.

18. Cite at least two examples of assets classified as investments on the balance sheet.

19. Explain the operating cycle for a service company.

GLOBAL VIEW

We explained that accounting under U.S. GAAP is similar, but not identical, to that under IFRS. This section discusses differences in adjusting accounts, preparing financial statements, and reporting assets and liabilities on a balance sheet.

Adjusting Accounts   Both U.S. GAAP and IFRS include broad and similar guidance for adjusting accounts. Although some variations exist in revenue and expense recognition and other principles, all of the adjustments in this chapter are accounted for identically under the two systems. In later chapters we describe how certain assets and liabilities can result in different adjusted amounts using fair value measurements.

Preparing Financial Statements   Both U.S. GAAP and IFRS prepare the same four basic financial statements following the same process discussed in this chapter. Chapter 2 explained how both U.S. GAAP and IFRS require current items to be separated from noncurrent items on the balance sheet (yielding a classified balance sheet). U.S. GAAP balance sheets report current items first. Assets are listed from most liquid to least liquid, where liquid refers to the ease of converting an asset to cash. Liabilities are listed from nearest to maturity to furthest from maturity, maturity refers to the nearness of paying off the liability. IFRS balance sheets normally present noncurrent items first (and equity before liabilities), but this is not a requirement. Other differences with financial statements exist, which we identify in later chapters. Piaggio provides the following example of IFRS reporting for its assets, liabilities, and equity within the balance sheet:

PIAGGIO

PIAGGIO Balance Sheet (in thousands of Euro) December 31, 2011				
Assets			**Equity and Liabilities**	
Noncurrent assets			Total equity	446,218
Intangible assets	649,420		Noncurrent liabilities	
Property, plant and equipment. . . .	274,871		Financial liabilities falling due after one year.	329,200
Other noncurrent assets	86,185		Other long-term liabilities	100,489
Total noncurrent assets	1,010,476		Total noncurrent liabilities	429,689
Current assets			Current liabilities	
Trade receivables	65,560		Financial liabilities falling due within one year	170,261
Other receivables	28,028		Trade payables	375,263
Short-term tax receivables	27,245		Tax payables	20,920
Inventories	236,988		Other short-term payables	64,718
Cash and cash equivalents	151,887		Current portion of other long-term provisions . . .	13,115
Total current assets	509,708		Total current liabilities	644,277
Total assets	1,520,184		Total equity and liabilities	1,520,184

Point: IASB and FASB are working to improve financial statements. One proposal would reorganize the balance sheet to show assets and liabilities classified as operating, investing, or financing.

IFRS: New revenue recognition rules proposed by the FASB and the IASB reduce variation between U.S. GAAP and IFRS when accounting for revenue.

Closing Process   The closing process is identical under U.S. GAAP and IFRS. Although unique accounts can arise under either system, the closing process remains the same.

Financial Pressure

IFRS

Revenue and expense recognition are key to recording accounting adjustments. IFRS tends to be more *principles-based* relative to U.S. GAAP, which is viewed as more *rules-based*. A principles-based system depends heavily on control procedures to reduce the potential for fraud or misconduct. Failure in judgment led to improper accounting adjustments at Fannie Mae, Xerox, WorldCom, and others. A KPMG survey of accounting and finance employees found that more than 10% of them had witnessed falsification or manipulation of accounting data within the past year. Internal controls and governance processes are directed at curtailing such behavior. Yet, a 2011 KPMG fraud survey found that one in seven frauds was uncovered by chance, which emphasizes our need to improve internal controls and governance. ■

Profit Margin and Current Ratio   **Decision Analysis**

Profit Margin

A useful measure of a company's operating results is the ratio of its net income to net sales. This ratio is called **profit margin,** or *return on sales,* and is computed as in Exhibit 3.22.

A2 Compute profit margin and describe its use in analyzing company performance.

$$\text{Profit margin} = \frac{\text{Net income}}{\text{Net sales}}$$

EXHIBIT 3.22

Profit Margin

This ratio is interpreted as reflecting the percent of profit in each dollar of sales. To illustrate how we compute and use profit margin, let's look at the results of Limited Brands, Inc., in Exhibit 3.23 for its fiscal years 2007 through 2011.

$ in millions	2011	2010	2009	2008	2007
Net income	$ 805	$ 448	$ 220	$ 718	$ 676
Net sales	$9,613	$8,632	$9,043	$10,134	$10,671
Profit margin	8.4%	5.2%	2.4%	7.1%	6.3%
Industry profit margin	2.1%	0.9%	0.3%	1.1%	1.6%

EXHIBIT 3.23

Limited Brands' Profit Margin

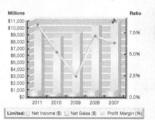

The Limited's average profit margin is 5.9% during this 5-year period. This favorably compares to the average industry profit margin of 1.2%. However, Limited's profit margin has rebounded in the most recent two years—from 2.4% in 2009 to 5.2% and 8.4% for the recent recovery periods (see margin graph). Future success depends on Limited maintaining its market share and increasing its profit margin.

Current Ratio

An important use of financial statements is to help assess a company's ability to pay its debts in the near future. Such analysis affects decisions by suppliers when allowing a company to buy on credit. It also affects decisions by creditors when lending money to a company, including loan terms such as interest rate, due date, and collateral requirements. It can also affect a manager's decisions about using cash to pay debts when they come due. The **current ratio** is one measure of a company's ability to pay its short-term obligations. It is defined in Exhibit 3.24 as current assets divided by current liabilities.

A3 Compute the current ratio and describe what it reveals about a company's financial condition.

$$\text{Current ratio} = \frac{\text{Current assets}}{\text{Current liabilities}}$$

EXHIBIT 3.24

Current Ratio

Using financial information from Limited Brands, Inc., we compute its current ratio for the recent five-year period. The results are in Exhibit 3.25.

$ in millions	2012	2011	2010	2009	2008	2007
Current assets	$2,368	$2,592	$3,250	$2,867	$2,919	$2,771
Current liabilities	$1,526	$1,504	$1,322	$1,255	$1,374	$1,709
Current ratio	1.6	1.7	2.5	2.3	2.1	1.6
Industry current ratio	1.6	1.7	1.9	2.0	2.1	2.3

EXHIBIT 3.25

Limited Brands' Current Ratio

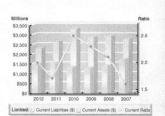

Limited Brands' current ratio averaged 2.0 for its fiscal years 2007 through 2012. The current ratio for each of these years suggests that the company's short-term obligations can be covered with its short-term assets. However, if its ratio would approach 1.0, Limited would expect to face challenges in covering liabilities. If the ratio were *less* than 1.0, current liabilities would exceed current assets, and the company's ability to pay short-term obligations could be in doubt. Limited Brand's liquidity, as evidenced by its current ratio, declines in 2011 and 2012, after growing steadily from 2008–2010.

■ Decision Maker

Analyst   You are analyzing the financial condition of a company to assess its ability to meet upcoming loan payments. You compute its current ratio as 1.2. You also find that a major portion of accounts receivable is due from one client who has not made any payments in the past 12 months. Removing this receivable from current assets lowers the current ratio to 0.7. What do you conclude? ■   [Answer—p. 132]

DEMONSTRATION PROBLEM 1

The following information relates to Fanning's Electronics on December 31, 2013. The company, which uses the calendar year as its annual reporting period, initially records prepaid and unearned items in balance sheet accounts (assets and liabilities, respectively).

a. The company's weekly payroll is $8,750, paid each Friday for a five-day workweek. Assume December 31, 2013, falls on a Monday, but the employees will not be paid their wages until Friday, January 4, 2014.

b. Eighteen months earlier, on July 1, 2012, the company purchased equipment that cost $20,000. Its useful life is predicted to be five years, at which time the equipment is expected to be worthless (zero salvage value).

c. On October 1, 2013, the company agreed to work on a new housing development. The company is paid $120,000 on October 1 in advance of future installation of similar alarm systems in 24 new homes. That amount was credited to the Unearned Services Revenue account. Between October 1 and December 31, work on 20 homes was completed.

d. On September 1, 2013, the company purchased a 12-month insurance policy for $1,800. The transaction was recorded with an $1,800 debit to Prepaid Insurance.

e. On December 29, 2013, the company completed a $7,000 service that has not been billed and not recorded as of December 31, 2013.

Required

1. Prepare any necessary adjusting entries on December 31, 2013, in relation to transactions and events *a* through *e*.

2. Prepare T-accounts for the accounts affected by adjusting entries, and post the adjusting entries. Determine the adjusted balances for the Unearned Revenue and the Prepaid Insurance accounts.

3. Complete the following table and determine the amounts and effects of your adjusting entries on the year 2013 income statement and the December 31, 2013, balance sheet. Use up (down) arrows to indicate an increase (decrease) in the Effect columns.

Entry	Amount in the Entry	Effect on Net Income	Effect on Total Assets	Effect on Total Liabilities	Effect on Total Equity

PLANNING THE SOLUTION

- Analyze each situation to determine which accounts need to be updated with an adjustment.
- Calculate the amount of each adjustment and prepare the necessary journal entries.
- Show the amount of each adjustment in the designated accounts, determine the adjusted balance, and identify the balance sheet classification of the account.
- Determine each entry's effect on net income for the year and on total assets, total liabilities, and total equity at the end of the year.

SOLUTION TO DEMONSTRATION PROBLEM 1

1. Adjusting journal entries.

(a) Dec. 31	Wages Expense	1,750	
	Wages Payable		1,750
	To accrue wages for the last day of the year ($8,750 × 1/5).		
(b) Dec. 31	Depreciation Expense—Equipment	4,000	
	Accumulated Depreciation—Equipment		4,000
	To record depreciation expense for the year ($20,000/5 years = $4,000 per year).		
(c) Dec. 31	Unearned Services Revenue	100,000	
	Services Revenue		100,000
	To recognize services revenue earned ($120,000 × 20/24).		
(d) Dec. 31	Insurance Expense	600	
	Prepaid Insurance		600
	To adjust for expired portion of insurance ($1,800 × 4/12).		
(e) Dec. 31	Accounts Receivable	7,000	
	Services Revenue		7,000
	To record services revenue earned.		

2. T-accounts for adjusting journal entries *a* through *e*.

Wages Expense			**Wages Payable**	
(a)	1,750		(a)	1,750

Depreciation Expense—Equipment			**Accumulated Depreciation— Equipment**	
(b)	4,000		(b)	4,000

Unearned Services Revenue			**Services Revenue**	
		Unadj. Bal. 120,000	(c)	100,000
(c)	100,000		(e)	7,000
		Adj. Bal. 20,000	Adj. Bal.	107,000

Insurance Expense			**Prepaid Insurance**	
(d)	600		Unadj. Bal. 1,800	
			(d)	600

Accounts Receivable				
(e)	7,000		Adj. Bal. 1,200	

3. Financial statement effects of adjusting journal entries.

Entry	Amount in the Entry	Effect on Net Income	Effect on Total Assets	Effect on Total Liabilities	Effect on Total Equity
a	$ 1,750	$ 1,750 ↓	No effect	$ 1,750 ↑	$ 1,750 ↓
b	4,000	4,000 ↓	$4,000 ↓	No effect	4,000 ↓
c	100,000	100,000 ↑	No effect	$100,000 ↓	100,000 ↑
d	600	600 ↓	$ 600 ↓	No effect	600 ↓
e	7,000	7,000 ↑	$7,000 ↑	No effect	7,000 ↑

DEMONSTRATION PROBLEM 2

Use the following adjusted trial balance to answer questions 1–3.

CHOI COMPANY Adjusted Trial Balance December 31		
	Debit	Credit
Cash	$ 3,050	
Accounts receivable	400	
Prepaid insurance	830	
Supplies	80	
Equipment	217,200	
Accumulated depreciation—Equipment		$ 29,100
Wages payable		880
Interest payable		3,600
Unearned rent		460
Long-term notes payable		150,000
Common stock		10,000
Retained earnings		30,340
Dividends	21,000	
Rent earned		57,500
Wages expense	25,000	
Utilities expense	1,900	
Insurance expense	3,200	
Supplies expense	250	
Depreciation expense—Equipment	5,970	
Interest expense	3,000	
Totals	$281,880	$281,880

1. Prepare the annual income statement from the adjusted trial balance of Choi Company.

Answer:

CHOI COMPANY Income Statement For Year Ended December 31		
Revenues		
Rent earned		$57,500
Expenses		
Wages expense	$25,000	
Utilities expense	1,900	
Insurance expense	3,200	
Supplies expense	250	
Depreciation expense—Equipment	5,970	
Interest expense	3,000	
Total expenses		39,320
Net income		$18,180

2. Prepare a statement of retained earnings from the adjusted trial balance of Choi Company.

Answer:

CHOI COMPANY	
Statement of Retained Earnings	
For Year Ended December 31	
Retained earnings, December 31 prior year-end	$30,340
Plus: Net income	18,180
	48,520
Less: Dividends	21,000
Retained earnings, December 31 current year-end	$27,520

3. Prepare a balance sheet from the adjusted trial balance of Choi Company.

Answer:

CHOI COMPANY		
Balance Sheet		
December 31		
Assets		
Cash		$ 3,050
Accounts receivable		400
Prepaid insurance		830
Supplies		80
Equipment	$217,200	
Less accumulated depreciation	29,100	188,100
Total assets		$192,460
Liabilities		
Wages payable		$ 880
Interest payable		3,600
Unearned rent		460
Long-term notes payable		150,000
Total liabilities		154,940
Equity		
Common stock		10,000
Retained earnings		27,520
Total equity		37,520
Total liabilities and equity		$192,460

APPENDIX

Alternative Accounting for Prepayments

3A

This appendix explains an alternative in accounting for prepaid expenses and unearned revenues.

RECORDING PREPAYMENT OF EXPENSES IN EXPENSE ACCOUNTS

An alternative method is to record *all* prepaid expenses with debits to expense accounts. If any prepaids remain unused or unexpired at the end of an accounting period, then adjusting entries must transfer the cost of the unused portions from expense accounts to prepaid expense (asset) accounts. This alternative method is acceptable. The financial statements are identical under either method, but the adjusting entries

P6 Explain the alternatives in accounting for prepaids.

are different. To illustrate the differences between these two methods, let's look at FastForward's cash payment of December 6 for 24 months of insurance coverage beginning on December 1. FastForward recorded that payment with a debit to an asset account, but it could have recorded a debit to an expense account. These alternatives are shown in Exhibit 3A.1.

EXHIBIT 3A.1

Alternative Initial Entries for Prepaid Expenses

		Payment Recorded as Asset	Payment Recorded as Expense
Dec. 6	Prepaid Insurance	2,400	
	Cash		2,400	
Dec. 6	Insurance Expense		2,400
	Cash		2,400

At the end of its accounting period on December 31, insurance protection for one month has expired. This means $100 ($2,400/24) of insurance coverage expired and is an expense for December. The adjusting entry depends on how the original payment was recorded. This is shown in Exhibit 3A.2.

EXHIBIT 3A.2

Adjusting Entry for Prepaid Expenses for the Two Alternatives

		Payment Recorded as Asset	Payment Recorded as Expense
Dec. 31	Insurance Expense	100	
	Prepaid Insurance	100	
Dec. 31	Prepaid Insurance		2,300
	Insurance Expense		2,300

When these entries are posted to the accounts in the ledger, we can see that these two methods give identical results. The December 31 adjusted account balances in Exhibit 3A.3 show Prepaid Insurance of $2,300 and Insurance Expense of $100 for both methods.

EXHIBIT 3A.3

Account Balances under Two Alternatives for Recording Prepaid Expenses

Payment Recorded as Asset				Payment Recorded as Expense			

Prepaid Insurance			128
Dec. 6	2,400	Dec. 31	100
Balance	2,300		

Prepaid Insurance			128
Dec. 31	2,300		

Insurance Expense			637
Dec. 31	100		

Insurance Expense			637
Dec. 6	2,400	Dec. 31	2,300
Balance	100		

RECORDING PREPAYMENT OF REVENUES IN REVENUE ACCOUNTS

As with prepaid expenses, an alternative method is to record *all* unearned revenues with credits to revenue accounts. If any revenues are unearned at the end of an accounting period, then adjusting entries must transfer the unearned portions from revenue accounts to unearned revenue (liability) accounts. This alternative method is acceptable. The adjusting entries are different for these two alternatives, but the financial statements are identical. To illustrate the accounting differences between these two methods, let's look at FastForward's December 26 receipt of $3,000 for consulting services covering the period December 27 to February 24. FastForward recorded this transaction with a credit to a liability account. The alternative is to record it with a credit to a revenue account, as shown in Exhibit 3A.4.

EXHIBIT 3A.4

Alternative Initial Entries for Unearned Revenues

		Receipt Recorded as Liability	Receipt Recorded as Revenue
Dec. 26	Cash	3,000	
	Unearned Consulting Revenue	3,000	
Dec. 26	Cash		3,000
	Consulting Revenue		3,000

By the end of its accounting period on December 31, FastForward has earned $250 of this revenue. This means $250 of the liability has been satisfied. Depending on how the initial receipt is recorded, the adjusting entry is as shown in Exhibit 3A.5.

			Receipt Recorded as Liability	Receipt Recorded as Revenue
Dec. 31	Unearned Consulting Revenue		250	
	Consulting Revenue			250
Dec. 31	Consulting Revenue			2,750
	Unearned Consulting Revenue			2,750

EXHIBIT 3A.5

Adjusting Entry for Unearned Revenues for the Two Alternatives

After adjusting entries are posted, the two alternatives give identical results. The December 31 adjusted account balances in Exhibit 3A.6 show unearned consulting revenue of $2,750 and consulting revenue of $250 for both methods.

Receipt Recorded as Liability			Receipt Recorded as Revenue		

EXHIBIT 3A.6

Account Balances under Two Alternatives for Recording Unearned Revenues

Unearned Consulting Revenue		236		Unearned Consulting Revenue		236
Dec. 31	250	Dec. 26	3,000		Dec. 31	2,750
		Balance	2,750			

Consulting Revenue		403		Consulting Revenue		403
	Dec. 31	250	Dec. 31	2,750	Dec. 26	3,000
					Balance	250

APPENDIX

Work Sheet as a Tool

3B

Information preparers use various analyses and internal documents when organizing information for internal and external decision makers. Internal documents are often called **working papers.** One widely used working paper is the **work sheet,** which is a useful tool for preparers in working with accounting information. It is usually not available to external decision makers.

Benefits of a Work Sheet (Spreadsheet)   A work sheet is *not* a required report, yet using a manual or electronic work sheet has several potential benefits. Specifically, a work sheet:

P7 Prepare a work sheet and explain its usefulness.

- Aids the preparation of financial statements.
- Reduces the possibility of errors when working with many accounts and adjustments.
- Links accounts and adjustments to their impacts in financial statements.
- Assists in planning and organizing an audit of financial statements—as it can be used to reflect any adjustments necessary.
- Helps in preparing interim (monthly and quarterly) financial statements when the journalizing and posting of adjusting entries are postponed until the year-end.
- Shows the effects of proposed or "what if" transactions.

Use of a Work Sheet (Spreadsheet)   When a work sheet is used to prepare financial statements, it is constructed at the end of a period before the adjusting process. The complete work sheet includes a list of the accounts, their balances and adjustments, and their sorting into financial statement columns. It provides two columns each for the unadjusted trial balance, the adjustments, the adjusted trial balance, the income statement, and the balance sheet. To describe and interpret the work sheet, we

Point: Since a work sheet is *not* a required report or an accounting record, its format is flexible and can be modified by its user to fit his/her preferences.

use the information from FastForward. Preparing the work sheet has five important steps. Each step, 1 through 5, is color-coded and explained with reference to Exhibit 3B.1.

1 Step 1. Enter Unadjusted Trial Balance

The first step in preparing a work sheet is to list the title of every account and its account number that is expected to appear on its financial statements. This includes all accounts in the ledger plus any new ones from adjusting entries. Most adjusting entries—including expenses from salaries, supplies, depreciation, and insurance—are predictable and recurring. The unadjusted balance for each account is then entered in the appropriate Debit or Credit column of the unadjusted trial balance columns. The totals of these two columns must be equal. Exhibit 3B.1 shows FastForward's work sheet after completing this first step. Sometimes blank lines are left on the work sheet based on past experience to indicate where lines will be needed for adjustments to certain accounts. Exhibit 3B.1 shows Consulting Revenue as one example. An alternative is to squeeze adjustments on one line or to combine the effects of two or more adjustments in one amount. In the unusual case when an account is not predicted, we can add a new line for such an account following the *Totals* line.

2 Step 2. Enter Adjustments

The second step in preparing a work sheet is to enter adjustments in the Adjustments columns. The adjustments shown are the same ones shown in Exhibit 3.13. An identifying letter links the debit and credit of each adjusting entry. This is called *keying* the adjustments. After preparing a work sheet, adjusting entries must still be entered in the journal and posted to the ledger. The Adjustments columns provide the information for those entries.

3 Step 3. Prepare Adjusted Trial Balance

Point: To avoid omitting the transfer of an account balance, start with the first line (cash) and continue in account order.

The adjusted trial balance is prepared by combining the adjustments with the unadjusted balances for each account. As an example, the Prepaid Insurance account has a $2,400 debit balance in the Unadjusted Trial Balance columns. This $2,400 debit is combined with the $100 credit in the Adjustments columns to give Prepaid Insurance a $2,300 debit in the Adjusted Trial Balance columns. The totals of the Adjusted Trial Balance columns confirm the equality of debits and credits.

4 Step 4. Sort Adjusted Trial Balance Amounts to Financial Statements

This step involves sorting account balances from the adjusted trial balance to their proper financial statement columns. Expenses go to the Income Statement Debit column and revenues to the Income Statement Credit column. Assets and Dividends go to the Balance Sheet Debit column. Liabilities, Retained Earnings, and Common Stock go to the Balance Sheet Credit column.

5 Step 5. Total Statement Columns, Compute Income or Loss, and Balance Columns

Each financial statement column (from Step 4) is totaled. The difference between the totals of the Income Statement columns is net income or net loss. This occurs because revenues are entered in the Credit column and expenses in the Debit column. If the Credit total exceeds the Debit total, there is net income. If the Debit total exceeds the Credit total, there is a net loss. For FastForward, the Credit total exceeds the Debit total, giving a $3,785 net income.

The net income from the Income Statement columns is then entered in the Balance Sheet Credit column. Adding net income to the last Credit column implies that it is to be added to retained earnings. If a loss occurs, it is added to the Debit column. This implies that it is to be subtracted from retained earnings. The ending balance of retained earnings does not appear in the last two columns as a single amount, but it is computed in the statement of retained earnings using these account balances. When net income or net loss is added to the proper Balance Sheet column, the totals of the last two columns must balance. If they do not, one or more errors have been made. The error can either be mathematical or involve sorting one or more amounts to incorrect columns.

Work Sheet Applications and Analysis   A work sheet does not substitute for financial statements. It is a tool we can use at the end of an accounting period to help organize data and prepare financial statements. FastForward's financial statements are shown in Exhibit 3.14. Its income statement amounts are taken from the Income Statement columns of the work sheet. Similarly, amounts for its balance sheet and its statement of retained earnings are taken from the Balance Sheet columns of the work sheet.

Work sheets are also useful in analyzing the effects of proposed, or what-if, transactions. This is done by entering financial statement amounts in the Unadjusted (what-if) columns. Proposed transactions are then entered in the Adjustments columns. We then compute "adjusted" amounts from these proposed transactions. The extended amounts in the financial statement columns show the effects of these proposed transactions. These financial statement columns yield **pro forma financial statements** because they show the statements *as if* the proposed transactions occurred.

EXHIBIT 3B.1

Work Sheet

File Edit View Insert Format Tools Data Window Help

FASTFORWARD
Work Sheet
For Month Ended December 31, 2013

No.	Account	Unadjusted Trial Balance Dr.	Cr.	Adjustments Dr.	Cr.	Adjusted Trial Balance Dr.	Cr.	Income Statement Dr.	Cr.	Balance Sheet Dr.	Cr.
101	Cash	4,350				4,350				4,350	
106	Accounts receivable	0		(f)1,800		1,800				1,800	
126	Supplies	9,720			(b)1,050	8,670				8,670	
128	Prepaid insurance	2,400			(a) 100	2,300				2,300	
167	Equipment	26,000				26,000				26,000	
168	Accumulated depreciation—Equip.		0		(c) 375		375				375
201	Accounts payable		6,200				6,200				6,200
209	Salaries payable		0		(e) 210		210				210
236	Unearned consulting revenue		3,000	(d) 250			2,750				2,750
307	Common stock		30,000				30,000				30,000
318	Retained earnings		0				0				0
319	Dividends	200				200				200	
403	Consulting revenue		5,800		(d) 250		7,850		7,850		
					(f)1,800						
406	Rental revenue		300				300		300		
612	Depreciation expense—Equip.	0		(c) 375		375		375			
622	Salaries expense	1,400		(e) 210		1,610		1,610			
637	Insurance expense	0		(a) 100		100		100			
640	Rent expense	1,000				1,000		1,000			
652	Supplies expense	0		(b)1,050		1,050		1,050			
690	Utilities expense	230				230		230			
	Totals	45,300	45,300	3,785	3,785	47,685	47,685	4,365	8,150	43,320	39,535
	Net income							3,785			3,785
	Totals							8,150	8,150	43,320	43,320

List all accounts from the ledger and those expected to arise from adjusting entries.

Enter all amounts available from ledger accounts. Column totals must be equal.

A work sheet collects and summarizes information used to prepare adjusting entries, financial statements, and closing entries.

APPENDIX

Reversing Entries

3C

Reversing entries are optional. They are recorded in response to accrued assets and accrued liabilities that were created by adjusting entries at the end of a reporting period. The purpose of reversing entries is to simplify a company's recordkeeping. Exhibit 3C.1 shows an example of FastForward's reversing entries. The top of the exhibit shows the adjusting entry FastForward recorded on December 31 for its employee's earned but unpaid salary. The entry recorded three days' salary of $210, which increased December's total salary expense to $1,610. The entry also recognized a liability of $210. The expense is reported on December's income statement. The expense account is then closed. The ledger on January 1, 2014, shows a $210 liability and a zero balance in the Salaries Expense account. At this point, the choice is made between using or not using reversing entries.

Point: As a general rule, adjusting entries that create new asset or liability accounts are likely candidates for reversing.

EXHIBIT 3C.1

Reversing Entries for an
Accrued Expense

Accrue salaries expense on December 31, 2013

Salaries Expense 210
    Salaries Payable 210

Salaries Expense

Date	Expl.	Debit	Credit	Balance
2013				
Dec. 12	(7)	700		700
26	(16)	700		1,400
31	(e)	210		1,610

Salaries Payable

Date	Expl.	Debit	Credit	Balance
2013				
Dec. 31	(e)		210	210

WITHOUT Reversing Entries	— OR —	**WITH Reversing Entries**
No reversing entry recorded on January 1, 2014		*Reversing entry recorded on January 1, 2014*

WITHOUT Reversing Entries

NO ENTRY

Salaries Expense

Date	Expl.	Debit	Credit	Balance
2014				

Salaries Payable

Date	Expl.	Debit	Credit	Balance
2013				
Dec. 31	(e)		210	210
2014				

WITH Reversing Entries

Salaries Payable 210
    Salaries Expense 210

Salaries Expense*

Date	Expl.	Debit	Credit	Balance
2014				
Jan. 1			210	(210)

Salaries Payable

Date	Expl.	Debit	Credit	Balance
2013				
Dec. 31	(e)		210	210
2014				
Jan. 1		210		0

Pay the accrued and current salaries on January 9, the first payday in 2014

WITHOUT Reversing Entries

Salaries Expense 490
Salaries Payable 210
    Cash.. 700

Salaries Expense

Date	Expl.	Debit	Credit	Balance
2014				
Jan. 9		490		490

Salaries Payable

Date	Expl.	Debit	Credit	Balance
2013				
Dec. 31	(e)		210	210
2014				
Jan. 9		210		0

WITH Reversing Entries

Salaries Expense 700
    Cash.. 700

Salaries Expense*

Date	Expl.	Debit	Credit	Balance
2014				
Jan. 1			210	(210)
Jan. 9		700		490

Salaries Payable

Date	Expl.	Debit	Credit	Balance
2013				
Dec. 31	(e)		210	210
2014				
Jan. 1		210		0

Under both approaches, the expense and liability accounts have
identical balances after the cash payment on January 9.

Salaries Expense $490
Salaries Payable .... $ 0

*Circled numbers in the *Balance* column indicate abnormal balances.*

Accounting *without* Reversing Entries The path down the left side of Exhibit 3C.1 is described in the chapter. To summarize here, when the next payday occurs on January 9, we record payment with a compound entry that debits both the expense and liability accounts and credits Cash. Posting that entry creates a $490 balance in the expense account and reduces the liability account balance to zero because the debt has been settled. The disadvantage of this approach is the slightly more complex entry required on January 9. Paying the accrued liability means that this entry differs from the routine entries made on all other paydays. To construct the proper entry on January 9, we must recall the effect of the December 31 adjusting entry. Reversing entries overcome this disadvantage.

Point: Firms that use reversing entries hope that this simplification will reduce errors.

Accounting *with* Reversing Entries   The right side of Exhibit 3C.1 shows how a reversing entry on January 1 overcomes the disadvantage of the January 9 entry when not using reversing entries. A reversing entry is the exact opposite of an adjusting entry. For FastForward, the Salaries Payable liability account is debited for $210, meaning that this account now has a zero balance after the entry is posted. The Salaries Payable account temporarily understates the liability, but this is not a problem since financial statements are not prepared before the liability is settled on January 9. The credit to the Salaries Expense account is unusual because it gives the account an *abnormal credit balance*. We highlight an abnormal balance by circling it. Because of the reversing entry, the January 9 entry to record payment is straightforward. This entry debits the Salaries Expense account and credits Cash for the full $700 paid. It is the same as all other entries made to record 10 days' salary for the employee. Notice that after the payment entry is posted, the Salaries Expense account has a $490 balance that reflects seven days' salary of $70 per day (see the lower right side of Exhibit 3C.1). The zero balance in the Salaries Payable account is now correct. The lower section of Exhibit 3C.1 shows that the expense and liability accounts have exactly the same balances whether reversing entries are used or not. This means that both approaches yield identical results.

> **P8** Prepare reversing entries and explain their purpose.

Summary

C1 Explain the importance of periodic reporting and the time period assumption. The value of information is often linked to its timeliness. To provide timely information, accounting systems prepare periodic reports at regular intervals. The time period assumption presumes that an organization's activities can be divided into specific time periods for periodic reporting.

C2 Explain accrual accounting and how it improves financial statements. Accrual accounting recognizes revenue when earned and expenses when incurred—not necessarily when cash inflows and outflows occur. This information is valuable in assessing a company's financial position and performance.

C3 Identify steps in the accounting cycle. The accounting cycle consists of 10 steps: (1) analyze transactions, (2) journalize, (3) post, (4) prepare an unadjusted trial balance, (5) adjust accounts, (6) prepare an adjusted trial balance, (7) prepare statements, (8) close, (9) prepare a post-closing trial balance, and (10) prepare (optional) reversing entries.

C4 Explain and prepare a classified balance sheet. Classified balance sheets report assets and liabilities in two categories: current and noncurrent. Noncurrent assets often include long-term investments, plant assets, and intangible assets. A corporation separates equity into common stock and retained earnings.

A1 Explain how accounting adjustments link to financial statements. Accounting adjustments bring an asset or liability account balance to its correct amount. They also update related expense or revenue accounts. Every adjusting entry affects one or more income statement accounts *and* one or more balance sheet accounts. An adjusting entry never affects cash.

A2 Compute profit margin and describe its use in analyzing company performance. *Profit margin* is defined as the reporting period's net income divided by its net sales. Profit margin reflects on a company's earnings activities by showing how much income is in each dollar of sales.

A3 Compute the current ratio and describe what it reveals about a company's financial condition. A company's current ratio is defined as current assets divided by current liabilities. We use it to evaluate a company's ability to pay its current liabilities out of current assets.

P1 Prepare and explain adjusting entries. *Prepaid expenses* refer to items paid for in advance of receiving their benefits. Prepaid expenses are assets. Adjusting entries for prepaids involve increasing (debiting) expenses and decreasing (crediting) assets. *Unearned* (or *prepaid*) *revenues* refer to cash received in advance of providing products and services. Unearned revenues are liabilities. Adjusting entries for unearned revenues involve increasing (crediting) revenues and decreasing (debiting) unearned revenues. *Accrued expenses* refer to costs incurred in a period that are both unpaid and unrecorded. Adjusting entries for recording accrued expenses involve increasing (debiting) expenses and increasing (crediting) liabilities. *Accrued revenues* refer to revenues earned in a period that are both unrecorded and not yet received in cash. Adjusting entries for recording accrued revenues involve increasing (debiting) assets and increasing (crediting) revenues.

P2 Explain and prepare an adjusted trial balance. An adjusted trial balance is a list of accounts and balances prepared after recording and posting adjusting entries. Financial statements are often prepared from the adjusted trial balance.

P3 Prepare financial statements from an adjusted trial balance. Revenue and expense balances are reported on the income statement. Asset, liability, and equity balances are reported on the balance sheet. We usually prepare statements in the following order: income statement, statement of retained earnings, balance sheet, and statement of cash flows.

P4 Describe and prepare closing entries. Closing entries involve four steps: (1) close credit balances in revenue (and gain) accounts to Income Summary, (2) close debit balances in expense (and loss) accounts to Income Summary, (3) close Income Summary to the retained earnings, and (4) close dividends account to retained earnings.

P5 Explain and prepare a post-closing trial balance. A post-closing trial balance is a list of permanent accounts and their balances after all closing entries have been journalized and posted. Its purpose is to verify that (1) total debits equal total credits for permanent accounts and (2) all temporary accounts have zero balances.

P6A Explain the alternatives in accounting for prepaids. Charging all prepaid expenses to expense accounts when they are purchased is acceptable. When this is done, adjusting entries must transfer any unexpired amounts from expense accounts to asset accounts. Crediting all unearned revenues to revenue accounts when cash is received is also acceptable. In this case, the adjusting entries must transfer any unearned amounts from revenue accounts to unearned revenue accounts.

P7ᴮ Prepare a work sheet and explain its usefulness. A work sheet can be a useful tool in preparing and analyzing financial statements. It is helpful at the end of a period in preparing adjusting

entries, an adjusted trial balance, and financial statements. A work sheet usually contains five pairs of columns: Unadjusted Trial Balance, Adjustments, Adjusted Trial Balance, Income Statement, and Balance Sheet & Statement of Equity.

P8ᶜ Prepare reversing entries and explain their purpose. Reversing entries are an optional step. They are applied to accrued expenses and revenues. The purpose of reversing entries is to simplify subsequent journal entries. Financial statements are unaffected by the choice to use or not use reversing entries.

Guidance Answers to Decision Maker and Decision Ethics

Investor Prepaid expenses are items paid for in advance of receiving their benefits. They are assets and are expensed as they are used up. The publishing company's treatment of the signing bonus is acceptable provided future book sales can at least match the $500,000 expense. As an investor, you are concerned about the risk of future book sales. The riskier the likelihood of future book sales is, the more likely your analysis is to treat the $500,000, or a portion of it, as an expense, not a prepaid expense (asset).

Entrepreneur Depreciation is a process of cost allocation, not asset valuation. Knowing the depreciation schedule is not especially useful in your estimation of what the building and equipment are currently worth. Your own assessment of the age, quality, and usefulness of the building and equipment is more important.

Loan Officer Your concern in lending to this store arises from analysis of current-year sales. While increased revenues and income are fine, your concern is with collectibility of these promotional sales. If the owner sold products to customers with poor records of

paying bills, then collectibility of these sales is low. Your analysis must assess this possibility and recognize any expected losses.

Financial Officer Omitting accrued expenses and recognizing revenue early can mislead financial statement users. One action is to request a second meeting with the president so you can explain that accruing expenses when incurred and recognizing revenue when earned are required practices. If the president persists, you might discuss the situation with legal counsel and any auditors involved. Your ethical action might cost you this job, but the potential pitfalls for falsification of statements, reputation and personal integrity loss, and other costs are too great.

Analyst A current ratio of 1.2 suggests that current assets are sufficient to cover current liabilities, but it implies a minimal buffer in case of errors in measuring current assets or current liabilities. Removing the past due receivable reduces the current ratio to 0.7. Your assessment is that the company will have some difficulty meeting its loan payments.

Guidance Answers to Quick Checks

1. An annual reporting (or accounting) period covers one year and refers to the preparation of annual financial statements. The annual reporting period is not always a calendar year that ends on December 31. An organization can adopt a fiscal year consisting of any consecutive 12 months or 52 weeks.

2. Interim financial statements (covering less than one year) are prepared to provide timely information to decision makers.

3. The revenue recognition principle and the expense recognition (matching) principle lead most directly to the adjusting process.

4. No. Cash basis accounting is not consistent with the matching principle because it reports revenue when received, not necessarily when earned, and expenses when paid, not necessarily in the period when the expenses were incurred as a result of the revenues earned.

5. No expense is reported in 2014. Under cash basis accounting, the entire $4,800 is reported as an expense in April 2013 when the premium is paid.

6. If the accrued revenues adjustment of $200 is not made, then both revenues and net income are understated by $200 on the current year's income statement, and both assets and equity are understated by $200 on the balance sheet.

7. A contra account is an account that is subtracted from the balance of a related account. Use of a contra account provides more information than simply reporting a net amount.

8. An accrued expense is a cost incurred in a period that is both unpaid and unrecorded prior to adjusting entries. One example is salaries earned but not yet paid at period-end.

9. An unearned revenue arises when a firm receives cash (or other assets) from a customer before providing the services or products to the customer. A magazine subscription paid in advance is one example; season ticket sales is another.

10.

Salaries Payable	1,000	
Salaries Expense	6,000	
Cash		7,000
Paid salary including accrual from December.		

11. The probable adjusting entries of Jordan Air are:

Insurance Expense	300	
Prepaid Insurance		300
To record insurance expired.		
Salaries Expense	1,400	
Salaries Payable		1,400
To record accrued salaries.		

12. Revenue accounts and expense accounts.

13. Statement of retained earnings.

14. The major steps in preparing closing entries are to close (1) credit balances in revenue accounts to Income Summary, (2) debit balances in expense accounts to Income Summary, (3) Income Summary to retained earnings, and (4) any dividends account to retained earnings.

15. Revenue (and gain) and expense (and loss) accounts are called *temporary* because they are opened and closed each period. The Income Summary and Dividends accounts are also temporary.

16. Permanent accounts make up the post-closing trial balance, which consist of asset, liability, and equity accounts.

17. Current assets: (*b*), (*c*), (*d*). Plant assets: (*a*), (*e*). Item (*f*) is an intangible asset.

18. Investment in common stock, investment in bonds, and land held for future expansion.

19. For a service company, the operating cycle is the usual time between (1) paying employees who do the services and (2) receiving cash from customers for services provided.

Key Terms

Accounting cycle (p. 116)	Current liabilities (p. 119)	Post-closing trial balance (p. 114)
Accounting periods (p. 98)	Current ratio (p. 121)	Prepaid expenses (p. 101)
Accrual basis accounting (p. 99)	Depreciation (p. 103)	Profit margin (p. 121)
Accrued expenses (p. 105)	Expense recognition (or matching)	Pro forma financial statements (p. 128)
Accrued revenues (p. 107)	principle (p. 100)	Reversing entries (p. 129)
Adjusted trial balance (p. 110)	Fiscal year (p. 99)	Straight-line depreciation method (p. 103)
Adjusting entry (p. 101)	Income Summary (p. 113)	Temporary accounts (p. 112)
Annual financial statements (p. 98)	Intangible assets (p. 119)	Time period assumption (p. 98)
Book value (p. 104)	Interim financial statements (p. 98)	Unadjusted trial balance (p. 110)
Cash basis accounting (p. 99)	Long-term investments (p. 119)	Unclassified balance sheet (p. 117)
Classified balance sheet (p. 117)	Long-term liabilities (p. 119)	Unearned revenues (p. 104)
Closing entries (p. 112)	Natural business year (p. 99)	Working papers (p. 127)
Closing process (p. 112)	Operating cycle (p. 117)	Work sheet (p. 127)
Contra account (p. 103)	Permanent accounts (p. 112)	
Current assets (p. 118)	Plant assets (p. 103)	

Multiple Choice Quiz   Answers on p. 159   mhhe.com/wildFINMAN5e

Additional Quiz Questions are available at the book's Website.

1. A company forgot to record accrued and unpaid employee wages of $350,000 at period-end. This oversight would
   a. Understate net income by $350,000.
   b. Overstate net income by $350,000.
   c. Have no effect on net income.
   d. Overstate assets by $350,000.
   e. Understate assets by $350,000.

2. Prior to recording adjusting entries, the Supplies account has a $450 debit balance. A physical count of supplies shows $125 of unused supplies still available. The required adjusting entry is:
   a. Debit Supplies $125; Credit Supplies Expense $125.
   b. Debit Supplies $325; Credit Supplies Expense $325.
   c. Debit Supplies Expense $325; Credit Supplies $325.
   d. Debit Supplies Expense $325; Credit Supplies $125.
   e. Debit Supplies Expense $125; Credit Supplies $125.

3. On May 1, 2013, a two-year insurance policy was purchased for $24,000 with coverage to begin immediately. What is the amount of insurance expense that appears on the company's income statement for the year ended December 31, 2013?
   a. $4,000
   b. $8,000

   c. $12,000
   d. $20,000
   e. $24,000

4. On November 1, 2013, Stockton Co. receives $3,600 cash from Hans Co. for consulting services to be provided evenly over the period November 1, 2013, to April 30, 2014—at which time Stockton credited $3,600 to Unearned Consulting Fees. The adjusting entry on December 31, 2013 (Stockton's year-end) would include a
   a. Debit to Unearned Consulting Fees for $1,200.
   b. Debit to Unearned Consulting Fees for $2,400.
   c. Credit to Consulting Fees Earned for $2,400.
   d. Debit to Consulting Fees Earned for $1,200.
   e. Credit to Cash for $3,600.

5. If a company had $15,000 in net income for the year, and its sales were $300,000 for the same year, what is its profit margin?
   a. 20%
   b. 2,000%
   c. $285,000
   d. $315,000
   e. 5%

6. Based on the following information from Repicor Company's balance sheet, what is Repicor Company's current ratio?

Current assets	$ 75,000	Current liabilities	50,000
Investments	30,000	Long-term liabilities . . .	60,000
Plant assets	300,000	Common stock	295,000

a. 2.10
b. 1.50
c. 1.00
d. 0.95
e. 0.67

A(B,C)   *Superscript letter A(B,C) denotes assignments based on Appendix 3A(3B,3C).*

🔘 Icon denotes assignments that involve decision making.

Discussion Questions

1. What is the difference between the cash basis and the accrual basis of accounting?

2. 🔘 Why is the accrual basis of accounting generally preferred over the cash basis?

3. What type of business is most likely to select a fiscal year that corresponds to its natural business year instead of the calendar year?

4. What is a prepaid expense and where is it reported in the financial statements?

5. 🔘 What type of assets require adjusting entries to record depreciation?

6. 🔘 What contra account is used when recording and reporting the effects of depreciation? Why is it used?

7. 🌐 Assume Piaggio has unearned revenue. **PIAGGIO** What is unearned revenue and where is it reported in financial statements?

8. What is an accrued revenue? Give an example.

9.A If a company initially records prepaid expenses with debits to expense accounts, what type of account is debited in the adjusting entries for those prepaid expenses?

10. 🔘 Review the balance sheet of Polaris in **Polaris** Appendix A. Identify one asset account that requires adjustment before annual financial statements can be prepared. What would be the effect on the income statement if this asset account were not adjusted? (Number not required, but comment on over- or understating of net income.)

11. 🔘 Review the balance sheet of Arctic Cat in **Arctic Cat** Appendix A. Identify the amount for property and equipment. What adjusting entry is necessary (no numbers required) for this account when preparing financial statements?

12. 🌐 Refer to KTM's balance sheet in Appendix A. **KTM** If it made an adjustment for unpaid wages at year-end, where would the accrued wages be reported on its balance sheet?

13. What are the steps in recording closing entries?

14. What accounts are affected by closing entries? What accounts are not affected?

15. 🔘 What two purposes are accomplished by recording closing entries?

16. What is the purpose of the Income Summary account?

17. 🔘 Explain whether an error has occurred if a post-closing trial balance includes a Depreciation Expense account.

18.B What tasks are aided by a work sheet?

19.B Why are the debit and credit entries in the Adjustments columns of the work sheet identified with letters?

20. What is a company's operating cycle?

21. What classes of assets and liabilities are shown on a typical classified balance sheet?

22. How is unearned revenue classified on the balance sheet?

23. What are the characteristics of plant assets?

24.C How do reversing entries simplify recordkeeping?

25.C If a company recorded accrued salaries expense of $500 at the end of its fiscal year, what reversing entry could be made? When would it be made?

26. 🔘 Refer to the most recent balance sheet for **Polaris** Polaris in Appendix A. What five main noncurrent asset categories are used on its classified balance sheet?

27. Refer to KTM's most recent balance sheet in **KTM** Appendix A. Identify and list its 7 current assets.

28. 🔘 Refer to Arctic Cat's most recent balance **Arctic Cat** sheet in Appendix A. Identify the three accounts listed as current liabilities.

29. 🔘 Refer to Piaggio's financial statements in **PIAGGIO** Appendix A. What journal entry was likely recorded as of December 31, 2011, to close its Income Summary account?

🔲 connect

QUICK STUDY

QS 3-1

Adjusting prepaid expenses

P1

a. On July 1, 2013, Lamis Company paid $1,200 for six months of insurance coverage. No adjustments have been made to the Prepaid Insurance account, and it is now December 31, 2013. Prepare the journal entry to reflect expiration of the insurance as of December 31, 2013.

b. Shandi Company has a Supplies account balance of $5,000 on January 1, 2013. During 2013, it purchased $2,000 of supplies. As of December 31, 2013, a supplies inventory shows $800 of supplies available. Prepare the adjusting journal entry to correctly report the balance of the Supplies account and the Supplies Expense account as of December 31, 2013.

a. Bargains Company purchases $20,000 of equipment on January 1, 2013. The equipment is expected to last five years and be worth $2,000 at the end of that time. Prepare the entry to record one year's depreciation expense of $3,600 for the equipment as of December 31, 2013.

b. Welch Company purchases $10,000 of land on January 1, 2013. The land is expected to last indefinitely. What depreciation adjustment, if any, should be made with respect to the Land account as of December 31, 2013?

QS 3-2

Adjusting for depreciation

P1

Classify the following adjusting entries as involving prepaid expenses (PE), unearned revenues (UR), accrued expenses (AE), or accrued revenues (AR).

a. _____ To record expiration of prepaid insurance.

b. _____ To record revenue earned but not yet billed (nor recorded).

c. _____ To record wages expense incurred but not yet paid (nor recorded).

d. _____ To record annual depreciation expense.

e. _____ To record revenue earned that was previously received as cash in advance.

QS 3-3

Identifying accounting adjustments

P1

Jasmine Culpepper employs one college student every summer in her coffee shop. The student works the five weekdays and is paid on the following Monday. (For example, a student who works Monday through Friday, June 1 through June 5, is paid for that work on Monday, June 8.) Culpepper adjusts her books monthly, if needed, to show salaries earned but unpaid at month-end. The student works the last week of July—Friday is August 1. If the student earns $100 per day, what adjusting entry must Culpepper make on July 31 to correctly record accrued salaries expense for July?

QS 3-4

Accruing salaries

A1 P1

---

a. Tao Co. receives $10,000 cash in advance for 4 months of legal services on October 1, 2013, and records it by debiting Cash and crediting Unearned Revenue both for $10,000. It is now December 31, 2013, and Tao has provided legal services as planned. What adjusting entry should Tao make to account for the work performed from October 1 through December 31, 2013?

b. A. Caden started a new publication called *Contest News*. Its subscribers pay $24 to receive 12 monthly issues. With every new subscriber, Caden debits Cash and credits Unearned Subscription Revenue for the amounts received. The company has 100 new subscribers as of July 1, 2013. It sends *Contest News* to each of these subscribers every month from July through December. Assuming no changes in subscribers, prepare the journal entry that Caden must make as of December 31, 2013, to adjust the Subscription Revenue account and the Unearned Subscription Revenue account.

QS 3-5

Adjusting for unearned revenues

A1 P1

In its first year of operations, Roma Co. earned $45,000 in revenues and received $37,000 cash from these customers. The company incurred expenses of $25,500 but had not paid $5,250 of them at year-end. The company also prepaid $6,750 cash for expenses that would be incurred the next year. Calculate the first year's net income under both the cash basis and the accrual basis of accounting.

QS 3-6

Computing accrual and cash income C2 A1

Adjusting entries affect at least one balance sheet account and at least one income statement account. For the following entries, identify the account to be debited and the account to be credited. Indicate which of the accounts is the income statement account and which is the balance sheet account.

a. Entry to record revenue earned that was previously received as cash in advance.

b. Entry to record wage expenses incurred but not yet paid (nor recorded).

c. Entry to record revenue earned but not yet billed (nor recorded).

d. Entry to record expiration of prepaid insurance.

e. Entry to record annual depreciation expense.

QS 3-7

Recording and analyzing adjusting entries

A1

During the year, Sereno Co. recorded prepayments of expenses in asset accounts, and cash receipts of unearned revenues in liability accounts. At the end of its annual accounting period, the company must make three adjusting entries: (1) accrue salaries expense, (2) adjust the Unearned Services Revenue account to recognize earned revenue, and (3) record services revenue earned for which cash will be received the following period. For each of these adjusting entries (1), (2), and (3), indicate the account from *a* through *i* to be debited and the account to be credited.

QS 3-8

Preparing adjusting entries

P1

a. Prepaid Salaries   **d.** Unearned Services Revenue   **g.** Accounts Receivable

b. Cash   **e.** Salaries Expense   **h.** Accounts Payable

c. Salaries Payable   **f.** Services Revenue   **i.** Equipment

QS 3-9
Interpreting adjusting entries
C2 P2

The following information is taken from Brooke Company's unadjusted and adjusted trial balances.

	Unadjusted		Adjusted	
	Debit	Credit	Debit	Credit
Prepaid insurance.........	$4,100		$3,700	
Interest payable		$ 0		$800

Given this information, which of the following is likely included among its adjusting entries?

a. A $400 debit to Insurance Expense and an $800 debit to Interest Payable.

b. A $400 debit to Insurance Expense and an $800 debit to Interest Expense.

c. A $400 credit to Prepaid Insurance and an $800 debit to Interest Payable.

QS 3-10
Determining effects of
adjusting entries

A1

In making adjusting entries at the end of its accounting period, Chao Consulting failed to record $3,200 of insurance coverage that had expired. This $3,200 cost had been initially debited to the Prepaid Insurance account. The company also failed to record accrued salaries expense of $2,000. As a result of these two oversights, the financial statements for the reporting period will [choose one] (1) understate assets by $3,200; (2) understate expenses by $5,200; (3) understate net income by $2,000; or (4) overstate liabilities by $2,000.

QS 3-11
Analyzing profit margin

A2

Deklin Company reported net income of $48,025 and net sales of $425,000 for the current year. Calculate the company's profit margin and interpret the result. Assume that its competitors earn an average profit margin of 15%.

QS 3-12ᴬ
Preparing adjusting entries
P6

Calvin Consulting initially records prepaid and unearned items in income statement accounts. Given this company's accounting practices, which of the following applies to the preparation of adjusting entries at the end of its first accounting period?

a. Unearned fees (on which cash was received in advance earlier in the period) are recorded with a debit to Consulting Fees Earned and a credit to Unearned Consulting Fees.

b. Unpaid salaries are recorded with a debit to Prepaid Salaries and a credit to Salaries Expense.

c. The cost of unused office supplies is recorded with a debit to Supplies Expense and a credit to Office Supplies.

d. Earned but unbilled (and unrecorded) consulting fees are recorded with a debit to Unearned Consulting Fees and a credit to Consulting Fees Earned.

QS 3-13
International accounting
standards

P3

Answer each of the following questions related to international accounting standards.

a. Do financial statements prepared under IFRS normally present assets from least liquid to most liquid or vice-versa?

b. Do financial statements prepared under IFRS normally present liabilities from furthest from maturity to nearest to maturity or vice-versa?

QS 3-14
Prepaid (deferred) expenses
adjustments
P1

For each separate case below, follow the 3-step process for adjusting the prepaid asset account: Step 1: Determine what the current account balance equals. Step 2: Determine what the current account balance should equal. Step 3: Record an adjusting entry to get from step 1 to step 2. *Assume no other adjusting entries are made during the year.*

a. Prepaid Insurance. The Prepaid Insurance account has a $4,700 debit balance to start the year. A review of insurance policies and payments shows that $900 of unexpired insurance remains at year-end.

b. Prepaid Insurance. The Prepaid Insurance account has a $5,890 debit balance at the start of the year. A review of insurance policies and payments shows $1,040 of insurance has expired by year-end.

c. Prepaid Rent. On September 1 of the current year, the company prepaid $24,000 for 2 years of rent for facilities being occupied that day. The company debited Prepaid Rent and credited Cash for $24,000.

For each separate case below, follow the 3-step process for adjusting the supplies asset account: Step 1: Determine what the current account balance equals. Step 2: Determine what the current account balance should equal. Step 3: Record an adjusting entry to get from step 1 to step 2. *Assume no other adjusting entries are made during the year.*

QS 3-15
Prepaid (deferred) expenses adjustments
P1

a. **Supplies.** The Supplies account has a $300 debit balance to start the year. No supplies were purchased during the current year. A December 31 physical count shows $110 of supplies remaining.

b. **Supplies.** The Supplies account has an $800 debit balance to start the year. Supplies of $2,100 were purchased during the current year and debited to the Supplies account. A December 31 physical count shows $650 of supplies remaining.

c. **Supplies.** The Supplies account has a $4,000 debit balance to start the year. During the current year, supplies of $9,400 were purchased and debited to the Supplies account. The inventory of supplies available at December 31 totaled $2,660.

For each separate case below, follow the 3-step process for adjusting the accumulated depreciation account: Step 1: Determine what the current account balance equals. Step 2: Determine what the current account balance should equal. Step 3: Record an adjusting entry to get from step 1 to step 2. *Assume no other adjusting entries are made during the year.*

QS 3-16
Accumulated depreciation adjustments
P1

a. **Accumulated Depreciation.** The Krug Company's Accumulated Depreciation account has a $13,500 balance to start the year. A review of depreciation schedules reveals that $14,600 of depreciation expense must be recorded for the year.

b. **Accumulated Depreciation.** The company has only one fixed asset (truck) that it purchased at the start of this year. That asset had cost $44,000, had an estimated life of 5 years, and is expected to have zero value at the end of the 5 years.

c. **Accumulated Depreciation.** The company has only one fixed asset (equipment) that it purchased at the start of this year. That asset had cost $32,000, had an estimated life of 7 years, and is expected to be valued at $4,000 at the end of the 7 years.

For each separate case below, follow the 3-step process for adjusting the unearned revenue liability account: Step 1: Determine what the current account balance equals. Step 2: Determine what the current account balance should equal. Step 3: Record an adjusting entry to get from step 1 to step 2. *Assume no other adjusting entries are made during the year.*

QS 3-17
Unearned (deferred) revenues adjustments
P1

a. **Unearned Rent Revenue.** The Krug Company collected $6,000 rent in advance on November 1, debiting Cash and crediting Unearned Rent Revenue. The tenant was paying twelve months rent in advance and occupancy began November 1.

b. **Unearned Services Revenue.** The company charges $75 per month to spray a house for insects. A customer paid $300 on October 1 in advance for four treatments, which was recorded with a debit to Cash and a credit to Unearned Services Revenue. At year-end, the company has applied three treatments for the customer.

c. **Unearned Rent Revenue.** On September 1, a client paid the company $24,000 cash for six months of rent in advance (the client leased a building and took occupancy immediately). The company recorded the cash as Unearned Rent Revenue.

For each separate case below, follow the 3-step process for adjusting the accrued expense account: Step 1: Determine what the current account balance equals. Step 2: Determine what the current account balance should equal. Step 3: Record an adjusting entry to get from step 1 to step 2. *Assume no other adjusting entries are made during the year.*

QS 3-18
Accrued expenses adjustments
P1

a. **Salaries Payable.** At year-end, salaries expense of $15,500 has been incurred by the company, but is not yet paid to employees.

b. **Interest Payable.** At its December 31 year-end, the company owes $250 of interest on a line-of-credit loan. That interest will not be paid until sometime in January of the next year.

c. **Interest Payable.** At its December 31 year-end, the company holds a mortgage payable that has incurred $875 in annual interest that is neither recorded nor paid. The company intends to pay the interest on January 7 of the next year.

QS 3-19

Accrued revenues adjustments

P1

For each separate case below, follow the 3-step process for adjusting the accrued revenue account: Step 1: Determine what the current account balance equals. Step 2: Determine what the current account balance should equal. Step 3: Record an adjusting entry to get from step 1 to step 2. *Assume no other adjusting entries are made during the year.*

a. **Accounts Receivable.** At year-end, the Krug Company has completed services of $19,000 for a client, but the client has not yet been billed for those services.

b. **Interest Receivable.** At year-end, the company has earned, but not yet recorded, $390 of interest earned from its investments in government bonds.

c. **Accounts Receivable.** A painting company collects fees when jobs are complete. The work for one customer, whose job was bid at $1,300, has been completed, but the customer has not yet been billed.

QS 3-20

Identifying the accounting cycle

C3

List the following steps of the accounting cycle in their proper order.

a. Posting the journal entries.

b. Journalizing and posting adjusting entries.

c. Preparing the adjusted trial balance.

d. Journalizing and posting closing entries.

e. Analyzing transactions and events.

f. Preparing the financial statements.

g. Preparing the unadjusted trial balance.

h. Journalizing transactions and events.

i. Preparing the post-closing trial balance.

QS 3-21

Classifying balance sheet items

C4

The following are common categories on a classified balance sheet.

A. Current assets

B. Long-term investments

C. Plant assets

D. Intangible assets

E. Current liabilities

F. Long-term liabilities

For each of the following items, select the letter that identifies the balance sheet category where the item typically would appear.

_____ **1.** Land not currently used in operations

_____ **2.** Notes payable (due in five years)

_____ **3.** Accounts receivable

_____ **4.** Trademarks

_____ **5.** Accounts payable

_____ **6.** Store equipment

_____ **7.** Wages payable

_____ **8.** Cash

QS 3-22

Identifying current accounts and computing the current ratio

A3

Compute Chavez Company's current ratio using the following information.

Accounts receivable	$18,000	Long-term notes payable	$21,000
Accounts payable	11,000	Office supplies	2,800
Buildings	45,000	Prepaid insurance	3,560
Cash	7,000	Unearned services revenue	3,000

QS 3-23

Prepare closing entries from the ledger   P4

The ledger of Mai Company includes the following accounts with normal balances: Common Stock $9,000; Dividends $800; Services Revenue $13,000; Wages Expense $8,400; and Rent Expense $1,600. Prepare the necessary closing entries from the available information at December 31.

QS 3-24

Identify post-closing accounts   P5

Identify the accounts listed in QS 3-23 that would be included in a post-closing trial balance.

QS 3-25ᴮ

Preparing a partial work sheet

P7

The ledger of Claudell Company includes the following unadjusted normal balances: Prepaid Rent $1,000, Services Revenue $55,600, and Wages Expense $5,000. Adjusting entries are required for (a) prepaid rent expired, $200; (b) accrued services revenue $900; and (c) accrued wages expense $700. Enter these unadjusted balances and the necessary adjustments on a work sheet and complete the work sheet for these accounts. *Note:* Also include the following accounts: Accounts Receivable, Wages Payable, and Rent Expense.

QS 3-26ᶜ

Reversing entries

P8

On December 31, 2012, Yates Co. prepared an adjusting entry for $12,000 of earned but unrecorded management fees. On January 16, 2013, Yates received $26,700 cash in management fees, which included the accrued fees earned in 2012. Assuming the company uses reversing entries, prepare the January 1, 2013, reversing entry and the January 16, 2013, cash receipt entry.

⊟connect

Prepare adjusting journal entries for the year ended (date of) December 31, 2013, for each of these separate situations. Assume that prepaid expenses are initially recorded in asset accounts. Also assume that fees collected in advance of work are initially recorded as liabilities.

a. Depreciation on the company's equipment for 2013 is computed to be $18,000.

b. The Prepaid Insurance account had a $6,000 debit balance at December 31, 2013, before adjusting for the costs of any expired coverage. An analysis of the company's insurance policies showed that $1,100 of unexpired insurance coverage remains.

c. The Office Supplies account had a $700 debit balance on December 31, 2012; and $3,480 of office supplies were purchased during the year. The December 31, 2013, physical count showed $298 of supplies available.

d. Two-thirds of the work related to $15,000 of cash received in advance was performed this period.

e. The Prepaid Insurance account had a $6,800 debit balance at December 31, 2013, before adjusting for the costs of any expired coverage. An analysis of insurance policies showed that $5,800 of coverage had expired.

f. Wage expenses of $3,200 have been incurred but are not paid as of December 31, 2013.

EXERCISES

Exercise 3-1
Preparing adjusting entries
P1

Check (c) Dr. Office Supplies Expense, $3,882; (e) Dr. Insurance Expense, $5,800

For each of the following separate cases, prepare adjusting entries required of financial statements for the year ended (date of) December 31, 2013. (Assume that prepaid expenses are initially recorded in asset accounts and that fees collected in advance of work are initially recorded as liabilities.)

a. One-third of the work related to $15,000 cash received in advance is performed this period.

b. Wages of $8,000 are earned by workers but not paid as of December 31, 2013.

c. Depreciation on the company's equipment for 2013 is $18,531.

d. The Office Supplies account had a $240 debit balance on December 31, 2012. During 2013, $5,239 of office supplies are purchased. A physical count of supplies at December 31, 2013, shows $487 of supplies available.

e. The Prepaid Insurance account had a $4,000 balance on December 31, 2012. An analysis of insurance policies shows that $1,200 of unexpired insurance benefits remain at December 31, 2013.

f. The company has earned (but not recorded) $1,050 of interest from investments in CDs for the year ended December 31, 2013. The interest revenue will be received on January 10, 2014.

g. The company has a bank loan and has incurred (but not recorded) interest expense of $2,500 for the year ended December 31, 2013. The company must pay the interest on January 2, 2014.

Exercise 3-2
Preparing adjusting entries
P1

Check (e) Dr. Insurance Expense, $2,800; (f) Cr. Interest Revenue, $1,050

Pablo Management has five part-time employees, each of whom earns $250 per day. They are normally paid on Fridays for work completed Monday through Friday of the same week. Assume that December 28, 2013, was a Friday, and that they were paid in full on that day. The next week, the five employees worked only four days because New Year's Day was an unpaid holiday. (a) Assuming that December 31, 2013, was a Monday, prepare the adjusting entry that would be recorded at the close of that day. (b) Assuming that January 4, 2014, was a Friday, prepare the journal entry that would be made to record payment of the employees' wages.

Exercise 3-3
Adjusting and paying accrued wages
C1   P1

The following three separate situations require adjusting journal entries to prepare financial statements as of April 30. For each situation, present both the April 30 adjusting entry and the subsequent entry during May to record the payment of the accrued expenses.

a. On April 1, the company retained an attorney for a flat monthly fee of $3,500. Payment for April legal services was made by the company on May 12.

b. A $900,000 note payable requires 10% annual interest, or $9,000 to be paid at the 20th day of each month. The interest was last paid on April 20 and the next payment is due on May 20. As of April 30, $3,000 of interest expense has accrued.

c. Total weekly salaries expense for all employees is $10,000. This amount is paid at the end of the day on Friday of each five-day workweek. April 30 falls on Tuesday of this year, which means that the employees had worked two days since the last payday. The next payday is May 3.

Exercise 3-4
Adjusting and paying accrued expenses
A1

Check (b) May 20 Dr. Interest Expense, $6,000

Exercise 3-5
Determining cost flows
through accounts

C1 A1

Determine the missing amounts in each of these four separate situations *a* through *d*.

	a	b	c	d
Supplies available—prior year-end	$ 400	$1,200	$1,260	?
Supplies purchased during the current year	2,800	6,500	?	$3,000
Supplies available—current year-end	650	?	1,350	700
Supplies expense for the current year	?	1,200	8,400	4,588

Exercise 3-6
Analyzing and preparing
adjusting entries

A1 P3

Following are two income statements for Alexis Co. for the year ended December 31. The left column is prepared before any adjusting entries are recorded, and the right column includes the effects of adjusting entries. The company records cash receipts and payments related to unearned and prepaid items in balance sheet accounts. Analyze the statements and prepare the eight adjusting entries that likely were recorded. (*Note:* 30% of the $7,000 adjustment for Fees Earned has been earned but not billed, and the other 70% has been earned by performing services that were paid for in advance.)

ALEXIS CO. Income Statements For Year Ended December 31		
	Unadjusted	**Adjusted**
Revenues		
Fees earned	$18,000	$25,000
Commissions earned	36,500	36,500
Total revenues	$54,500	61,500
Expenses		
Depreciation expense—Computers	0	1,600
Depreciation expense—Office furniture	0	1,850
Salaries expense	13,500	15,750
Insurance expense	0	1,400
Rent expense	3,800	3,800
Office supplies expense	0	580
Advertising expense	2,500	2,500
Utilities expense	1,245	1,335
Total expenses	21,045	28,815
Net income	$33,455	$32,685

Exercise 3-7
Computing and interpreting
profit margin

A2

Use the following information to compute profit margin for each separate company *a* through *e*.

	Net Income	**Net Sales**		**Net Income**	**Net Sales**
a.	$ 4,361	$ 44,500	**d.**	$65,646	$1,458,800
b.	97,706	398,800	**e.**	80,142	435,500
c.	111,281	257,000			

Which of the five companies is the most profitable according to the profit margin ratio? Interpret that company's profit margin ratio.

Exercise 3-8^A
Adjusting for prepaids recorded
as expenses and unearned
revenues recorded as revenues

P6

Ricardo Construction began operations on December 1. In setting up its accounting procedures, the company decided to debit expense accounts when it prepays its expenses and to credit revenue accounts when customers pay for services in advance. Prepare journal entries for items *a* through *d* and the adjusting entries as of its December 31 period-end for items *e* through *g*.

a. Supplies are purchased on December 1 for $2,000 cash.
b. The company prepaid its insurance premiums for $1,540 cash on December 2.
c. On December 15, the company receives an advance payment of $13,000 cash from a customer for remodeling work.
d. On December 28, the company receives $3,700 cash from another customer for remodeling work to be performed in January.
e. A physical count on December 31 indicates that the Company has $1,840 of supplies available.

f. An analysis of the insurance policies in effect on December 31 shows that $340 of insurance coverage had expired.

g. As of December 31, only one remodeling project has been worked on and completed. The $5,570 fee for this project had been received in advance and recorded as remodeling fees earned.

Check   (f) Cr. Insurance Expense, $1,200; (g) Dr. Remodeling Fees Earned, $11,130

Costanza Company experienced the following events and transactions during July.

July   1   Received $3,000 cash in advance of performing work for Vivian Solana.
     6   Received $7,500 cash in advance of performing work for Iris Haru.
   12   Completed the job for Solana.
   18   Received $8,500 cash in advance of performing work for Amina Jordan.
   27   Completed the job for Haru.
   31   None of the work for Jordan has been performed.

a. Prepare journal entries (including any adjusting entries as of the end of the month) to record these events using the procedure of initially crediting the Unearned Fees account when payment is received from a customer in advance of performing services.

b. Prepare journal entries (including any adjusting entries as of the end of the month) to record these events using the procedure of initially crediting the Fees Earned account when payment is received from a customer in advance of performing services.

c. Under each method, determine the amount of earned fees reported on the income statement for July and the amount of unearned fees reported on the balance sheet as of July 31.

Exercise 3-9ᴬ
Recording and reporting
revenues received in advance
P6

Check   (c) Fees Earned—using entries from part b, $10,500

---

adidas AG reports the following balance sheet accounts for the year ended December 31, 2011 (euros in millions). Prepare the balance sheet for this company as of December 31, 2011, following usual IFRS practices.

Exercise 3-10
Preparing a balance sheet
following IFRS
P3

Tangible and other assets	€ 255		Intangible assets	€ 154
Total equity	2,322		Total current liabilities	345
Receivables and other assets	1,767		Inventories	30
Total noncurrent liabilities	3,379		Total liabilities	3,724
Cash and cash equivalents	383		Other current assets	28
Total current assets	2,208		Total noncurrent assets	3,838
Other noncurrent assets	3,429			

Use the following adjusted trial balance of Wilson Trucking Company to prepare the (1) income statement and (2) statement of retained earnings, for the year ended December 31, 2013. The retained earnings account balance is $145,000 at December 31, 2012.

Exercise 3-11
Preparing financial statements
C3   P3

Account Title	Debit	Credit
Cash	$ 8,000	
Accounts receivable	17,500	
Office supplies	3,000	
Trucks	172,000	
Accumulated depreciation—Trucks		$ 36,000
Land	85,000	
Accounts payable		12,000
Interest payable		4,000
Long-term notes payable		53,000
Common stock		30,000
Retained earnings		145,000
Dividends	20,000	
Trucking fees earned		130,000
Depreciation expense—Trucks	23,500	
Salaries expense	61,000	
Office supplies expense	8,000	
Repairs expense—Trucks	12,000	
Totals	$410,000	$410,000

Exercise 3-12

Preparing a classified balance sheet   **C4**

Check Total assets, $249,500

Use the information in the adjusted trial balance reported in Exercise 3-11 to prepare Wilson Trucking Company's classified balance sheet as of December 31, 2013.

Exercise 3-13

Computing the current ratio

A3

Use the information in the adjusted trial balance reported in Exercise 3-11 to compute the current ratio as of the balance sheet date (round the ratio to two decimals). Interpret the current ratio for the Wilson Trucking Company. (Assume that the industry average for the current ratio is 1.5.)

Exercise 3-14

Computing and analyzing the current ratio

A3

Calculate the current ratio in each of the following separate cases (round the ratio to two decimals). Identify the company case with the strongest liquidity position. (These cases represent competing companies in the same industry.)

	Current Assets	Current Liabilities
Case 1	$ 79,040	$ 32,000
Case 2	104,880	76,000
Case 3	45,080	49,000
Case 4	85,680	81,600
Case 5	61,000	100,000

Exercise 3-15[A]

Preparing reversing entries

P8

The following two events occurred for Trey Co. on October 31, 2013, the end of its fiscal year.

a. Trey rents a building from its owner for $2,800 per month. By a prearrangement, the company delayed paying October's rent until November 5. On this date, the company paid the rent for both October and November.

b. Trey rents space in a building it owns to a tenant for $850 per month. By prearrangement, the tenant delayed paying the October rent until November 8. On this date, the tenant paid the rent for both October and November.

Required

1. Prepare adjusting entries that the company must record for these events as of October 31.

2. Assuming Trey does *not* use reversing entries, prepare journal entries to record Trey's payment of rent on November 5 and the collection of the tenant's rent on November 8.

3. Assuming that the company uses reversing entries, prepare reversing entries on November 1 and the journal entries to record Trey's payment of rent on November 5 and the collection of the tenant's rent on November 8.

Exercise 3-16

Preparing closing entries

P4

Following are Nintendo's revenue and expense accounts for a recent calendar year (yen in millions). Prepare the company's closing entries for its revenues and its expenses.

Net sales	¥1,014,345
Cost of sales	626,379
Advertising expense	96,359
Other expense, net	213,986

Exercise 3-17

Completing a worksheet

P7

The following data are taken from the unadjusted trial balance of the Westcott Company at December 31, 2013. Each account carries a normal balance and the accounts are shown here in alphabetical order.

Accounts Payable	$ 6	Prepaid Insurance	$18	Retained earnings	$32
Accounts Receivable...............	12	Revenue	75	Dividends	6
Accumulated Depreciation—Equip.	15	Salaries Expense......	18	Unearned Revenue	12
Cash............................	21	Supplies	24	Utilities Expense	12
Equipment........................	39	Common stock	10		

1. Use the data above to prepare a worksheet. Enter the accounts in proper order and enter their balances in the correct debit or credit column.

2. Use the following adjustment information to complete the worksheet.

    a. Depreciation on equipment, $3

    b. Accrued salaries, $6

    c. The $12 of unearned revenue has been earned

    d. Supplies available at December 31, 2013, $15

    e. Expired insurance, $15

⊟ connect

For each of the following entries, enter the letter of the explanation that most closely describes it in the space beside each entry. (You can use letters more than once.)

  A. To record receipt of unearned revenue.

  B. To record this period's earning of prior unearned revenue.

  C. To record payment of an accrued expense.

  D. To record receipt of an accrued revenue.

  E. To record an accrued expense.

  F. To record an accrued revenue.

  G. To record this period's use of a prepaid expense.

  H. To record payment of a prepaid expense.

  I. To record this period's depreciation expense.

PROBLEM SET A

Problem 3-1A
Identifying adjusting entries with explanations
P1

____	1.	Interest Expense	1,000
		Interest Payable	1,000
____	2.	Depreciation Expense	4,000
		Accumulated Depreciation	4,000
____	3.	Unearned Professional Fees	3,000
		Professional Fees Earned	3,000
____	4.	Insurance Expense	4,200
		Prepaid Insurance	4,200
____	5.	Salaries Payable	1,400
		Cash	1,400
____	6.	Prepaid Rent	4,500
		Cash	4,500
____	7.	Salaries Expense	6,000
		Salaries Payable	6,000
____	8.	Interest Receivable	5,000
		Interest Revenue	5,000
____	9.	Cash	9,000
		Accounts Receivable (from consulting)	9,000
____	10.	Cash	7,500
		Unearned Professional Fees	7,500
____	11.	Cash	2,000
		Interest Receivable	2,000
____	12.	Rent Expense	2,000
		Prepaid Rent	2,000

Arnez Co. follows the practice of recording prepaid expenses and unearned revenues in balance sheet accounts. The company's annual accounting period ends on December 31, 2013. The following information concerns the adjusting entries to be recorded as of that date.

    a. The Office Supplies account started the year with a $4,000 balance. During 2013, the company purchased supplies for $13,400, which was added to the Office Supplies account. The inventory of supplies available at December 31, 2013, totaled $2,554.

Problem 3-2A
Preparing adjusting and subsequent journal entries
C1 A1 P1

b. An analysis of the company's insurance policies provided the following facts.

Policy	Date of Purchase	Months of Coverage	Cost
A	April 1, 2011	24	$14,400
B	April 1, 2012	36	12,960
C	August 1, 2013	12	2,400

The total premium for each policy was paid in full (for all months) at the purchase date, and the Prepaid Insurance account was debited for the full cost. (Year-end adjusting entries for Prepaid Insurance were properly recorded in all prior years.)

c. The company has 15 employees, who earn a total of $1,960 in salaries each working day. They are paid each Monday for their work in the five-day workweek ending on the previous Friday. Assume that December 31, 2013, is a Tuesday, and all 15 employees worked the first two days of that week. Because New Year's Day is a paid holiday, they will be paid salaries for five full days on Monday, January 6, 2014.

d. The company purchased a building on January 1, 2013. It cost $960,000 and is expected to have a $45,000 salvage value at the end of its predicted 30-year life. Annual depreciation is $30,500.

e. Since the company is not large enough to occupy the entire building it owns, it rented space to a tenant at $3,000 per month, starting on November 1, 2013. The rent was paid on time on November 1, and the amount received was credited to the Rent Earned account. However, the tenant has not paid the December rent. The company has worked out an agreement with the tenant, who has promised to pay both December and January rent in full on January 15. The tenant has agreed not to fall behind again.

f. On November 1, the company rented space to another tenant for $2,800 per month. The tenant paid five months' rent in advance on that date. The payment was recorded with a credit to the Unearned Rent account.

Required

Check   (1b) Dr. Insurance Expense,
$7,120 (1d) Dr. Depreciation Expense,
$30,500

1. Use the information to prepare adjusting entries as of December 31, 2013.

2. Prepare journal entries to record the first subsequent cash transaction in 2014 for parts *c* and *e*.

Problem 3-3A

Preparing adjusting entries, adjusted trial balance, and financial statements

A1 P1 P2 P3

mhhe.com/wildFINMAN5e

Wells Technical Institute (WTI), a school owned by Tristana Wells, provides training to individuals who pay tuition directly to the school. WTI also offers training to groups in off-site locations. Its unadjusted trial balance as of December 31, 2013, follows. WTI initially records prepaid expenses and unearned revenues in balance sheet accounts. Descriptions of items *a* through *h* that require adjusting entries on December 31, 2013, follow.

Additional Information Items

a. An analysis of WTI's insurance policies shows that $2,400 of coverage has expired.

b. An inventory count shows that teaching supplies costing $2,800 are available at year-end 2013.

c. Annual depreciation on the equipment is $13,200.

d. Annual depreciation on the professional library is $7,200.

e. On November 1, WTI agreed to do a special six-month course (starting immediately) for a client. The contract calls for a monthly fee of $2,500, and the client paid the first five months' fees in advance. When the cash was received, the Unearned Training Fees account was credited. The fee for the sixth month will be recorded when it is collected in 2014.

f. On October 15, WTI agreed to teach a four-month class (beginning immediately) for an individual for $3,000 tuition per month payable at the end of the class. The class started on October 15, but no payment has yet been received. (WTI's accruals are applied to the nearest half-month; for example, October recognizes one-half month accrual.)

g. WTI's two employees are paid weekly. As of the end of the year, two days' salaries have accrued at the rate of $100 per day for each employee.

h. The balance in the Prepaid Rent account represents rent for December.

WELLS TECHNICAL INSTITUTE		
Unadjusted Trial Balance		
December 31, 2013		
	Debit	**Credit**
Cash	$ 34,000	
Accounts receivable	0	
Teaching supplies	8,000	
Prepaid insurance	12,000	
Prepaid rent	3,000	
Professional library	35,000	
Accumulated depreciation—Professional library		$ 10,000
Equipment	80,000	
Accumulated depreciation—Equipment		15,000
Accounts payable		26,000
Salaries payable		0
Unearned training fees		12,500
Common stock		10,000
Retained earnings		80,000
Dividends	50,000	
Tuition fees earned		123,900
Training fees earned		40,000
Depreciation expense—Professional library	0	
Depreciation expense—Equipment	0	
Salaries expense	50,000	
Insurance expense	0	
Rent expense	33,000	
Teaching supplies expense	0	
Advertising expense	6,000	
Utilities expense	6,400	
Totals	$ 317,400	$ 317,400

Required

1. Prepare T-accounts (representing the ledger) with balances from the unadjusted trial balance.
2. Prepare the necessary adjusting journal entries for items *a* through *h* and post them to the T-accounts. Assume that adjusting entries are made only at year-end.
3. Update balances in the T-accounts for the adjusting entries and prepare an adjusted trial balance.
4. Prepare Wells Technical Institute's income statement and statement of retained earnings for the year 2013 and prepare its balance sheet as of December 31, 2013.

Check   (2e) Cr. Training Fees Earned, $5,000; (2f) Cr. Tuition Fees Earned, $7,500; (3) Adj. Trial balance totals, $345,700; (4) Net income, $49,600

A six-column table for JKL Company follows. The first two columns contain the unadjusted trial balance for the company as of July 31, 2013. The last two columns contain the adjusted trial balance as of the same date.

Required

Analysis Component

1. Analyze the differences between the unadjusted and adjusted trial balances to determine the eight adjustments that likely were made. Show the results of your analysis by inserting these adjustment amounts in the table's two middle columns. Label each adjustment with a letter *a* through *h* and provide a short description of it at the bottom of the table.

Preparation Component

2. Use the information in the adjusted trial balance to prepare the company's (*a*) income statement and its statement of retained earnings for the year ended July 31, 2013 (*Note:* retained earnings at July 31, 2012, was $25,000, and the current-year dividends were $5,000), and (*b*) the balance sheet as of July 31, 2013.

Problem 3-4A
Interpreting unadjusted and adjusted trial balances, and preparing financial statements

A1 P1 P2 P3

mhhe.com/wildFINMAN5e

Check   (2) Net income, $4,960; Total assets, $124,960

	Unadjusted Trial Balance		Adjustments		Adjusted Trial Balance	
Cash	$ 34,000				$ 34,000	
Accounts receivable	14,000				22,000	
Office supplies	16,000				2,000	
Prepaid insurance	8,540				2,960	
Office equipment	84,000				84,000	
Accum. depreciation— Office equip.		$ 14,000				$ 20,000
Accounts payable		9,100				10,000
Interest payable		0				1,000
Salaries payable		0				7,000
Unearned consulting fees		18,000				15,000
Long-term notes payable		52,000				52,000
Common stock		15,000				15,000
Retained earnings..............		25,000				25,000
Dividends	5,000				5,000	
Consulting fees earned		123,240				134,240
Depreciation expense— Office equip.	0				6,000	
Salaries expense	67,000				74,000	
Interest expense	1,200				2,200	
Insurance expense	0				5,580	
Rent expense	14,500				14,500	
Office supplies expense	0				14,000	
Advertising expense	12,100				13,000	
Totals	$256,340	$256,340			$279,240	$279,240

Problem 3-5A
Preparing financial statements from the adjusted trial balance and calculating profit margin
P3 A1 A2

The adjusted trial balance for Chiara Company as of December 31, 2013, follows.

	Debit	Credit
Cash	$ 30,000	
Accounts receivable	52,000	
Interest receivable	18,000	
Notes receivable (due in 90 days)	168,000	
Office supplies	16,000	
Automobiles	168,000	
Accumulated depreciation—Automobiles		$ 50,000
Equipment	138,000	
Accumulated depreciation—Equipment		18,000
Land	78,000	
Accounts payable		96,000
Interest payable		20,000
Salaries payable		19,000
Unearned fees		30,000
Long-term notes payable		138,000
Common stock		20,000
Retained earnings.........................		235,800
Dividends	46,000	
Fees earned		484,000
Interest earned		24,000
Depreciation expense—Automobiles	26,000	
Depreciation expense—Equipment	18,000	
Salaries expense	188,000	
Wages expense	40,000	
Interest expense	32,000	
Office supplies expense	34,000	
Advertising expense	58,000	
Repairs expense—Automobiles	24,800	
Totals	$1,134,800	$1,134,800

Required

1. Use the information in the adjusted trial balance to prepare (*a*) the income statement for the year ended December 31, 2013; (*b*) the statement of retained earnings for the year ended December 31, 2013; and (*c*) the balance sheet as of December 31, 2013.

Check (1) Total assets, $600,000

2. Calculate the profit margin for year 2013.

In the blank space beside each numbered balance sheet item, enter the letter of its balance sheet classification. If the item should not appear on the balance sheet, enter a *Z* in the blank.

Problem 3-6A
Determining balance sheet classifications
C4

A. Current assets   **D.** Intangible assets   **F.** Long-term liabilities
B. Long-term investments **E.** Current liabilities   **G.** Equity
C. Plant assets

_____ **1.** Long-term investment in stock	_____ **12.** Accumulated depreciation—Trucks
_____ **2.** Depreciation expense—Building	_____ **13.** Cash
_____ **3.** Prepaid rent	_____ **14.** Buildings
_____ **4.** Interest receivable	_____ **15.** Store supplies
_____ **5.** Taxes payable	_____ **16.** Office equipment
_____ **6.** Automobiles	_____ **17.** Land (used in operations)
_____ **7.** Notes payable (due in 3 years)	_____ **18.** Repairs expense
_____ **8.** Accounts payable	_____ **19.** Office supplies
_____ **9.** Prepaid insurance	_____ **20.** Current portion of long-term note payable
_____ **10.** Common stock	
_____ **11.** Unearned services revenue	

On April 1, 2013, Jiro Nozomi created a new travel agency, Adventure Travel. The following transactions occurred during the company's first month.

Problem 3-7A
Applying the accounting cycle
P1 P2 P3 P4 P5

mhhe.com/wildFINMAN5e

April 1	Nozomi invested $30,000 cash and computer equipment worth $20,000 in the company in exchange for common stock.
2	The company rented furnished office space by paying $1,800 cash for the first month's (April) rent.
3	The company purchased $1,000 of office supplies for cash.
10	The company paid $2,400 cash for the premium on a 12-month insurance policy. Coverage begins on April 11.
14	The company paid $1,600 cash for two weeks' salaries earned by employees.
24	The company collected $8,000 cash on commissions from airlines on tickets obtained for customers.
28	The company paid $1,600 cash for two weeks' salaries earned by employees.
29	The company paid $350 cash for minor repairs to the company's computer.
30	The company paid $750 cash for this month's telephone bill.
30	The company paid $1,500 cash for dividends.

The company's chart of accounts follows:

101	Cash	405	Commissions Earned
106	Accounts Receivable	612	Depreciation Expense—Computer Equip.
124	Office Supplies	622	Salaries Expense
128	Prepaid Insurance	637	Insurance Expense
167	Computer Equipment	640	Rent Expense
168	Accumulated Depreciation—Computer Equip.	650	Office Supplies Expense
209	Salaries Payable	684	Repairs Expense
307	Common Stock	688	Telephone Expense
318	Retained Earnings	901	Income Summary
319	Dividends		

Required

1. Use the balance column format to set up each ledger account listed in its chart of accounts.

2. Prepare journal entries to record the transactions for April and post them to the ledger accounts. The company records prepaid and unearned items in balance sheet accounts.

3. Prepare an unadjusted trial balance as of April 30.

Check (3) Unadj. trial balance totals, $58,000

148

(4a) Dr. Insurance
Expense, $133

4. Use the following information to journalize and post adjusting entries for the month:

   a. Two-thirds (or $133) of one month's insurance coverage has expired.

   b. At the end of the month, $600 of office supplies are still available.

   c. This month's depreciation on the computer equipment is $500.

   d. Employees earned $420 of unpaid and unrecorded salaries as of month-end.

   e. The company earned $1,750 of commissions that are not yet billed at month-end.

(5) Net income, $2,197;
Total assets, $51,117

5. Prepare the adjusted trial balance as of April 30. Prepare the income statement and the statement of retained earnings for the month of April and the balance sheet at April 30, 2013.

(7) P-C trial balance totals,
$51,617

6. Prepare journal entries to close the temporary accounts and post these entries to the ledger.

7. Prepare a post-closing trial balance.

Problem 3-8A
Preparing closing entries,
financial statements, and ratios

C4 A2 A3 P3 P4

Sage 50
QB

The adjusted trial balance for Tybalt Construction as of December 31, 2013, follows.

No.	Account Title	Debit	Credit
	TYBALT CONSTRUCTION		
	Adjusted Trial Balance		
	December 31, 2013		
101	Cash	$ 5,000	
104	Short-term investments	23,000	
126	Supplies	8,100	
128	Prepaid insurance	7,000	
167	Equipment	40,000	
168	Accumulated depreciation—Equipment		$ 20,000
173	Building	150,000	
174	Accumulated depreciation—Building		50,000
183	Land	55,000	
201	Accounts payable		16,500
203	Interest payable		2,500
208	Rent payable		3,500
210	Wages payable		2,500
213	Property taxes payable		900
233	Unearned professional fees		7,500
251	Long-term notes payable		67,000
307	Common stock...........................		5,000
318	Retained earnings		121,400
319	Dividends	13,000	
401	Professional fees earned		97,000
406	Rent earned		14,000
407	Dividends earned		2,000
409	Interest earned		2,100
606	Depreciation expense—Building	11,000	
612	Depreciation expense—Equipment	6,000	
623	Wages expense	32,000	
633	Interest expense	5,100	
637	Insurance expense	10,000	
640	Rent expense	13,400	
652	Supplies expense	7,400	
682	Postage expense	4,200	
683	Property taxes expense	5,000	
684	Repairs expense	8,900	
688	Telephone expense	3,200	
690	Utilities expense	4,600	
	Totals	$411,900	$411,900

O. Tybalt invested $5,000 cash in the business in exchange for more common stock during year 2013 (the December 31, 2012, credit balance of retained earnings was $121,400). Tybalt Construction is required to make a $7,000 payment on its long-term notes payable during 2014.

Required

Check　(1) Total assets (12/31/2013),
$218,100; Net income, $4,300

1. Prepare the income statement and the statement of retained earnings for the calendar year 2013 and the classified balance sheet at December 31, 2013.

2. Prepare the necessary closing entries at December 31, 2013.

3. Use the information in the financial statements to compute these ratios: (*a*) return on assets (total assets at December 31, 2012, was $200,000), (*b*) debt ratio, (*c*) profit margin ratio (use total revenues as the denominator), and (*d*) current ratio. Round ratios to three decimals for parts *a* and *c,* and to two decimals for parts *b* and *d*.

For each of the following entries, enter the letter of the explanation that most closely describes it in the space beside each entry. (You can use letters more than once.)

PROBLEM SET B

Problem 3-1B
Identifying adjusting entries with explanations
P1

A. To record payment of a prepaid expense.

B. To record this period's use of a prepaid expense.

C. To record this period's depreciation expense.

D. To record receipt of unearned revenue.

E. To record this period's earning of prior unearned revenue.

F. To record an accrued expense.

G. To record payment of an accrued expense.

H. To record an accrued revenue.

I. To record receipt of accrued revenue.

_____ 1.	Interest Receivable	3,500	
	Interest Revenue		3,500
_____ 2.	Salaries Payable	9,000	
	Cash		9,000
_____ 3.	Depreciation Expense	8,000	
	Accumulated Depreciation		8,000
_____ 4.	Cash	9,000	
	Unearned Professional Fees		9,000
_____ 5.	Insurance Expense	4,000	
	Prepaid Insurance		4,000
_____ 6.	Interest Expense	5,000	
	Interest Payable		5,000
_____ 7.	Cash	1,500	
	Accounts Receivable (from services)		1,500
_____ 8.	Salaries Expense	7,000	
	Salaries Payable		7,000
_____ 9.	Cash	1,000	
	Interest Receivable		1,000
_____ 10.	Prepaid Rent	3,000	
	Cash		3,000
_____ 11.	Rent Expense	7,500	
	Prepaid Rent		7,500
_____ 12.	Unearned Professional Fees	6,000	
	Professional Fees Earned		6,000

Natsu Co. follows the practice of recording prepaid expenses and unearned revenues in balance sheet accounts. The company's annual accounting period ends on October 31, 2013. The following information concerns the adjusting entries that need to be recorded as of that date.

Problem 3-2B
Preparing adjusting and subsequent journal entries
C1 A1 P1

a. The Office Supplies account started the fiscal year with a $600 balance. During the fiscal year, the company purchased supplies for $4,570, which was added to the Office Supplies account. The supplies available at October 31, 2013, totaled $800.

b. An analysis of the company's insurance policies provided the following facts.

Policy	Date of Purchase	Months of Coverage	Cost
A	April 1, 2012	24	$6,000
B	April 1, 2013	36	7,200
C	August 1, 2013	12	1,320

The total premium for each policy was paid in full (for all months) at the purchase date, and the Prepaid Insurance account was debited for the full cost. (Year-end adjusting entries for Prepaid Insurance were properly recorded in all prior fiscal years.)

c. The company has four employees, who earn a total of $1,000 for each workday. They are paid each Monday for their work in the five-day workweek ending on the previous Friday. Assume that October 31, 2013, is a Monday, and all four employees worked the first day of that week. They will be paid salaries for five full days on Monday, November 7, 2013.

d. The company purchased a building on November 1, 2010, that cost $175,000 and is expected to have a $40,000 salvage value at the end of its predicted 25-year life. Annual depreciation is $5,400.

e. Since the company does not occupy the entire building it owns, it rented space to a tenant at $1,000 per month, starting on September 1, 2013. The rent was paid on time on September 1, and the amount received was credited to the Rent Earned account. However, the October rent has not been paid. The company has worked out an agreement with the tenant, who has promised to pay both October and November rent in full on November 15. The tenant has agreed not to fall behind again.

f. On September 1, the company rented space to another tenant for $725 per month. The tenant paid five months' rent in advance on that date. The payment was recorded with a credit to the Unearned Rent account.

Check   (1*b*) Dr. Insurance Expense, $4,730; (1*d*) Dr. Depreciation Expense, $5,400.

Required

1. Use the information to prepare adjusting entries as of October 31, 2013.

2. Prepare journal entries to record the first subsequent cash transaction in November 2013 for parts *c* and *e*.

Problem 3-3B
Preparing adjusting entries, adjusted trial balance, and financial statements
A1 P1 P2 P3

Following is the unadjusted trial balance for Augustus Institute as of December 31, 2013, which initially records prepaid expenses and unearned revenues in balance sheet accounts. The Institute provides one-on-one training to individuals who pay tuition directly to the business and offers extension training to groups in off-site locations. Shown after the trial balance are items *a* through *h* that require adjusting entries as of December 31, 2013.

AUGUSTUS INSTITUTE
Unadjusted Trial Balance
December 31, 2013

	Debit	Credit
Cash	$ 60,000	
Accounts receivable	0	
Teaching supplies	70,000	
Prepaid insurance	19,000	
Prepaid rent	3,800	
Professional library	12,000	
Accumulated depreciation—Professional library		$ 2,500
Equipment	40,000	
Accumulated depreciation—Equipment		20,000
Accounts payable		11,200
Salaries payable		0
Unearned training fees		28,600
Common stock		11,000
Retained earnings		60,500
Dividends	20,000	
Tuition fees earned		129,200
Training fees earned		68,000
Depreciation expense—Professional library	0	
Depreciation expense—Equipment	0	
Salaries expense	44,200	
Insurance expense	0	
Rent expense	29,600	
Teaching supplies expense	0	
Advertising expense	19,000	
Utilities expense	13,400	
Totals	$ 331,000	$331,000

Additional Information Items

a. An analysis of the Institute's insurance policies shows that $9,500 of coverage has expired.

b. An inventory count shows that teaching supplies costing $20,000 are available at year-end 2013.

c. Annual depreciation on the equipment is $5,000.

d. Annual depreciation on the professional library is $2,400.

e. On November 1, the Institute agreed to do a special five-month course (starting immediately) for a client. The contract calls for a $14,300 monthly fee, and the client paid the first two months' fees in advance. When the cash was received, the Unearned Training Fees account was credited. The last two month's fees will be recorded when collected in 2014.

f. On October 15, the Institute agreed to teach a four-month class (beginning immediately) to an individual for $2,300 tuition per month payable at the end of the class. The class started on October 15, but no payment has yet been received. (The Institute's accruals are applied to the nearest half-month; for example, October recognizes one-half month accrual.)

g. The Institute's only employee is paid weekly. As of the end of the year, three days' salaries have accrued at the rate of $150 per day.

h. The balance in the Prepaid Rent account represents rent for December.

Required

1. Prepare T-accounts (representing the ledger) with balances from the unadjusted trial balance.

2. Prepare the necessary adjusting journal entries for items *a* through *h*, and post them to the T-accounts. Assume that adjusting entries are made only at year-end.

3. Update balances in the T-accounts for the adjusting entries and prepare an adjusted trial balance.

4. Prepare the company's income statement and statement of retained earnings for the year 2013, and prepare its balance sheet as of December 31, 2013.

Check (2*e*) Cr. Training Fees Earned, $28,600; (2*f*) Cr. Tuition Fees Earned, $5,750; (3) Adj. trial balance totals, $344,600; (4) Net income, $54,200

A six-column table for Yan Consulting Company follows. The first two columns contain the unadjusted trial balance for the company as of December 31, 2013, and the last two columns contain the adjusted trial balance as of the same date.

Problem 3-4B
Interpreting unadjusted and adjusted trial balances, and preparing financial statements

A1 P1 P2 P3

	Unadjusted Trial Balance		Adjustments		Adjusted Trial Balance	
Cash	$ 45,000				$ 45,000	
Accounts receivable	60,000				66,660	
Office supplies	40,000				17,000	
Prepaid insurance	8,200				3,600	
Office equipment	120,000				120,000	
Accumulated depreciation— Office equip.		$ 20,000				$ 30,000
Accounts payable		26,000				32,000
Interest payable		0				2,150
Salaries payable		0				16,000
Unearned consulting fees		40,000				27,800
Long-term notes payable		75,000				75,000
Common stock		4,000				4,000
Retained earnings.............		76,200				76,200
Dividends....................	20,000				20,000	
Consulting fees earned		234,600				253,460
Depreciation expense— Office equip.	0				10,000	
Salaries expense	112,000				128,000	
Interest expense	8,600				10,750	
Insurance expense	0				4,600	
Rent expense	20,000				20,000	
Office supplies expense	0				23,000	
Advertising expense	42,000				48,000	
Totals	$475,800	$475,800			$516,610	$516,610

Required

Analysis Component

1. Analyze the differences between the unadjusted and adjusted trial balances to determine the eight adjustments that likely were made. Show the results of your analysis by inserting these adjustment amounts in the table's two middle columns. Label each adjustment with a letter *a* through *h* and provide a short description of it at the bottom of the table.

Preparation Component

Check   (2) Net income, $9,110;
Total assets, $222,260

2. Use the information in the adjusted trial balance to prepare this company's (*a*) income statement and its statement of retained earnings for the year ended December 31, 2013 (*Note:* retained earnings at December 31, 2012, was $76,200, and the current-year dividends were $20,000), and (*b*) the balance sheet as of December 31, 2013.

Problem 3-5B
Preparing financial statements
from the adjusted trial balance
and calculating profit margin

P3 A1 A2

The adjusted trial balance for Speedy Courier as of December 31, 2013, follows.

	Debit	Credit
Cash	$ 58,000	
Accounts receivable	120,000	
Interest receivable	7,000	
Notes receivable (due in 90 days)	210,000	
Office supplies	22,000	
Trucks	134,000	
Accumulated depreciation—Trucks		$ 58,000
Equipment	270,000	
Accumulated depreciation—Equipment		200,000
Land	100,000	
Accounts payable		134,000
Interest payable		20,000
Salaries payable		28,000
Unearned delivery fees		120,000
Long-term notes payable		200,000
Common stock		15,000
Retained earnings		110,000
Dividends	50,000	
Delivery fees earned		611,800
Interest earned		34,000
Depreciation expense—Trucks	29,000	
Depreciation expense—Equipment	48,000	
Salaries expense	74,000	
Wages expense	300,000	
Interest expense	15,000	
Office supplies expense	31,000	
Advertising expense	27,200	
Repairs expense—Trucks	35,600	
Totals	$1,530,800	$1,530,800

Required

Check   (1) Total assets, $663,000

1. Use the information in the adjusted trial balance to prepare (*a*) the income statement for the year ended December 31, 2013, (*b*) the statement of retained earnings for the year ended December 31, 2013, and (*c*) the balance sheet as of December 31, 2013.

2. Calculate the profit margin for year 2013.

In the blank space beside each numbered balance sheet item, enter the letter of its balance sheet classification. If the item should not appear on the balance sheet, enter a *Z* in the blank.

Problem 3-6B

Determining balance sheet classifications

C4

A. Current assets   **E.** Current liabilities
B. Long-term investments **F.** Long-term liabilities
C. Plant assets   **G.** Equity
D. Intangible assets

_____ **1.** Commissions earned
_____ **2.** Interest receivable
_____ **3.** Long-term investment in stock
_____ **4.** Prepaid insurance
_____ **5.** Machinery
_____ **6.** Notes payable (due in 15 years)
_____ **7.** Copyrights
_____ **8.** Current portion of long-term note payable
_____ **9.** Accumulated depreciation—Trucks
_____ **10.** Office equipment

_____ **11.** Rent receivable
_____ **12.** Salaries payable
_____ **13.** Income taxes payable
_____ **14.** Common stock
_____ **15.** Office supplies
_____ **16.** Interest payable
_____ **17.** Rent revenue
_____ **18.** Notes receivable (due in 120 days)
_____ **19.** Land (used in operations)
_____ **20.** Depreciation expense—Trucks

On July 1, 2013, Lula Plume created a new self-storage business, Safe Storage Co. The following transactions occurred during the company's first month.

Problem 3-7B

Applying the accounting cycle

P1 P2 P3 P4 P5

July	1	Plume invested $30,000 cash and buildings worth $150,000 in the company in exchange for common stock.
	2	The company rented equipment by paying $2,000 cash for the first month's (July) rent.
	5	The company purchased $2,400 of office supplies for cash.
	10	The company paid $7,200 cash for the premium on a 12-month insurance policy. Coverage begins on July 11.
	14	The company paid an employee $1,000 cash for two weeks' salary earned.
	24	The company collected $9,800 cash for storage fees from customers.
	28	The company paid $1,000 cash for two weeks' salary earned by an employee.
	29	The company paid $950 cash for minor repairs to a leaking roof.
	30	The company paid $400 cash for this month's telephone bill.
	31	The company paid $2,000 cash for dividends.

The company's chart of accounts follows:

101	Cash	401	Storage Fees Earned
106	Accounts Receivable	606	Depreciation Expense—Buildings
124	Office Supplies	622	Salaries Expense
128	Prepaid Insurance	637	Insurance Expense
173	Buildings	640	Rent Expense
174	Accumulated Depreciation—Buildings	650	Office Supplies Expense
209	Salaries Payable	684	Repairs Expense
307	Common Stock	688	Telephone Expense
318	Retained Earnings	901	Income Summary
319	Dividends		

Required

1. Use the balance column format to set up each ledger account listed in its chart of accounts.

2. Prepare journal entries to record the transactions for July and post them to the ledger accounts. Record prepaid and unearned items in balance sheet accounts.

3. Prepare an unadjusted trial balance as of July 31.

Check (3) Unadj. trial balance totals, $189,800

4. Use the following information to journalize and post adjusting entries for the month:

(4a) Dr. Insurance
Expense, $400

   a. Two-thirds of one month's insurance coverage has expired.

   b. At the end of the month, $1,525 of office supplies are still available.

   c. This month's depreciation on the buildings is $1,500.

   d. An employee earned $100 of unpaid and unrecorded salary as of month-end.

   e. The company earned $1,150 of storage fees that are not yet billed at month-end.

(5) Net income, $2,725;
Total assets, $180,825

5. Prepare the adjusted trial balance as of July 31. Prepare the income statement and the statement of retained earnings for the month of July and the balance sheet at July 31, 2013.

(7) P-C trial balance
totals, $182,325

6. Prepare journal entries to close the temporary accounts and post these entries to the ledger.

7. Prepare a post-closing trial balance.

Problem 3-8B
Preparing closing entries,
financial statements, and ratios
C4 A2 A3 P3 P4

The adjusted trial balance for Anara Co. as of December 31, 2013, follows.

	ANARA COMPANY		
	Adjusted Trial Balance		
	December 31, 2013		
No.	**Account Title**	**Debit**	**Credit**
101	Cash	$ 7,400	
104	Short-term investments	11,200	
126	Supplies	4,600	
128	Prepaid insurance	1,000	
167	Equipment	24,000	
168	Accumulated depreciation—Equipment		$ 4,000
173	Building	100,000	
174	Accumulated depreciation—Building		10,000
183	Land	30,500	
201	Accounts payable		3,500
203	Interest payable		1,750
208	Rent payable		400
210	Wages payable		1,280
213	Property taxes payable		3,330
233	Unearned professional fees		750
251	Long-term notes payable		40,000
307	Common stock............................		40,000
318	Retained earnings		52,800
319	Dividends	8,000	
401	Professional fees earned		59,600
406	Rent earned		4,500
407	Dividends earned		1,000
409	Interest earned		1,320
606	Depreciation expense—Building	2,000	
612	Depreciation expense—Equipment	1,000	
623	Wages expense	18,500	
633	Interest expense	1,550	
637	Insurance expense	1,525	
640	Rent expense	3,600	
652	Supplies expense	1,000	
682	Postage expense	410	
683	Property taxes expense	4,825	
684	Repairs expense	679	
688	Telephone expense	521	
690	Utilities expense..........................	1,920	
	Totals	$224,230	$224,230

P. Anara invested $40,000 cash in the business in exchange for more common stock during year 2013 (the December 31, 2012, credit balance of retained earnings was $52,800). Anara Company is required to make a $8,400 payment on its long-term notes payable during 2014.

Required

1. Prepare the income statement and the statement of retained earnings for the calendar year 2013 and the classified balance sheet at December 31, 2013.

2. Prepare the necessary closing entries at December 31, 2013.

3. Use the information in the financial statements to calculate these ratios: (*a*) return on assets (total assets at December 31, 2012, were $160,000), (*b*) debt ratio, (*c*) profit margin ratio (use total revenues as the denominator), and (*d*) current ratio. Round ratios to three decimals for parts *a* and *c*, and to two decimals for parts *b* and *d*.

This serial problem began in Chapter 1 and continues through most of the book. If previous chapter segments were not completed, the serial problem can still begin at this point. It is helpful, but not necessary, to use the Working Papers that accompany the book.

SERIAL PROBLEM
Success Systems
P1 P2 P3 P4 P5

Sage 50 QB

SP 3   After the success of the company's first two months, Adria Lopez continues to operate Success Systems. (Transactions for the first two months are described in the serial problem of Chapter 2.) The November 30, 2013, unadjusted trial balance of Success Systems (reflecting its transactions for October and November of 2013) follows.

No.	Account Title	Debit	Credit
101	Cash	$ 48,052	
106	Accounts receivable	12,618	
126	Computer supplies	2,545	
128	Prepaid insurance	2,220	
131	Prepaid rent	3,300	
163	Office equipment	8,000	
164	Accumulated depreciation—Office equipment		$ 0
167	Computer equipment	20,000	
168	Accumulated depreciation—Computer equipment		0
201	Accounts payable		0
210	Wages payable		0
236	Unearned computer services revenue		0
307	Common stock		83,000
318	Retained earnings		0
319	Dividends	5,600	
403	Computer services revenue		25,659
612	Depreciation expense—Office equipment	0	
613	Depreciation expense—Computer equipment	0	
623	Wages expense	2,625	
637	Insurance expense	0	
640	Rent expense	0	
652	Computer supplies expense	0	
655	Advertising expense	1,940	
676	Mileage expense	704	
677	Miscellaneous expenses	250	
684	Repairs expense—Computer	805	
	Totals	$108,659	$108,659

Success Systems had the following transactions and events in December 2013.

Dec.   2   Paid $1,025 cash to Hillside Mall for Success Systems' share of mall advertising costs.
      3   Paid $500 cash for minor repairs to the company's computer.
      4   Received $3,950 cash from Alex's Engineering Co. for the receivable from November.
    10   Paid cash to Lyn Addie for six days of work at the rate of $125 per day.
    14   Notified by Alex's Engineering Co. that Success Systems' bid of $7,000 on a proposed project has been accepted. Alex's paid a $1,500 cash advance to Success Systems.
    15   Purchased $1,100 of computer supplies on credit from Harris Office Products.
    16   Sent a reminder to Gomez Co. to pay the fee for services recorded on November 8.
    20   Completed a project for Liu Corporation and received $5,625 cash.

22–26   Took the week off for the holidays.
   28   Received $3,000 cash from Gomez Co. on its receivable.
   29   Reimbursed A. Lopez for business automobile mileage (600 miles at $0.32 per mile).
   31   The business paid $1,500 cash for dividends.

The following additional facts are collected for use in making adjusting entries prior to preparing financial statements for the company's first three months:

a. The December 31 inventory count of computer supplies shows $580 still available.

b. Three months have expired since the 12-month insurance premium was paid in advance.

c. As of December 31, Lyn Addie has not been paid for four days of work at $125 per day.

d. The computer system, acquired on October 1, is expected to have a four-year life with no salvage value.

e. The office equipment, acquired on October 1, is expected to have a five-year life with no salvage value.

f. Three of the four months' prepaid rent has expired.

Required

1. Prepare journal entries to record each of the December transactions and events for Success Systems. Post those entries to the accounts in the ledger.
2. Prepare adjusting entries to reflect *a* through *f*. Post those entries to the accounts in the ledger.
3. Prepare an adjusted trial balance as of December 31, 2013.
4. Prepare an income statement for the three months ended December 31, 2013.
5. Prepare a statement of retained earnings for the three months ended December 31, 2013.
6. Prepare a balance sheet as of December 31, 2013.
7. Record and post the necessary closing entries for Success Systems.
8. Prepare a post-closing trial balance as of December 31, 2013.

Check   (3) Adjusted trial balance totals, $119,034

(6) Total assets, $93,248

Check   Post-closing trial balance totals, $94,898

Beyond the Numbers

REPORTING IN ACTION

C1 C2 A1 A2 P4

Polaris

BTN 3-1   Refer to Polaris's financial statements in Appendix A to answer the following.

1. Identify and write down the revenue recognition principle as explained in the chapter.
2. Review Polaris's footnotes to discover how it applies the revenue recognition principle and when it recognizes revenue. Report what you discover.
3. What is Polaris's profit margin for fiscal years ended December 31, 2011 and 2010.
4. For the year ended December 31, 2011, what amount is credited to Income Summary to summarize its revenues earned?
5. For the year ended December 31, 2011, what amount is debited to Income Summary to summarize its expenses incurred?
6. For the year ended December 31, 2011, what is the balance of its Income Summary account before it is closed?

Fast Forward

7. Access Polaris's annual report (10-K) for fiscal years ending after December 31, 2011, at its Website (Polaris.com) or the SEC's EDGAR database (www.SEC.gov). Assess and compare the December 31, 2011, fiscal year profit margin to any subsequent year's profit margin that you compute.

COMPARATIVE ANALYSIS

A2 A3

Polaris
Arctic Cat

BTN 3-2   Key figures for the recent two years of both Polaris and Arctic Cat follow.

($ thousands)	Polaris		Arctic Cat	
	Current Year	Prior Year	Current Year	Prior Year
Net income	$ 227,575	$ 147,138	$ 13,007	$ 1,875
Net sales	2,656,949	1,991,139	363,015	350,871
Current assets	878,676	808,145	232,040	201,015
Current liabilities	615,531	584,210	87,444	75,320

Required

1. Compute profit margins for (*a*) Polaris and (*b*) Arctic Cat for the two years of data shown.
2. Which company is more successful on the basis of profit margin? Explain.
3. Compute the current ratio for both years for both companies.
4. Which company has the better ability to pay short-term obligations according to the current ratio?
5. Analyze and comment on each company's current ratios for the past two years.
6. How do Polaris's and Arctic Cat's current ratios compare to their industry (assumed) average ratio of 2.4?

BTN 3-3 Jessica Boland works for Sea Biscuit Co. She and Farah Smith, her manager, are preparing adjusting entries for annual financial statements. Boland computes depreciation and records it as

ETHICS CHALLENGE

C1 C2 A1

Depreciation Expense—Equipment	123,000	
Accumulated Depreciation—Equipment		123,000

Smith agrees with her computation but says the credit entry should be directly to the Equipment account. Smith argues that while accumulated depreciation is technically correct, "it is less hassle not to use a contra account and just credit the Equipment account directly. And besides, the balance sheet shows the same amount for total assets under either method."

Required

1. How should depreciation be recorded? Do you support Boland or Smith?
2. Evaluate the strengths and weaknesses of Smith's reasons for preferring her method.
3. Indicate whether the situation Boland faces is an ethical problem. Explain.

BTN 3-4 Assume that one of your classmates states that a company's books should be ongoing and therefore not closed until that business is terminated. Write a half-page memo to this classmate explaining the concept of the closing process by drawing analogies between (1) a scoreboard for an athletic event and the revenue and expense accounts of a business or (2) a sports team's record book and retained earnings. (*Hint:* Think about what would happen if the scoreboard is not cleared before the start of a new game.)

COMMUNICATING IN PRACTICE

P4

BTN 3-5 Access EDGAR online (www.SEC.gov) and locate the 10-K report of The Gap, Inc., (ticker GPS) filed on March 26, 2012. Review its financial statements reported for the year ended January 28, 2012, to answer the following questions.

TAKING IT TO THE NET

C1 A2

Required

1. What are Gap's main brands?
2. What is Gap's fiscal year-end?
3. What is Gap's net sales for the period ended January 28, 2012?
4. What is Gap's net income for the period ended January 28, 2012?
5. Compute Gap's profit margin for the year ended January 28, 2012.
6. Do you believe Gap's decision to use a year-end of late January or early February relates to its natural business year? Explain.

BTN 3-6 Four types of adjustments are described in the chapter: (1) prepaid expenses, (2) unearned revenues, (3) accrued expenses, and (4) accrued revenues.

Required

1. Form *learning teams* of four (or more) members. Each team member must select one of the four adjustments as an area of expertise (each team must have at least one expert in each area).
2. Form *expert teams* from the individuals who have selected the same area of expertise. Expert teams are to discuss and write a report that each expert will present to his or her learning team addressing the following:
   a. Description of the adjustment and why it's necessary.
   b. Example of a transaction or event, with dates and amounts, that requires adjustment.
   c. Adjusting entry(ies) for the example in requirement *b*.
   d. Status of the affected account(s) before and after the adjustment in requirement *c*.
   e. Effects on financial statements of not making the adjustment.
3. Each expert should return to his or her learning team. In rotation, each member should present his or her expert team's report to the learning team. Team discussion is encouraged.

BTN 3-7 Review the opening feature of this chapter dealing with ash&dans and the entrepreneurial owners, Ashley Cook and Danielle Dankner.

Required

1. Assume that ash&dans sells a $300 gift certificate to a customer, collecting the $300 cash in advance. Prepare the journal entry for the (*a*) collection of the cash for delivery of the gift certificate to the customer and (*b*) revenue from the subsequent delivery of merchandise when the gift certificate is used.
2. How can keeping less inventory help to improve ash&dans's profit margin?
3. Ashley Cook and Danielle Dankner understand that many companies carry considerable inventory, and they are thinking of carrying additional inventory of merchandise for sale. Ashley and Danielle desire your advice on the pros and cons of carrying such inventory. Provide at least one reason for and one reason against carrying additional inventory.

BTN 3-8 Select a company that you can visit in person or interview on the telephone. Call ahead to the company to arrange a time when you can interview an employee (preferably an accountant) who helps prepare the annual financial statements. Inquire about the following aspects of its *accounting cycle:*

1. Does the company prepare interim financial statements? What time period(s) is used for interim statements?
2. Does the company use the cash or accrual basis of accounting?
3. Does the company use a work sheet in preparing financial statements? Why or why not?
4. Does the company use a spreadsheet program? If so, which software program is used?
5. How long does it take after the end of its reporting period to complete annual statements?

BTN 3-9 Piaggio (Piaggio.com) manufactures two-, three- and four-wheel vehicles and is Europe's leading manufacturer of motorcycles and scooters. The following selected information is available from Piaggio's financial statements.

(Euro thousands)	Current Year	Prior Year
Current assets	509,708	575,897
Current liabilities	644,277	616,166

Required

1. Locate the notes to its December 31, 2011, financial statements at the company's Website, and read note *2.2 Accounting Principles—Recognition of Revenues,* first paragraph only. When is revenue recognized by Piaggio?

2. Refer to Piaggio's financials in Appendix A. What is Piaggio's profit margin for the year ended December 31, 2011?

3. Compute Piaggio's current ratio for both the current year and the prior year.

4. Comment on any change from the prior year to the current year for the current ratio.

ANSWERS TO MULTIPLE CHOICE QUIZ

1. b; the forgotten adjusting entry is: *dr.* Wages Expense, *cr.* Wages Payable.

2. c; Supplies used = $450 − $125 = $325

3. b; Insurance expense = $24,000 × (8/24) = $8,000; adjusting entry is: *dr.* Insurance Expense for $8,000, *cr.* Prepaid Insurance for $8,000.

4. a; Consulting fees earned = $3,600 × (2/6) = $1,200; adjusting entry is: *dr.* Unearned Consulting Fee for $1,200, *cr.* Consulting Fees Earned for $1,200.

5. e; Profit margin = $15,000/$300,000 = 5%

6. b

Cash and Internal Controls

A Look Back

Chapters 4 and 5 focused on merchandising activities and accounting for inventory. We explained inventory systems, accounting for inventory transactions, and assigning costs to inventory.

A Look at This Chapter

This chapter extends our study of accounting to internal control and the analysis of cash. We describe procedures that are good for internal control. We also explain the control of and the accounting for cash, including control features of banking activities.

A Look Ahead

Chapter 7 focuses on receivables. We explain how to account and report on receivables and their related accounts. This includes estimating uncollectible receivables and computing interest earned.

Learning Objectives

CONCEPTUAL

C1 Define internal control and identify its purpose and principles. (p. 258)

C2 Define cash and cash equivalents and explain how to report them. (p. 263)

ANALYTICAL

A1 Compute the days' sales uncollected ratio and use it to assess liquidity. (p. 277)

PROCEDURAL

P1 Apply internal control to cash receipts and disbursements. (p. 264)

P2 Explain and record petty cash fund transactions. (p. 268)

P3 Prepare a bank reconciliation. (p. 273)

P4 *Appendix 6A*—Describe the use of documentation and verification to control cash disbursements. (p. 280)

P5 *Appendix 6B—Apply the net method to control purchase discounts. (p. 283)*

Decision Insight

Cheese Wiz

"Entrepreneurship is the antithesis of stability."
—MICHAEL INWALD

BOSTON—Michael Inwald did his research: 2.2 billion grilled cheese sandwiches are consumed by Americans each year. His conclusion: The country is one big cheeseball! Given the cheese wiz he is, Michael, known to his friends as *Cheeseboy,* opened a fast-food grilled cheese take-out joint named CHEESEBOY (**CheeseBoy.com**). "I'm somewhat obsessed with cheese!" admits Michael. That obsession has led to several CHEESEBOY locations, and he is readying for a national franchise program.

"Giving our customers an amazing grilled cheese experience, all-around, is very critical to us," insists Michael. He currently offers customers a grilled cheese experience with four bread options, five cheese options, and a range of toppings. He also provides the classic tomato soup combo, along with other soup options. "The most challenging part of my business is . . . to create the perfect experience," explains Michael.

Although the grilled cheese experience is key to his success, Michael's management of internal controls and cash is equally impressive. Several control procedures monitor business activities and safeguard assets. An example is his inventory control system. Explains Michael, quality ingredients are crucial to

customer satisfaction, and monitoring controls ensure the quality of his ingredients. Similar controls are applied throughout his store. Michael explains that such controls raise productivity, cut expenses, and enhance the customer experience.

His store's cash management practices are equally impressive, including controls over cash receipts, disbursements, and petty cash. The use of bank reconciliations further helps with his store's control and management of cash. "Take basic accounting," explains Michael, "I was able to say, 'I'm going to need to know how to balance my books.'" Michael explains that he takes advantage of available banking services to enhance controls over cash.

Internal controls are crucial when on a busy day his stores bring in thousands of customers, and their cash. "We have put the infrastructure in place to ensure that (the growth) goes as smoothly as possible," explains Michael. "We're definitely going to be moving at what feels like light speed."

[Sources: *CHEESEBOY Website,* January 2013; *CNNMoney,* July 2011; *BOLDFACERS,* August 2011; *The Patriot Ledger,* November 2011; *Boston Business Journal,* December 2011; *The New Journal,* February 2012.]

Chapter Preview

We all are aware of theft and fraud. They affect us in several ways: We lock doors, chain bikes, review credit card statements, and acquire alarm systems. A company also takes actions to safeguard, control, and manage what it owns. Experience tells us that small companies are most vulnerable, usually due to weak internal controls. It is management's responsibility to set up policies and procedures to safeguard a company's assets, especially cash. To do so, management *and* employees must understand and apply principles of internal control. This chapter describes these principles and how to apply them. It focuses special attention on cash because it is easily transferable and is often at high risk of loss.

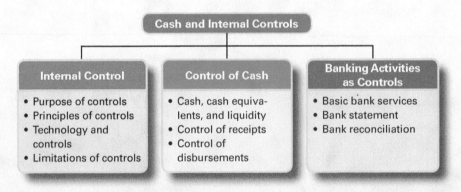

Cash and Internal Controls

Internal Control	Control of Cash	Banking Activities as Controls
• Purpose of controls • Principles of controls • Technology and controls • Limitations of controls	• Cash, cash equivalents, and liquidity • Control of receipts • Control of disbursements	• Basic bank services • Bank statement • Bank reconciliation

INTERNAL CONTROL

This section describes internal control and its fundamental principles. We also discuss the impact of technology on internal control and the limitations of control procedures.

Purpose of Internal Control

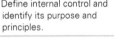

C1 Define internal control and identify its purpose and principles.

Managers (or owners) of small businesses often control the entire operation. These managers usually purchase all assets, hire and manage employees, negotiate all contracts, and sign all checks. They know from personal contact and observation whether the business is actually receiving the assets and services paid for. Most companies, however, cannot maintain this close personal supervision. They must delegate responsibilities and rely on formal procedures rather than personal contact in controlling business activities.

Internal Control System   Managers use an internal control system to monitor and control business activities. An **internal control system** consists of the policies and procedures managers use to

- Protect assets.
- Ensure reliable accounting.
- Promote efficient operations.
- Urge adherence to company policies.

A properly designed internal control system is a key part of systems design, analysis, and performance. Managers place a high priority on internal control systems because they can prevent avoidable losses, help managers plan operations, and monitor company and employee performance. For example, internal controls for health care must protect patient records and privacy. Internal controls do not provide guarantees, but they lower the company's risk of loss.

Sarbanes-Oxley Act (SOX)   The **Sarbanes-Oxley Act (SOX)** requires the managers and auditors of companies whose stock is traded on an exchange (called *public companies*) to document and certify the system of internal controls. Following are some of the specific requirements:

- Auditors must evaluate internal controls and issue an internal control report.
- Auditors of a client are restricted as to what consulting services they can provide that client.
- The person leading an audit can serve no more than seven years without a two-year break.
- Auditors' work is overseen by the *Public Company Accounting Oversight Board* (PCAOB).
- Harsh penalties exist for violators—sentences up to 25 years in prison with severe fines.

SOX has markedly impacted companies, and the costs of its implementation are high. Importantly, **Section 404** of SOX requires that managers document and assess the effectiveness of all internal control processes that can impact financial reporting. The benefits include greater confidence in accounting systems and their related reports. However, the public continues to debate the costs versus the benefits of SOX as nearly all business activities of these companies are impacted by SOX. Section 404 of SOX requires that managers document and assess their internal controls *and* that auditors provide an opinion on managers' documentation and assessment. Costs of complying with Section 404 for companies is reported to average $4 million (source: Financial Executives Institute).

Principles of Internal Control

Internal control policies and procedures vary from company to company according to such factors as the nature of the business and its size. Certain fundamental internal control principles apply to all companies. The **principles of internal control** are to

1. Establish responsibilities.
2. Maintain adequate records.
3. Insure assets and bond key employees.
4. Separate recordkeeping from custody of assets.
5. Divide responsibility for related transactions.
6. Apply technological controls.
7. Perform regular and independent reviews.

...a control system is only as strong as its weakest link

This section explains these seven principles and describes how internal control procedures minimize the risk of fraud and theft. These procedures also increase the reliability and accuracy of accounting records. A framework for how these seven principles improve the quality of financial reporting is provided by the **Committee of Sponsoring Organizations (COSO)** (www.COSO.org). Specifically, these principles link to five aspects of internal control: control activities, control environment, risk assessment, monitoring, and communication.

Point: Sarbanes-Oxley Act (SOX) requires that each annual report contain an *internal control report,* which must: (1) state managers' responsibility for establishing and maintaining adequate internal controls for financial reporting; and (2) assess the effectiveness of those controls.

Establish Responsibilities Proper internal control means that responsibility for a task is clearly established and assigned to one person. When a problem occurs in a company where responsibility is not identified, determining who is at fault is difficult. For instance, if two sales-clerks share the same cash register and there is a cash shortage, neither clerk can be held accountable. To prevent this problem, one clerk might be given responsibility for handling all cash sales. Alternately, a company can use a register with separate cash drawers for each clerk. Most of us have waited at a retail counter during a shift change while employees swap cash drawers.

Point: Many companies have a mandatory vacation policy for employees who handle cash. When another employee must cover for the one on vacation, it is more difficult to hide cash frauds.

Maintain Adequate Records Good recordkeeping is part of an internal control system. It helps protect assets and ensures that employees use prescribed procedures. Reliable records are also a source of information that managers use to monitor company activities. When detailed records of equipment are kept, for instance, items are unlikely to be lost or stolen without detection. Similarly, transactions are less likely to be entered in wrong accounts if a chart of accounts is set up and carefully used. Many preprinted forms and internal documents are also designed for use in a good internal control system. When sales slips are properly designed, for instance, sales personnel can record needed information efficiently with less chance of errors or delays to customers. When sales slips are prenumbered and controlled, each one issued is the responsibility of one salesperson, preventing the salesperson from pocketing cash by making a sale and destroying the sales slip. Computerized point-of-sale systems achieve the same control results.

Insure Assets and Bond Key Employees Good internal control means that assets are adequately insured against casualty and that employees handling large amounts of cash and easily transferable assets are bonded. An employee is *bonded* when a company purchases an insurance policy, or a bond, against losses from theft by that employee. Bonding reduces the risk of loss. It also discourages theft because bonded employees know an independent bonding company will be involved when theft is uncovered and is unlikely to be sympathetic with an employee involved in theft. (A common question on job applications is whether you are bonded or bondable.)

260   Chapter 6   Cash and Internal Controls

Decision Insight

Tagging Assets   A novel technique exists for marking physical assets. It involves embedding a less than one-inch-square tag of fibers that creates a unique optical signature recordable by scanners. Manufacturers hope to embed tags in everything from compact discs and credit cards to designer clothes for purposes of internal control and efficiency. ■

Point: The Association of Certified Fraud Examiners (**acfe.com**) estimates that employee fraud costs small companies more than $100,000 per incident.

Separate Recordkeeping from Custody of Assets   A person who controls or has access to an asset must not keep that asset's accounting records. This principle reduces the risk of theft or waste of an asset because the person with control over it knows that another person keeps its records. Also, a recordkeeper who does not have access to the asset has no reason to falsify records. This means that to steal an asset and hide the theft from the records, two or more people must *collude*—or agree in secret to commit the fraud. Some payroll cash checking services require fingerprint ID before the payroll check is cashed.

Divide Responsibility for Related Transactions   Good internal control divides responsibility for a transaction or a series of related transactions between two or more individuals or departments. This is to ensure that the work of one individual acts as a check on the other. This principle, often called *separation of duties,* is not a call for duplication of work. Each employee or department should perform unduplicated effort. Examples of transactions with divided responsibility are placing purchase orders, receiving merchandise, and paying vendors. These tasks should not be given to one individual or department. Assigning responsibility for two or more of these tasks to one party increases mistakes and perhaps fraud. Having an independent person, for example, check incoming goods for quality and quantity encourages more care and attention to detail than having the person who placed the order do the checking. Added protection can result from identifying a third person to approve payment of the invoice. A company can even designate a fourth person with authority to write checks as another protective measure.

Point: There's a new security device—a person's ECG (electrocardiogram) reading—that is as unique as a fingerprint and a lot harder to lose or steal than a PIN. ECGs can be read through fingertip touches. An ECG also shows that a living person is actually there, whereas fingerprint and facial recognition software can be fooled.

Apply Technological Controls   Cash registers, check protectors, time clocks, and personal identification scanners are examples of devices that can improve internal control. Technology often improves the effectiveness of controls. A cash register with a locked-in tape or electronic file makes a record of each cash sale. A check protector perforates the amount of a check into its face and makes it difficult to alter the amount. A time clock registers the exact time an employee both arrives at and departs from the job. Mechanical change and currency counters quickly and accurately count amounts, and personal scanners limit access to only authorized individuals. Each of these and other technological controls are an effective part of many internal control systems. Some companies video record workers as they clock in and out, which discourages them from clocking in or out for others.

Decision Insight

Face Reading   Face-recognition software snaps a digital picture of the face and converts key facial features—say, the distance between the eyes—into a series of numerical values. These can be stored on an ID or ATM card as a simple bar code to prohibit unauthorized access. ■

Perform Regular and Independent Reviews   Changes in personnel, stress of time pressures, and technological advances present opportunities for shortcuts and lapses. To counter these factors, regular reviews of internal control systems are needed to ensure that procedures are followed. These reviews are preferably done by internal auditors not directly involved in the activities. Their impartial perspective encourages an evaluation of the efficiency as well as the effectiveness of the internal control system. Many companies also pay for audits by independent, external auditors. These external auditors test the company's financial records to give an opinion as to whether its financial statements are presented fairly. Before external auditors decide on how much testing is needed, they evaluate the effectiveness of the internal control system. This evaluation is often helpful to a client. Independent, external audits are usually performed by auditors who work for public accounting firms.

Point: COSO organizes control components into five types:

* Control environment
* Control activities
* Risk assessment
* Monitoring
* Information and communication

◼ Decision Maker

Entrepreneur   As owner of a start-up information services company, you hire a systems analyst. The analyst sees that your company only employs two workers. She recommends you improve controls and says that as owner you must serve as a compensating control. What does the analyst mean? ◼   [Answer—p. 285]

Technology and Internal Control

The fundamental principles of internal control are relevant no matter what the technological state of the accounting system, from purely manual to fully automated systems. Technology impacts an internal control system in several important ways. Perhaps the most obvious is that technology allows us quicker access to databases and information. Used effectively, technology greatly improves managers' abilities to monitor and control business activities. This section describes some technological impacts we must be alert to.

Reduced Processing Errors   Technologically advanced systems reduce the number of errors in processing information. Provided the software and data entry are correct, the risk of mechanical and mathematical errors is nearly eliminated. However, we must remember that erroneous software or data entry does exist. Also, less human involvement in data processing can cause data entry errors to go undiscovered. Moreover, errors in software can produce consistent but erroneous processing of transactions. Continually checking and monitoring all types of systems are important.

More Extensive Testing of Records   A company's review and audit of electronic records can include more extensive testing when information is easily and rapidly accessed. When accounting records are kept manually, auditors and others likely select only small samples of data to test. When data are accessible with computer technology, however, auditors can quickly analyze large samples or even the entire database.

Limited Evidence of Processing   Many data processing steps are increasingly done by computer. Accordingly, fewer hard-copy items of documentary evidence are available for review. Yet technologically advanced systems can provide new evidence. They can, for instance, record who made the entries, the date and time, the source of the entry, and so on. Technology can also be designed to require the use of passwords or other identification before access to the system is granted. This means that internal control depends more on the design and operation of the information system and less on the analysis of its resulting documents.

Crucial Separation of Duties   Technological advances in accounting information systems often yield some job eliminations or consolidations. While those who remain have the special skills necessary to operate advanced programs and equipment, a company with a reduced workforce risks losing its crucial separation of duties. The company must establish ways to control and monitor employees to minimize risk of error and fraud. For instance, the person who designs and programs the information system must not be the one who operates it. The company must also separate control over programs and files from the activities related to cash receipts and disbursements. For instance, a computer operator should not control check-writing activities. Achieving acceptable separation of duties can be especially difficult and costly in small companies with few employees.

Increased E-Commerce   Technology has encouraged the growth of e-commerce. Amazon.com and eBay are examples of companies that have successfully exploited e-commerce. Most companies have some e-commerce transactions. All such transactions involve at least three risks. (1) *Credit card number theft* is a risk of using, transmitting, and storing such data online. This increases the cost of e-commerce. (2) *Computer viruses* are malicious programs that attach themselves to innocent files for purposes of infecting and harming other files and programs. (3) *Impersonation* online can result in charges of sales to bogus accounts, purchases of inappropriate materials, and the unknowing giving up of confidential information to hackers. Companies use both firewalls and encryption to

Point: Information on Internet fraud can be found at these Websites: sec.gov/investor/pubs/cyberfraud.htm ftc.gov/bcp/consumer.shtm www.fraud.org

Point: Evidence of any internal control failure for a company reduces user confidence in its financial statements.

Point: We look to several sources when assessing a company's internal controls. Sources include the auditor's report, management report on controls (if available), management discussion and analysis, and financial press.

"Worst case of identity theft I've ever seen!"

Copyright 2004 by Randy Glasbergen. www.glasbergen.com

combat some of these risks—firewalls are points of entry to a system that require passwords to continue, and encryption is a mathematical process to rearrange contents that cannot be read without the process code. Nearly 5% of Americans already report being victims of identity theft, and roughly 10 million say their privacy has been compromised.

Decision Insight

Winnings and Controls   Certified Fraud Examiners Website reports the following: Andrew Cameron stole Jacqueline Boanson's credit card. Cameron headed to the racetrack and promptly charged two bets for $150 on the credit card—winning $400. Unfortunately for Cameron the racetrack refused to pay him cash as its internal control policy is to credit winnings from bets made on a credit card to that same card. Cameron was later nabbed; and the racetrack let Ms. Boanson keep the winnings. ◼

Limitations of Internal Control

All internal control policies and procedures have limitations that usually arise from either (1) the human element or (2) the cost–benefit principle.

Internal control policies and procedures are applied by people. This human element creates several potential limitations that we can categorize as either (1) human error or (2) human fraud. *Human error* can occur from negligence, fatigue, misjudgment, or confusion. *Human fraud* involves intent by people to defeat internal controls, such as *management override,* for personal gain. Fraud also includes collusion to thwart the separation of duties. The human element highlights the importance of establishing an *internal control environment* to convey management's commitment to internal control policies and procedures. Human fraud is driven by the *triple-threat* of fraud:

- **Opportunity**—refers to internal control deficiencies in the workplace.
- **Pressure**—refers to financial, family, society, and other stresses to succeed.
- **Rationalization**—refers to employees justifying fraudulent behavior.

The second major limitation on internal control is the *cost–benefit principle,* which dictates that the costs of internal controls must not exceed their benefits. Analysis of costs and benefits must consider all factors, including the impact on morale. Most companies, for instance, have a legal right to read employees' e-mails, yet companies seldom exercise that right unless they are confronted with evidence of potential harm to the company. The same holds for drug testing, phone tapping, and hidden cameras. The bottom line is that managers must establish internal control policies and procedures with a net benefit to the company.

Point: **Cybercrime.gov** pursues computer and intellectual property crimes, including that of e-commerce.

Hacker's Guide to Cyberspace

Pharming   Viruses attached to e-mails and Websites load software onto your PC that monitors keystrokes; when you sign on to financial Websites, it steals your passwords.

Phishing   Hackers send e-mails to you posing as banks; you are asked for information using fake Websites where they reel in your passwords and personal data.

WI-Phishing   Cybercrooks set up wireless networks hoping you use them to connect to the Web; your passwords and data are stolen as you use their network.

Bot-Networking   Hackers send remote-control programs to your PC that take control to send out spam and viruses; they even rent your bot to other cybercrooks.

Typo-Squatting   Hackers set up Websites with addresses similar to legit outfits; when you make a typo and hit their sites, they infect your PC with viruses or take them over as bots.

Hackers also have their own self-identification system...
- *Hackers,* or *external attackers,* crack systems and take data for illicit gains (as unauthorized users).
- *Rogue insiders,* or *internal attackers,* crack systems and take data for illicit gains or revenge (as authorized users).
- *Ethical hackers,* or *good-guys* or *white-hat hackers,* crack systems and reveal vulnerabilities to enhance controls.
- *Crackers,* or *criminal hackers,* crack systems illegally for illicit gains, fame, or revenge.

■ **Decision** Insight

Ball Control   Ryan Braun of the Milwaukee Brewers won an appeal of a 50-game Major League Baseball (MLB) suspension for a positive drug test. Ryan maintained that MLB did not maintain control over his sample through the testing process and raised the risk that his sample was tainted. This control failure led to dismissal of that particular test result and him winning the appeal. Controls are crucial when people's livelihoods and reputations are on the line. ■

Quick Check Answers — p. 285

1. Principles of internal control suggest that (choose one): (*a*) Responsibility for a series of related transactions (such as placing orders, receiving and paying for merchandise) should be assigned to one employee; (*b*) Responsibility for individual tasks should be shared by more than one employee so that one serves as a check on the other; or (*c*) Employees who handle considerable cash and easily transferable assets should be bonded.
2. What are some impacts of computing technology on internal control?
3. Many companies require each employee to take at least one week (five consecutive days) of vacation per year. Why is a "forced vacation" policy good for internal control?

CONTROL OF CASH

Cash is a necessary asset of every company. Most companies also own *cash equivalents* (defined below), which are assets similar to cash. Cash and cash equivalents are the most liquid of all assets and are easily hidden and moved. Cash is also the most desired asset as other assets must be *fenced* (sold in a secondary market). An effective system of internal controls protects cash assets and it should meet three basic guidelines:

1. Handling cash is separate from recordkeeping of cash.
2. Cash receipts are promptly deposited in a bank.
3. Cash disbursements are made by check.

The first guideline applies separation of duties to minimize errors and fraud. When duties are separated, two or more people must collude to steal cash and conceal this action in the accounting records. The second guideline uses immediate (say, daily) deposits of all cash receipts to produce a timely independent record of the cash received. It also reduces the likelihood of cash theft (or loss) and the risk that an employee could personally use the money before depositing it. The third guideline uses payments by check to develop an independent bank record of cash disbursements. This guideline also reduces the risk of cash theft (or loss).

This section begins with definitions of cash and cash equivalents. Discussion then focuses on controls and accounting for both cash receipts and disbursements. The exact procedures used to achieve control over cash vary across companies. They depend on factors such as company size, number of employees, volume of cash transactions, and sources of cash.

Cash, Cash Equivalents, and Liquidity

Good accounting systems help in managing the amount of cash and controlling who has access to it. Cash is the usual means of payment when paying for assets, services, or liabilities. **Liquidity** refers to a company's ability to pay for its near-term obligations. Cash and similar assets are called **liquid assets** because they can be readily used to settle such obligations. A company needs liquid assets to effectively operate.

C2 Define cash and cash equivalents and explain how to report them.

Cash includes currency and coins along with the amounts on deposit in bank accounts, checking accounts (called *demand deposits*), and many savings accounts (called *time deposits*). Cash also

Point: The most liquid assets are usually reported first on a balance sheet; the least liquid assets are reported last.

Point: Google reports cash and cash equivalents of $9,983 million in its balance sheet. This amount makes up nearly 15% of its total assets.

includes items that are acceptable for deposit in these accounts such as customer checks, cashier's checks, certified checks, and money orders. **Cash equivalents** are short-term, highly liquid investment assets meeting two criteria: (1) readily convertible to a known cash amount and (2) sufficiently close to their due date so that their market value is not sensitive to interest rate changes. Only investments purchased within three months of their due date usually satisfy these criteria. Examples of cash equivalents are short-term investments in assets such as U.S. Treasury bills and money market funds. To increase their return, many companies invest idle cash in cash equivalents. Most companies combine cash equivalents with cash as a single item on the balance sheet.

Cash Management

When companies fail, one of the most common causes is their inability to manage cash. Companies must plan both cash receipts and cash payments. The goals of cash management are twofold:

1. Plan cash receipts to meet cash payments when due.
2. Keep a minimum level of cash necessary to operate.

The *treasurer* of the company is responsible for cash management. Effective cash management involves applying the following cash management principles.

- **Encourage collection of receivables.** The more quickly customers and others pay the company, the more quickly that company can use the money. Some companies have cash-only sales policies. Others might offer discounts for payments received early.
- **Delay payment of liabilities.** The more delayed a company is in paying others, the more time it has to use the money. Some companies regularly wait to pay their bills until the last possible day allowed—although, a company must take care not to hurt its credit standing.
- **Keep only necessary levels of assets.** The less money tied up in idle assets, the more money to invest in productive assets. Some companies maintain *just-in-time* inventory; meaning they plan inventory to be available at the same time orders are filled. Others might lease out excess warehouse space or rent equipment instead of buying it.
- **Plan expenditures.** Money should be spent only when it is available. Companies must look at seasonal and business cycles to plan expenditures.
- **Invest excess cash.** Excess cash earns no return and should be invested. Excess cash from seasonal cycles can be placed in a bank account or other short-term investment for income. Excess cash beyond what's needed for regular business should be invested in productive assets like factories and inventories.

Decision Insight

Days' Cash Expense Coverage The ratio of *cash (and cash equivalents) to average daily cash expenses* indicates the number of days a company can operate without additional cash inflows. It reflects on company liquidity and on the potential of excess cash. ▪

Control of Cash Receipts

P1 Apply internal control to cash receipts and disbursements.

Internal control of cash receipts ensures that cash received is properly recorded and deposited. Cash receipts can arise from transactions such as cash sales, collections of customer accounts, receipts of interest earned, bank loans, sales of assets, and owner investments. This section explains internal control over two important types of cash receipts: over-the-counter and by mail.

Over-the-Counter Cash Receipts For purposes of internal control, over-the-counter cash receipts from sales should be recorded on a cash register at the time of each sale. To help ensure that correct amounts are entered, each register should be located so customers can read the amounts entered. Clerks also should be required to enter each sale before wrapping merchandise and to give the customer a receipt for each sale. The design of each cash register should provide a permanent, locked-in record of each transaction. In many systems, the register is directly linked with computing and accounting services. Less advanced registers simply print a record of each transaction on a paper tape or electronic file locked inside the register.

Proper internal control prescribes that custody over cash should be separate from its recordkeeping. For over-the-counter cash receipts, this separation begins with the cash sale. The clerk who has access to cash in the register should not have access to its locked-in record. At the end of the clerk's work period, the clerk should count the cash in the register, record the amount, and turn over the cash and a record of its amount to the company cashier. The cashier, like the clerk, has access to the cash but should not have access to accounting records (or the register tape or file). A third employee, often a supervisor, compares the record of total register transactions (or the register tape or file) with the cash receipts reported by the cashier. This record is the basis for a journal entry recording over-the-counter cash receipts. The third employee has access to the records for cash but not to the actual cash. The clerk and the cashier have access to cash but not to the accounting records. None of them can make a mistake or divert cash without the difference being revealed—see the following diagram.

Point: Convenience stores sometimes display a sign: *Cashier has no access to cash in locked floor (or wall) safe.* Such signs help thwart theft and holdups because of lack of access to the floor (or wall) safe.

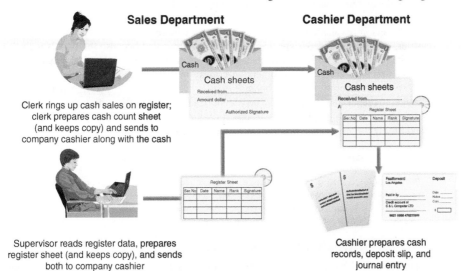

Sales Department

Clerk rings up cash sales on **register**; clerk prepares cash count **sheet** (and keeps copy) and sends to company cashier along with **the cash**

Supervisor reads register data, **prepares register sheet (and keeps copy), and sends** both to company cashier

Cashier Department

Cashier prepares cash records, deposit slip, and journal entry

Cash over and short. Sometimes errors in making change are discovered from differences between the cash in a cash register and the record of the amount of cash receipts. Although a clerk is careful, one or more customers can be given too much or too little change. This means that at the end of a work period, the cash in a cash register might not equal the record of cash receipts. This difference is reported in the **Cash Over and Short** account, also called *Cash Short and Over,* which is an income statement account recording the income effects of cash overages and cash shortages. To illustrate, if a cash register's record shows $550 but the count of cash in the register is $555, the entry to record cash sales and its overage is

Point: Retailers often require cashiers to restrictively endorse checks immediately on receipt by stamping them "For deposit only."

Cash	555	
Cash Over and Short		5
Sales		550
To record cash sales and a cash overage.		

Assets = Liabilities + Equity
+555   + 5
                +550

On the other hand, if a cash register's record shows $625 but the count of cash in the register is $621, the entry to record cash sales and its shortage is

Cash	621	
Cash Over and Short	4	
Sales		625
To record cash sales and a cash shortage.		

Assets = Liabilities + Equity
+621   − 4
                +625

Since customers are more likely to dispute being shortchanged than being given too much change, the Cash Over and Short account usually has a debit balance at the end of an accounting period. A debit balance reflects an expense. It is reported on the income statement as part of general and administrative expenses. (Since the amount is usually small, it is often combined

Point: Merchants begin a business day with a *change fund* in their cash register. The accounting for a change fund is similar to that for petty cash, including that for cash shortages or overages.

with other small expenses and reported as part of *miscellaneous expenses*—or as part of *miscellaneous revenues* if it has a credit balance.)

Cash Receipts by Mail   Control of cash receipts that arrive through the mail starts with the person who opens the mail. Preferably, two people are assigned the task of, and are present for, opening the mail. In this case, theft of cash receipts by mail requires collusion between these two employees. Specifically, the person(s) opening the mail enters a list (in triplicate) of money received. This list should contain a record of each sender's name, the amount, and an explanation of why the money is sent. The first copy is sent with the money to the cashier. A second copy is sent to the recordkeeper in the accounting area. A third copy is kept by the clerk(s) who opened the mail. The cashier deposits the money in a bank, and the recordkeeper records the amounts received in the accounting records.

Point: Collusion implies that two or more individuals are knowledgeable or involved with the activities of the other(s).

This process reflects good internal control. That is, when the bank balance is reconciled by another person (explained later in the chapter), errors or acts of fraud by the mail clerks, the cashier, or the recordkeeper are revealed. They are revealed because the bank's record of cash deposited must agree with the records from each of the three. Moreover, if the mail clerks do not report all receipts correctly, customers will question their account balances. If the cashier does not deposit all receipts, the bank balance does not agree with the recordkeeper's cash balance. The recordkeeper and the person who reconciles the bank balance do not have access to cash and therefore have no opportunity to divert cash to themselves. This system makes errors and fraud highly unlikely. The exception is employee collusion.

Decision Insight

Perpetual Accounting   Walmart uses a network of information links with its point-of-sale cash registers to coordinate sales, purchases, and distribution. Its supercenters, for instance, ring up 15,000 separate sales on heavy days. By using cash register information, the company can fix pricing mistakes quickly and capitalize on sales trends. Interestingly, Sam Walton, the founder, was a self-described distruster of computers.

Control of Cash Disbursements

Control of cash disbursements is especially important as most large thefts occur from payment of fictitious invoices. One key to controlling cash disbursements is to require all expenditures to be made by check. The only exception is small payments made from petty cash. Another key is to deny access to the accounting records to anyone other than the owner who has the authority to sign checks. A small business owner often signs checks and knows from personal contact that the items being paid for are actually received. This arrangement is impossible in large businesses. Instead, internal control procedures must be substituted for personal contact. Such procedures are designed to assure the check signer that the obligations recorded are properly incurred and should be paid. This section describes these and other internal control procedures, including the voucher system and petty cash system. A method for management of cash disbursements for purchases is described in Appendix 6B.

Cash Budget   Projected cash receipts and cash disbursements are often summarized in a *cash budget*. Provided that sufficient cash exists for effective operations, companies wish to minimize the cash they hold because of its risk of theft and its low return versus other investment opportunities.

Decision Insight

Lock Box   Some companies do not receive cash in the mail but, instead, elect to have customers send deposits directly to the bank using a *lock box* system. Bank employees are charged with receipting the cash and depositing it in the correct business bank account.

Voucher System of Control   A **voucher system** is a set of procedures and approvals designed to control cash disbursements and the acceptance of obligations. The voucher system of control establishes procedures for

- Verifying, approving, and recording obligations for eventual cash disbursement.
- Issuing checks for payment of verified, approved, and recorded obligations.

A reliable voucher system follows standard procedures for every transaction. This applies even when multiple purchases are made from the same supplier.

A voucher system's control over cash disbursements begins when a company incurs an obligation that will result in payment of cash. A key factor in this system is that only approved departments and individuals are authorized to incur such obligations. The system often limits the type of obligations that a department or individual can incur. In a large retail store, for instance, only a purchasing department should be authorized to incur obligations for merchandise inventory. Another key factor is that procedures for purchasing, receiving, and paying for merchandise are divided among several departments (or individuals). These departments include the one requesting the purchase, the purchasing department, the receiving department, and the accounting department. To coordinate and control responsibilities of these departments, a company uses several different business documents. Exhibit 6.1 shows how documents are accumulated in a **voucher,** which is an internal document (or file) used to accumulate information to control cash disbursements and to ensure that a transaction is properly recorded. This specific example begins with a *purchase requisition* and concludes with a *check* drawn against cash. Appendix 6A describes the documentation and verification necessary for a voucher system of control. It also describes the internal control objective served by each document.

Point: MCI, formerly **WorldCom,** paid a whopping $500 million in SEC fines for accounting fraud. Among the charges were that it inflated earnings by as much as $10 billion. Its CEO, Bernard Ebbers, was sentenced to 25 years.

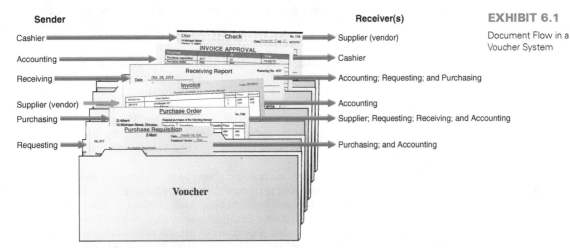

Sender		Receiver(s)
Cashier		Supplier (vendor)
Accounting		Cashier
Receiving		Accounting; Requesting; and Purchasing
Supplier (vendor)		Accounting
Purchasing		Supplier; Requesting; Receiving; and Accounting
Requesting		Purchasing; and Accounting

EXHIBIT 6.1

Document Flow in a Voucher System

A voucher system should be applied not only to purchases of inventory but to all expenditures. To illustrate, when a company receives a monthly telephone bill, it should review and verify the charges, prepare a voucher (file), and insert the bill. This transaction is then recorded with a journal entry. If the amount is currently due, a check is issued. If not, the voucher is filed for payment on its due date. If no voucher is prepared, verifying the invoice and its amount after several days or weeks can be difficult. Also, without records, a dishonest employee could collude with a dishonest supplier to get more than one payment for an obligation, payment for excessive amounts, or payment for goods and services not received. An effective voucher system helps prevent such frauds.

Point: A *voucher* is an internal document (or file).

Point: The basic purposes of paper and electronic documents are similar. However, the internal control system must change to reflect different risks, including confidential and competitive-sensitive information that is at greater risk in electronic systems.

■ **Decision** Insight ━━━━━━━━━━━━━━━━━━━━━━━▶

Cyber Setup The FTC is on the cutting edge of cybersleuthing. Opportunists in search of easy money are lured to <u>WeMarket4U. net/SundaeStation</u> and <u>WeMarket4U.net/FatFoe</u>. Take the bait and you get warned. The top 5 fraud complaints as compiled by the Federal Trade Commission are shown to the right. ■

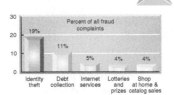

268   Chapter 6   Cash and Internal Controls

Quick Check
Answers — p. 285

4. Why must a company hold liquid assets?
5. Why does a company hold cash equivalent assets in addition to cash?
6. Identify at least two assets that are classified as cash equivalents.
7. Good internal control procedures for cash include which of the following? (a) All cash disbursements, other than those for very small amounts, are made by check; (b) One employee counts cash received from sales and promptly deposits cash receipts; or (c) Cash receipts by mail are opened by one employee who is then responsible for recording and depositing them.
8. Should all companies require a voucher system? At what point in a company's growth would you recommend a voucher system?

P2 Explain and record petty cash fund transactions.

Petty Cash System of Control   A basic principle for controlling cash disbursements is that all payments must be made by check. An exception to this rule is made for *petty cash disbursements,* which are the small payments required for items such as postage, courier fees, minor repairs, and low-cost supplies. To avoid the time and cost of writing checks for small amounts, a company sets up a petty cash fund to make small payments. (**Petty cash** activities are part of an *imprest system,* which designates advance money to establish the fund, to withdraw from the fund, and to reimburse the fund.)

Operating a petty cash fund.   Establishing a petty cash fund requires estimating the total amount of small payments likely to be made during a short period such as a week or month. A check is then drawn by the company cashier for an amount slightly in excess of this estimate. This check is recorded with a debit to the Petty Cash account (an asset) and a credit to Cash. The check is cashed, and the currency is given to an employee designated as the *petty cashier* or *petty cash custodian.* The petty cashier is responsible for keeping this cash safe, making payments from the fund, and keeping records of it in a secure place referred to as the *petty cashbox.*

Point: A petty cash fund is used only for business expenses.

When each cash disbursement is made, the person receiving payment should sign a prenumbered *petty cash receipt,* also called *petty cash ticket*—see Exhibit 6.2. The petty cash receipt is then placed in the petty cashbox with the remaining money. Under this system, the sum of all receipts plus the remaining cash equals the total fund amount. A $100 petty cash fund, for instance, contains any combination of cash and petty cash receipts that totals $100 (examples are $80 cash plus $20 in receipts, or $10 cash plus $90 in receipts). Each disbursement reduces cash and increases the amount of receipts in the petty cashbox.

EXHIBIT 6.2

Petty Cash Receipt

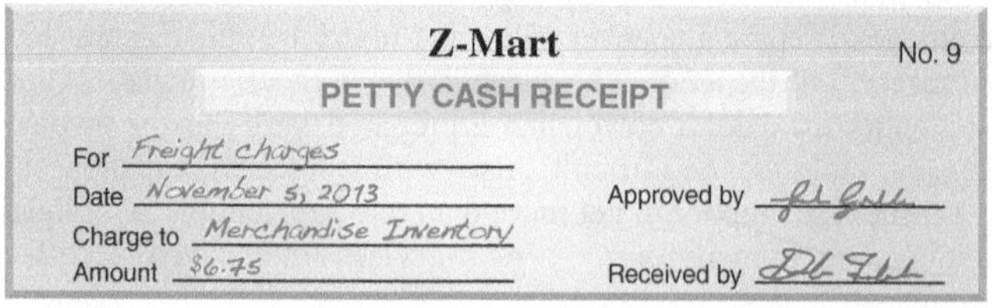

Z-Mart   No. 9

PETTY CASH RECEIPT

For _Freight charges_
Date _November 5, 2013_   Approved by _R.L. Gull_
Charge to _Merchandise Inventory_
Amount _$6.75_   Received by _D.L. Fill_

Point: Petty cash receipts with either no signature or a forged signature usually indicate misuse of petty cash. Companies respond with surprise petty cash counts for verification.

The petty cash fund should be reimbursed when it is nearing zero and at the end of an accounting period when financial statements are prepared. For this purpose, the petty cashier sorts the paid receipts by the type of expense or account and then totals the receipts. The petty cashier presents all paid receipts to the company cashier, who stamps all receipts *paid* so they cannot be reused, files them for recordkeeping, and gives the petty cashier a check for their sum. When this check is cashed and the money placed in the cashbox, the total money in the cashbox is restored to its original amount. The fund is now ready for a new cycle of petty cash payments.

Illustrating a petty cash fund.   To illustrate, assume Z-Mart establishes a petty cash fund on November 1 and designates one of its office employees as the petty cashier. A $75 check is drawn, cashed, and the proceeds given to the petty cashier. The entry to record the setup of this petty cash fund is

Nov. 1	Petty Cash	75	
	Cash		75
	To establish a petty cash fund.		

Assets = Liabilities + Equity
+75
−75

After the petty cash fund is established, the Petty Cash account is not debited or credited again unless the amount of the fund is changed. (A fund should be increased if it requires reimbursement too frequently. On the other hand, if the fund is too large, some of its money should be redeposited in the Cash account.)

Next, assume that Z-Mart's petty cashier makes several November payments from petty cash. Each person who received payment is required to sign a receipt. On November 27, after making a $26.50 cash payment for tile cleaning, only $3.70 cash remains in the fund. The petty cashier then summarizes and totals the petty cash receipts as shown in Exhibit 6.3.

Z-MART			
Petty Cash Payments Report			
Miscellaneous Expenses			
Nov. 2	Cleaning of LCD panels	$20.00	
Nov. 27	Tile cleaning	26.50	$ 46.50
Merchandise Inventory (transportation-in)			
Nov. 5	Transport of merchandise purchased	6.75	
Nov. 20	Transport of merchandise purchased	8.30	15.05
Delivery Expense			
Nov. 18	Customer's package delivered		5.00
Office Supplies Expense			
Nov. 15	Purchase of office supplies immediately used		4.75
Total			$71.30

EXHIBIT 6.3

Petty Cash Payments Report

The petty cash payments report and all receipts are given to the company cashier in exchange for a $71.30 check to reimburse the fund. The petty cashier cashes the check and puts the $71.30 cash in the petty cashbox. The company records this reimbursement as follows.

Nov. 27	Miscellaneous Expenses	46.50	
	Merchandise Inventory	15.05	
	Delivery Expense	5.00	
	Office Supplies Expense	4.75	
	Cash		71.30
	To reimburse petty cash.		

Assets = Liabilities + Equity
−71.30   −46.50
                −15.05
                − 5.00
                − 4.75

A petty cash fund is usually reimbursed at the end of an accounting period so that expenses are recorded in the proper period, even if the fund is not low on money. If the fund is not reimbursed at the end of a period, the financial statements would show both an overstated cash asset and understated expenses (or assets) that were paid out of petty cash. Some companies do not reimburse the petty cash fund at the end of each period under the notion that this amount is immaterial to users of financial statements.

Increasing or decreasing a petty cash fund.   A decision to increase or decrease a petty cash fund is often made when reimbursing it. To illustrate, assume Z-Mart decides to *increase* its petty cash fund from $75 to $100 on November 27 when it reimburses the fund. The entries

270   Chapter 6   Cash and Internal Controls

required are to (1) reimburse the fund as usual (see the preceding November 27 entry) and (2) increase the fund amount as follows.

Nov. 27	Petty Cash	25	
	Cash		25
	To increase the petty cash fund amount.		

Summary of Petty Cash Accounting

Event	Petty Cash	Cash	Expenses
Set up fund	Dr.	Cr.	—
Reimburse fund ..	—	Cr.	Dr.
Increase fund	Dr.	Cr.	—
Decrease fund ...	Cr.	Dr.	—

Alternatively, if Z-Mart *decreases* the petty cash fund from $75 to $55 on November 27, the entry is to (1) credit Petty Cash for $20 (decreasing the fund from $75 to $55) and (2) debit Cash for $20 (reflecting the $20 transfer from Petty Cash to Cash).

Cash over and short.   Sometimes a petty cashier fails to get a receipt for payment or overpays for the amount due. When this occurs and the fund is later reimbursed, the petty cash payments report plus the cash remaining will not total to the fund balance. This mistake causes the fund to be *short.* This shortage is recorded as an expense in the reimbursing entry with a debit to the Cash Over and Short account. (An overage in the petty cash fund is recorded with a credit to Cash Over and Short in the reimbursing entry.) To illustrate, prepare the June 1 entry to reimburse a $200 petty cash fund when its payments report shows $178 in miscellaneous expenses and $15 cash remains.

$200 Petty Cash Fund

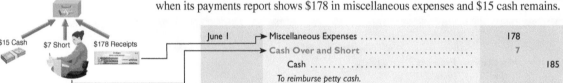

$15 Cash $7 Short $178 Receipts

June 1	Miscellaneous Expenses	178	
	Cash Over and Short	7	
	Cash		185
	To reimburse petty cash.		

Decision Insight

Warning Signs There are clues to internal control violations. Warning signs from accounting include (1) an increase in customer refunds—could be fake, (2) missing documents—could be used for fraud, (3) differences between bank deposits and cash receipts—could be cash embezzled, and (4) delayed recording—could reflect fraudulent records. Warning signs from employees include (1) lifestyle change—could be embezzlement, (2) too close with suppliers—could signal fraudulent transactions, and (3) failure to leave job, even for vacations—could conceal fraudulent activities. ■

Quick Check   Answers — pp. 285–286

9. Why are some cash payments made from a petty cash fund and not by check?
10. Why should a petty cash fund be reimbursed at the end of an accounting period?
11. Identify at least two results of reimbursing a petty cash fund.
12. Assume that we are auditing a company for the first time. Our audit procedures for petty cash require a surprise audit of the petty cash fund. We approach the petty cash custodian to conduct the audit and she says: "I'm busy right now. Can we do this after lunch?" Do we accommodate the request?

BANKING ACTIVITIES AS CONTROLS

Banks (and other financial institutions) provide many services, including helping companies control cash. Banks safeguard cash, provide detailed and independent records of cash transactions, and are a source of cash financing. This section describes these services and the documents provided by banking activities that increase managers' control over cash.

Basic Bank Services

This section explains basic bank services—such as the bank account, the bank deposit, and checking—that contribute to the control of cash.

Bank Account, Deposit, and Check A *bank account* is a record set up by a bank for a customer. It permits a customer to deposit money for safekeeping and helps control withdrawals. To limit access to a bank account, all persons authorized to write checks on the account must sign a **signature card,** which bank employees use to verify signatures on checks. Many companies have more than one bank account to serve different needs and to handle special transactions such as payroll.

Each bank deposit is supported by a **deposit ticket,** which lists items such as currency, coins, and checks deposited along with their corresponding dollar amounts. The bank gives the customer a copy of the deposit ticket or a deposit receipt as proof of the deposit. Exhibit 6.4 shows one type of deposit ticket.

Point: Online banking services include the ability to stop payment on a check, move money between accounts, get up-to-date balances, and identify cleared checks and deposits.

EXHIBIT 6.4

Deposit Ticket

Front

Back

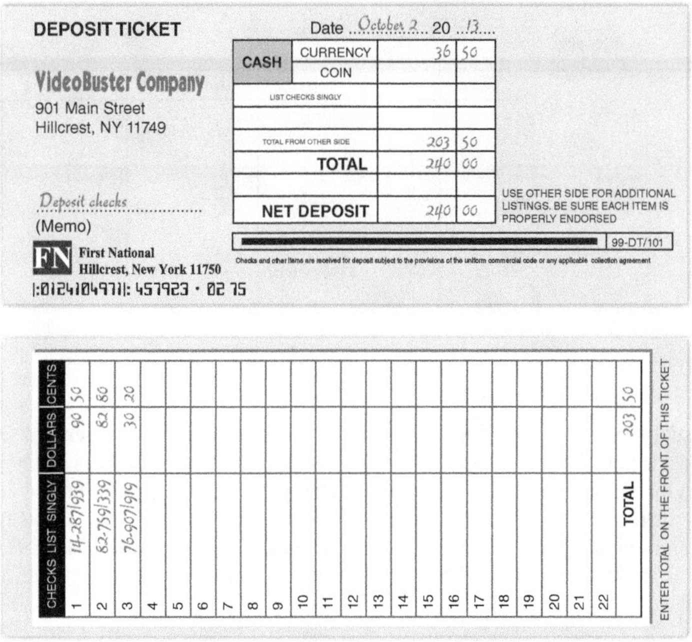
DEPOSIT TICKET

Date October 2 20 13

VideoBuster Company
901 Main Street
Hillcrest, NY 11749

CASH	CURRENCY	36	50
	COIN		
LIST CHECKS SINGLY			
TOTAL FROM OTHER SIDE		203	50
TOTAL		240	00
NET DEPOSIT		240	00

USE OTHER SIDE FOR ADDITIONAL LISTINGS. BE SURE EACH ITEM IS PROPERLY ENDORSED

Deposit checks
(Memo)

99-DT/101

FN First National
Hillcrest, New York 11750

Checks and other items are received for deposit subject to the provisions of the uniform commercial code or any applicable collection agreement

|:012410497|: 457923 • 02 75

CHECKS LIST SINGLY		DOLLARS	CENTS
1	14-287/939	90	50
2	82-759/339	82	80
3	76-907/919	30	20
4			
5			
6			
7			
8			
9			
10			
11			
12			
13			
14			
15			
16			
17			
18			
19			
20			
21			
22			
TOTAL		203	50

ENTER TOTAL ON THE FRONT OF THIS TICKET

To withdraw money from an account, the depositor can use a **check,** which is a document signed by the depositor instructing the bank to pay a specified amount of money to a designated recipient. A check involves three parties: a *maker* who signs the check, a *payee* who is the recipient, and a *bank* (or *payer*) on which the check is drawn. The bank provides a depositor the checks that are serially numbered and imprinted with the name and address of both the depositor and bank. Both checks and deposit tickets are imprinted with identification codes in magnetic ink for computer processing. Exhibit 6.5 shows one type of check. It is accompanied with an optional *remittance advice* explaining the payment. When a remittance advice is unavailable, the *memo* line is often used for a brief explanation.

Electronic Funds Transfer **Electronic funds transfer (EFT)** is the electronic transfer of cash from one party to another. No paper documents are necessary. Banks simply transfer cash from one account to another with a journal entry. Companies are increasingly using EFT because of its convenience and low cost. For instance, it can cost up to 50 cents to process a check through the banking system, whereas EFT cost is near zero. We now commonly see items such as payroll, rent, utilities, insurance, and interest payments being handled by EFT. The bank statement lists cash withdrawals by EFT with the checks and other deductions. Cash receipts by EFT are listed with deposits and other additions. A bank statement is sometimes a depositor's only notice of an EFT. *Automated teller machines (ATMs)* are one form of EFT, which allows bank customers to deposit, withdraw, and transfer cash.

EXHIBIT 6.5

Check with Remittance Advice

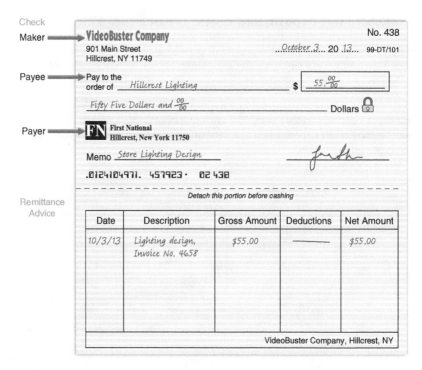

Bank Statement

Usually once a month, the bank sends each depositor a **bank statement** showing the activity in the account. Although a monthly statement is common, companies often regularly access information on their banking transactions. (Companies can choose to record any accounting adjustments required from the bank statement immediately or later, say, at the end of each day, week, month, or when reconciling a bank statement.) Different banks use different formats for their bank statements, but all of them include the following items of information:

1. Beginning-of-period balance of the depositor's account.
2. Checks and other debits decreasing the account during the period.
3. Deposits and other credits increasing the account during the period.
4. End-of-period balance of the depositor's account.

This information reflects the bank's records. Exhibit 6.6 shows one type of bank statement. Identify each of these four items in that statement. Part Ⓐ of Exhibit 6.6 summarizes changes in the account. Part Ⓑ lists paid checks along with other debits. Part Ⓒ lists deposits and credits to the account, and part Ⓓ shows the daily account balances.

In reading a bank statement note that a depositor's account is a liability on the bank's records. This is so because the money belongs to the depositor, not the bank. When a depositor increases the account balance, the bank records it with a *credit* to that liability account. This means that debit memos from the bank produce *credits* on the depositor's books, and credit memos from the bank produce *debits* on the depositor's books.

Enclosed with a bank statement is a list of the depositor's canceled checks (or the actual canceled checks) along with any debit or credit memoranda affecting the account. Increasingly, banks are showing canceled checks electronically via online access to accounts. **Canceled checks** are checks the bank has paid and deducted from the customer's account during the period. Other deductions that can appear on a bank statement include (1) service charges and fees assessed by the bank, (2) checks deposited that are uncollectible, (3) corrections of previous errors, (4) withdrawals through automated teller machines (ATMs), and (5) periodic payments arranged in advance by a depositor. (Most company checking accounts do not allow ATM withdrawals because of the company's desire to make all disbursements by check.) Except for service charges, the bank notifies the depositor of each deduction with a debit memorandum when the bank

EXHIBIT 6.6

Bank Statement

FN First National
Hillcrest, New York 11750   **Bank Statement**

Member FDIC

VideoBuster **Company**   October 31, 2013
901 Main Street   Statement Date
Hillcrest, NY 11749
                                                              494 504 2
                                                              Account Number

Previous Balance	Total Checks and Debits	Total Deposits and Credits	Current Balance
1,609.58	723.00	1,163.42	2,050.00

Checks and Debits			Deposits and Credits		Daily Balance	
Date	No.	Amount	Date	Amount	Date	Amount
10/03	119	55.00	10/02	240.00	10/01	1,609.58
10/09	120	200.00	10/09	180.00	10/02	1,849.58
10/10	121	120.00	10/15	100.00 EFT	10/03	1,794.58
10/12		23.00 DM	10/16	150.00	10/09	1,774.58
10/14	122	70.00	10/23	485.00 CM	10/10	1,654.58
10/16	123	25.00	10/31	8.42 IN	10/12	1,631.58
10/23	125	15.00			10/14	1,561.58
10/25		20.00 NSF			10/15	1,661.58
		10.00 DM			10/16	1,786.58
10/26	127	50.00			10/23	2,256.58
10/29	128	135.00			10/25	2,226.58
					10/26	2,176.58
					10/29	2,041.58
					10/31	2,050.00

Symbols: **CM**–Credit Memo   **EC**–Error Correction   **NSF**–Non-Sufficient Funds   **SC**–Service Charge
          DM–Debit Memo   **IN**–Interest Earned   **EFT**–Electronic Funds Transfer   **OD**–Overdraft

< Reconcile the account immediately. >

Point: Many banks separately report other debits and credits apart from checks and deposits.

reduces the balance. A copy of each debit memorandum is usually sent with the statement (again, this information is often available earlier via online access and notifications).

Transactions that increase the depositor's account include amounts the bank collects on behalf of the depositor and the corrections of previous errors. Credit memoranda notify the depositor of all increases when they are recorded. A copy of each credit memorandum is often sent with the bank statement. Banks that pay interest on checking accounts often compute the amount of interest earned on the average cash balance and credit it to the depositor's account each period. In Exhibit 6.6, the bank credits $8.42 of interest to the account.

Bank Reconciliation

When a company deposits all cash receipts and makes all cash payments (except petty cash) by check, it can use the bank statement for proving the accuracy of its cash records. This is done using a **bank reconciliation,** which is a report explaining any differences between the checking account balance according to the depositor's records and the balance reported on the bank statement. The figure below reflects this process, which we describe in the following sections.

P3 Prepare a bank
     reconciliation.

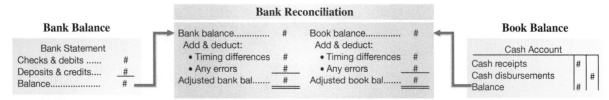

Bank Reconciliation

Bank Balance

Bank Statement
Checks & debits ......   #
Deposits & credits....   #
Balance...................   #

Bank balance.............   #
Add & deduct:
 • Timing differences   #
 • Any errors   #
Adjusted bank bal.......   #

Book balance.............   #
Add & deduct:
 • Timing differences   #
 • Any errors   #
Adjusted book bal.......   #

Book Balance

Cash Account
Cash receipts   #
Cash disbursements   #
Balance   #

Purpose of Bank Reconciliation   The balance of a checking account reported on the bank statement rarely equals the balance in the depositor's accounting records. This is usually due to information that one party has that the other does not. We must therefore prove the accuracy of both the depositor's records and those of the bank. This means we must *reconcile* the

274 Chapter 6 Cash and Internal Controls

two balances and explain or account for any differences in them. Among the factors causing the bank statement balance to differ from the depositor's book balance are these:

- **Outstanding checks.** **Outstanding checks** are checks written (or drawn) by the depositor, deducted on the depositor's records, and sent to the payees but not yet received by the bank for payment at the bank statement date.

- **Deposits in transit** (also called outstanding deposits). **Deposits in transit** are deposits made and recorded by the depositor but not yet recorded on the bank statement. For example, companies can make deposits (in the night depository) at the end of a business day after the bank is closed. If such a deposit occurred on a bank statement date, it would not appear on this period's statement. The bank would record such a deposit on the next business day, and it would appear on the next period's bank statement. Deposits mailed to the bank near the end of a period also can be in transit and unrecorded when the statement is prepared.

- **Deductions for uncollectible items and for services.** A company sometimes deposits another party's check that is uncollectible (usually meaning the balance in that party's account is not large enough to cover the check). This check is called a *nonsufficient funds (NSF)* check. The bank would have initially credited the depositor's account for the amount of the check. When the bank learns the check is uncollectible, it debits (reduces) the depositor's account for the amount of that check. The bank may also charge the depositor a fee for processing an uncollectible check and notify the depositor of the deduction by sending a debit memorandum. The depositor should record each deduction when a debit memorandum is received, but an entry is sometimes not made until the bank reconciliation is prepared. Other possible bank charges to a depositor's account that are first reported on a bank statement include printing new checks and service fees.

- **Additions for collections and for interest.** Banks sometimes act as collection agents for their depositors by collecting notes and other items. Banks can also receive electronic funds transfers to the depositor's account. When a bank collects an item, it is added to the depositor's account, less any service fee. The bank also sends a credit memorandum to notify the depositor of the transaction. When the memorandum is received, the depositor should record it; yet it sometimes remains unrecorded until the bank reconciliation is prepared. The bank statement also includes a credit for any interest earned.

- **Errors.** Both banks and depositors can make errors. Bank errors might not be discovered until the depositor prepares the bank reconciliation. Also, depositor errors are sometimes discovered when the bank balance is reconciled. Error testing includes: (a) comparing deposits on the bank statement with deposits in the accounting records and (b) comparing canceled checks on the bank statement with checks recorded in the accounting records.

Illustration of a Bank Reconciliation We follow nine steps in preparing the bank reconciliation. It is helpful to refer to the bank reconciliation in Exhibit 6.7 when studying steps ① through ⑨.

Forms of Check Fraud (CkFraud.org)

- Forged signatures—legitimate blank checks with fake payer signature
- Forged endorsements—stolen check that is endorsed and cashed by someone other than the payee
- Counterfeit checks—fraudulent checks with fake payer signature
- Altered checks—legitimate check altered (such as changed payee or amount) to benefit perpetrator
- Check kiting—deposit check from one bank account (without sufficient funds) into a second bank account

Point: Small businesses with few employees often allow recordkeepers to both write checks and keep the general ledger. If this is done, it is essential that the owner do the bank reconciliation.

Point: The person preparing the bank reconciliation should not be responsible for processing cash receipts, managing checks, or maintaining cash records.

EXHIBIT 6.7

Bank Reconciliation

	VIDEOBUSTER Bank Reconciliation October 31, 2013						
①	Bank statement balance		$ 2,050.00	⑤	Book balance		$ 1,404.58
②	Add			⑥	Add		
	Deposit of Oct. 31 in transit		145.00		Collect $500 note less $15 fee	$485.00	
			2,195.00		Interest earned	8.42	493.42
③	Deduct						1,898.00
	Outstanding checks			⑦	Deduct		
	No. 124	$150.00			Check printing charge	23.00	
	No. 126	200.00	350.00		NSF check plus service fee	30.00	53.00
④	**Adjusted bank balance**		$1,845.00	⑧	Adjusted book balance		$1,845.00
			↑		⑨ Balances are equal (reconciled)		↑

1 Identify the bank statement balance of the cash account (*balance per bank*). VideoBuster's bank balance is $2,050.

2 Identify and list any unrecorded deposits and any bank errors understating the bank balance. Add them to the bank balance. VideoBuster's $145 deposit placed in the bank's night depository on October 31 is not recorded on its bank statement.

3 Identify and list any outstanding checks and any bank errors overstating the bank balance. Deduct them from the bank balance. VideoBuster's comparison of canceled checks with its books shows two checks outstanding: No. 124 for $150 and No. 126 for $200.

4 Compute the *adjusted bank balance,* also called the *corrected* or *reconciled balance.*

5 Identify the company's book balance of the cash account (*balance per book*). VideoBuster's book balance is $1,404.58.

6 Identify and list any unrecorded credit memoranda from the bank, any interest earned, and errors understating the book balance. Add them to the book balance. VideoBuster's bank statement includes a credit memorandum showing the bank collected a note receivable for the company on October 23. The note's proceeds of $500 (minus a $15 collection fee) are credited to the company's account. VideoBuster's bank statement also shows a credit of $8.42 for interest earned on the average cash balance. There was no prior notification of this item, and it is not yet recorded.

7 Identify and list any unrecorded debit memoranda from the bank, any service charges, and errors overstating the book balance. Deduct them from the book balance. Debits on Video-Buster's bank statement that are not yet recorded include (a) a $23 charge for check printing and (b) an NSF check for $20 plus a related $10 processing fee. (The NSF check is dated October 16 and was included in the book balance.)

8 Compute the *adjusted book balance,* also called *corrected* or *reconciled balance.*

9 Verify that the two adjusted balances from steps 4 and 8 are equal. If so, they are reconciled. If not, check for accuracy and missing data to achieve reconciliation.

Point: Outstanding checks are identified by comparing canceled checks on the bank statement with checks recorded. This includes identifying any outstanding checks listed on the *previous* period's bank reconciliation that are not included in the canceled checks on this period's bank statement.

Point: Adjusting entries can be combined into one compound entry.

Adjusting Entries from a Bank Reconciliation A bank reconciliation often identifies unrecorded items that need recording by the company. In VideoBuster's reconciliation, the adjusted balance of $1,845 is the correct balance as of October 31. But the company's accounting records show a $1,404.58 balance. We must prepare journal entries to adjust the book balance to the correct balance. It is important to remember that only the items reconciling the *book balance* require adjustment. A review of Exhibit 6.7 indicates that four entries are required for VideoBuster.

Collection of note. The first entry is to record the proceeds of its note receivable collected by the bank less the expense of having the bank perform that service.

Oct. 31	Cash	485	
	Collection Expense	15	
	Notes Receivable.........................		500
	To record the collection fee and proceeds		
	for a note collected by the bank.		

Assets = Liabilities + Equity
+485   −15
−500

Interest earned. The second entry records interest credited to its account by the bank.

Oct. 31	Cash	8.42	
	Interest Revenue		8.42
	To record interest earned on the cash		
	balance in the checking account.		

Assets = Liabilities + Equity
+8.42   +8.42

Check printing. The third entry records expenses for the check printing charge.

Oct. 31	Miscellaneous Expenses..........................	23	
	Cash		23
	Check printing charge.		

Assets = Liabilities + Equity
−23   −23

NSF check. The fourth entry records the NSF check that is returned as uncollectible. The $20 check was originally received from T. Woods in payment of his account and then deposited. The

276   Chapter 6   Cash and Internal Controls

Point: The company will try to collect the entire NSF amount of $30 from customer.

Assets = Liabilities + Equity
+30
−30

Point: The Demo Problem 1 shows an adjusting entry for an error correction.

bank charged $10 for handling the NSF check and deducted $30 total from VideoBuster's account. This means the entry must reverse the effects of the original entry made when the check was received and must record (add) the $10 bank fee.

Oct. 31	Accounts Receivable—T. Woods	30	
	Cash		30
	To charge Woods' account for $20 NSF check and $10 bank fee.		

Cash			
Unadj. bal.	1,404.58		
⑥	485.00	⑦	23.00
⑥	8.42	⑦	30.00
Adj. bal.	1,845.00		

After these four entries are recorded, the book balance of cash is adjusted to the correct amount of $1,845 (computed as $1,404.58 + $485 + $8.42 − $23 − $30). The Cash T-account to the side shows the same computation, where entries are keyed to the numerical codes in Exhibit 6.7.

Decision Insight

Fraud   A survey reports that 74% of employees had 'personally seen' or had 'firsthand knowledge of' fraud or misconduct within the past year. Another survey found that fraudsters exploited weak internal controls in 74% of the frauds—up from 47% four years earlier—see graphic (KPMG 2011). ▨

Percent Citing These Root Causes to Override Controls

	2007 Survey	2011 Survey
Weak internal controls exploited	49%	74%
Reckless dishonesty regardless of controls	36%	15%
Collusion to circumvent good controls	15%	11%

Quick Check

    Answers — p. 286

13. What is a bank statement?
14. What is the meaning of the phrase *to reconcile a bank balance?*
15. Why do we reconcile the bank statement balance of cash and the depositor's book balance of cash?
16. List at least two items affecting the *bank balance* side of a bank reconciliation and indicate whether the items are added or subtracted.
17. List at least three items affecting the *book balance* side of a bank reconciliation and indicate whether the items are added or subtracted.

 GLOBAL VIEW

This section discusses similarities and differences between U.S. GAAP and IFRS regarding internal controls and in the accounting and reporting of cash.

Internal Control Purposes, Principles, and Procedures   Both U.S. GAAP and IFRS aim for high-quality financial reporting. That aim translates into enhanced internal controls worldwide. Specifically, the purposes and principles of internal control systems are fundamentally the same across the globe. However, culture and other realities suggest different emphases on the mix of control procedures, and some sensitivity to different customs and environments when establishing that mix. Nevertheless, the discussion in this chapter applies internationally. Nokia provides the following description of its control activities.

NOKIA

> Nokia has an internal audit function that acts as an independent appraisal function by examining and evaluating the adequacy and effectiveness of the company's system of internal control.

Control of Cash Accounting definitions for cash are similar for U.S. GAAP and IFRS. The need for control of cash is universal and applies globally. This means that companies worldwide desire to apply cash management procedures as explained in this chapter and aim to control both cash receipts and disbursements. Accordingly, systems that employ tools such as cash monitoring mechanisms, verification of documents, and petty cash processes are applied worldwide. The basic techniques explained in this chapter are part of those control procedures.

Banking Activities as Controls There is a global demand for banking services, bank statements, and bank reconciliations. To the extent feasible, companies utilize banking services as part of their effective control procedures. Further, bank statements are similarly used along with bank reconciliations to control and monitor cash.

 IFRS

Internal controls are crucial to companies that convert from U.S. GAAP to IFRS. Major risks include misstatement of financial information and fraud. Other risks are ineffective communication of the impact of this change for investors, creditors and others, and management's inability to certify the effectiveness of controls over financial reporting. ■

Days' Sales Uncollected **Decision Analysis**

An important part of cash management is monitoring the receipt of cash from receivables. If customers and others who owe money to a company are delayed in payment, then that company can find it difficult to pay its obligations when they are due. A company's customers are crucial partners in its cash management. Many companies attract customers by selling to them on credit. This means that cash receipts from customers are delayed until accounts receivable are collected.

One measure of how quickly a company can convert its accounts receivable into cash is the **days' sales uncollected,** also called *days' sales in receivables*. This measure is computed by dividing the current balance of receivables by net credit sales over the year just completed and then multiplying by 365 (number of days in a year). Since net credit sales usually are not reported to external users, the net sales (or revenues) figure is commonly used in the computation as in Exhibit 6.8.

A1 Compute the days' sales uncollected ratio and use it to assess liquidity.

$$\text{Days' sales uncollected} = \frac{\text{Accounts receivable}}{\text{Net sales}} \times 365$$

EXHIBIT 6.8

Days' Sales Uncollected

We use days' sales uncollected to estimate how much time is likely to pass before the current amount of accounts receivable is received in cash. For evaluation purposes, we need to compare this estimate to that for other companies in the same industry. We also make comparisons between current and prior periods.

To illustrate, we select data from the annual reports of two toy manufacturers, Hasbro and Mattel. Their days' sales uncollected figures are shown in Exhibit 6.9.

EXHIBIT 6.9

Analysis Using Days' Sales Uncollected

Company	Figure ($ millions)	2011	2010	2009	2008	2007
Hasbro	Accounts receivable	$1,035	$961	$1,039	$612	$655
	Net sales	$4,286	$4,002	$4,068	$4,022	$3,838
	Days' sales uncollected	88 days	88 days	93 days	56 days	62 days
Mattel	Accounts receivable	$1,247	$1,146	$749	$874	$991
	Net sales	$6,266	$5,856	$5,431	$5,918	$5,970
	Days' sales uncollected	73 days	71 days	50 days	54 days	61 days

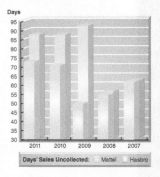

Days' sales uncollected for Hasbro in 2011 is computed as ($1,035/$4,286) × 365 days = 88 days. This means that it will take about 88 days to collect cash from ending accounts receivable. This number reflects one or more of the following factors: a company's ability to collect receivables, customer financial health, customer payment strategies, and discount terms. To further assess days' sales uncollected for Hasbro, we compare it to four prior years and to those of Mattel. We see that Hasbro's days' sales uncollected has worsened since 2008 as it takes much longer to collect its receivables relative to 2007 and 2008. In comparison, Mattel has also worsened from 50 days in 2009 up to 73 days in 2011. For all years, Mattel is superior to Hasbro on this measure of cash management. The less time that money is tied up in receivables often translates into increased profitability.

Decision Maker

Sales Representative   The sales staff is told to take action to help reduce days' sales uncollected for cash management purposes. What can you, a salesperson, do to reduce days' sales uncollected? ■   [Answer—p. 285]

DEMONSTRATION PROBLEM 1

Prepare a bank reconciliation for Jamboree Enterprises for the month ended November 30, 2013. The following information is available to reconcile Jamboree Enterprises' book balance of cash with its bank statement balance as of November 30, 2013:

a. After all posting is complete on November 30, the company's book balance of Cash has a $16,380 debit balance, but its bank statement shows a $38,520 balance.

b. Checks No. 2024 for $4,810 and No. 2026 for $5,000 are outstanding.

c. In comparing the canceled checks on the bank statement with the entries in the accounting records, it is found that Check No. 2025 in payment of rent is correctly drawn for $1,000 but is erroneously entered in the accounting records as $880.

Point: Generally, the party that is not the initial recorder of an item, but is later informed, includes that item on its "book" of the bank reconciliation. For example, the bank records an NSF check and then informs the company. The company, as not the initial recorder of the item, reports it on the book side of its reconciliation.

d. The November 30 deposit of $17,150 was placed in the night depository after banking hours on that date, and this amount does not appear on the bank statement.

e. In reviewing the bank statement, a check written by Jumbo Enterprises in the amount of $160 was erroneously drawn against Jamboree's account.

f. A credit memorandum enclosed with the bank statement indicates that the bank collected a $30,000 note and $900 of related interest on Jamboree's behalf. This transaction was not recorded by Jamboree prior to receiving the statement.

g. A debit memorandum for $1,100 lists a $1,100 NSF check received from a customer, Marilyn Welch. Jamboree had not recorded the return of this check before receiving the statement.

h. Bank service charges for November total $40. These charges were not recorded by Jamboree before receiving the statement.

PLANNING THE SOLUTION

- Set up a bank reconciliation with a bank side and a book side (as in Exhibit 6.7). Leave room to both add and deduct items. Each column will result in a reconciled, equal balance.
- Examine each item *a* through *h* to determine whether it affects the book or the bank balance and whether it should be added or deducted from the bank or book balance.
- After all items are analyzed, complete the reconciliation and arrive at a reconciled balance between the bank side and the book side.
- For each reconciling item on the book side, prepare an adjusting entry. Additions to the book side require an adjusting entry that debits Cash. Deductions on the book side require an adjusting entry that credits Cash.

SOLUTION TO DEMONSTRATION PROBLEM 1

JAMBOREE ENTERPRISES
Bank Reconciliation
November 30, 2013

Bank statement balance		$ 38,520	Book balance			$ 16,380
Add			Add			
Deposit of Nov. 30	$17,150		Collection of note	$30,000		
Bank error (Jumbo)	160	17,310	Interest earned	900	30,900	
		55,830			47,280	
Deduct			Deduct			
Outstanding checks			NSF check (M. Welch)	1,100		
No. 2024	4,810		Recording error (# 2025) ...	120		
No. 2026	5,000	9,810	Service charge	40	1,260	
Adjusted bank balance ...		$46,020	Adjusted book balance		$46,020	

Required Adjusting Entries for Jamboree

Nov. 30	Cash	30,900	
	Notes Receivable		30,000
	Interest Earned		900
	To record collection of note with interest.		
Nov. 30	Accounts Receivable—M. Welch	1,100	
	Cash		1,100
	To reinstate account due from an NSF check.		
Nov. 30	Rent Expense	120	
	Cash		120
	To correct recording error on check no. 2025.		
Nov. 30	Bank Service Charges	40	
	Cash		40
	To record bank service charges.		

Point: Error correction can alternatively involve (1) reversing the error entry, and (2) recording the correct entry.

DEMONSTRATION PROBLEM 2

Bacardi Company established a $150 petty cash fund with Eminem as the petty cashier. When the fund balance reached $19 cash, Eminem prepared a petty cash payment report, which follows.

Petty Cash Payments Report				
Receipt No.	**Account Charged**		**Approved by**	**Received by**
12	Delivery Expense	$ 29	Eminem	A. Smirnoff
13	Merchandise Inventory	18	Eminem	J. Daniels
15	(Omitted)	32	Eminem	C. Carlsberg
16	Miscellaneous Expense	41	(Omitted)	J. Walker
	Total	$120		

Required

1. Identify four internal control weaknesses from the payment report.

2. Prepare general journal entries to record:
   a. Establishment of the petty cash fund.
   b. Reimbursement of the fund. (Assume for this part only that petty cash receipt no. 15 was issued for miscellaneous expenses.)

3. What is the Petty Cash account balance immediately before reimbursement? Immediately after reimbursement?

SOLUTION TO DEMONSTRATION PROBLEM 2

1. Four internal control weaknesses are
   a. Petty cash ticket no. 14 is missing. Its omission raises questions about the petty cashier's management of the fund.
   b. The $19 cash balance means that $131 has been withdrawn ($150 − $19 = $131). However, the total amount of the petty cash receipts is only $120 ($29 + $18 + $32 + $41). The fund is $11 short of cash ($131 − $120 = $11). Was petty cash receipt no. 14 issued for $11? Management should investigate.
   c. The petty cashier (Eminem) did not sign petty cash receipt no. 16. This omission could have been an oversight on his part or he might not have authorized the payment. Management should investigate.
   d. Petty cash receipt no. 15 does not indicate which account to charge. This omission could have been an oversight on the petty cashier's part. Management could check with C. Carlsberg and the petty cashier (Eminem) about the transaction. Without further information, debit Miscellaneous Expense.

2. Petty cash general journal entries.

a. Entry to establish the petty cash fund.

Petty Cash	150	
Cash		150

b. Entry to reimburse the fund.

Delivery Expense	29	
Merchandise Inventory	18	
Miscellaneous Expense ($41 + $32)	73	
Cash Over and Short	11	
Cash		131

3. The Petty Cash account balance *always* equals its fund balance, in this case $150. This account balance does not change unless the fund is increased or decreased.

APPENDIX

6A

Documentation and Verification

This appendix describes the important business documents of a voucher system of control.

Purchase Requisition   Department managers are usually not allowed to place orders directly with suppliers for control purposes. Instead, a department manager must inform the purchasing department of its needs by preparing and signing a **purchase requisition,** which lists the merchandise needed and requests that it be purchased—see Exhibit 6A.1. Two copies of the purchase requisition are sent to the purchasing department, which then sends one copy to the accounting department. When the accounting department receives a purchase requisition, it creates and maintains a voucher for this transaction. The requesting department keeps the third copy.

EXHIBIT 6A.1

Purchase Requisition

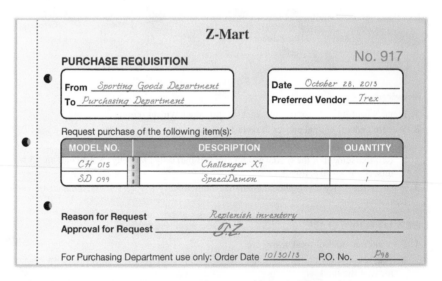

Purchase Order   A **purchase order** is a document the purchasing department uses to place an order with a **vendor** (seller or supplier). A purchase order authorizes a vendor to ship ordered merchandise at the stated price and terms—see Exhibit 6A.2. When the purchasing department receives a purchase requisition, it prepares at least five copies of a purchase order. The copies are distributed as follows: *copy 1* to the vendor as a purchase request and as authority to ship merchandise; *copy 2,* along with a copy of the purchase requisition, to the accounting department, where it is entered in the voucher and used in approving payment of the invoice; *copy 3* to the requesting department to inform its manager that action is being taken; *copy 4* to the receiving department without order quantity so it can compare with goods received and provide independent count of goods received; and *copy 5* retained on file by the purchasing department.

Z-Mart
10 Michigan Street
Chicago, Illinois 60521

PURCHASE ORDER

No. P98

To: Trex	
W9797 Cherry Road	
Antigo, Wisconsin 54409	

Date	10/30/13
FOB	Destination
Ship by	As soon as possible
Terms	2/15, n/30

Request shipment of the following item(s):

Model No.	Description	Quantity	Price	Amount
CH 015	Challenger X7	1	490	490
SD 099	SpeedDemon	1	710	710

All shipments and invoices must include purchase order number

J.W.

ORDERED BY

EXHIBIT 6A.2

Purchase Order

Point: Shipping terms and credit terms are shown on the purchase order.

Invoice   An **invoice** is an itemized statement of goods prepared by the vendor listing the customer's name, items sold, sales prices, and terms of sale. An invoice is also a bill sent to the buyer from the supplier. From the vendor's point of view, it is a *sales invoice*. The buyer, or **vendee,** treats it as a *purchase invoice*. When receiving a purchase order, the vendor ships the ordered merchandise to the buyer and includes or mails a copy of the invoice covering the shipment to the buyer. The invoice is sent to the buyer's accounting department where it is placed in the voucher. (Refer back to Exhibit 4.5, which shows Z-Mart's purchase invoice.)

Receiving Report   Many companies maintain a separate department to receive all merchandise and purchased assets. When each shipment arrives, this receiving department counts the goods and checks them for damage and agreement with the purchase order. It then prepares four or more copies of a **receiving report,** which is used within the company to notify the appropriate persons that ordered goods have been received and to describe the quantities and condition of the goods. One copy is sent to accounting and placed in the voucher. Copies are also sent to the requesting department and the purchasing department to notify them that the goods have arrived. The receiving department retains a copy in its files.

Invoice Approval   When a receiving report arrives, the accounting department should have copies of the following documents in the voucher: purchase requisition, purchase order, and invoice. With the information in these documents, the accounting department can record the purchase and approve its payment. In approving an invoice for payment, it checks and compares information across all documents. To facilitate this checking and to ensure that no step is omitted, it often uses an **invoice approval,** also called *check authorization*—see Exhibit 6A.3. An invoice approval is a checklist of steps necessary for approving an invoice for recording and payment. It is a separate document either filed in the voucher or preprinted (or stamped) on the voucher.

INVOICE APPROVAL

DOCUMENT		BY	DATE
Purchase requisition	917	TZ	10/28/13
Purchase order	P98	JW	10/30/13
Receiving report	R85	SK	11/03/13
Invoice:	4657		11/12/13
Price		JK	11/12/13
Calculations		JK	11/12/13
Terms		JK	11/12/13
Approved for payment		BC	

EXHIBIT 6A.3

Invoice Approval

As each step in the checklist is approved, the person initials the invoice approval and records the current date. Final approval implies the following steps have occurred:

1. **Requisition check:** Items on invoice are requested per purchase requisition.
2. **Purchase order check:** Items on invoice are ordered per purchase order.
3. **Receiving report check:** Items on invoice are received per receiving report.
4. **Invoice check: Price:** Invoice prices are as agreed with the vendor.
   Calculations: Invoice has no mathematical errors.
   Terms: Terms are as agreed with the vendor.

Voucher   Once an invoice has been checked and approved, the voucher is complete. A complete voucher is a record summarizing a transaction. Once the voucher certifies a transaction, it authorizes recording an obligation. A voucher also contains approval for paying the obligation on an appropriate date. The physical form of a voucher varies across companies. Many are designed so that the invoice and other related source documents are placed inside the voucher, which can be a folder.

Completion of a voucher usually requires a person to enter certain information on both the inside and outside of the voucher. Typical information required on the inside of a voucher is shown in Exhibit 6A.4, and that for the outside is shown in Exhibit 6A.5. This information is taken from the invoice and the supporting documents filed in the voucher. A complete voucher is sent to an authorized individual (often called an *auditor*). This person performs a final review, approves the accounts and amounts for debiting (called the *accounting distribution*), and authorizes recording of the voucher.

EXHIBIT 6A.4

Inside of a Voucher

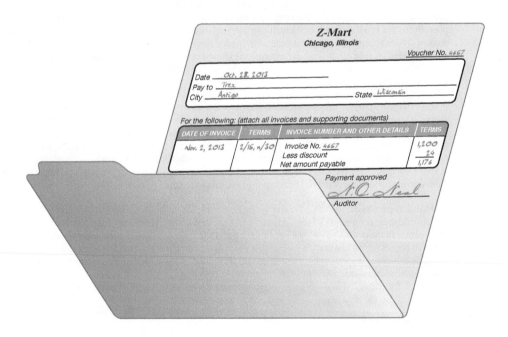

After a voucher is approved and recorded (in a journal called a **voucher register**), it is filed by its due date. A check is then sent on the payment date from the cashier, the voucher is marked "paid," and the voucher is sent to the accounting department and recorded (in a journal called the **check register**). The person issuing checks relies on the approved voucher and its signed supporting documents as proof that an obligation has been incurred and must be paid. The purchase requisition and purchase order confirm the purchase was authorized. The receiving report shows that items have been received, and the invoice approval form verifies that the invoice has been checked for errors. There is little chance for error and even less chance for fraud without collusion unless all the documents and signatures are forged.

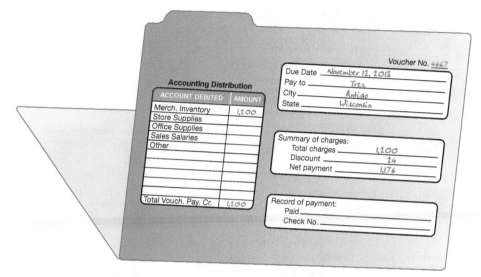

EXHIBIT 6A.5

Outside of a Voucher

Control of Purchase Discounts

6B

This appendix explains how a company can better control its cash *disbursements* to take advantage of favorable purchases discounts. Chapter 4 described the entries to record the receipt and payment of an invoice for a merchandise purchase with and without discount terms. Those entries were prepared under what is called the **gross method** of recording purchases, which initially records the invoice at its *gross* amount ignoring any cash discount.

P5 Apply the net method to control purchase discounts.

The **net method** is another means of recording purchases, which initially records the invoice at its *net* amount of any cash discount. The net method gives management an advantage in controlling and monitoring cash payments involving purchase discounts.

To explain, when invoices are recorded at *gross* amounts, the amount of any discounts taken is deducted from the balance of the Merchandise Inventory account when cash payment is made. This means that the amount of any discounts lost is not reported in any account or on the income statement. Lost discounts recorded in this way are unlikely to come to the attention of management. When purchases are recorded at *net* amounts, a **Discounts Lost** expense account is recorded and brought to management's attention. Management can then seek to identify the reason for discounts lost such as oversight, carelessness, or unfavorable terms. (Chapter 4 explains how managers assess whether a discount is favorable or not.)

Perpetual Inventory System   To illustrate, assume that a company purchases merchandise on November 2 at a $1,200 invoice price with terms of 2/10, n/30. Its November 2 entries under the gross and net methods are

Gross Method—Perpetual			Net Method—Perpetual		
Merchandise Inventory	1,200		Merchandise Inventory	1,176	
Accounts Payable		1,200	Accounts Payable		1,176

If the invoice is paid on November 12 within the discount period, it records the following:

Gross Method—Perpetual			Net Method—Perpetual		
Accounts Payable	1,200		Accounts Payable	1,176	
Merchandise Inventory		24	Cash		1,176
Cash		1,176			

If the invoice is *not* paid within the discount period, it records the following November 12 entry (which is the date corresponding to the end of the discount period):

Gross Method—Perpetual			Net Method—Perpetual		
No entry			Discounts Lost	24	
			Accounts Payable		24

Then, when the invoice is later paid on December 2, outside the discount period, it records the following:

Gross Method—Perpetual			Net Method—Perpetual		
Accounts Payable	1,200		Accounts Payable	1,200	
Cash......................		1,200	Cash		1,200

(The discount lost can be recorded when the cash payment is made with a single entry. However, in this case, when financial statements are prepared after a discount is lost and before the cash payment is made, an adjusting entry is required to recognize any unrecorded discount lost in the period when incurred.)

Periodic Inventory System   The preceding entries assume a perpetual inventory system. If a company is using a periodic system, its November 2 entries under the gross and net methods are

Gross Method—Periodic			Net Method—Periodic		
Purchases......................	1,200		Purchases	1,176	
Accounts Payable		1,200	Accounts Payable		1,176

If the invoice is paid on November 12 within the discount period, it records the following:

Gross Method—Periodic			Net Method—Periodic		
Accounts Payable	1,200		Accounts Payable	1,176	
Purchases Discounts		24	Cash		1,176
Cash......................		1,176			

If the invoice is *not* paid within the discount period, it records the following November 12 entry:

Gross Method—Periodic			Net Method—Periodic		
No entry			Discounts Lost	24	
			Accounts Payable		24

Then, when the invoice is later paid on December 2, outside the discount period, it records the following:

Gross Method—Periodic			Net Method—Periodic		
Accounts Payable	1,200		Accounts Payable	1,200	
Cash		1,200	Cash		1,200

Summary

C1   Define internal control and identify its purpose and principles. An internal control system consists of the policies and procedures managers use to protect assets, ensure reliable accounting, promote efficient operations, and urge adherence to company policies. It can prevent avoidable losses and help managers both plan operations and monitor company and human performance. Principles of good internal control include establishing responsibilities, maintaining adequate records, insuring assets and bonding employees, separating recordkeeping from custody of assets, dividing responsibilities for related transactions, applying technological controls, and performing regular independent reviews.

C2   Define cash and cash equivalents and explain how to report them. Cash includes currency, coins, and amounts on (or acceptable for) deposit in checking and savings accounts. Cash equivalents are short-term, highly liquid investment assets readily convertible to a known cash amount and sufficiently close to their maturity date so that market value is not sensitive to interest rate changes. Cash and cash equivalents are liquid assets because they are readily converted into other assets or can be used to pay for goods, services, or liabilities.

A1   Compute the days' sales uncollected ratio and use it to assess liquidity. Many companies attract customers by selling to them on credit. This means that cash receipts from customers are delayed until accounts receivable are collected. Users want to know how quickly a company can convert its accounts receivable into cash. The days' sales uncollected ratio, one measure reflecting company liquidity, is computed by dividing the ending balance of receivables by annual net sales, and then multiplying by 365.

P1 **Apply internal control to cash receipts and disbursements.** Internal control of cash receipts ensures that all cash received is properly recorded and deposited. Attention focuses on two important types of cash receipts: over-the-counter and by mail. Good internal control for over-the-counter cash receipts includes use of a cash register, customer review, use of receipts, a permanent transaction record, and separation of the custody of cash from its record-keeping. Good internal control for cash receipts by mail includes at least two people assigned to open mail and a listing of each sender's name, amount, and explanation. (Banks offer several services that promote the control and safeguarding of cash.)

P2 **Explain and record petty cash fund transactions.** Petty cash disbursements are payments of small amounts for items such as postage, courier fees, minor repairs, and supplies. A company usually sets up one or more petty cash funds. A petty cash fund cashier is responsible for safekeeping the cash, making payments from this fund, and keeping receipts and records. A Petty Cash account is debited only when the fund is established or increased in amount. When the fund is replenished, petty cash disbursements are recorded with debits to expense (or asset) accounts and a credit to cash.

P3 **Prepare a bank reconciliation.** A bank reconciliation proves the accuracy of the depositor's and the bank's records. The bank statement balance is adjusted for items such as outstanding checks and unrecorded deposits made on or before the bank statement date but not reflected on the statement. The book balance is adjusted for items such as service charges, bank collections for the depositor, and interest earned on the account.

P4ᴬ **Describe the use of documentation and verification to control cash disbursements.** A voucher system is a set of procedures and approvals designed to control cash disbursements and acceptance of obligations. The voucher system of control relies on several important documents, including the voucher and its supporting files. A key factor in this system is that only approved departments and individuals are authorized to incur certain obligations.

P5ᴮ **Apply the net method to control purchase discounts.** The net method aids management in monitoring and controlling purchase discounts. When invoices are recorded at gross amounts, the amount of discounts taken is deducted from the balance of the Inventory account. This means that the amount of any discounts lost is not reported in any account and is unlikely to come to the attention of management. When purchases are recorded at net amounts, a Discounts Lost account is brought to management's attention as an operating expense. Management can then seek to identify the reason for discounts lost, such as oversight, carelessness, or unfavorable terms.

Guidance Answers to Decision Maker and Decision Ethics

Entrepreneur To achieve proper separation of duties, a minimum of three employees are required. Transaction authorization, recording, and asset custody are ideally handled by three employees. Many small businesses do not employ three workers. In such cases, an owner must exercise more oversight to make sure that the lack of separation of duties does not result in fraudulent transactions.

Sales Representative A salesperson can take several steps to reduce days' sales uncollected. These include (1) decreasing the ratio of sales on account to total sales by encouraging more cash sales, (2) identifying customers most delayed in their payments and encouraging earlier payments or cash sales, and (3) applying stricter credit policies to eliminate credit sales to customers that never pay.

Guidance Answers to Quick Checks

1. (c)
2. Technology reduces processing errors. It also allows more extensive testing of records, limits the amount of hard evidence, and highlights the importance of separation of duties.
3. When employees are forced to take vacations, their ability to hide any fraudulent behavior decreases because others must perform the vacationers' duties. A replacement employee potentially can uncover fraudulent behavior or falsified records. A forced vacation policy is especially important for employees in sensitive positions of handling money or in control of easily transferable assets.
4. A company holds liquid assets so that it can purchase other assets, buy services, and pay obligations.
5. It owns cash equivalents because they yield a return greater than what cash earns (and are readily exchanged for cash).
6. Examples of cash equivalents are 90-day (or less) U.S. Treasury bills, money market funds, and commercial paper (notes).
7. (a)
8. A voucher system is used when an owner/manager can no longer control purchasing procedures through personal supervision and direct participation.
9. If all cash payments are made by check, numerous checks for small amounts must be written. Since this practice is expensive and time-consuming, a petty cash fund is often established for making small (immaterial) cash payments.
10. If the petty cash fund is not reimbursed at the end of an accounting period, the transactions involving petty cash are not yet recorded and the petty cash asset is overstated.
11. First, petty cash transactions are recorded when the petty cash fund is reimbursed. Second, reimbursement provides cash to allow the fund to continue being used. Third, reimbursement identifies any cash shortage or overage in the fund.

12. If we accommodate the custodian's request, we reduce effectiveness of this audit procedure. If the custodian uses the lunch period to fix any shortages or irregularities in the petty cash fund, we risk not discovering such problems when we defer our audit.

13. A bank statement is a report prepared by the bank describing the activities in a depositor's account.

14. To reconcile a bank balance means to explain the difference between the cash balance in the depositor's accounting records and the cash balance on the bank statement.

15. The purpose of the bank reconciliation is to determine whether the bank or the depositor has made any errors and whether the

bank has entered any transactions affecting the account that the depositor has not recorded.

16. Unrecorded deposits—added
Outstanding checks—subtracted

17. Interest earned—added   Debit memos—subtracted
Credit memos—added   NSF checks—subtracted
                            Bank service charges—subtracted

Key Terms

Bank reconciliation (p. 273)	Deposits in transit (p. 274)	Principles of internal control (p. 259)
Bank statement (p. 272)	Discounts lost (p. 283)	Purchase order (p. 280)
Canceled checks (p. 272)	Electronic funds transfer (EFT) (p. 271)	Purchase requisition (p. 280)
Cash (p. 263)	Gross method (p. 283)	Receiving report (p. 281)
Cash equivalents (p. 264)	Internal control system (p. 258)	Sarbanes-Oxley Act (p. 258)
Cash Over and Short (p. 265)	Invoice (p. 281)	Section 404 (of SOX) (p. 259)
Check (p. 271)	Invoice approval (p. 281)	Signature card (p. 271)
Check register (p. 282)	Liquid assets (p. 263)	Vendee (p. 281)
Committee of Sponsoring Organizations (COSO) (p. 259)	Liquidity (p. 263)	Vendor (p. 280)
Days' sales uncollected (p. 277)	Net method (p. 283)	Voucher (p. 267)
Deposit ticket (p. 271)	Outstanding checks (p. 274)	Voucher register (p. 282)
	Petty cash (p. 268)	Voucher system (p. 266)

Multiple Choice Quiz   Answers on p. 299   mhhe.com/wildFINMAN5e

Additional Quiz Questions are available at the book's Website.

1. A company needs to replenish its $500 petty cash fund. Its petty cash box has $75 cash and petty cash receipts of $420. The journal entry to replenish the fund includes
   a. A debit to Cash for $75.
   b. A credit to Cash for $75.
   c. A credit to Petty Cash for $420.
   d. A credit to Cash Over and Short for $5.
   e. A debit to Cash Over and Short for $5.

2. The following information is available for Hapley Company:
   • The November 30 bank statement shows a $1,895 balance.
   • The general ledger shows a $1,742 balance at November 30.
   • A $795 deposit placed in the bank's night depository on November 30 does not appear on the November 30 bank statement.
   • Outstanding checks amount to $638 at November 30.
   • A customer's $335 note was collected by the bank in November. A collection fee of $15 was deducted by the bank and the difference deposited in Hapley's account.
   • A bank service charge of $10 is deducted by the bank and appears on the November 30 bank statement.

   How will the customer's note appear on Hapley's November 30 bank reconciliation?
   a. $320 appears as an addition to the book balance of cash.
   b. $320 appears as a deduction from the book balance of cash.
   c. $320 appears as an addition to the bank balance of cash.

   d. $320 appears as a deduction from the bank balance of cash.
   e. $335 appears as an addition to the bank balance of cash.

3. Using the information from question 2, what is the reconciled balance on Hapley's November 30 bank reconciliation?
   a. $2,052
   b. $1,895
   c. $1,742
   d. $2,201
   e. $1,184

4. A company had net sales of $84,000 and accounts receivable of $6,720. Its days' sales uncollected is
   a. 3.2 days
   b. 18.4 days
   c. 230.0 days
   d. 29.2 days
   e. 12.5 days

5.[B] A company records its purchases using the net method. On August 1, it purchases merchandise on account for $6,000 with terms of 2/10, n/30. The August 1 journal entry to record this transaction includes a
   a. Debit to Merchandise Inventory for $6,000.
   b. Debit to Merchandise Inventory for $5,880.
   c. Debit to Merchandise Inventory for $120.
   d. Debit to Accounts Payable for $5,880.
   e. Credit to Accounts Payable for $6,000.

A(B) *Superscript letter A(B) denotes assignments based on Appendix 6A (6B).*

Icon denotes assignments that involve decision making.

Discussion Questions

1. List the seven broad principles of internal control.
2. Internal control procedures are important in every business, but at what stage in the development of a business do they become especially critical?
3. Why should responsibility for related transactions be divided among different departments or individuals?
4. Why should the person who keeps the records of an asset not be the person responsible for its custody?
5. When a store purchases merchandise, why are individual departments not allowed to directly deal with suppliers?
6. What are the limitations of internal controls?
7. Which of the following assets is most liquid? Which is least liquid? Inventory, building, accounts receivable, or cash.
8. What is a petty cash receipt? Who should sign it?
9. Why should cash receipts be deposited on the day of receipt?
10. Polaris' statement of cash flows in Appendix A **Polaris** describes changes in cash and cash equivalents for the year ended December 31, 2011. What total amount is provided (used) by investing activities? What amount is provided (used) by financing activities?
11. Refer to **Arctic Cat**'s financial statements in **Arctic Cat** Appendix A. Identify Arctic Cat's net earnings (income) for the year ended March 31, 2011. Is its net earnings equal to the increase in cash and cash equivalents for the year? Explain the difference between net earnings and the increase in cash and cash equivalents.
12. Refer to **KTM**'s balance sheet in Appendix A. **KTM** How does its cash (titled "liquid assets") compare with its other current assets (both in amount and percent) as of December 31, 2011? Compare and assess its cash at December 31, 2011, with its cash at December 31, 2010.
13. **Piaggio**'s balance sheet in Appendix A re- **PIAGGIO** ports that cash and equivalents decreased during the year ended December 31, 2011. Identify the cash generated (or used) by operating activities, by investing activities, and by financing (funding) activities.

connect

An internal control system consists of all policies and procedures used to protect assets, ensure reliable accounting, promote efficient operations, and urge adherence to company policies.

1. What is the main objective of internal control procedures? How is that objective achieved?
2. Why should recordkeeping for assets be separated from custody over those assets?
3. Why should the responsibility for a transaction be divided between two or more individuals or departments?

QUICK STUDY

QS 6-1
Internal control objectives
C1

Good accounting systems help in managing cash and controlling who has access to it.

1. What items are included in the category of cash?
2. What items are included in the category of cash equivalents?
3. What does the term *liquidity* refer to?

QS 6-2
Cash and equivalents
C2

A good system of internal control for cash provides adequate procedures for protecting both cash receipts and cash disbursements.

1. What are three basic guidelines that help achieve this protection?
2. Identify two control systems or procedures for cash disbursements.

QS 6-3
Internal control for cash
P1

---

1. For each of the following items, indicate whether its amount (i) affects the bank or book side of a bank reconciliation and (ii) represents an addition or a subtraction in a bank reconciliation.

   a. Interest on cash balance   d. Outstanding checks   g. Outstanding deposits
   b. Bank service charges   e. Credit memos
   c. Debit memos   f. NSF checks
2. Which of the items in part 1 require an adjusting journal entry?

QS 6-4
Bank reconciliation
P3

---

1. The petty cash fund of the Brooks Agency is established at $150. At the end of the current period, the fund contained $28 and had the following receipts: film rentals, $24, refreshments for meetings, $46 (both expenditures to be classified as Entertainment Expense); postage, $30; and printing, $22. Prepare journal entries to record (*a*) establishment of the fund and (*b*) reimbursement of the fund at the end of the current period.
2. Identify the two events that cause a Petty Cash account to be credited in a journal entry.

QS 6-5
Petty cash accounting
P2

QS 6-6

Bank reconciliation

P3

Nolan Company deposits all cash receipts on the day when they are received and it makes all cash payments by check. At the close of business on June 30, 2013, its Cash account shows an $22,352 debit balance. Nolan's June 30 bank statement shows $21,332 on deposit in the bank. Prepare a bank reconciliation for the Company using the following information.

a. Outstanding checks as of June 30 total $3,713.

b. The June 30 bank statement included a $41 debit memorandum for bank services; the company has not yet recorded the cost of these services.

c. In reviewing the bank statement, a $90 check written by the Company was mistakenly recorded in the company's books at $99.

d. June 30 cash receipts of $4,724 were placed in the bank's night depository after banking hours and were not recorded on the June 30 bank statement.

e. The bank statement included a $23 credit for interest earned on the cash in the bank.

QS 6-7

Reviewing bank statements

P3

An entrepreneur commented that a bank reconciliation may not be necessary as she regularly reviews her online bank statement for any unusual items and errors.

a. Describe how a bank reconciliation and an online review (or reading) of the bank statement are not equivalent.

b. Identify and explain at least two frauds or errors that would be uncovered through a bank reconciliation and that would *not* be uncovered through an online review of the bank statement.

QS 6-8

Days' sales uncollected

A1

The following annual account balances are taken from Armour Sports at December 31.

	2013	2012
Accounts receivable	$ 85,692	$ 80,485
Net sales	2,691,855	2,396,858

What is the change in the number of days' sales uncollected between years 2012 and 2013? (Round the number of days to one decimal.) According to this analysis, is the company's collection of receivables improving? Explain.

QS 6-9ᴬ

Documents in a voucher system

P4

Management uses a voucher system to help control and monitor cash disbursements. Identify and describe at least four key documents that are part of a voucher system of control.

QS 6-10ᴮ

Purchase discounts   P5

An important part of cash management is knowing when, and if, to take purchase discounts.

a. Which accounting method uses a Discounts Lost account?

b. What is the advantage of this method for management?

QS 6-11

International accounting and internal controls

C1   P1

Answer each of the following related to international accounting standards.

a. Explain how the purposes and principles of internal controls are different between accounting systems reporting under IFRS versus U.S. GAAP.

b. Cash presents special internal control challenges. How do internal controls for cash differ for accounting systems reporting under IFRS versus U.S. GAAP? How do the procedures applied differ across those two accounting systems?

EXERCISES

Exercise 6-1

Analyzing internal control

C1

Franco Company is a rapidly growing start-up business. Its recordkeeper, who was hired six months ago, left town after the company's manager discovered that a large sum of money had disappeared over the past three months. An audit disclosed that the recordkeeper had written and signed several checks made payable to her fiancé and then recorded the checks as salaries expense. The fiancé, who cashed the checks but never worked for the company, left town with the recordkeeper. As a result, the company incurred an uninsured loss of $184,000. Evaluate Franco's internal control system and indicate which principles of internal control appear to have been ignored.

Some of Crown Company's cash receipts from customers are received by the company with the regular mail. The company's recordkeeper opens these letters and deposits the cash received each day. (*a*) Identify any internal control problem(s) in this arrangement. (*b*) What changes to its internal control system do you recommend?

Exercise 6-2
Control of cash receipts by mail
P1

What internal control procedures would you recommend in each of the following situations?

1. A concession company has one employee who sells towels, coolers, and sunglasses at the beach. Each day, the employee is given enough towels, coolers, and sunglasses to last through the day and enough cash to make change. The money is kept in a box at the stand.
2. An antique store has one employee who is given cash and sent to garage sales each weekend. The employee pays cash for any merchandise acquired that the antique store resells.

Exercise 6-3
Internal control recommendations
C1

Good accounting systems help with the management and control of cash and cash equivalents.

1. Define and contrast the terms *liquid asset* and *cash equivalent*.
2. Why would companies invest their idle cash in cash equivalents?
3. Identify five principles of effective cash management.

Exercise 6-4
Cash, liquidity, and return
C2

Palmona Co. establishes a $200 petty cash fund on January 1. On January 8, the fund shows $38 in cash along with receipts for the following expenditures: postage, $74; transportation-in, $29; delivery expenses, $16; and miscellaneous expenses, $43. Palmona uses the perpetual system in accounting for merchandise inventory. Prepare journal entries to (1) establish the fund on January 1, (2) reimburse it on January 8, and (3) both reimburse the fund and increase it to $450 on January 8, assuming no entry in part 2. (*Hint*: Make two separate entries for part 3.)

Exercise 6-5
Petty cash fund accounting
P2

Check (3) Cr. Cash $162 (total)

Waupaca Company establishes a $350 petty cash fund on September 9. On September 30, the fund shows $104 in cash along with receipts for the following expenditures: transportation-in, $40; postage expenses, $123; and miscellaneous expenses, $80. The petty cashier could not account for a $3 shortage in the fund. The company uses the perpetual system in accounting for merchandise inventory. Prepare (1) the September 9 entry to establish the fund, (2) the September 30 entry to reimburse the fund, and (3) an October 1 entry to increase the fund to $400.

Exercise 6-6
Petty cash fund with a shortage
P2

Check (2) Cr. Cash $246 and (3) Cr. Cash $50

Prepare a table with the following headings for a monthly bank reconciliation dated September 30.

Exercise 6-7
Bank reconciliation and adjusting entries
P3

Bank Balance		Book Balance			Not Shown on the Reconciliation
Add	Deduct	Add	Deduct	Adjust	

For each item 1 through 12, place an *x* in the appropriate column to indicate whether the item should be added to or deducted from the book or bank balance, or whether it should not appear on the reconciliation. If the book balance is to be adjusted, place a *Dr.* or *Cr.* in the Adjust column to indicate whether the Cash balance should be debited or credited. At the left side of your table, number the items to correspond to the following list.

1. NSF check from customer is returned on September 25 but not yet recorded by this company.
2. Interest earned on the September cash balance in the bank.
3. Deposit made on September 5 and processed by the bank on September 6.
4. Checks written by another depositor but charged against this company's account.
5. Bank service charge for September.
6. Checks outstanding on August 31 that cleared the bank in September.
7. Check written against the company's account and cleared by the bank; erroneously not recorded by the company's recordkeeper.
8. Principal and interest on a note receivable to this company is collected by the bank but not yet recorded by the company.
9. Checks written and mailed to payees on October 2.
10. Checks written by the company and mailed to payees on September 30.
11. Night deposit made on September 30 after the bank closed.
12. Special bank charge for collection of note in part 8 on this company's behalf.

Exercise 6-8

Voucher system

P1

The voucher system of control is designed to control cash disbursements and the acceptance of obligations.

1. The voucher system of control establishes procedures for what two processes?

2. What types of expenditures should be overseen by a voucher system of control?

3. When is the voucher initially prepared? Explain.

Exercise 6-9

Bank reconciliation

P3

Wright Company deposits all cash receipts on the day when they are received and it makes all cash payments by check. At the close of business on May 31, 2013, its Cash account shows a $27,500 debit balance. The company's May 31 bank statement shows $25,800 on deposit in the bank. Prepare a bank reconciliation for the company using the following information.

a. The May 31 bank statement included a $100 debit memorandum for bank services; the company has not yet recorded the cost of these services.

b. Outstanding checks as of May 31 total $5,600.

c. May 31 cash receipts of $6,200 were placed in the bank's night depository after banking hours and were not recorded on the May 31 bank statement.

d. In reviewing the bank statement, a $400 check written by Smith Company was mistakenly drawn against Wright's account.

Check Reconciled bal., $26,800

e. A debit memorandum for $600 refers to a $600 NSF check from a customer; the company has not yet recorded this NSF check.

Exercise 6-10

Bank reconciliation

P3

Del Gato Clinic deposits all cash receipts on the day when they are received and it makes all cash payments by check. At the close of business on June 30, 2013, its Cash account shows a $11,589 debit balance. Del Gato Clinic's June 30 bank statement shows $10,555 on deposit in the bank. Prepare a bank reconciliation for Del Gato Clinic using the following information:

a. Outstanding checks as of June 30 total $1,829.

b. The June 30 bank statement included a $16 debit memorandum for bank services.

c. Check No. 919, listed with the canceled checks, was correctly drawn for $467 in payment of a utility bill on June 15. Del Gato Clinic mistakenly recorded it with a debit to Utilities Expense and a credit to Cash in the amount of $476.

Check Reconciled bal., $11,582

d. The June 30 cash receipts of $2,856 were placed in the bank's night depository after banking hours and were not recorded on the June 30 bank statement.

Exercise 6-11

Adjusting entries from bank reconciliation   P3

Prepare the adjusting journal entries that Del Gato Clinic must record as a result of preparing the bank reconciliation in Exercise 6-10.

Exercise 6-12

Liquid assets and accounts receivable

A1

Bargains Co. reported annual net sales for 2012 and 2013 of $665,000 and $747,000, respectively. Its year-end balances of accounts receivable follow: December 31, 2012, $61,000; and December 31, 2013, $93,000. (*a*) Calculate its days' sales uncollected at the end of each year. Round the number of days to one decimal. (*b*) Evaluate and comment on any changes in the amount of liquid assets tied up in receivables.

Exercise 6-13^A

Documents in a voucher system

P4

Match each document in a voucher system in column one with its description in column two.

Document	**Description**
1. Purchase requisition	**A.** An itemized statement of goods prepared by the vendor listing the customer's name, items sold, sales prices, and terms of sale.
2. Purchase order	**B.** An internal file used to store documents and information to control cash disbursements and to ensure that a transaction is properly authorized and recorded.
3. Invoice	
4. Receiving report	
5. Invoice approval	**C.** A document used to place an order with a vendor that authorizes the vendor to ship ordered merchandise at the stated price and terms.
6. Voucher	**D.** A checklist of steps necessary for the approval of an invoice for recording and payment; also known as a check authorization.
	E. A document used by department managers to inform the purchasing department to place an order with a vendor.
	F. A document used to notify the appropriate persons that ordered goods have arrived, including a description of the quantities and condition of goods.

Piere Imports uses the perpetual system in accounting for merchandise inventory and had the following transactions during the month of October. Prepare entries to record these transactions assuming that Piere Imports records invoices (*a*) at gross amounts and (*b*) at net amounts.

Oct. 2   Purchased merchandise at a $3,000 price, invoice dated October 2, terms 2/10, n/30.
10   Received a $500 credit memorandum (at full invoice price) for the return of merchandise that it purchased on October 2.
17   Purchased merchandise at a $5,400 price, invoice dated October 17, terms 2/10, n/30.
27   Paid for the merchandise purchased on October 17, less the discount.
31   Paid for the merchandise purchased on October 2. Payment was delayed because the invoice was mistakenly filed for payment today. This error caused the discount to be lost.

Exercise 6-14[8]

Record invoices at gross or net amounts

P5

connect

For each of these five separate cases, identify the principle(s) of internal control that is violated. Recommend what the business should do to ensure adherence to principles of internal control.

1. Chi Han records all incoming customer cash receipts for her employer and posts the customer payments to their respective accounts.

2. At Tico Company, Julia and Justine alternate lunch hours. Julia is the petty cash custodian, but if someone needs petty cash when he is at lunch, Jose fills in as custodian.

3. Nori Nozumi posts all patient charges and payments at the Hopeville Medical Clinic. Each night Nori backs up the computerized accounting system to a tape and stores the tape in a locked file at her desk.

4. Benedict Shales prides himself on hiring quality workers who require little supervision. As office manager, Benedict gives his employees full discretion over their tasks and for years has seen no reason to perform independent reviews of their work.

5. Carla Farah's manager has told her to reduce costs. Cala decides to raise the deductible on the plant's property insurance from $5,000 to $10,000. This cuts the property insurance premium in half. In a related move, she decides that bonding the plant's employees is a waste of money since the company has not experienced any losses due to employee theft. Cala saves the entire amount of the bonding insurance premium by dropping the bonding insurance.

PROBLEM SET A

Problem 6-1A
Analyzing internal control

C1

Nakashima Gallery had the following petty cash transactions in February of the current year.

Feb. 2   Wrote a $400 check, cashed it, and gave the proceeds and the petty cashbox to Chloe Addison, the petty cashier.
5   Purchased bond paper for the copier for $14.15 that is immediately used.
9   Paid $32.50 COD shipping charges on merchandise purchased for resale, terms FOB shipping point. Nakashima uses the perpetual system to account for merchandise inventory.
12   Paid $7.95 postage to express mail a contract to a client.
14   Reimbursed Adina Sharon, the manager, $68 for business mileage on her car.
20   Purchased stationery for $67.77 that is immediately used.
23   Paid a courier $20 to deliver merchandise sold to a customer, terms FOB destination.
25   Paid $13.10 COD shipping charges on merchandise purchased for resale, terms FOB shipping point.
27   Paid $54 for postage expenses.
28   The fund had $120.42 remaining in the petty cash box. Sorted the petty cash receipts by accounts affected and exchanged them for a check to reimburse the fund for expenditures.
28   The petty cash fund amount is increased by $100 to a total of $500.

Problem 6-2A
Establish, reimburse, and increase petty cash

P2

Required

1. Prepare the journal entry to establish the petty cash fund.

2. Prepare a petty cash payments report for February with these categories: delivery expense, mileage expense, postage expense, merchandise inventory (for transportation-in), and office supplies expense. Sort the payments into the appropriate categories and total the expenditures in each category.

3. Prepare the journal entries (in dollars and cents) for part 2 to both (*a*) reimburse and (*b*) increase the fund amount.

Check   (3a & 3b) Total Cr. to Cash $379.58

Problem 6-3A

Establish, reimburse, and adjust petty cash

P2 Sage 50

Kiona Co. set up a petty cash fund for payments of small amounts. The following transactions involving the petty cash fund occurred in May (the last month of the company's fiscal year).

May 1   Prepared a company check for $300 to establish the petty cash fund.

     15   Prepared a company check to replenish the fund for the following expenditures made since May 1.
- *a.*   Paid $88 for janitorial services.
- *b.*   Paid $53.68 for miscellaneous expenses.
- *c.*   Paid postage expenses of $53.50.
- *d.*   Paid $47.15 to *The County Gazette* (the local newspaper) for an advertisement.
- *e.*   Counted $62.15 remaining in the petty cash box.

     16   Prepared a company check for $200 to increase the fund to $500.

     31   The petty cashier reports that $288.20 cash remains in the fund. A company check is drawn to replenish the fund for the following expenditures made since May 15.
- *f.*   Paid postage expenses of $147.36.
- *g.*   Reimbursed the office manager for business mileage, $23.50.
- *h.*   Paid $34.75 to deliver merchandise to a customer, terms FOB destination.

     31   The company decides that the May 16 increase in the fund was too large. It reduces the fund by $100, leaving a total of $400.

Required

Check (1) Cr. to Cash: May 15, $237.85; May 16, $200.00

1. Prepare journal entries (in dollars and cents) to establish the fund on May 1, to replenish it on May 15 and on May 31, and to reflect any increase or decrease in the fund balance on May 16 and May 31.

Analysis Component

2. Explain how the company's financial statements are affected if the petty cash fund is not replenished and no entry is made on May 31.

Problem 6-4A

Prepare a bank reconciliation and record adjustments

P3

mhhe.com/wildFINMAN5e

The following information is available to reconcile Branch Company's book balance of cash with its bank statement cash balance as of July 31, 2013.

- **a.** On July 31, the company's Cash account has a $27,497 debit balance, but its July bank statement shows a $27,233 cash balance.
- **b.** Check No. 3031 for $1,482 and Check No. 3040 for $558 were outstanding on the June 30 bank reconciliation. Check No. 3040 is listed with the July canceled checks, but Check No. 3031 is not. Also, Check No. 3065 for $382 and Check No. 3069 for $2,281, both written in July, are not among the canceled checks on the July 31 statement.
- **c.** In comparing the canceled checks on the bank statement with the entries in the accounting records, it is found that Check No. 3056 for July rent was correctly written and drawn for $1,270 but was erroneously entered in the accounting records as $1,250.
- **d.** A credit memorandum enclosed with the July bank statement indicates the bank collected $8,000 cash on a non-interest-bearing note for Branch, deducted a $45 collection fee, and credited the remainder to its account. Branch had not recorded this event before receiving the statement.
- **e.** A debit memorandum for $805 lists a $795 NSF check plus a $10 NSF charge. The check had been received from a customer, Evan Shaw. Branch has not yet recorded this check as NSF.
- **f.** Enclosed with the July statement is a $25 debit memorandum for bank services. It has not yet been recorded because no previous notification had been received.
- **g.** Branch's July 31 daily cash receipts of $11,514 were placed in the bank's night depository on that date, but do not appear on the July 31 bank statement.

Required

Check (1) Reconciled balance, $34,602; (2) Cr. Note Receivable $8,000

1. Prepare the bank reconciliation for this company as of July 31, 2013.

2. Prepare the journal entries necessary to bring the company's book balance of cash into conformity with the reconciled cash balance as of July 31, 2013.

Analysis Component

3. Assume that the July 31, 2013, bank reconciliation for this company is prepared and some items are treated incorrectly. For each of the following errors, explain the effect of the error on (i) the adjusted bank statement cash balance and (ii) the adjusted cash account book balance.
- **a.** The company's unadjusted cash account balance of $27,497 is listed on the reconciliation as $27,947.
- **b.** The bank's collection of the $8,000 note less the $45 collection fee is added to the bank statement cash balance on the reconciliation.

Chavez Company most recently reconciled its bank statement and book balances of cash on August 31 and it reported two checks outstanding, No. 5888 for $1,028.05 and No. 5893 for $494.25. The following information is available for its September 30, 2013, reconciliation.

Problem 6-5A

Prepare a bank reconciliation and record adjustments

P3

mhhe.com/wildFINMAN5e

Sage 50

From the September 30 Bank Statement

PREVIOUS BALANCE	TOTAL CHECKS AND DEBITS	TOTAL DEPOSITS AND CREDITS	CURRENT BALANCE
16,800.45	9,620.05	11,272.85	18,453.25

CHECKS AND DEBITS			DEPOSITS AND CREDITS		DAILY BALANCE	
Date	No.	Amount	Date	Amount	Date	Amount
09/03	5888	1,028.05	09/05	1,103.75	08/31	16,800.45
09/04	5902	719.90	09/12	2,226.90	09/03	15,772.40
09/07	5901	1,824.25	09/21	4,093.00	09/04	15,052.50
09/17		600.25 NSF	09/25	2,351.70	09/05	16,156.25
09/20	5905	937.00	09/30	12.50 IN	09/07	14,332.00
09/22	5903	399.10	09/30	1,485.00 CM	09/12	16,558.90
09/22	5904	2,090.00			09/17	15,958.65
09/28	5907	213.85			09/20	15,021.65
09/29	5909	1,807.65			09/21	19,114.65
					09/22	16,625.55
					09/25	18,977.25
					09/28	18,763.40
					09/29	16,955.75
					09/30	18,453.25

From Chavez Company's Accounting Records

Cash Receipts Deposited			
Date			Cash Debit
Sept.	5		1,103.75
	12		2,226.90
	21		4,093.00
	25		2,351.70
	30		1,682.75
			11,458.10

Cash Disbursements		
Check No.		Cash Credit
5901		1,824.25
5902		719.90
5903		399.10
5904		2,060.00
5905		937.00
5906		982.30
5907		213.85
5908		388.00
5909		1,807.65
		9,332.05

Cash						Acct. No. 101
Date		Explanation	PR	Debit	Credit	Balance
Aug.	31	Balance				15,278.15
Sept.	30	Total receipts	R12	11,458.10		26,736.25
	30	Total disbursements	D23		9,332.05	17,404.20

Additional Information

Check No. 5904 is correctly drawn for $2,090 to pay for computer equipment; however, the recordkeeper misread the amount and entered it in the accounting records with a debit to Computer Equipment and a credit to Cash of $2,060. The NSF check shown in the statement was originally received from a customer, S. Nilson, in payment of her account. Its return has not yet been recorded by the company. The credit

294   Chapter 6   Cash and Internal Controls

memorandum is from the collection of a $1,500 note for Chavez Company by the bank. The bank deducted a $15 collection fee. The collection and fee are not yet recorded.

Required

1. Prepare the September 30, 2013, bank reconciliation for this company.
2. Prepare the journal entries (in dollars and cents) to adjust the book balance of cash to the reconciled balance.

Analysis Component

3. The bank statement reveals that some of the prenumbered checks in the sequence are missing. Describe three situations that could explain this.

Check (1) Reconciled balance, $18,271.45 (2) Cr. Note Receivable $1,500.00

PROBLEM SET B

Problem 6-1B
Analyzing internal control

C1

For each of these five separate cases, identify the principle(s) of internal control that is violated. Recommend what the business should do to ensure adherence to principles of internal control.

1. Latisha Tally is the company's computer specialist and oversees its computerized payroll system. Her boss recently asked her to put password protection on all office computers. Latisha has put a password in place that allows only the boss access to the file where pay rates are changed and personnel are added or deleted from the payroll.
2. Marker Theater has a computerized order-taking system for its tickets. The system is active all week and backed up every Friday night.
3. Sutton Company has two employees handling acquisitions of inventory. One employee places purchase orders and pays vendors. The second employee receives the merchandise.
4. The owner of Super Pharmacy uses a check protector to perforate checks, making it difficult for anyone to alter the amount of the check. The check protector is on the owner's desk in an office that contains company checks and is normally unlocked.
5. Lavina Company is a small business that has separated the duties of cash receipts and cash disbursements. The employee responsible for cash disbursements reconciles the bank account monthly.

Problem 6-2B
Establish, reimburse, and increase petty cash

P2

Blues Music Center had the following petty cash transactions in March of the current year.

March	5	Wrote a $250 check, cashed it, and gave the proceeds and the petty cashbox to Jen Rouse, the petty cashier.
	6	Paid $12.50 COD shipping charges on merchandise purchased for resale, terms FOB shipping point. Blues uses the perpetual system to account for merchandise inventory.
	11	Paid $10.75 delivery charges on merchandise sold to a customer, terms FOB destination.
	12	Purchased file folders for $14.13 that are immediately used.
	14	Reimbursed Bob Geldof, the manager, $11.65 for office supplies purchased and used.
	18	Purchased printer paper for $20.54 that is immediately used.
	27	Paid $45.10 COD shipping charges on merchandise purchased for resale, terms FOB shipping point.
	28	Paid postage expenses of $18.
	30	Reimbursed Geldof $56.80 for business car mileage.
	31	Cash of $61.53 remained in the fund. Sorted the petty cash receipts by accounts affected and exchanged them for a check to reimburse the fund for expenditures.
	31	The petty cash fund amount is increased by $50 to a total of $300.

Required

1. Prepare the journal entry to establish the petty cash fund.
2. Prepare a petty cash payments report for March with these categories: delivery expense, mileage expense, postage expense, merchandise inventory (for transportation-in), and office supplies expense. Sort the payments into the appropriate categories and total the expenses in each category.
3. Prepare the journal entries (in dollars and cents) for part 2 to both (*a*) reimburse and (*b*) increase the fund amount.

Check (2) Total expenses $189.47

(3a & 3b) Total Cr. to Cash $238.47

Problem 6-3B
Establishing, reimbursing, and adjusting petty cash

P2

Moya Co. establishes a petty cash fund for payments of small amounts. The following transactions involving the petty cash fund occurred in January (the last month of the company's fiscal year).

Jan. 3   A company check for $150 is written and made payable to the petty cashier to establish the petty cash fund.

14   A company check is written to replenish the fund for the following expenditures made since January 3.
  a.   Purchased office supplies for $14.29 that are immediately used up.
  b.   Paid $19.60 COD shipping charges on merchandise purchased for resale, terms FOB shipping point. Moya uses the perpetual system to account for inventory.
  c.   Paid $38.57 to All-Tech for minor repairs to a computer.
  d.   Paid $12.82 for items classified as miscellaneous expenses.
  e.   Counted $62.28 remaining in the petty cash box.
15   Prepared a company check for $50 to increase the fund to $200.
31   The petty cashier reports that $17.35 remains in the fund. A company check is written to replenish the fund for the following expenditures made since January 14.
  f.   Paid $50 to *The Smart Shopper* for an advertisement in January's newsletter.
  g.   Paid $48.19 for postage expenses.
  h.   Paid $78 to Smooth Delivery for delivery of merchandise, terms FOB destination.
31   The company decides that the January 15 increase in the fund was too little. It increases the fund by another $50, leaving a total of $250.

Required

1.   Prepare journal entries (in dollars and cents) to establish the fund on January 3, to replenish it on January 14 and January 31, and to reflect any increase or decrease in the fund balance on January 15 and 31.

Check (1) Cr. to Cash: Jan. 14, $87.72; Jan. 31 (total), $232.65

Analysis Component

2.   Explain how the company's financial statements are affected if the petty cash fund is not replenished and no entry is made on January 31.

The following information is available to reconcile Severino Co.'s book balance of cash with its bank statement cash balance as of December 31, 2013.

a. The December 31 cash balance according to the accounting records is $32,878.30, and the bank statement cash balance for that date is $46,822.40.

b. Check No. 1273 for $4,589.30 and Check No. 1282 for $400, both written and entered in the accounting records in December, are not among the canceled checks. Two checks, No. 1231 for $2,289 and No. 1242 for $410.40, were outstanding on the most recent November 30 reconciliation. Check No. 1231 is listed with the December canceled checks, but Check No. 1242 is not.

c. When the December checks are compared with entries in the accounting records, it is found that Check No. 1267 had been correctly drawn for $3,456 to pay for office supplies but was erroneously entered in the accounting records as $3,465.

d. Two debit memoranda are enclosed with the statement and are unrecorded at the time of the reconciliation. One debit memorandum is for $762.50 and dealt with an NSF check for $745 received from a customer, Titus Industries, in payment of its account. The bank assessed a $17.50 fee for processing it. The second debit memorandum is a $99 charge for check printing. Severino did not record these transactions before receiving the statement.

e. A credit memorandum indicates that the bank collected $19,000 cash on a note receivable for the company, deducted a $20 collection fee, and credited the balance to the company's Cash account. Severino did not record this transaction before receiving the statement.

f. Severino's December 31 daily cash receipts of $9,583.10 were placed in the bank's night depository on that date, but do not appear on the December 31 bank statement.

Problem 6-4B
Prepare a bank reconciliation and record adjustments

P3

Required

1.   Prepare the bank reconciliation for this company as of December 31, 2013.

2.   Prepare the journal entries (in dollars and cents) necessary to bring the company's book balance of cash into conformity with the reconciled cash balance as of December 31, 2013.

Check (1) Reconciled balance, $51,005.80; (2) Cr. Note Receivable $19,000.00

Analysis Component

3.   Explain the nature of the communications conveyed by a bank when the bank sends the depositor (*a*) a debit memorandum and (*b*) a credit memorandum.

Problem 6-5B
Prepare a bank reconciliation
and record adjustments

P3

Shamara Systems most recently reconciled its bank balance on April 30 and reported two checks outstanding at that time, No. 1771 for $781 and No. 1780 for $1,425.90. The following information is available for its May 31, 2013, reconciliation.

From the May 31 Bank Statement

PREVIOUS BALANCE	TOTAL CHECKS AND DEBITS	TOTAL DEPOSITS AND CREDITS	CURRENT BALANCE
18,290.70	13,094.80	16,566.80	21,762.70

CHECKS AND DEBITS			DEPOSITS AND CREDITS		DAILY BALANCE	
Date	No.	Amount	Date	Amount	Date	Amount
05/01	1771	781.00	05/04	2,438.00	04/30	18,290.70
05/02	1783	382.50	05/14	2,898.00	05/01	17,509.70
05/04	1782	1,285.50	05/22	1,801.80	05/02	17,127.20
05/11	1784	1,449.60	05/25	7,350.00 CM	05/04	18,279.70
05/18		431.80 NSF	05/26	2,079.00	05/11	16,830.10
05/25	1787	8,032.50			05/14	19,728.10
05/26	1785	63.90			05/18	19,296.30
05/29	1788	654.00			05/22	21,098.10
05/31		14.00 SC			05/25	20,415.60
					05/26	22,430.70
					05/29	21,776.70
					05/31	21,762.70

From Shamara Systems' Accounting Records

Cash Receipts Deposited				Cash Disbursements		
Date		Cash Debit		Check No.		Cash Credit
May	4	2,438.00		1782		1,285.50
	14	2,898.00		1783		382.50
	22	1,801.80		1784		1,449.60
	26	2,079.00		1785		63.90
	31	2,727.30		1786		353.10
		11,944.10		1787		8,032.50
				1788		644.00
				1789		639.50
						12,850.60

Cash						Acct. No. 101
Date		Explanation	PR	Debit	Credit	Balance
Apr.	30	Balance				16,083.80
May	31	Total receipts	R7	11,944.10		28,027.90
	31	Total disbursements	D8		12,850.60	15,177.30

Additional Information

Check No. 1788 is correctly drawn for $654 to pay for May utilities; however, the recordkeeper misread the amount and entered it in the accounting records with a debit to Utilities Expense and a credit to Cash for $644. The bank paid and deducted the correct amount. The NSF check shown in the statement was originally received from a customer, W. Sox, in payment of her account. The company has not yet recorded its return. The credit memorandum is from a $7,400 note that the bank collected for the company.

The bank deducted a $50 collection fee and deposited the remainder in the company's account. The collection and fee have not yet been recorded.

Required

1. Prepare the May 31, 2013, bank reconciliation for Shamara Systems.

2. Prepare the journal entries (in dollars and cents) to adjust the book balance of cash to the reconciled balance.

Analysis Component

3. The bank statement reveals that some of the prenumbered checks in the sequence are missing. Describe three possible situations to explain this.

Check (1) Reconciled balance, $22,071.50; (2) Cr. Note Receivable $7,400.00

(This serial problem began in Chapter 1 and continues through most of the book. If previous chapter segments were not completed, the serial problem can begin at this point. It is helpful, but not necessary, to use the Working Papers that accompany the book.)

SERIAL PROBLEM
Success Systems

P3

Sage 50

SP 6   Adria Lopez receives the March bank statement for Success Systems on April 11, 2014. The March 31 bank statement shows an ending cash balance of $77,354. A comparison of the bank statement with the general ledger Cash account, No. 101, reveals the following.

a. A. Lopez notices that the bank erroneously cleared a $500 check against her account in March that she did not issue. The check documentation included with the bank statement shows that this check was actually issued by a company named Sierra Systems.

b. On March 25, the bank issued a $50 debit memorandum for the safety deposit box that Success Systems agreed to rent from the bank beginning March 25.

c. On March 26, the bank issued a $102 debit memorandum for printed checks that Success Systems ordered from the bank.

d. On March 31, the bank issued a credit memorandum for $33 interest earned on Success Systems' checking account for the month of March.

e. A. Lopez notices that the check she issued for $128 on March 31, 2014, has not yet cleared the bank.

f. A. Lopez verifies that all deposits made in March do appear on the March bank statement.

g. The general ledger Cash account, No. 101, shows an ending cash balance per books of $77,845 as of March 31 (prior to any reconciliation).

Required

1. Prepare a bank reconciliation for Success Systems for the month ended March 31, 2014.

2. Prepare any necessary adjusting entries. Use Miscellaneous Expenses, No. 677, for any bank charges. Use Interest Revenue, No. 404, for any interest earned on the checking account for the month of March.

Check (1) Adj. bank bal. $77,726

Beyond the Numbers

BTN 6-1   Refer to Polaris' financial statements in Appendix A to answer the following.

1. For both years ended December 31, 2011 and 2010, identify the total amount of cash and cash equivalents. Determine the percent (rounded to one decimal) that this amount represents of total current assets, total current liabilities, total shareholders' equity, and total assets for both years. Comment on any trends.

2. For years ended December 31, 2011 and 2010, use the information in the statement of cash flows to determine the percent change (rounded to one decimal) between the beginning and ending year amounts of cash and cash equivalents.

3. Compute the days' sales uncollected (rounded to two decimals) as of December 31, 2011 and 2010. Has the collection of receivables improved? Are accounts receivable an important asset for Polaris? Explain.

**REPORTING IN
ACTION**

C2 A1

Polaris

Fast Forward

4. Access Polaris' financial statements for fiscal years ending after December 31, 2011, from its Website (Polaris.com) or the SEC's EDGAR database (www.sec.gov). Recompute its days' sales uncollected for years ending after December 31, 2011. Compare this to the days' sales uncollected for 2011 and 2010.

COMPARATIVE ANALYSIS

A1

Polaris

Arctic Cat

BTN 6-2   Key comparative figures for Polaris and Arctic Cat follow.

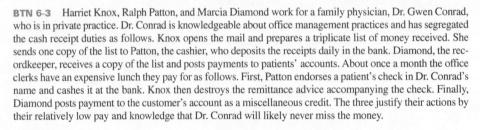

($ thousands)	Polaris		Arctic Cat	
	Current Year	Prior Year	Current Year	Prior Year
Accounts receivable	$ 115,302	$ 89,294	$ 23,732	$ 29,227
Net sales	2,656,949	1,991,139	363,015	350,871

Required

Compute days' sales uncollected (rounded to two decimals) for these companies for each of the two years shown. Comment on any trends for the companies. Which company has the largest percent change (rounded to two decimals) in days' sales uncollected?

ETHICS CHALLENGE

C1

BTN 6-3   Harriet Knox, Ralph Patton, and Marcia Diamond work for a family physician, Dr. Gwen Conrad, who is in private practice. Dr. Conrad is knowledgeable about office management practices and has segregated the cash receipt duties as follows. Knox opens the mail and prepares a triplicate list of money received. She sends one copy of the list to Patton, the cashier, who deposits the receipts daily in the bank. Diamond, the recordkeeper, receives a copy of the list and posts payments to patients' accounts. About once a month the office clerks have an expensive lunch they pay for as follows. First, Patton endorses a patient's check in Dr. Conrad's name and cashes it at the bank. Knox then destroys the remittance advice accompanying the check. Finally, Diamond posts payment to the customer's account as a miscellaneous credit. The three justify their actions by their relatively low pay and knowledge that Dr. Conrad will likely never miss the money.

Required

1. Who is the best person in Dr. Conrad's office to reconcile the bank statement?
2. Would a bank reconciliation uncover this office fraud?
3. What are some procedures to detect this type of fraud?
4. Suggest additional internal controls that Dr. Conrad could implement.

COMMUNICATING IN PRACTICE

P5

BTN 6-4[B]   Assume you are a business consultant. The owner of a company sends you an e-mail expressing concern that the company is not taking advantage of its discounts offered by vendors. The company currently uses the gross method of recording purchases. The owner is considering a review of all invoices and payments from the previous period. Due to the volume of purchases, however, the owner recognizes that this is time-consuming and costly. The owner seeks your advice about monitoring purchase discounts in the future. Provide a response in memorandum form.

TAKING IT TO THE NET

C1 P1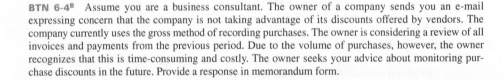

BTN 6-5   Visit the Association of Certified Fraud Examiners Website at acfe.com. Find and open the file "2010 Report to the Nation." Read the two-page Executive Summary and fill in the following blanks. (The report is under its *Fraud Resources* tab or under its *About the ACFE* tab [under Press Room]; we can also use the *Search* tab.)

1. The median loss caused by occupational frauds was $_____.
2. Nearly _____ of fraud cases involved losses of at least $1 million in losses.
3. Companies lose ___% of their annual revenues to fraud; this figure translates to a potential total fraud loss of more than $_____ trillion.
4. The typical length of fraud schemes was _____ months from the time the fraud began until it was detected.
5. Less than ___% of victim organizations conducted surprise audits, however these organizations have lower fraud losses and detect fraud more quickly than those without surprise audits.
6. Asset misappropriation schemes were most common at ___% of cases with a median loss of $_____.
7. Financial statement fraud schemes made up less than ___% of cases with a median loss of more than $_____ million.
8. Corruption schemes comprised ___% of cases with a median loss of $_____.
9. Less than ___% of the perpetrators had convictions prior to committing their frauds.

BTN 6-6   Organize the class into teams. Each team must prepare a list of 10 internal controls a consumer could observe in a typical retail department store. When called upon, the team's spokesperson must be prepared to share controls identified by the team that have not been shared by another team's spokesperson.

TEAMWORK IN ACTION

C1

BTN 6-7   Review the opening feature of this chapter that highlights Michael Inwald and his company CHEESEBOY.

Required

1. List the seven principles of internal control and explain how Michael could implement each of them in his stores.
2. Do you believe that Michael will need to add controls as his business expands? Explain.

ENTREPRENEURIAL DECISION

C1   P1

BTN 6-8   Visit an area of your college that serves the student community with either products or services. Some examples are food services, libraries, and bookstores. Identify and describe between four and eight internal controls being implemented.

HITTING THE ROAD

C1

BTN 6-9   The following information is from Piaggio (www.Piaggio.com), which manufactures two-, three- and four-wheel vehicles, and is Europe's leading manufacturer of motorcycles and scooters.

GLOBAL DECISION

C2   A1

 PIAGGIO

Euro in thousands	Current Year	Prior Year
Cash	151,887	154,859
Accounts receivable	65,560	90,421
Current assets	509,708	575,897
Total assets	1,520,184	1,545,722
Current liabilities	644,277	616,166
Shareholders' equity	446,218	442,890
Net sales	1,516,463	1,485,351

Required

1. For each year, compute the percentage (rounded to one decimal) that cash represents of current assets, total assets, current liabilities, and shareholders' equity. Comment on any trends in these percentages.
2. Determine the percentage change (rounded to one decimal) between the current and prior year cash balances.
3. Compute the days' sales uncollected (rounded to one decimal) at the end of both the current year and the prior year. Has the collection of receivables improved? Explain.

ANSWERS TO MULTIPLE CHOICE QUIZ

1. e; The entry follows.

Debits to expenses (or assets)	420	
Cash Over and Short	5	
Cash		425

2. a; recognizes cash collection of note by bank.
3. a; the bank reconciliation follows.

4. d; ($6,720/$84,000) × 365 = 29.2 days
5. b; The entry follows.

| Merchandise Inventory* | 5,880 | |
| Accounts Payable | | 5,880 |

*$6,000 × 98%

Bank Reconciliation November 30				
Balance per bank statement	$1,895		Balance per books	$1,742
Add: Deposit in transit	795		Add: Note collected less fee	320
Deduct: Outstanding checks	(638)		Deduct: Service charge	(10)
Reconciled balance	$2,052		Reconciled balance	$2,052

Managerial Accounting Concepts and Principles

A Look Back

Chapter 13 described the analysis and interpretation of financial statement information. We applied horizontal, vertical, and ratio analyses to better understand company performance and financial condition.

A Look at This Chapter

We begin our study of managerial accounting by explaining its purpose and describing its major characteristics. We also discuss cost concepts and describe how they help managers gather and organize information for making decisions. The reporting of manufacturing activities is also discussed.

A Look Ahead

The remaining chapters discuss the types of decisions managers must make and how managerial accounting helps with those decisions. The first of these chapters, Chapter 15, considers how we measure costs assigned to certain types of projects.

Learning Objectives

CONCEPTUAL

C1 Explain the purpose and nature of, and the role of ethics in, managerial accounting. (p. 610)

C2 Describe accounting concepts useful in classifying costs. (p. 614)

C3 Define product and period costs and explain how they impact financial statements. (p. 616)

C4 Explain how balance sheets and income statements for manufacturing and merchandising companies differ. (p. 619)

C5 Explain manufacturing activities and the flow of manufacturing costs. (p. 622)

C6 Describe trends in managerial accounting. (p. 625)

ANALYTICAL

A1 Assess raw materials inventory management using raw materials inventory turnover and days' sales in raw materials inventory. (p. 628)

PROCEDURAL

P1 Compute cost of goods sold for a manufacturer. (p. 620)

P2 Prepare a manufacturing statement and explain its purpose and links to financial statements. (p. 623)

Decision Insight

Fun-guys

"We didn't even know what a good mushroom tasted like."
—**NIKHIL ARORA** (on right)

OAKLAND, CA—Nearing college graduation, Alex Velez and Nikhil Arora spurned the glamor of investment banking for a more down-to-earth calling: urban mushroom farming using coffee grounds. Complete strangers, each was intrigued by the idea of turning waste into food (and wages). "We both fell in love with the idea of using coffee waste and started doing research and brainstorming," says Nikhil. After researching mushroom-growing techniques and determining there was a demand for their product, the duo wrote up a business plan, set up a managerial accounting system, and began farming. The result is **Back to the Roots (backtotheroots.com),** a socially conscious company with estimated 2012 revenues of over $5 million.

The company's production process begins with several thousand pounds of used coffee grounds that local coffee shops would typically discard. The company's second key raw material, mushroom seeds, is then added to the coffee grounds. The passage of time and moisture combine with the coffee grounds and mushroom seeds to yield delicious mushrooms in as little as 10 days. Then, the used coffee grounds and mushroom roots are packaged and sold as mulch for landscaping. This simple, sustainable production process "starts with waste and creates delicious food and fertile mulch," explains Alex.

Alex and Nikhil stress that college is the best time to start a new business. Risk is low, and "if the owners are passionate and have a good plan, someone will provide financing to get the business going," says Nikhil. In Back to the Roots' case, $5,000 of start-up financing was provided by a contest for social innovation sponsored by their college. In addition to passion and seed money, the owners stress that understanding basic managerial principles, product and period costs, manufacturing statements, and cost flow is critical. Managerial accounting information enables the owners to monitor and control costs and make good decisions. An understanding of costs and a keen eye for demand led the owners to ask, as Alex explains, "whether we could take this one step more and enable people to grow mushrooms at home." The company now sells Grow-Your-Own Mushroom Gardens for home use.

Alex and Nikhil believe that entrepreneurs fill a void by creating a niche. While financial success depends on monitoring and controlling operations to best meet customers' needs, the owners measure success by more than just profits. "For 2011, we collected and diverted over 1 million pounds of coffee grounds from landfill and enabled families to grow over 250,000 pounds of fresh food. In 2012, we've already been collecting 40,000 lbs. per week," exclaims Nikhil. Now, Alex and Nikhil hope to continue to grow their business, while staying focused on sustainability, healthy communities, and green development. Insists Nikhil, "our goal is to show people that you can create a successful company and create a positive impact in the community."

[Sources: *Back to the Roots* Website, January 2013; *Bloomberg Business Week,* http://images.businessweek.com/ss/09/10/1009_entrepreneurs_25_and_under/4.htm; *Whole Foods Market Blog,* August 20, 2011; *White House Champions of Change* blog, August 8, 2011, posted by Ari Matusiak.]

Chapter Preview

Managerial accounting, like financial accounting, provides information to help users make better decisions. However, managerial accounting and financial accounting differ in important ways, which this chapter explains. This chapter also compares the accounting and reporting practices used by manufacturing and merchandising companies. A merchandising company sells products without changing their condition. A manufacturing company buys raw materials and turns them into finished products for sale to customers. A third type of company earns revenues by providing services rather than products. The skills, tools, and techniques developed for measuring a manufacturing company's activities apply to service companies as well. The chapter concludes by explaining the flow of manufacturing activities and preparing the manufacturing statement.

Managerial Accounting Concepts and Principles

Managerial Accounting Basics	Managerial Cost Concepts	Reporting Manufacturing Activities
• Purpose of managerial accounting • Nature of managerial accounting • Managerial decisions • Fraud and ethics in managerial accounting	• Types of cost classifications • Identification of cost classifications • Cost concepts for service companies	• Manufacturer costs • Balance sheet • Income statement • Flow of activities • Manufacturing statement • Managerial accounting trends

MANAGERIAL ACCOUNTING BASICS

Managerial accounting is an activity that provides financial and nonfinancial information to an organization's managers and other internal decision makers. This section explains the purpose of managerial accounting (also called *management accounting*) and compares it with financial accounting. The main purpose of the financial accounting system is to prepare general-purpose financial statements. That information is incomplete for internal decision makers who manage organizations.

Purpose of Managerial Accounting

C1 Explain the purpose and nature of, and the role of ethics in, managerial accounting.

The purpose of both managerial accounting and financial accounting is providing useful information to decision makers. They do this by collecting, managing, and reporting information in demand by their users. Both areas of accounting also share the common practice of reporting monetary information, although managerial accounting usually includes the reporting of more nonmonetary information. They even report some of the same information. For instance, a company's financial statements contain information useful for both its managers (insiders) and other persons interested in the company (outsiders).

The remainder of this book looks carefully at managerial accounting information, how to gather it, and how managers use it. We consider the concepts and procedures used to determine the costs of products and services as well as topics such as budgeting, break-even analysis, product costing, profit planning, and cost analysis. Information about the costs of products and services is important for many decisions that managers make. These decisions include predicting the future costs of a product or service. Predicted costs are used in product pricing, profitability analysis, and in deciding whether to make or buy a product or component. More generally, much of managerial accounting involves gathering information about costs for planning and control decisions.

Planning is the process of setting goals and making plans to achieve them. Companies formulate long-term strategic plans that usually span a 5- to 10-year horizon and then refine them with medium-term and short-term plans. Strategic plans usually set a firm's long-term direction by developing a road map based on opportunities such as new products, new markets, and capital investments. A strategic plan's goals and objectives are broadly defined given its long-term

Point: Nonfinancial information, also called nonmonetary information, includes customer and employee satisfaction data, the percentage of on-time deliveries, and product defect rates.

Point: Costs are important to managers because they impact both the financial position and profitability of a business. Managerial accounting assists in analysis, planning, and control of costs.

orientation. Medium- and short-term plans are more operational in nature. They translate the strategic plan into actions. These plans are more concrete and consist of better defined objectives and goals. A short-term plan often covers a one-year period that, when translated in monetary terms, is known as a budget.

Control is the process of monitoring planning decisions and evaluating an organization's activities and employees. It includes the measurement and evaluation of actions, processes, and outcomes. Feedback provided by the control function allows managers to revise their plans. Measurement of actions and processes also allows managers to take corrective actions to avoid undesirable outcomes. For example, managers periodically compare actual results with planned results. Exhibit 14.1 portrays the important management functions of planning and control.

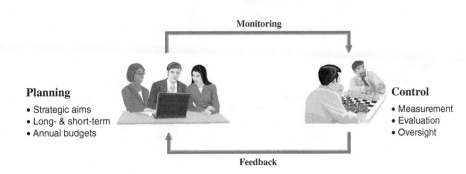

Monitoring

Planning
- Strategic aims
- Long- & short-term
- Annual budgets

Control
- Measurement
- Evaluation
- Oversight

Feedback

EXHIBIT 14.1

Planning and Control (including monitoring and feedback)

Managers use information to plan and control business activities. In later chapters, we explain how managers also use this information to direct and improve business operations.

Nature of Managerial Accounting

Managerial accounting has its own special characteristics. To understand these characteristics, we compare managerial accounting to financial accounting; they differ in at least seven important ways. These differences are summarized in Exhibit 14.2. This section discusses each of these characteristics.

EXHIBIT 14.2

Key Differences between Managerial Accounting and Financial Accounting

"This company's outlook is good. I'll buy its stock."

"This department is doing well. We'll expand its product line."

	Financial Accounting	Managerial Accounting
1. Users and decision makers	Investors, creditors, and other users external to the organization	Managers, employees, and decision makers internal to the organization
2. Purpose of information	Assist external users in making investment, credit, and other decisions	Assist managers in making planning and control decisions
3. Flexibility of practice	Structured and often controlled by GAAP	Relatively flexible (no GAAP constraints)
4. Timeliness of information	Often available only after an audit is complete	Available quickly without the need to wait for an audit
5. Time dimension	Focus on historical information with some predictions	Many projections and estimates; historical information also presented
6. Focus of information	Emphasis on whole organization	Emphasis on an organization's projects, processes, and subdivisions
7. Nature of information	Monetary information	Mostly monetary; but also nonmonetary information

Users and Decision Makers   Companies accumulate, process, and report financial accounting and managerial accounting information for different groups of decision makers. Financial accounting information is provided primarily to external users including investors, creditors, analysts, and regulators. External users rarely have a major role in managing a company's daily activities. Managerial accounting information is provided primarily to internal users who are responsible for making and implementing decisions about a company's business activities.

Point: It is desirable to accumulate certain information for management reports in a database separate from financial accounting records.

Purpose of Information   Investors, creditors, and other external users of financial accounting information must often decide whether to invest in or lend to a company. If they have already done so, they must decide whether to continue owning the company or carrying the loan. Internal decision makers must plan a company's future. They seek to take advantage of opportunities or to overcome obstacles. They also try to control activities and ensure their effective and efficient implementation. Managerial accounting information helps these internal users make both planning and control decisions.

Flexibility of Practice   External users compare companies by using financial reports and need protection against false or misleading information. Accordingly, financial accounting relies on accepted principles that are enforced through an extensive set of rules and guidelines, or GAAP. Internal users need managerial accounting information for planning and controlling their company's activities rather than for external comparisons. They require different types of information depending on the activity. This makes standardizing managerial accounting systems across companies difficult. Instead, managerial accounting systems are flexible. The design of a company's managerial accounting system depends largely on the nature of the business and the arrangement of its internal operations. Managers can decide for themselves what information they want and how they want it reported. Even within a single company, different managers often design their own systems to meet their special needs. The important question a manager must ask is whether the information being collected and reported is useful for planning, decision making, and control purposes.

Point: The *Institute of Management Accountants* issues statements that govern the practice of managerial accounting. Accountants who pass a qualifying exam are awarded the CMA.

Timeliness of Information   Formal financial statements reporting past transactions and events are not immediately available to outside parties. Independent certified public accountants often must *audit* a company's financial statements before it provides them to external users. Thus, because audits often take several weeks to complete, financial reports to outsiders usually are not available until well after the period-end. However, managers can quickly obtain managerial accounting information. External auditors need not review it. Estimates and projections are acceptable. To get information quickly, managers often accept less precision in reports. As an example, an early internal report to management prepared right after the year-end could report net income for the year between $4.2 and $4.8 million. An audited income statement could later show net income for the year at $4.6 million. The internal report is not precise, but its information can be more useful because it is available earlier.

Point: Financial statements are usually issued several weeks after the period-end. GAAP requires the reporting of important events that occur while the statements are being prepared. These events are called *subsequent events*.

Point: Independent auditors test the integrity of managerial accounting records when they are used in preparing financial statements.

Internal auditing plays an important role in managerial accounting. Internal auditors evaluate the flow of information not only inside but also outside the company. Managers are responsible for preventing and detecting fraudulent activities in their companies.

Time Dimension   To protect external users from false expectations, financial reports deal primarily with results of both past activities and current conditions. While some predictions such as service lives and salvage values of plant assets are necessary, financial accounting avoids predictions whenever possible. Managerial accounting regularly includes predictions of conditions and events. As an example, one important managerial accounting report is a budget, which predicts revenues, expenses, and other items. If managerial accounting reports were restricted to the past and present, managers would be less able to plan activities and less effective in managing and evaluating current activities.

EXHIBIT 14.3

Focus of External Reports

Reports to external users focus on company as a whole

Focus of Information   Companies often organize into divisions and departments, but investors rarely can buy shares in one division or department. Nor do creditors lend money to a company's single division or department. Instead, they own shares in or make loans to the entire company. Financial accounting focuses primarily on a company as a whole as depicted in Exhibit 14.3. The focus of managerial accounting is different. While top-level managers are responsible for managing the whole company, most other managers are responsible for much smaller sets of activities. These middle-level and lower-level managers need managerial accounting reports dealing with specific activities, projects, and subdivisions for which they are responsible. For instance, division sales managers are directly responsible only for the results achieved in their divisions. Accordingly, division sales managers need information about results achieved in their own divisions to improve their performance. This information includes the level of success achieved by each individual, product, or department in each division of the whole company as depicted in Exhibit 14.4.

Nature of Information   Both financial and managerial accounting systems report monetary information. Managerial accounting systems also report considerable nonmonetary information. Monetary information is an important part of managerial decisions, and nonmonetary information plays a crucial role, especially when monetary effects are difficult to measure. Common examples of nonmonetary information are the quality and delivery criteria of purchasing decisions.

EXHIBIT 14.4

Focus of Internal Reports

Reports to internal users focus on company units and divisions, along with the company as a whole

♟ Decision Ethics

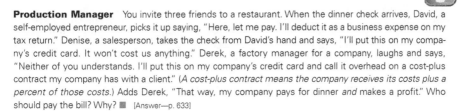

Production Manager   You invite three friends to a restaurant. When the dinner check arrives, David, a self-employed entrepreneur, picks it up saying, "Here, let me pay. I'll deduct it as a business expense on my tax return." Denise, a salesperson, takes the check from David's hand and says, "I'll put this on my company's credit card. It won't cost us anything." Derek, a factory manager for a company, laughs and says, "Neither of you understands. I'll put this on my company's credit card and call it overhead on a cost-plus contract my company has with a client." (*A cost-plus contract means the company receives its costs plus a percent of those costs.*) Adds Derek, "That way, my company pays for dinner *and* makes a profit." Who should pay the bill? Why? ■   [Answer—p. 633]

Managerial Decision Making

The previous section emphasized differences between financial and managerial accounting, but they are not entirely separate. Similar information is useful to both external and internal users. For instance, information about costs of manufacturing products is useful to all users in making decisions. Also, both financial and managerial accounting affect peoples' actions. For example, Trek's design of a sales compensation plan affects the behavior of its salesforce when selling its manufactured bikes. It also must estimate the dual effects of promotion and sales compensation plans on buying patterns of customers. These estimates impact the equipment purchase decisions for manufacturing and can affect the supplier selection criteria established by purchasing. Thus, financial and managerial accounting systems do more than measure; they also affect people's decisions and actions.

Fraud and Ethics in Managerial Accounting

Fraud, and the role of ethics in reducing fraud, are important factors in running business operations. Fraud involves the use of one's job for personal gain through the deliberate misuse of the employer's assets. Examples include theft of the employer's cash or other assets, overstating reimbursable expenses, payroll schemes, and financial statement fraud. Three factors must exist for a person to commit fraud: opportunity, pressure, and rationalization. This is known as the *fraud triangle.* Fraud affects all business and it is costly: A 2010 *Report to the Nation* from the Association of Certified Fraud Examiners (ACFE) estimates the average U.S. business loses 5% of its annual revenues to fraud. This report also shows that the frequency and average loss from fraud vary by industry; the mining industry has a relatively small number of frauds but a high ($1 million) average loss per fraud. The banking industry has the highest number (16.6%) of the total frauds reported in the current ACFE report.

The most common type of fraud, where employees steal or misuse the employer's resources, results in an average loss of $135,000 per occurrence. For example, in a billing fraud, an employee sets up a bogus supplier. The employee then prepares bills from the supplier and pays these bills from the employer's checking account. The employee cashes the checks sent to the bogus supplier and uses them for his or her own personal benefit.

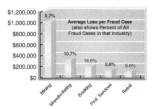

More generally, although there are many types of fraud schemes, all fraud:

- Is done to provide direct or indirect benefit to the employee.
- Violates the employee's obligations to the employer.
- Costs the employer money or loss of other assets.
- Is hidden from the employer.

Implications for Managerial Accounting   Fraud increases a business's costs. Left undetected, these inflated costs can result in poor pricing decisions, an improper product mix, and faulty performance evaluations. Management can develop accounting systems to closely track costs and identify deviations from expected amounts. In addition, managers rely on an **internal control system** to monitor and control business activities. An internal control system is the policies and procedures managers use to:

- Urge adherence to company policies.
- Promote efficient operations.
- Ensure reliable accounting.
- Protect assets.

Combating fraud and other dilemmas requires ethics in accounting. **Ethics** are beliefs that distinguish right from wrong. They are accepted standards of good and bad behavior. Identifying the ethical path can be difficult. The preferred path is a course of action that avoids casting doubt on one's decisions.

The **Institute of Management Accountants** (IMA), the professional association for management accountants, has issued a code of ethics to help accountants involved in solving ethical dilemmas. The IMA's Statement of Ethical Professional Practice requires that management accountants be competent, maintain confidentiality, act with integrity, and communicate information in a fair and credible manner.

The IMA provides a "road map" for resolving ethical conflicts. It suggests that an employee follow the company's policies on how to resolve such conflicts. If the conflict remains unresolved, an employee should contact the next level of management (such as the immediate supervisor) who is not involved in the ethical conflict.

Point: The IMA also issues the Certified Management Accountant (CMA) and the Certified Financial Manager (CFM) certifications. Employees with the CMA or CFM certifications typically earn higher salaries than those without.

Point: The Sarbanes-Oxley Act requires each issuer of securities to disclose whether it has adopted a code of ethics for its senior officers and the content of that code.

Quick Check   Answers — p. 634

1. Managerial accounting produces information (a) to meet internal users' needs, (b) to meet a user's specific needs, (c) often focusing on the future, or (d) all of these.
2. What is the difference between the intended users of financial and managerial accounting?
3. Do generally accepted accounting principles (GAAP) control and dictate managerial accounting?

MANAGERIAL COST CONCEPTS

 C2   Describe accounting concepts useful in classifying costs.

An organization incurs many different types of costs that are classified differently, depending on management needs (different costs for different purposes). We can classify costs on the basis of their (1) behavior, (2) traceability, (3) controllability, (4) relevance, and (5) function. This section explains each concept for assigning costs to products and services.

Types of Cost Classifications

Classification by Behavior   At a basic level, a cost can be classified as fixed or variable. A **fixed cost** does not change with changes in the volume of activity (within a range of activity known as an activity's *relevant range*). For example, straight-line depreciation on equipment is a fixed cost. A **variable cost** changes in proportion to changes in the volume of activity. Sales commissions computed as a percent of sales revenue are variable costs. Additional examples of fixed and variable costs for a bike manufacturer are provided in Exhibit 14.5. When cost items are combined, total cost can be fixed, variable, or mixed. *Mixed* refers to a combination of fixed and variable costs. Equipment rental often includes a fixed cost for some minimum amount and a variable cost based on amount of usage. Classification of costs by behavior is helpful in cost-volume-profit analyses and short-term decision making. We discuss these in Chapters 18 and 23.

EXHIBIT 14.5

Fixed and Variable Costs

Fixed Cost: Rent for Rocky Mountain Bikes' building is $22,000, and it doesn't change with the number of bikes produced.

Variable Cost: Cost of bicycle tires is variable with the number of bikes produced—this cost is $15 per pair.

Classification by Traceability   A cost is often traced to a **cost object,** which is a product, process, department, or customer to which costs are assigned. **Direct costs** are those traceable to a single cost object. For example, if a product is a cost object, its material and labor costs are usually directly traceable. Direct costs for a bicycle, when it is the cost object, include raw materials such as wheels, brakes, chains, and wages and benefits of employees who work directly on making bikes. **Indirect costs** are those that cannot be easily and cost–beneficially traced to a single cost object. An example of an indirect cost is a maintenance department that benefits two or more departments. Salaries of Rocky Mountain Bikes' maintenance department employees are considered indirect if the cost object is bicycles. However, these salaries are direct if the cost object is the maintenance department. Exhibit 14.6 identifies examples of both direct and indirect costs for the maintenance department, when the maintenance department is considered the cost object. Classification of costs by traceability is useful for cost allocation. This is discussed in Chapter 22.

EXHIBIT 14.6

Direct and Indirect Costs of a Maintenance Department

Direct Costs (to a Maintenance Department)

- Salaries of maintenance department employees
- Equipment purchased by maintenance department
- Materials purchased by maintenance department
- Maintenance department equipment depreciation

Indirect Costs (to a Maintenance Department)

- Factory accounting
- Factory administration
- Factory rent
- Factory manager's salary
- Factory light and heat
- Factory internal audit
- Factory intranet
- Insurance on factory

 **Decision** Maker

Entrepreneur   You wish to trace as many of your assembly department's direct costs as possible. You can trace 90% of them in an economical manner. To trace the other 10%, you need sophisticated and costly accounting software. Do you purchase this software? ■ [Answer—p. 633]

Classification by Controllability   A cost can be defined as **controllable** or **not controllable.** Whether a cost is controllable or not depends on the employee's responsibilities, as shown in Exhibit 14.7. This is referred to as *hierarchical levels* in management, or *pecking order.* For example, investments in machinery are controllable by upper-level managers but not lower-level managers. Many daily operating expenses such as overtime often are controllable by lower-level managers. Classification of costs by controllability is especially useful for assigning responsibility to and evaluating managers.

EXHIBIT 14.7

Controllability of Costs

Senior Manager
Controls costs of investments in land, buildings, and equipment.

Supervisor
Controls daily expenses such as supplies, maintenance, and overtime.

Classification by Relevance   A cost can be classified by relevance by identifying it as either a sunk cost or an out-of-pocket cost. A **sunk cost** has already been incurred and cannot be avoided or changed. It is irrelevant to future decisions. One example is the cost of a company's office equipment previously purchased. An **out-of-pocket cost** requires a future outlay of cash and is relevant for decision making. Future purchases of equipment involve out-of-pocket costs. A discussion of relevant costs must also consider opportunity costs. An **opportunity cost** is the potential benefit lost by choosing a specific action from two or more alternatives. One example is a student giving up wages from a job to attend evening classes. Consideration of opportunity cost is important when, for example, an insurance company must decide whether to outsource its payroll function or maintain it internally. This is discussed in Chapter 23.

Point: Opportunity costs are not recorded by the accounting system.

C3 Define product and period costs and explain how they impact financial statements.

Classification by Function   Another cost classification (for manufacturers) is capitalization as inventory or to expense as incurred. Costs capitalized as inventory are called **product costs,** which refer to expenditures necessary and integral to finished products. They include direct materials, direct labor, and indirect manufacturing costs called *overhead costs*. Product costs pertain to activities carried out to manufacture the product. Costs expensed are called **period costs,** which refer to expenditures identified more with a time period than with finished products. They include selling and general administrative expenses. Period costs pertain to activities that are not part of the manufacturing process. A distinction between product and period costs is important because period costs are expensed in the income statement and product costs are assigned to inventory on the balance sheet until that inventory is sold. An ability to understand and identify product costs and period costs is crucial to using and interpreting a *manufacturing statement* described later in this chapter.

Exhibit 14.8 shows the different effects of product and period costs. Period costs flow directly to the current income statement as expenses. They are not reported as assets. Product costs are first assigned to inventory. Their final treatment depends on when inventory is sold or disposed of. Product costs assigned to finished goods that are sold in year 2013 are reported on the 2013 income statement as part of cost of goods sold. Product costs assigned to unsold inventory are carried forward on the balance sheet at the end of year 2013. If this inventory is sold in year 2014, product costs assigned to it are reported as part of cost of goods sold in that year's income statement.

Point: Only costs of production and purchases are classed as product costs.

Point: Product costs are either in the income statement as part of cost of goods sold or in the balance sheet as inventory. Period costs appear only on the income statement under operating expenses. See Exhibit 14.8.

The difference between period and product costs explains why the year 2013 income statement does not report operating expenses related to either factory workers' wages or depreciation on factory buildings and equipment. Instead, both costs are combined with the cost of raw materials to compute the product cost of finished goods. A portion of these manufacturing costs

EXHIBIT 14.8

Period and Product Costs in Financial Statements

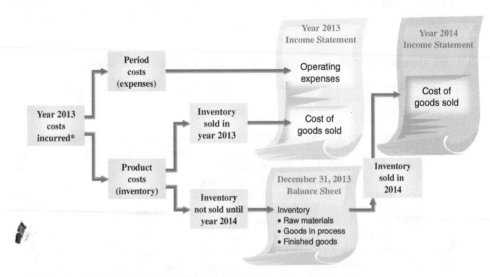

* This diagram excludes costs to acquire assets other than inventory.

(related to the goods sold) is reported in the year 2013 income statement as part of cost of goods sold. The other portion is reported on the balance sheet at the end of that year as part of inventory. The portion assigned to inventory could be included in any or all of raw materials, goods in process, or finished goods inventories.

Exhibit 14.9 summarizes typical managerial decisions for various cost classifications.

Costs Classified By	Example Managerial Decision
Behavior (variable or fixed)	How many units must we sell to break even?
	What will profit be if we raise the selling price?
	Should we add a new line of business?
Traceability (direct or indirect)	How well did our departments perform?
Controllability (controllable or not)	How well did our division managers perform?
Relevance (sunk, out-of-pocket, opportunity)	Should we make or buy a product?
	Should we keep or replace equipment?

Point: For a team approach to identifying period and product costs, see *Teamwork in Action* in the *Beyond the Numbers* section.

EXHIBIT 14.9

Summary of Cost Classifications and Example Managerial Decisions

 **Decision Maker**

Purchase Manager   You are evaluating two potential suppliers of seats for the manufacturing of motorcycles. One supplier (A) quotes a $145 price per seat and ensures 100% quality standards and on-time delivery. The second supplier (B) quotes a $115 price per seat but does not give any written assurances on quality or delivery. You decide to contract with the second supplier (B), saving $30 per seat. Does this decision have opportunity costs? ■   [Answer—p. 634]

Identification of Cost Classifications

It is important to understand that a cost can be classified using any one (or combination) of the five different means described here. To do this we must understand costs and operations. Specifically, for the five classifications, we must be able to identify the *activity* for behavior, *cost object* for traceability, *management hierarchical level* for controllability, *opportunity cost* for relevance, and *benefit period* for function. Factory rent, for instance, can be classified as a product cost; it is fixed with respect to number of units produced, it is indirect with respect to the product, and it is not controllable by a production supervisor. Potential multiple classifications are shown in Exhibit 14.10 using different cost items incurred in manufacturing mountain bikes. The finished bike is the cost object. Proper allocation of these costs and the managerial decisions based on cost data depend on a correct cost classification.

Cost Item	By Behavior	By Traceability	By Function
Bicycle tires	Variable	Direct	Product
Wages of assembly worker*	Variable	Direct	Product
Advertising	Fixed	Indirect	Period
Production manager's salary	Fixed	Indirect	Product
Office depreciation	Fixed	Indirect	Period

EXHIBIT 14.10

Examples of Multiple Cost Classifications

* Although an assembly worker's wages are classified as variable costs, their actual behavior depends on how workers are paid and whether their wages are based on a union contract (such as piece rate or monthly wages).

Cost Concepts for Service Companies

The cost concepts described are generally applicable to service organizations. For example, consider Southwest Airlines. Its cost of beverages for passengers is a variable cost based on number of passengers. The cost of leasing an aircraft is fixed with respect to number of passengers. We can also trace a flight crew's salary to a specific flight whereas we likely cannot trace wages for the ground crew to a specific flight. Classification by function (such as product

Point: All expenses of service companies are period costs because these companies do not have inventory.

Service Costs
- Beverages and snacks
- Cleaning fees
- Pilot and copilot salaries
- Attendant salaries
- Fuel and oil costs
- Travel agent fees
- Ground crew salaries

versus period costs) is not relevant to service companies because services are not inventoried. Instead, costs incurred by a service firm are expensed in the reporting period when incurred.

Managers in service companies must understand and apply cost concepts. They seek and rely on accurate cost estimates for many decisions. For example, an airline manager must often decide between canceling or rerouting flights. The manager must also be able to estimate costs saved by canceling a flight versus rerouting. Knowledge of fixed costs is equally important. We explain more about the cost requirements for these and other managerial decisions in Chapter 23.

Quick Check   Answers — p. 634

4. Which type of cost behavior increases total costs when volume of activity increases?

5. How could traceability of costs improve managerial decisions?

REPORTING MANUFACTURING ACTIVITIES

Companies with manufacturing activities differ from both merchandising and service companies. The main difference between merchandising and manufacturing companies is that merchandisers buy goods ready for sale while manufacturers produce goods from materials and labor. Payless is an example of a merchandising company. It buys and sells shoes without physically changing them. Adidas is primarily a manufacturer of shoes, apparel, and accessories. It purchases materials such as leather, cloth, dye, plastic, rubber, glue, and laces and then uses employees' labor to convert these materials to products. Southwest Airlines is a service company that transports people and items.

Manufacturer's Costs

Direct Materials   **Direct materials** are tangible components of a finished product. **Direct material costs** are the expenditures for direct materials that are separately and readily traced through the manufacturing process to finished goods. Examples of direct materials in manufacturing a mountain bike include its tires, seat, frame, pedals, brakes, cables, gears, and handlebars. The chart in the margin shows that direct materials generally make up about 45% of manufacturing costs in today's products, but this amount varies across industries and companies.

Typical Manufacturing Costs in Today's Products

- Direct labor 15%
- Direct materials 45%
- Factory overhead 40%

Direct Labor   **Direct labor** refers to the efforts of employees who physically convert materials to finished product. **Direct labor costs** are the wages and salaries for direct labor that are separately and readily traced through the manufacturing process to finished goods. Examples of direct labor in manufacturing a mountain bike include operators directly involved in converting raw materials into finished products (welding, painting, forming) and assembly workers who attach materials such as tires, seats, pedals, and brakes to the bike frames. Costs of other workers on the assembly line who assist direct laborers are classified as **indirect labor costs. Indirect labor** refers to manufacturing workers' efforts not linked to specific units or batches of the product.

Point: Indirect labor costs are part of factory overhead.

Factory Overhead   **Factory overhead** consists of all manufacturing costs that are not direct materials or direct labor. **Factory overhead costs** cannot be separately or readily traced to finished goods. These costs include indirect materials and indirect labor, costs not directly traceable to the product. Overtime paid to direct laborers is also included in overhead because overtime

Point: Factory overhead is also called *manufacturing overhead.*

is due to delays, interruptions, or constraints not necessarily identifiable to a specific product or batches of product. Factory overhead costs also include maintenance of the mountain bike factory, supervision of its employees, repairing manufacturing equipment, factory utilities (water, gas, electricity), production manager's salary, factory rent, depreciation on factory buildings and equipment, factory insurance, property taxes on factory buildings and equipment, and factory accounting and legal services. Factory overhead does *not* include selling and administrative expenses because they are not incurred in manufacturing products. These expenses are called *period costs* and are recorded as expenses on the income statement when incurred.

EXHIBIT 14.11

Prime and Conversion Costs and Their Makeup

Prime costs = Direct materials + Direct labor.
Conversion costs = Direct labor + Factory overhead.

Prime and Conversion Costs   Direct material costs and direct labor costs are also called **prime costs**—expenditures directly associated with the manufacture of finished goods. Direct labor costs and overhead costs are called **conversion costs**—expenditures incurred in the process of converting raw materials to finished goods. Direct labor costs are considered both prime costs and conversion costs. Exhibit 14.11 conveys the relation between prime and conversion costs and their components of direct material, direct labor, and factory overhead.

Since manufacturing activities differ from both selling merchandise and providing services, the financial statements differ slightly between these companies. This section considers some of these differences and compares them to accounting for a merchandising or service company. First we use the cost classification concept of traceability to discuss a manufacturer's costs.

Manufacturer's Balance Sheet

Manufacturers carry several unique assets and usually have three inventories instead of the single inventory that merchandisers carry. Exhibit 14.12 shows three different inventories in the current asset section of the balance sheet for Rocky Mountain Bikes, a manufacturer. The three inventories are raw materials, goods in process, and finished goods.

C4 Explain how balance sheets and income statements for manufacturing and merchandising companies differ.

EXHIBIT 14.12

Balance Sheet for a Manufacturer

ROCKY MOUNTAIN BIKES				
Balance Sheet				
December 31, 2013				
Assets			**Liabilities and Equity**	
Current assets			Current liabilities	
Cash	$ 11,000		Accounts payable	$ 14,000
Accounts receivable, net	30,150		Wages payable	540
Raw materials inventory	9,000		Interest payable	2,000
Goods in process inventory	7,500		Income taxes payable	32,600
Finished goods inventory	10,300		Total current liabilities	49,140
Factory supplies	350			
Prepaid insurance	300			
Total current assets	68,600		Long-term liabilities	
Plant assets			Long-term notes payable	50,000
Small tools, net	1,100		Total liabilities	99,140
Delivery equipment, net	5,000			
Office equipment, net	1,300			
Factory machinery, net	65,500		Stockholders' equity	
Factory building, net	86,700		Common stock, $1.2 par	24,000
Land	9,500		Paid-in capital	76,000
Total plant assets, net	169,100		Retained earnings	49,760
Intangible assets (patents), net	11,200		Total stockholders' equity	149,760
Total assets	$248,900		Total liabilities and equity	$248,900

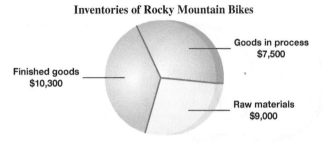

Inventories of Rocky Mountain Bikes

Goods in process
$7,500

Finished goods
$10,300

Raw materials
$9,000

Point: Reducing the size of inventories saves storage costs and frees money for other uses.

Raw Materials Inventory   Raw materials inventory refers to the goods a company acquires to use in making products. It uses raw materials in two ways: directly and indirectly. Most raw materials physically become part of a product and are identified with specific units or batches of a product. Raw materials used directly in a product are called *direct materials.* Other materials used to support production processes are sometimes not as clearly identified with specific units or batches of product. These materials are called **indirect materials** because they are not clearly identified with specific product units or batches. Items used as indirect materials often appear on a balance sheet as factory supplies or are included in raw materials. Some direct materials are classified as indirect materials when their costs are low (insignificant). Examples include screws and nuts used in assembling mountain bikes and staples and glue used in manufacturing shoes. Using the *materiality principle,* individually tracing the costs of each of these materials and classifying them separately as direct materials does not make much economic sense. For instance, keeping detailed records of the amount of glue used to manufacture one shoe is not cost beneficial.

Goods in Process Inventory   Another inventory held by manufacturers is **goods in process inventory,** also called *work in process inventory.* It consists of products in the process of being manufactured but not yet complete. The amount of goods in process inventory depends on the type of production process. If the time required to produce a unit of product is short, the goods in process inventory is likely small; but if weeks or months are needed to produce a unit, the goods in process inventory is usually larger.

Finished Goods Inventory   A third inventory owned by a manufacturer is **finished goods inventory,** which consists of completed products ready for sale. This inventory is similar to merchandise inventory owned by a merchandising company. Manufacturers also often own unique plant assets such as small tools, factory buildings, factory equipment, and patents to manufacture products. The balance sheet in Exhibit 14.12 shows that Rocky Mountain Bikes owns all of these assets. Some manufacturers invest millions or even billions of dollars in production facilities and patents. Briggs & Stratton's recent balance sheet shows about $1 billion net investment in land, buildings, machinery, and equipment, much of which involves production facilities. It manufactures more racing engines than any other company in the world.

Balance Sheets for Merchandising and Service Companies   The current assets section of the balance sheet will look different for merchandising and service companies as compared to manufacturing companies. A merchandiser will report only merchandise inventory rather than the three types of inventory reported by a manufacturer. A service company's balance sheet does not have any inventory held for sale.

Manufacturer's Income Statement

P1   Compute cost of goods sold for a manufacturer.

The main difference between the income statement of a manufacturer and that of a merchandiser involves the items making up cost of goods sold. Exhibit 14.13 compares the components of cost of goods sold for a manufacturer and a merchandiser. A merchandiser adds cost of goods purchased to beginning merchandise inventory and then subtracts ending merchandise inventory to get cost of goods sold. A manufacturer adds cost of goods manufactured to beginning finished goods inventory and then subtracts ending finished goods inventory to get cost of goods sold.

A merchandiser often uses the term *merchandise* inventory; a manufacturer often uses the term *finished goods* inventory. A manufacturer's inventories of raw materials and goods in process are not included in finished goods because they are not available for sale. A manufacturer also shows cost of goods *manufactured* instead of cost of goods *purchased.* This difference

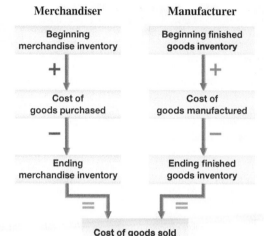

Merchandiser	Manufacturer
Beginning merchandise inventory	Beginning finished goods inventory
+	+
Cost of goods purchased	Cost of goods manufactured
−	−
Ending merchandise inventory	Ending finished goods inventory
=	=

Cost of goods sold

EXHIBIT 14.13

Cost of Goods Sold Computation

occurs because a manufacturer produces its goods instead of purchasing them ready for sale. We show later in this chapter how to derive cost of goods manufactured from the manufacturing statement.

The Cost of Goods Sold sections for both a merchandiser (Tele-Mart) and a manufacturer (Rocky Mountain Bikes) are shown in Exhibit 14.14 to highlight these differences. The remaining income statement sections are similar.

EXHIBIT 14.14

Cost of Goods Sold for a Merchandiser and Manufacturer

Merchandising (Tele-Mart) Company		Manufacturing (Rocky Mtn. Bikes) Company	
Cost of goods sold		Cost of goods sold	
Beginning *merchandise* inventory	$ 14,200	Beginning *finished goods* inventory	$ 11,200
Cost of merchandise *purchased*	234,150	Cost of goods *manufactured**	170,500
Goods available for sale	248,350	Goods available for sale	181,700
Less ending *merchandise* inventory	12,100	Less ending *finished goods* inventory	10,300
Cost of goods sold	$236,250	Cost of goods sold	$171,400

* Cost of goods manufactured is reported in the income statement of Exhibit 14.15.

Although the cost of goods sold computations are similar, the numbers in these computations reflect different activities. A merchandiser's cost of goods purchased is the cost of buying products to be sold. A manufacturer's cost of goods manufactured is the sum of direct materials, direct labor, and factory overhead costs incurred in producing products. Next we show a manufacturer's income statement.

Reporting Performance   Exhibit 14.15 shows the income statement for Rocky Mountain Bikes. Its operating expenses include sales salaries, office salaries, and depreciation of delivery and office equipment. Operating expenses do not include manufacturing costs such as factory workers' wages and depreciation of production equipment and the factory buildings. These manufacturing costs are reported as part of cost of goods manufactured and included in cost of goods sold. We explained why and how this is done in the section "Classification by Function."

Point: Manufacturers treat costs such as depreciation and rent as product costs if they are related to manufacturing.

Income Statement for Service Company   Since a service provider does not make or buy inventory to be sold, it does not report cost of goods manufactured or cost of goods sold. Instead, its operating expenses include all of the costs it incurred in providing its service. Southwest Airlines reports large operating expenses for employee pay and benefits, fuel and oil, and depreciation.

EXHIBIT 14.15

Income Statement for a Manufacturer

ROCKY MOUNTAIN BIKES		
Income Statement		
For Year Ended December 31, 2013		

Sales		$310,000
Cost of goods sold		
Finished goods inventory, Dec. 31, 2012	$ 11,200	
Cost of goods manufactured	170,500	
Goods available for sale	181,700	
Less finished goods inventory, Dec. 31, 2013	10,300	
Cost of goods sold		171,400
Gross profit		138,600
Operating expenses		
Selling expenses		
Sales salaries expense	18,000	
Advertising expense	5,500	
Delivery wages expense	12,000	
Shipping supplies expense	250	
Insurance expense—Delivery equipment	300	
Depreciation expense—Delivery equipment	2,100	
Total selling expenses		38,150
General and administrative expenses		
Office salaries expense	15,700	
Miscellaneous expense	200	
Bad debts expense	1,550	
Office supplies expense	100	
Depreciation expense—Office equipment	200	
Interest expense	4,000	
Total general and administrative expenses		21,750
Total operating expenses		59,900
Income before income taxes		78,700
Income taxes expense		32,600
Net income		$ 46,100

Quick Check   Answers — p. 634

6. What are the three types of inventory on a manufacturing company's balance sheet?

7. How does cost of goods sold differ for merchandising versus manufacturing companies?

Flow of Manufacturing Activities

C5 Explain manufacturing activities and the flow of manufacturing costs.

To understand manufacturing and its reports, we must first understand the flow of manufacturing activities and costs. Exhibit 14.16 shows the flow of manufacturing activities for a manufacturer. This exhibit has three important sections: *materials activity, production activity,* and *sales activity.* We explain each activity in this section.

Point: Knowledge of managerial accounting provides us a means of measuring manufacturing costs and is a sound foundation for studying advanced business topics.

Materials Activity   The far left side of Exhibit 14.16 shows the flow of raw materials. Manufacturers usually start a period with some beginning raw materials inventory carried over from the previous period. The company then acquires additional raw materials in the current period. Adding these purchases to beginning inventory gives total raw materials available for use in production. These raw materials are then either used in production in the current period or remain in inventory at the end of the period for use in future periods.

Production Activity   The middle section of Exhibit 14.16 describes production activity. Four factors come together in production: beginning goods in process inventory, direct materials,

EXHIBIT 14.16

Activities and Cost Flows in Manufacturing

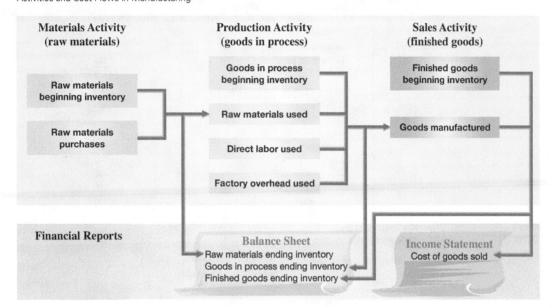

direct labor, and overhead. Beginning goods in process inventory consists of partly assembled products from the previous period. Production activity results in products that are either finished or remain unfinished. The cost of finished products makes up the cost of goods manufactured for the current period. Unfinished products are identified as ending goods in process inventory. The cost of unfinished products consists of direct materials, direct labor, and factory overhead, and is reported on the current period's balance sheet. The costs of both finished goods manufactured and goods in process are *product costs.*

Sales Activity   The company's sales activity is portrayed in the far right side of Exhibit 14.16. Newly completed units are combined with beginning finished goods inventory to make up total finished goods available for sale in the current period. The cost of finished products sold is reported on the income statement as cost of goods sold. The cost of products not sold is reported on the current period's balance sheet as ending finished goods inventory.

Manufacturing Statement

A company's manufacturing activities are described in a **manufacturing statement,** also called the *schedule of manufacturing activities* or the *schedule of cost of goods manufactured.* The manufacturing statement summarizes the types and amounts of costs incurred in a company's manufacturing process. Exhibit 14.17 shows the manufacturing statement for Rocky Mountain Bikes. The statement is divided into four parts: *direct materials, direct labor, overhead,* and *computation of cost of goods manufactured.* We describe each of these parts in this section.

P2 Prepare a manufacturing statement and explain its purpose and links to financial statements.

① The manufacturing statement begins by computing direct materials used. We start by adding beginning raw materials inventory of $8,000 to the current period's purchases of $86,500. This yields $94,500 of total raw materials available for use. A physical count of inventory shows $9,000 of ending raw materials inventory. This implies a total cost of raw materials used during the period of $85,500 ($94,500 total raw materials available for use − $9,000 ending inventory). (*Note:* All raw materials are direct materials for Rocky Mountain Bikes.)

② The second part of the manufacturing statement reports direct labor costs. Rocky Mountain Bikes had total direct labor costs of $60,000 for the period. This amount includes payroll taxes and fringe benefits.

Point: Direct material and direct labor costs increase with increases in production volume and are called *variable costs.* Overhead can be both variable and fixed. When overhead costs vary with production, they are called *variable overhead.* When overhead costs don't vary with production, they are called *fixed overhead.*

EXHIBIT 14.17

Manufacturing Statement

ROCKY MOUNTAIN BIKES		
Manufacturing Statement		
For Year Ended December 31, 2013		
Direct materials		
① Raw materials inventory, Dec. 31, 2012	$ 8,000	
Raw materials purchases	86,500	
Raw materials available for use	94,500	
Less raw materials inventory, Dec. 31, 2013	9,000	
Direct materials used		$ 85,500
② Direct labor		60,000
Factory overhead		
Indirect labor	9,000	
Factory supervision	6,000	
Factory utilities	2,600	
Repairs—Factory equipment	2,500	
Property taxes—Factory building	1,900	
③ Factory supplies used	600	
Factory insurance expired	1,100	
Depreciation expense—Small tools	200	
Depreciation expense—Factory equipment	3,500	
Depreciation expense—Factory building	1,800	
Amortization expense—Patents	800	
Total factory overhead		30,000
Total manufacturing costs		175,500
Add goods in process inventory, Dec. 31, 2012		2,500
④ Total cost of goods in process		178,000
Less goods in process inventory, Dec. 31, 2013		7,500
Cost of goods manufactured		$170,500

Point: Manufacturers sometimes report variable and fixed overhead separately in the manufacturing statement to provide more information to managers about cost behavior.

③ The third part of the manufacturing statement reports overhead costs. The statement lists each important factory overhead item and its cost. Total factory overhead cost for the period is $30,000. Some companies report only *total* factory overhead on the manufacturing statement and attach a separate schedule listing individual overhead costs.

④ The final section of the manufacturing statement computes and reports the *cost of goods manufactured.* (Total manufacturing costs for the period are $175,500 [$85,500 + $60,000 + $30,000], the sum of direct materials used and direct labor and overhead costs incurred.) This amount is first added to beginning goods in process inventory. This gives the total goods in process inventory of $178,000 ($175,500 + $2,500). We then compute the current period's cost of goods manufactured of $170,500 by taking the $178,000 total goods in process and subtracting the $7,500 cost of ending goods in process inventory that consists of direct materials, direct labor, and factory overhead. The cost of goods manufactured amount is also called *net cost of goods manufactured* or *cost of goods completed.* Exhibit 14.15 shows that this item and amount are listed in the Cost of Goods Sold section of Rocky Mountain Bikes' income statement and the balance sheet.

A managerial accounting system records costs and reports them in various reports that eventually determine financial statements. Exhibit 14.18 shows how overhead costs flow through the system: from an initial listing of specific costs, to a section of the manufacturing statement, to the reporting on the income statement and the balance sheet.

. Management uses information in the manufacturing statement to plan and control the company's manufacturing activities. To provide timely information for decision making, the statement is often prepared monthly, weekly, or even daily. In anticipation of release of its much-hyped iPad, Apple grew its inventory of critical components, and its finished goods

EXHIBIT 14.18

Overhead Cost Flows across Accounting Reports

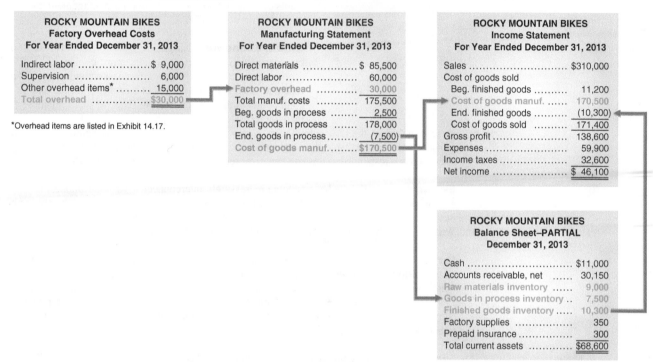

ROCKY MOUNTAIN BIKES
Factory Overhead Costs
For Year Ended December 31, 2013

Indirect labor	$ 9,000
Supervision	6,000
Other overhead items*	15,000
Total overhead	$30,000

*Overhead items are listed in Exhibit 14.17.

ROCKY MOUNTAIN BIKES
Manufacturing Statement
For Year Ended December 31, 2013

Direct materials	$ 85,500
Direct labor	60,000
Factory overhead	30,000
Total manuf. costs	175,500
Beg. goods in process	2,500
Total goods in process	178,000
End. goods in process	(7,500)
Cost of goods manuf.	$170,500

ROCKY MOUNTAIN BIKES
Income Statement
For Year Ended December 31, 2013

Sales	$310,000
Cost of goods sold	
Beg. finished goods	11,200
Cost of goods manuf.	170,500
End. finished goods	(10,300)
Cost of goods sold	171,400
Gross profit	138,600
Expenses	59,900
Income taxes	32,600
Net income	$ 46,100

ROCKY MOUNTAIN BIKES
Balance Sheet–PARTIAL
December 31, 2013

Cash	$11,000
Accounts receivable, net	30,150
Raw materials inventory	9,000
Goods in process inventory	7,500
Finished goods inventory	10,300
Factory supplies	350
Prepaid insurance	300
Total current assets	$68,600

inventory. The manufacturing statement contains information useful to external users but is not a general-purpose financial statement. Companies rarely publish the manufacturing statement because managers view this information as proprietary and potentially harmful to them if released to competitors.

Quick Check   Answers — p. 634

8. A manufacturing statement (a) computes cost of goods manufactured for the period, (b) computes cost of goods sold for the period, or (c) reports operating expenses incurred for the period.

9. Are companies required to report a manufacturing statement?

10. How are both beginning and ending goods in process inventories reported on a manufacturing statement?

Trends in Managerial Accounting

The analytical tools and techniques of managerial accounting have always been useful, and their relevance and importance continue to increase. This is so because of changes in the business environment. This section describes some of these changes and their impact on managerial accounting.

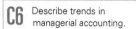

C6   Describe trends in managerial accounting.

Customer Orientation   There is an increased emphasis on *customers* as the most important constituent of a business. Customers expect to derive a certain value for the money they spend to buy products and services. Specifically, they expect that their suppliers will offer them the right service (or product) at the right time and the right price. This implies that

companies accept the notion of **customer orientation,** which means that employees understand the changing needs and wants of their customers and align their management and operating practices accordingly.

Global Economy Our *global economy* expands competitive boundaries and provides customers more choices. The global economy also produces changes in business activities. One notable case that reflects these changes in customer demand and global competition is auto manufacturing. The top three Japanese auto manufacturers (Honda, Nissan, and Toyota) once controlled more than 40% of the U.S. auto market. Customers perceived that Japanese auto manufacturers provided value not available from other manufacturers. Many European and North American auto manufacturers responded to this challenge and regained much of the lost market share.

E-Commerce People have become increasingly interconnected via smartphones, text messaging, and other electronic applications. Consumers thus expect and demand to be able to buy items electronically, whenever and wherever they want. Many businesses have enhanced their Websites to allow for online transactions. Online sales now make up over 7% of total retail sales.

Service Economy Businesses that provide services, such as telecommunications and health care, constitute an ever-growing part of our economy. In developed economies like the United States, service businesses typically account for over 60% to 70% of total economic activity.

Companies must be alert to these and other factors. Many companies have responded by adopting the **lean business model,** whose goal is to *eliminate waste* while "satisfying the customer" and "providing a positive return" to the company.

Lean Practices **Continuous improvement** rejects the notions of "good enough" or "acceptable" and challenges employees and managers to continuously experiment with new and improved business practices. This has led companies to adopt practices such as total quality management (TQM) and just-in-time (JIT) manufacturing. The philosophy underlying both practices is continuous improvement; the difference is in the focus.

Point: Goals of a TQM process include reduced waste, better inventory control, fewer defects, and continuous improvement. Just-in-time concepts have similar goals.

Total quality management focuses on quality improvement and applies this standard to all aspects of business activities. In doing so, managers and employees seek to uncover waste in business activities including accounting activities such as payroll and disbursements. To encourage an emphasis on quality, the U.S. Congress established the Malcolm Baldrige National Quality Award (MBNQA). Entrants must conduct a thorough analysis and evaluation of their business using guidelines from the Baldrige committee. Ritz Carlton Hotel is a recipient of the Baldrige award in the service category. The company applies a core set of values, collectively called *The Gold Standards,* to improve customer service.

Point: The time between buying raw materials and selling finished goods is called *throughput time.*

Just-in-time manufacturing is a system that acquires inventory and produces only when needed. An important aspect of JIT is that companies manufacture products only after they receive an order (a *demand-pull* system) and then deliver the customer's requirements on time. This means that processes must be aligned to eliminate any delays and inefficiencies including inferior inputs and outputs. Companies must also establish good relations and communications with their suppliers. On the downside, JIT is more susceptible to disruption than traditional systems. As one example, several General Motors plants were temporarily shut down due to a strike at an assembly division; the plants supplied components *just in time* to the assembly division.

"My boss wants us to appeal to a younger and hipper crowd. So, I'd like to get a tattoo that says-- 'Accounting rules!'"

Value Chain The **value chain** refers to the series of activities that add value to a company's products or services. Exhibit 14.19 illustrates a possible value chain for a retail cookie company. Companies can use lean practices to increase efficiency and profits.

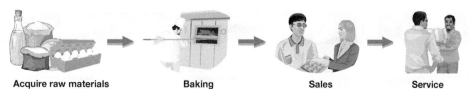

EXHIBIT 14.19

Typical Value Chain (Cookie Retailer)

Acquire raw materials   Baking   Sales   Service

 Decision Insight

Global Lean   Toyota Motor Corporation pioneered lean manufacturing, and it has since spread to other manufacturers throughout the world. The goals include improvements in quality, reliability, inventory turnover, productivity, exports, and—above all—sales and income. ■

Implications for Managerial Accounting   Adopting the lean business model can be challenging because to foster its implementation, all systems and procedures that a company follows must be realigned. Managerial accounting has an important role to play by providing accurate cost and performance information. Companies must understand the nature and sources of cost and must develop systems that capture costs accurately. Developing such a system is important to measuring the "value" provided to customers. The price that customers pay for acquiring goods and services is an important determinant of value. In turn, the costs a company incurs are key determinants of price. All else being equal, the better a company is at controlling its costs, the better its performance.

Decision Insight

Balanced Scorecard   The *balanced scorecard* aids continuous improvement by augmenting financial measures with information on the "drivers" (indicators) of future financial performance along four dimensions: (1) *financial*—profitability and risk, (2) *customer*—value creation and product and service differentiation, (3) *internal business processes*—business activities that create customer and owner satisfaction, and (4) *learning and growth*—organizational change, innovation, and growth. ■

GLOBAL VIEW

Managerial accounting is more flexible than financial accounting and does not follow a set of strict rules. However, many international businesses use the managerial accounting concepts and principles described in this chapter.

Customer Focus   Nestlé, one of the world's leading nutrition and wellness companies, adopts a customer focus and strives to understand its customers' tastes. For example, Nestlé employees spent three days living with people in Lima, Peru, to understand their motivations, routines, buying habits, and everyday lives. This allowed Nestlé to adjust its products to suit local tastes.

Reporting Manufacturing Activities   Nestlé must classify and report costs. In reporting inventory, Nestlé includes direct production costs, production overhead, and factory depreciation. A recent Nestlé annual report shows the following:

(in millions of Swiss francs)	Ending Inventory	Beginning Inventory
Raw materials, work in progress, and sundry supplies	3,243	3,175
Finished goods	4,182	4,741

Nestlé managers use this information, along with the more detailed information found in a manufacturing statement, to plan and control manufacturing activities.

Decision Analysis   Raw Materials Inventory Turnover and Days' Sales in
Raw Materials Inventory

 A1 Assess raw materials inventory management using raw materials inventory turnover and days' sales in raw materials inventory.

Managerial accounting information helps business managers perform detailed analyses that are not readily available to external users of accounting information. Inventory management is one example. Using publicly available financial statements, an external user can compute the *inventory turnover* ratio. However, a managerial accountant can go much further.

Raw Materials Inventory Turnover

A business manager can assess how effectively a company manages its *raw materials* inventory by computing the **raw materials inventory turnover ratio** as shown in Exhibit 14.20.

EXHIBIT 14.20

Raw Materials Inventory Turnover

> **Raw materials inventory turnover = Raw materials used/Average raw materials inventory**

This ratio reveals how many times a company turns over (uses in production) its raw materials inventory during a period. Generally, a high ratio of raw materials inventory turnover is preferred, as long as raw materials inventory levels are adequate to meet demand. To illustrate, Rocky Mountain Bikes reports direct (raw) materials used of $85,500 for a year, with a beginning raw materials inventory of $8,000 and an ending raw materials inventory of $9,000 (see Exhibit 14.17). Raw materials inventory turnover for Rocky Mountain Bikes for that year is computed as in Exhibit 14.21.

EXHIBIT 14.21

Raw Materials Inventory Turnover
Computed

> Raw materials inventory turnover = $85,500/[($8,000 + $9,000)/2] = 10.06 (rounded).

Days' Sales in Raw Materials Inventory

To further assess raw materials inventory management, a manager can measure the adequacy of raw materials inventory to meet production demand. **Days' sales in raw materials inventory** reveals how much raw materials inventory is available in terms of the number of days' sales. It is a measure of how long it takes raw materials to be used in production. It is defined and computed for Rocky Mountain Bikes in Exhibit 14.22.

EXHIBIT 14.22

Days' Sales in Raw Materials
Inventory Turnover

> **Days' sales in raw materials inventory = Ending raw materials inventory/Raw materials used × 365**
> = $9,000/$85,500 × 365 = 38.4 days (rounded)

This computation suggests that it will take 38 days for Rocky Mountain Bikes' raw materials inventory to be used in production. Assuming production needs can be met, companies usually prefer a *lower* number of days' sales in raw materials inventory. Just-in-time manufacturing techniques can be useful in lowering days' sales in raw materials inventory; for example, Dell keeps less than seven days of production needs in raw materials inventory for most of its computer components.

DEMONSTRATION PROBLEM 1: COST BEHAVIOR AND CLASSIFICATION

Understanding the classification and assignment of costs is important. Consider a company that manufactures computer chips. It incurs the following costs in manufacturing chips and in operating the company.

1. Plastic board used to mount the chip, $3.50 each.
2. Assembly worker pay of $15 per hour to attach chips to plastic board.
3. Salary for factory maintenance workers who maintain factory equipment.
4. Factory supervisor pay of $55,000 per year to supervise employees.
5. Real estate taxes paid on the factory, $14,500.
6. Real estate taxes paid on the company office, $6,000.
7. Depreciation costs on machinery used by workers, $30,000.
8. Salary paid to the chief financial officer, $95,000.
9. Advertising costs of $7,800 paid to promote products.

10. Salespersons' commissions of $0.50 for each assembled chip sold.

11. Management has the option to rent the manufacturing plant to six local hospitals to store medical records instead of producing and assembling chips.

Classify each cost in the following table according to the categories listed in the table header. A cost can be classified under more than one category. For example, the plastic board used to mount chips is classified as a direct material product cost and as a direct unit cost.

Cost	Period Costs Selling and Administrative	Product Costs Direct Material (Prime Cost)	Product Costs Direct Labor (Prime and Conversion)	Product Costs Factory Overhead (Conversion Cost)	Unit Cost Classification Direct	Unit Cost Classification Indirect	Sunk Cost	Opportunity Cost
1. Plastic board used to mount the chip, $3.50 each		✔			✔			

SOLUTION TO DEMONSTRATION PROBLEM 1

Cost*	Period Costs Selling and Administrative	Product Costs Direct Material (Prime Cost)	Product Costs Direct Labor (Prime and Conversion)	Product Costs Factory Overhead (Conversion Cost)	Unit Cost Classification Direct	Unit Cost Classification Indirect	Sunk Cost	Opportunity Cost
1.		✔			✔			
2.			✔		✔			
3.				✔		✔		
4.				✔		✔		
5.				✔		✔		
6.	✔							
7.				✔		✔	✔	
8.	✔							
9.	✔							
10.	✔							
11.								✔

* Costs 1 through 11 refer to the 11 cost items described at the beginning of the problem.

DEMONSTRATION PROBLEM 2: REPORTING FOR MANUFACTURERS

A manufacturing company's balance sheet and income statement differ from those for a merchandising or service company.

Required

1. Fill in the [BLANK] descriptors on the partial balance sheets for both the manufacturing company and the merchandising company. Explain why a different presentation is required.

Manufacturing Company

ADIDAS GROUP Partial Balance Sheet December 31, 2013	
Current assets	
Cash........................	$10,000
[BLANK]................	8,000
[BLANK]................	5,000
[BLANK]................	7,000
Supplies	500
Prepaid insurance	500
Total current assets.........	$31,000

Merchandising Company

PAYLESS SHOE OUTLET Partial Balance Sheet December 31, 2013	
Current assets	
Cash......................	$ 5,000
[BLANK]................	12,000
Supplies	500
Prepaid insurance	500
Total current assets	$18,000

2. Fill in the [BLANK] descriptors on the income statements for the manufacturing company and the merchandising company. Explain why a different presentation is required.

Manufacturing Company

ADIDAS GROUP Partial Income Statement For Year Ended December 31, 2013	
Sales	$200,000
Cost of goods sold	
Finished goods inventory, Dec. 31, 2012.........	10,000
[BLANK]..............................	120,000
Goods available for sale	130,000
Finished goods inventory, Dec. 31, 2013	(7,000)
Cost of goods sold	123,000
Gross profit..................................	$ 77,000

Merchandising Company

PAYLESS SHOE OUTLET Partial Income Statement For Year Ended December 31, 2013	
Sales	$190,000
Cost of goods sold	
Merchandise inventory, Dec. 31, 2012	8,000
[BLANK]..............................	108,000
Goods available for sale	116,000
Merchandise inventory, Dec. 31, 2013	(12,000)
Cost of goods sold	104,000
Gross profit..................................	$ 86,000

3. A manufacturer's cost of goods manufactured is the sum of (a) _____, (b) _____, and (c) _____ costs incurred in producing the product.

SOLUTION TO DEMONSTRATION PROBLEM 2

1. Inventories for a manufacturer and for a merchandiser.

Manufacturing Company

ADIDAS GROUP Partial Balance Sheet December 31, 2013	
Current assets	
Cash	$10,000
Raw materials inventory...........	8,000
Goods in process inventory	5,000
Finished goods inventory	7,000
Supplies	500
Prepaid insurance	500
Total current assets	$31,000

Merchandising Company

PAYLESS SHOE OUTLET Partial Balance Sheet December 31, 2013	
Current assets	
Cash	$ 5,000
Merchandise inventory	12,000
Supplies	500
Prepaid insurance	500
Total current assets	$18,000

Explanation: A manufacturing company must control and measure three types of inventories: raw materials, goods in process, and finished goods. In the sequence of making a product, the raw materials move into production—called *goods in process inventory*—and then to finished goods. All raw materials and goods in process inventory at the end of each accounting period are considered current assets. All unsold finished inventory is considered a current asset at the end of each accounting period. The merchandising company must control and measure only one type of inventory, purchased goods.

2. Cost of goods sold for a manufacturer and for a merchandiser.

Manufacturing Company

ADIDAS GROUP Partial Income Statement For Year Ended December 31, 2013	
Sales	$ 200,000
Cost of goods sold	
Finished goods inventory, Dec. 31, 2012	10,000
Cost of goods manufactured	120,000
Goods available for sale	130,000
Finished goods inventory, Dec. 31, 2013	(7,000)
Cost of goods sold	123,000
Gross profit	$ 77,000

Merchandising Company

PAYLESS SHOE OUTLET Partial Income Statement For Year Ended December 31, 2013	
Sales	$ 190,000
Cost of goods sold	
Merchandise inventory, Dec. 31, 2012	8,000
Cost of purchases	108,000
Goods available for sale	116,000
Merchandise inventory, Dec. 31, 2013	(12,000)
Cost of goods sold	104,000
Gross profit	$ 86,000

Explanation: Manufacturing and merchandising companies use different reporting terms. In particular, the terms *finished goods* and *cost of goods manufactured* are used to reflect the production of goods, yet the concepts and techniques of reporting cost of goods sold for a manufacturing company and merchandising company are similar.

3. A manufacturer's cost of goods manufactured is the sum of (a) *direct material,* (b) *direct labor,* and (c) *factory overhead* costs incurred in producing the product.

DEMONSTRATION PROBLEM 3: MANUFACTURING STATEMENT

The following account balances and other information are from SUNN Corporation's accounting records for year-end December 31, 2013. Use this information to prepare (1) a table listing factory overhead costs, (2) a manufacturing statement (show only the total factory overhead cost), and (3) an income statement.

Advertising expense	$ 85,000	Goods in process inventory, Dec. 31, 2012	$ 8,000
Amortization expense—Factory Patents	16,000	Goods in process inventory, Dec. 31, 2013	9,000
Bad debts expense	28,000	Income taxes	53,400
Depreciation expense—Office equipment	37,000	Indirect labor	26,000
Depreciation expense—Factory building	133,000	Interest expense	25,000
Depreciation expense—Factory equipment	78,000	Miscellaneous expense	55,000
Direct labor	250,000	Property taxes on factory equipment	14,000
Factory insurance expired	62,000	Raw materials inventory, Dec. 31, 2012	60,000
Factory supervision	74,000	Raw materials inventory, Dec. 31, 2013	78,000
Factory supplies used	21,000	Raw materials purchases	313,000
Factory utilities	115,000	Repairs expense—Factory equipment	31,000
Finished goods inventory, Dec. 31, 2012	15,000	Salaries expense	150,000
Finished goods inventory, Dec. 31, 2013	12,500	Sales	1,630,000

PLANNING THE SOLUTION

- Analyze the account balances and select those that are part of factory overhead costs.
- Arrange these costs in a table that lists factory overhead costs for the year.
- Analyze the remaining costs and select those related to production activity for the year; selected costs should include the materials and goods in process inventories and direct labor.

● Prepare a manufacturing statement for the year showing the calculation of the cost of materials used in production, the cost of direct labor, and the total factory overhead cost. When presenting overhead cost on this statement, report only total overhead cost from the table of overhead costs for the year. Show the costs of beginning and ending goods in process inventory to determine cost of goods manufactured.

● Organize the remaining revenue and expense items into the income statement for the year. Combine cost of goods manufactured from the manufacturing statement with the finished goods inventory amounts to compute cost of goods sold for the year.

SOLUTION TO DEMONSTRATION PROBLEM 3

SUNN CORPORATION
Factory Overhead Costs
For Year Ended December 31, 2013

Amortization expense—Factory patents	$ 16,000
Depreciation expense—Factory building	133,000
Depreciation expense—Factory equipment	78,000
Factory insurance expired	62,000
Factory supervision	74,000
Factory supplies used	21,000
Factory utilities	115,000
Indirect labor	26,000
Property taxes on factory equipment	14,000
Repairs expense—Factory equipment	31,000
Total factory overhead	$570,000

SUNN CORPORATION
Manufacturing Statement
For Year Ended December 31, 2013

Direct materials		
Raw materials inventory, Dec. 31, 2012	$ 60,000	
Raw materials purchase	313,000	
Raw materials available for use	373,000	
Less raw materials inventory, Dec. 31, 2013	78,000	
Direct materials used		295,000
Direct labor		250,000
Factory overhead		570,000
Total manufacturing costs		1,115,000
Goods in process inventory, Dec. 31, 2012		8,000
Total cost of goods in process		1,123,000
Less goods in process inventory, Dec. 31, 2013		9,000
Cost of goods manufactured		$1,114,000

SUNN CORPORATION
Income Statement
For Year Ended December 31, 2013

Sales			$1,630,000
Cost of goods sold			
Finished goods inventory, Dec. 31, 2012	$ 15,000		
Cost of goods manufactured	1,114,000		
Goods available for sale	1,129,000		
Less finished goods inventory, Dec. 31, 2013	12,500		
Cost of goods sold		1,116,500	
Gross profit		513,500	
Operating expenses			
Advertising expense	85,000		
Bad debts expense	28,000		
Depreciation expense—Office equipment	37,000		
Interest expense	25,000		
Miscellaneous expense	55,000		
Salaries expense	150,000		
Total operating expenses		380,000	
Income before income taxes		133,500	
Income taxes		53,400	
Net income		$ 80,100	

Summary

C1 Explain the purpose and nature of, and the role of ethics in, managerial accounting. The purpose of managerial accounting is to provide useful information to management and other internal decision makers. It does this by collecting, managing, and reporting both monetary and nonmonetary information in a manner useful to internal users. Major characteristics of managerial accounting include (1) focus on internal decision makers, (2) emphasis on planning and control, (3) flexibility, (4) timeliness, (5) reliance on forecasts and estimates, (6) focus on segments and projects, and (7) reporting both monetary and nonmonetary information. Ethics are beliefs that distinguish right from wrong. Ethics can be important in reducing fraud in business operations.

C2 Describe accounting concepts useful in classifying costs. We can classify costs on the basis of their (1) behavior—fixed vs. variable, (2) traceability—direct vs. indirect, (3) controllability—controllable vs. uncontrollable, (4) relevance—sunk vs. out of pocket, and (5) function—product vs. period. A cost can be classified in more than one way, depending on the purpose for which the cost is being determined. These classifications help us understand cost patterns, analyze performance, and plan operations.

C3 Define product and period costs and explain how they impact financial statements. Costs that are capitalized because they are expected to have future value are called *product costs;* costs that are expensed are called *period costs.* This classification is important because it affects the amount of costs expensed in the income statement and the amount of costs assigned to inventory on the balance sheet. Product costs are commonly made up of direct materials, direct labor, and overhead. Period costs include selling and administrative expenses.

C4 Explain how balance sheets and income statements for manufacturing and merchandising companies differ. The main difference is that manufacturers usually carry three inventories on their balance sheets—raw materials, goods in process, and finished goods—instead of one inventory that merchandisers carry. The main difference between income statements of manufacturers and merchandisers is the items making up cost of goods sold. A merchandiser adds beginning merchandise inventory to cost of goods purchased and then subtracts ending merchandise inventory to get cost of goods sold. A manufacturer adds beginning finished goods inventory to cost of goods

manufactured and then subtracts ending finished goods inventory to get cost of goods sold.

C5 Explain manufacturing activities and the flow of manufacturing costs. Manufacturing activities consist of materials, production, and sales activities. The materials activity consists of the purchase and issuance of materials to production. The production activity consists of converting materials into finished goods. At this stage in the process, the materials, labor, and overhead costs have been incurred and the manufacturing statement is prepared. The sales activity consists of selling some or all of finished goods available for sale. At this stage, the cost of goods sold is determined.

C6 Describe trends in managerial accounting. Important trends in managerial accounting include an increased focus on satisfying customers, the impact of a global economy, and the growing presence of e-commerce and service-based businesses. The lean business model, designed to eliminate waste and satisfy customers, can be useful in responding to recent trends. Concepts such as total quality management, just-in-time production, and the value chain often aid in application of the lean business model.

A1 Assess raw materials inventory management using raw materials inventory turnover and days' sales in raw materials inventory. A high raw materials inventory turnover suggests a business is more effective in managing its raw materials inventory. We use days' sales in raw materials inventory to assess the likelihood of production being delayed due to inadequate levels of raw materials. We prefer a high raw materials inventory turnover ratio and a small number of days' sales in raw materials inventory, provided that raw materials inventory levels are adequate to keep production steady.

P1 Compute cost of goods sold for a manufacturer. A manufacturer adds beginning finished goods inventory to cost of goods manufactured and then subtracts ending finished goods inventory to get cost of goods sold.

P2 Prepare a manufacturing statement and explain its purpose and links to financial statements. The manufacturing statement reports computation of cost of goods manufactured for the period. It begins by showing the period's costs for direct materials, direct labor, and overhead and then adjusts these numbers for the beginning and ending inventories of the goods in process to yield cost of goods manufactured.

Guidance Answers to Decision Maker and Decision Ethics

Production Manager It appears that all three friends want to pay the bill with someone else's money. David is using money belonging to the tax authorities, Denise is taking money from her company, and Derek is defrauding the client. To prevent such practices, companies have internal audit mechanisms. Many companies also adopt ethical codes of conduct to help guide employees. We must recognize that some entertainment expenses are justifiable and even encouraged. For example, the tax law allows certain deductions for

entertainment that have a business purpose. Corporate policies also sometimes allow and encourage reimbursable spending for social activities, and contracts can include entertainment as allowable costs. Nevertheless, without further details, payment for this bill should be made from personal accounts.

Entrepreneur Tracing all costs directly to cost objects is always desirable, but you need to be able to do so in an economically feasible manner. In this case, you are able to trace 90% of the assembly department's direct costs. It may not be economical to spend more money on a new software to trace the final 10% of costs. You need to make a cost–benefit trade-off. If the software offers benefits beyond tracing the remaining 10% of the assembly department's costs, your decision should consider this.

Purchase Manager   Opportunity costs relate to the potential quality and delivery benefits given up by not choosing supplier (A).

Selecting supplier (B) might involve future costs of poor-quality seats (inspection, repairs, and returns). Also, potential delivery delays could interrupt work and increase manufacturing costs. Your company could also incur sales losses if the product quality of supplier (B) is low. As purchase manager, you are responsible for these costs and must consider them in making your decision.

Guidance Answers to Quick Checks

1. *d*
2. Financial accounting information is intended for users external to an organization such as investors, creditors, and government authorities. Managerial accounting focuses on providing information to managers, officers, and other decision makers within the organization.
3. No, GAAP do not control the practice of managerial accounting. Unlike external users, the internal users need managerial accounting information for planning and controlling business activities rather than for external comparison. Different types of information are required, depending on the activity. Therefore it is difficult to standardize managerial accounting.
4. Variable costs increase when volume of activity increases.
5. By being able to trace costs to cost objects (say, to products and departments), managers better understand the total costs associated with a cost object. This is useful when managers

consider making changes to the cost object (such as when dropping the product or expanding the department).
6. Raw materials inventory, goods in process inventory, and finished goods inventory.
7. The cost of goods sold for merchandising companies includes all costs of acquiring the merchandise; the cost of goods sold for manufacturing companies includes the three costs of manufacturing: direct materials, direct labor, and overhead.
8. *a*
9. No; companies rarely report a manufacturing statement.
10. Beginning goods in process inventory is added to total manufacturing costs to yield total goods in process. Ending goods in process inventory is subtracted from total goods in process to yield cost of goods manufactured for the period.

Key Terms

Continuous improvement (p. 626)
Control (p. 611)
Controllable or not controllable cost (p. 615)
Conversion costs (p. 619)
Cost object (p. 615)
Customer orientation (p. 626)
Days' sales in raw materials inventory (p. 628)
Direct costs (p. 615)
Direct labor (p. 618)
Direct labor costs (p. 618)
Direct materials (p. 618)
Direct material costs (p. 618)
Ethics (p. 614)

Factory overhead (p. 618)
Factory overhead costs (p. 618)
Finished goods inventory (p. 620)
Fixed cost (p. 614)
Goods in process inventory (p. 620)
Indirect costs (p. 615)
Indirect labor (p. 618)
Indirect labor costs (p. 618)
Indirect material (p. 620)
Institute of Management Accountants (IMA) (p. 614)
Internal control system (p. 614)
Just-in-time (JIT) manufacturing (p. 626)
Lean business model (p. 626)
Managerial accounting (p. 610)

Manufacturing statement (p. 623)
Opportunity cost (p. 616)
Out-of-pocket cost (p. 616)
Period costs (p. 616)
Planning (p. 610)
Prime costs (p. 619)
Product costs (p. 616)
Raw materials inventory (p. 620)
Raw materials inventory turnover ratio (p. 628)
Sunk cost (p. 616)
Total quality management (TQM) (p. 626)
Value chain (p. 626)
Variable cost (p. 614)

Multiple Choice Quiz   Answers on p. 651   mhhe.com/wildFINMAN5e

Additional Quiz Questions are available at the book's Website.

1. Continuous improvement
  a. Is used to reduce inventory levels.
  b. Is applicable only in service businesses.
  c. Rejects the notion of "good enough."
  d. Is used to reduce ordering costs.
  e. Is applicable only in manufacturing businesses.

2. A direct cost is one that is
  a. Variable with respect to the cost object.
  b. Traceable to the cost object.
  c. Fixed with respect to the cost object.
  d. Allocated to the cost object.
  e. A period cost.

3. Costs that are incurred as part of the manufacturing process, but are not clearly traceable to the specific unit of product or batches of product, are called
  a. Period costs.
  b. Factory overhead.
  c. Sunk costs.
  d. Opportunity costs.
  e. Fixed costs.

4. The three major cost components of manufacturing a product are
  a. Direct materials, direct labor, and factory overhead.
  b. Period costs, product costs, and sunk costs.
  c. Indirect labor, indirect materials, and fixed expenses.
  d. Variable costs, fixed costs, and period costs.
  e. Opportunity costs, sunk costs, and direct costs.

5. A company reports the following for the current year.

Finished goods inventory, beginning year	$6,000
Finished goods inventory, ending year	3,200
Cost of goods sold	7,500

Its cost of goods manufactured for the current year is
  a. $1,500.
  b. $1,700.
  c. $7,500.
  d. $2,800.
  e. $4,700.

🔲 Icon denotes assignments that involve decision making.

Discussion Questions

1. Describe the managerial accountant's role in business planning, control, and decision making.

2. Distinguish between managerial and financial accounting on
  a. Users and decision makers.   **b.** Purpose of information.
  c. Flexibility of practice.   **d.** Time dimension.
  e. Focus of information.   **f.** Nature of information.

3. 🔲 Identify the usual changes that a company must make when it adopts a customer orientation.

4. Distinguish between direct labor and indirect labor.

5. Distinguish between (a) factory overhead and (b) selling and administrative overhead.

6. Distinguish between direct material and indirect material.

7. What product cost is listed as both a prime cost and a conversion cost?

8. 🔲 Assume that we tour **Polaris**' factory where **Polaris** it makes its products. List three direct costs and three indirect costs that we are likely to see.

9. 🔲 Should we evaluate a manager's performance on the basis of controllable or noncontrollable costs? Why?

10. 🔲 Explain why knowledge of cost behavior is useful in product performance evaluation.

11. Explain why product costs are capitalized but period costs are expensed in the current accounting period.

12. 🔲 Explain how business activities and inventories for a manufacturing company, a merchandising company, and a service company differ.

13. 🔲 Why does managerial accounting often involve working with numerous predictions and estimates?

14. How do an income statement and a balance sheet for a manufacturing company and a merchandising company differ?

15. Besides inventories, what other assets often appear on manufacturers' balance sheets but not on merchandisers' balance sheets?

16. Why does a manufacturing company require three different inventory categories?

17. Manufacturing activities of a company are described in the _____. This statement summarizes the types and amounts of costs incurred in its manufacturing _____.

18. What are the three categories of manufacturing costs?

19. List several examples of factory overhead.

20. 🔲 List the four components of a manufacturing **Polaris** statement and provide specific examples of each for **Polaris**.

21. ⬛ Prepare a proper title for the annual "manufacturing statement" of Arctic Cat. Does the date match the balance sheet or income statement? Why?   Arctic Cat

22. ⬛ Describe the relations among the income statement, the manufacturing statement, and a detailed listing of factory overhead costs.

23. ⬛ Define and describe two measures to assess raw materials inventory management.

24. ⬛ Can management of a company such as Polaris use cycle time and cycle efficiency as useful measures of performance? Explain.   **Polaris**

25. Access Dell's annual report (10-K) for the fiscal year ended February 3, 2012, at the SEC's EDGAR database (SEC.gov) or its Website (Dell.com). From its financial statement notes, identify the titles and amounts of its inventory components.

⬛ connect

QUICK STUDY

QS 14-1

Managerial accounting defined

C1

Managerial accounting (choose one)

1. Is directed at reporting aggregate data on the company as a whole.

2. Provides information that is widely available to all interested parties.

3. Must follow generally accepted accounting principles.

4. Provides information to aid management in planning and controlling business activities.

QS 14-2

Managerial accounting versus financial accounting

C1

Identify whether each description most likely applies to managerial or financial accounting.

1. _____ Its primary users are company managers.

2. _____ Its information is often available only after an audit is complete.

3. _____ Its primary focus is on the organization as a whole.

4. _____ Its principles and practices are very flexible.

5. _____ It is directed at external users in making investment, credit, and other decisions.

QS 14-3

Product and period costs

C3

Which of these statements is true regarding product and period costs?

1. Factory maintenance is a product cost and sales commission is a period cost.

2. Sales commission is a product cost and depreciation on factory equipment is a product cost.

3. Sales commission is a product cost and factory rent is a period cost.

4. Factory wages are a product cost and direct material is a period cost.

QS 14-4

Fixed and variable costs

C2

Which of these statements is true regarding fixed and variable costs?

1. Fixed costs stay the same and variable costs increase in total as activity volume increases.

2. Both fixed and variable costs increase as activity volume increases.

3. Both fixed and variable costs stay the same in total as activity volume increases.

4. Fixed costs increase and variable costs decrease in total as activity volume decreases.

QS 14-5

Direct and indirect costs

C2

Verdi Company produces sporting equipment, including leather footballs. Identify each of the following costs as direct or indirect if the cost object is a football produced by Verdi.

1. Electricity used in the production plant.

2. Labor used on the football production line.

3. Salary of manager who supervises the entire plant.

4. Depreciation on equipment used to produce footballs.

5. Leather used to produce footballs.

Three inventory categories are reported on a manufacturing company's balance sheet: (a) raw materials, (b) goods in process, and (c) finished goods. Identify the usual order in which these inventory items are reported on the balance sheet.

1. (b)(c)(a)　　　**2.** (c)(b)(a)　　　**3.** (a)(b)(c)　　　**4.** (b)(a)(c)

QS 14-6
Inventory reporting for manufacturers C4

Compute cost of goods sold for year 2013 using the following information.

Finished goods inventory, Dec. 31, 2012	$345,000
Goods in process inventory, Dec. 31, 2012	83,500
Goods in process inventory, Dec. 31, 2013	72,300
Cost of goods manufactured, year 2013	918,700
Finished goods inventory, Dec. 31, 2013	283,600

QS 14-7
Cost of goods sold
P1

A company has year-end cost of goods manufactured of $4,000, beginning finished goods inventory of $500, and ending finished goods inventory of $750. Its cost of goods sold is

1. $4,250　　**2.** $4,000　　**3.** $3,750　　**4.** $3,900

QS 14-8
Cost of goods sold P1

Identify the usual sequence of manufacturing activities by filling in the blank (1, 2 or 3) corresponding to its order: _____ Production activities; _____ sales activities; _____ materials activities.

QS 14-9
Manufacturing flows identified
C5

Prepare the 2013 manufacturing statement for Briton Company using the following information.

Direct materials	$190,500
Direct labor	63,150
Factory overhead costs	24,000
Goods in process, Dec. 31, 2012	157,600
Goods in process, Dec. 31, 2013	142,750

QS 14-10
Cost of goods manufactured
P2

Match each lean business concept with its best description by entering its letter in the blank.

1. _____ Just-in-time manufacturing
2. _____ Continuous improvements
3. _____ Customer orientation
4. _____ Total quality management

A. Focuses on quality throughout the production process.
B. Flexible product designs can be modified to accommodate customer choices.
C. Every manager and employee constantly looks for ways to improve company operations.
D. Inventory is acquired or produced only as needed.

QS 14-11
Lean business concepts
C6

Nestlé reports beginning raw materials inventory of 3,243 and ending raw materials inventory of 3,904 (both numbers in millions of Swiss francs). If Nestlé purchased 16,200 (in millions of Swiss francs) of raw materials during the year, what is the amount of raw materials it used during the year?

QS 14-12
Direct materials used
C5

Refer to QS 14-12 and compute raw materials inventory turnover and the number of days' sales in raw materials inventory.

QS 14-13
Raw materials inventory management A1

connect

EXERCISES

Exercise 14-1
Characteristics of financial accounting and managerial accounting

C1

In the following chart, compare financial accounting and managerial accounting by describing how each differs for the items listed. Be specific in your responses.

	Financial Accounting	Managerial Accounting
1. Time dimension	_____	_____
2. Users and decision makers	_____	_____
3. Timeliness of information	_____	_____
4. Purpose of information	_____	_____
5. Nature of information	_____	_____
6. Flexibility of practice	_____	_____
7. Focus of information	_____	_____

Exercise 14-2
Planning and control descriptions

C1

Complete the following statements by filling in the blanks.
1. _____ _____ usually covers a period of one year.
2. _____ is the process of monitoring planning decisions and evaluating an organization's activities and employees.
3. _____ is the process of setting goals and making plans to achieve them.
4. _____ _____ usually covers a period of 5 to 10 years.

Exercise 14-3
Sources of accounting information

C1

Both managerial accounting and financial accounting provide useful information to decision makers. Indicate in the following chart the most likely source of information for each business decision (a decision can require major input from both sources, in which case both can be marked).

Business Decision	Primary Information Source	
	Managerial	Financial
1. Determine amount of dividends to pay stockholders	___	___
2. Evaluate a purchasing department's performance	___	___
3. Report financial performance to board of directors	___	___
4. Estimate product cost for a new line of shoes	___	___
5. Plan the budget for next quarter	___	___
6. Measure profitability of all individual stores..............	___	___
7. Prepare financial reports according to GAAP	___	___
8. Determine location and size for a new plant	___	___

Exercise 14-4
Cost classifications   C2

(1) Identify each of the five cost classifications discussed in the chapter. (2) List two purposes of identifying these separate cost classifications.

Exercise 14-5
Cost analysis and classification

C2

Listed here are product costs for the production of soccer balls. (1) Classify each cost (a) as either variable or fixed and (b) as either direct or indirect. (2) What pattern do you see regarding the relation between costs classified by behavior and costs classified by traceability?

Product Cost	Cost by Behavior		Cost by Traceability	
	Variable	Fixed	Direct	Indirect
1. Leather covers for soccer balls	___	___	___	___
2. Annual flat fee paid for office security	___	___	___	___
3. Coolants for machinery	___	___	___	___
4. Wages of assembly workers	___	___	___	___
5. Lace to hold leather together	___	___	___	___
6. Taxes on factory	___	___	___	___
7. Machinery depreciation	___	___	___	___

Georgia Pacific, a manufacturer, incurs the following costs. (1) Classify each cost as either a product or a period cost. If a product cost, identify it as direct materials, direct labor, or factory overhead, and then as a prime and/or conversion cost. (2) Classify each product cost as either a direct cost or an indirect cost using the product as the cost object.

Exercise 14-6
Cost analysis and identification
C3

| | Product Cost | | | | | | |
| | Prime | | Conversion | | | | |
Cost	Direct Material	Direct Labor	Direct Labor	Overhead	Period Cost	Direct Cost	Indirect Cost
1. Factory utilities	___	___	___	___	___	___	___
2. Advertising	___	___	___	___	___	___	___
3. Amortization of patents on factory machine	___	___	___	___	___	___	___
4. State and federal income taxes	___	___	___	___	___	___	___
5. Office supplies used	___	___	___	___	___	___	___
6. Bad debts expense	___	___	___	___	___	___	___
7. Small tools used	___	___	___	___	___	___	___
8. Payroll taxes for production supervisor	___	___	___	___	___	___	___
9. Accident insurance on factory workers	___	___	___	___	___	___	___
10. Depreciation—Factory building	___	___	___	___	___	___	___
11. Wages to assembly workers	___	___	___	___	___	___	___
12. Direct materials used	___	___	___	___	___	___	___

Current assets for two different companies at calendar year-end 2013 are listed here. One is a manufacturer, Salomon Skis Mfg., and the other, Sun Fresh Foods, is a grocery distribution company. (1) Identify which set of numbers relates to the manufacturer and which to the merchandiser. (2) Prepare the current asset section for each company from this information. Discuss why the current asset section for these two companies is different.

Exercise 14-7
Balance sheet identification and preparation
C4

Account	Company 1	Company 2
Cash	$ 7,000	$ 5,000
Raw materials inventory	—	42,000
Merchandise inventory	45,000	—
Goods in process inventory	—	30,000
Finished goods inventory	—	50,000
Accounts receivable, net	62,000	75,000
Prepaid expenses	1,500	900

Using the following data, compute (1) the cost of goods manufactured and (2) the cost of goods sold for both Garcia Company and Culpepper Company.

Exercise 14-8
Cost of goods manufactured and cost of goods sold computation
P1 P2

	Garcia Company	Culpepper Company
Beginning finished goods inventory	$12,000	$16,450
Beginning goods in process inventory	14,500	19,950
Beginning raw materials inventory	7,250	9,000
Rental cost on factory equipment	27,000	22,750
Direct labor	19,000	35,000
Ending finished goods inventory	17,650	13,300
Ending goods in process inventory	22,000	16,000
Ending raw materials inventory	5,300	7,200
Factory utilities	9,000	12,000
Factory supplies used	8,200	3,200
General and administrative expenses	21,000	43,000
Indirect labor	1,250	7,660
Repairs—Factory equipment	4,780	1,500
Raw materials purchases	33,000	52,000
Sales salaries	50,000	46,000

Check Garcia COGS, $91,030

Exercise 14-9
Cost of goods sold computation
P1

Compute cost of goods sold for each of these two companies for the year ended December 31, 2013.

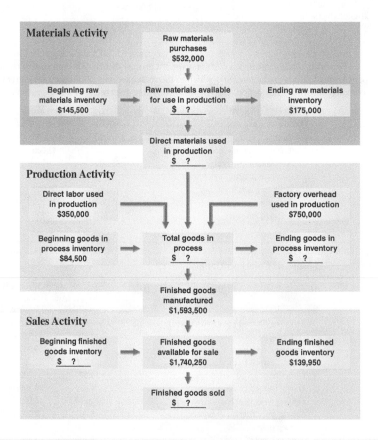

	Viking Retail	Log Homes Manufacturing
Beginning inventory		
Merchandise	$275,000	
Finished goods		$450,000
Cost of purchases	500,000	
Cost of goods manufactured		900,000
Ending inventory		
Merchandise	115,000	
Finished goods		375,000

Check   Viking COGS, $660,000

Exercise 14-10
Cost flows in manufacturing
C5

The following chart shows how costs flow through a business as a product is manufactured. Some boxes in the flowchart show cost amounts. Compute the cost amounts for the boxes that contain question marks.

Materials Activity

Raw materials purchases
$532,000

Beginning raw materials inventory $145,500 → Raw materials available for use in production $? → Ending raw materials inventory $175,000

Direct materials used in production $?

Production Activity

Direct labor used in production $350,000

Factory overhead used in production $750,000

Beginning goods in process inventory $84,500 → Total goods in process $? → Ending goods in process inventory $?

Finished goods manufactured $1,593,500

Sales Activity

Beginning finished goods inventory $? → Finished goods available for sale $1,740,250 → Ending finished goods inventory $139,950

Finished goods sold $?

Exercise 14-11
Components of accounting reports
P2

For each of the following accounts for a manufacturing company, place a ✔ in the appropriate column indicating that it appears on the balance sheet, the income statement, the manufacturing statement, and/or a detailed listing of factory overhead costs. Assume that the income statement shows the calculation of cost of goods sold and the manufacturing statement shows only the total amount of factory overhead. (An account can appear on more than one report.)

Chapter 14   Managerial Accounting Concepts and Principles   **641**

	Balance Sheet	Income Statement	Manufacturing Statement	Overhead Report
Account				
3 Accounts receivable				
4 Computer supplies used in office				
5 Beginning finished goods inventory				
6 Beginning goods in process inventory				
7 Beginning raw materials inventory				
8 Cash				
9 Depreciation expense—Factory building				
10 Depreciation expense—Factory equipment				
11 Depreciation expense—Office building				
12 Depreciation expense—Office equipment				
13 Direct labor				
14 Ending finished goods inventory				
15 Ending goods in process inventory				
16 Ending raw materials inventory				
17 Factory maintenance wages				
18 Computer supplies used in factory				
19 Income taxes				
20 Insurance on factory building				
21 Rent cost on office building				
22 Office supplies used				
23 Property taxes on factory building				
24 Raw materials purchases				
25 Sales				

Given the following selected account balances of Shanta Company, prepare its manufacturing statement for the year ended on December 31, 2013. Include a listing of the individual overhead account balances in this statement.

Sales	$1,250,000
Raw materials inventory, Dec. 31, 2012	37,000
Goods in process inventory, Dec. 31, 2012	53,900
Finished goods inventory, Dec. 31, 2012	62,750
Raw materials purchases	175,600
Direct labor	225,000
Factory computer supplies used	17,840
Indirect labor	47,000
Repairs—Factory equipment	5,250
Rent cost of factory building	57,000
Advertising expense	94,000
General and administrative expenses	129,300
Raw materials inventory, Dec. 31, 2013	42,700
Goods in process inventory, Dec. 31, 2013	41,500
Finished goods inventory, Dec. 31, 2013	67,300

Exercise 14-12
Manufacturing statement preparation

P2

Check Cost of goods manufactured, $534,390

Use the information in Exercise 14-12 to prepare an income statement for Shanta Company (a manufacturer). Assume that its cost of goods manufactured is $534,390.

Exercise 14-13
Income statement preparation

P2

Following are three separate events affecting the managerial accounting systems for different companies. Match the management concept(s) that the company is likely to adopt for the event identified. There is some overlap in the meaning of customer orientation and total quality management and, therefore, some responses can include more than one concept.

Exercise 14-14
Management concepts

C6

Event	Management Concept
_____ 1. The company starts reporting measures such as the percent of defective products and the number of units scrapped.	a. Continuous improvement (CI)
	b. Total quality management (TQM)
_____ 2. The company starts reporting measures on customer complaints and product returns from customers.	c. Just-in-time (JIT) system
_____ 3. The company starts measuring inventory turnover and discontinues elaborate inventory records. Its new focus is to pull inventory through the system.	d. Customer orientation (CO)

Exercise 14-15
Customer orientation in practice
C6

Customer orientation means that a company's managers and employees respond to customers' changing wants and needs. A manufacturer of metal parts has created a customer satisfaction survey that it asks each of its customers to complete. The survey asks about the following factors: (A) product performance; (B) price; (C) lead time; (D) delivery. Each factor is to be rated as unsatisfactory, marginal, average, satisfactory, or very satisfied.

a. Match the competitive forces 1 through 4 to the factors on the survey. A factor can be matched to more than one competitive force.

Survey Factor	Competitive Force
A. Product performance	_____ **1.** Time
B. Price	_____ **2.** Quality
C. Lead time	_____ **3.** Cost
D. Delivery	_____ **4.** Flexibility of service

b. How can managers of this company use the information from this customer satisfaction survey to better meet competitive forces and satisfy their customers?

Exercise 14-16
Cost classifications for a service company
C2

Listed below are costs of providing an airline service. Classify each cost as (a) either variable or fixed and (b) as either direct or indirect. Consider the cost object to be a flight.

Cost	Cost by Behavior		Cost by Traceability	
	Variable	Fixed	Direct	Indirect
1. Advertising..........................	____	____	____	____
2. Beverages and snacks..................	____	____	____	____
3. Regional vice-president salary.............	____	____	____	____
4. Depreciation on ground equipment.......	____	____	____	____
5. Fuel and oil used in planes..............	____	____	____	____
6. Flight attendant salaries.................	____	____	____	____
7. Pilot salaries.........................	____	____	____	____
8. Ground crew wages.....................	____	____	____	____
9. Travel agent salaries..................	____	____	____	____

connect

PROBLEM SET A

Problem 14-1A
Managerial accounting role
C1

This chapter explained the purpose of managerial accounting in the context of the current business environment. Review the *automobile* section of your local newspaper; the Sunday paper is often best. Review advertisements of sport-utility vehicles and identify the manufacturers that offer these products and the factors on which they compete.

Required

Discuss the potential contributions and responsibilities of the managerial accounting professional in helping an automobile manufacturer succeed. (*Hint:* Think about information and estimates that a managerial accountant might provide new entrants into the sport-utility market.)

Refer to *Decision Maker,* **Purchase Manager,** in this chapter. Assume that you are the motorcycle manu-facturer's managerial accountant. The purchasing manager asks you about preparing an estimate of the related costs for buying motorcycle seats from supplier (B). She tells you this estimate is needed because unless dollar estimates are attached to nonfinancial factors, such as lost production time, her supervisor will not give it full attention. The manager also shows you the following information.

Problem 14-2A
Opportunity cost estimation and application

C1 C2

- Production output is 1,000 motorcycles per year based on 250 production days a year.
- Production time per day is 8 hours at a cost of $2,000 per hour to run the production line.
- Lost production time due to poor quality is 1%.
- Satisfied customers purchase, on average, three motorcycles during a lifetime.
- Satisfied customers recommend the product, on average, to 5 other people.
- Marketing predicts that using seat (B) will result in 5 lost customers per year from repeat business and referrals.
- Average gross profit per motorcycle is $3,000.

Required

Estimate the costs (including opportunity costs) of buying motorcycle seats from supplier (B). This problem requires that you think creatively and make reasonable estimates; thus there could be more than one correct answer. (*Hint:* Reread the answer to *Decision Maker* and compare the cost savings for buying from supplier [B] to the sum of lost customer revenue from repeat business and referrals and the cost of lost production time.)

Check   Estimated cost of lost production time, $40,000

Listed here are the total costs associated with the 2013 production of 1,000 drum sets manufactured by DrumBeat. The drum sets sell for $500 each.

Problem 14-3A
Cost computation, classification, and analysis

C2 C3

Costs	Cost by Behavior		Cost by Function	
	Variable	Fixed	Product	Period
1. Plastic for casing—$17,000............................	$17,000	____	$17,000	____
2. Wages of assembly workers—$82,000....................	____	____	____	____
3. Property taxes on factory—$5,000	____	____	____	____
4. Accounting staff salaries—$35,000	____	____	____	____
5. Drum stands (1,000 stands outsourced)—$26,000	____	____	____	____
6. Rent cost of equipment for sales staff—$10,000	____	____	____	____
7. Upper management salaries—$125,000	____	____	____	____
8. Annual flat fee for maintenance service—$10,000	____	____	____	____
9. Sales commissions—$15 per unit	____	____	____	____
10. Machinery depreciation, straight-line—$40,000	____	____	____	____

Required

1. Classify each cost and its amount as (*a*) either variable or fixed and (*b*) either product or period. (The first cost is completed as an example.)

2. Compute the manufacturing cost per drum set.

Check   (1) Total variable production cost, $125,000

Analysis Component

3. Assume that 1,200 drum sets are produced in the next year. What do you predict will be the total cost of plastic for the casings and the per unit cost of the plastic for the casings? Explain.

4. Assume that 1,200 drum sets are produced in the next year. What do you predict will be the total cost of property taxes and the per unit cost of the property taxes? Explain.

Assume that you must make a presentation to the marketing staff explaining the difference between prod-uct and period costs. Your supervisor tells you the marketing staff would also like clarification regarding prime and conversion costs and an explanation of how these terms fit with product and period cost. You are told that many on the staff are unable to classify costs in their merchandising activities.

Problem 14-4A
Cost classification and explanation

C2 C3

Required

Prepare a one-page memorandum to your supervisor outlining your presentation to the marketing staff.

Problem 14-5A
Ending inventory computation
and evaluation

C4

Notaro's Boot Company makes specialty boots for the rodeo circuit. On December 31, 2012, the company had (a) 300 pairs of boots in finished goods inventory and (b) 1,200 heels at a cost of $8 each in raw materials inventory. During 2013, the company purchased 35,000 additional heels at $8 each and manufactured 16,600 pairs of boots.

Required

1. Determine the unit and dollar amounts of raw materials inventory in heels at December 31, 2013.

Analysis Component

2. Write a one-half page memorandum to the production manager explaining why a just-in-time inventory system for heels should be considered. Include the amount of working capital that can be reduced at December 31, 2013, if the ending heel raw material inventory is cut by half.

Problem 14-6A
Inventory computation
and reporting

C4 P1

mhhe.com/wildFINMAN5e

Shown here are annual financial data at December 31, 2013, taken from two different companies.

	Sports World Retail	Sno-Board Manufacturing
Beginning inventory		
Merchandise	$200,000	
Finished goods		$500,000
Cost of purchases	300,000	
Cost of goods manufactured		875,000
Ending inventory		
Merchandise	175,000	
Finished goods		225,000

Required

1. Compute the cost of goods sold section of the income statement at December 31, 2013, for each company. Include the proper title and format in the solution.

2. Write a half-page memorandum to your instructor (a) identifying the inventory accounts and (b) describing where each is reported on the income statement and balance sheet for both companies.

Problem 14-7A
Manufacturing and income
statements; inventory analysis

P2   A1

The following calendar year-end information is taken from the December 31, 2013, adjusted trial balance and other records of DeLeon Company.

Advertising expense	$ 28,750	Direct labor	$ 675,480
Depreciation expense—Office equipment	7,250	Income taxes expense	233,725
Depreciation expense—Selling equipment	8,600	Indirect labor	56,875
Depreciation expense—Factory equipment	33,550	Miscellaneous production costs	8,425
Factory supervision	102,600	Office salaries expense	63,000
Factory supplies used	7,350	Raw materials purchases	925,000
Factory utilities	33,000	Rent expense—Office space	22,000
Inventories		Rent expense—Selling space	26,100
Raw materials, December 31, 2012	166,850	Rent expense—Factory building	76,800
Raw materials, December 31, 2013	182,000	Maintenance expense—Factory equipment	35,400
Goods in process, December 31, 2012	15,700	Sales	4,525,000
Goods in process, December 31, 2013	19,380	Sales discounts	62,500
Finished goods, December 31, 2012	167,350	Sales salaries expense	392,560
Finished goods, December 31, 2013	136,490		

Required

1. Prepare the company's 2013 manufacturing statement.

2. Prepare the company's 2013 income statement that reports separate categories for (*a*) selling expenses and (*b*) general and administrative expenses.

Analysis Component

3. Compute the (*a*) inventory turnover, defined as cost of goods sold divided by average inventory, and (*b*) days' sales in inventory, defined as 365 times ending inventory divided by cost of goods sold, for both its raw materials inventory and its finished goods inventory. (To compute turnover and days' sales in inventory for raw materials, use raw materials used rather than cost of goods sold.) Discuss some possible reasons for differences between these ratios for the two types of inventories. Round answers to one decimal place.

Many fast-food restaurants compete on lean business concepts. Match each of the following activities at a fast-food restaurant with the lean business concept it strives to achieve. Some activities might relate to more than one lean business concept.

_____ **1.** Courteous employees
_____ **2.** Food produced to order
_____ **3.** Clean tables and floors
_____ **4.** Orders filled within three minutes
_____ **5.** Standardized food making processes
_____ **6.** New product development
_____ **7.** Customer satisfaction surveys
_____ **8.** Standardized menus from location to location
_____ **9.** Drive-through windows
_____ **10.** Continually changing menus

a. Just-in-time (JIT)
b. Continuous improvement (CI)
c. Total quality management (TQM)

Problem 14-8A
Lean business concepts
C6

This chapter described the purpose of managerial accounting in the context of the current business environment. Review the *home electronics* section of your local newspaper; the Sunday paper is often best. Review advertisements of home electronics and identify the manufacturers that offer these products and the factors on which they compete.

PROBLEM SET B

Problem 14-1B
Managerial accounting role
C1

Required

Discuss the potential contributions and responsibilities of the managerial accounting professional in helping a home electronics manufacturer succeed. (*Hint:* Think about information and estimates that a managerial accountant might provide new entrants into the home electronics market.)

Refer to *Decision Maker,* **Purchase Manager,** in this chapter. Assume that you are the motorcycle manufacturer's managerial accountant. The purchasing manager asks you about preparing an estimate of the related costs for buying motorcycle seats from supplier (B). She tells you this estimate is needed because unless dollar estimates are attached to nonfinancial factors such as lost production time, her supervisor will not give it full attention. The manager also shows you the following information.

Problem 14-2B
Opportunity cost estimation and application
C1 C2

- Production output is 1,000 motorcycles per year based on 250 production days a year.
- Production time per day is 8 hours at a cost of $500 per hour to run the production line.
- Lost production time due to poor quality is 1%.
- Satisfied customers purchase, on average, three motorcycles during a lifetime.
- Satisfied customers recommend the product, on average, to four other people.
- Marketing predicts that using seat (B) will result in four lost customers per year from repeat business and referrals.
- Average gross profit per motorcycle is $4,000.

Required

Check Cost of lost gross profit, $16,000

Estimate the costs (including opportunity costs) of buying motorcycle seats from supplier (B). This problem requires that you think creatively and make reasonable estimates; thus there could be more than one correct answer. (*Hint:* Reread the answer to *Decision Maker,* and compare the cost savings for buying from supplier [B] to the sum of lost customer revenue from repeat business and referrals and the cost of lost production time.)

Problem 14-3B
Cost computation, classification, and analysis

C2 C3

Listed here are the total costs associated with the 2013 production of 15,000 Blu-ray Discs (BDs) manufactured by Nextgen. The BDs sell for $18 each.

Costs	Cost by Behavior		Cost by Function	
	Variable	Fixed	Product	Period
1. Plastic for BDs—$1,500	$1,500		$1,500	
2. Wages of assembly workers—$30,000				
3. Cost of factory rent—$6,750				
4. Systems staff salaries—$15,000				
5. Labeling (12,000 outsourced)—$3,750				
6. Cost of office equipment rent—$1,050				
7. Upper management salaries—$120,000				
8. Annual fixed fee for cleaning service—$4,520				
9. Sales commissions—$0.50 per BD				
10. Machinery depreciation, straight-line—$18,000				

Required

1. Classify each cost and its amount as (*a*) either variable or fixed and (*b*) either product or period. (The first cost is completed as an example.)

Check (2) Total variable production cost, $35,250

2. Compute the manufacturing cost per BD.

Analysis Component

3. Assume that 10,000 BDs are produced in the next year. What do you predict will be the total cost of plastic for the BDs and the per unit cost of the plastic for the BDs? Explain.

4. Assume that 10,000 BDs are produced in the next year. What do you predict will be the total cost of factory rent and the per unit cost of the factory rent? Explain.

Problem 14-4B
Cost classification and explanation

C2 C3

Assume that you must make a presentation to a client explaining the difference between prime and conversion costs. The client makes and sells 200,000 cookies per week. The client tells you that her sales staff also would like a clarification regarding product and period costs. She tells you that most of the staff lack training in managerial accounting.

Required

Prepare a one-page memorandum to your client outlining your planned presentation to her sales staff.

Problem 14-5B
Ending inventory computation and evaluation

C4

Sharp Edges makes specialty skates for the ice skating circuit. On December 31, 2012, the company had (*a*) 1,500 skates in finished goods inventory and (*b*) 2,500 blades at a cost of $20 each in raw materials inventory. During 2013, Sharp Edges purchased 45,000 additional blades at $20 each and manufactured 20,750 pairs of skates.

Required

1. Determine the unit and dollar amounts of raw materials inventory in blades at December 31, 2013.

Check (1) Ending (blade) inventory, 6,000 units; $120,000

Analysis Component

2. Write a one-half page memorandum to the production manager explaining why a just-in-time inventory system for blades should be considered. Include the amount of working capital that can be reduced at December 31, 2013, if the ending blade raw materials inventory is cut in half.

Shown here are annual financial data at December 31, 2013, taken from two different companies.

Problem 14-6B
Inventory computation and reporting

C4 P1

	Badger (Retail)	Naima (Manufacturing)
Beginning inventory		
Merchandise	$100,000	
Finished goods		$300,000
Cost of purchases	250,000	
Cost of goods manufactured		586,000
Ending inventory		
Merchandise	150,000	
Finished goods		200,000

Required

1. Compute the cost of goods sold section of the income statement at December 31, 2013, for each company. Include the proper title and format in the solution.

Check (1) Badger cost of goods sold, $200,000

2. Write a half-page memorandum to your instructor (*a*) identifying the inventory accounts and (*b*) identifying where each is reported on the income statement and balance sheet for both companies.

The following calendar year-end information is taken from the December 31, 2013, adjusted trial balance and other records of Elegant Furniture.

Problem 14-7B
Manufacturing and income statements; analysis of inventories P2 A1

Advertising expense	$ 20,250	Direct labor	$ 562,500
Depreciation expense—Office equipment	8,440	Income taxes expense	136,700
Depreciation expense—Selling equipment	10,125	Indirect labor	59,000
Depreciation expense—Factory equipment	35,400	Miscellaneous production costs	8,440
Factory supervision	121,500	Office salaries expense	70,875
Factory supplies used	6,060	Raw materials purchases	894,375
Factory utilities	37,500	Rent expense—Office space	23,625
Inventories		Rent expense—Selling space	27,000
Raw materials, December 31, 2012	40,375	Rent expense—Factory building	93,500
Raw materials, December 31, 2013	70,430	Maintenance expense—Factory equipment	30,375
Goods in process, December 31, 2012	12,500	Sales	5,000,000
Goods in process, December 31, 2013	14,100	Sales discounts	57,375
Finished goods, December 31, 2012	177,200	Sales salaries expense	295,300
Finished goods, December 31, 2013	141,750		

Required

1. Prepare the company's 2013 manufacturing statement.

Check (1) Cost of goods manufactured, $1,816,995

2. Prepare the company's 2013 income statement that reports separate categories for (*a*) selling expenses and (*b*) general and administrative expenses.

Analysis Component

3. Compute the (*a*) inventory turnover, defined as cost of goods sold divided by average inventory, and (*b*) days' sales in inventory, defined as 365 times ending inventory divided by cost of goods sold, for both its raw materials inventory and its finished goods inventory. (To compute turnover and days' sales in inventory for raw materials, use raw materials used rather than cost of goods sold.) Discuss some possible reasons for differences between these ratios for the two types of inventories. Round answers to one decimal place.

Problem 14-8B

Lean business concepts

C6

Canon manufactures digital cameras and must compete on lean manufacturing concepts. Match each of the following activities that it engages in with the lean manufacturing concept it strives to achieve. (Some activities might relate to more than one lean manufacturing concept.)

_____ **1.** Manufacturing facilities are arranged to reduce move time and wait time.

_____ **2.** Canon conducts focus groups to determine new features that customers want in digital cameras.

_____ **3.** Canon monitors the market to determine what features its competitors are offering on digital cameras.

_____ **4.** Canon asks production workers for ideas to improve production.

_____ **5.** The manufacturing process is standardized and documented.

_____ **6.** Cameras are produced in small lots, and only to customer order.

_____ **7.** Lenses are received daily based on customer orders.

_____ **8.** Customers receive a satisfaction survey with each camera purchased.

_____ **9.** Orders received are filled within two business days.

_____ **10.** Canon works with suppliers to reduce inspection time of incoming materials.

a. Just-in-time (JIT)
b. Continuous improvement (CI)
c. Total quality management (TQM)

SERIAL PROBLEM

Success Systems

C2 C4 P2

(This serial problem begins in Chapter 1 and continues through most of the book. If previous chapter segments were not completed, the serial problem can begin at this point. It is helpful, but not necessary, to use the Working Papers that accompany the book.)

SP 14 Adria Lopez, owner of Success Systems, decides to diversify her business by also manufacturing computer workstation furniture.

Required

1. Classify the following manufacturing costs of Success Systems by behavior and traceability.

Product Costs	Cost by Behavior		Cost by Traceability	
	Variable	Fixed	Direct	Indirect
1. Monthly flat fee to clean workshop	___	___	___	___
2. Laminate coverings for desktops	___	___	___	___
3. Taxes on assembly workshop	___	___	___	___
4. Glue to assemble workstation component parts	___	___	___	___
5. Wages of desk assembler	___	___	___	___
6. Electricity for workshop	___	___	___	___
7. Depreciation on tools	___	___	___	___

2. Prepare a manufacturing statement for Success Systems for the month ended January 31, 2014. Assume the following manufacturing costs:

Direct materials: $2,200

Factory overhead: $490

Direct labor: $900

Beginning goods in process: none (December 31, 2013)

Ending goods in process: $540 (January 31, 2014)

Beginning finished goods inventory: none (December 31, 2013)

Ending finished goods inventory: $350 (January 31, 2014)

3. Prepare the cost of goods sold section of a partial income statement for Success Systems for the month ended January 31, 2014.

Check   (3) COGS, $2,700

Beyond the Numbers

BTN 14-1   Managerial accounting is more than recording, maintaining, and reporting financial results. Managerial accountants must provide managers with both financial and nonfinancial information including estimates, projections, and forecasts. An important estimate for Polaris is its reserve for warranty claims, and the company must provide shareholders information on these estimates.

REPORTING IN ACTION

C1

Polaris

Required

1. Access and read Polaris's "Product warranties" section of the "Organization and Significant Accounting Policies" footnote to its financial statements, from Appendix A. What is the warranty period for Polaris's products? How does management establish and adjust the warranty reserve? What are some of the effects if the company's actual results differ from its estimates?

2. What is the management accountant's role in determining those estimates?

3. What are some factors that could impact the warranty accrual in a given year?

Fast Forward

4. Access Polaris's annual report for a fiscal year ending after December 31, 2011, from either its Website [Polaris.com] or the SEC's EDGAR database [www.sec.gov]. Answer the questions in parts (1), (2), and (3) after reading the current "Organization and Significant Accounting Policies". Identify any major changes.

BTN 14-2   Both Polaris and Arctic Cat provide warranties on the products they sell. Accurate estimates of these future warranty claims are important. Access the annual report or 10-K for both Polaris (from Appendix A) and Arctic Cat. The Polaris report is for the year ended December 31, 2011, and the Arctic Cat report is for the year ended March 31, 2011.

COMPARATIVE ANALYSIS

C2

Polaris

Arctic Cat

Required

1. Read the "Product warranties" section of the "Organization and Significant Accounting Policies" footnote for Polaris. For each of the three years reported, compare the dollar amounts of the annual warranty expense and actual warranty claims paid. Is Polaris' warranty expense higher, lower, or about the same as its warranty claims paid?

2. Read the "Product Warranties" section of the "Summary of Significant Accounting Policies" footnote for Arctic Cat. For each of the three years reported, compare the dollar amounts of the annual warranty expense and actual warranty claims paid. Is Arctic Cat's warranty expense higher, lower, or about the same as its warranty claims paid?

3. Using the answers from parts (1) and (2), which company made more accurate estimates of warranty costs over the most recent three years?

BTN 14-3   Assume that you are the managerial accountant at Infostore, a manufacturer of hard drives, CDs, and DVDs. Its reporting year-end is December 31. The chief financial officer is concerned about having enough cash to pay the expected income tax bill because of poor cash flow management. On November 15, the purchasing department purchased excess inventory of CD raw materials in anticipation of rapid growth of this product beginning in January. To decrease the company's tax liability, the chief financial officer tells you to record the purchase of this inventory as part of supplies and expense it in the current year; this would decrease the company's tax liability by increasing expenses.

ETHICS CHALLENGE

C1 C3

650   Chapter 14   Managerial Accounting Concepts and Principles

Required

1. In which account should the purchase of CD raw materials be recorded?
2. How should you respond to this request by the chief financial officer?

**COMMUNICATING
IN PRACTICE**
C6

BTN 14-4   Write a one-page memorandum to a prospective college student about salary expectations for graduates in business. Compare and contrast the expected salaries for accounting (including different subfields such as public, corporate, tax, audit, and so forth), marketing, management, and finance majors. Prepare a graph showing average starting salaries (and those for experienced professionals in those fields if available). To get this information, stop by your school's career services office; libraries also have this information. The Website JobStar.org (click on *Salary Info*) also can get you started.

**TAKING IT TO
THE NET**
C1

BTN 14-5   Managerial accounting professionals follow a code of ethics. As a member of the Institute of Management Accountants, the managerial accountant must comply with Standards of Ethical Conduct.

Required

1. Identify, print, and read the *Statement of Ethical Professional Practice* posted at www.IMAnet.org. (Search using "statement of ethical professional practice and select the Ethics Center and Helpline link. Under Ethical Practices, select Learn More.")
2. What four overarching ethical principles underlie the IMA's statement?
3. Describe the courses of action the IMA recommends in resolving ethical conflicts.

**TEAMWORK IN
ACTION**
C5 P2

BTN 14-6   The following calendar-year information is taken from the December 31, 2013, adjusted trial balance and other records of Dahlia Company.

Advertising expense	$ 19,125	Direct labor	$ 650,750
Depreciation expense—Office equipment	8,750	Indirect labor	60,000
Depreciation expense—Selling equipment	10,000	Miscellaneous production costs	8,500
Depreciation expense—Factory equipment	32,500	Office salaries expense	100,875
Factory supervision	122,500	Raw materials purchases	872,500
Factory supplies used	15,750	Rent expense—Office space	21,125
Factory utilities	36,250	Rent expense—Selling space	25,750
Inventories		Rent expense—Factory building	79,750
Raw materials, December 31, 2012	177,500	Maintenance expense—Factory equipment	27,875
Raw materials, December 31, 2013	168,125	Sales	3,275,000
Goods in process, December 31, 2012	15,875	Sales discounts	57,500
Goods in process, December 31, 2013	14,000	Sales salaries expense	286,250
Finished goods, December 31, 2012	164,375		
Finished goods, December 31, 2013	129,000		

Required

1. *Each* team member is to be responsible for computing **one** of the following amounts. You are not to duplicate your teammates' work. Get any necessary amounts from teammates. Each member is to explain the computation to the team in preparation for reporting to class.

   a. Materials used.   **d.** Total cost of goods in process.
   b. Factory overhead.   **e.** Cost of goods manufactured.
   c. Total manufacturing costs.

2. Check your cost of goods manufactured with the instructor. If it is correct, proceed to part (3).

3. *Each* team member is to be responsible for computing **one** of the following amounts. You are not to duplicate your teammates' work. Get any necessary amounts from teammates. Each member is to explain the computation to the team in preparation for reporting to class.

a. Net sales.	**d.** Total operating expenses.
b. Cost of goods sold.	**e.** Net income or loss before taxes.
c. Gross profit.	

Point: Provide teams with transparencies and markers for presentation purposes.

BTN 14-7   Alex Velez and Nikhil Arora of Back to the Roots must understand manufacturing costs to effectively operate and succeed as a profitable and efficient business.

ENTREPRENEURIAL DECISION

C1 C2 C6

Required

1. What are the three main categories of manufacturing costs the owners must monitor and control? Provide examples of each.

2. What are four goals of a total quality management process? How can Back to the Roots use TQM to improve its business activities?

BTN 14-8   Visit your favorite fast-food restaurant. Observe its business operations.

HITTING THE ROAD

C1 C2

Required

1. Describe all business activities from the time a customer arrives to the time that customer departs.

2. List all costs you can identify with the separate activities described in part 1.

3. Classify each cost from part 2 as fixed or variable, and explain your classification.

BTN 14-9   Access Piaggio's Website (www.piaggiogroup.com) and select "Governance" and then select "Company boards." Read the section dealing with the role of its board of directors.

GLOBAL DECISION

C1

PIAGGIO

Required

1. Identify the role of Piaggio's board of directors.

2. How would management accountants be involved in assisting the board of directors in carrying out their responsibilities? Explain.

ANSWERS TO MULTIPLE CHOICE QUIZ

1. c
2. b
3. b
4. a

5. Beginning finished goods + Cost of goods manufactured (COGM) − Ending finished goods = Cost of goods sold
$6,000 + COGM − $3,200 = $7,500
COGM = $4,700

Job Order Costing and Analysis

A Look Back

Chapter 14 introduced managerial accounting and explained basic cost concepts. We also described the lean business model and the reporting of manufacturing activities, including the manufacturing statement.

A Look at This Chapter

We begin this chapter by describing a cost accounting system. We then explain the procedures used to determine costs using a job order costing system. We conclude with a discussion of over- and underapplied overhead.

A Look Ahead

Chapter 16 focuses on measuring costs in process production companies. We explain process production, describe how to assign costs to processes, and compute and analyze cost per equivalent unit.

Learning Objectives

CONCEPTUAL

C1 Describe important features of job order production. (p. 654)

C2 Explain job cost sheets and how they are used in job order cost accounting. (p. 656)

ANALYTICAL

A1 Apply job order costing in pricing services. (p. 667)

PROCEDURAL

P1 Describe and record the flow of materials costs in job order cost accounting. (p. 658)

P2 Describe and record the flow of labor costs in job order cost accounting. (p. 660)

P3 Describe and record the flow of overhead costs in job order cost accounting. (p. 661)

P4 Determine adjustments for overapplied and underapplied factory overhead. (p. 666)

Decision Insight

Suit Yourself!

"Be fearless!"

—DAVID SCHOTTENSTEIN

COLUMBUS, OH—Watching Italian tailors hand-sew high-quality men's suits, David Schottenstein decided to start his own men's clothing store. David's aspirations were high: Sell custom-made mens' suits, hand-sewn and made from the finest fabrics, at prices up to 80 percent less than competitor's clothes. David recalls thinking, "If I have to crawl around on my hands and knees to measure people's inseams to get this business started, I'm going to do it." The result is **Astor and Black** (**AstorandBlack.com**), a startup international company with sales in 2010 of over $20 million.

David's employees travel to customers' homes, offices, and clubs around the world to do personal fittings. Customers select the fabrics, buttons, stitching, and other details, and then tailors hand-sew each suit to exact customer specifications. "I like to pick out my own stuff, and it's easier than going to a store," says Malcolm Jenkins, All-Pro NFL cornerback and owner of over 30 Astor and Black suits. David stresses that "customer service and satisfying each customer's individual needs" are what drive success.

David's business model is based on selling a higher volume of suits than competitors, but at lower margins per suit. This requires David to carefully monitor costs. Astor and Black, like other makers of custom products, uses a state-of-the-art job order cost accounting system to track costs. Such a system tracks the cost of materials, labor, and overhead for each suit, enabling David to make quick business decisions regarding costs and selling prices. Job order costing allows entrepreneurs like David to better isolate costs and avoid the run away costs often experienced by startups that fail to use such costing techniques. "We keep our fixed costs low by not stocking inventory," explains David, "and we use minimal office space as our sales mainly occur in customer's homes or offices."

David encourages young entrepreneurs to believe in themselves. "People have great ideas all the time but find all the [wrong] reasons not to do it. You have to be fearless," says David. In David's case, that fearlessness began with selling rare cigars and trading stocks as a teenager. "It was bizarre," says his father Tom. "He was a kid on a mission." With attention to detail and insights gained from job order costing information, David's business continues to expand, now offering women's suits and online tailoring, allowing customers to create a simulated version of the outfit they want. "Be brazen or you will be done on the day you start," says David.

[Sources: *Astor and Black* Website, January 2013; *Yourhiddenpotential.co.uk* Website, May 8, 2011; *The Columbus Dispatch*, June 22, 2008; *Forbes*, May 9, 2011; *Smart Business Online*, www.sbonline.com, June 2009.]

This chapter introduces a system for assigning costs to the flow of goods through a production process. We then describe the details of a *job order cost accounting system*. Job order costing is frequently used by manufacturers of custom products or providers of custom services. Manufacturers that use job order costing typically base it on a perpetual inventory system, which provides a continuous record of materials, goods in process, and finished goods inventories.

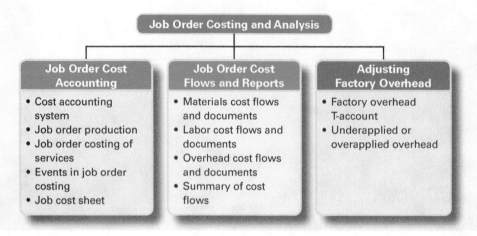

Job Order Costing and Analysis

Job Order Cost Accounting	Job Order Cost Flows and Reports	Adjusting Factory Overhead
• Cost accounting system • Job order production • Job order costing of services • Events in job order costing • Job cost sheet	• Materials cost flows and documents • Labor cost flows and documents • Overhead cost flows and documents • Summary of cost flows	• Factory overhead T-account • Underapplied or overapplied overhead

JOB ORDER COST ACCOUNTING

This section describes a cost accounting system and job order production and costing.

Cost Accounting System

Point: Cost accounting systems accumulate costs and then assign them to products and services.

An ever-increasing number of companies use a cost accounting system to generate timely and accurate inventory information. A **cost accounting system** records manufacturing activities using a *perpetual* inventory system, which continuously updates records for costs of materials, goods in process, and finished goods inventories. A cost accounting system also provides timely information about inventories and manufacturing costs per unit of product. This is especially helpful for managers' efforts to control costs and determine selling prices. (A **general accounting system** records manufacturing activities using a *periodic* inventory system. Some companies still use a general accounting system, but its use is declining as competitive forces and customer demands have increased pressures on companies to better manage inventories.)

C1 Describe important features of job order production.

The two basic types of cost accounting systems are *job order cost accounting* and *process cost accounting*. We describe job order cost accounting in this chapter. Process cost accounting is explained in the next chapter.

Job Order Production

Many companies produce products individually designed to meet the needs of a specific customer. Each customized product is manufactured separately and its production is called **job order production,** or *job order manufacturing* (also called *customized production,* which is the production of products in response to special orders). Examples of such products include synthetic football fields, special-order machines, a factory building, custom jewelry, wedding invitations, and artwork. The production activities for a customized product represent a **job.**

Boeing's aerospace division is one example of a job order production system. Its primary business is twofold: (1) design, develop, and integrate space carriers and (2) provide systems engineering and integration of Department of Defense (DoD) systems. Many of its orders are customized and produced through job order operations.

When a job involves producing more than one unit of a custom product, it is often called a **job lot.** Products produced as job lots could include benches for a church, imprinted T-shirts for a 10K race or company picnic, or advertising signs for a chain of stores. Although these orders involve more than one unit, the volume of production is typically low, such as 50 benches, 200 T-shirts, or 100 signs. Another feature of job order production is the diversity, often called *heterogeneity,* of the products produced. Namely, each customer order is likely to differ from another in some important respect. These variations can be minor or major.

 Decision Insight

Custom Design   Managers once saw companies as the center of a solar system orbited by suppliers and customers. Now the customer has become the center of the business universe. Nike allows custom orders over the Internet, enabling customers to select materials, colors, and to personalize their shoes with letters and numbers. Soon consumers may be able to personalize almost any product, from cellular phones to appliances to furniture. ▪

Job Order Costing of Services

The principle of customization is equally applicable to both manufacturing *and* service companies. Most service companies meet customers' needs by performing a custom service for a specific customer. Examples of such services include an accountant auditing a client's financial statements, an interior designer remodeling an office, a wedding consultant planning and supervising a reception, and a lawyer defending a client. Whether the setting is manufacturing or services, job order operations involve meeting the needs of customers by producing or performing custom jobs. We show an example of job order costing for an advertising service in the Decision Analysis section of this chapter.

Events in Job Order Costing

The initial event in a normal job order operation is the receipt of a customer order for a custom product. This causes the company to begin work on a job. A less common case occurs when management decides to begin work on a job before it has a signed contract. This is referred to as *jobs produced on speculation.*

Step 1: **Predict the cost to complete the job.** This cost depends on the product design prepared by either the customer or the producer.

Step 2: **Negotiate price and decide whether to pursue the job.** Other than for government or other cost-plus contracts, the selling price is determined by market factors. Producers evaluate the market price, compare it to cost, and determine whether the profit on the job is reasonable. If the profit is not reasonable, the producer would determine a desired **target cost.**

Step 3: **Schedule production of the job.** This must meet the customer's needs and fit within the company's own production constraints. Preparation of this work schedule should consider workplace facilities including equipment, personnel, and supplies. Once this schedule is complete, the producer can place orders for raw materials. Production occurs as materials and labor are applied to the job.

An overview of job order production activity is shown in Exhibit 15.1. This exhibit shows the March production activity of Road Warriors, which installs security devices into cars and trucks. The company converts any vehicle by adding alarms, reinforced exterior, bulletproof glass, and bomb detectors. The company began by catering to high-profile celebrities, but it now caters to anyone who desires added security in a vehicle.

Job order production for Road Warriors requires materials, labor, and overhead costs. Recall that direct materials are goods used in manufacturing that are clearly identified with a particular job. Similarly, direct labor is effort devoted to a particular job. Overhead costs support production of more than one job. Common overhead items are depreciation on factory buildings and equipment, factory supplies, supervision, maintenance, cleaning, and utilities.

Exhibit 15.1 shows that materials, labor, and overhead are added to Jobs B15, B16, B17, B18, and B19, which were started during March. Special tires and bulletproof glass are added to Jobs B15 and B16, while Job B17 receives a reinforced exterior and bulletproof glass. Road Warriors completed Jobs B15, B16, and B17 in March and delivered Jobs B15 and B16 to

Point: Some jobs are priced on a *cost-plus basis:* The customer pays the manufacturer for costs incurred on the job plus a negotiated amount or rate of profit.

Point: Many professional examinations including the CPA and CMA exams require knowledge of job order and process cost accounting.

EXHIBIT 15.1

Job Order Production Activities

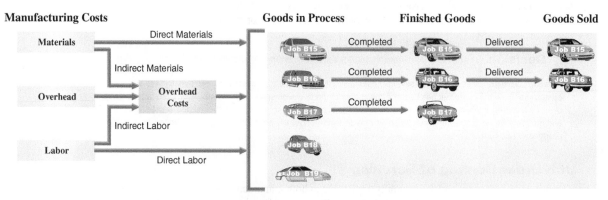

customers. At the end of March, Jobs B18 and B19 remain in goods in process inventory and Job B17 is in finished goods inventory. Both labor and materials costs are also separated into their direct and indirect components. Their indirect amounts are added to overhead. Total overhead cost is then allocated to the various jobs.

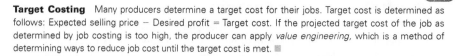

Decision Insight

Target Costing   Many producers determine a target cost for their jobs. Target cost is determined as follows: Expected selling price − Desired profit = Target cost. If the projected target cost of the job as determined by job costing is too high, the producer can apply *value engineering,* which is a method of determining ways to reduce job cost until the target cost is met. ■

Job Cost Sheet

C2 Explain job cost sheets and how they are used in job order cost accounting.

General ledger accounts usually do not provide the accounting information that managers of job order cost operations need to plan and control production activities. This is so because the needed information often requires more detailed data. Such detailed data are usually stored in subsidiary records controlled by general ledger accounts. Subsidiary records store information about raw materials, overhead costs, jobs in process, finished goods, and other items. This section describes the use of these records.

A major aim of a **job order cost accounting system** is to determine the cost of producing each job or job lot. In the case of a job lot, the system also aims to compute the cost per unit. The accounting system must include separate records for each job to accomplish this, and it must capture information about costs incurred and charge these costs to each job.

A **job cost sheet** is a separate record maintained for each job. Exhibit 15.2 shows a job cost sheet for an alarm system that Road Warriors produced for a customer. This job cost sheet identifies the customer, the job number assigned, the product, and key dates. Costs incurred on the job are immediately recorded on this sheet. When each job is complete, the supervisor enters the date of completion, records any remarks, and signs the sheet. The job cost sheet in Exhibit 15.2 classifies costs as direct materials, direct labor, or overhead. It shows that a total of $600 in direct materials is added to Job B15 on four different dates. It also shows seven entries for direct labor costs that total $1,000. Road Warriors *allocates* (also termed *applies, assigns,* or *charges*) factory overhead costs of $1,600 to this job using an allocation rate of 160% of direct labor cost (160% × $1,000)—we discuss overhead allocation later in this chapter.

Point: Factory overhead consists of costs (other than direct materials and direct labor) that ensure the production activities are carried out.

Cost Flows: During Production   While a job is being produced, its accumulated costs are kept in **Goods in Process Inventory.** The collection of job cost sheets for all jobs in process makes up a subsidiary ledger controlled by the Goods in Process Inventory account in the general ledger. Managers use job cost sheets to monitor costs incurred to date and to predict and control costs for each job.

EXHIBIT 15.2

Job Cost Sheet

```
┌─────────────────────────────────────────────────────────────────────────────┐
│ Accounting System: Exhibit 15-2                                    [_][□][X]  │
│ File  Edit  Maintain  Tasks  Analysis  Options  Reports  Window  Help         │
│ Road Warriors, Los Angeles, California                       JOB COST SHEET   │
└─────────────────────────────────────────────────────────────────────────────┘
```

Customer's Name Carroll Connor	**Job No.** B15	
Address 1542 High Point Dr.	**City & State** Malibu, California	
Job Description Level 1 Alarm System on Ford Expedition		
Date promised March 15	**Date started** March 3	**Date completed** March 11

Direct Materials			Direct Labor			Overhead		
Date	Requisition	Cost	Date	Time Ticket	Cost	Date	Rate	Cost
3/3/2013	R-4698	100.00	3/3/2013	L-3393	120.00	3/11/2013	160% of	1,600.00
3/7/2013	R-4705	225.00	3/4/2013	L-3422	150.00		Direct	
3/9/2013	R-4725	180.00	3/5/2013	L-3456	180.00		Labor	
3/10/2013	R-4777	95.00	3/8/2013	L-3479	60.00		Cost	
			3/9/2013	L-3501	90.00			
			3/10/2013	L-3535	240.00			
			3/11/2013	L-3559	160.00			
	Total	600.00		**Total**	1,000.00		**Total**	1,600.00

REMARKS: Completed job on March 11, and shipped to customer on March 15. Met all specifications and requirements.	**SUMMARY:**
	Materials 600.00
	Labor 1,000.00
	Overhead 1,600.00
Signed: *C. Luther, Supervisor*	Total cost 3,200.00

Cost Flows: Job Completion   When a job is finished, its job cost sheet is completed and moved from the jobs in process file to the finished jobs file. This latter file acts as a subsidiary ledger controlled by the **Finished Goods Inventory** account.

Cost Flows: Job Delivery   When a finished job is delivered to a customer, the job cost sheet is moved to a permanent file supporting the total cost of goods sold. This permanent file contains records from both current and prior periods. When the job is finished, the company also prepares a journal entry that credits Sales and debits Cash (or Accounts Receivable).

Point: Documents (electronic and paper) are crucial in a job order system, and the job cost sheet is a cornerstone. Understanding it aids in grasping concepts of capitalizing product costs and product cost flow.

◼ Decision Maker

Management Consultant   One of your tasks is to control and manage costs for a consulting company. At the end of a recent month, you find that three consulting jobs were completed and two are 60% complete. Each unfinished job is estimated to cost $10,000 and to earn a revenue of $12,000. You are unsure how to recognize goods in process inventory and record costs and revenues. Do you recognize any inventory? If so, how much? How much revenue is recorded for unfinished jobs this month? ◼   [Answer—p. 671]

Quick Check   Answers — p. 671

1. Which of these products is likely to involve job order production? (*a*) inexpensive watches, (*b*) racing bikes, (*c*) bottled soft drinks, or (*d*) athletic socks.
2. What is the difference between a job and a job lot?
3. Which of these statements is correct? (*a*) The collection of job cost sheets for unfinished jobs makes up a subsidiary ledger controlled by the Goods in Process Inventory account, (*b*) Job cost sheets are financial statements provided to investors, or (*c*) A separate job cost sheet is maintained in the general ledger for each job in process.
4. What three costs are normally accumulated on job cost sheets?

JOB ORDER COST FLOWS AND REPORTS

Materials

| P1 | Describe and record the flow of materials costs in job order cost accounting. |

Point: Some companies certify certain suppliers based on the quality of their materials. Goods received from these suppliers are not always inspected by the purchaser to save costs.

Materials Cost Flows and Documents

This section focuses on the flow of materials costs and the related documents in a job order cost accounting system. We begin analysis of the flow of materials costs by examining Exhibit 15.3. When materials are first received from suppliers, the employees count and inspect them and record the items' quantity and cost on a receiving report. The receiving report serves as the *source document* for recording materials received in both a materials ledger card and in the general ledger. In nearly all job order cost systems, **materials ledger cards** (or files) are perpetual records that are updated each time units are purchased and each time units are issued for use in production.

To illustrate the purchase of materials, Road Warriors acquired $450 of wiring and related materials on March 4, 2013. This purchase is recorded as follows.

Assets = Liabilities + Equity
+450   +450

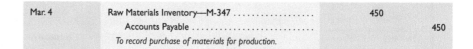

Mar. 4	Raw Materials Inventory—M-347	450	
	Accounts Payable		450
	To record purchase of materials for production.		

EXHIBIT 15.3

Materials Cost Flows through Subsidiary Records

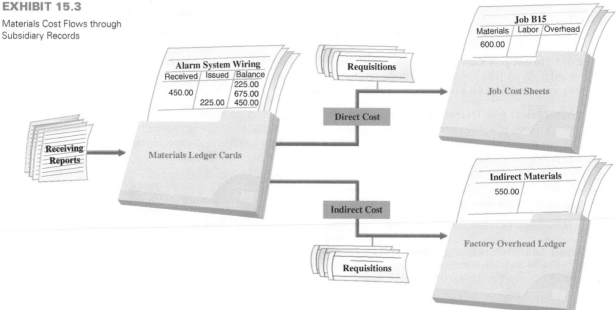

Exhibit 15.3 shows that materials can be requisitioned for use either on a specific job (direct materials) or as overhead (indirect materials). Cost of direct materials flows from the materials ledger card to the job cost sheet. The cost of indirect materials flows from the materials ledger card to the Indirect Materials account in the factory overhead ledger, which is a subsidiary ledger controlled by the Factory Overhead account in the general ledger.

Exhibit 15.4 shows a materials ledger card for material received and issued by Road Warriors. The card identifies the item as alarm system wiring and shows the item's stock number, its location in the storeroom, information about the maximum and minimum quantities that should be available, and the reorder quantity. For example, alarm system wiring is issued

EXHIBIT 15.4

Materials Ledger Card

MATERIALS LEDGER CARD

Road Warriors
Los Angeles, California

| Item | Alarm system wiring | Stock No. | M–347 | Location in Storeroom | Bin 137 |
| Maximum quantity | 5 units | Minimum quantity | 1 unit | Quantity to reorder | 2 units |

	Received				Issued				Balance		
Date	Receiving Report Number	Units	Unit Price	Total Price	Requi-sition Number	Units	Unit Price	Total Price	Units	Unit Price	Total Price
3/4/2013	C-7117	2	225.00	450.00					1	225.00	225.00
									3	225.00	675.00
3/7/2013					R–4705	1	225.00	225.00	2	225.00	450.00

and recorded on March 7, 2013. The job cost sheet in Exhibit 15.2 showed that Job B15 used this wiring.

When materials are needed in production, a production manager prepares a **materials requisition** and sends it to the materials manager. The requisition shows the job number, the type of material, the quantity needed, and the signature of the manager authorized to make the requisition. Exhibit 15.5 shows the materials requisition for alarm system wiring for Job B15. To see how this requisition ties to the flow of costs, compare the information on the requisition with the March 7, 2013, data in Exhibits 15.2 and 15.4.

Point: Requisitions are often accumulated and recorded in one entry. The frequency of entries depends on the job, the industry, and management procedures.

EXHIBIT 15.5

Materials Requisition

MATERIALS REQUISITION   No. R–4705

Road Warriors
Los Angeles, California

Job No.	B15	Date	3/7/2013
Material Stock No.	M–347	Material Description	Alarm system wiring
Quantity Requested	1	Requested By	C. Luther
Quantity Provided	1	Date Provided	3/7/2013
Filled By	M. Bateman	Material Received By	C. Luther
Remarks			

The use of alarm system wiring on Job B15 yields the following entry (locate this cost item in the job cost sheet shown in Exhibit 15.2).

Mar. 7	Goods in Process Inventory—Job B15	225	
	Raw Materials Inventory—M-347		225
	To record use of material on Job B15.		

Assets = Liabilities + Equity
+225
−225

This entry is posted both to its general ledger accounts and to subsidiary records. Posting to subsidiary records includes a debit to a job cost sheet and a credit to a materials ledger card. (*Note:* An entry to record use of indirect materials is the same as that for direct materials *except* the debit is to Factory Overhead. In the subsidiary factory overhead ledger, this entry is posted to Indirect Materials.)

Point: Exhibit 15.12 shows this entry.

P2	Describe and record the flow of labor costs in job order cost accounting.

Labor

Labor Cost Flows and Documents

Exhibit 15.6 shows the flow of labor costs from clock cards and the Factory Payroll account to subsidiary records of the job order cost accounting system. Recall that costs in subsidiary records give detailed information needed to manage and control operations.

EXHIBIT 15.6

Labor Cost Flows through Subsidiary Records

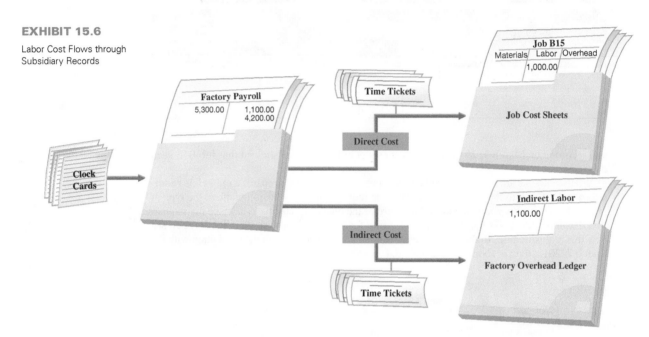

Point: In the accounting equation, we treat accounts such as Factory Payroll and Factory Overhead as temporary accounts, which hold various expenses until they are allocated to balance sheet or income statement accounts.

The flow of costs in Exhibit 15.6 begins with **clock cards.** Employees commonly use these cards to record the number of hours worked, and they serve as source documents for entries to record labor costs. Clock card data on the number of hours worked is used at the end of each pay period to determine total labor cost. This amount is then debited to the Factory Payroll account, a temporary account containing the total payroll cost (both direct and indirect). Payroll cost is later allocated to both specific jobs and overhead.

According to clock card data, workers earned $1,500 for the week ended March 5. Illustrating the flow of labor costs, the accrual and payment of these wages are recorded as follows.

Assets = Liabilities + Equity				
−1,500	−1,500			

Mar. 6	Factory Payroll	1,500	
	Cash		1,500
	To record the weekly payroll.		

Point: Many employee fraud schemes involve payroll, including overstated hours on clock cards.

To assign labor costs to specific jobs and to overhead, we must know how each employee's time is used and its costs. Source documents called **time tickets** usually capture these data. Employees regularly fill out time tickets to report how much time they spent on each job. An employee who works on several jobs during a day completes a separate time ticket for each job. Tickets are also prepared for time charged to overhead as indirect labor. A supervisor signs an employee's time ticket to confirm its accuracy.

Exhibit 15.7 shows a time ticket reporting the time a Road Warrior employee spent working on Job B15. The employee's supervisor signed the ticket to confirm its accuracy. The hourly rate and total labor cost are computed after the time ticket is turned in. To see the effect of this time ticket on the job cost sheet, look at the entry dated March 8, 2013, in Exhibit 15.2.

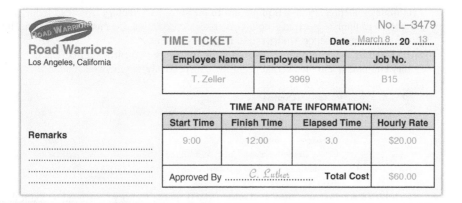

EXHIBIT 15.7

Time Ticket

When time tickets report labor used on a specific job, this cost is recorded as direct labor. The following entry records the data from the time ticket in Exhibit 15.7.

Mar. 8	Goods in Process Inventory—Job B15	60	
	Factory Payroll		60
	To record direct labor used on Job B15.		

Assets = Liabilities + Equity
+60   +60

The debit in this entry is posted both to the general ledger account and to the appropriate job cost sheet. (*Note:* An entry to record indirect labor is the same as for direct labor *except* that it debits Factory Overhead and credits Factory Payroll. In the subsidiary factory overhead ledger, the debit in this entry is posted to the Indirect Labor account.)

Point: Exhibit 15.12 shows this entry.

Overhead Cost Flows and Documents

Factory overhead (or simply overhead) cost flows are shown in Exhibit 15.8. Factory overhead includes all production costs other than direct materials and direct labor. Two sources of overhead costs are indirect materials and indirect labor. These costs are recorded from requisitions for indirect materials and time tickets for indirect labor. Two other sources of overhead are (1) vouchers authorizing payments for items such as supplies or utilities and (2) adjusting entries for costs such as depreciation on factory assets.

Overhead

P3 Describe and record the flow of overhead costs in job order cost accounting.

Factory overhead usually includes many different costs and, thus, a separate account for each is often maintained in a subsidiary factory overhead ledger. This ledger is controlled by the Factory Overhead account in the general ledger. Factory Overhead is a temporary account that accumulates costs until they are allocated to jobs.

Recording Overhead   Recall that overhead costs are recorded with debits to the Factory Overhead account and with credits to other accounts such as Cash, Accounts Payable, and

Point: Companies also incur *nonmanufacturing* costs, such as advertising, salesperson's salaries, and depreciation on assets not used in production. These types of costs are not considered overhead, but instead are treated as period costs and charged directly to the income statement. These period costs can be relevant to managers' pricing decisions.

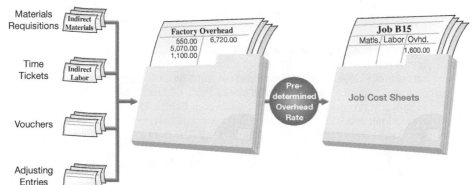

EXHIBIT 15.8

Overhead Cost Flows through Subsidiary Records

Accumulated Depreciation—Equipment. In the subsidiary factory overhead ledger, the debits are posted to their respective accounts such as Depreciation Expense—Equipment, Insurance Expense—Warehouse, or Amortization Expense—Patents.

To illustrate the recording of overhead, the following two entries reflect the depreciation of factory equipment and the accrual of utilities, respectively, for the week ended March 6.

Assets = Liabilities + Equity
−600   −600

Assets = Liabilities + Equity
            +250   −250

Mar. 6	Factory Overhead	600	
	Accumulated Depreciation—Equipment		600
	To record depreciation on factory equipment.		
Mar. 6	Factory Overhead	250	
	Utilities Payable		250
	To record the accrual of factory utilities.		

Entries to record indirect materials and indirect labor follow:

Factory Overhead .... $
    Raw Materials Inventory .... $
Factory Overhead .... $
    Factory Payroll............ $

In the subsidiary factory overhead ledger, these entries are posted to Indirect Materials and Indirect Labor, respectively.

Exhibit 15.8 shows that overhead costs flow from the Factory Overhead account to job cost sheets. Because overhead is made up of costs not directly associated with specific jobs or job lots, we cannot determine the dollar amount incurred on a specific job. We know, however, that overhead costs represent a necessary part of business activities. If a job cost is to include all costs needed to complete the job, some amount of overhead must be included. Given the difficulty in determining the overhead amount for a specific job, however, we allocate overhead to individual jobs in some reasonable manner.

Overhead Allocation Bases   We generally allocate overhead by linking it to another factor used in production, such as direct labor or machine hours. The factor to which overhead costs are linked is known as the *allocation base*. A manager must think carefully about how many and which allocation bases to use. This managerial decision influences the accuracy with which overhead costs are allocated to individual jobs. In turn, the cost of individual jobs might impact a manager's decisions for pricing or performance evaluation. In Exhibit 15.2, overhead is expressed as 160% of direct labor. We then allocate overhead by multiplying 160% by the estimated amount of direct labor on the jobs.

Point: The predetermined overhead rate is computed at the start of the period and is used throughout the period to allocate overhead to jobs. Predetermined overhead rates can be estimated using mathematical equations, statistical analysis, or professional experience.

Overhead Allocation Rates   We cannot wait until the end of a period to allocate overhead to jobs because perpetual inventory records are part of the job order costing system (demanding up-to-date costs). Instead, we must predict overhead in advance and assign it to jobs so that a job's total costs can be estimated prior to its completion. This estimated cost is useful for managers in many decisions including setting prices and identifying costs that are out of control. Being able to estimate overhead in advance requires a **predetermined overhead rate,** also called *predetermined overhead allocation* (or *application*) *rate*. This rate requires an estimate of total overhead cost and an allocation factor such as total direct labor cost before the start of the period. Exhibit 15.9 shows the usual formula for computing a predetermined overhead rate (estimates are commonly based on annual amounts). This rate is used during the period to allocate overhead to jobs. It is common for companies to use multiple activity (allocation) bases and multiple predetermined overhead rates for different types of products and services.

EXHIBIT 15.9

Predetermined Overhead Allocation Rate Formula

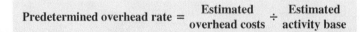

$$\text{Predetermined overhead rate} = \frac{\text{Estimated overhead costs}}{\text{Estimated activity base}}$$

Example: If management predicts total direct labor costs of $100,000 and total overhead costs of $200,000, what is its predetermined overhead rate? *Answer:* 200% of direct labor cost.

Recording Allocated Overhead   To illustrate, Road Warriors allocates overhead by linking it to direct labor. At the start of the current period, management predicts total direct labor costs of $125,000 and total overhead costs of $200,000. Using these estimates, management computes its predetermined overhead rate as 160% of direct labor cost ($200,000 ÷ $125,000). Specifically, reviewing the job order cost sheet in Exhibit 15.2, we see that $1,000 of direct labor went into Job B15. We then use the predetermined overhead rate of 160% to allocate $1,600 (equal to $1,000 × 1.60) of overhead to this job. The entry to record this allocation is

Assets = Liabilities + Equity
+1,600   +1,600

Mar. 11	Goods in Process Inventory—Job B15..............	1,600	
	Factory Overhead		1,600
	To assign overhead to Job B15.		

Since the allocation rate for overhead is estimated at the start of a period, the total amount assigned to jobs during a period rarely equals the amount actually incurred. We explain how this difference is treated later in this chapter.

■ Decision Ethics

Web Consultant   You are working on seven client engagements. Two clients reimburse your firm for actual costs plus a 10% markup. The other five pay a fixed fee for services. Your firm's costs include overhead allocated at $47 per labor hour. The managing partner of your firm instructs you to record as many labor hours as possible to the two markup engagements by transferring labor hours from the other five. What do you do? ■   [Answer—p. 671]

Summary of Cost Flows

We showed journal entries for charging Goods in Process Inventory (Job B15) with the cost of (1) direct materials requisitions, (2) direct labor time tickets, and (3) factory overhead. We made separate entries for each of these costs, but they are usually recorded in one entry. Specifically, materials requisitions are often collected for a day or a week and recorded with a single entry summarizing them. The same is done with labor time tickets. When summary entries are made, supporting schedules of the jobs charged and the types of materials used provide the basis for postings to subsidiary records.

Point: Study the flow of manufacturing costs through general ledger accounts and job cost sheets. Use Exhibit 15.11 as reinforcement.

To show all production cost flows for a period and their related entries, we again look at Road Warriors' activities. Exhibit 15.10 shows costs linked to all of Road Warriors' production activities for March. Road Warriors did not have any jobs in process at the beginning of March, but it did apply materials, labor, and overhead costs to five new jobs in March. Jobs B15 and B16 are completed and delivered to customers in March, Job B17 is completed but not delivered, and Jobs B18 and B19 are still in process. Exhibit 15.10 also shows purchases of raw materials for $2,750, labor costs incurred for $5,300, and overhead costs of $6,720.

EXHIBIT 15.10

Job Order Costs of All Production Activities

| | | | Overhead | | Goods in | Finished | Cost of Goods |
Explanation	Materials	Labor	Incurred	Allocated	Process	Goods	Sold
Job B15	$ 600	$1,000		$1,600			$3,200
Job B16	300	800		1,280			2,380
Job B17	500	1,100		1,760		$3,360	
Job B18	150	700		1,120	$1,970		
Job B19	250	600		960	1,810		
Total job costs	1,800	4,200		→$6,720	$3,780	$3,360	$5,580
Indirect materials	550		$ 550				
Indirect labor		1,100	1,100				
Other overhead			5,070				
Total costs used in production...........	2,350	$5,300	$6,720 ◄				
Ending materials inventory..............	1,400						
Materials available	3,750						
Less beginning materials inventory	(1,000)						
Materials purchased	$2,750						

ROAD WARRIORS
Job Order Manufacturing Costs
For Month Ended March 31, 2013

The upper part of Exhibit 15.11 shows the flow of these costs through general ledger accounts and the end-of-month balances in key subsidiary records. Arrow lines are numbered to show the flows of costs for March. Each numbered cost flow reflects several entries made in March. The lower part of Exhibit 15.11 shows summarized job cost sheets and their status at the end of March. The sum of costs assigned to the jobs in process ($1,970 + $1,810) equals the

EXHIBIT 15.11

Job Order Cost Flows and Ending Job Cost Sheets

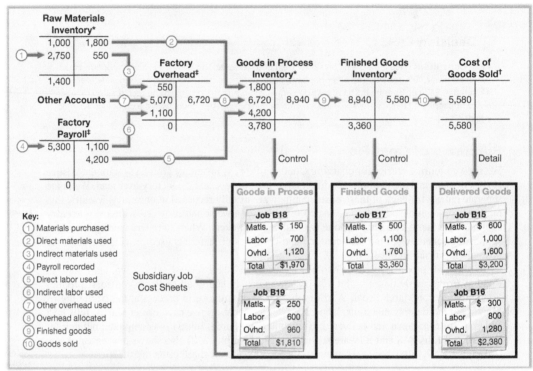

* The ending balances in the inventory accounts are carried to the balance sheet.
† The Cost of Goods Sold balance is carried to the income statement.
‡ Factory Payroll and Factory Overhead are considered temporary accounts; when these costs are allocated to jobs, the balances in these accounts are reduced.

$3,780 balance in Goods in Process Inventory shown in Exhibit 15.10. Also, costs assigned to Job B17 equal the $3,360 balance in Finished Goods Inventory. The sum of costs assigned to Jobs B15 and B16 ($3,200 + $2,380) equals the $5,580 balance in Cost of Goods Sold.

Exhibit 15.12 shows each cost flow with a single entry summarizing the actual individual entries made in March. Each entry is numbered to link with the arrow lines in Exhibit 15.11.

Decision Maker ▬▬▬▬▬▬▬▬▬▬▬▬▬▬▬▬▬▬▬▬▬▬▬

Entrepreneur   Competitors' prices on one of your product segments are lower than yours. Of the total product cost used in setting your prices, 53% is overhead allocated using direct labor hours. You believe that product costs are distorted and wonder whether there is a better way to allocate overhead and to set product price. What do you suggest? ■   [Answer—p. 671]

Quick Check   Answers — p. 671

5. In job order cost accounting, which account is debited in recording a raw materials requisition? (a) Raw Materials Inventory, (b) Raw Materials Purchases, (c) Goods in Process Inventory if for a job, or (d) Goods in Process Inventory if they are indirect materials.

6. What are four sources of information for recording costs in the Factory Overhead account?

7. Why does job order cost accounting require a predetermined overhead rate?

8. What events result in a debit to Factory Payroll? What events result in a credit?

EXHIBIT 15.12

Entries for Job Order Production Costs*

①	Raw Materials Inventory	2,750	
	Accounts Payable		2,750
	Acquired materials on credit for factory use.		
②	Goods in Process Inventory	1,800	
	Raw Materials Inventory		1,800
	To assign costs of direct materials used.		
③	Factory Overhead	550	
	Raw Materials Inventory		550
	To record use of indirect materials.		
④	Factory Payroll	5,300	
	Cash (and other accounts)		5,300
	To record salaries and wages of factory workers (including various payroll liabilities).		
⑤	Goods in Process Inventory	4,200	
	Factory Payroll		4,200
	To assign costs of direct labor used.		
⑥	Factory Overhead	1,100	
	Factory Payroll		1,100
	To record indirect labor costs as overhead.		
⑦	Factory Overhead	5,070	
	Cash (and other accounts)		5,070
	To record factory overhead costs such as insurance, utilities, rent, and depreciation.		
⑧	Goods in Process Inventory	6,720	
	Factory Overhead		6,720
	To apply overhead at 160% of direct labor.		
⑨	Finished Goods Inventory	8,940	
	Goods in Process Inventory		8,940
	To record completion of Jobs B15, B16, and B17.		
⑩	Cost of Goods Sold	5,580	
	Finished Goods Inventory		5,580
	To record sale of Jobs B15 and B16.		

* Exhibit 15.12 provides summary journal entries. *Actual* overhead is debited to Factory Overhead. *Allocated* overhead is credited to Factory Overhead.

ADJUSTING FACTORY OVERHEAD

Refer to the debits in the Factory Overhead account in Exhibit 15.11 (or Exhibit 15.12). The total cost of factory overhead incurred during March is $6,720 ($550 + $5,070 + $1,100). The $6,720 exactly equals the amount assigned to goods in process inventory (see ⑧). Therefore, the overhead incurred equals the overhead applied in March. The amount of overhead incurred rarely equals the amount of overhead applied, however, because estimates rarely equal the exact amounts actually incurred. This section explains what we do when too much or too little overhead is applied to jobs.

Factory Overhead T-Account

Exhibit 15.13 shows a Factory Overhead T-account. The company applies overhead using a predetermined rate estimated at the beginning of the period. At the end of the period, the company receives bills for its actual overhead costs.

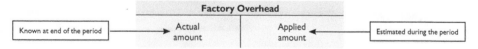

EXHIBIT 15.13

Factory Overhead T-account

Exhibit 15.14 shows what to do when actual overhead does not equal applied overhead. When less overhead is applied than is actually incurred, the remaining debit balance in the Factory Overhead account is called **underapplied overhead.** When the overhead applied in a period exceeds the overhead incurred, the resulting credit balance in the Factory Overhead account is called **overapplied overhead.** In either case, a journal entry is needed to adjust Factory Overhead and Cost of Goods Sold. Exhibit 15.14 summarizes this entry.

EXHIBIT 15.14

Adjusting Factory Overhead

Overhead Costs	Factory Overhead Balance Is	Overhead Is	Journal Entry Required	
Actual > Applied	Debit	Underapplied	Cost of Goods Sold ...... #	
			Factory Overhead	#
Actual < Applied	Credit	Overapplied	Factory Overhead .... #	
			Cost of Goods Sold	#

Underapplied or Overapplied Overhead

EXHIBIT 15.15

Underapplied Overhead in the Factory Overhead Ledger Account

To illustrate, assume that Road Warriors actually incurred *other overhead costs* of $5,550 instead of the $5,070 shown in Exhibit 15.11. This yields an actual total overhead cost of $7,200 in March. Since the amount of overhead applied was only $6,720, the Factory Overhead account is left with a $480 debit balance as shown in the ledger account in Exhibit 15.15.

	Factory Overhead			Acct. No. 540
Date	Explanation	Debit	Credit	Balance
Mar. 31	Indirect materials cost	550		550 Dr.
31	Indirect labor cost	1,100		1,650 Dr.
31	Other overhead cost	5,550		7,200 Dr.
31	Overhead costs applied to jobs		6,720	480 Dr.

Example: If we do not adjust for underapplied overhead, will net income be overstated or understated? *Answer:* Overstated.

Assets = Liabilities + Equity
                    −480
                    +480

The $480 debit balance reflects manufacturing costs not assigned to jobs. This means that the balances in Goods in Process Inventory, Finished Goods Inventory, and Cost of Goods Sold do not include all production costs incurred. When the underapplied overhead amount is immaterial, it is allocated (closed) to the Cost of Goods Sold account with the following adjusting entry.

Mar. 31	Cost of Goods Sold	480	
	Factory Overhead		480
	To adjust for underapplied overhead costs.		

The $480 debit (increase) to Cost of Goods Sold reduces income by $480. (When the underapplied (or overapplied) overhead is material, the amount is normally allocated to the Cost of Goods Sold, Finished Goods Inventory, and Goods in Process Inventory accounts. This process is covered in advanced courses.)

We treat overapplied overhead at the end of the period in the same way we treat underapplied overhead, except that we debit Factory Overhead and credit Cost of Good Sold for the amount.

Decision Insight

Job Order Learning   Many companies invest in their employees, and the demand for executive education is strong. Annual spending on training and education exceeds $20 billion. Annual revenues for providers of executive education continue to rise, with about 40% of revenues coming from custom programs designed for one or a select group of companies. ▪

Quick Check   Answers — p. 672

9. In a job order cost accounting system, why does the Factory Overhead account usually have an overapplied or underapplied balance at period-end?
10. When the Factory Overhead account has a debit balance at period-end, does this reflect overapplied or underapplied overhead?

GLOBAL VIEW

Porsche AG manufactures high-performance cars. Each car is built according to individual customer specifications. Customers can use the Internet to place orders for their dream cars. Porsche employs just-in-time inventory techniques to ensure a flexible production process that can respond rapidly to customer orders. For a recent year, Porsche reported €33,781 million in costs of materials and €9,038 million in personnel costs, which helped generate €57,081 million in revenue.

Pricing for Services   **Decision Analysis**

The chapter described job order costing mainly using a manufacturing setting. However, these concepts and procedures are applicable to a service setting. Consider AdWorld, an advertising agency that develops Web-based ads for small firms. Each of its customers has unique requirements, so costs for each individual job must be tracked separately.

A1	Apply job order costing in pricing services.

AdWorld uses two types of labor: Web designers ($65 per hour) and computer staff ($50 per hour). It also incurs overhead costs that it assigns using two different predetermined overhead allocation rates: $125 per designer hour and $96 per staff hour. For each job, AdWorld must estimate the number of designer and staff hours needed. Then total costs pertaining to each job are determined using the procedures in the chapter. (*Note:* Most service firms have neither the category of materials cost nor inventory.)

To illustrate, a manufacturer of golf balls requested a quote from AdWorld for an advertising engagement. AdWorld estimates that the job will require 43 designer hours and 61 staff hours, with the following total estimated cost for this job.

Direct Labor		
Designers (43 hours × $65)	$ 2,795	
Staff (61 hours × $50)	3,050	
Total direct labor		$ 5,845
Overhead		
Designer related (43 hours × $125)	5,375	
Staff related (61 hours × $96)	5,856	
Total overhead		11,231
Total estimated job cost		$17,076

AdWorld can use this cost information to help determine the price quote for the job (see *Decision Maker,* **Sales Manager,** scenario in this chapter).

Another source of information that AdWorld must consider is the market, that is, how much competitors will quote for this job. Competitor information is often unavailable; therefore, AdWorld's managers must use estimates based on their assessment of the competitive environment.

■ Decision Maker ━━━━━━━━━━━━━━━━━━━━━━━━━━━

Sales Manager   As AdWorld's sales manager, assume that you estimate costs pertaining to a proposed job as $17,076. Your normal pricing policy is to apply a markup of 18% from total costs. However, you learn that three other agencies are likely to bid for the same job, and that their quotes will range from $16,500 to $22,000. What price should you quote? What factors other than cost must you consider? ■   [Answer—p. 671]

⸢ DEMONSTRATION PROBLEM—JOB ORDER COSTING ⸣

The following information reflects Walczak Company's job order production activities for May.

Raw materials purchases	$16,000
Factory payroll cost	15,400
Overhead costs incurred	
Indirect materials	5,000
Indirect labor	3,500
Other factory overhead	9,500

Walczak's predetermined overhead rate is 150% of direct labor cost. Costs are allocated to the three jobs worked on during May as follows.

	Job 401	Job 402	Job 403
In-process balances on April 30			
Direct materials	$3,600		
Direct labor	1,700		
Applied overhead	2,550		
Costs during May			
Direct materials	3,550	$3,500	$1,400
Direct labor	5,100	6,000	800
Applied overhead	?	?	?
Status on May 31	Finished (sold)	Finished (unsold)	In process

Required

1. Determine the total cost of:

   a. The April 30 inventory of jobs in process.

   b. Materials used during May.

   c. Labor used during May.

   d. Factory overhead incurred and applied during May and the amount of any over- or underapplied overhead on May 31.

   e. Each job as of May 31, the May 31 inventories of both goods in process and finished goods, and the goods sold during May.

2. Prepare summarized journal entries for the month to record:

   a. Materials purchases (on credit), the factory payroll (paid with cash), indirect materials, indirect labor, and the other factory overhead (paid with cash).

   b. Assignment of direct materials, direct labor, and overhead costs to the Goods in Process Inventory account. (Use separate debit entries for each job.)

   c. Transfer of each completed job to the Finished Goods Inventory account.

   d. Cost of goods sold.

   e. Removal of any underapplied or overapplied overhead from the Factory Overhead account. (Assume the amount is not material.)

3. Prepare a manufacturing statement for May.

PLANNING THE SOLUTION

- Determine the cost of the April 30 goods in process inventory by totaling the materials, labor, and applied overhead costs for Job 401.
- Compute the cost of materials used and labor by totaling the amounts assigned to jobs and to overhead.
- Compute the total overhead incurred by summing the amounts for the three components. Compute the amount of applied overhead by multiplying the total direct labor cost by the predetermined overhead rate. Compute the underapplied or overapplied amount as the difference between the actual cost and the applied cost.
- Determine the total cost charged to each job by adding the costs incurred in April (if any) to the cost of materials, labor, and overhead applied during May.
- Group the costs of the jobs according to their completion status.
- Record the direct materials costs assigned to the three jobs, using a separate Goods in Process Inventory account for each job; do the same for the direct labor and the applied overhead.
- Transfer costs of Jobs 401 and 402 from Goods in Process Inventory to Finished Goods.
- Record the costs of Job 401 as cost of goods sold.
- Record the transfer of underapplied overhead from the Factory Overhead account to the Cost of Goods Sold account.
- On the manufacturing statement, remember to include the beginning and ending goods in process inventories and to deduct the underapplied overhead.

SOLUTION TO DEMONSTRATION PROBLEM

1. Total cost of

a. April 30 inventory of jobs in process (Job 401).

Direct materials..........	$3,600
Direct labor.............	1,700
Applied overhead	2,550
Total cost..............	$7,850

b. Materials used during May.

Direct materials	
Job 401.................	$ 3,550
Job 402.................	3,500
Job 403.................	1,400
Total direct materials	8,450
Indirect materials	5,000
Total materials used	$13,450

c. Labor used during May.

Direct labor	
Job 401................	$ 5,100
Job 402................	6,000
Job 403................	800
Total direct labor.........	11,900
Indirect labor............	3,500
Total labor used..........	$15,400

d. Factory overhead incurred in May.

Actual overhead	
Indirect materials......................	$ 5,000
Indirect labor........................	3,500
Other factory overhead	9,500
Total actual overhead	18,000
Overhead applied (150% × $11,900)	17,850
Underapplied overhead	$ 150

e. Total cost of each job.

	401	402	403
In-process costs from April			
Direct materials................	$ 3,600		
Direct labor...................	1,700		
Applied overhead*.............	2,550		
Cost incurred in May			
Direct materials................	3,550	$ 3,500	$1,400
Direct labor...................	5,100	6,000	800
Applied overhead*.............	7,650	9,000	1,200
Total costs	$24,150	$18,500	$3,400

* Equals 150% of the direct labor cost.

Total cost of the May 31 inventory of goods in process (Job 403) = $3,400

Total cost of the May 31 inventory of finished goods (Job 402) = $18,500

Total cost of goods sold during May (Job 401) = $24,150

2. Journal entries.

a.

Raw Materials Inventory	16,000	
Accounts Payable		16,000
To record materials purchases.		
Factory Payroll..................................	15,400	
Cash		15,400
To record factory payroll.		
Factory Overhead	5,000	
Raw Materials Inventory		5,000
To record indirect materials.		
Factory Overhead	3,500	
Factory Payroll		3,500
To record indirect labor.		
Factory Overhead	9,500	
Cash		9,500
To record other factory overhead.		

670   Chapter 15   Job Order Costing and Analysis

b. Assignment of costs to Goods in Process Inventory.

Goods in Process Inventory (Job 401)	3,550	
Goods in Process Inventory (Job 402)	3,500	
Goods in Process Inventory (Job 403)	1,400	
Raw Materials Inventory		8,450
To assign direct materials to jobs.		
Goods in Process Inventory (Job 401)	5,100	
Goods in Process Inventory (Job 402)	6,000	
Goods in Process Inventory (Job 403)	800	
Factory Payroll		11,900
To assign direct labor to jobs.		
Goods in Process Inventory (Job 401)	7,650	
Goods in Process Inventory (Job 402)	9,000	
Goods in Process Inventory (Job 403)	1,200	
Factory Overhead		17,850
To apply overhead to jobs.		

c. Transfer of completed jobs to Finished Goods Inventory.

Finished Goods Inventory	42,650	
Goods in Process Inventory (Job 401)		24,150
Goods in Process Inventory (Job 402)		18,500
To record completion of jobs.		

d.

Cost of Goods Sold	24,150	
Finished Goods Inventory		24,150
To record sale of Job 401.		

e.

Cost of Goods Sold	150	
Factory Overhead		150
To assign underapplied overhead.		

3.

WALCZAK COMPANY
Manufacturing Statement
For Month Ended May 31

Direct materials		$ 8,450
Direct labor		11,900
Factory overhead		
Indirect materials	$5,000	
Indirect labor	3,500	
Other factory overhead	9,500	18,000
Total production costs		38,350
Add goods in process, April 30.		7,850
Total cost of goods in process		46,200
Less goods in process, May 31		3,400
Less underapplied overhead		150
Cost of goods manufactured		$42,650

Note how underapplied overhead is reported. Overapplied overhead is similarly reported, but is added.

Summary

C1 **Describe important features of job order production.** Certain companies called *job order manufacturers* produce custom-made products for customers. These customized products are produced in response to a customer's orders. A job order manufacturer produces products that usually are different and, typically, produced in low volumes. The production systems of job order companies are flexible and are not highly standardized.

C2 **Explain job cost sheets and how they are used in job order cost accounting.** In a job order cost accounting system, the costs of producing each job are accumulated on a separate job cost sheet. Costs of direct materials, direct labor, and overhead are accumulated separately on the job cost sheet and then added to determine the total cost of a job. Job cost sheets for jobs in process, finished jobs, and jobs sold make up subsidiary records controlled by general ledger accounts.

A1 **Apply job order costing in pricing services.** Job order costing can usefully be applied to a service setting. The resulting job cost estimate can then be used to help determine a price for services.

P1 **Describe and record the flow of materials costs in job order cost accounting.** Costs of materials flow from receiving reports to materials ledger cards and then to either job cost sheets or the Indirect Materials account in the factory overhead ledger.

P2 **Describe and record the flow of labor costs in job order cost accounting.** Costs of labor flow from clock cards to the Factory Payroll account and then to either job cost sheets or the Indirect Labor account in the factory overhead ledger.

P3 **Describe and record the flow of overhead costs in job order cost accounting.** Overhead costs are accumulated in the Factory Overhead account that controls the subsidiary factory overhead ledger. Then, using a predetermined overhead rate, overhead costs are charged to jobs.

P4 **Determine adjustments for overapplied and underapplied factory overhead.** At the end of each period, the Factory Overhead account usually has a residual debit (underapplied overhead) or credit (overapplied overhead) balance. If the balance is not material, it is transferred to Cost of Goods Sold, but if it is material, it is allocated to Goods in Process Inventory, Finished Goods Inventory, and Cost of Goods Sold.

Guidance Answers to Decision Maker and Decision Ethics

Management Consultant Service companies (such as this consulting firm) do not recognize goods in process inventory or finished goods inventory—an important difference between service and manufacturing companies. For the two jobs that are 60% complete, you could recognize revenues and costs at 60% of the total expected amounts. This means you could recognize revenue of $7,200 (0.60 × $12,000) and costs of $6,000 (0.60 × $10,000), yielding net income of $1,200 from each job.

Web Consultant The partner has a monetary incentive to *manage* the numbers and assign more costs to the two cost-plus engagements. This also would reduce costs on the fixed-price engagements. To act in such a manner is unethical. As a professional and an honest person, it is your responsibility to engage in ethical behavior. You must not comply with the partner's instructions. If the partner insists you act in an unethical manner, you should report the matter to a higher authority in the organization.

Entrepreneur An inadequate cost system can distort product costs. You should review overhead costs in detail. Once you know the different cost elements in overhead, you can classify them into groups such as material related, labor related, or machine related. Other groups can also be formed (we discuss this in Chapter 22). Once you have classified overhead items into groups, you can better establish overhead allocation bases and use them to compute predetermined overhead rates. These multiple rates and bases can then be used to assign overhead costs to products. This will likely improve product pricing.

Sales Manager The price based on AdWorld's normal pricing policy is $20,150 ($17,076 × 1.18), which is within the price range offered by competitors. One option is to apply normal pricing policy and quote a price of $20,150. On the other hand, assessing the competition, particularly in terms of their service quality and other benefits they might offer, would be useful. Although price is an input customers use to select suppliers, factors such as quality and timeliness (responsiveness) of suppliers are important. Accordingly, your price can reflect such factors.

Guidance Answers to Quick Checks

1. *b*

2. A job is a special order for a custom product. A job lot consists of a quantity of identical, special-order items.

3. *a*

4. Three costs normally accumulated on a job cost sheet are direct materials, direct labor, and factory overhead.

5. *c*

6. Four sources of factory overhead are materials requisitions, time tickets, vouchers, and adjusting entries.

7. Since a job order cost accounting system uses perpetual inventory records, overhead costs must be assigned to jobs before the end of a period. This requires the use of a predetermined overhead rate.

8. Debits are recorded when wages and salaries of factory employees are paid or accrued. Credits are recorded when direct labor costs are assigned to jobs and when indirect labor costs are transferred to the Factory Overhead account.

9. Overapplied or underapplied overhead usually exists at the end of a period because application of overhead is based on

estimates of overhead and another variable such as direct labor. Estimates rarely equal actual amounts incurred.

10. A debit balance reflects underapplied factory overhead.

Key Terms

Clock card (p. 660)
Cost accounting system (p. 654)
Finished Goods Inventory (p. 657)
General accounting system (p. 654)
Goods in Process Inventory (p. 656)
Job (p. 654)

Job cost sheet (p. 656)
Job lot (p. 654)
Job order cost accounting system (p. 656)
Job order production (p. 654)
Materials ledger card (p. 658)

Materials requisition (p. 659)
Overapplied overhead (p. 665)
Predetermined overhead rate (p. 662)
Target cost (p. 655)
Time ticket (p. 660)
Underapplied overhead (p. 665)

Multiple Choice Quiz   Answers on p. 689   mhhe.com/wildFINMAN5e

Additional Quiz Questions are available at the book's Website.

1. A company's predetermined overhead allocation rate is 150% of its direct labor costs. How much overhead is applied to a job that requires total direct labor costs of $30,000?
   a. $15,000
   b. $30,000
   c. $45,000
   d. $60,000
   e. $75,000

2. A company's cost accounting system uses direct labor costs to apply overhead to goods in process and finished goods inventories. Its production costs for the period are: direct materials, $45,000; direct labor, $35,000; and overhead applied, $38,500. What is its predetermined overhead allocation rate?
   a. 10%
   b. 110%
   c. 86%
   d. 91%
   e. 117%

3. A company's ending inventory of finished goods has a total cost of $10,000 and consists of 500 units. If the overhead applied to these goods is $4,000, and the predetermined overhead rate is 80% of direct labor costs, how much direct materials cost was incurred in producing these 500 units?
   a. $10,000
   b. $ 6,000
   c. $ 4,000
   d. $ 5,000
   e. $ 1,000

4. A company's Goods in Process Inventory T-account follows.

Goods in Process Inventory			
Beginning balance	9,000		
Direct materials	94,200		
Direct labor	59,200		
Overhead applied	31,600	?	Finished goods
Ending balance	17,800		

The cost of units transferred to Finished Goods inventory is
   a. $193,000
   b. $211,800
   c. $185,000
   d. $144,600
   e. $176,200

5. At the end of its current year, a company learned that its overhead was underapplied by $1,500 and that this amount is not considered material. Based on this information, the company should
   a. Close the $1,500 to Finished Goods Inventory.
   b. Close the $1,500 to Cost of Goods Sold.
   c. Carry the $1,500 to the next period.
   d. Do nothing about the $1,500 because it is not material and it is likely that overhead will be overapplied by the same amount next year.
   e. Carry the $1,500 to the Income Statement as "Other Expense."

🚹 Icon denotes assignments that involve decision making.

Discussion Questions

1. Why must a company estimate the amount of factory overhead assigned to individual jobs or job lots?

2. 🚹 The chapter used a percent of labor cost to assign factory overhead to jobs. Identify another factor (or base) a company might reasonably use to assign overhead costs.

3. What information is recorded on a job cost sheet? How do management and employees use job cost sheets?

4. In a job order cost accounting system, what records serve as a subsidiary ledger for Goods in Process Inventory? For Finished Goods Inventory?

5. What journal entry is recorded when a materials manager receives a materials requisition and then issues materials (both direct and indirect) for use in the factory?

6. How does the materials requisition help safeguard a company's assets?

7. Polaris uses a "time ticket" for some employees. What is the difference between a clock card and a time ticket?   **Polaris**

8. What events cause debits to be recorded in the Factory Overhead account? What events cause credits to be recorded in the Factory Overhead account?

9. Piaggio applies overhead to product costs. What account(s) is(are) used to eliminate overapplied   **PIAGGIO**

or underapplied overhead from the Factory Overhead account, assuming the amount is not material?

10. Assume that Arctic Cat produces a batch of 1,000 snowmobile helmets. Does it account   Arctic Cat for this as 1,000 individual jobs or as a job lot? Explain (consider costs and benefits).

11. Why must a company prepare a predetermined overhead rate when using job order cost accounting?

12. How would a hospital apply job order costing? Explain.

13. Harley-Davidson manufactures 30 custom-made, luxury-model motorcycles. Does it account for these motorcycles as 30 individual jobs or as a job lot? Explain.   Harley-Davidson

14. Assume Sprint will install and service a server to link all of a customer's employees' smartphones to a centralized company server, for an upfront flat price. How can Sprint use a job order costing system?   Sprint

connect

Determine which products are most likely to be manufactured as a job and which as a job lot.

1. Hats imprinted with company logo.
2. Little League trophies.
3. A hand-crafted table.
4. A 90-foot motor yacht.
5. Wedding dresses for a chain of stores.
6. A custom-designed home.

QUICK STUDY

QS 15-1
Jobs and job lots   C1

List the three types of costs that are typically recorded on a job cost sheet. How can managers use job cost sheets?

QS 15-2
Job cost sheets   C2

Clemens Cars' job cost sheet for job A40 shows that the cost to add security features to a car was $10,500. The car was delivered to the customer, who paid $14,900 in cash for the added features. What journal entries should Clemens record for the completion and delivery of job A40?

QS 15-3
Job cost sheets   C2

During the current month, a company that uses a job order cost accounting system purchases $50,000 in raw materials for cash. It then uses $12,000 of raw materials indirectly as factory supplies and uses $32,000 of raw materials as direct materials. Prepare entries to record these three transactions.

QS 15-4
Direct materials journal entries
P1

During the current month, a company that uses a job order cost accounting system incurred a monthly factory payroll of $180,000, paid in cash. Of this amount, $40,000 is classified as indirect labor and the remainder as direct. Prepare entries to record these transactions.

QS 15-5
Direct labor journal entries   P2

During the current month, a company that uses a job order cost accounting system incurred a monthly factory payroll of $175,000, paid in cash. Of this amount, $44,000 is classified as indirect labor and the remainder as direct for the production of Job 65A. Factory overhead is applied at 90% of direct labor. Prepare the entry to apply factory overhead to this job lot.

QS 15-6
Factory overhead journal entries
P3

A company incurred the following manufacturing costs this period: direct labor, $468,000; direct materials, $354,000; and factory overhead, $117,000. Compute its overhead cost as a percent of (1) direct labor and (2) direct materials. Express your answers as percents, rounded to the nearest whole number.

QS 15-7
Factory overhead rates   P3

A company's Factory Overhead T-account shows total debits of $624,000 and total credits of $646,000 at the end of a period. Prepare the journal entry to close the balance in the Factory Overhead account to Cost of Goods Sold.

QS 15-8
Entry for over- or underapplied overhead   P4

QS 15-9

Entry for over- or underapplied overhead   P4

A company allocates overhead at a rate of 150% of direct labor cost. Actual overhead cost for the current period is $950,000, and direct labor cost is $600,000. Prepare the entry to close over- or underapplied overhead to cost of goods sold.

QS 15-10

Predetermined overhead rate

P3

At the beginning of a period a company predicts total direct materials costs of $900,000 and total overhead costs of $1,170,000. If the company uses direct materials costs as its activity base to allocate overhead, what is the predetermined overhead rate it should use during the period?

QS 15-11

Pricing services   A1

An advertising agency is estimating costs for advertising a music festival. The job will require 200 direct labor hours at a cost of $50 per hour. Overhead costs are applied at a rate of $65 per direct labor hour. What is the total estimated cost for this job?

QS 15-12

Job order production   C1

Refer to this chapter's Global View. Porsche AG is the manufacturer of the Porsche automobile line. Does Porsche produce in jobs or in job lots? Explain.

---

connect

EXERCISES

Exercise 15-1

Job order production

C1

Match the terms below with their definitions.

1. Cost accounting system
2. Target cost
3. General accounting system
4. Job
5. Job order production
6. Job lot

a. Production of products in response to customer orders.
b. A system that records manufacturing costs using a periodic inventory system.
c. A system that records manufacturing costs using a perpetual inventory system.
d. The expected selling price of a job minus its desired profit.
e. Production of more than one unit of a custom product.
f. Production activities for a customized product.

Exercise 15-2

Job cost computation

C2

The following information is from the materials requisitions and time tickets for Job 9-1005 completed by Great Bay Boats. The requisitions are identified by code numbers starting with the letter Q and the time tickets start with W. At the start of the year, management estimated that overhead cost would equal 110% of direct labor cost for each job. Determine the total cost on the job cost sheet for Job 9-1005.

Date	Document	Amount
7/1/2013	Q-4698	$1,250
7/1/2013	W-3393	600
7/5/2013	Q-4725	1,000
7/5/2013	W-3479	450
7/10/2013	W-3559	300

Exercise 15-3

Documents in job order cost accounting

P1 P2 P3

The left column lists the titles of documents and accounts used in job order cost accounting. The right column presents short descriptions of the purposes of the documents. Match each document in the left column to its numbered description in the right column.

A. Time ticket
B. Materials ledger card
C. Factory Payroll account
D. Clock card
E. Materials requisition
F. Factory Overhead account
G. Voucher

_____ 1. Shows amount of time an employee works on a job.
_____ 2. Temporarily accumulates the cost of incurred overhead until the cost is assigned to specific jobs.
_____ 3. Temporarily accumulates incurred labor costs until they are assigned to specific jobs or to overhead.
_____ 4. Communicates the need for materials to complete a job.
_____ 5. Shows only total time an employee works each day.
_____ 6. Shows amount approved for payment of an overhead or other cost.
_____ 7. Perpetual inventory record of raw materials received, used, and available for use.

As of the end of June, the job cost sheets at Racing Wheels, Inc., show the following total costs accumulated on three custom jobs.

Exercise 15-4
Analysis of cost flows
C2 P1 P2 P3

	Job 102	Job 103	Job 104
Direct materials.........	$15,000	$33,000	$27,000
Direct labor.............	8,000	14,200	21,000
Overhead..............	4,000	7,100	10,500

Job 102 was started in production in May and the following costs were assigned to it in May: direct materials, $6,000; direct labor, $1,800; and overhead, $900. Jobs 103 and 104 are started in June. Overhead cost is applied with a predetermined rate based on direct labor cost. Jobs 102 and 103 are finished in June, and Job 104 is expected to be finished in July. No raw materials are used indirectly in June. Using this information, answer the following questions. (Assume this company's predetermined overhead rate did not change across these months).

1. What is the cost of the raw materials requisitioned in June for each of the three jobs?

2. How much direct labor cost is incurred during June for each of the three jobs?

3. What predetermined overhead rate is used during June?

4. How much total cost is transferred to finished goods during June?

Check (4) $81,300

In December 2012, Shire Computer's management establishes the year 2013 predetermined overhead rate based on direct labor cost. The information used in setting this rate includes estimates that the company will incur $747,500 of overhead costs and $575,000 of direct labor cost in year 2013. During March 2013, Shire began and completed Job No. 13-56.

Exercise 15-5
Overhead rate; costs assigned to jobs
P3

1. What is the predetermined overhead rate for year 2013?

2. Use the information on the following job cost sheet to determine the total cost of the job.

Check (2) $22,710

JOB COST SHEET

Customer's Name	Keiser Co.			Job No.	13-56	
Job Description	5 plasma monitors—61 inch					

| | **Direct Materials** | | **Direct Labor** | | **Overhead Costs Applied** | |
Date	Requisition No.	Amount	Time-Ticket No.	Amount	Rate	Amount
Mar. 8	4-129	$5,000	T-306	$ 700		
Mar. 11	4-142	7,020	T-432	1,250		
Mar. 18	4-167	3,330	T-456	1,250		
Totals						

Lorenzo Company uses a job order cost accounting system that charges overhead to jobs on the basis of direct material cost. At year-end, the Goods in Process Inventory account shows the following.

Exercise 15-6
Analysis of costs assigned to goods in process
P3

Accounting System

File Edit Maintain Tasks Analysis Options Reports Window Help

Goods in Process Inventory   Acct. No. 121

Date	Explanation	Debit	Credit	Balance
2013				
Dec. 31	Direct materials cost	1,500,000		1,500,000
31	Direct labor cost	300,000		1,800,000
31	Overhead costs	600,000		2,400,000
31	To finished goods		2,350,000	50,000

Sales   Purchases   General Ledger   Payroll   Inventory   Company   Analysis

1. Determine the overhead rate used (based on direct material cost).

2. Only one job remained in the goods in process inventory at December 31, 2013. Its direct materials cost is $30,000. How much direct labor cost and overhead cost are assigned to it?

Check (2) Direct labor cost, $8,000

Exercise 15-7

Cost flows in a job order
cost system

P1 P2 P3 P4

The following information is available for Lock-Safe Company, which produces special-order security products and uses a job order cost accounting system.

	April 30	May 31
Inventories		
Raw materials	$43,000	$ 52,000
Goods in process	10,200	21,300
Finished goods	63,000	35,600
Activities and information for May		
Raw materials purchases (paid with cash)		210,000
Factory payroll (paid with cash)		345,000
Factory overhead		
Indirect materials		15,000
Indirect labor		80,000
Other overhead costs		120,000
Sales (received in cash)		1,400,000
Predetermined overhead rate based on direct labor cost		70%

Compute the following amounts for the month of May.

1. Cost of direct materials used.   4. Cost of goods sold.*
2. Cost of direct labor used.   5. Gross profit.

Check (3) $625,400

3. Cost of goods manufactured.   6. Overapplied or underapplied overhead.

*Do not consider any underapplied or overapplied overhead.

Exercise 15-8

Journal entries for materials

P1

Use information in Exercise 15-7 to prepare journal entries for the following events for the month of May.

1. Raw materials purchases for cash.   3. Indirect materials usage.
2. Direct materials usage.

Exercise 15-9

Journal entries for labor

P2

Use information in Exercise 15-7 to prepare journal entries for the following events for the month of May.

1. Factory payroll costs in cash.   3. Indirect labor usage.
2. Direct labor usage.

Exercise 15-10

Journal entries for overhead

P3

Use information in Exercise 15-7 to prepare journal entries for the following events for the month of May.

1. Factory overhead excluding indirect materials and indirect labor (record credit to Other Accounts).
2. Application of overhead to goods in process.

Exercise 15-11

Adjusting factory overhead P4

Refer to information in Exercise 15-7. Prepare the journal entry to allocate (close) overapplied or underapplied overhead to Cost of Goods Sold.

Exercise 15-12

Adjusting factory overhead

P4

Record the journal entry to close over- or underapplied factory overhead to Cost of Goods Sold for each of the independent cases below.

	Marsh Concert Promotions	Ellis Home Builders
Actual indirect materials costs	$22,000	$ 12,500
Actual indirect labor costs	46,000	46,500
Other overhead costs	17,000	47,000
Overhead applied	88,200	105,200

Exercise 15-13

Recording events in job order
costing

P1 P2 P3 P4

Using Exhibit 15.12 as a guide, prepare summary journal entries to record the following transactions and events *a* through *h* for a company in its first month of operations.

a. Raw materials purchased on account, $90,000.

b. Direct materials used in production, $36,500. Indirect materials used in production, $19,200.

c. Paid cash for factory payroll, $50,000. Of this total, $38,000 is for direct labor and $12,000 is for indirect labor.

d. Paid cash for other actual overhead costs, $11,475.

e. Applied overhead at the rate of 125 percent of direct labor cost.

f. Transferred cost of jobs completed to finished goods, $56,800.

g. Sold jobs on account for $82,000. The jobs had a cost of $56,800.

h. Close underapplied or overapplied overhead to cost of goods sold.

In December 2012, Infovision established its predetermined overhead rate for movies produced during year 2013 by using the following cost predictions: overhead costs, $1,680,000, and direct labor costs, $480,000. At year end 2013, the company's records show that actual overhead costs for the year are $1,652,000. Actual direct labor cost had been assigned to jobs as follows.

> **Exercise 15-14**
> Factory overhead computed, applied, and adjusted
> P3 P4

Movies completed and released	$425,000
Movies still in production	50,000
Total actual direct labor cost	$475,000

1. Determine the predetermined overhead rate for year 2013.

2. Set up a T-account for overhead and enter the overhead costs incurred and the amounts applied to movies during the year using the predetermined overhead rate.

3. Determine whether overhead is overapplied or underapplied (and the amount) during the year.

> **Check** (3) $10,500 overapplied

4. Prepare the adjusting entry to allocate any over- or underapplied overhead to Cost of Goods Sold.

In December 2012, Cardozo Company established its predetermined overhead rate for jobs produced during year 2013 by using the following cost predictions: overhead costs, $750,000, and direct labor costs, $625,000. At year end 2013, the company's records show that actual overhead costs for the year are $830,000. Actual direct labor cost had been assigned to jobs as follows.

> **Exercise 15-15**
> Factory overhead computed, applied, and adjusted
> P3 P4

Jobs completed and sold	$513,750
Jobs in finished goods inventory	102,750
Jobs in goods in process inventory	68,500
Total actual direct labor cost	$685,000

1. Determine the predetermined overhead rate for year 2013.

2. Set up a T-account for Factory Overhead and enter the overhead costs incurred and the amounts applied to jobs during the year using the predetermined overhead rate.

3. Determine whether overhead is overapplied or underapplied (and the amount) during the year.

> **Check** (3) $8,000 underapplied

4. Prepare the adjusting entry to allocate any over- or underapplied overhead to Cost of Goods Sold.

Sunrise Company applies factory overhead based on direct labor costs. The company incurred the following costs during 2013: direct materials costs, $650,000; direct labor costs, $3,000,000; and factory overhead costs applied, $1,800,000.

> **Exercise 15-16**
> Overhead rate calculation, allocation, and analysis
> P3

1. Determine the company's predetermined overhead rate for year 2013.

2. Assuming that the company's $71,000 ending Goods in Process Inventory account for year 2013 had $20,000 of direct labor costs, determine the inventory's direct materials costs.

3. Assuming that the company's $490,000 ending Finished Goods Inventory account for year 2013 had $250,000 of direct materials costs, determine the inventory's direct labor costs and its overhead costs.

> **Check** (3) $90,000 overhead costs

Deschamps Company's ending Goods in Process Inventory account consists of 5,000 units of partially completed product, and its Finished Goods Inventory account consists of 12,000 units of product. The factory manager determines that Goods in Process Inventory includes direct materials cost of $10 per unit and direct labor cost of $7 per unit. Finished goods are estimated to have $12 of direct materials cost per unit and $9 of direct labor cost per unit. The company established the predetermined overhead rate using the following predictions: estimated direct labor cost, $300,000, and estimated factory overhead, $375,000. The company allocates factory overhead to its goods in process and finished goods inventories based on direct labor cost. During the period, the company incurred these costs: direct materials, $535,000; direct labor, $290,000; and factory overhead applied, $362,500.

> **Exercise 15-17**
> Costs allocated to ending inventories
> P1 P2 P3

1. Determine the predetermined overhead rate.

2. Compute the total cost of the two ending inventories.

3. Compute cost of goods sold for the year (assume no beginning inventories and no underapplied or overapplied overhead).

> **Check** (3) Cost of goods sold, $671,750

678   Chapter 15   Job Order Costing and Analysis

Hansel Corporation has requested bids from several architects to design its new corporate headquarters. Frey Architects is one of the firms bidding on the job. Frey estimates that the job will require the following direct labor.

Labor	Estimated Hours	Hourly Rate
Architects	150	$300
Staff	300	75
Clerical	500	20

Frey applies overhead to jobs at 175% of direct labor cost. Frey would like to earn at least $80,000 profit on the architectural job. Based on past experience and market research, it estimates that the competition will bid between $285,000 and $350,000 for the job.

Check   (1) $213,125

1. What is Frey's estimated cost of the architectural job?

2. What bid would you suggest that Frey submit?

A recent balance sheet for Porsche AG shows beginning raw materials inventory of €83 million and ending raw materials inventory of €85 million. Assume the company purchased raw materials (on account) for €3,108 million during the year. (1) Prepare journal entries to record (a) the purchase of raw materials and (b) the use of raw materials in production. (2) What do you notice about the € amounts in your journal entries?

Ciolino Co.'s March 31 inventory of raw materials is $80,000. Raw materials purchases in April are $500,000, and factory payroll cost in April is $363,000. Overhead costs incurred in April are: indirect materials, $50,000; indirect labor, $23,000; factory rent, $32,000; factory utilities, $19,000; and factory equipment depreciation, $51,000. The predetermined overhead rate is 50% of direct labor cost. Job 306 is sold for $635,000 cash in April. Costs of the three jobs worked on in April follow.

	Job 306	Job 307	Job 308
Balances on March 31			
Direct materials............	$ 29,000	$ 35,000	
Direct labor...............	20,000	18,000	
Applied overhead..........	10,000	9,000	
Costs during April			
Direct materials............	135,000	220,000	$100,000
Direct labor...............	85,000	150,000	105,000
Applied overhead..........	?	?	?
Status on April 30...........	Finished (sold)	Finished (unsold)	In process

Required

1. Determine the total of each production cost incurred for April (direct labor, direct materials, and applied overhead), and the total cost assigned to each job (including the balances from March 31).

2. Prepare journal entries for the month of April to record the following.

    a. Materials purchases (on credit), factory payroll (paid in cash), and actual overhead costs including indirect materials and indirect labor. (Factory rent and utilities are paid in cash.)

    b. Assignment of direct materials, direct labor, and applied overhead costs to the Goods in Process Inventory.

    c. Transfer of Jobs 306 and 307 to the Finished Goods Inventory.

    d. Cost of goods sold for Job 306.

    e. Revenue from the sale of Job 306.

Check   (2f) $5,000 underapplied

    f. Assignment of any underapplied or overapplied overhead to the Cost of Goods Sold account. (The amount is not material.)

(3) Cost of goods
     manufactured, $828,500

3. Prepare a manufacturing statement for April (use a single line presentation for direct materials and show the details of overhead cost).

4. Compute gross profit for April. Show how to present the inventories on the April 30 balance sheet.

5. The over- or underapplied overhead is closed to Cost of Goods Sold. Discuss how this adjustment impacts business decision making regarding individual jobs or batches of jobs.

Farina Bay's computer system generated the following trial balance on December 31, 2013. The company's manager knows something is wrong with the trial balance because it does not show any balance for Goods in Process Inventory but does show balances for the Factory Payroll and Factory Overhead accounts.

Problem 15-2A

Source documents, journal entries, overhead, and financial reports

P1 P2 P3 P4

Sage 50

	Debit	Credit
Cash	$102,000	
Accounts receivable	75,000	
Raw materials inventory	80,000	
Goods in process inventory	0	
Finished goods inventory	15,000	
Prepaid rent	3,000	
Accounts payable		$ 17,000
Notes payable		25,000
Common stock		50,000
Retained earnings		271,000
Sales		373,000
Cost of goods sold	218,000	
Factory payroll	68,000	
Factory overhead	115,000	
Operating expenses	60,000	
Totals	$736,000	$736,000

After examining various files, the manager identifies the following six source documents that need to be processed to bring the accounting records up to date.

Materials requisition 21-3010:	$10,200 direct materials to Job 402
Materials requisition 21-3011:	$18,600 direct materials to Job 404
Materials requisition 21-3012:	$5,600 indirect materials
Labor time ticket 6052:	$36,000 direct labor to Job 402
Labor time ticket 6053:	$23,800 direct labor to Job 404
Labor time ticket 6054:	$8,200 indirect labor

Jobs 402 and 404 are the only units in process at year-end. The predetermined overhead rate is 200% of direct labor cost.

Required

1. Use information on the six source documents to prepare journal entries to assign the following costs.
  a. Direct materials costs to Goods in Process Inventory.
  b. Direct labor costs to Goods in Process Inventory.
  c. Overhead costs to Goods in Process Inventory.
  d. Indirect materials costs to the Factory Overhead account.
  e. Indirect labor costs to the Factory Overhead account.

2. Determine the revised balance of the Factory Overhead account after making the entries in part 1. Determine whether there is any under- or overapplied overhead for the year. Prepare the adjusting entry to allocate any over- or underapplied overhead to Cost of Goods Sold, assuming the amount is not material.

Check (2) $9,200 underapplied overhead

3. Prepare a revised trial balance.

4. Prepare an income statement for year 2013 and a balance sheet as of December 31, 2013.

(3) T. B. totals, $736,000

(4) Net income, $85,800

Analysis Component

5. Assume that the $5,600 on materials requisition 21-3012 should have been direct materials charged to Job 404. Without providing specific calculations, describe the impact of this error on the income statement for 2013 and the balance sheet at December 31, 2013.

Problem 15-3A

Source documents, journal entries, and accounts in job order cost accounting

P1 P2 P3

Widmer Watercraft's predetermined overhead rate for year 2013 is 200% of direct labor. Information on the company's production activities during May 2013 follows.

a. Purchased raw materials on credit, $200,000.

b. Paid $126,000 cash for factory wages.

c. Paid $15,000 cash to a computer consultant to reprogram factory equipment.

d. Materials requisitions record use of the following materials for the month.

Job 136	$ 48,000
Job 137	32,000
Job 138	19,200
Job 139	22,400
Job 140	6,400
Total direct materials	128,000
Indirect materials	19,500
Total materials used	$147,500

e. Time tickets record use of the following labor for the month.

Job 136	$ 12,000
Job 137	10,500
Job 138	37,500
Job 139	39,000
Job 140	3,000
Total direct labor	102,000
Indirect labor	24,000
Total	$126,000

f. Applied overhead to Jobs 136, 138, and 139.

g. Transferred Jobs 136, 138, and 139 to Finished Goods.

h. Sold Jobs 136 and 138 on credit at a total price of $525,000.

i. The company incurred the following overhead costs during the month (credit Prepaid Insurance for expired factory insurance).

Depreciation of factory building	$68,000
Depreciation of factory equipment	36,500
Expired factory insurance	10,000
Accrued property taxes payable	35,000

j. Applied overhead at month-end to the Goods in Process (Jobs 137 and 140) using the predetermined overhead rate of 200% of direct labor cost.

Required

1. Prepare a job cost sheet for each job worked on during the month. Use the following simplified form.

Job No. _____	
Materials	$ _____
Labor	_____
Overhead	_____
Total cost	$ _____

Check (2f) Cr. Factory Overhead, $177,000

2. Prepare journal entries to record the events and transactions *a* through *j*.

3. Set up T-accounts for each of the following general ledger accounts, each of which started the month with a zero balance: Raw Materials Inventory; Goods in Process Inventory; Finished Goods Inventory;

Factory Payroll; Factory Overhead; Cost of Goods Sold. Then post the journal entries to these T-accounts and determine the balance of each account.

4. Prepare a report showing the total cost of each job in process and prove that the sum of their costs equals the Goods in Process Inventory account balance. Prepare similar reports for Finished Goods Inventory and Cost of Goods Sold.

Check   (4) Finished Goods Inventory, $139,400

In December 2012, Yerbury Company's manager estimated next year's total direct labor cost assuming 50 persons working an average of 2,000 hours each at an average wage rate of $25 per hour. The manager also estimated the following manufacturing overhead costs for year 2013.

Problem 15-4A
Overhead allocation and adjustment using a predetermined overhead rate

P3 P4

Indirect labor	$ 319,200
Factory supervision	240,000
Rent on factory building	140,000
Factory utilities	88,000
Factory insurance expired	68,000
Depreciation—Factory equipment	480,000
Repairs expense—Factory equipment	60,000
Factory supplies used	68,800
Miscellaneous production costs	36,000
Total estimated overhead costs	$1,500,000

mhhe.com/wildFINMAN5e

At the end of 2013, records show the company incurred $1,520,000 of actual overhead costs. It completed and sold five jobs with the following direct labor costs: Job 201, $604,000; Job 202, $563,000; Job 203, $298,000; Job 204, $716,000; and Job 205, $314,000. In addition, Job 206 is in process at the end of 2013 and had been charged $17,000 for direct labor. No jobs were in process at the end of 2012. The company's predetermined overhead rate is based on direct labor cost.

Required

1. Determine the following.

  a. Predetermined overhead rate for year 2013.

  b. Total overhead cost applied to each of the six jobs during year 2013.

  c. Over- or underapplied overhead at year-end 2013.

Check   (1c) 12,800 underapplied

(2) Cr. Factory Overhead $12,800

2. Assuming that any over- or underapplied overhead is not material, prepare the adjusting entry to allocate any over- or underapplied overhead to Cost of Goods Sold at the end of year 2013.

Sager Company manufactures variations of its product, a technopress, in response to custom orders from its customers. On May 1, the company had no inventories of goods in process or finished goods but held the following raw materials.

Problem 15-5A
Production transactions, subsidiary records, and source documents

P1 P2 P3 P4

Material M	200 units @ $250 =		$50,000
Material R	95 units @ 180 =		17,100
Paint	55 units @ 75 =		4,125
Total cost			$71,225

On May 4, the company began working on two technopresses: Job 102 for Worldwide Company and Job 103 for Reuben Company.

Required

Using Exhibit 15.2 as a guide, prepare job cost sheets for jobs 102 and 103. Using Exhibit 15.4 as a guide, prepare materials ledger cards for Material M, Material R, and paint. Enter the beginning raw materials inventory dollar amounts for each of these materials on their respective ledger cards. Then, follow the instructions in this list of activities.

a. Purchased raw materials on credit and recorded the following information from receiving reports and invoices.

Receiving Report No. 426, Material M, 250 units at $250 each.
Receiving Report No. 427, Material R, 90 units at $180 each.

Instructions: Record these purchases with a single journal entry. Enter the receiving report information on the materials ledger cards.

b. Requisitioned the following raw materials for production.

> Requisition No. 35, for Job 102, 135 units of Material M.
> Requisition No. 36, for Job 102, 72 units of Material R.
> Requisition No. 37, for Job 103, 70 units of Material M.
> Requisition No. 38, for Job 103, 38 units of Material R.
> Requisition No. 39, for 15 units of paint.

Instructions: Enter amounts for direct materials requisitions on the materials ledger cards and the job cost sheets. Enter the indirect material amount on the materials ledger card. Do not record a journal entry at this time.

c. Received the following employee time tickets for work in May.

> Time tickets Nos. 1 to 10 for direct labor on Job 102, $90,000.
> Time tickets Nos. 11 to 30 for direct labor on Job 103, $65,000.
> Time tickets Nos. 31 to 36 for equipment repairs, $19,250.

Instructions: Record direct labor from the time tickets on the job cost sheets. Do not record a journal entry at this time.

d. Paid cash for the following items during the month: factory payroll, $174,250, and miscellaneous overhead items, $102,000.

Instructions: Record these payments with journal entries.

e. Finished Job 102 and transferred it to the warehouse. The company assigns overhead to each job with a predetermined overhead rate equal to 80% of direct labor cost.

Instructions: Enter the allocated overhead on the cost sheet for Job 102, fill in the cost summary section of the cost sheet, and then mark the cost sheet "Finished." Prepare a journal entry to record the job's completion and its transfer to Finished Goods.

f. Delivered Job 102 and accepted the customer's promise to pay $400,000 within 30 days.

Instructions: Prepare journal entries to record the sale of Job 102 and the cost of goods sold.

g. Applied overhead to Job 103 based on the job's direct labor to date.

Instructions: Enter overhead on the job cost sheet but do not make a journal entry at this time.

Check (h) Dr. Goods in Process Inventory, $71,050

h. Recorded the total direct and indirect materials costs as reported on all the requisitions for the month.

Instructions: Prepare a journal entry to record these costs.

i. Recorded the total direct and indirect labor costs as reported on all time tickets for the month.

Instructions: Prepare a journal entry to record these costs.

Check Balance in Factory Overhead, $1,625 Cr., overapplied

j. Recorded the total overhead costs applied to jobs.

Instructions: Prepare a journal entry to record the allocation of these overhead costs.

k. Compute the balance in the Factory Overhead account as of the end of May.

PROBLEM SET B

Problem 15-1B
Production costs computed and recorded; reports prepared

C2 P1 P2 P3 P4

Tavella Co.'s August 31 inventory of raw materials is $150,000. Raw materials purchases in September are $400,000, and factory payroll cost in September is $232,000. Overhead costs incurred in September are: indirect materials, $30,000; indirect labor, $14,000; factory rent, $20,000; factory utilities, $12,000; and factory equipment depreciation, $30,000. The predetermined overhead rate is 50% of direct labor cost. Job 114 is sold for $380,000 cash in September. Costs for the three jobs worked on in September follow.

	Job 114	Job 115	Job 116
Balances on August 31			
Direct materials.............	$ 14,000	$ 18,000	
Direct labor................	18,000	16,000	
Applied overhead............	9,000	8,000	
Costs during September			
Direct materials.............	100,000	170,000	$ 80,000
Direct labor................	30,000	68,000	120,000
Applied overhead............	?	?	?
Status on September 30	Finished (sold)	Finished (unsold)	In process

Required

1. Determine the total of each production cost incurred for September (direct labor, direct materials, and applied overhead), and the total cost assigned to each job (including the balances from August 31).

2. Prepare journal entries for the month of September to record the following.

    a. Materials purchases (on credit), factory payroll (paid in cash), and actual overhead costs including indirect materials and indirect labor. (Factory rent and utilities are paid in cash.)

    b. Assignment of direct materials, direct labor, and applied overhead costs to Goods in Process Inventory.

    c. Transfer of Jobs 114 and 115 to the Finished Goods Inventory.

    d. Cost of Job 114 in the Cost of Goods Sold account.

    e. Revenue from the sale of Job 114.

    f. Assignment of any underapplied or overapplied overhead to the Cost of Goods Sold account. (The amount is not material.)

Check (2f) $3,000 overapplied

3. Prepare a manufacturing statement for September (use a single line presentation for direct materials and show the details of overhead cost).

(3) Cost of goods manufactured, $500,000

4. Compute gross profit for September. Show how to present the inventories on the September 30 balance sheet.

Analysis Component

5. The over- or underapplied overhead adjustment is closed to Cost of Goods Sold. Discuss how this adjustment impacts business decision making regarding individual jobs or batches of jobs.

Swisher Company's computer system generated the following trial balance on December 31, 2013. The company's manager knows that the trial balance is wrong because it does not show any balance for Goods in Process Inventory but does show balances for the Factory Payroll and Factory Overhead accounts.

Problem 15-2B
Source documents, journal entries, overhead, and financial reports

P1 P2 P3 P4

	Debit	Credit
Cash..........................	$ 48,000	
Accounts receivable	42,000	
Raw materials inventory	26,000	
Goods in process inventory	0	
Finished goods inventory	9,000	
Prepaid rent	3,000	
Accounts payable		$ 10,500
Notes payable		13,500
Common stock		30,000
Retained earnings		87,000
Sales...........................		180,000
Cost of goods sold	105,000	
Factory payroll	16,000	
Factory overhead	27,000	
Operating expenses	45,000	
Totals	$321,000	$321,000

After examining various files, the manager identifies the following six source documents that need to be processed to bring the accounting records up to date.

Materials requisition 94-231:	$4,600 direct materials to Job 603
Materials requisition 94-232:	$7,600 direct materials to Job 604
Materials requisition 94-233:	$2,100 indirect materials
Labor time ticket 765:	$5,000 direct labor to Job 603
Labor time ticket 766:	$8,000 direct labor to Job 604
Labor time ticket 777:	$3,000 indirect labor

Jobs 603 and 604 are the only units in process at year-end. The predetermined overhead rate is 200% of direct labor cost.

Required

1. Use information on the six source documents to prepare journal entries to assign the following costs.
   a. Direct materials costs to Goods in Process Inventory.
   b. Direct labor costs to Goods in Process Inventory.
   c. Overhead costs to Goods in Process Inventory.
   d. Indirect materials costs to the Factory Overhead account.
   e. Indirect labor costs to the Factory Overhead account.

Check (2) $6,100 underapplied overhead

(3) T. B. totals, $321,000

(4) Net income, $23,900

2. Determine the revised balance of the Factory Overhead account after making the entries in part 1. Determine whether there is under- or overapplied overhead for the year. Prepare the adjusting entry to allocate any over- or underapplied overhead to Cost of Goods Sold, assuming the amount is not material.
3. Prepare a revised trial balance.
4. Prepare an income statement for year 2013 and a balance sheet as of December 31, 2013.

Analysis Component

5. Assume that the $2,100 indirect materials on materials requisition 94-233 should have been direct materials charged to Job 604. Without providing specific calculations, describe the impact of this error on the income statement for 2013 and the balance sheet at December 31, 2013.

Problem 15-3B
Source documents, journal entries, and accounts in job order cost accounting
P1 P2 P3

Prescott Company's predetermined overhead rate is 200% of direct labor. Information on the company's production activities during September 2013 follows.
a. Purchased raw materials on credit, $125,000.
b. Paid $84,000 cash for factory wages.
c. Paid $11,000 cash for miscellaneous factory overhead costs.
d. Materials requisitions record use of the following materials for the month.

Job 487...................	$30,000
Job 488...................	20,000
Job 489...................	12,000
Job 490...................	14,000
Job 491...................	4,000
Total direct materials.........	80,000
Indirect materials............	12,000
Total materials used..........	$92,000

e. Time tickets record use of the following labor for the month.

Job 487................	$ 8,000
Job 488................	7,000
Job 489................	25,000
Job 490................	26,000
Job 491................	2,000
Total direct labor.........	68,000
Indirect labor............	16,000
Total.................	$84,000

f. Allocated overhead to Jobs 487, 489, and 490.

g. Transferred Jobs 487, 489, and 490 to Finished Goods.

h. Sold Jobs 487 and 489 on credit for a total price of $340,000.

i. The company incurred the following overhead costs during the month (credit Prepaid Insurance for expired factory insurance).

Depreciation of factory building	$37,000
Depreciation of factory equipment	21,000
Expired factory insurance	7,000
Accrued property taxes payable	31,000

j. Applied overhead at month-end to the Goods in Process (Jobs 488 and 491) using the predetermined overhead rate of 200% of direct labor cost.

Required

1. Prepare a job cost sheet for each job worked on in the month. Use the following simplified form.

Job No. _____	
Materials	$ _____
Labor	_____
Overhead	_____
Total cost	$ _____

2. Prepare journal entries to record the events and transactions *a* through *j*.

3. Set up T-accounts for each of the following general ledger accounts, each of which started the month with a zero balance: Raw Materials Inventory, Goods in Process Inventory, Finished Goods Inventory, Factory Payroll, Factory Overhead, Cost of Goods Sold. Then post the journal entries to these T-accounts and determine the balance of each account.

4. Prepare a report showing the total cost of each job in process and prove that the sum of their costs equals the Goods in Process Inventory account balance. Prepare similar reports for Finished Goods Inventory and Cost of Goods Sold.

Check (2f) Cr. Factory Overhead, $118,000

(3) Finished goods inventory, $92,000 bal.

In December 2012, Pavelka Company's manager estimated next year's total direct labor cost assuming 50 persons working an average of 2,000 hours each at an average wage rate of $15 per hour. The manager also estimated the following manufacturing overhead costs for year 2013.

Problem 15-4B
Overhead allocation and adjustment using a predetermined overhead rate

P3 P4

Indirect labor	$159,600
Factory supervision	120,000
Rent on factory building	70,000
Factory utilities	44,000
Factory insurance expired	34,000
Depreciation—Factory equipment	240,000
Repairs expense—Factory equipment	30,000
Factory supplies used	34,400
Miscellaneous production costs	18,000
Total estimated overhead costs	$750,000

At the end of 2013, records show the company incurred $725,000 of actual overhead costs. It completed and sold five jobs with the following direct labor costs: Job 625, $354,000; Job 626, $330,000; Job 627, $175,000; Job 628, $420,000; and Job 629, $184,000. In addition, Job 630 is in process at the end of 2013 and had been charged $10,000 for direct labor. No jobs were in process at the end of 2012. The company's predetermined overhead rate is based on direct labor cost.

Required

1. Determine the following.

    a. Predetermined overhead rate for year 2013.

    b. Total overhead cost applied to each of the six jobs during year 2013.

    c. Over- or underapplied overhead at year-end 2013.

2. Assuming that any over- or underapplied overhead is not material, prepare the adjusting entry to allocate any over- or underapplied overhead to Cost of Goods Sold at the end of year 2013.

Check (1c) $11,500 overapplied

    (2) Dr. Factory Overhead, $11,500

Problem 15-5B
Production transactions, subsidiary records, and source documents

P1 P2 P3 P4

King Company produces variations of its product, a megatron, in response to custom orders from its customers. On June 1, the company had no inventories of goods in process or finished goods but held the following raw materials.

Material M	120 units @ $200 =	$24,000
Material R	80 units @ 160 =	12,800
Paint	44 units @ 72 =	3,168
Total cost		$39,968

On June 3, the company began working on two megatrons: Job 450 for Encinita Company and Job 451 for Fargo, Inc.

Required

Using Exhibit 15.2 as a guide, prepare job cost sheets for jobs 20 and 21. Using Exhibit 15.4 as a guide, prepare materials ledger cards for Material M, Material R, and paint. Enter the beginning raw materials inventory dollar amounts for each of these materials on their respective ledger cards. Then, follow instructions in this list of activities.

a. Purchased raw materials on credit and recorded the following information from receiving reports and invoices.

> Receiving Report No. 20, Material M, 150 units at $200 each.
> Receiving Report No. 21, Material R, 70 units at $160 each.

Instructions: Record these purchases with a single journal entry. Enter the receiving report information on the materials ledger cards.

b. Requisitioned the following raw materials for production.

> Requisition No. 223, for Job 450, 80 units of Material M.
> Requisition No. 224, for Job 450, 60 units of Material R.
> Requisition No. 225, for Job 451, 40 units of Material M.
> Requisition No. 226, for Job 451, 30 units of Material R.
> Requisition No. 227, for 12 units of paint.

Instructions: Enter amounts for direct materials requisitions on the materials ledger cards and the job cost sheets. Enter the indirect material amount on the materials ledger card. Do not record a journal entry at this time.

c. Received the following employee time tickets for work in June.

> Time tickets Nos. 1 to 10 for direct labor on Job 450, $40,000.
> Time tickets Nos. 11 to 20 for direct labor on Job 451, $32,000.
> Time tickets Nos. 21 to 24 for equipment repairs, $12,000.

Instructions: Record direct labor from the time tickets on the job cost sheets. Do not record a journal entry at this time.

d. Paid cash for the following items during the month: factory payroll, $84,000, and miscellaneous overhead items, $36,800.

Instructions: Record these payments with journal entries.

e. Finished Job 450 and transferred it to the warehouse. The company assigns overhead to each job with a predetermined overhead rate equal to 70% of direct labor cost.

Instructions: Enter the allocated overhead on the cost sheet for Job 450, fill in the cost summary section of the cost sheet, and then mark the cost sheet "Finished." Prepare a journal entry to record the job's completion and its transfer to Finished Goods.

f. Delivered Job 450 and accepted the customer's promise to pay $290,000 within 30 days.

Instructions: Prepare journal entries to record the sale of Job 450 and the cost of goods sold.

g. Applied overhead cost to Job 451 based on the job's direct labor used to date.

Instructions: Enter overhead on the job cost sheet but do not make a journal entry at this time.

h. Recorded the total direct and indirect materials costs as reported on all the requisitions for the month.

Instructions: Prepare a journal entry to record these.

> **Check** (h) Dr. Goods in Process Inventory, $38,400

i. Recorded the total direct and indirect labor costs as reported on all time tickets for the month.

Instructions: Prepare a journal entry to record these costs.

j. Recorded the total overhead costs applied to jobs.

Instructions: Prepare a journal entry to record the allocation of these overhead costs.

> **Check** Balance in Factory Overhead, $736 Cr., overapplied

k. Compute the balance in the Factory Overhead account as of the end of June.

(This serial problem began in Chapter 1 and continues through most of the book. If previous chapter segments were not completed, the serial problem can begin at this point. It is helpful, but not necessary, to use the Working Papers that accompany the book.)

SERIAL PROBLEM
Success Systems
P1 P2 P3

SP 15 The computer workstation furniture manufacturing that Adria Lopez started in January is progressing well. As of the end of June, Success Systems' job cost sheets show the following total costs accumulated on three furniture jobs.

	Job 6.02	Job 6.03	Job 6.04
Direct materials.........	$1,500	$3,300	$2,700
Direct labor............	800	1,420	2,100
Overhead.............	400	710	1,050

Job 6.02 was started in production in May, and these costs were assigned to it in May: direct materials, $600; direct labor, $180; and overhead, $90. Jobs 6.03 and 6.04 were started in June. Overhead cost is applied with a predetermined rate based on direct labor costs. Jobs 6.02 and 6.03 are finished in June, and Job 6.04 is expected to be finished in July. No raw materials are used indirectly in June. (Assume this company's predetermined overhead rate did not change over these months).

Required

1. What is the cost of the raw materials used in June for each of the three jobs and in total?

> **Check** (1) Total materials, $6,900

2. How much total direct labor cost is incurred in June?

3. What predetermined overhead rate is used in June?

> (3) 50%

4. How much cost is transferred to finished goods inventory in June?

Beyond the Numbers

BTN 15-1 Polaris' financial statements and notes in Appendix A provide evidence of growth potential in its sales.

REPORTING IN ACTION

C1

Required

1. Identify at least two types of costs that will predictably increase as a percent of sales with growth in sales.

Polaris

2. Explain why you believe the types of costs identified for part 1 will increase, and describe how you might assess Polaris' success with these costs. (*Hint:* You might consider the gross margin ratio.)

Fast Forward

3. Access Polaris' annual report for a fiscal year ending after December 31, 2011, from its Website [Polaris.com] or the SEC's EDGAR database [www.sec.gov]. Review and report its growth in sales along with its cost and income levels (including its gross margin ratio).

COMPARATIVE ANALYSIS

C1

Polaris

Arctic Cat

BTN 15-2   Manufacturers and merchandisers can apply just-in-time (JIT) to their inventory management. Both Polaris and Arctic Cat want to know the impact of a JIT inventory system for their operating cash flows. Review each company's statement of cash flows in Appendix A to answer the following.

Required

1. Identify the impact on operating cash flows (increase or decrease) for changes in inventory levels (increase or decrease) for both companies for each of the three most recent years.

2. What impact would a JIT inventory system have on both Polaris' and Arctic Cat's operating income? Link the answer to your response for part 1.

3. Would the move to a JIT system have a one-time or recurring impact on operating cash flow?

ETHICS CHALLENGE

P3

BTN 15-3   An accounting professional requires at least two skill sets. The first is to be technically competent. Knowing how to capture, manage, and report information is a necessary skill. Second, the ability to assess manager and employee actions and biases for accounting analysis is another skill. For instance, knowing how a person is compensated helps anticipate information biases. Draw on these skills and write a one-half page memo to the financial officer on the following practice of allocating overhead.

Background: Assume that your company sells portable housing to both general contractors and the government. It sells jobs to contractors on a bid basis. A contractor asks for three bids from different manufacturers. The combination of low bid and high quality wins the job. However, jobs sold to the government are bid on a cost-plus basis. This means price is determined by adding all costs plus a profit based on cost at a specified percent, such as 10%. You observe that the amount of overhead allocated to government jobs is higher than that allocated to contract jobs. These allocations concern you and motivate your memo.

Point: Students could compare responses and discuss differences in concerns with allocating overhead.

COMMUNICATING IN PRACTICE

C1 C2

BTN 15-4   Assume that you are preparing for a second interview with a manufacturing company. The company is impressed with your credentials but has indicated that it has several qualified applicants. You anticipate that in this second interview, you must show what you offer over other candidates. You learn the company currently uses a periodic inventory system and is not satisfied with the timeliness of its information and its inventory management. The company manufactures custom-order holiday decorations and display items. To show your abilities, you plan to recommend that it use a cost accounting system.

Required

In preparation for the interview, prepare notes outlining the following:

1. Your cost accounting system recommendation and why it is suitable for this company.

2. A general description of the documents that the proposed cost accounting system requires.

3. How the documents in part 2 facilitate the operation of the cost accounting system.

Point: Have students present a mock interview, one assuming the role of the president of the company and the other the applicant.

TAKING IT TO THE NET

C1

BTN 15-5   Many contractors work on custom jobs that require a job order costing system.

Required

Access the Website AMSI.com and click on *Construction Management Software,* and then on STARBUILDER. Prepare a one-page memorandum for the CEO of a construction company providing information about the job order costing software this company offers. Would you recommend that the company purchase this software?

BTN 15-6   Consider the activities undertaken by a medical clinic in your area.

Required

1. Do you consider a job order cost accounting system appropriate for the clinic?

2. Identify as many factors as possible to lead you to conclude that it uses a job order system.

BTN 15-7   Refer to the chapter opener regarding David Schottenstein and his company, Astor and Black. All successful businesses track their costs, and it is especially important for start-up businesses to monitor and control costs.

Required

1. Assume that Astor and Black uses a job order costing system. For the basic cost category of direct materials, explain how a job cost sheet for Astor and Black would differ from a job cost sheet for a service company.

2. For the basic cost categories of direct labor and overhead, provide examples of the types of costs that would fall into each category for Astor and Black.

BTN 15-8   Job order cost accounting is frequently used by home builders.

Required

1. You (or your team) are to prepare a job cost sheet for a single-family home under construction. List four items of both direct materials and direct labor. Explain how you think overhead should be applied.

2. Contact a builder and compare your job cost sheet to this builder's job cost sheet. If possible, speak to that company's accountant. Write your findings in a short report.

BTN 15-9   KTM and Piaggio are competitors in the global marketplace. KTM's and Piaggio's financial statements are in Appendix A.

Required

1. Determine the change in KTM's and Piaggio's inventories for the most recent year reported. Then identify the impact on net resources generated by operating activities (increase or decrease) for the change in inventory level (increase or decrease) for KTM and Piaggio for that same year.

2. How would the move to a just-in-time (JIT) system likely impact future operating cash flows and operating income?

3. Would a move to a JIT system likely impact KTM more than it would Piaggio? Explain.

ANSWERS TO MULTIPLE CHOICE QUIZ

1. c; $30,000 \times 150\% = \underline{\$45,000}$

2. b; $38,500/\$35,000 = \underline{110\%}$

3. e; Direct materials + Direct labor + Overhead = Total cost;
   Direct materials + ($4,000/.80) + $4,000 = $10,000
   Direct materials = $\underline{\$1,000}$

4. e; $9,000 + $94,200 + $59,200 + $31,600 − Finished goods = $17,800
   Thus, finished goods = $\underline{\$176,200}$

5. b

Cost Behavior and Cost-Volume-Profit Analysis

A Look Back

Chapter 17 introduced the activity-based costing (ABC) system, which has the potential for greater accuracy of cost allocations and for providing managers with better cost information for strategic decisions.

A Look at This Chapter

This chapter shows how information on both costs and sales behavior is useful to managers in performing cost-volume-profit analysis. This analysis is an important part of successful management and sound business decisions.

A Look Ahead

Chapter 19 compares reports prepared under variable costing with those under absorption costing, and it explains how variable costing can improve managerial decisions.

Learning Objectives

CONCEPTUAL

C1 Describe different types of cost behavior in relation to production and sales volume. (p. 778)

C2 Describe several applications of cost-volume-profit analysis. (p. 789)

ANALYTICAL

A1 Compute the contribution margin and describe what it reveals about a company's cost structure. (p. 785)

A2 Analyze changes in sales using the degree of operating leverage. (p. 795)

PROCEDURAL

P1 Determine cost estimates using the scatter diagram, high-low, and regression methods of estimating costs. (p. 781)

P2 Compute the break-even point for a single product company. (p. 785)

P3 Graph costs and sales for a single product company. (p. 787)

P4 Compute the break-even point for a multiproduct company. (p. 793)

Decision Insight

Sporting Success

"Put passion into your work"

—PAUL

GLEN ROCK, NJ—Most quarterbacks in backyard football games have a glaring weakness: They can't throw good passes. Paul Cunningham, lifelong sports fan and master craftsman, set out to make "an exceptional quality football, slightly smaller than an NFL ball, so that the average person can throw it." As a result, what started as a side project in his home workshop turned into a full-fledged business, Leather Head Sports (**Leather-headsports.com**). As Paul notes, "I've been able to leave the corporate world and do this full-time."

Paul's forays began when he crafted leather baseballs for the Major League Baseball Hall of Fame to use in recreating 19th century baseball games. Now, Paul makes leather baseballs, which he sells as Lemon Balls™, along with a line of Leather Head™ footballs and medicine balls. Paul makes every Leather Head™ ball himself. "I want someone to look at my football and see the passion that went into it," says Paul.

Paul stresses that he, like many entrepreneurs, had to learn through a process of trial and error. "Every hide is different, and I tried many different approaches to making a football." Now, upon receiving an order, Paul begins his production process by grabbing a side of top-quality leather. Using custom-made cutting dies, he hand cuts the leather panels. He then sews the leather panels together, inserts a rubber bladder, and laces the ball with rawhide lace. The result is what Paul calls the "official football of collegiate tailgating."

Operating at a small scale and using exp materials require Paul to understand and con cessful entrepreneurs must understand succeed. Identifying fixed and variable cos standing break-even points and maintaining mix. Paul's small but diverse product line has ent selling prices and costs. Contribution ma ments, which separate fixed and variab entrepreneurs like Paul to quickly see how prices, variable costs, or fixed costs impact ing contribution margins and cost-volume-p ables small businesses to profit and grow.

Paul encourages young entrepreneurs to g happen. His sights are set on growing his co bringing in additional craftsmen. Scaling hi way would make understanding how costs and profit even more important. "I work har love working with my hands and creating thi perfect pass.

[Sources: *Leather Head Sports Website,* January 20 youtube.com/watch?v=GaL3qxV4UzQ; http://video. v/1404850982001/investors-consider-adding-fine-ar ?playlist_id=87185; http://video.foxbusiness.com/v/3

Chapter Preview

This chapter describes different types of costs and shows how changes in a company's operating volume affect these costs. The chapter also analyzes a company's costs and sales to explain how different operating strategies affect profit or loss. Managers use this type of analysis to forecast what will happen if changes are made to costs, sales volume, selling prices, or product mix. They then use these forecasts to select the best business strategy for the company.

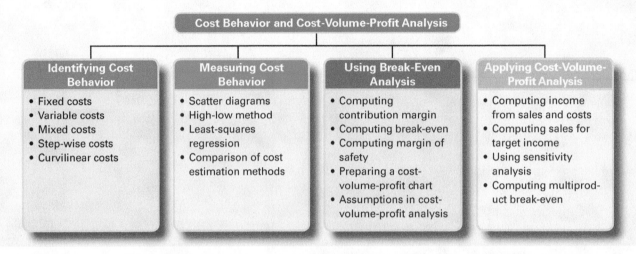

Cost Behavior and Cost-Volume-Profit Analysis

Identifying Cost Behavior	Measuring Cost Behavior	Using Break-Even Analysis	Applying Cost-Volume-Profit Analysis
• Fixed costs • Variable costs • Mixed costs • Step-wise costs • Curvilinear costs	• Scatter diagrams • High-low method • Least-squares regression • Comparison of cost estimation methods	• Computing contribution margin • Computing break-even • Computing margin of safety • Preparing a cost-volume-profit chart • Assumptions in cost-volume-profit analysis	• Computing income from sales and costs • Computing sales for target income • Using sensitivity analysis • Computing multiproduct break-even

IDENTIFYING COST BEHAVIOR

Point: *Profit* is another term for *income.*

Planning a company's future activities and events is crucial to successful management. One of the first steps in planning is to predict the volume of activity, the costs to be incurred, sales to be made, and profit to be received. An important tool to help managers carry out this step is **cost-volume-profit (CVP) analysis,** which helps them predict how changes in costs and sales levels affect income. In its basic form, CVP analysis involves computing the sales level at which a company neither earns an income nor incurs a loss, called the *break-even point*. For this reason, this basic form of cost-volume-profit analysis is often called *break-even analysis*. Managers use variations of CVP analysis to answer questions like:

- What sales volume is needed to earn a target income?
- What is the change in income if selling prices decline and sales volume increases?
- How much does income increase if we install a new machine to reduce labor costs?
- How will income change if we change the sales mix of our products or services?

Consequently, cost-volume-profit analysis is useful in a wide range of business decisions.

Conventional cost-volume-profit analysis requires management to classify all costs as either *fixed* or *variable* with respect to production or sales volume. The remainder of this section discusses the concepts of fixed and variable cost behavior as they relate to CVP analysis.

Decision Insight

No Free Lunch   Hardly a week goes by without a company advertising a free product with the purchase of another. Examples are a free printer with a digital camera purchase or a free monitor with a computer purchase. Can these companies break even, let alone earn profits? We are reminded of the *no-free-lunch* adage, meaning that companies expect profits from the companion or add-on purchase to make up for the free product. ∎

C1   Describe different types of cost behavior in relation to production and sales volume.

Fixed Costs

A *fixed cost* remains unchanged in amount when the volume of activity varies from period to period within a relevant range. For example, $32,000 in monthly rent paid for a factory building remains the same whether the factory operates with a single eight-hour shift or around the clock with three shifts. This means that rent cost is the same each month at any level of output from zero to the plant's full productive capacity. Notice that while *total* fixed cost does not change as the level of production changes, the fixed cost *per unit* of output decreases as volume increases. For instance, if 200 units are produced when monthly rent is $32,000, the average rent cost per unit is $160 (computed as $32,000/200 units); and when 100 units are produced, the average rent cost per unit is $320 (computed as $32,000/100 units). When production increases to 1,000 units per month, the average rent cost per unit decreases to $32 (computed as $32,000/1,000 units). The average rent cost decreases to $16 per unit if production increases to 2,000 units per month. Common examples of fixed costs include depreciation, property taxes, office salaries, and many service department costs.

When production volume and costs are graphed, units of product are usually plotted on the *horizontal axis* and dollars of cost are plotted on the *vertical axis*. Fixed costs then are represented as a horizontal line because they remain constant at all levels of production. To illustrate, the top graph in Exhibit 18.1 shows that fixed costs remain at $32,000 at all production levels up to the company's monthly capacity of 2,000 units of output. The bottom graph in Exhibit 18.1 shows that fixed costs per unit fall as production levels increase. This drop in costs per unit as production levels increase is known as *economies of scale*. The *relevant range* for fixed costs in Exhibit 18.1 is 0 to 2,000 units. If the relevant range changes (that is, production capacity extends beyond this range), the amount of fixed costs will likely change.

Example: If the fixed cost line in Exhibit 18.1 is shifted upward, does the total cost line shift up, down, or remain in the same place? *Answer:* It shifts up by the same amount.

EXHIBIT 18.1

Relations of Total and Per-Unit Costs to Volume

Example: If the level of fixed costs in Exhibit 18.1 changes, does the slope of the total cost line change? *Answer:* No, the slope doesn't change. The total cost line is simply shifted upward or downward.

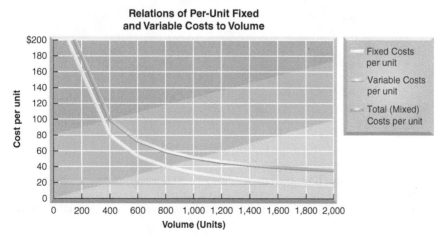

Variable Costs

A *variable cost* changes in proportion to changes in volume of activity. The direct materials cost of a product is one example of a variable cost. If one unit of product requires materials costing $20, total materials costs are $200 when 10 units of product are manufactured, $400 for 20 units, $600 for 30 units, and so on. Notice that variable cost *per unit* remains constant but the *total* amount of variable cost changes with the level of production. In addition to direct materials, common variable costs include direct labor (if employees are paid per unit), sales commissions, shipping costs, and some overhead costs.

When variable costs are plotted on a graph of cost and volume, they appear as a straight line starting at the zero cost level. This straight line is upward (positive) sloping. The line rises as volume of activity increases. A variable cost line using a $20 per unit cost is graphed in Exhibit 18.1. The bottom graph in Exhibit 18.1 shows that variable cost per unit is constant as production levels change.

Mixed Costs

A **mixed cost** includes both fixed and variable cost components. For example, compensation for sales representatives often includes a fixed monthly salary and a variable commission based on sales. Like a fixed cost, a mixed cost is greater than zero when volume is zero; but unlike a fixed cost, it increases steadily in proportion to increases in volume. The mixed cost line in the top graph Exhibit 18.1 starts on the vertical axis at the $32,000 fixed cost point. Thus, at the zero volume level, total (mixed) cost equals the fixed costs. As the activity level increases, the mixed cost line increases at an amount equal to the variable cost per unit. This line is highest when the volume of activity is at 2,000 units (the end point of the relevant range). In CVP analysis, mixed costs are often separated into fixed and variable components. The fixed component is added to other fixed costs, and the variable component is added to other variable costs.

Step-Wise Costs

A **step-wise cost** reflects a step pattern in costs. Salaries of production supervisors often behave in a step-wise manner in that their salaries are fixed within a *relevant range* of the current production volume. However, if production volume expands significantly (for example, with the addition of another shift), additional supervisors must be hired. This means that the total cost for supervisory salaries goes up by a lump-sum amount. Similarly, if volume takes another significant step up, supervisory salaries will increase by another lump sum. This behavior reflects a step-wise cost, also known as a *stair-step cost,* which is graphed in Exhibit 18.2. See how the step-wise cost line is flat within ranges (steps). Then, when volume significantly changes, it shifts to another level for that range (step).

EXHIBIT 18.2

Step-Wise and
Curvilinear Costs

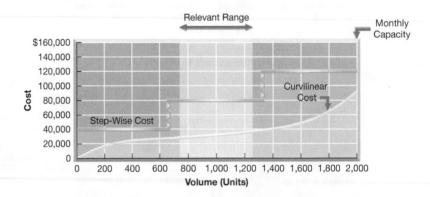

In a conventional CVP analysis, a step-wise cost is usually treated as either a fixed cost or a variable cost. This treatment involves manager judgment and depends on the width of the range and the expected volume. To illustrate, suppose after the production of every 25 snowboards, an operator lubricates the finishing machine. The cost of this lubricant reflects a step-wise pattern. Also, suppose that after the production of every 1,000 units, the snowboard cutting tool is replaced. Again, this is a step-wise cost. Note that the range of 25 snowboards is much narrower than the range of 1,000 snowboards. Some managers might treat the lubricant cost as a variable cost and the cutting tool cost as a fixed cost.

Point: Computer spreadsheets are important and effective tools for CVP analysis and for analyzing alternative "what-if" strategies.

Curvilinear Costs

A variable cost, as explained, is a *linear* cost; that is, it increases at a constant rate as volume of activity increases. A **curvilinear cost,** also called a *nonlinear cost,* increases at a nonconstant rate as volume increases. When graphed, curvilinear costs appear as a curved line. Exhibit 18.2 shows a curvilinear cost beginning at zero when production is zero and then increasing at different rates.

An example of a curvilinear cost is total direct labor cost when workers are paid by the hour. At low to medium levels of production, adding more employees allows each of them to specialize by doing certain tasks repeatedly instead of doing several different tasks. This often yields additional units of output at lower costs. A point is eventually reached at which adding more employees creates inefficiencies. For instance, a large crew demands more time and effort in communicating and coordinating their efforts. While adding employees in this case increases output, the labor cost per unit increases, and the total labor cost goes up at a steeper slope. This pattern is seen in Exhibit 18.2 where the curvilinear cost curve starts at zero, rises, flattens out, and then increases at a faster rate as output nears the maximum.

Point: Cost-volume-profit analysis helped Rod Canion, Jim Harris, and Bill Murto raise start-up capital of $20 million to launch **Compaq Computer.** They showed that break-even volumes were attainable within the first year.

Quick Check   Answers – p. 799

1. Which of the following statements is typically true? (*a*) Variable cost per unit increases as volume increases, (*b*) fixed cost per unit decreases as volume increases, or (*c*) a curvilinear cost includes both fixed and variable elements.
2. Describe the behavior of a fixed cost.
3. If cost per unit of activity remains constant (fixed), why is it called a variable cost?

MEASURING COST BEHAVIOR

Identifying and measuring cost behavior requires careful analysis and judgment. An important part of this process is to identify costs that can be classified as either fixed or variable, which often requires analysis of past cost behavior. Three methods are commonly used to analyze past costs: scatter diagrams, the high-low method, and least-squares regression. Each method is discussed in this section using the unit and cost data shown in Exhibit 18.3, which

P1 Determine cost estimates using the scatter diagram, high-low, and regression methods of estimating costs.

EXHIBIT 18.3

Data for Estimating Cost Behavior

Month	Units Produced	Total Cost
January	27,500	$21,500
February.......	17,500	20,500
March	25,000	25,000
April	35,000	21,500
May	47,500	25,500
June	22,500	18,500
July	30,000	23,500
August	52,500	28,500
September	37,500	26,000
October	67,500	29,000
November	62,500	31,000
December	57,500	26,000

are taken from a start-up company that uses units produced as the activity base in estimating cost behavior.

Scatter Diagrams

Scatter diagrams display past cost and unit data in graphical form. In preparing a scatter diagram, units are plotted on the horizontal axis and cost is plotted on the vertical axis. Each individual point on a scatter diagram reflects the cost and number of units for a prior period. In Exhibit 18.4, the prior 12 months' costs and numbers of units are graphed. Each point reflects total costs incurred and units produced for one of those months. For instance, the point labeled March had units produced of 25,000 and costs of $25,000.

EXHIBIT 18.4

Scatter Diagram

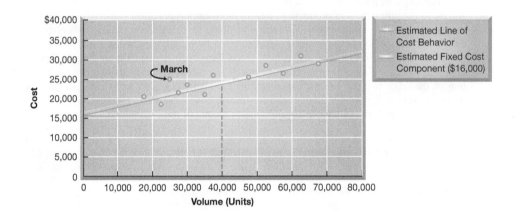

The **estimated line of cost behavior** is drawn on a scatter diagram to reflect the relation between cost and unit volume. This line best visually "fits" the points in a scatter diagram. Fitting this line demands judgment. The line drawn in Exhibit 18.4 intersects the vertical axis at approximately $16,000, which reflects fixed cost. To compute variable cost per unit, or the slope, we perform three steps. First, we select any two points on the horizontal axis (units), say 0 and 40,000. Second, we draw a vertical line from each of these points to intersect the estimated line of cost behavior. The point on the vertical axis (cost) corresponding to the 40,000 units point that intersects the estimated line is roughly $24,000. Similarly, the cost corresponding to zero units is $16,000 (the fixed cost point). Third, we compute the slope of the line, or variable cost, as the change in cost divided by the change in units. Exhibit 18.5 shows this computation.

EXHIBIT 18.5

Variable Cost per Unit
(Scatter Diagram)

$$\frac{\text{Change in cost}}{\text{Change in units}} = \frac{\$24,000 - \$16,000}{40,000 - 0} = \frac{\$8,000}{40,000} = \$0.20 \text{ per unit}$$

Example: In Exhibits 18.4 and 18.5, if units are projected at 30,000, what is the predicted cost? *Answer:* Approximately $22,000.

Variable cost is $0.20 per unit. Thus, the cost equation that management will use to estimate costs for different unit levels is $16,000 plus $0.20 per unit.

High-Low Method

The **high-low method** is a way to estimate the cost equation by graphically connecting the two cost amounts at the highest and lowest unit volumes. In our case, the lowest number of units is 17,500, and the highest is 67,500. The costs corresponding to these unit volumes are $20,500 and $29,000, respectively (see the data in Exhibit 18.3). The estimated line of cost behavior for the high-low method is then drawn by connecting these two points on the scatter diagram corresponding to the lowest and highest unit volumes as follows.

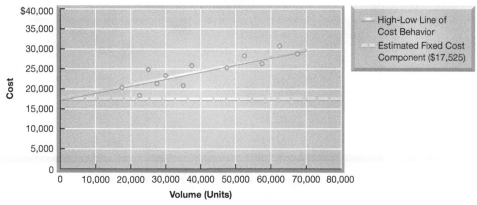

The variable cost per unit is determined as the change in cost divided by the change in units and uses the data from the high and low unit volumes. This results in a slope, or variable cost per unit, of $0.17 as computed in Exhibit 18.6.

Point: Note that the high-low method identifies the high and low points of the volume (activity) base, and the costs linked with those extremes—which may not be the highest and lowest costs.

$$\frac{\text{Change in cost}}{\text{Change in units}} = \frac{\$29{,}000 - \$20{,}500}{67{,}500 - 17{,}500} = \frac{\$8{,}500}{50{,}000} = \$0.17 \text{ per unit}$$

EXHIBIT 18.6

Variable Cost per Unit
(High-Low Method)

To estimate the fixed cost for the high-low method, we use the knowledge that total cost equals fixed cost plus variable cost per unit times the number of units. Then we pick either the high or low point to determine the fixed cost. This computation is shown in Exhibit 18.7—where we use the high point (67,500 units) in determining the fixed cost of $17,525. Use of the low point (17,500 units) yields the same fixed cost estimate: $20,500 = Fixed cost + ($0.17 per unit × 17,500), or Fixed cost = $17,525.

Total cost = Fixed cost + (Variable cost × Units)

$29,000 = Fixed cost + ($0.17 per unit × 67,500 units)

Then,   Fixed cost = $17,525

EXHIBIT 18.7

Fixed Cost (High-Low Method)

Thus, the cost equation used to estimate costs at different units is $17,525 plus $0.17 per unit. This cost equation differs slightly from that determined from the scatter diagram method. A deficiency of the high-low method is that it ignores all cost points except the highest and lowest. The result is less precision because the high-low method uses the most extreme points rather than the more usual conditions likely to recur.

Least-Squares Regression

Least-squares regression is a statistical method for identifying cost behavior. For our purposes, we use the cost equation estimated from this method but leave the computational details for more advanced courses. Such computations for least-squares regression are readily done using most spreadsheet programs or calculators. We illustrate this using Excel® in Appendix 18A.

The regression cost equation for the data presented in Exhibit 18.3 is $16,947 plus $0.19 per unit; that is, the fixed cost is estimated as $16,947 and the variable cost at $0.19 per unit. Both costs are reflected in the following graph.

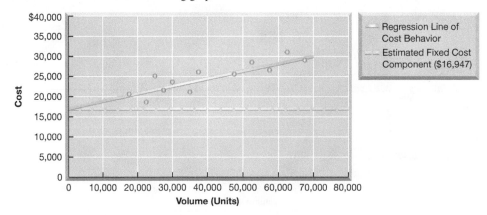

Comparison of Cost Estimation Methods

The three cost estimation methods result in slightly different estimates of fixed and variable costs as summarized in Exhibit 18.8. Estimates from the scatter diagram are based on a visual fit of the cost line and are subject to interpretation. Estimates from the high-low method use only two sets of values corresponding to the lowest and highest unit volumes. Estimates from least-squares regression use a statistical technique and all available data points.

EXHIBIT 18.8

Comparison of Cost
Estimation Methods

Estimation Method	Fixed Cost	Variable Cost
Scatter diagram	$16,000	$0.20 per unit
High-low method	17,525	0.17 per unit
Least-squares regression	16,947	0.19 per unit

We must remember that all three methods use *past data*. Thus, cost estimates resulting from these methods are only as good as the data used for estimation. Managers must establish that the data are reliable in deriving cost estimates for the future. If the data are reliable, the use of more data points, as in the regression or scatter diagram methods, should yield more accurate estimates than the high-low method. However, the high-low method is easier to apply than the regression method and less subject to interpretation than the scatter diagram approach.

Quick Check   Answers — p. 799

4. Which of the following methods is likely to yield the most precise estimated line of cost behavior? (*a*) High-low, (*b*) least-squares regression, or (*c*) scatter diagram.
5. What is the primary weakness of the high-low method?
6. Using conventional CVP analysis, a mixed cost should be (*a*) disregarded, (*b*) treated as a fixed cost, or (*c*) separated into fixed and variable components.

USING BREAK-EVEN ANALYSIS

Break-even analysis is a special case of cost-volume-profit analysis. This section describes break-even analysis by computing the break-even point and preparing a CVP (or break-even) chart.

Contribution Margin and Its Measures

We explained how managers classify costs by behavior. This often refers to classifying costs as being fixed or variable with respect to volume of activity. In manufacturing companies, volume of activity usually refers to the number of units produced. We then classify a cost as either fixed or variable, depending on whether total cost changes as the number of units produced changes. Once we separate costs by behavior, we can then compute a product's contribution margin. **Contribution margin per unit,** or *unit contribution margin,* is the amount by which a product's unit selling price exceeds its total variable cost per unit. This excess amount contributes to covering fixed costs and generating profits on a per unit basis. Exhibit 18.9 shows the contribution margin per unit formula.

A1 | Compute the contribution margin and describe what it reveals about a company's cost structure.

Contribution margin per unit = Sales price per unit − Total variable cost per unit

EXHIBIT 18.9

Contribution Margin per Unit

The **contribution margin ratio,** which is the percent of a unit's selling price that exceeds total unit variable cost, is also useful for business decisions. It can be interpreted as the percent of each sales dollar that remains after deducting the total unit variable cost. Exhibit 18.10 shows the formula for the contribution margin ratio.

$$\text{Contribution margin ratio} = \frac{\text{Contribution margin per unit}}{\text{Sales price per unit}}$$

EXHIBIT 18.10

Contribution Margin Ratio

To illustrate the use of contribution margin, let's consider **Rydell,** which sells footballs for $100 each and incurs variable costs of $70 per football sold. Its fixed costs are $24,000 per month with monthly capacity of 1,800 units (footballs). Rydell's contribution margin per unit is $30, which is computed as follows.

Selling price per unit	$100
Variable cost per unit	70
Contribution margin per unit	$ 30

Its contribution margin ratio is 30%, computed as $30/$100. This reveals that for each unit sold, Rydell has $30 that contributes to covering fixed cost and profit. If we consider sales in dollars, a contribution margin of 30% implies that for each $1 in sales, Rydell has $0.30 that contributes to fixed cost and profit.

▉ Decision Maker

Sales Manager   You are evaluating orders from two customers but can accept only one of the orders because of your company's limited capacity. The first order is for 100 units of a product with a contribution margin ratio of 60% and a selling price of $1,000. The second order is for 500 units of a product with a contribution margin ratio of 20% and a selling price of $800. The incremental fixed costs are the same for both orders. Which order do you accept? ▉   [Answer—p. 798]

Computing the Break-Even Point

The **break-even point** is the sales level at which a company neither earns a profit nor incurs a loss. The concept of break-even is applicable to nearly all organizations, activities, and events. One of the most important items of information when launching a project is whether it will break even—that is, whether sales will at least cover total costs. The break-even point can be expressed in either units or dollars of sales.

P2 | Compute the break-even point for a single product company.

To illustrate break-even analysis, let's again look at Rydell, which sells footballs for $100 per unit and incurs $70 of variable costs per unit sold. Its fixed costs are $24,000 per month. Rydell breaks even for the month when it sells 800 footballs (sales volume of $80,000). We compute this break-even point using the formula in Exhibit 18.11. This formula uses the contribution margin per unit, which for Rydell is $30 ($100 − $70). From this we can compute the break-even sales volume as $24,000/$30, or 800 units per month.

EXHIBIT 18.11

Formula for Computing
Break-Even Sales (in Units)

$$\text{Break-even point in units} = \frac{\text{Fixed costs}}{\text{Contribution margin per unit}}$$

At a price of $100 per unit, monthly sales of 800 units yield sales dollars of $80,000 (called *break-even sales dollars*). This $80,000 break-even sales can be computed directly using the formula in Exhibit 18.12.

EXHIBIT 18.12

Formula for Computing
Break-Even Sales (in Dollars)

$$\text{Break-even point in dollars} = \frac{\text{Fixed costs}}{\text{Contribution margin ratio}}$$

Point: Even if a company operates at a level in excess of its break-even point, management may decide to stop operating because it is not earning a reasonable return on investment.

Rydell's break-even point in dollars is computed as $24,000/0.30, or $80,000 of monthly sales. To verify that Rydell's break-even point equals $80,000 (or 800 units), we prepare a simplified income statement in Exhibit 18.13. It shows that the $80,000 revenue from sales of 800 units exactly equals the sum of variable and fixed costs.

EXHIBIT 18.13

Contribution Margin
Income Statement for
Break-Even Sales

RYDELL COMPANY	
Contribution Margin Income Statement (at Break-Even)	
For Month Ended January 31, 2013	
Sales (800 units at $100 each)	$80,000
Variable costs (800 units at $70 each)	56,000
Contribution margin	24,000
Fixed costs	24,000
Net income	$ 0

Point: A contribution margin income statement is also referred to as a *variable costing income statement.* This differs from the traditional *absorption costing* approach where all product costs are assigned to units sold and to units in ending inventory. Recall that variable costing expenses all fixed product costs. Thus, income for the two approaches differs depending on the level of finished goods inventory; the lower inventory is, the more similar the two approaches are.

The statement in Exhibit 18.13 is called a *contribution margin income statement.* It differs in format from a conventional income statement in two ways. First, it separately classifies costs and expenses as variable or fixed. Second, it reports contribution margin (Sales − Variable costs). The contribution margin income statement format is used in this chapter's assignment materials because of its usefulness in CVP analysis.

Computing the Margin of Safety

All companies wish to sell more than the break-even number of units. The excess of expected sales over the break-even sales level is called a company's **margin of safety,** the amount that sales can drop before the company incurs a loss. It can be expressed in units, dollars, or even as a percent of the predicted level of sales. To illustrate, if Rydell's expected sales are $100,000, the margin of safety is $20,000 above break-even sales of $80,000. As a percent, the margin of safety is 20% of expected sales as shown in Exhibit 18.14.

EXHIBIT 18.14

Computing Margin of Safety
(in Percent)

$$\text{Margin of safety (in percent)} = \frac{\text{Expected sales} - \text{Break-even sales}}{\text{Expected sales}}$$

$$= \frac{\$100,000 - \$80,000}{\$100,000} = 20\%$$

Management must assess whether the margin of safety is adequate in light of factors such as sales variability, competition, consumer tastes, and economic conditions.

Preparing a Cost-Volume-Profit Chart

Exhibit 18.15 is a graph of Rydell's cost-volume-profit relations. This graph is called a **cost-volume-profit (CVP) chart,** or a *break-even chart* or *break-even graph.* The horizontal axis is the number of units produced and sold and the vertical axis is dollars of sales and costs. The lines in the chart depict both sales and costs at different output levels.

P3   Graph costs and sales for a single product company.

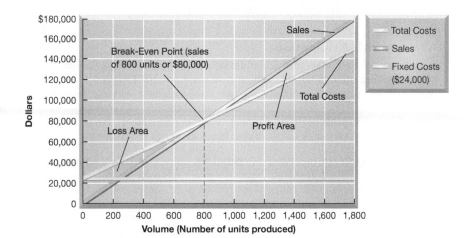

EXHIBIT 18.15

Cost-Volume-Profit Chart

We follow three steps to prepare a CVP chart, which can also be drawn with computer programs that convert numeric data to graphs:

1. Plot fixed costs on the vertical axis ($24,000 for Rydell). Draw a horizontal line at this level to show that fixed costs remain unchanged regardless of output volume (drawing this fixed cost line is not essential to the chart).

2. Draw the total (variable plus fixed) cost line for a relevant range of volume levels. This line starts at the fixed costs level on the vertical axis because total costs equal fixed costs at zero volume. The slope of the total cost line equals the variable cost per unit ($70). To draw the line, compute the total costs for any volume level, and connect this point with the vertical axis intercept ($24,000). Do not draw this line beyond the productive capacity for the planning period (1,800 units for Rydell).

   Point: CVP analysis is often based on *sales volume,* using either units sold or dollar sales. Other output measures, such as the number of units produced, can also be used.

3. Draw the sales line. Start at the origin (zero units and zero dollars of sales) and make the slope of this line equal to the selling price per unit ($100). To sketch the line, compute dollar sales for any volume level and connect this point with the origin. Do not extend this line beyond the productive capacity. Total sales will be at the highest level at maximum capacity.

The total cost line and the sales line intersect at 800 units in Exhibit 18.15, which is the break-even point—the point where total dollar sales of $80,000 equals the sum of both fixed and variable costs ($80,000).

On either side of the break-even point, the vertical distance between the sales line and the total cost line at any specific volume reflects the profit or loss expected at that point. At volume levels to the left of the break-even point, this vertical distance is the amount of the expected loss because the total costs line is above the total sales line. At volume levels to the right of the break-even point, the vertical distance represents the expected profit because the total sales line is above the total cost line.

Example: In Exhibit 18.15, the sales line intersects the total cost line at 800 units. At what point would the two lines intersect if selling price is increased by 20% to $120 per unit? *Answer:* $24,000/($120 − $70) = 480 units

 Decision Maker ━━━━━━━━━━━━━━━━━━━━━━━━━

Operations Manager   As a start-up manufacturer, you wish to identify the behavior of manufacturing costs to develop a production cost budget. You know three methods can be used to identify cost behavior from past data, but past data are unavailable because this is a start-up. What do you do? ■ [Answer—p. 799]

Making Assumptions in Cost-Volume-Profit Analysis

Cost-volume-profit analysis assumes that relations can normally be expressed as simple lines similar to those in Exhibits 18.4 and 18.15. CVP analysis assumes that selling prices per unit, variable costs per unit, and total fixed costs are all held constant. If the expected costs and sales behavior differ from the assumptions, the results of CVP analysis can be limited. While the behavior of individual costs and sales may not be perfectly consistent with CVP assumptions, we can still perform useful analyses in spite of these assumptions' limitations, for reasons we describe next.

Working with Assumptions

Summing costs can offset individual deviations. Deviations from assumptions with individual costs are often minor when these costs are summed. That is, individual variable cost items may not be perfectly variable, but when we sum these variable costs, their individual deviations can offset each other. This means the assumption of variable cost behavior can be proper for total variable costs. Similarly, an assumption that total fixed costs are constant can be proper even when individual fixed cost items are not exactly constant.

CVP is applied to a relevant range of operations. Sales, variable costs, and fixed costs often are reasonably reflected in straight lines on a graph when the assumptions are applied over a relevant range. The **relevant range of operations** is the normal operating range for a business. Except for unusually difficult or prosperous times, management typically plans for operations within a range of volume neither close to zero nor at maximum capacity. The relevant range excludes extremely high and low operating levels that are unlikely to occur. The validity of assuming that a specific cost is fixed or variable is more acceptable when operations are within the relevant range. As shown in Exhibit 18.2, a curvilinear cost can be treated as variable and linear if the relevant range covers volumes where it has a nearly constant slope. If the normal range of activity changes, some costs might need reclassification.

CVP analysis yields estimates. CVP analysis yields approximate answers to questions about costs, volumes, and profits. These answers do not have to be precise because the analysis makes rough estimates about the future. For example, to simplify analysis, we sometimes assume that the production level is the same as the sales level. That is, inventory levels do not change. This often is justified by arguing that CVP analysis provides only approximations. With just-in-time inventory systems, production levels should approximate sales levels, thus CVP estimates should be more accurate. As long as managers understand that CVP analysis gives estimates, it can be a useful tool for starting the planning process. Other qualitative factors also must be considered.

Example: If the selling price declines, what happens to the break-even point? *Answer:* It increases.

Quick Check

Answers — p. 799

7. Fixed cost divided by the contribution margin ratio yields the (a) break-even point in dollars, (b) contribution margin per unit, or (c) break-even point in units.

8. A company sells a product for $90 per unit with variable costs of $54 per unit. What is the contribution margin ratio?

9. Refer to Quick Check (8). If fixed costs for the period are $90,000, what is the break-even point in dollars?

10. What is a company's margin of safety?

11. What three basic assumptions are used in CVP analysis?

Working with Changes in Estimates Because CVP analysis uses estimates, knowing how changes in those estimates impact break-even is useful. For example, a manager might form three estimates for each of the components of break-even: optimistic, most likely, and pessimistic. Then ranges of break-even points in units can be computed using the formula in Exhibit 18.11.

To illustrate, assume Rydell's managers provide the set of estimates in Exhibit 18.16.

	Selling Price per Unit	Variable Cost per Unit	Total Fixed Costs
Optimistic	$105	$68	$21,000
Most likely	100	70	24,000
Pessimistic	95	72	27,000

EXHIBIT 18.16

Alternative Estimates for Break-Even Analysis

If, for example, Rydell's managers believe they can raise the selling price of a football to $105, without any change in unit variable or total fixed costs, then the revised contribution margin per football is $35, and the revised break-even in units follows in Exhibit 18.17.

$$\text{Revised break-even point in units} = \frac{\$24,000}{\$35} = 686 \text{ units (rounded)}$$

EXHIBIT 18.17

Revised Break-Even in Units

Repeating this calculation using each of the other eight separate estimates above, and graphing the results, yields the three scatter diagrams in Exhibit 18.18.

EXHIBIT 18.18

Scatter Diagrams—Break-Even Points for Alternative Estimates

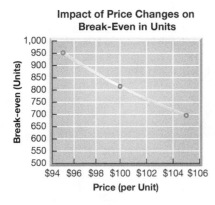

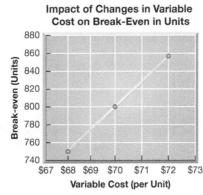

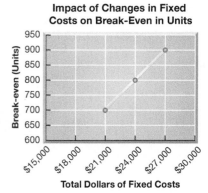

These scatter diagrams show how changes in selling prices, variable costs, and fixed costs impact break-even. When selling prices can be increased without impacting unit variable costs or total fixed costs, break-even decreases. When competition drives selling prices down, and the company cannot reduce costs, break-even increases. Increases in either variable or fixed costs, if they cannot be passed on to customers via higher selling prices, will increase break-even. If costs can be reduced and selling prices held constant, the break-even decreases.

Point: This analysis changed only one estimate at a time; managers can examine how combinations of changes in estimates will impact break-even.

APPLYING COST-VOLUME-PROFIT ANALYSIS

Managers consider a variety of strategies in planning business operations. Cost-volume-profit analysis is useful in helping managers evaluate the likely effects of these strategies, which is the focus of this section.

Computing Income from Sales and Costs

An important question managers often ask is "What is the predicted income from a predicted level of sales?" To answer this, we look at four variables in CVP analysis. These variables and their relations to income (pretax) are shown in Exhibit 18.19. We use these relations to compute expected income from predicted sales and cost levels.

 C2 Describe several applications of cost-volume-profit analysis.

EXHIBIT 18.19

Income Relations in
CVP Analysis

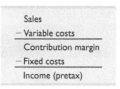

Sales
− Variable costs
Contribution margin
− Fixed costs
Income (pretax)

To illustrate, let's assume that Rydell's management expects to sell 1,500 units in January 2013. What is the amount of income if this sales level is achieved? Following Exhibit 18.19, we compute Rydell's expected income in Exhibit 18.20.

EXHIBIT 18.20

Computing Expected Pretax
Income from Expected Sales

RYDELL COMPANY Contribution Margin Income Statement For Month Ended January 31, 2013	
Sales (1,500 units at $100 each)	$150,000
Variable costs (1,500 units at $70 each)	105,000
Contribution margin	45,000
Fixed costs	24,000
Income (pretax)	$ 21,000

The $21,000 income is pretax. To find the amount of *after-tax* income from selling 1,500 units, management must apply the proper tax rate. Assume that the tax rate is 25%. Then we can prepare the after-tax income statement shown in Exhibit 18.21. We can also compute pretax income as after-tax income divided by (1 − tax rate); for Rydell, this is $15,750/(1 − 0.25), or $21,000.

EXHIBIT 18.21

Computing Expected After-Tax
Income from Expected Sales

RYDELL COMPANY Contribution Margin Income Statement For Month Ended January 31, 2013	
Sales (1,500 units at $100 each)	$150,000
Variable costs (1,500 units at $70 each)	105,000
Contribution margin	45,000
Fixed costs	24,000
Pretax income	21,000
Income taxes (25%)	5,250
Net income (after tax)	$ 15,750

"How many units must we sell to earn $50,000?"

Management then assesses whether this income is an adequate return on assets invested. Management should also consider whether sales and income can be increased by raising or lowering prices. CVP analysis is a good tool for addressing these kinds of "what-if" questions.

Computing Sales for a Target Income

Many companies' annual plans are based on certain income targets (sometimes called *budgets*). Rydell's income target for this year is to increase income by 10% over the prior year. When prior year income is known, Rydell easily computes its target income. CVP analysis helps to determine the sales level needed to achieve the target income. Planning for the year is then based on this level.

We use the formula shown in Exhibit 18.22 to compute sales for a target *after-tax* income. To illustrate, Rydell has monthly fixed costs of $24,000 and a 30% contribution margin ratio. Assume that it sets a target monthly after-tax income of $9,000 when the tax rate is 25%. This means the pretax income is targeted at $12,000 [$9,000/(1 − 0.25)] with a tax expense of $3,000. Using the formula in Exhibit 18.22, we find that $120,000 of sales are needed to produce a $9,000 after-tax income.

$$\text{Dollar sales at target after-tax income} = \frac{\text{Fixed costs} + \text{Target pretax income}}{\text{Contribution margin ratio}}$$

$$= \frac{\$24{,}000 + \$12{,}000}{30\%} = \$120{,}000$$

EXHIBIT 18.22

Computing Sales (Dollars) for a Target After-Tax Income

We can alternatively compute *unit sales* instead of dollar sales. To do this, we substitute *contribution margin per unit* for the contribution margin ratio in the denominator. This gives the number of units to sell to reach the target after-tax income. Exhibit 18.23 illustrates this for Rydell. The two computations in Exhibits 18.22 and 18.23 are equivalent because sales of 1,200 units at $100 per unit equal $120,000 of sales.

Point: Break-even is a special case of the formulas in Exhibits 18.22 and 18.23; simply set target pretax income to $0 and the formulas reduce to those in Exhibits 18.11 and 18.12.

$$\text{Unit sales at target after-tax income} = \frac{\text{Fixed costs} + \text{Target pretax income}}{\text{Contribution margin per unit}}$$

$$= \frac{\$24{,}000 + \$12{,}000}{\$30} = 1{,}200 \text{ units}$$

EXHIBIT 18.23

Computing Sales (Units) for a Target After-Tax Income

▣ Decision Ethics

Supervisor   Your team is conducting a cost-volume-profit analysis for a new product. Different sales projections have different incomes. One member suggests picking numbers yielding favorable income because any estimate is "as good as any other." Another member points to a scatter diagram of 20 months' production on a comparable product and suggests dropping unfavorable data points for cost estimation. What do you do? ▣ [Answer—p. 799]

We can also use the contribution margin income statement approach to compute sales for a target income. In step 1, we insert the fixed costs ($24,000) and the desired after tax profit level ($9,000) into a contribution margin income statement, as shown in Exhibit 18.24. To achieve an after tax profit of $9,000, Rydell's pretax income must be $12,000, computed as $9,000/(1 − 0.25). We insert this as step 2 in the pretax income row in the contribution margin income statement and solve for Rydell's income taxes ($12,000 − $9,000), or $3,000. To cover its fixed costs of $24,000 and yield a pretax income of $12,000, Rydell must generate a contribution margin of $36,000 (computed as $24,000 plus $12,000). We enter this in the contribution margin row as step 3. With a contribution margin ratio of 30%, sales must be $120,000, computed as $36,000/0.30, to yield a contribution margin of $36,000. We enter this in the sales row of the contribution margin income statement as step 3 and solve for variable costs of $84,000 (computed as $120,000 − $36,000). At a selling price of $100 per unit, Rydell must sell 1,200 units ($120,000/$100) to earn after tax net income of $9,000.

EXHIBIT 18.24

Using the Contribution Margin Income Statement to Find Target Sales

RYDELL COMPANY
Contribution Margin Income Statement
For Month Ended January 31, 2013

	Step 1	Step 2	Step 3
Sales	?	?	$120,000
Variable costs	?	?	84,000
Contribution margin	?	?	36,000
Fixed costs	24,000	24,000	24,000
Income (pretax)	?	12,000	12,000
Incomes taxes (25%)	?	3,000	3,000
Net income (after tax)	$ 9,000	$ 9,000	$ 9,000

| $9,000/(1 − 0.25) | $24,000 + $12,000 | $36,000/0.30 |

Using Sensitivity Analysis

Earlier we showed how changing one of the estimates in a CVP analysis impacts break-even. We can also examine strategies that impact several estimates in the CVP analysis. For instance, we might want to know what happens to income if we automate a currently manual process. We can use CVP analysis to predict income if we can describe how these changes affect a company's fixed costs, variable costs, selling price, and volume.

To illustrate, assume that Rydell Company is looking into buying a new machine that would increase monthly fixed costs from $24,000 to $30,000 but decrease variable costs from $70 per unit to $60 per unit. The machine is used to produce output whose selling price will remain unchanged at $100. This results in increases in both the unit contribution margin and the contribution margin ratio. The revised contribution margin per unit is $40 ($100 − $60), and the revised contribution margin ratio is 40% of selling price ($40/$100). Using CVP analysis, Rydell's revised break-even point in dollars would be $75,000 as computed in Exhibit 18.25.

Example: If fixed costs decline, what happens to the break-even point? *Answer:* It decreases.

EXHIBIT 18.25

Revising Break-even When Changes Occur

$$\text{Revised break-even point in dollars} = \frac{\text{Revised fixed costs}}{\text{Revised contribution margin ratio}} = \frac{\$30,000}{40\%} = \$75,000$$

We can also use the contribution margin income statement approach in sensitivity analysis, as we show in Exhibit 18.26. The revised fixed costs and the revised contribution margin ratio can be used to address other issues including computation of (1) expected income for a given sales level and (2) the sales level needed to earn a target income. Once again, we can use sensitivity analysis to generate different sets of revenue and cost estimates that are *optimistic, pessimistic,* and *most likely.* Different CVP analyses based on these estimates provide different scenarios that management can analyze and use in planning business strategy.

EXHIBIT 18.26

Using the Contribution Margin Income Statement in Sensitivity Analysis

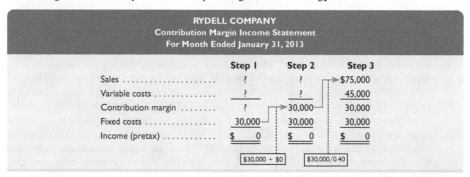

RYDELL COMPANY			
Contribution Margin Income Statement			
For Month Ended January 31, 2013			
	Step 1	Step 2	Step 3
Sales	?	?	$75,000
Variable costs	?	?	45,000
Contribution margin	?	30,000	30,000
Fixed costs	30,000	30,000	30,000
Income (pretax)	$ 0	$ 0	$ 0

$30,000 + $0 $30,000/0.40

■ Decision Insight

RFID-CVP Companies are increasingly using radio-frequency identification (RFID) tags to control inventory. Affixed to products, RFID tags enable companies to reduce costs of inventory theft and scanning errors. Are RFID systems economically feasible? Railroad companies have long used RFID tags on rail cars. While expensive, these tags can be reused thousands of times, thus the cost per tag falls as railroad traffic increases. Such economies of scale and other cost savings make RFID a better-than break-even investment for railroad companies. ■

Quick Check   Answers — p. 799

12. A company has fixed costs of $50,000 and a 25% contribution margin ratio. What dollar sales are necessary to achieve an after-tax net income of $120,000 if the tax rate is 20%? (a) $800,000, (b) $680,000, or (c) $600,000.

13. If a company's contribution margin ratio decreases from 50% to 25%, what can be said about the unit sales needed to achieve the same target income level?

Computing a Multiproduct Break-Even Point

P4 Compute the break-even point for a multiproduct company.

To this point, we have looked only at cases where the company sells a single product or service. This was to keep the basic CVP analysis simple. However, many companies sell multiple products or services, and we can modify the CVP analysis for use in these cases. An important assumption in a multiproduct setting is that the sales mix of different products is known and remains constant during the planning period. **Sales mix** is the ratio (proportion) of the sales volumes for the various products. For instance, if a company normally sells 10,000 footballs, 5,000 softballs, and 4,000 basketballs per month, its sales mix can be expressed as 10:5:4 for footballs, softballs, and basketballs.

To apply multiproduct CVP analysis, we can estimate the break-even point by using a **composite unit,** which consists of a specific number of units of each product in proportion to their expected sales mix. Multiproduct CVP analysis treats this composite unit as a single product. To illustrate, let's look at Hair-Today, a styling salon that offers three cuts: basic, ultra, and budget in the ratio of 4 basic units to 2 ultra units to 1 budget unit (expressed as 4:2:1). Management wants to estimate its break-even point for next year. Unit selling prices for these three cuts are basic, $20; ultra, $32; and budget, $16. Using the 4:2:1 sales mix, the selling price of a composite unit of the three products is computed as follows.

4 units of basic @ $20 per unit	$ 80
2 units of ultra @ $32 per unit	64
1 unit of budget @ $16 per unit	16
Selling price of a composite unit	**$160**

Hair-Today's fixed costs are $192,000 per year, and its variable costs of the three products are basic, $13; ultra, $18.00; and budget, $8.00. Variable costs for a composite unit of these products follow.

Point: Selling prices and variable costs are usually expressed in per unit amounts. Fixed costs are usually expressed in total amounts.

4 units of basic @ $13 per unit	$52
2 units of ultra @ $18 per unit	36
1 unit of budget @ $8 per unit	8
Variable costs of a composite unit	**$96**

Hair-Today's $64 contribution margin for a composite unit is computed by subtracting the variable costs of a composite unit ($96) from its selling price ($160). We then use the contribution margin to determine Hair-Today's break-even point in composite units in Exhibit 18.27.

$$\text{Break-even point in composite units} = \frac{\text{Fixed costs}}{\text{Contribution margin per composite unit}}$$

$$= \frac{\$192,000}{\$64} = 3,000 \text{ composite units}$$

EXHIBIT 18.27

Break-Even Point in Composite Units

This computation implies that Hair-Today breaks even when it sells 3,000 composite units. To determine how many units of each product it must sell to break even, we multiply the number of units of each product in the composite by 3,000 as follows.

Point: The break-even point in dollars for Exhibit 18.27 is $192,000/($64/$160) = $480,000.

Basic:	4 × 3,000	12,000 units
Ultra:	2 × 3,000	6,000 units
Budget:	1 × 3,000	3,000 units

Instead of computing contribution margin per composite unit, a company can compute a **weighted-average contribution margin.** Given the 4:2:1 product mix, basic cuts comprise 57.14% (computed as 4/7) of the company's haircuts, ultra makes up 28.57% of its business, and budget cuts comprise 14.29%. The weighted-average contribution margin follows in Exhibit 18.28.

EXHIBIT 18.28

Weighted-Average
Contribution Margin

	Unit contribution margin	× Percentage of sales mix	= Weighted unit contribution margin
Basic..	$ 7	57.14%	$4.000
Ultra	14	28.57	4.000
Budget	8	14.29	1.143
Weighted-average contribution margin			$9.143

The company's break-even point in units is computed in Exhibit 18.29 as follows:

EXHIBIT 18.29

Break-Even in Units using
Weighted-Average
Contribution Margin

$$\text{Break-even point in units} = \frac{\text{Fixed costs}}{\text{Weighted-average contribution margin}}$$

$$= \frac{\$192,000}{\$9.143} = 21,000 \text{ units}$$

We see that the weighted-average contribution margin method yields 21,000 whole units as the break-even amount, the same total as the composite unit approach.

Exhibit 18.30 verifies the results for composite units by showing Hair-Today's sales and costs at this break-even point using a contribution margin income statement.

EXHIBIT 18.30

Multiproduct Break-Even
Income Statement

HAIR-TODAY Forecasted Contribution Margin Income Statement (at Break-Even)				
	Basic	Ultra	Budget	Totals
Sales				
Basic (12,000 @ $20)..........	$240,000			
Ultra (6,000 @ $32)...........		$192,000		
Budget (3,000 @ $16).........			$48,000	
Total sales				$480,000
Variable costs				
Basic (12,000 @ $13)..........	156,000			
Ultra (6,000 @ $18)...........		108,000		
Budget (3,000 @ $8)			24,000	
Total variable costs				288,000
Contribution margin	$ 84,000	$ 84,000	$24,000	192,000
Fixed costs				192,000
Net income				$ 0

A CVP analysis using composite units can be used to answer a variety of planning questions. Once a product mix is set, all answers are based on the assumption that the mix remains constant at all relevant sales levels as other factors in the analysis do. We also can vary the sales mix to see what happens under alternative strategies.

Point: Enterprise resource planning (ERP) systems can quickly generate multiproduct break-even analyses.

Decision Maker

Entrepreneur A CVP analysis indicates that your start-up, which markets electronic products, will break even with the current sales mix and price levels. You have a target income in mind. What analysis might you perform to assess the likelihood of achieving this income? ■ [Answer—p. 799]

Quick Check

Answers — p. 799

14. The sales mix of a company's two products, X and Y, is 2:1. Unit variable costs for both products are $2, and unit sales prices are $5 for X and $4 for Y. What is the contribution margin per composite unit? (a) $5, (b) $10, or (c) $8.

15. What additional assumption about sales mix must be made in doing a conventional CVP analysis for a company that produces and sells more than one product?

GLOBAL VIEW

Survey evidence shows that many German companies have elaborate and detailed cost accounting systems. Over 90 percent of companies surveyed report their systems focus on *contribution margin*. This focus helps German companies like Volkswagen control costs and plan their production levels. Recently, Volkswagen announced it expects its Spanish brand *Seat* to break even within five years. For 2010, the *Seat* brand lost €311 million on revenue of €5.038 billion (349,000 units).

Degree of Operating Leverage **Decision Analysis**

CVP analysis is especially useful when management begins the planning process and wishes to predict outcomes of alternative strategies. These strategies can involve changes in selling prices, fixed costs, variable costs, sales volume, and product mix. Managers are interested in seeing the effects of changes in some or all of these factors.

One goal of all managers is to get maximum benefits from their fixed costs. Managers would like to use 100% of their output capacity so that fixed costs are spread over the largest number of units. This would decrease fixed cost per unit and increase income. The extent, or relative size, of fixed costs in the total cost structure is known as **operating leverage.** Companies having a higher proportion of fixed costs in their total cost structure are said to have higher operating leverage. An example of this is a company that chooses to automate its processes instead of using direct labor, increasing its fixed costs and lowering its variable costs. A useful managerial measure to help assess the effect of changes in the level of sales on income is the **degree of operating leverage (DOL)** defined in Exhibit 18.31.

> **A2** Analyze changes in sales using the degree of operating leverage.

$$\textbf{DOL = Total contribution margin (in dollars)/Pretax income}$$

EXHIBIT 18.31
Degree of Operating Leverage

To illustrate, let's return to Rydell Company. At a sales level of 1,200 units, Rydell's total contribution margin is $36,000 (1,200 units × $30 contribution margin per unit). Its pretax income, after subtracting fixed costs of $24,000, is $12,000 ($36,000 − $24,000). Rydell's degree of operating leverage at this sales level is 3.0, computed as contribution margin divided by pretax income ($36,000/$12,000). We then use DOL to measure the effect of changes in the level of sales on pretax income. For instance, suppose Rydell expects sales to increase by 10%. If this increase is within the relevant range of operations, we can expect this 10% increase in sales to result in a 30% increase in pretax income computed as DOL multiplied by the increase in sales (3.0 × 10%). Similar analyses can be done for expected decreases in sales.

DEMONSTRATION PROBLEM

Sport Caps Co. manufactures and sells caps for different sporting events. The fixed costs of operating the company are $150,000 per month, and the variable costs for caps are $5 per unit. The caps are sold for $8 per unit. The fixed costs provide a production capacity of up to 100,000 caps per month.

Required

1. Use the formulas in the chapter to compute the following:

  a. Contribution margin per cap.

  b. Break-even point in terms of the number of caps produced and sold.

  c. Amount of net income at 30,000 caps sold per month (ignore taxes).

  d. Amount of net income at 85,000 caps sold per month (ignore taxes).

  e. Number of caps to be produced and sold to provide $45,000 of after-tax income, assuming an income tax rate of 25%.

2. Draw a CVP chart for the company, showing cap output on the horizontal axis. Identify (*a*) the break-even point and (*b*) the amount of pretax income when the level of cap production is 70,000. (Omit the fixed cost line.)

3. Use the formulas in the chapter to compute the

   a. Contribution margin ratio.

   b. Break-even point in terms of sales dollars.

   c. Amount of net income at $250,000 of sales per month (ignore taxes).

   d. Amount of net income at $600,000 of sales per month (ignore taxes).

   e. Dollars of sales needed to provide $45,000 of after-tax income, assuming an income tax rate of 25%.

PLANNING THE SOLUTION

- Identify the formulas in the chapter for the required items expressed in units and solve them using the data given in the problem.
- Draw a CVP chart that reflects the facts in the problem. The horizontal axis should plot the volume in units up to 100,000, and the vertical axis should plot the total dollars up to $800,000. Plot the total cost line as upward sloping, starting at the fixed cost level ($150,000) on the vertical axis and increasing until it reaches $650,000 at the maximum volume of 100,000 units. Verify that the break-even point (where the two lines cross) equals the amount you computed in part 1.
- Identify the formulas in the chapter for the required items expressed in dollars and solve them using the data given in the problem.

SOLUTION TO DEMONSTRATION PROBLEM

1. a. Contribution margin per cap   = Selling price per unit − Variable cost per unit
         = \$8 − \$5 = <u>\$3</u>

   b. Break-even point in caps $= \dfrac{\text{Fixed costs}}{\text{Contribution margin per cap}} = \dfrac{\$150{,}000}{\$3} = \underline{50{,}000 \text{ caps}}$

   c. Net income at 30,000 caps sold   = (Units × Contribution margin per unit) − Fixed costs
         = (30,000 × \$3) − \$150,000 = <u>\$(60,000) loss</u>

   d. Net income at 85,000 caps sold   = (Units × Contribution margin per unit) − Fixed costs
         = (85,000 × \$3) − \$150,000 = <u>\$105,000 profit</u>

   e. Pretax income   = \$45,000/(1 − 0.25) = \$60,000
      Income taxes   = \$60,000 × 25% = \$15,000

      Units needed for \$45,000 income $= \dfrac{\text{Fixed costs} + \text{Target pretax income}}{\text{Contribution margin per cap}}$

                 $= \dfrac{\$150{,}000 + \$60{,}000}{\$3} = \underline{70{,}000 \text{ caps}}$

2. CVP chart.

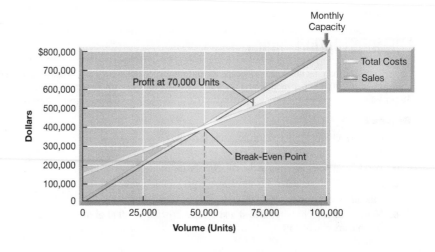

3. a. Contribution margin ratio $= \dfrac{\text{Contribution margin per unit}}{\text{Selling price per unit}} = \dfrac{\$3}{\$8} = \underline{0.375}, \text{ or } \underline{37.5\%}$

b. Break-even point in dollars $= \dfrac{\text{Fixed costs}}{\text{Contribution margin ratio}} = \dfrac{\$150,000}{37.5\%} = \underline{\$400,000}$

c. Net income at sales of \$250,000 $= (\text{Sales} \times \text{Contribution margin ratio}) - \text{Fixed costs}$
$= (\$250,000 \times 37.5\%) - \$150,000 = \underline{\$(56,250) \text{ loss}}$

d. Net income at sales of \$600,000 $= (\text{Sales} \times \text{Contribution margin ratio}) - \text{Fixed costs}$
$= (\$600,000 \times 37.5\%) - \$150,000 = \underline{\$75,000 \text{ income}}$

e. Dollars of sales to yield \$45,000 after-tax income $= \dfrac{\text{Fixed costs} + \text{Target pretax income}}{\text{Contribution margin ratio}}$

$= \dfrac{\$150,000 + \$60,000}{37.5\%} = \underline{\$560,000}$

APPENDIX

Using Excel to Estimate Least-Squares Regression

18A

Microsoft Excel® and other spreadsheet software can be used to perform least-squares regressions to identify cost behavior. In Excel®, the INTERCEPT and SLOPE functions are used. The following screen shot reports the data from Exhibit 18.3 in cells A1 through C13 and shows the cell contents to find the intercept (cell B15) and slope (cell B16). Cell B15 uses Excel® to find the intercept from a least-squares regression of total cost (shown as C2:C13 in cell B15) on units produced (shown as B2:B13 in cell B15). Spreadsheet software is useful in understanding cost behavior when many data points (such as monthly total costs and units produced) are available.

	File	Home	Insert	Page Layout	Formulas	Data	Review	View	Datastream

	A	B	C
1	**Month**	**Units Produced**	**Total Cost**
2	January	27500	21500
3	February	17500	20500
4	March	25000	25000
5	April	35000	21500
6	May	47500	25500
7	June	22500	18500
8	July	30000	23500
9	August	52500	28500
10	September	37500	26000
11	October	67500	29000
12	November	62500	31000
13	December	57500	26000
14			
15	**Intercept**	=INTERCEPT(C2:C13, B2:B13)	
16	**Slope**	=SLOPE(C2:C13,B2:B13)	

Excel® can also be used to create scatter diagrams such as that in Exhibit 18.4. In contrast to visually drawing a line that "fits" the data, Excel® more precisely fits the regression line. To draw a scatter diagram with a line of fit, follow these steps:

1. Highlight the data cells you wish to diagram; in this example, start from cell C13 and highlight through cell B2.
2. Then select "Insert" and "Scatter" from the drop-down menus. Selecting the chart type in the upper left corner of the choices under Scatter will produce a diagram that looks like that in Exhibit 18.4, without a line of fit.
3. To add a line of fit (also called trend line), select "Layout" and "Trendline" from the drop-down menus. Selecting "Linear Trendline" will produce a diagram that looks like that in Exhibit 18.4, including the line of fit.

Summary

C1 **Describe different types of cost behavior in relation to production and sales volume.** Cost behavior is described in terms of how its amount changes in relation to changes in volume of activity within a relevant range. Fixed costs remain constant to changes in volume. Total variable costs change in direct proportion to volume changes. Mixed costs display the effects of both fixed and variable components. Step-wise costs remain constant over a small volume range, then change by a lump sum and remain constant over another volume range, and so on. Curvilinear costs change in a nonlinear relation to volume changes.

C2 **Describe several applications of cost-volume-profit analysis.** Cost-volume-profit analysis can be used to predict what can happen under alternative strategies concerning sales volume, selling prices, variable costs, or fixed costs. Applications include "what-if" analysis, computing sales for a target income, and break-even analysis.

A1 **Compute the contribution margin and describe what it reveals about a company's cost structure.** Contribution margin per unit is a product's sales price less its total variable costs. Contribution margin ratio is a product's contribution margin per unit divided by its sales price. Unit contribution margin is the amount received from each sale that contributes to fixed costs and income. The contribution margin ratio reveals what portion of each sales dollar is available as contribution to fixed costs and income.

A2 **Analyze changes in sales using the degree of operating leverage.** The extent, or relative size, of fixed costs in a company's total cost structure is known as *operating leverage*. One tool useful in assessing the effect of changes in sales on income is the degree of operating leverage, or DOL. DOL is the ratio of the contribution margin divided by pretax income. This ratio can be used to determine the expected percent change in income given a percent change in sales.

P1 **Determine cost estimates using the scatter diagram, high-low, and regression methods of estimating costs.** Three different methods used to estimate costs are the scatter diagram, the high-low method, and least-squares regression. All three methods use past data to estimate costs. Cost estimates from a scatter diagram are based on a visual fit of the cost line. Estimates from the high-low method are based only on costs corresponding to the lowest and highest sales. The least-squares regression method is a statistical technique and uses all data points.

P2 **Compute the break-even point for a single product company.** A company's break-even point for a period is the sales volume at which total revenues equal total costs. To compute a break-even point in terms of sales units, we divide total fixed costs by the contribution margin per unit. To compute a break-even point in terms of sales dollars, divide total fixed costs by the contribution margin ratio.

P3 **Graph costs and sales for a single product company.** The costs and sales for a company can be graphically illustrated using a CVP chart. In this chart, the horizontal axis represents the number of units sold and the vertical axis represents dollars of sales or costs. Straight lines are used to depict both costs and sales on the CVP chart.

P4 **Compute the break-even point for a multiproduct company.** CVP analysis can be applied to a multiproduct company by expressing sales volume in terms of composite units. A composite unit consists of a specific number of units of each product in proportion to their expected sales mix. Multiproduct CVP analysis treats this composite unit as a single product.

Guidance Answers to Decision Maker and Decision Ethics

Sales Manager The contribution margin per unit for the first order is $600 (60% of $1,000); the contribution margin per unit for the second order is $160 (20% of $800). You are likely tempted to accept the first order based on its high contribution margin per unit, but you must compute the total contribution margin based on the number of units sold for each order. Total contribution margin is $60,000 ($600 per unit × 100 units) and $80,000 ($160 per unit × 500 units) for the two orders, respectively. The second order provides the largest return in absolute dollars and is the order you would accept. Another factor to consider in your selection is the potential for a long-term relationship with these customers including repeat sales and growth.

Operations Manager   Without the availability of past data, none of the three methods described in the chapter can be used to measure cost behavior. Instead, the manager must investigate whether data from similar manufacturers can be accessed. This is likely difficult due to the sensitive nature of such data. In the absence of data, the manager should develop a list of the different production inputs and identify input-output relations. This provides guidance to the manager in measuring cost behavior. After several months, actual cost data will be available for analysis.

Supervisor   Your dilemma is whether to go along with the suggestions to "manage" the numbers to make the project look like it will achieve sufficient profits. You should not succumb to these suggestions. Many people will likely be affected negatively if you manage the predicted numbers and the project eventually is unprofitable. Moreover, if it does fail, an investigation would likely reveal

that data in the proposal were "fixed" to make it look good. Probably the only benefit from managing the numbers is the short-term payoff of pleasing those who proposed the product. One way to deal with this dilemma is to prepare several analyses showing results under different assumptions and then let senior management make the decision.

Entrepreneur   You must first compute the level of sales required to achieve the desired net income. Then you must conduct sensitivity analysis by varying the price, sales mix, and cost estimates. Results from the sensitivity analysis provide information you can use to assess the possibility of reaching the target sales level. For instance, you might have to pursue aggressive marketing strategies to push the high-margin products, or you might have to cut prices to increase sales and profits, or another strategy might emerge.

Guidance Answers to Quick Checks

1. *b*
2. A fixed cost remains unchanged in total amount regardless of output levels. However, fixed *cost per unit* declines with increased output.
3. Such a cost is considered variable because the *total* cost changes in proportion to volume changes.
4. *b*
5. The high-low method ignores all costs and sales (activity base) volume data points except the costs corresponding to the highest and lowest (most extreme) sales (activity base) volume.
6. *c*
7. *a*
8. ($90 − $54)/$90 = 40%
9. $90,000/40% = $225,000
10. A company's margin of safety is the excess of the predicted sales level over its break-even sales level.
11. Three basic CVP assumptions are that (1) selling price per unit is constant, (2) variable costs per unit are constant, and (3) total fixed costs are constant.

12. a; Two steps are required for explanation:
    (1) Pretax income = $120,000/(1 − 0.20) = $150,000
    (2) $\dfrac{\$50,000 + \$150,000}{25\%} = \$800,000$

13. If the contribution margin ratio decreases from 50% to 25%, unit sales would have to double.

14. *c*; Selling price of a composite unit:

2 units of X @ $5 per unit	$10
1 unit of Y @ $4 per unit	4
Selling price of a composite unit	$14

Variable costs of a composite unit:	
2 units of X @ $2 per unit	$4
1 unit of Y @ $2 per unit	2
Variable costs of a composite unit	$6

    Therefore, the contribution margin per composite unit is $8.

15. It must be assumed that the sales mix remains unchanged at all sales levels in the relevant range.

Key Terms

Multiple Choice Quiz   Answers on p. 813   mhhe.com/wildFINMAN5e

Additional Quiz Questions are available at the book's Website.

1. A company's only product sells for $150 per unit. Its variable costs per unit are $100, and its fixed costs total $75,000. What is its contribution margin per unit?
   a. $50
   b. $250
   c. $100
   d. $150
   e. $25

2. Using information from question 1, what is the company's contribution margin ratio?
   a. 66⅔%
   b. 100%
   c. 50%
   d. 0%
   e. 33⅓%

3. Using information from question 1, what is the company's break-even point in units?
   a. 500 units
   b. 750 units

   c. 1,500 units
   d. 3,000 units
   e. 1,000 units

4. A company's forecasted sales are $300,000 and its sales at break-even are $180,000. Its margin of safety in dollars is
   a. $180,000.
   b. $120,000.
   c. $480,000.
   d. $60,000.
   e. $300,000.

5. A product sells for $400 per unit and its variable costs per unit are $260. The company's fixed costs are $840,000. If the company desires $70,000 pretax income, what is the required dollar sales?
   a. $2,400,000
   b. $200,000
   c. $2,600,000
   d. $2,275,000
   e. $1,400,000

A   *Superscript letter A denotes assignments based on Appendix 18A*
🎲 Icon denotes assignments that involve decision making.

Discussion Questions

1. What is a variable cost? Identify two variable costs.
2. 🎲 When output volume increases, do variable costs per unit increase, decrease, or stay the same within the relevant range of activity? Explain.
3. 🎲 When output volume increases, do fixed costs per unit increase, decrease, or stay the same within the relevant range of activity? Explain.
4. 🎲 How is cost-volume-profit analysis useful?
5. How do step-wise costs and curvilinear costs differ?
6. Describe the contribution margin ratio in layperson's terms.
7. Define and explain the *contribution margin ratio*.
8. Define and describe *contribution margin* per unit.
9. In performing CVP analysis for a manufacturing company, what simplifying assumption is usually made about the volume of production and the volume of sales?
10. What two arguments tend to justify classifying all costs as either fixed or variable even though individual costs might not behave exactly as classified?
11. 🎲 How does assuming that operating activity occurs within a relevant range affect cost-volume-profit analysis?
12. List three methods to measure cost behavior.
13. How is a scatter diagram used to identify and measure the behavior of a company's costs?
14. In cost-volume-profit analysis, what is the estimated profit at the break-even point?

15. 🎲 Assume that a straight line on a CVP chart intersects the vertical axis at the level of fixed costs and has a positive slope that rises with each additional unit of volume by the amount of the variable costs per unit. What does this line represent?
16. **KTM** has both fixed and variable costs. Why are fixed costs depicted as a horizontal line on a CVP chart?   **KTM**
17. 🎲 Each of two similar companies has sales of $20,000 and total costs of $15,000 for a month. Company A's total costs include $10,000 of variable costs and $5,000 of fixed costs. If Company B's total costs include $4,000 of variable costs and $11,000 of fixed costs, which company will enjoy more profit if sales double?
18. _____ of _____ reflects expected sales in excess of the level of break-even sales.
19. 🎲 **Arctic Cat** produces snowmobiles for sale. Identify some of the variable and fixed product costs associated with that production. [*Hint:* Limit costs to product costs.]   Arctic Cat
20. 🎲 Should **Polaris** use single product or multi-product break-even analysis? Explain.   **Polaris**
21. 🎲 **Piaggio** is thinking of expanding sales of its most popular scooter model by 65%. Should we expect its variable and fixed costs for this model to stay within the relevant range? Explain.   **PIAGGIO**

≣connect

Listed here are four series of separate costs measured at various volume levels. Examine each series and identify whether it is best described as a fixed, variable, step-wise, or curvilinear cost. (It can help to graph the cost series.)

Volume (Units)	Series 1	Series 2	Series 3	Series 4
0	$ 0	$450	$ 800	$100
100	800	450	800	105
200	1,600	450	800	120
300	2,400	450	1,600	145
400	3,200	450	1,600	190
500	4,000	450	2,400	250
600	4,800	450	2,400	320

Determine whether each of the following is best described as a fixed, variable, or mixed cost with respect to product units.

1. Rubber used to manufacture athletic shoes.
2. Maintenance of factory machinery.
3. Packaging expense.
4. Wages of an assembly-line worker paid on the basis of acceptable units produced.

5. Factory supervisor's salary.
6. Taxes on factory building.
7. Depreciation expense of warehouse.

The following information is available for a company's maintenance cost over the last seven months. Using the high-low method, estimate both the fixed and variable components of its maintenance cost.

Month	Maintenance Hours	Maintenance Cost
June.............	9	$5,450
July	18	6,900
August	12	5,100
September	15	6,000
October..........	21	6,900
November	24	8,100
December	6	3,600

This scatter diagram reflects past maintenance hours and their corresponding maintenance costs.

1. Draw an estimated line of cost behavior.
2. Estimate the fixed and variable components of maintenance costs.

Compute and interpret the contribution margin ratio using the following data: sales, $5,000; total variable cost, $3,000.

QS 18-6

Contribution margin per unit and break-even units   P2

SBD Phone Company sells its cordless phone for $90 per unit. Fixed costs total $162,000, and variable costs are $36 per unit. Determine the (1) contribution margin per unit and (2) break-even point in units.

QS 18-7

Assumptions in CVP analysis

C2

Refer to the information from QS 18-6. How will the break-even point in units change in response to each of the following independent changes in selling price per unit, variable cost per unit, or total fixed costs? Use I for increase and D for decrease. (It is not necessary to compute new break-even points.)

Change	Break-even in Units Will
1. Total fixed cost to $190,000	_____
2. Variable cost to $34 per unit	_____
3. Selling price per unit to $80	_____
4. Variable cost to $67 per unit	_____
5. Total fixed cost to $150,000	_____
6. Selling price per unit to $120	_____

QS 18-8

Contribution margin ratio and break-even dollars   P2

Refer to QS 18-6. Determine the (1) contribution margin ratio and (2) break-even point in dollars.

QS 18-9

CVP analysis and target income

P2

Refer to QS 18-6. Assume that SBD Phone Co. is subject to a 30% income tax rate. Compute the units of product that must be sold to earn after-tax income of $140,000. (Round to the nearest whole unit.)

QS 18-10

CVP assumptions

C2

Which one of the following is an assumption that underlies cost-volume-profit analysis?
1. The selling price per unit must change in proportion to the number of units sold.
2. All costs have approximately the same relevant range.
3. For costs classified as variable, the costs per unit of output must change constantly.
4. For costs classified as fixed, the costs per unit of output must remain constant.

QS 18-11

Operating leverage analysis   A2

A high proportion of Company A's total costs are variable with respect to units sold; a high proportion of Company B's total costs are fixed with respect to units sold. Which company is likely to have a higher degree of operating leverage (DOL)? Explain.

QS 18-12

Multiproduct break-even   P4

US-Mobile Company manufactures and sells two products, conventional phones and smart phones, in the ratio of 5:3. Fixed costs are $105,000, and the contribution margin per composite unit is $125. What number of both conventional and smart phones is sold at the break-even point?

QS 18-13

CVP graph   P3

Corme Company expects sales of $34 million (400,000 units). The company's total fixed costs are $17.5 million and its variable costs are $35 per unit. Prepare a CVP chart from this information.

QS 18-14

Contribution margin   A1

A recent income statement for Volkswagen reports the following (in € millions). Assume 75 percent of the cost of sales and 75 percent of the selling and administrative costs are variable costs, and the remaining 25 percent of each is fixed. Compute the contribution margin (in € millions). (Round computations using percentages to the nearest whole euro.)

Sales	€126,875
Cost of sales	105,431
Selling and administrative expenses	15,500

📊 connect

A company reports the following information about its sales and its cost of sales. Each unit of its product sells for $500. Use these data to prepare a scatter diagram. Draw an estimated line of cost behavior and determine whether the cost appears to be variable, fixed, or mixed.

EXERCISES

Exercise 18-1
Measurement of cost behavior using a scatter diagram
P1

Period	Sales	Cost of Sales	Period	Sales	Cost of Sales
1	$22,500	$15,150	4	11,250	8,250
2	17,250	11,250	5	13,500	9,000
3	15,750	10,500	6	18,750	14,250

Following are five graphs representing various cost behaviors. (1) Identify whether the cost behavior in each graph is mixed, step-wise, fixed, variable, or curvilinear. (2) Identify the graph (by number) that best illustrates each cost behavior: (a) Factory policy requires one supervisor for every 30 factory workers; (b) real estate taxes on factory; (c) electricity charge that includes the standard monthly charge plus a charge for each kilowatt hour; (d) commissions to salespersons; and (e) costs of hourly paid workers that provide substantial gains in efficiency when a few workers are added but gradually smaller gains in efficiency when more workers are added.

Exercise 18-2
Cost behavior in graphs
C1

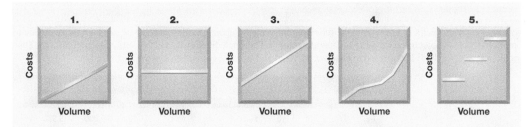

The left column lists several cost classifications. The right column presents short definitions of those costs. In the blank space beside each of the numbers in the right column, write the letter of the cost best described by the definition.

Exercise 18-3
Cost behavior defined
C1

A. Total cost
B. Mixed cost
C. Variable cost
D. Curvilinear cost
E. Step-wise cost
F. Fixed cost

_____ **1.** This cost is the combined amount of all the other costs.

_____ **2.** This cost remains constant over a limited range of volume; when it reaches the end of its limited range, it changes by a lump sum and remains at that level until it exceeds another limited range.

_____ **3.** This cost has a component that remains the same over all volume levels and another component that increases in direct proportion to increases in volume.

_____ **4.** This cost increases when volume increases, but the increase is not constant for each unit produced.

_____ **5.** This cost remains constant over all volume levels within the productive capacity for the planning period.

_____ **6.** This cost increases in direct proportion to increases in volume; its amount is constant for each unit produced.

Following are five series of costs A through E measured at various volume levels. Examine each series and identify which is fixed, variable, mixed, step-wise, or curvilinear.

Exercise 18-4
Cost behavior identification
C1

	Volume (Units)	Series A	Series B	Series C	Series D	Series E
1	0	$ 0	$2,500	$ 0	$1,000	$5,000
2	400	3,600	3,100	6,000	1,000	5,000
3	800	7,200	3,700	6,600	2,000	5,000
4	1,200	10,800	4,300	7,200	2,000	5,000
5	1,600	14,400	4,900	8,200	3,000	5,000
6	2,000	18,000	5,500	9,600	3,000	5,000
7	2,400	21,600	6,100	13,500	4,000	5,000

Exercise 18-5

Predicting sales and variable costs using contribution margin   C2

Bloom Company management predicts that it will incur fixed costs of $160,000 and earn pretax income of $164,000 in the next period. Its expected contribution margin ratio is 25%. Use this information to compute the amounts of (1) total dollar sales and (2) total variable costs.

Exercise 18-6

Scatter diagram and measurement of cost behavior

P1

Use the following information about sales and costs to prepare a scatter diagram. Draw a cost line that reflects the behavior displayed by this cost. Determine whether the cost is variable, step-wise, fixed, mixed, or curvilinear.

Period	Sales	Costs	Period	Sales	Costs
1	$760	$590	9	$580	$390
2	800	560	10	320	240
3	200	230	11	240	230
4	400	400	12	720	550
5	480	390	13	280	260
6	620	550	14	440	410
7	680	590	15	380	260
8	540	430			

Exercise 18-7

Cost behavior estimation— scatter diagram and high-low

P1

Felix & Co. reports the following information about its sales and cost of sales. Draw an estimated line of cost behavior using a scatter diagram, and compute fixed costs and variable costs per unit sold. Then use the high-low method to estimate the fixed and variable components of the cost of sales.

Period	Units Sold	Cost of Sales	Period	Units Sold	Cost of Sales
1	0	$2,500	6	2,000	5,500
2	400	3,100	7	2,400	6,100
3	800	3,700	8	2,800	6,700
4	1,200	4,300	9	3,200	7,300
5	1,600	4,900	10	3,600	7,900

Exercise 18-8[A]

Measurement of cost behavior using regression   P1

Refer to the information from Exercise 18-7. Use spreadsheet software to use ordinary least-squares regression to estimate the cost equation, including fixed and variable cost amounts.

Exercise 18-9

Contribution margin

A2

A jeans maker is designing a new line of jeans called the Slims. The jeans will sell for $205 per pair and cost $164 per pair in variable costs to make. (1) Compute the contribution margin per pair. (2) Compute the contribution margin ratio. (3) Describe what the contribution margin ratio reveals about this new jeans line.

Exercise 18-10

Contribution margin and break-even   P2

Blanchard Company manufactures a single product that sells for $180 per unit and whose total variable costs are $135 per unit. The company's annual fixed costs are $562,500. (1) Use this information to compute the company's (a) contribution margin, (b) contribution margin ratio, (c) break-even point in units, and (d) break-even point in dollars of sales.

Exercise 18-11

CVP chart   P3

Refer to the information in Exercise 18-10. Prepare a CVP chart for the company.

Exercise 18-12

Income reporting and break-even analysis   C2

Refer to Exercise 18-10. (1) Prepare a contribution margin income statement for Blanchard Company showing sales, variable costs, and fixed costs at the break-even point. (2) If the company's fixed costs increase by $135,000, what amount of sales (in dollars) is needed to break even? Explain.

Exercise 18-13

Computing sales to achieve target income   C2

Blanchard Company management (in Exercise 18-10) targets an annual after-tax income of $810,000. The company is subject to a 20% income tax rate. Assume that fixed costs remain at $562,500. Compute the (1) unit sales to earn the target after-tax net income and (2) dollar sales to earn the target after-tax net income.

Blanchard Company's sales manager (in Exercise 18-10) predicts that annual sales of the company's product will soon reach 40,000 units and its price will increase to $200 per unit. According to the production manager, the variable costs are expected to increase to $140 per unit but fixed costs will remain at $562,500. The income tax rate is 20%. What amounts of pretax and after-tax income can the company expect to earn from these predicted changes? (*Hint:* Prepare a forecasted contribution margin income statement as in Exhibit 18.21.)

Exercise 18-14
Forecasted income statement
C2

Check   Forecasted income,
$1,470,000

Nombre Company management predicts $390,000 of variable costs, $430,000 of fixed costs, and a pretax income of $155,000 in the next period. Management also predicts that the contribution margin per unit will be $9. Use this information to compute the (1) total expected dollar sales for next period and (2) number of units expected to be sold next period.

Exercise 18-15
Predicting unit and dollar sales
C2

Cooper Company expects to sell 200,000 units of its product next year, which would generate total sales of $17 million. Management predicts that pretax net income for next year will be $1,250,000 and that the contribution margin per unit will be $25. Use this information to compute next year's total expected (a) variable costs and (b) fixed costs.

Exercise 18-16
Computation of variable and fixed costs
C2

Handy Home sells windows and doors in the ratio of 8:2 (windows:doors). The selling price of each window is $200 and of each door is $500. The variable cost of a window is $125 and of a door is $350. Fixed costs are $900,000. Use this information to determine the (1) selling price per composite unit, (2) variable costs per composite unit, (3) break-even point in composite units, and (4) number of units of each product that will be sold at the break-even point.

Exercise 18-17
CVP analysis using
composite units   P4

Check   (3) 1,000 composite units

Refer to the information from Exercise 18-17. Use the information to determine the (1) weighted-average contribution margin, (2) break-even point in units, and (3) number of units of each product that will be sold at the break-even point.

Exercise 18-18
CVP analysis using weighted-average contribution margin
P4

R&R Tax Service offers tax and consulting services to individuals and small businesses. Data for fees and costs of three types of tax returns follow. R&R provides services in the ratio of 5:3:2 (easy, moderate, business). Fixed costs total $18,000 for the tax season. Use this information to determine the (1) selling price per composite unit, (2) variable costs per composite unit, (3) break-even point in composite units, and (4) number of units of each product that will be sold at the break-even point.

Exercise 18-19
CVP analysis using
composite units
P4

Type of Return	Fee Charged	Variable Cost per Return
Easy (form 1040EZ)	$ 50	$ 30
Moderate (form 1040)	125	75
Business	275	100

Refer to the information from Exercise 18-19. Use the information to determine the (1) weighted-average contribution margin, (2) break-even point in units, and (3) number of units of each product that will be sold at the break-even point.

Exercise 18-20
CVP analysis using weighted-average contribution margin
P4

Company A is a manufacturer with current sales of $6,000,000 and a 60% contribution margin. Its fixed costs equal $2,600,000. Company B is a consulting firm with current service revenues of $4,500,000 and a 25% contribution margin. Its fixed costs equal $375,000. Compute the degree of operating leverage (DOL) for each company. Identify which company benefits more from a 20% increase in sales and explain why.

Exercise 18-21
Operating leverage computed and applied

A2

≣connect

PROBLEM SET A

Problem 18-1A
Contribution margin income
statement and contribution
margin ratio
A1

The following costs result from the production and sale of 1,000 drum sets manufactured by Tom Thompson Company for the year ended December 31, 2013. The drum sets sell for $500 each. The company has a 25% income tax rate.

Variable production costs	
Plastic for casing	$ 17,000
Wages of assembly workers	82,000
Drum stands	26,000
Variable selling costs	
Sales commissions	15,000
Fixed manufacturing costs	
Taxes on factory	5,000
Factory maintenance	10,000
Factory machinery depreciation	40,000
Fixed selling and administrative costs	
Lease of equipment for sales staff	10,000
Accounting staff salaries	35,000
Administrative management salaries	125,000

Required

Check (1) Net income, $101,250

1. Prepare a contribution margin income statement for the company.

2. Compute its contribution margin per unit and its contribution margin ratio.

Analysis Component

3. Interpret the contribution margin and contribution margin ratio from part 2.

Problem 18-2A
CVP analysis and charting
P2 P3

mhhe.com/wildFINMAN5e

Check (1) Break-even sales, 4,500 units

Xcite Equipment Co. manufactures and markets a number of rope products. Management is considering the future of Product XT, a special rope for hang gliding, that has not been as profitable as planned. Since Product XT is manufactured and marketed independently of the other products, its total costs can be precisely measured. Next year's plans call for a $200 selling price per 100 yards of XT rope. Its fixed costs for the year are expected to be $270,000, up to a maximum capacity of 700,000 yards of rope. Forecasted variable costs are $140 per 100 yards of XT rope.

Required

1. Estimate Product XT's break-even point in terms of (a) sales units and (b) sales dollars.

2. Prepare a CVP chart for Product XT like that in Exhibit 18.15. Use 7,000 units (700,000 yards/100 yards) as the maximum number of sales units on the horizontal axis of the graph, and $1,400,000 as the maximum dollar amount on the vertical axis.

3. Prepare a contribution margin income statement showing sales, variable costs, and fixed costs for Product XT at the break-even point.

Problem 18-3A
Scatter diagram and cost
behavior estimation
P1

Alden Co.'s monthly sales and cost data for its operating activities of the past year follow. Management wants to use these data to predict future fixed and variable costs.

Month	Sales	Total Cost	Month	Sales	Total Cost
1	$320,000	$160,000	7	$340,000	$220,000
2	160,000	100,000	8	280,000	160,000
3	280,000	220,000	9	80,000	64,000
4	200,000	100,000	10	160,000	140,000
5	300,000	230,000	11	100,000	100,000
6	200,000	120,000	12	110,000	80,000

Required

1. Prepare a scatter diagram for these data with sales volume (in $) plotted on the horizontal axis and total cost plotted on the vertical axis.

2. Estimate both the variable costs per sales dollar and the total monthly fixed costs using the high-low method. Draw the total costs line on the scatter diagram in part 1.

3. Use the estimated line of cost behavior and results from part 2 to predict future total costs when sales volume is (a) $200,000 and (b) $300,000.

Check   (2) Variable costs, $0.60 per sales dollar; fixed costs, $16,000

Astro Co. sold 20,000 units of its only product and incurred a $50,000 loss (ignoring taxes) for the current year as shown here. During a planning session for year 2014's activities, the production manager notes that variable costs can be reduced 50% by installing a machine that automates several operations. To obtain these savings, the company must increase its annual fixed costs by $200,000. The maximum output capacity of the company is 40,000 units per year.

Problem 18-4A
Break-even analysis; income targeting and forecasting

C2   P2   A1

ASTRO COMPANY	
Contribution Margin Income Statement	
For Year Ended December 31, 2013	
Sales	$1,000,000
Variable costs	800,000
Contribution margin	200,000
Fixed costs	250,000
Net loss	$ (50,000)

Required

1. Compute the break-even point in dollar sales for year 2013.

2. Compute the predicted break-even point in dollar sales for year 2014 assuming the machine is installed and there is no change in the unit sales price.

3. Prepare a forecasted contribution margin income statement for 2014 that shows the expected results with the machine installed. Assume that the unit sales price and the number of units sold will not change, and no income taxes will be due.

Check   (3) Net income, $150,000

4. Compute the sales level required in both dollars and units to earn $140,000 of after-tax income in 2014 with the machine installed and no change in the unit sales price. Assume that the income tax rate is 30%. (*Hint:* Use the procedures in Exhibits 18.22 and 18.23.) (Round answers to whole dollars or units.)

(4) Required sales, $1,083,333 or 21,667 units

5. Prepare a forecasted contribution margin income statement that shows the results at the sales level computed in part 4. Assume an income tax rate of 30%.

Vanna Co. produces and sells two products, T and O. It manufactures these products in separate factories and markets them through different channels. They have no shared costs. This year, the company sold 50,000 units of each product. Sales and costs for each product follow.

Problem 18-5A
Break-even analysis, different cost structures, and income calculations

C2   A1   P4

	Product T	Product O
Sales	$2,000,000	$2,000,000
Variable costs	1,600,000	250,000
Contribution margin	400,000	1,750,000
Fixed costs	125,000	1,475,000
Income before taxes	275,000	275,000
Income taxes (32% rate)	88,000	88,000
Net income	$ 187,000	$ 187,000

Required

1. Compute the break-even point in dollar sales for each product. (Round the answer to whole dollars.)

2. Assume that the company expects sales of each product to decline to 30,000 units next year with no change in unit sales price. Prepare forecasted financial results for next year following the format of the contribution margin income statement as just shown with columns for each of the two products (assume a 32% tax rate). Also, assume that any loss before taxes yields a 32% tax savings.

3. Assume that the company expects sales of each product to increase to 60,000 units next year with no change in unit sales price. Prepare forecasted financial results for next year following the format of the contribution margin income statement shown with columns for each of the two products (assume a 32% tax rate).

Analysis Component

4. If sales greatly decrease, which product would experience a greater loss? Explain.

5. Describe some factors that might have created the different cost structures for these two products.

Problem 18-6A

Analysis of price, cost, and volume changes for contribution margin and net income

P2 A1

mhhe.com/wildFINMAN5e

This year Bertrand Company sold 40,000 units of its only product for $25 per unit. Manufacturing and selling the product required $200,000 of fixed manufacturing costs and $325,000 of fixed selling and administrative costs. Its per unit variable costs follow.

Material	$8.00
Direct labor (paid on the basis of completed units)..........	5.00
Variable overhead costs	1.00
Variable selling and administrative costs	0.50

Next year the company will use new material, which will reduce material costs by 50% and direct labor costs by 60% and will not affect product quality or marketability. Management is considering an increase in the unit sales price to reduce the number of units sold because the factory's output is nearing its annual output capacity of 45,000 units. Two plans are being considered. Under plan 1, the company will keep the price at the current level and sell the same volume as last year. This plan will increase income because of the reduced costs from using the new material. Under plan 2, the company will increase price by 20%. This plan will decrease unit sales volume by 10%. Under both plans 1 and 2, the total fixed costs and the variable costs per unit for overhead and for selling and administrative costs will remain the same.

Required

1. Compute the break-even point in dollar sales for both (a) plan 1 and (b) plan 2.

2. Prepare a forecasted contribution margin income statement with two columns showing the expected results of plan 1 and plan 2. The statements should report sales, total variable costs, contribution margin, total fixed costs, income before taxes, income taxes (30% rate), and net income.

Problem 18-7A

Break-even analysis with composite units

P4

Patriot Co. manufactures and sells three products: red, white, and blue. Their unit sales prices are red, $20; white, $35; and blue, $65. The per unit variable costs to manufacture and sell these products are red, $12; white, $22; and blue, $50. Their sales mix is reflected in a ratio of 5:4:2 (red:white:blue). Annual fixed costs shared by all three products are $250,000. One type of raw material has been used to manufacture all three products. The company has developed a new material of equal quality for less cost. The new material would reduce variable costs per unit as follows: red, by $6; white, by $12; and blue, by $10. However, the new material requires new equipment, which will increase annual fixed costs by $50,000. (Round answers to whole composite units.)

Required

1. If the company continues to use the old material, determine its break-even point in both sales units and sales dollars of each individual product.

2. If the company uses the new material, determine its new break-even point in both sales units and sales dollars of each individual product.

Analysis Component

3. What insight does this analysis offer management for long-term planning?

The following costs result from the production and sale of 12,000 CD sets manufactured by Gilmore Company for the year ended December 31, 2013. The CD sets sell for $18 each. The company has a 25% income tax rate.

PROBLEM SET B

Problem 18-1B
Contribution margin income statement and contribution margin ratio

A1

Variable manufacturing costs	
Plastic for CD sets	$ 1,500
Wages of assembly workers	30,000
Labeling	3,000
Variable selling costs	
Sales commissions	6,000
Fixed manufacturing costs	
Rent on factory	6,750
Factory cleaning service	4,520
Factory machinery depreciation	20,000
Fixed selling and administrative costs	
Lease of office equipment	1,050
Systems staff salaries	15,000
Administrative management salaries	120,000

Required

1. Prepare a contribution margin income statement for the company.

2. Compute its contribution margin per unit and its contribution margin ratio.

Check   (1) Net income, $6,135

Analysis Component

3. Interpret the contribution margin and contribution margin ratio from part 2.

Hip-Hop Co. manufactures and markets several products. Management is considering the future of one product, electronic keyboards, that has not been as profitable as planned. Since this product is manufactured and marketed independently of the other products, its total costs can be precisely measured. Next year's plans call for a $350 selling price per unit. The fixed costs for the year are expected to be $42,000, up to a maximum capacity of 700 units. Forecasted variable costs are $210 per unit.

Problem 18-2B
CVP analysis and charting

P2   P3

Required

1. Estimate the keyboards' break-even point in terms of (a) sales units and (b) sales dollars.

2. Prepare a CVP chart for keyboards like that in Exhibit 18.15. Use 700 keyboards as the maximum number of sales units on the horizontal axis of the graph, and $250,000 as the maximum dollar amount on the vertical axis.

3. Prepare a contribution margin income statement showing sales, variable costs, and fixed costs for keyboards at the break-even point.

Check   (1) Break-even sales, 300 units

Kyo Co.'s monthly sales and costs data for its operating activities of the past year follow. Management wants to use these data to predict future fixed and variable costs. (Dollar amounts are in thousands.)

Problem 18-3B
Scatter diagram and cost behavior estimation

P1

Month	Sales	Total Cost	Month	Sales	Total Cost
1	$195	$ 97	7	$145	$ 93
2	125	87	8	185	105
3	105	73	9	135	85
4	155	89	10	85	58
5	95	81	11	175	95
6	215	110	12	115	79

Required

1. Prepare a scatter diagram for these data with sales volume (in $) plotted on the horizontal axis and total costs plotted on the vertical axis.

810   Chapter 18   Cost Behavior and Cost-Volume-Profit Analysis

2. Estimate both the variable costs per sales dollar and the total monthly fixed costs using the high-low method. Draw the total costs line on the scatter diagram in part 1.

3. Use the estimated line of cost behavior and results from part 2 to predict future total costs when sales volume is (a) $100 and (b) $170.

Problem 18-4B

Break-even analysis; income targeting and forecasting

C2 P2 A1

Rivera Co. sold 20,000 units of its only product and incurred a $50,000 loss (ignoring taxes) for the current year as shown here. During a planning session for year 2014's activities, the production manager notes that variable costs can be reduced 50% by installing a machine that automates several operations. To obtain these savings, the company must increase its annual fixed costs by $150,000. The maximum output capacity of the company is 40,000 units per year.

RIVERA COMPANY Contribution Margin Income Statement For Year Ended December 31, 2013	
Sales	$750,000
Variable costs.	600,000
Contribution margin	150,000
Fixed costs	200,000
Net loss	$ (50,000)

Required

1. Compute the break-even point in dollar sales for year 2013.

2. Compute the predicted break-even point in dollar sales for year 2014 assuming the machine is installed and no change occurs in the unit sales price. (Round the change in variable costs to a whole number.)

3. Prepare a forecasted contribution margin income statement for 2014 that shows the expected results with the machine installed. Assume that the unit sales price and the number of units sold will not change, and no income taxes will be due.

4. Compute the sales level required in both dollars and units to earn $140,000 of after-tax income in 2014 with the machine installed and no change in the unit sales price. Assume that the income tax rate is 30%. (*Hint:* Use the procedures in Exhibits 18.22 and 18.23.) (Round sales in dollars to whole dollars and round sales in units to the next whole unit.)

5. Prepare a forecasted contribution margin income statement that shows the results at the sales level computed in part 4. Assume an income tax rate of 30%.

Problem 18-5B

Break-even analysis, different cost structures, and income calculations

C2 P4 A1

Mingei Co. produces and sells two products, BB and TT. It manufactures these products in separate factories and markets them through different channels. They have no shared costs. This year, the company sold 50,000 units of each product. Sales and costs for each product follow.

	Product BB	Product TT
Sales	$800,000	$800,000
Variable costs.	560,000	100,000
Contribution margin	240,000	700,000
Fixed costs	100,000	560,000
Income before taxes	140,000	140,000
Income taxes (32% rate)	44,800	44,800
Net income	$ 95,200	$ 95,200

Required

1. Compute the break-even point in dollar sales for each product. (Round the answer to the next whole dollar.)

2. Assume that the company expects sales of each product to decline to 33,000 units next year with no change in the unit sales price. Prepare forecasted financial results for next year following the format of the contribution margin income statement as shown here with columns for each of the two products (assume a 32% tax rate, and that any loss before taxes yields a 32% tax savings).

3. Assume that the company expects sales of each product to increase to 64,000 units next year with no change in the unit sales prices. Prepare forecasted financial results for next year following the format of the contribution margin income statement as shown here with columns for each of the two products (assume a 32% tax rate).

Analysis Component

4. If sales greatly increase, which product would experience a greater increase in profit? Explain.

5. Describe some factors that might have created the different cost structures for these two products.

This year Best Company earned a disappointing 5.6% after-tax return on sales (net income/sales) from marketing 100,000 units of its only product. The company buys its product in bulk and repackages it for resale at the price of $20 per unit. Best incurred the following costs this year.

Total variable unit costs..............	$800,000
Total variable packaging costs	$100,000
Fixed costs......................	$950,000
Income tax rate	25%

Problem 18-6B
Analysis of price, cost, and volume changes for contribution margin and net income

A1   P2

The marketing manager claims that next year's results will be the same as this year's unless some changes are made. The manager predicts the company can increase the number of units sold by 80% if it reduces the selling price by 20% and upgrades the packaging. This change would increase variable packaging costs by 20%. Increased sales would allow the company to take advantage of a 25% quantity purchase discount on the cost of the bulk product. Neither the packaging change nor the volume discount would affect fixed costs, which provide an annual output capacity of 200,000 units.

Required

1. Compute the break-even point in dollar sales under the (a) existing business strategy and (b) new strategy that alters both unit sales price and variable costs. (Round answers to the next whole dollar.)

2. Prepare a forecasted contribution margin income statement with two columns showing the expected results of (a) the existing strategy and (b) changing to the new strategy. The statements should report sales, total variable costs (unit and packaging), contribution margin, fixed costs, income before taxes, income taxes, and net income. Also determine the after-tax return on sales for these two strategies.

Check   (1) Break-even sales for new strategy, $1,727,273

(2) Net income: Existing strategy, $112,500; new strategy, $475,500

Milano Co. manufactures and sells three products: product 1, product 2, and product 3. Their unit sales prices are product 1, $40; product 2, $30; and product 3, $20. The per unit variable costs to manufacture and sell these products are product 1, $30; product 2, $15; and product 3, $8. Their sales mix is reflected in a ratio of 6:4:2. Annual fixed costs shared by all three products are $270,000. One type of raw material has been used to manufacture products 1 and 2. The company has developed a new material of equal quality for less cost. The new material would reduce variable costs per unit as follows: product 1 by $10, and product 2, by $5. However, the new material requires new equipment, which will increase annual fixed costs by $50,000.

Problem 18-7B
Break-even analysis with composite units

P4

Required

1. If the company continues to use the old material, determine its break-even point in both sales units and sales dollars of each individual product.

2. If the company uses the new material, determine its new break-even point in both sales units and sales dollars of each individual product.

Check   (1) Old plan break-even, 1,875 composite units (rounded)

(2) New plan break-even, 1,429 composite units (rounded)

Analysis Component

3. What insight does this analysis offer management for long-term planning?

(This serial problem began in Chapter 1 and continues through most of the book. If previous chapter segments were not completed, the serial problem can begin at this point. It is helpful, but not necessary, to use the working papers that accompany the book.)

SERIAL PROBLEM
Success Systems

P4

SP 18   Success Systems sells upscale modular desk units and office chairs in the ratio of 3:2 (desk unit:chair). The selling prices are $1,250 per desk unit and $500 per chair. The variable costs are $750 per desk unit and $250 per chair. Fixed costs are $120,000.

Required

1. Compute the selling price per composite unit.

2. Compute the variable costs per composite unit.

3. Compute the break-even point in composite units.

4. Compute the number of units of each product that would be sold at the break-even point.

Check   (3) 60 composite units

Beyond the Numbers

REPORTING IN ACTION

C1

Polaris

BTN 18-1 Polaris offers extended service contracts that provide repair and maintenance coverage over its products. As you complete the following requirements, assume that the Polaris services department uses many of Polaris's existing resources such as its facilities, repair machinery, and computer systems.

Required

1. Identify several of the variable, mixed, and fixed costs that the Polaris services department is likely to incur in carrying out its services.
2. Assume that Polaris's services revenues are expected to grow by 25% in the next year. How would we expect the costs identified in part 1 to change, if at all?
3. Based on the answer to part 2, can Polaris use the contribution margin ratio to predict how income will change in response to increases in Polaris's services revenues?

COMPARATIVE ANALYSIS

P2 A2

Polaris
Arctic Cat

BTN 18-2 Both Polaris and Arctic Cat sell motorized vehicles, and each of these companies has a different product mix.

Required

1. Assume the following data are available for both companies. Compute each company's break-even point in unit sales. (Each company sells many motorized vehicles at many different selling prices, and each has its own variable costs. This assignment assumes an *average* selling price per unit and an *average* cost per item.)

	Polaris	Arctic Cat
Average selling price per item sold	$10,500	$11,200
Average variable cost per item sold	$4,200	$5,100
Total fixed costs ($ in thousands)	$146,570	$133,570

2. If unit sales were to decline, which company would experience the larger decline in operating profit? Explain.

ETHICS CHALLENGE

C1

BTN 18-3 Labor costs of an auto repair mechanic are seldom based on actual hours worked. Instead, the amount paid a mechanic is based on an industry average of time estimated to complete a repair job. The repair shop bills the customer for the industry average amount of time at the repair center's billable cost per hour. This means a customer can pay, for example, $120 for two hours of work on a car when the actual time worked was only one hour. Many experienced mechanics can complete repair jobs faster than the industry average. The average data are compiled by engineering studies and surveys conducted in the auto repair business. Assume that you are asked to complete such a survey for a repair center. The survey calls for objective input, and many questions require detailed cost data and analysis. The mechanics and owners know you have the survey and encourage you to complete it in a way that increases the average billable hours for repair work.

Required

Write a one-page memorandum to the mechanics and owners that describes the direct labor analysis you will undertake in completing this survey.

COMMUNICATING IN PRACTICE

C2

BTN 18-4 Several important assumptions underlie CVP analysis. Assumptions often help simplify and focus our analysis of sales and costs. A common application of CVP analysis is as a tool to forecast sales, costs, and income.

Required

Assume that you are actively searching for a job. Prepare a one-half page report identifying (1) three assumptions relating to your expected revenue (salary) and (2) three assumptions relating to your expected costs for the first year of your new job. Be prepared to discuss your assumptions in class.

BTN 18-5   Access and review the entrepreneurial information at Business Owner's Toolkit [Toolkit.com]. Access and review its *New Business Cash Needs Checklist* under the Start Up menu bar or similar worksheets related to controls of cash and costs.

TAKING IT TO THE NET

C1

Required

Write a one-half page report that describes the information and resources available at the Business Owner's Toolkit to help the owner of a start-up business to control and monitor its cash flows and costs.

BTN 18-6   A local movie theater owner explains to you that ticket sales on weekends and evenings are strong, but attendance during the weekdays, Monday through Thursday, is poor. The owner proposes to offer a contract to the local grade school to show educational materials at the theater for a set charge per student during school hours. The owner asks your help to prepare a CVP analysis listing the cost and sales projections for the proposal. The owner must propose to the school's administration a charge per child. At a minimum, the charge per child needs to be sufficient for the theater to break even.

TEAMWORK IN ACTION

C2

Required

Your team is to prepare two separate lists of questions that enable you to complete a reliable CVP analysis of this situation. One list is to be answered by the school's administration, the other by the owner of the movie theater.

BTN 18-7   Leather Head Sports, launched by entrepreneur Paul Cunningham, produces balls for various sports. Selling prices typically range from $40 per ball to $295 per ball.

ENTREPRENEURIAL DECISION

C1 A1

Required

1. Identify at least two fixed costs that will not change regardless of how many footballs Leather Head Sports produces.
2. How could overly optimistic sales estimates potentially hurt Paul Cunningham's business?
3. Explain how cost-volume-profit analysis can help Paul Cunningham manage Leather Head Sports.

BTN 18-8   Multiproduct break-even analysis is often viewed differently when actually applied in practice. You are to visit a local fast-food restaurant and count the number of items on the menu. To apply multiproduct break-even analysis to the restaurant, similar menu items must often be fit into groups. A reasonable approach is to classify menu items into approximately five groups. We then estimate average selling price and average variable cost to compute average contribution margin. (*Hint:* For fast-food restaurants, the highest contribution margin is with its beverages, at about 90%.)

HITTING THE ROAD

P4

Required

1. Prepare a one-year multiproduct break-even analysis for the restaurant you visit. Begin by establishing groups. Next, estimate each group's volume and contribution margin. These estimates are necessary to compute each group's contribution margin. Assume that annual fixed costs in total are $500,000 per year. (*Hint:* You must develop your own estimates on volume and contribution margin for each group to obtain the break-even point and sales.)
2. Prepare a one-page report on the results of your analysis. Comment on the volume of sales necessary to break even at a fast-food restaurant.

BTN 18-9   Access and review Piaggio's Website (www.piaggio.com) to answer the following questions.

GLOBAL DECISION

P4

Required

1. Do you believe that Piaggio's managers use single product CVP analysis or multiproduct break-even analysis? Explain.
2. How does the addition of a new product line affect Piaggio's CVP analysis?

PIAGGIO

ANSWERS TO MULTIPLE CHOICE QUIZ

1. a; $150 − $100 = $50
2. e; ($150 − $100)/$150 = 33⅓%
3. c; $75,000/$50 CM per unit = 1,500 units

4. b; $300,000 − $180,000 = $120,000
5. c; Contribution margin ratio = ($400 − $260)/$400 = 0.35
   Targeted sales = ($840,000 + $70,000)/0.35 = $2,600,000

Master Budgets and Performance Planning

A Look Back

Chapter 19 compared reports prepared under variable costing with those under absorption costing, and it explained how variable costing can improve managerial decisions.

A Look at This Chapter

This chapter explains the importance of budgeting and describes the master budget and its preparation. It also discusses the value of the master budget to the planning of future business activities.

A Look Ahead

Chapter 21 focuses on flexible budgets, standard costs, and variance reporting. It explains the usefulness of these procedures and reports for business decisions.

Learning Objectives

CONCEPTUAL

C1 Describe the importance and benefits of budgeting and the process of budget administration. (p. 848)

C2 Describe a master budget and the process of preparing it. (p. 852)

ANALYTICAL

A1 Analyze expense planning using activity-based budgeting. (p. 862)

PROCEDURAL

P1 Prepare each component of a master budget and link each to the budgeting process. (p. 854)

P2 Link both operating and capital expenditures budgets to budgeted financial statements. (p. 858)

P3 *Appendix 20A*—Prepare production and manufacturing budgets. (p. 863)

Decision Insight

Fresh Profits

"Talk is cheap . . . execution sets you apart"
—MATTHEW CORRIN

CHICAGO, IL—Matthew Corrin was tired of eating typical lunch fare. Stuck in a greasy deli, Matthew realized "the service and food was lackluster. I needed an alternative." The then 22-year-old budding entrepreneur set off to build a restaurant based on fresh, healthy foods served in an environmentally sustaining environment. Today, Matthew's company, Freshii **(Freshii.com),** has over 60 stores across several countries.

Matthew admits he was "totally naïve. Restaurants are one of the hardest businesses. A thousand things have to go right every day." Unfortunately, many things did go wrong at the beginning. "The first day we ran out of food at lunch. We ordered more but ran out again on the second day," recalls Matt. Making accurate sales forecasts is one of the most important, but most difficult, parts of preparing business budgets. Sales forecasts are especially challenging for new businesses. Through hard work and help from his girlfriend (now wife), Matthew's business broke sales records every day for its first six months. "Those first days were a turning point for me. I realized if I could get through that, I could survive anything" says Matthew.

Matthew learned his business by doing "whatever needed to be done." "This isn't rocket science," he says, "just hard work." In addition to learning the nuances of the restaurant business, Matthew had to learn budgeting and cost concepts. As Matthew explains, the perishability of food items is a key variable. Food costs can vary due to weather, supply disruptions, and other factors. Matthew updates his budgets frequently to factor in changing costs and customer tastes.

Matthew advises young entrepreneurs to "go for it." "Some might say starting a restaurant with no previous food or retail experience wasn't the smartest move. But, isn't that the entrepreneurial spirit, to just jump in and figure it out on the fly?" As his company continues to grow, the budgeting process and master budgets become even more important. Budgets help formalize plans and goals, and help direct and monitor employees. Matthew also uses budgeted income statements to determine how changes in the cost of food, labor, and overhead will impact his bottom line.

While linking budgeted data to budgeted financial statements and using that information to control costs is important, Matthew stresses "you have to execute every day and generate a buzz." From humble beginnings, Freshii has over 400 new locations in development, forecasted sales of $50 million, and, in Matthew's words, "a vision to be the Starbucks of the fresh food business." Bold and fresh.

[Sources: *Freshii Website,* January 2013; *Inc.com,* March 16, 2011, and June 27, 2011; *Canada Restaurant News,* January 31, 2011; *Under30ceo. com,* October 25, 2010.]

Chapter Preview

Management seeks to turn its strategies into action plans. These action plans include financial details that are compiled in a master budget. The budgeting process serves several purposes, including motivating employees and communicating with them. The budget process also helps coordinate a company's activities toward common goals and is useful in evaluating results and management performance. This chapter explains how to prepare a master budget and use it as a formal plan of a company's future activities. The ability to prepare this type of plan is of enormous help in starting and operating a company. Such planning gives managers a glimpse into the future, and it can help translate ideas into actions.

Master Budgets and Performance Planning

Budget Process	**Budget Administration**	**Master Budget**
• Strategic budgeting • Benchmarking budgets • Budgeting and human behavior • Budgeting as a management tool • Budgeting communication	• Budget committee • Budget reporting • Budget timing	• Master budget components • Operating budgets • Capital expenditures budget • Financial budgets

BUDGET PROCESS

Strategic Budgeting

C1 Describe the importance and benefits of budgeting and the process of budget administration.

Most companies prepare long-term strategic plans spanning 5 to 10 years. They then fine-tune them in preparing medium-term and short-term plans. Strategic plans usually set a company's long-term direction. They provide a road map for the future about potential opportunities such as new products, markets, and investments. The strategic plan can be inexact, given its long-term focus. Medium- and short-term plans are more operational and translate strategic plans into actions. These action plans are fairly concrete and consist of defined objectives and goals.

Short-term financial plans are called *budgets* and typically cover a one-year period. A **budget** is a formal statement of a company's future plans. It is usually expressed in monetary terms because the economic or financial aspects of the business are the primary factors driving management's decisions. All managers should be involved in **budgeting,** the process of planning future business actions and expressing them as formal plans. Managers who plan carefully and formalize plans in a budgeting process increase the likelihood of both personal and company success. (Although most firms prepare annual budgets, it is not unusual for organizations to prepare three-year and five-year budgets that are revised at least annually.)

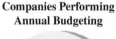
Companies Performing Annual Budgeting

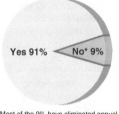

Yes 91%   No* 9%

*Most of the 9% have eliminated annual budgeting in favor of rolling or continual budgeting.

The relevant focus of a budgetary analysis is the future. Management must focus on future transactions and events and the opportunities available. A focus on the future is important because the pressures of daily operating problems often divert management's attention and take precedence over planning. A good budgeting system counteracts this tendency by formalizing the planning process and demanding relevant input. Budgeting makes planning an explicit management responsibility.

Benchmarking Budgets

The control function requires management to evaluate (benchmark) business operations against some norm. Evaluation involves comparing actual results against one of two usual alternatives: (1) past performance or (2) expected performance.

An evaluation assists management in identifying problems and taking corrective actions if necessary. Evaluation using expected, or budgeted, performance is potentially superior to using past performance to decide whether actual results trigger a need for corrective actions. This is so because past performance fails to consider several changes that can affect current and future activities. Changes in economic conditions, shifts in competitive advantages within the industry, new product developments, increased or decreased advertising, and other factors reduce the usefulness of comparisons with past results. In hi-tech industries, for instance, increasing competition, technological advances, and other innovations often reduce the usefulness of performance comparisons across years.

Budgeted performance is computed after careful analysis and research that attempts to anticipate and adjust for changes in important company, industry, and economic factors. Therefore, budgets usually provide management an effective control and monitoring system.

Budgeting and Human Behavior

Budgeting provides standards for evaluating performance and can affect the attitudes of employees evaluated by them. It can be used to create a positive effect on employees' attitudes, but it can also create negative effects if not properly applied. Budgeted levels of performance, for instance, must be realistic to avoid discouraging employees. Personnel who will be evaluated should be consulted and involved in preparing the budget to increase their commitment to meeting it. Performance evaluations must allow the affected employees to explain the reasons for apparent performance deficiencies.

The budgeting process has three important guidelines: (1) Employees affected by a budget should be consulted when it is prepared (*participatory budgeting*), (2) goals reflected in a budget should be attainable, and (3) evaluations should be made carefully with opportunities to explain any failures. Budgeting can be a positive motivating force when these guidelines are followed. Budgeted performance levels can provide goals for employees to attain or even exceed as they carry out their responsibilities. This is especially important in organizations that consider the annual budget a "sacred" document.

Managers must also be aware of potential negative outcomes of budgeting. Under participatory budgeting, some employees might understate sales budgets and overstate expense budgets to allow them a cushion, or *budgetary slack,* to aid in meeting targets. For some businesses, pressure to meet budgeted results might lead employees to engage in unethical behavior or commit fraud. Finally, some employees might always spend their budgeted amounts, even on unnecessary items, to ensure their budgets aren't reduced for the next period.

Point: The practice of involving employees in the budgeting process is known as *participatory budgeting*.

Example: Assume a company's sales force receives a bonus when sales exceed the budgeted amount. How would this arrangement affect the participatory sales forecasts? *Answer:* Sales reps may understate their budgeted sales.

■ Decision Ethics

Budget Staffer   Your company's earnings for the current period will be far below the budgeted amount reported in the press. One of your superiors, who is aware of the upcoming earnings shortfall, has accepted a management position with a competitor. This superior is selling her shares of the company. What are your ethical concerns, if any? ■   [Answer—p. 870]

Budgeting as a Management Tool

An important management objective in large companies is to ensure that activities of all departments contribute to meeting the company's overall goals. This requires coordination. Budgeting helps to achieve this coordination.

We describe later in this chapter that a company's budget, or operating plan, is based on its objectives. This operating plan starts with the sales budget, which drives all other budgets including production, materials, labor, and overhead. The budgeting process coordinates the activities of these various departments to meet the company's overall goals.

Budgeting Communication

Managers of small companies can adequately explain business plans directly to employees through conversations and other informal communications. However, conversations can create uncertainty and confusion if not supported by clear documentation of the plans. A written budget is preferred and can inform employees in all types of organizations about management's plans. The budget can also communicate management's specific action plans for the employees in the budget period.

Decision Insight

Budgets Exposed When companies go public and their securities trade on an organized stock exchange, management usually develops specific future plans and budgets. For this purpose, companies often develop detailed six- to twelve-month budgets and less-detailed budgets spanning two to five years. ■

BUDGET ADMINISTRATION

Budget Committee

The task of preparing a budget should not be the sole responsibility of any one department. Similarly, the budget should not be simply handed down as top management's final word. Instead, budget figures and budget estimates developed through a *bottom-up* process

usually are more useful. This includes, for instance, involving the sales department in preparing sales estimates. Likewise, the production department should have initial responsibility for preparing its own expense budget. Without active employee involvement in preparing budget figures, there is a risk these employees will feel that the numbers fail to reflect their special problems and needs.

Most budgets should be developed by a bottom-up process, but the budgeting system requires central guidance. This guidance is supplied by a budget committee of department heads and other executives responsible for seeing that budgeted amounts are realistic and coordinated. If a de-

Point: In a large company, developing a budget through a bottom-up process can involve hundreds of employees and take several weeks to finalize.

partment submits initial budget figures not reflecting efficient performance, the budget committee should return them with explanatory comments on how to improve them. Then the originating department must either adjust its proposals or explain why they are acceptable. Communication between the originating department and the budget committee should continue as needed to ensure that both parties accept the budget as reasonable, attainable, and desirable.

The concept of continuous improvement applies to budgeting as well as production. For example, one of the world's largest energy companies streamlined its monthly budget report from a one-inch-thick stack of monthly control reports to a tidy, two-page flash report on monthly earnings and key production statistics. The key to this efficiency gain was the integration of new budgeting and cost allocation processes with its strategic planning process. Its controller explained the new role of the finance department with respect to the budgetary control process as follows: "there's less of an attitude that finance's job is to control. People really have come to see that our job is to help attain business objectives."

Budget Reporting

The budget period usually coincides with the accounting period. Most companies prepare at least an annual budget, which reflects the objectives for the next year. To provide specific guidance, the annual budget usually is separated into quarterly or monthly budgets. These short-term budgets allow management to periodically evaluate performance and take needed corrective action.

Managers can compare actual results to budgeted amounts in a report such as that shown in Exhibit 20.1. This report shows actual amounts, budgeted amounts, and their differences. A difference is called a *variance*. Management examines variances, particularly large ones, to identify areas for improvement and corrective action.

ECCENTRIC MUSIC Income Statement with Variances from Budget For Month Ended April 30, 2013			
	Actual	Budget	Variance
Net sales	$60,500	$57,150	$+3,350
Cost of goods sold	41,350	39,100	+2,250
Gross profit	19,150	18,050	+1,100
Operating expenses			
Selling expenses			
Sales salaries	6,250	6,000	+250
Advertising	900	800	+100
Store supplies	550	500	+50
Depreciation—Store equipment	1,600	1,600	
Total selling expenses	9,300	8,900	+400
General and administrative expenses			
Office salaries	2,000	2,000	
Office supplies used	165	150	+15
Rent	1,100	1,100	
Insurance	200	200	
Depreciation—Office equipment	100	100	
Total general and administrative expenses	3,565	3,550	+15
Total operating expenses	12,865	12,450	+415
Net income	$ 6,285	$ 5,600	$ +685

EXHIBIT 20.1

Comparing Actual Performance with Budgeted Performance

Example: Assume that you must explain variances to top management. Which variances in Exhibit 20.1 would you research and why? *Answer:* Sales and cost of goods sold—due to their large variances.

Budget Timing

The time period required for the annual budgeting process can vary considerably. For example, budgeting for 2014 can begin as early as January 2013 or as late as December 2013. Large, complex organizations usually require a longer time to prepare their budgets than do smaller organizations. This is so because considerable effort is required to coordinate the different units (departments) within large organizations.

Many companies apply **continuous budgeting** by preparing **rolling budgets.** As each monthly or quarterly budget period goes by, these companies revise their entire set of budgets for the months or quarters remaining and add new monthly or quarterly budgets to replace the ones that have lapsed. At any point in time, monthly or quarterly budgets are available for the next 12 months or four quarters. Exhibit 20.2 shows rolling budgets prepared at the end of five consecutive

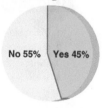

Companies Using Rolling Budgets

No 55%   Yes 45%

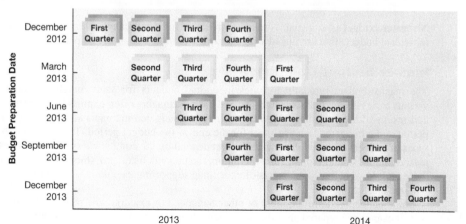

EXHIBIT 20.2

Rolling Budgets

periods. The first set (at top) is prepared in December 2012 and covers the four calendar quarters of 2013. In March 2013, the company prepares another rolling budget for the next four quarters through March 2014. This same process is repeated every three months. As a result, management is continuously planning ahead.

Exhibit 20.2 reflects an annual budget composed of four quarters prepared four times per year using the most recent information available. For example, the budget for the fourth quarter of 2013 is prepared in December 2012 and revised in March, June, and September of 2013. When continuous budgeting is not used, the fourth-quarter budget is nine months old and perhaps out of date when applied.

Decision Insight

Budget Calendar Many companies use long-range operating budgets. For large companies, three groups usually determine or influence the budgets: creditors, directors, and management. All three are interested in the companies' future cash flows and earnings. The annual budget process often begins six months or more before the budget is due to the board of directors. A typical budget calendar, shown here, provides insight into the budget process during a typical calendar year. ■

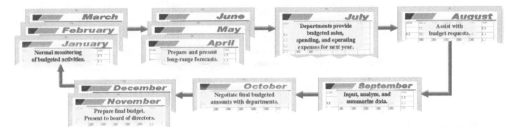

Quick Check

Answers — p. 870

1. What are the major benefits of budgeting?
2. What is the main responsibility of the budget committee?
3. What is the usual time period covered by a budget?
4. What are rolling budgets?

MASTER BUDGET

C2 Describe a master budget and the process of preparing it.

A **master budget** is a formal, comprehensive plan for a company's future. It contains several individual budgets that are linked with each other to form a coordinated plan.

Master Budget Components

The master budget typically includes individual budgets for sales, purchases, production, various expenses, capital expenditures, and cash. Managers often express the expected financial results of these planned activities with both a budgeted income statement for the budget period and a budgeted balance sheet for the end of the budget period. The usual number and types of budgets included in a master budget depend on the company's size and complexity. A master budget should include, at a minimum, the budgets listed in Exhibit 20.3. In addition to these individual budgets, managers often include supporting calculations and additional tables with the master budget.

Some budgets require the input of other budgets. For example, the merchandise purchases budget cannot be prepared until the sales budget has been prepared because the number of units

EXHIBIT 20.3

Basic Components of a Master Budget

Operating budgets
- *Sales budget*
- For merchandisers add: *Merchandise purchases budget* (units to be purchased)
- For manufacturers add: *Production budget* (units to be produced)
                          Manufacturing budget (manufacturing costs)
- *Selling expense budget*
- *General and administrative expense budget*

Capital expenditures budget (expenditures for plant assets)

Financial budgets
- *Cash budget* (cash receipts and disbursements)
- *Budgeted income statement*
- *Budgeted balance sheet*

to be purchased depends on how many units are expected to be sold. As a result, we often must sequentially prepare budgets within the master budget.

A typical sequence for a master budget consists of the five steps in Exhibit 20.4. Any stage in this budgeting process might reveal undesirable outcomes, so changes often must be made to prior budgets by repeating the previous steps. For instance, an early version of the cash budget could show an insufficient amount of cash unless cash outlays are reduced. This could yield a reduction in planned equipment purchases. A preliminary budgeted balance sheet could also reveal too much debt from an ambitious capital expenditures budget. Findings such as these often result in revised plans and budgets.

EXHIBIT 20.4

Master Budget Sequence

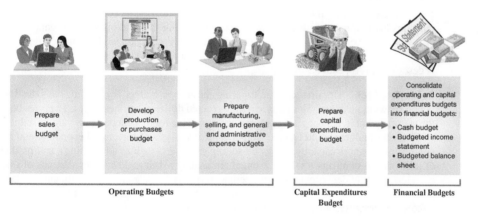

The remainder of this section explains how Hockey Den (HD), a retailer of youth hockey sticks, prepares its master budget. Its master budget includes operating, capital expenditures, and cash budgets for each month in each quarter. It also includes a budgeted income statement for each quarter and a budgeted balance sheet as of the last day of each quarter. We show how HD prepares budgets for October, November, and December 2013. Exhibit 20.5 presents HD's balance sheet at the start of this budgeting period, which we often refer to as we prepare the component budgets.

Decision Insight

Incentive Pay Budgets are important in determining managers' pay. A recent survey shows that 82% of large companies tie managers' bonus payments to beating budget goals. For these companies, bonus payments are frequently more than 20% of total manager pay. ■

EXHIBIT 20.5

Balance Sheet Prior to the
Budgeting Periods

HOCKEY DEN Balance Sheet September 30, 2013		
Assets		
Cash		$ 20,000
Accounts receivable		42,000
Inventory (900 units @ $60)		54,000
Equipment*	$200,000	
Less accumulated depreciation	36,000	164,000
Total assets		$280,000
Liabilities and Equity		
Liabilities		
Accounts payable	$ 58,200	
Income taxes payable (due 10/31/2013)	20,000	
Note payable to bank	10,000	$ 88,200
Stockholders' equity		
Common stock	150,000	
Retained earnings	41,800	191,800
Total liabilities and equity		$280,000

* Equipment is depreciated on a straight-line basis over 10 years (salvage value is $20,000).

Operating Budgets

P1 Prepare each component of a master budget and link each to the budgeting process.

This section explains HD's preparation of operating budgets. Its operating budgets consist of the sales budget, merchandise purchases budget, selling expense budget, and general and administrative expense budget. HD does not prepare production and manufacturing budgets because it is a merchandiser. (The preparation of production budgets and manufacturing budgets is described in Appendix 20A.)

Sales Budget   The first step in preparing the master budget is planning the **sales budget,** which shows the planned sales units and the expected dollars from these sales. The sales budget is the starting point in the budgeting process because plans for most departments are linked to sales.

The sales budget should emerge from a careful analysis of forecasted economic and market conditions, business capacity, proposed selling expenses (such as advertising), and predictions of unit sales. A company's sales personnel are usually asked to develop predictions of sales for each territory and department because people normally feel a greater commitment to goals they help set. Another advantage to this participatory budgeting approach is that it draws on knowledge and experience of people involved in the activity.

To illustrate, in September 2013, HD sold 700 hockey sticks at $100 per unit. After considering sales predictions and market conditions, HD prepares its sales budget for the next quarter (three months) plus one extra month (see Exhibit 20.6). The sales budget includes

EXHIBIT 20.6

Sales Budget for Planned Unit
and Dollar Sales

HOCKEY DEN Monthly Sales Budget October 2013–January 2014	Budgeted Unit Sales	Budgeted Unit Price	Budgeted Total Sales
September 2013 (actual)	700	$100	$ 70,000
October 2013	1,000	$100	$100,000
November 2013	800	100	80,000
December 2013	1,400	100	140,000
Totals for the quarter	3,200	100	$320,000
January 2014	900	100	$ 90,000

January 2014 because the purchasing department relies on estimated January sales to decide on December 2013 inventory purchases. The sales budget in Exhibit 20.6 includes forecasts of both unit sales and unit prices. Some sales budgets are expressed only in total sales dollars, but most are more detailed. Management finds it useful to know budgeted units and unit prices for many different products, regions, departments, and sales representatives.

Decision Maker

Entrepreneur   You run a start-up that manufactures designer clothes. Business is seasonal, and fashions and designs quickly change. How do you prepare reliable annual sales budgets? ■   [Answer—p. 870]

Merchandise Purchases Budget   Companies use various methods to help managers make inventory purchasing decisions. These methods recognize that the number of units added to inventory depends on budgeted sales volume. Whether a company manufactures or purchases the product it sells, budgeted future sales volume is the primary factor in most inventory management decisions. A company must also consider its inventory system and other factors that we discuss next.

Just-in-time inventory systems.   Managers of *just-in-time* (JIT) inventory systems use sales budgets for short periods (often as few as one or two days) to order just enough merchandise or materials to satisfy the immediate sales demand. This keeps the amount of inventory to a minimum (or zero in an ideal situation). A JIT system minimizes the costs of maintaining inventory, but it is practical only if customers are content to order in advance or if managers can accurately determine short-term sales demand. Suppliers also must be able and willing to ship small quantities regularly and promptly.

Point: Accurate estimates of future sales are crucial in a JIT system.

Safety stock inventory systems.   Market conditions and manufacturing processes for some products do not allow use of a just-in-time system. Companies in these cases maintain sufficient inventory to reduce the risk and cost of running short. This practice requires enough purchases to satisfy the budgeted sales amounts and to maintain a **safety stock,** a quantity of inventory that provides protection against lost sales caused by unfulfilled demands from customers or delays in shipments from suppliers.

Merchandise purchases budget preparation.   A merchandiser usually expresses a **merchandise purchases budget** in both units and dollars. Exhibit 20.7 shows the general layout for this budget in equation form. If this formula is expressed in units and only one product is involved, we can compute the number of dollars of inventory to be purchased for the budget by multiplying the units to be purchased by the cost per unit.

$$\boxed{\begin{array}{c}\text{Inventory}\\\text{to be}\\\text{purchased}\end{array}} = \boxed{\begin{array}{c}\text{Budgeted}\\\text{ending}\\\text{inventory}\end{array}} + \boxed{\begin{array}{c}\text{Budgeted}\\\text{cost of sales}\\\text{for the period}\end{array}} - \boxed{\begin{array}{c}\text{Budgeted}\\\text{beginning}\\\text{inventory}\end{array}}$$

EXHIBIT 20.7

General Formula for a Merchandise Purchases Budget

To illustrate, after assessing the cost of keeping inventory along with the risk and cost of inventory shortages, HD decided that the number of units in its inventory at each month-end should equal 90% of next month's predicted sales. For example, inventory at the end of October should equal 90% of budgeted November sales, and the November ending inventory should equal 90% of budgeted December sales, and so on. Also, HD's suppliers expect the September 2013 per unit cost of $60 to remain unchanged through January 2014. This information along with knowledge of 900 units in inventory at September 30 (see Exhibit 20.5) allows the company to prepare the merchandise purchases budget shown in Exhibit 20.8.

The first three lines of HD's merchandise purchases budget determine the required ending inventories (in units). Budgeted unit sales are then added to the desired ending inventory to give the required units of available merchandise. We then subtract beginning inventory to

Example: Assume Hockey Den adopts a JIT system in purchasing merchandise. How will its sales budget differ from its merchandise purchases budget? *Answer:* The two budgets will be similar because future inventory should be near zero.

EXHIBIT 20.8

Merchandise Purchases Budget

Example: If ending inventory in Exhibit 20.8 is required to equal 80% of next month's predicted sales, how many units must be purchased each month? *Answer:* Budgeted ending inventory: Oct. = 640 units; Nov. = 1,120 units; Dec. = 720 units. Required purchases: Oct. = 740 units; Nov. = 1,280 units; Dec. = 1,000 units.

HOCKEY DEN Merchandise Purchases Budget October 2013–December 2013			
	October	November	December
Next month's budgeted sales (units)	800	1,400	900
Ratio of inventory to future sales	× 90%	× 90%	× 90%
Budgeted ending inventory (units)	720	1,260	810
Add budgeted sales (units)	1,000	800	1,400
Required units of available merchandise	1,720	2,060	2,210
Deduct beginning inventory (units)	900	720	1,260
Units to be purchased	820	1,340	950
Budgeted cost per unit	$ 60	$ 60	$ 60
Budgeted cost of merchandise purchases	$49,200	$80,400	$57,000

determine the budgeted number of units to be purchased. The last line is the budgeted cost of the purchases, computed by multiplying the number of units to be purchased by the predicted cost per unit.

We already indicated that some budgeting systems describe only the total dollars of budgeted sales. Likewise, a system can express a merchandise purchases budget only in terms of the total cost of merchandise to be purchased, omitting the number of units to be purchased. This method assumes a constant relation between sales and cost of goods sold. HD, for instance, might assume the expected cost of goods sold to be 60% of sales, computed from the budgeted unit cost of $60 and the budgeted sales price of $100. However, it still must consider the effects of changes in beginning and ending inventories in determining the amounts to be purchased.

Selling Expense Budget   The **selling expense budget** is a plan listing the types and amounts of selling expenses expected during the budget period. Its initial responsibility usually rests with the vice president of marketing or an equivalent sales manager. The selling expense budget is normally created to provide sufficient selling expenses to meet sales goals reflected in the sales budget. Predicted selling expenses are based on both the sales budget and the experience of previous periods. After some or all of the master budget is prepared, management might decide that projected sales volume is inadequate. If so, subsequent adjustments in the sales budget can require corresponding adjustments in the selling expense budget.

To illustrate, HD's selling expense budget is in Exhibit 20.9. The firm's selling expenses consist of commissions paid to sales personnel and a $2,000 monthly salary paid to the sales manager. Sales commissions equal 10% of total sales and are paid in the month sales occur. Sales commissions are variable with respect to sales volume, but the sales manager's salary is fixed. No advertising expenses are budgeted for this particular quarter.

EXHIBIT 20.9

Selling Expense Budget

Example: If sales commissions in Exhibit 20.9 are increased, which budgets are affected? *Answer:* Selling expenses budget, cash budget, and budgeted income statement.

HOCKEY DEN Selling Expense Budget October 2013–December 2013				
	October	November	December	Totals
Budgeted sales	$100,000	$80,000	$140,000	$320,000
Sales commission percent	× 10%	× 10%	× 10%	× 10%
Sales commissions	10,000	8,000	14,000	32,000
Salary for sales manager	2,000	2,000	2,000	6,000
Total selling expenses	$ 12,000	$10,000	$ 16,000	$ 38,000

General and Administrative Expense Budget   The **general and administrative expense budget** plans the predicted operating expenses not included in the selling expenses budget. General and administrative expenses can be either variable or fixed with respect to sales volume. The office manager responsible for general administration often is responsible for preparing the initial general and administrative expense budget.

Exhibit 20.10 shows HD's general and administrative expense budget. It includes salaries of $54,000 per year, or $4,500 per month (paid each month when they are earned). Using information in Exhibit 20.5, the depreciation on equipment is computed as $18,000 per year [($200,000 − $20,000)/10 years], or $1,500 per month ($18,000/12 months).

HOCKEY DEN General and Administrative Expense Budget October 2013–December 2013				
	October	November	December	Totals
Administrative salaries	$4,500	$4,500	$4,500	$13,500
Depreciation of equipment	1,500	1,500	1,500	4,500
Total general and administrative expenses	$6,000	$6,000	$6,000	$18,000

EXHIBIT 20.10

General and Administrative Expense Budget

Interest expense and income tax expense are often classified as general and administrative expenses in published income statements but normally cannot be planned at this stage of the budgeting process. The prediction of interest expense follows the preparation of the cash budget and the decisions regarding debt. The predicted income tax expense depends on the budgeted amount of pretax income. Both interest and income taxes are usually beyond the control of the office manager. As a result, they are not used in comparison to the budget to evaluate that person's performance.

Example: In Exhibit 20.10, how would a rental agreement of $5,000 per month plus 1% of sales affect the general and administrative expense budget? (Budgeted sales are in Exhibit 20.6.) *Answer:* Rent expense: Oct. = $6,000; Nov. = $5,800; Dec. = $6,400; Total = $18,200; *Revised total general and administrative expenses:* Oct. = $12,000; Nov. = $11,800; Dec. = $12,400; Total = $36,200.

 Decision Insight

No Biz Like Snow Biz   Ski resorts' costs of making snow are in the millions of dollars for equipment alone. Snowmaking involves spraying droplets of water into the air, causing them to freeze and come down as snow. Making snow can cost more than $2,000 an hour. Snowmaking accounts for 40 to 50 percent of the operating budgets for many ski resorts. ■

Quick Check   Answers — p. 870

5. What is a master budget?

6. A master budget (a) always includes a manufacturing budget specifying the units to be produced; (b) is prepared with a process starting with the operating budgets and continues with the capital expenditures budget and then financial budgets; or (c) is prepared with a process ending with the sales budget.

7. What are the three primary categories of budgets in the master budget?

8. In preparing monthly budgets for the third quarter, a company budgeted sales of 120 units for July and 140 units for August. Management wants each month's ending inventory to be 60% of next month's sales. The June 30 inventory consists of 50 units. How many units of product for July acquisition should the merchandise purchases budget specify for the third quarter? (a) 84, (b) 120, (c) 154, or (d) 204.

9. How do the operating budgets for merchandisers and manufacturers differ?

10. How does a just-in-time inventory system differ from a safety stock system?

Capital Expenditures Budget

The **capital expenditures budget** lists dollar amounts to be both received from plant asset disposals and spent to purchase additional plant assets to carry out the budgeted business activities. It is usually prepared after the operating budgets. Since a company's plant assets determine its productive capacity, this budget is usually affected by long-range plans for the business. Yet the process of preparing a sales or purchases budget can reveal that the company requires more (or less) capacity, which implies more (or less) plant assets.

Capital budgeting is the process of evaluating and planning for capital (plant asset) expenditures. This is an important management task because these expenditures often involve long-run commitments of large amounts, affect predicted cash flows, and impact future debt and equity financing. This means that the capital expenditures budget is often linked with management's evaluation of the company's ability to take on more debt. We describe capital budgeting in Chapter 24.

Hockey Den does not anticipate disposal of any plant assets through December 2013, but it does plan to acquire additional equipment for $25,000 cash near the end of December 2013. This is the only budgeted capital expenditure from October 2013 through January 2014. Thus, no separate budget is shown. Hockey Den's cash budget will reflect this $25,000 planned expenditure.

Financial Budgets

After preparing its operating and capital expenditures budgets, a company uses information from these budgets to prepare at least three financial budgets: the cash budget, budgeted income statement, and budgeted balance sheet.

P2 Link both operating and capital expenditures budgets to budgeted financial statements.

Cash Budget   After developing budgets for sales, merchandise purchases, expenses, and capital expenditures, the next step is to prepare the **cash budget,** which shows expected cash inflows and outflows during the budget period. It is especially important to maintain a cash balance necessary to meet ongoing obligations. By preparing a cash budget, management can prearrange loans to cover anticipated cash shortages before they are needed. A cash budget also helps management avoid a cash balance that is too large. Too much cash is undesirable because it earns a relatively low (if any) return. Exhibit 20.11 shows the general formula for the cash budget.

EXHIBIT 20.11

General Formula for Cash Budget

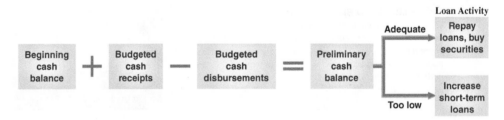

When preparing a cash budget, we add expected cash receipts to the beginning cash balance and deduct expected cash disbursements. If the expected (preliminary) ending cash balance is too low, additional cash requirements appear in the budget as planned increases from short-term loans. If the expected ending cash balance exceeds the desired balance, the excess is used to repay loans or to acquire short-term investments. Information for preparing the cash budget is mainly taken from the operating and capital expenditures budgets.

Cash Receipts from Sales   To illustrate, Exhibit 20.12 presents HD's budgeted cash receipts.

EXHIBIT 20.12

Computing Budgeted Cash Receipts

	September	October	November	December
Sales	$70,000	$100,000	$80,000	$140,000
Less ending accounts receivable (60%)	42,000	60,000	48,000	84,000
Cash receipts from				
Cash sales (40% of sales)		40,000	32,000	56,000
Collections of prior month's receivables		42,000	60,000	48,000
Total cash receipts		$ 82,000	$92,000	$104,000

We begin with reference to HD's budgeted sales (Exhibit 20.6). Analysis of past sales indicates that 40% of the firm's sales are for cash. The remaining 60% are credit sales; these customers are expected to pay in full in the month following the sales. We now can compute the budgeted cash receipts from customers as shown in Exhibit 20.12. October's budgeted cash receipts consist of $40,000 from expected cash sales ($100,000 × 40%) plus the anticipated collection of $42,000 of accounts receivable from the end of September.

Cash Disbursements for Merchandise   Next, we see that HD's merchandise purchases are entirely on account. It makes full payment during the month following its purchases. Therefore, cash disbursements for purchases can be computed from the September 30, 2013, balance sheet (Exhibit 20.5), for October disbursements, and the merchandise purchases budget (Exhibit 20.8), for November and December disbursements. This is shown in Exhibit 20.13.

	October	November	December
Purchases (from Exhibit 20.8)	$49,200	$80,400	$57,000
Cash disbursements for			
Current month purchases (0%)	0	0	0
Prior month purchases (100%)	58,200*	49,200	80,400
Total cash disbursements for purchases	$58,200	$49,200	$80,400

EXHIBIT 20.13

Computing Cash Disbursements for Purchases

*From September 30 balance sheet (Exhibit 20.5)

The schedule above can be modified for alternative payment timing. For example, if Hockey Den paid for 20% of its purchases in the month of purchase, and paid the remaining 80% of a month's purchases in the following month, its cash disbursements in December would equal $75,720, computed as (20% × $57,000) plus (80% × $80,400).

Exhibit 20.14 shows the full cash budget for Hockey Den, beginning with information on budgeted cash receipts from Exhibit 20.13 and budgeted cash purchases for merchandise from Exhibit 20.13. Next we discuss HD's other cash disbursements and loan activity on its cash budget.

HOCKEY DEN
Cash Budget
October 2013–December 2013

	October	November	December
Beginning cash balance	$ 20,000	$ 20,000	$ 22,272
Cash receipts from customers (Exhibit 20.12)	82,000	92,000	104,000
Total cash available	102,000	112,000	126,272
Cash disbursements			
Payments for merchandise (Exhibit 20.13)	58,200	49,200	80,400
Sales commissions (Exhibit 20.9)	10,000	8,000	14,000
Salaries			
Sales (Exhibit 20.9)	2,000	2,000	2,000
Administrative (Exhibit 20.10)	4,500	4,500	4,500
Income taxes payable (Exhibit 20.5)	20,000		
Dividends ($150,000 × 2%)		3,000	
Interest on bank loan			
October ($10,000 × 1%)*	100		
November ($22,800 × 1%)		228	
Purchase of equipment			25,000
Total cash disbursements	94,800	66,928	125,900
Preliminary cash balance	$ 7,200	$ 45,072	$ 372
Loan activity			
Additional loan from bank.......................	12,800		19,628
Repayment of loan to bank		22,800	
Ending cash balance	$ 20,000	$ 22,272	$ 20,000
Loan balance, end of month	$ 22,800	$ 0	$ 19,628

* Beginning loan balance from Exhibit 20.5

EXHIBIT 20.14

Cash Budget

Example: If the minimum ending cash balance in Exhibit 20.14 is changed to $25,000 for each month, what is the projected loan balance at Dec. 31, 2013? *Answer:*

Loan balance, Oct. 31	$27,800
November interest	278
November payment........	25,022
Loan balance, Nov. 30	2,778
December interest	28
Additional loan in Dec.	21,928
Loan balance, Dec. 31.......	$24,706

The monthly budgeted cash disbursements for sales commissions and salaries are taken from the selling expense budget (Exhibit 20.9) and the general and administrative expense budget (Exhibit 20.10). The cash budget is unaffected by depreciation as reported in the general and administrative expenses budget.

Cash Disbursements for Other Items   Income taxes are due and payable in October as shown in the September 30, 2013, balance sheet (Exhibit 20.5). The cash budget in Exhibit 20.14 shows this $20,000 expected payment in October. Predicted income tax expense for the quarter ending December 31 is 40% of net income and is due in January 2014. It is therefore not reported in the October–December 2013 cash budget but in the budgeted income statement as income tax expense and on the budgeted balance sheet as income tax liability.

Hockey Den also pays a cash dividend equal to 2% of the par value of common stock in the second month of each quarter. The cash budget in Exhibit 20.14 shows a November payment of $3,000 for this purpose (2% of $150,000; see Exhibit 20.5).

Loan Activity   Analyzing Hockey Den's loan activity is necessary in computing its budgeted cash disbursements for interest. Hockey Den has an agreement with its bank that promises additional loans at each month-end, if necessary, to keep a minimum cash balance of $20,000. If the cash balance exceeds $20,000 at a month-end, HD uses the excess to repay loans. Interest is paid at each month-end at the rate of 1% of the beginning balance of these loans. For October, this payment is 1% of the $10,000 amount reported in the balance sheet of Exhibit 20.5. For November, HD expects to pay interest of $228, computed as 1% of the $22,800 expected loan balance at October 31. No interest is budgeted for December because the company expects to repay the loans in full at the end of November. Exhibit 20.14 shows that the October 31 cash balance declines to $7,200 (before any loan-related activity). This amount is less than the $20,000 minimum. Hockey Den will bring this balance up to the minimum by borrowing $12,800 with a short-term note. At the end of November, the budget shows an expected cash balance of $45,072 before any loan activity. This means that HD expects to repay $22,800 of debt. The equipment purchase budgeted for December reduces the expected cash balance to $372, far below the $20,000 minimum. The company expects to borrow $19,628 in that month to reach the minimum desired ending balance.

Decision Insight

Cash Cushion   Why do some companies maintain a minimum cash balance when the budget shows extra cash is not needed? For example, iPhone sales have pushed Apple's cash and investments balance to over $97 billion. For Apple's CEO Tim Cook the cushion provides "flexibility and security," important in navigating uncertain economic times. ■

Budgeted Income Statement   One of the final steps in preparing the master budget is to summarize the income effects. The **budgeted income statement** is a managerial accounting report showing predicted amounts of sales and expenses for the budget period. Information needed for preparing a budgeted income statement is primarily taken from already prepared budgets. The volume of information summarized in the budgeted income statement is so large for some companies that they often use spreadsheets to accumulate the budgeted transactions and classify them by their effects on income. We condense HD's budgeted income statement and show it in Exhibit 20.15. All information in this exhibit is taken from earlier budgets. Also, we now can predict the amount of income tax expense for the quarter, computed as 40% of the budgeted pretax income. This amount is included in the cash budget and/or the budgeted balance sheet as necessary.

Point: Lenders often require potential borrowers to provide cash budgets, budgeted income statements, and budgeted balance sheets, as well as data on past performance.

Budgeted Balance Sheet   The final step in preparing the master budget is summarizing the company's financial position. The **budgeted balance sheet** shows predicted amounts for the

EXHIBIT 20.15

Budgeted Income Statement

HOCKEY DEN		
Budgeted Income Statement		
For Three Months Ended December 31, 2013		
Sales (Exhibit 20.6, 3,200 units @ $100)		$320,000
Cost of goods sold (3,200 units @ $60)		192,000
Gross profit		128,000
Operating expenses		
Sales commissions (Exhibit 20.9)	$32,000	
Sales salaries (Exhibit 20.9)	6,000	
Administrative salaries (Exhibit 20.10)	13,500	
Depreciation on equipment (Exhibit 20.10)	4,500	
Interest expense (Exhibit 20.14)	328	56,328
Income before income taxes		71,672
Income tax expense ($71,672 × 40%)		28,669
Net income		$ 43,003

company's assets, liabilities, and equity as of the end of the budget period. HD's budgeted balance sheet in Exhibit 20.16 is prepared using information from the other budgets. The sources of amounts are reported in the notes to the budgeted balance sheet.[1]

EXHIBIT 20.16

Budgeted Balance Sheet

HOCKEY DEN		
Budgeted Balance Sheet		
December 31, 2013		
Assets		
Cash[a]		$ 20,000
Accounts receivable[b]		84,000
Inventory[c]		48,600
Equipment[d]	$225,000	
Less accumulated depreciation[e]	40,500	184,500
Total assets		$337,100
Liabilities and Equity		
Liabilities		
Accounts payable[f]	$ 57,000	
Income taxes payable[g]	28,669	
Bank loan payable[h]	19,628	$105,297
Stockholders' equity		
Common stock[i]	150,000	
Retained earnings[j]	81,803	231,803
Total liabilities and equity		$337,100

[a] Ending balance for December from the cash budget in Exhibit 20.14.

[b] 60% of $140,000 sales budgeted for December from the sales budget in Exhibit 20.6.

[c] 810 units in budgeted December ending inventory at the budgeted cost of $60 per unit (from the purchases budget in Exhibit 20.8).

[d] September 30 balance of $200,000 from the beginning balance sheet in Exhibit 20.5 plus $25,000 cost of new equipment from the cash budget in Exhibit 20.14.

[e] September 30 balance of $36,000 from the beginning balance sheet in Exhibit 20.5 plus $4,500 expense from the general and administrative expense budget in Exhibit 20.10.

[f] Budgeted cost of purchases for December from the purchases budget in Exhibit 20.8.

[g] Income tax expense from the budgeted income statement for the fourth quarter in Exhibit 20.15.

[h] Budgeted December 31 balance from the cash budget in Exhibit 20.14.

[i] Unchanged from the beginning balance sheet in Exhibit 20.5.

[j] September 30 balance of $41,800 from the beginning balance sheet in Exhibit 20.5 plus budgeted net income of $43,003 from the budgeted income statement in Exhibit 20.15 minus budgeted cash dividends of $3,000 from the cash budget in Exhibit 20.14.

---

[1] An eight-column spreadsheet, or work sheet, can be used to prepare a budgeted balance sheet (and income statement). The first two columns show the ending balance sheet amounts from the period prior to the budget period. The budgeted transactions and adjustments are entered in the third and fourth columns in the same manner as adjustments are entered on an ordinary work sheet. After all budgeted transactions and adjustments have been entered, the amounts in the first two columns are combined with the budget amounts in the third and fourth columns and sorted to the proper Income Statement (fifth and sixth columns) and Balance Sheet columns (seventh and eighth columns). Amounts in these columns are used to prepare the budgeted income statement and balance sheet.

Decision Insight

Strategic Planning Most companies allocate dollars based on budgets submitted by department managers. These managers verify the numbers and monitor the budget. Managers must remember, however, that a budget is judged by its success in helping achieve the company's mission. One analogy is that a hiker must know the route to properly plan a hike and monitor hiking progress. ■

Quick Check

Answers — p. 870

11. In preparing a budgeted balance sheet, (a) plant assets are determined by analyzing the capital expenditures budget and the balance sheet from the beginning of the budget period, (b) liabilities are determined by analyzing the general and administrative expense budget, or (c) retained earnings are determined from information contained in the cash budget and the balance sheet from the beginning of the budget period.
12. What sequence is followed in preparing the budgets that constitute the master budget?

GLOBAL VIEW

Royal Phillips Electronics of the Netherlands is a diversified company. Preparing budgets and evaluating progress helps the company achieve its goals. In a recent annual report the company reports that it budgets sales to grow at a faster pace than overall economic growth. Based on this sales target, company managers prepare detailed operating, capital expenditure, and financial budgets.

Budgeted and actual results of companies that do global business are impacted by changes in foreign currency exchange rates. While most of Royal Phillips' cash disbursements are in euros, the company's sales are in euros, U.S. dollars, Chinese yuan, Brazilian real, and other currencies. Forecasting future exchange rates and their impact on sales budgets is difficult. In addition, global economic and political uncertainties add to budgeting challenges.

Decision Analysis Activity-Based Budgeting

A1   Analyze expense planning using activity-based budgeting.

Activity-based budgeting (ABB) is a budget system based on expected activities. Knowledge of expected activities and their levels for the budget period enables management to plan for resources required to perform the activities. To illustrate, we consider the budget of a company's accounting department. Traditional budgeting systems list items such as salaries, supplies, equipment, and utilities. Such an itemized budget informs management of the use of the funds budgeted (for example, salaries), but management cannot assess the basis for increases or decreases in budgeted amounts as compared to prior periods. Accordingly, management often makes across-the-board cuts or increases. In contrast, ABB requires management to list activities performed by, say, the accounting department such as auditing, tax reporting, financial reporting, and cost accounting. Exhibit 20.17 contrasts a traditional budget with an activity-based

EXHIBIT 20.17

Activity-Based Budgeting versus Traditional Budgeting (for an accounting department)

Activity-Based Budget		Traditional Budget	
Auditing	$ 58,000	Salaries	$152,000
Tax reporting	71,000	Supplies	22,000
Financial reporting	63,000	Depreciation	36,000
Cost accounting	32,000	Utilities	14,000
Total	$224,000	Total	$224,000

budget for a company's accounting department. An understanding of the resources required to perform the activities, the costs associated with these resources, and the way resource use changes with changes in activity levels allows management to better assess how expenses will change to accommodate changes in activity levels. Moreover, by knowing the relation between activities and costs, management can attempt to reduce costs by eliminating nonvalue-added activities.

■ Decision Maker

Environmental Manager   You hold the new position of environmental control manager for a chemical company. You are asked to develop a budget for your job and identify job responsibilities. How do you proceed? ■   [Answer—p. 870]

DEMONSTRATION PROBLEM

Wild Wood Company's management asks you to prepare its master budget using the following information. The budget is to cover the months of April, May, and June of 2013.

WILD WOOD COMPANY
Balance Sheet
March 31, 2013

Assets		Liabilities and Equity	
Cash	$ 50,000	Accounts payable	$156,000
Accounts receivable	175,000	Short-term notes payable	12,000
Inventory	126,000	Total current liabilities	168,000
Total current assets	351,000	Long-term note payable	200,000
Equipment, gross	480,000	Total liabilities	368,000
Accumulated depreciation	(90,000)	Common stock	235,000
Equipment, net	390,000	Retained earnings	138,000
		Total stockholders' equity	373,000
Total assets	$741,000	Total liabilities and equity	$741,000

Additional Information

a. Sales for March total 10,000 units. Each month's sales are expected to exceed the prior month's results by 5%. The product's selling price is $25 per unit.

b. Company policy calls for a given month's ending inventory to equal 80% of the next month's expected unit sales. The March 31 inventory is 8,400 units, which complies with the policy. The purchase price is $15 per unit.

c. Sales representatives' commissions are 12.5% of sales and are paid in the month of the sales. The sales manager's monthly salary will be $3,500 in April and $4,000 per month thereafter.

d. Monthly general and administrative expenses include $8,000 administrative salaries, $5,000 depreciation, and 0.9% monthly interest on the long-term note payable.

e. The company expects 30% of sales to be for cash and the remaining 70% on credit. Receivables are collected in full in the month following the sale (none is collected in the month of the sale).

f. All merchandise purchases are on credit, and no payables arise from any other transactions. One month's purchases are fully paid in the next month.

g. The minimum ending cash balance for all months is $50,000. If necessary, the company borrows enough cash using a short-term note to reach the minimum. Short-term notes require an interest payment of 1% at each month-end (before any repayment). If the ending cash balance exceeds the minimum, the excess will be applied to repaying the short-term notes payable balance.

h. Dividends of $100,000 are to be declared and paid in May.

i. No cash payments for income taxes are to be made during the second calendar quarter. Income taxes will be assessed at 35% in the quarter.

j. Equipment purchases of $55,000 are scheduled for June.

Required

Prepare the following budgets and other financial information as required:

1. Sales budget, including budgeted sales for July.

2. Purchases budget, the budgeted cost of goods sold for each month and quarter, and the cost of the June 30 budgeted inventory.

3. Selling expense budget.

4. General and administrative expense budget.

5. Expected cash receipts from customers and the expected June 30 balance of accounts receivable.

6. Expected cash payments for purchases and the expected June 30 balance of accounts payable.

7. Cash budget.

8. Budgeted income statement.

9. Budgeted statement of retained earnings.

10. Budgeted balance sheet.

PLANNING THE SOLUTION

● The sales budget shows expected sales for each month in the quarter. Start by multiplying March sales by 105% and then do the same for the remaining months. July's sales are needed for the purchases budget. To complete the budget, multiply the expected unit sales by the selling price of $25 per unit.

● Use these results and the 80% inventory policy to budget the size of ending inventory for April, May, and June. Add the budgeted sales to these numbers and subtract the actual or expected beginning inventory for each month. The result is the number of units to be purchased each month. Multiply these numbers by the per unit cost of $15. Find the budgeted cost of goods sold by multiplying the unit sales in each month by the $15 cost per unit. Compute the cost of the June 30 ending inventory by multiplying the expected units available at that date by the $15 cost per unit.

● The selling expense budget has only two items. Find the amount of the sales representatives' commissions by multiplying the expected dollar sales in each month by the 12.5% commission rate. Then include the sales manager's salary of $3,500 in April and $4,000 in May and June.

● The general and administrative expense budget should show three items. Administrative salaries are fixed at $8,000 per month, and depreciation is $5,000 per month. Budget the monthly interest expense on the long-term note by multiplying its $200,000 balance by the 0.9% monthly interest rate.

● Determine the amounts of cash sales in each month by multiplying the budgeted sales by 30%. Add to this amount the credit sales of the prior month (computed as 70% of prior month's sales). April's cash receipts from collecting receivables equals the March 31 balance of $175,000. The expected June 30 accounts receivable balance equals 70% of June's total budgeted sales.

● Determine expected cash payments on accounts payable for each month by making them equal to the merchandise purchases in the prior month. The payments for April equal the March 31 balance of accounts payable shown on the beginning balance sheet. The June 30 balance of accounts payable equals merchandise purchases for June.

● Prepare the cash budget by combining the given information and the amounts of cash receipts and cash payments on account that you computed. Complete the cash budget for each month by either borrowing enough to raise the preliminary balance to the minimum or paying off short-term debt as much as the balance allows without falling below the minimum. Show the ending balance of the short-term note in the budget.

● Prepare the budgeted income statement by combining the budgeted items for all three months. Determine the income before income taxes and multiply it by the 35% rate to find the quarter's income tax expense.

● The budgeted statement of retained earnings should show the March 31 balance plus the quarter's net income minus the quarter's dividends.

● The budgeted balance sheet includes updated balances for all items that appear in the beginning balance sheet and an additional liability for unpaid income taxes. Amounts for all asset, liability, and equity accounts can be found either in the budgets, other calculations, or by adding amounts found there to the beginning balances.

SOLUTION TO DEMONSTRATION PROBLEM

1. Sales budget

	April	May	June	July
Prior period's unit sales	10,000	10,500	11,025	11,576
Plus 5% growth	500	525	551	579
Projected unit sales	10,500	11,025	11,576	12,155

	April	May	June	Quarter
Projected unit sales	10,500	11,025	11,576	
Selling price per unit	× $25	× $25	× $25	
Projected sales	$262,500	$275,625	$289,400	$827,525

2. Purchases budget

	April	May	June	Quarter
Next period's unit sales (part 1)	11,025	11,576	12,155	
Ending inventory percent	× 80%	× 80%	× 80%	
Desired ending inventory	8,820	9,261	9,724	
Current period's unit sales (part 1)	10,500	11,025	11,576	
Units to be available	19,320	20,286	21,300	
Less beginning inventory	8,400	8,820	9,261	
Units to be purchased	10,920	11,466	12,039	
Budgeted cost per unit	× $15	× $15	× $15	
Projected purchases	$163,800	$171,990	$180,585	$516,375

Budgeted cost of goods sold

	April	May	June	Quarter
This period's unit sales (part 1)	10,500	11,025	11,576	
Budgeted cost per unit	× $15	× $15	× $15	
Projected cost of goods sold	$157,500	$165,375	$173,640	$496,515

Budgeted inventory for June 30

Units (part 2)	9,724
Cost per unit	× $15
Total	$145,860

3. Selling expense budget

	April	May	June	Quarter
Budgeted sales (part 1)	$262,500	$275,625	$289,400	$827,525
Commission percent	× 12.5%	× 12.5%	× 12.5%	× 12.5%
Sales commissions	32,813	34,453	36,175	103,441
Manager's salary	3,500	4,000	4,000	11,500
Projected selling expenses	$ 36,313	$ 38,453	$ 40,175	$114,941

4. General and administrative expense budget

	April	May	June	Quarter
Administrative salaries	$ 8,000	$ 8,000	$ 8,000	$24,000
Depreciation	5,000	5,000	5,000	15,000
Interest on long-term note payable (0.9% × $200,000)	1,800	1,800	1,800	5,400
Projected expenses	$14,800	$14,800	$14,800	$44,400

5. Expected cash receipts from customers

	April	May	June	Quarter
Budgeted sales (part 1)	$262,500	$275,625	$289,400	
Ending accounts receivable (70%)	$183,750	$192,938	$202,580	
Cash receipts				
Cash sales (30% of budgeted sales)	$ 78,750	$ 82,687	$ 86,820	$248,257
Collections of prior month's receivables	175,000	183,750	192,938	551,688
Total cash to be collected	$253,750	$266,437	$279,758	$799,945

6. Expected cash payments to suppliers

	April	May	June	Quarter
Cash payments (equal to prior month's purchases)	$156,000	$163,800	$171,990	$491,790
Expected June 30 balance of accounts payable (June purchases)			$180,585	

7. Cash budget

	April	May	June
Beginning cash balance	$ 50,000	$ 89,517	$ 50,000
Cash receipts (part 5)	253,750	266,437	279,758
Total cash available	303,750	355,954	329,758
Cash payments			
Payments for merchandise (part 6)	156,000	163,800	171,990
Sales commissions (part 3)	32,813	34,453	36,175
Salaries			
Sales (part 3)	3,500	4,000	4,000
Administrative (part 4)	8,000	8,000	8,000
Interest on long-term note (part 4)	1,800	1,800	1,800
Dividends		100,000	
Equipment purchase			55,000
Interest on short-term notes			
April ($12,000 × 1.0%)	120		
June ($6,099 × 1.0%)			61
Total cash payments	202,233	312,053	277,026
Preliminary balance	101,517	43,901	52,732
Loan activity			
Additional loan		6,099	
Loan repayment	(12,000)		(2,732)
Ending cash balance	$ 89,517	$ 50,000	$ 50,000
Ending short-term notes	$ 0	$ 6,099	$ 3,367

8.

WILD WOOD COMPANY		
Budgeted Income Statement		
For Quarter Ended June 30, 2013		
Sales (part 1)		$827,525
Cost of goods sold (part 2)		496,515
Gross profit		331,010
Operating expenses		
Sales commissions (part 3)	$103,441	
Sales salaries (part 3)	11,500	
Administrative salaries (part 4)	24,000	
Depreciation (part 4)	15,000	
Interest on long-term note (part 4)	5,400	
Interest on short-term notes (part 7)	181	
Total operating expenses		159,522
Income before income taxes		171,488
Income taxes (35%)		60,021
Net income		$111,467

9.

WILD WOOD COMPANY	
Budgeted Statement of Retained Earnings	
For Quarter Ended June 30, 2013	
Beginning retained earnings (given)	$138,000
Net income (part 8)	111,467
	249,467
Less cash dividends (given)	100,000
Ending retained earnings	$149,467

10.

WILD WOOD COMPANY		
Budgeted Balance Sheet		
June 30, 2013		
Assets		
Cash (part 7)		$ 50,000
Accounts receivable (part 5)		202,580
Inventory (part 2)		145,860
Total current assets		398,440
Equipment (given plus purchase)	$535,000	
Less accumulated depreciation (given plus expense)	105,000	430,000
Total assets		$828,440
Liabilities and Equity		
Accounts payable (part 6)		$180,585
Short-term notes payable (part 7)		3,367
Income taxes payable (part 8)		60,021
Total current liabilities		243,973
Long-term note payable (given)		200,000
Total liabilities		443,973
Common stock (given)		235,000
Retained earnings (part 9)		149,467
Total stockholders' equity		384,467
Total liabilities and equity		$828,440

20A

Production and Manufacturing Budgets

P3 Prepare production and manufacturing budgets.

Unlike a merchandising company, a manufacturer must prepare a **production budget** instead of a merchandise purchases budget. A production budget, which shows the number of units to be produced each month, is similar to merchandise purchases budgets except that the number of units to be purchased each month (as shown in Exhibit 20.8) is replaced by the number of units to be manufactured each month. A production budget does not show costs; it is *always expressed in units of product*. Exhibit 20A.1 shows the production budget for **Toronto Sticks Company (TSC),** a manufacturer of hockey sticks. TSC is an exclusive supplier of hockey sticks to Hockey Den, meaning that TSC uses HD's budgeted sales figures (Exhibit 20.6) to determine its production and manufacturing budgets.

EXHIBIT 20A.1

Production Budget

TSC Production Budget October 2013–December 2013			
	October	November	December
Next period's budgeted sales (units)	800	1,400	900
Ratio of inventory to future sales	× 90%	× 90%	× 90%
Budgeted ending inventory (units)	720	1,260	810
Add budgeted sales for the period (units)	1,000	800	1,400
Required units of available production	1,720	2,060	2,210
Deduct beginning inventory (units)	(900)	(720)	(1,260)
Units to be produced	820	1,340	950

A **manufacturing budget** shows the budgeted costs for direct materials, direct labor, and overhead. It is based on the budgeted production volume from the production budget. The manufacturing budget for most companies consists of three individual budgets: direct materials budget, direct labor budget, and overhead budget. Exhibits 20A.2–20A.4 show these three manufacturing budgets for TSC. These budgets yield the total expected cost of goods to be manufactured in the budget period.

The *direct materials budget* is driven by the budgeted materials needed to satisfy each month's production requirement. To this we must add the desired ending inventory requirements. The desired ending inventory of direct materials as shown in Exhibit 20A.2 is 50% of next month's budgeted materials requirements of wood. For instance, in October 2013, an ending inventory of 335 units of material is desired (50% of November's 670 units). The desired ending inventory for December 2013 is 225 units, computed from the direct material requirement of 450 units for a production level of 900 units in January 2014. The total materials requirements are computed by adding the desired ending inventory figures to that month's budgeted production material requirements. For October 2013, the total materials requirement is 745 units (335 + 410). From the total materials requirement, we then subtract the units of

EXHIBIT 20A.2

Direct Materials Budget

TSC Direct Materials Budget October 2013–December 2013			
	October	November	December
Budget production (units)	820	1,340	950
Materials requirements per unit	× 0.5	× 0.5	× 0.5
Materials needed for production (units)	410	670	475
Add budgeted ending inventory (units)	335	237.5	225
Total materials requirements (units)	745	907.5	700
Deduct beginning inventory (units)	(205)	(335)	(237.5)
Materials to be purchased (units)	540	572.5	462.5
Material price per unit	$ 20	$ 20	$ 20
Total cost of direct materials purchases	$10,800	$11,450	$9,250

materials available in beginning inventory. For October 2013, the materials available from September 2013 are computed as 50% of October's materials requirements to satisfy production, or 205 units (50% of 410). Therefore, direct materials purchases in October 2013 are budgeted at 540 units (745 − 205). See Exhibit 20A.2.

TSC's *direct labor budget* is shown in Exhibit 20A.3. About 15 minutes of labor time is required to produce one unit. Labor is paid at the rate of $12 per hour. Budgeted labor hours are computed by multiplying the budgeted production level for each month by one-quarter (0.25) of an hour. Direct labor cost is then computed by multiplying budgeted labor hours by the labor rate of $12 per hour.

TSC Direct Labor Budget October 2013–December 2013	October	November	December
Budgeted production (units)	820	1,340	950
Labor requirements per unit (hours)	× 0.25	× 0.25	× 0.25
Total labor hours needed	205	335	237.5
Labor rate (per hour)	$ 12	$ 12	$ 12
Labor dollars	$2,460	$4,020	$2,850

EXHIBIT 20A.3

Direct Labor Budget

TSC's *factory overhead budget* is shown in Exhibit 20A.4. The variable portion of overhead is assigned at the rate of $2.50 per unit of production. The fixed portion stays constant at $1,500 per month. The budget in Exhibit 20A.4 is in condensed form; most overhead budgets are more detailed, listing each overhead cost item. We explain these more detailed overhead budgets in the next chapter.

TSC Factory Overhead Budget October 2013–December 2013	October	November	December
Budgeted production (units)	820	1,340	950
Variable factory overhead rate	× $2.50	× $2.50	× $2.50
Budgeted variable overhead	2,050	3,350	2,375
Budgeted fixed overhead	1,500	1,500	1,500
Budgeted total overhead	$3,550	$4,850	$3,875

EXHIBIT 20A.4

Factory Overhead Budget

Summary

C1 **Describe the importance and benefits of budgeting and the process of budget administration.** Planning is a management responsibility of critical importance to business success. Budgeting is the process management uses to formalize its plans. Budgeting promotes management analysis and focuses its attention on the future. Budgeting also provides a basis for evaluating performance, serves as a source of motivation, is a means of coordinating activities, and communicates management's plans and instructions to employees. Budgeting is a detailed activity that requires administration. At least three aspects are important: budget committee, budget reporting, and budget timing. A budget committee oversees the budget preparation. The budget period pertains to the time period for which the budget is prepared such as a year or month.

C2 **Describe a master budget and the process of preparing it.** A master budget is a formal overall plan for a company. It consists of plans for business operations and capital expenditures, plus the financial results of those activities. The budgeting process begins with a sales budget. Based on expected sales volume, companies can budget purchases, selling expenses, and administrative expenses. Next, the capital expenditures budget is prepared, followed by the cash budget and budgeted financial statements. Manufacturers also must budget production quantities, materials purchases, labor costs, and overhead.

A1 **Analyze expense planning using activity-based budgeting.** Activity-based budgeting requires management to identify activities performed by departments, plan necessary activity levels, identify resources required to perform these activities, and budget the resources.

P1 **Prepare each component of a master budget and link each to the budgeting process.** The term *master budget* refers to a collection of individual component budgets. Each component budget is designed to guide persons responsible for activities covered by that component. A master budget must reflect the components of a company and their interaction in pursuit of company goals.

P2 Link both operating and capital expenditures budgets to budgeted financial statements. The operating budgets, capital expenditures budget, and cash budget contain much of the information to prepare a budgeted income statement for the budget period and a budgeted balance sheet at the end of the budget period. Budgeted financial statements show the expected financial consequences of the planned activities described in the budgets.

P3 Prepare production and manufacturing budgets. A manufacturer must prepare a *production budget* instead of a purchases budget. A *manufacturing budget* shows the budgeted production costs for direct materials, direct labor, and overhead.

Guidance Answers to Decision Maker and Decision Ethics

Budget Staffer Your superior's actions appear unethical because she is using private information for personal gain. As a budget staffer, you are low in the company's hierarchical structure and probably unable to confront this superior directly. You should inform an individual with a position of authority within the organization about your concerns.

Entrepreneur You must deal with two issues. First, because fashions and designs frequently change, you cannot heavily rely on previous budgets. As a result, you must carefully analyze the market to understand what designs are in vogue. This will help you plan the product mix and estimate demand. The second issue is the budgeting

period. An annual sales budget may be unreliable because tastes can quickly change. Your best bet might be to prepare monthly and quarterly sales budgets that you continuously monitor and revise.

Environmental Manager You are unlikely to have data on this new position to use in preparing your budget. In this situation, you can use activity-based budgeting. This requires developing a list of activities to conduct, the resources required to perform these activities, and the expenses associated with these resources. You should challenge yourself to be absolutely certain that the listed activities are necessary and that the listed resources are required.

Guidance Answers to Quick Checks

1. Major benefits include promoting a focus on the future; providing a basis for evaluating performance; providing a source of motivation; coordinating the departments of a business; and communicating plans and instructions.

2. The budget committee's responsibility is to provide guidance to ensure that budget figures are realistic and coordinated.

3. Budget periods usually coincide with accounting periods and therefore cover a month, quarter, or a year. Budgets can also be prepared for longer time periods, such as five years.

4. Rolling budgets are budgets that are periodically revised in the ongoing process of continuous budgeting.

5. A master budget is a comprehensive or overall plan for the company that is generally expressed in monetary terms.

6. *b*

7. The master budget includes operating budgets, the capital expenditures budget, and financial budgets.

8. *c*; Computed as $(60\% \times 140) + 120 - 50 = 154$.

9. Merchandisers prepare merchandise purchases budgets; manufacturers prepare production and manufacturing budgets.

10. A just-in-time system keeps the level of inventory to a minimum and orders merchandise or materials to meet immediate sales demand. A safety stock system maintains an inventory that is large enough to meet sales demands plus an amount to satisfy unexpected sales demands and an amount to cover delayed shipments from suppliers.

11. *a*

12. (a) Operating budgets (such as sales, selling expense, and administrative budgets), (b) capital expenditures budget, (c) financial budgets: cash budget, budgeted income statement, and budgeted balance sheet.

Key Terms

Activity-based budgeting (ABB) (p. 862)
Budget (p. 848)
Budgeted balance sheet (p. 860)
Budgeted income statement (p. 860)
Budgeting (p. 848)
Capital expenditures budget (p. 858)

Cash budget (p. 858)
Continuous budgeting (p. 851)
General and administrative expense budget (p. 857)
Manufacturing budget (p. 868)
Master budget (p. 852)

Merchandise purchases budget (p. 855)
Production budget (p. 868)
Rolling budgets (p. 851)
Safety stock (p. 855)
Sales budget (p. 854)
Selling expense budget (p. 856)

Additional Quiz Questions are available at the book's Website.

1. A plan that reports the units or costs of merchandise to be purchased by a merchandising company during the budget period is called a
 a. Capital expenditures budget.
 b. Cash budget.
 c. Merchandise purchases budget.
 d. Selling expenses budget.
 e. Sales budget.

2. A hardware store has budgeted sales of $36,000 for its power tool department in July. Management wants to have $7,000 in power tool inventory at the end of July. Its beginning inventory of power tools is expected to be $6,000. What is the budgeted dollar amount of merchandise purchases?
 a. $36,000
 b. $43,000
 c. $42,000
 d. $35,000
 e. $37,000

3. A store has the following budgeted sales for the next five months.

May	$210,000
June	186,000
July	180,000
August	220,000
September	240,000

Cash sales are 25% of total sales and all credit sales are expected to be collected in the month following the sale. The total amount of cash expected to be received from customers in September is

 a. $240,000
 b. $225,000
 c. $ 60,000
 d. $165,000
 e. $220,000

4. A plan that shows the expected cash inflows and cash outflows during the budget period, including receipts from loans needed to maintain a minimum cash balance and repayments of such loans, is called
 a. A rolling budget.
 b. An income statement.
 c. A balance sheet.
 d. A cash budget.
 e. An operating budget.

5.[A] The following sales are predicted for a company's next four months.

	September	October	November	December
Unit sales ..	480	560	600	480

Each month's ending inventory of finished goods should be 30% of the next month's sales. At September 1, the finished goods inventory is 140 units. The budgeted production of units for October is
 a. 572 units.
 b. 560 units.
 c. 548 units.
 d. 600 units.
 e. 180 units.

[A] *Superscript letter A denotes assignments based on Appendix 20A, relating to production, direct materials, direct labor, and factory overhead budgets.*

 Icon denotes assignments that involve decision making.

Discussion Questions

1. Identify at least three roles that budgeting plays in helping managers control and monitor a business.

2. What two common benchmarks can be used to evaluate actual performance? Which of the two is generally more useful?

3. What is the benefit of continuous budgeting?

4. Identify three usual time horizons for short-term planning and budgets.

5. Why should each department participate in preparing its own budget?

6. How does budgeting help management coordinate and plan business activities?

7. Why is the sales budget so important to the budgeting process?

8. What is a selling expense budget? What is a capital expenditures budget?

9. Budgeting promotes good decision making by requiring managers to conduct _____ and by focusing their attention on the _____.

10. Piaggio prepares a cash budget. What is a cash **PIAGGIO** budget? Why must operating budgets and the capital expenditures budget be prepared before the cash budget?

11. KTM regularly uses budgets. What is the difference **KTM** between a production budget and a manufacturing budget?

12. Would a manager of an Apple retail store partici- **Apple** pate more in budgeting than a manager at the corporate offices? Explain.

13. Does the manager of a Arctic Cat distribu- **Arctic Cat** tion center participate in long-term budgeting? Explain.

14. Assume that Polaris' snowmobile division **Polaris** is charged with preparing a master budget. Identify the participants—for example, the sales manager for the sales budget—and describe the information each person provides in preparing the master budget.

connect

QUICK STUDY

QS 20-1
Components of a master budget
C2

Which one of the following sets of items are all necessary components of the master budget?
1. Operating budgets, historical income statement, and budgeted balance sheet.
2. Prior sales reports, capital expenditures budget, and financial budgets.
3. Sales budget, operating budgets, and historical financial budgets.
4. Operating budgets, financial budgets, and capital expenditures budget.

QS 20-2
Budget motivation   C1

The motivation of employees is one goal of budgeting. Identify three guidelines that organizations should follow if budgeting is to serve effectively as a source of motivation for employees.

QS 20-3
Merchandising: Purchases budget   P1

Montel Company's July sales budget calls for sales of $600,000. The store expects to begin July with $50,000 of inventory and to end the month with $40,000 of inventory. Gross margin is typically 40% of sales. Determine the budgeted cost of merchandise purchases for July.

QS 20-4
Budgeting process   C1

Good management includes good budgeting. (1) Explain why the bottom-up approach to budgeting is considered a more successful management technique than a top-down approach. (2) Provide an example of implementation of the bottom-up approach to budgeting.

QS 20-5
Computing budgeted accounts receivable
P2

Lighthouse Company anticipates total sales for June and July of $420,000 and $398,000, respectively. Cash sales are normally 60% of total sales. Of the credit sales, 20% are collected in the same month as the sale, 70% are collected during the first month after the sale, and the remaining 10% are collected in the second month. Determine the amount of accounts receivable reported on the company's budgeted balance sheet as of July 31.

QS 20-6
Cash budget
P1

Use the following information to prepare a cash budget for the month ended on March 31 for Gado Merchandising Company. The budget should show expected cash receipts and cash disbursements for the month of March and the balance expected on March 31.
a. Beginning cash balance on March 1, $72,000.
b. Cash receipts from sales, $300,000.
c. Budgeted cash disbursements for purchases, $140,000.
d. Budgeted cash disbursements for salaries, $80,000.
e. Other budgeted cash expenses, $45,000.
f. Cash repayment of bank loan, $20,000.

QS 20-7
Activity-based budgeting
A1

Activity-based budgeting is a budget system based on *expected activities*. (1) Describe activity-based budgeting, and explain its preparation of budgets. (2) How does activity-based budgeting differ from traditional budgeting?

QS 20-8^A
Manufacturing: Production budget
P3

Forrest Company manufactures watches and has a JIT policy that ending inventory must equal 10% of the next month's sales. It estimates that October's actual ending inventory will consist of 40,000 watches. November and December sales are estimated to be 400,000 and 350,000 watches, respectively. Compute the number of watches to be produced that would appear on the company's production budget for the month of November.

QS 20-9^A
Manufacturing: Factory overhead budget   P3

Refer to information from QS 20-8. Forrest Company assigns variable overhead at the rate of $1.50 per unit of production. Fixed overhead equals $4,600,000 per month. Prepare a factory overhead budget for November.

QS 20-10
Sales budget   P1

Grace sells miniature digital cameras for $250 each. 1,000 units were sold in May, and it forecasts 4% growth in unit sales each month. Determine (a) the number of camera sales and (b) the dollar amount of camera sales for the month of June.

Refer to information from QS 20-10. Grace pays a sales manager a monthly salary of $6,000 and a commission of 8% of camera sales (in dollars). Prepare a selling expense budget for the month of June.

QS 20-11
Selling expense budget P1

Refer to information from QS 20-10. Assume 60% of Grace's sales are for cash. The remaining 40% are credit sales; these customers pay in the month following the sale. Compute the budgeted cash receipts for June.

QS 20-12
Cash budget P1

Following are selected accounts for a company. For each account, indicate whether it will appear on a budgeted income statement (BIS) or a budgeted balance sheet (BBS). If an item will not appear on either budgeted financial statement, label it NA.

QS 20-13
Budgeted financial statements
P2

Sales	_____	Interest paid on note payable	_____
Office salaries paid.	_____	Cash dividends paid	_____
Accumulated depreciation.	_____	Bank loan owed	_____
Amortization expense	_____	Cost of goods sold.	_____

The Candle Shoppe reports the following sales forecast: August, $150,000; September, $170,000. Cash sales are normally 40% of total sales and all credit sales are expected to be collected in the month following the date of sale. Prepare a schedule of cash receipts for September.

QS 20-14
Cash receipts P1

Wells Company reports the following sales forecast: September, $55,000; October, $66,000; and November, $80,000. All sales are on account. Collections of credit sales are received as follows: 20% in the month of sale, 70% in the first month after sale, and 10% in the second month after sale. Prepare a schedule of cash receipts for November.

QS 20-15
Cash receipts P1

Gordands purchased $600,000 of merchandise in August and expects to purchase $720,000 in September. Merchandise purchases are paid as follows: 25% in the month of purchase and 75% in the following month. Compute cash disbursements for merchandise for September.

QS 20-16
Merchandising: Cash disbursements for merchandise
P1

Meyer Co. forecasts merchandise purchases of $15,800 in January, $18,600 in February, and $20,200 in March; 40% of purchases are paid in the month of purchase and 60% are paid in the following month. At December 31 of the prior year, the balance of Accounts Payable (for December purchases) is $22,000. Prepare a schedule of cash disbursements for merchandise for each of the months of January, February, and March.

QS 20-17
Merchandising: Cash disbursements for merchandise
P1

Raider-X Company forecasts sales of 18,000 units for April. Beginning inventory is 3,000 units. The desired ending inventory is 30% higher than the beginning inventory. How many units should Raider-X purchase in April?

QS 20-18
Merchandising: Computing purchases
P1

Lexi Company forecasts unit sales of 1,040,000 in April, 1,220,000 in May, 980,000 in June, and 1,020,000 in July. Beginning inventory on April 1 is 280,000 units, and the company wants to have 30% of next month's sales in inventory at the end of each month. Prepare a merchandise purchases budget for the months of April, May, and June.

QS 20-19
Merchandising: Computing purchases
P1

Champ, Inc. predicts the following sales in units for the coming three months:

QS 20-20^A
Manufacturing: Production budget
P3

	May	June	July
Sales in units	180	200	240

Each month's ending inventory of finished units should be 60% of the next month's sales. The April 30 finished goods inventory is 50 units. Compute Champ's budgeted production (in units) for May.

Zortek Corp. budgets production of 400 units in January and 200 units in February. Each finished unit requires five pounds of raw material Z, which costs $2 per pound. Each month's ending inventory of raw materials should be 40% of the following month's budgeted production. The January 1 raw materials inventory has 130 pounds of Z. Prepare a direct materials budget for January.

QS 20-21^A
Manufacturing: Direct materials budget P3

QS 20-22^A

Manufacturing: Direct labor budget   P3

Tora Co. plans to produce 1,020 units in July. Each unit requires two hours of direct labor. The direct labor rate is $20 per hour. Prepare a direct labor budget for July.

QS 20-23

Sales budget   P1

Scora, Inc., is preparing its master budget for the quarter ending March 31. It sells a single product for $50 per unit. Budgeted sales for the next four months follow. Prepare a sales budget for the months of January, February, and March.

	January	February	March	April
Sales in units	1,200	2,000	1,600	1,400

QS 20-24

Cash receipts budget   P1

Refer to information in QS 20-23. In addition, sales are 40% cash and 60% on credit. All credit sales are collected in the month following the sale. The January 1 balance in accounts receivable is $15,000. Prepare a schedule of budgeted cash receipts for January, February, and March.

QS 20-25

Selling expense budget   P1

Refer to information in QS 20-23. In addition, sales commissions are 10% of sales and the company pays a sales manager a salary of $6,000 per month. Sales commissions and salaries are paid in the month incurred. Prepare a selling expense budget for January, February, and March.

QS 20-26

Budgeted loan activity

P1

Messers Company is preparing a cash budget for February. The company has $20,000 cash at the beginning of February and anticipates $75,000 in cash receipts and $100,250 in cash disbursements during February. What amount, if any, must the company borrow during February to maintain a $5,000 cash balance? The company has no loans outstanding on February 1.

QS 20-27

Operating budgets

P1

Royal Phillips Electronics of the Netherlands reports sales of €25,400 million for a recent year. Assume that the company expects sales growth of 3 percent for the next year. Also assume that selling expenses are typically 20 percent of sales, while general and administrative expenses are 4 percent of sales.

Required

1. Compute budgeted sales for the next year.

2. Assume budgeted sales for next year is €26,000 million, and then compute budgeted selling expenses and budgeted general and administrative expenses for the next year.

EXERCISES

Exercise 20-1

Preparation of cash budgets (for three periods)

P1

Kayak Co. budgeted the following cash receipts (excluding cash receipts from loans received) and cash disbursements (excluding cash disbursements for loan and interest payments) for the first three months of next year.

	Cash Receipts	Cash Disbursements
January	$525,000	$475,000
February.........	400,000	350,000
March	450,000	525,000

Check January ending cash balance, $30,000

According to a credit agreement with the company's bank, Kayak promises to have a minimum cash balance of $30,000 at each month-end. In return, the bank has agreed that the company can borrow up to $150,000 at an annual interest rate of 12%, paid on the last day of each month. The interest is computed based on the beginning balance of the loan for the month. The company has a cash balance of $30,000 and a loan balance of $60,000 at January 1. Prepare monthly cash budgets for each of the first three months of next year.

Exercise 20-2

Merchandising: Preparation of purchases budgets (for three periods)

P1

Walker Company prepares monthly budgets. The current budget plans for a September ending inventory of 30,000 units. Company policy is to end each month with merchandise inventory equal to a specified percent of budgeted sales for the following month. Budgeted sales and merchandise purchases for the three most recent months follow. (1) Prepare the merchandise purchases budget for the months of July, August, and September. (2) Compute the ratio of ending inventory to the next month's sales for each budget prepared in part 1. (3) How many units are budgeted for sale in October?

	Sales (Units)	Purchases (Units)
July	180,000	200,250
August	315,000	308,250
September	270,000	259,500

Use the following information to prepare the July cash budget for Acco Co. It should show expected cash receipts and cash disbursements for the month and the cash balance expected on July 31.

a. Beginning cash balance on July 1: $50,000.

b. Cash receipts from sales: 30% is collected in the month of sale, 50% in the next month, and 20% in the second month after sale (uncollectible accounts are negligible and can be ignored). Sales amounts are: May (actual), $1,720,000; June (actual), $1,200,000; and July (budgeted), $1,400,000.

c. Payments on merchandise purchases: 60% in the month of purchase and 40% in the month following purchase. Purchases amounts are: June (actual), $700,000; and July (budgeted), $750,000.

d. Budgeted cash disbursements for salaries in July: $275,000.

e. Budgeted depreciation expense for July: $36,000.

f. Other cash expenses budgeted for July: $200,000.

g. Accrued income taxes due in July: $80,000.

h. Bank loan interest due in July: $6,600.

Exercise 20-3
Merchandising: Preparation of a cash budget
P1

Check   Ending cash balance, $122,400

Use the information in Exercise 20-3 and the following additional information to prepare a budgeted income statement for the month of July and a budgeted balance sheet for July 31.

a. Cost of goods sold is 55% of sales.

b. Inventory at the end of June is $80,000 and at the end of July is $60,000.

c. Salaries payable on June 30 are $50,000 and are expected to be $60,000 on July 31.

d. The equipment account balance is $1,600,000 on July 31. On June 30, the accumulated depreciation on equipment is $280,000.

e. The $6,600 cash payment of interest represents the 1% monthly expense on a bank loan of $660,000.

f. Income taxes payable on July 31 are $30,720, and the income tax rate applicable to the company is 30%.

g. The only other balance sheet accounts are: Common Stock, with a balance of $600,000 on June 30; and Retained Earnings, with a balance of $964,000 on June 30.

Exercise 20-4
Merchandising: Preparing a budgeted income statement and balance sheet
P2

Check   Net income, $71,680; Total assets, $2,686,400

Hardy Company's cost of goods sold is consistently 60% of sales. The company plans to carry ending merchandise inventory for each month equal to 20% of the next month's budgeted cost of good sold. All merchandise is purchased on credit, and 50% of the purchases made during a month is paid for in that month. Another 35% is paid for during the first month after purchase, and the remaining 15% is paid for during the second month after purchase. Expected sales are: August (actual), $325,000; September (actual), $320,000; October (estimated), $250,000; November (estimated), $310,000. Use this information to determine October's expected cash payments for purchases. (*Hint:* Use the layout of Exhibit 20.8, but revised for the facts given here.)

Exercise 20-5
Merchandising: Computing budgeted cash payments for purchases
P1

Check   Budgeted purchases: August, $194,400; October, $157,200

Quick Dollar Company purchases all merchandise on credit. It recently budgeted the following month-end accounts payable balances and merchandise inventory balances. Cash payments on accounts payable during each month are expected to be: May, $1,600,000; June, $1,490,000; July, $1,425,000; and August, $1,495,000. Use the available information to compute the budgeted amounts of (1) merchandise purchases for June, July, and August and (2) cost of goods sold for June, July, and August.

Exercise 20-6
Merchandising: Computing budgeted purchases and costs of goods sold
P1

	Accounts Payable	Merchandise Inventory
May 31	$150,000	$250,000
June 30	200,000	400,000
July 31	235,000	300,000
August 31	195,000	330,000

Check   June purchases, $1,540,000; June cost of goods sold, $1,390,000

Exercise 20-7
Merchandising: Computing budgeted accounts payable and purchases—sales forecast in dollars

P1 P2

Check July purchases, $236,600;
Sept. payments on accts. pay.,
$214,235

Big Sound, a merchandising company specializing in home computer speakers, budgets its monthly cost of goods sold to equal 70% of sales. Its inventory policy calls for ending inventory in each month to equal 20% of the next month's budgeted cost of goods sold. All purchases are on credit, and 25% of the purchases in a month is paid for in the same month. Another 60% is paid for during the first month after purchase, and the remaining 15% is paid for in the second month after purchase. The following sales budgets are set: July, $350,000; August, $290,000; September, $320,000; October, $275,000; and November, $265,000. Compute the following: (1) budgeted merchandise purchases for July, August, September, and October; (2) budgeted payments on accounts payable for September and October; and (3) budgeted ending balances of accounts payable for September and October. (*Hint:* For part 1, refer to Exhibits 20.7 and 20.8 for guidance, but note that budgeted sales are in dollars for this assignment.)

Exercise 20-8ᴬ
Manufacturing: Preparing production budgets (for two periods) P3

Check Second quarter production, 480,000 units

Electro Company manufactures an innovative automobile transmission for electric cars. Management predicts that ending inventory for the first quarter will be 75,000 units. The following unit sales of the transmissions are expected during the rest of the year: second quarter, 450,000 units; third quarter, 525,000 units; and fourth quarter, 475,000 units. Company policy calls for the ending inventory of a quarter to equal 20% of the next quarter's budgeted sales. Prepare a production budget for both the second and third quarters that shows the number of transmissions to manufacture.

Exercise 20-9ᴬ
Manufacturing: Direct materials budget

P3

Refer to information from Exercise 20-8. Each transmission requires 0.80 pounds of a key raw material. Electro Company aims to end each quarter with an ending inventory of direct materials equal to 50% of next quarter's budgeted materials requirements. Direct materials cost $170 per unit. Prepare a direct materials budget for the second quarter.

Exercise 20-10ᴬ
Manufacturing: Direct labor budget P3

Refer to information from Exercise 20-8. Each transmission requires 4 direct labor hours, at a cost of $12 per hour. Prepare a direct labor budget for the second quarter.

Exercise 20-11
Merchandising: Budgeted cash disbursements

P1

Hector Company reports the following:

	July	August	September
Sales	$50,000	$72,000	$66,000
Purchases	14,400	19,200	21,600

Payments for purchases are made in the month after purchase. Selling expenses are 10% of sales, administrative expenses are 8% of sales, and both are paid in the month of sale. Rent expense of $7,400 is paid monthly. Depreciation expense is $2,300 per month. Prepare a schedule of budgeted cash disbursements for August and September.

Exercise 20-12
Budgeted cash receipts

P1

Jasper Company has sales on account and sales for cash. Specifically, 70% of its sales are on account and 30% are for cash. Credit sales are collected in full in the month following the sale. The company forecasts sales of $525,000 for April, $535,000 for May, and $560,000 for June. The beginning balance of Accounts Receivable is $400,000 on April 1. Prepare a schedule of budgeted cash receipts for April, May, and June.

Exercise 20-13
Cash budget

P1

Karim Corp. requires a minimum $8,000 cash balance. If necessary, loans are taken to meet this requirement at a cost of 1% interest per month (paid monthly). Any excess cash is used to repay loans at month-end. The cash balance on July 1 is $8,400 and the company has no outstanding loans. Forecasted cash receipts (other than for loans received) and forecasted cash payments (other than for loan or interest payments) are:

	July	August	September
Cash receipts	$20,000	$26,000	$40,000
Cash disbursements	28,000	30,000	22,000

Prepare a cash budget for July, August, and September. Round interest payments to the nearest whole dollar.

Foyert Corp. requires a minimum $30,000 cash balance. If necessary, loans are taken to meet this requirement at a cost of 1% interest per month (paid monthly). Any excess cash is used to repay loans at month-end. The cash balance on October 1 is $30,000 and the company has an outstanding loan of $10,000. Forecasted cash receipts (other than for loans received) and forecasted cash payments (other than for loan or interest payments) follow. Prepare a cash budget for October, November, and December. Round interest payments to the nearest whole dollar.

Exercise 20-14
Cash budget
P1

	October	November	December
Cash receipts	$110,000	$80,000	$100,000
Cash disbursements	120,000	75,000	80,000

Castor, Inc. is preparing its master budget for the quarter ended June 30. Budgeted sales and cash payments for merchandise for the next three months follow:

Exercise 20-15
Merchandising: Cash budget
P1

	April	May	June
Budgeted sales	$32,000	$40,000	$24,000
Budgeted cash payments for merchandise..................	20,200	16,800	17,200

Sales are 50% cash and 50% on credit. All credit sales are collected in the month following the sale. The March 30 balance sheet includes balances of $12,000 in cash, $12,000 in accounts receivable, $11,000 in accounts payable, and a $2,000 balance in loans payable. A minimum cash balance of $12,000 is required. Loans are obtained at the end of any month when a cash shortage occurs. Interest is 1% per month based on the beginning of the month loan balance and is paid at each month-end. If an excess balance of cash exists, loans are repaid at the end of the month. Operating expenses are paid in the month incurred and consist of sales commissions (10% of sales), shipping (2% of sales), office salaries ($5,000 per month) and rent ($3,000 per month). Prepare a cash budget for each of the months of April, May, and June (round all dollar amounts to the nearest whole dollar).

Kelsey is preparing its master budget for the quarter ended September 30. Budgeted sales and cash payments for merchandise for the next three months follow:

Exercise 20-16
Merchandising: Cash budget
P1

	July	August	September
Budgeted sales	$64,000	$80,000	$48,000
Budgeted cash payments for merchandise..................	40,400	33,600	34,400

Sales are 20% cash and 80% on credit. All credit sales are collected in the month following the sale. The June 30 balance sheet includes balances of $15,000 in cash; $45,000 in accounts receivable; $4,500 in accounts payable; and a $5,000 balance in loans payable. A minimum cash balance of $15,000 is required. Loans are obtained at the end of any month when a cash shortage occurs. Interest is 1% per month based on the beginning of the month loan balance and is paid at each month-end. If an excess balance of cash exists, loans are repaid at the end of the month. Operating expenses are paid in the month incurred and consist of sales commissions (10% of sales), office salaries ($4,000 per month), and rent ($6,500 per month). (1) Prepare a cash receipts budget for July, August, and September. (2) Prepare a cash budget for each of the months of July, August, and September. (Round all dollar amounts to the nearest whole dollar.)

Exercise 20-17

Merchandising: Budgeted balance sheet

P2

The following information is available for Zetrov Company:

a. The cash budget for March shows an ending bank loan of $10,000 and an ending cash balance of $50,000.

b. The sales budget for March indicates sales of $140,000. Accounts receivable are expected to be 70% of the current-month sales.

c. The merchandise purchases budget indicates that $89,000 in merchandise will be purchased on account in March. Purchases on account are paid 100% in the month following the purchase. Ending inventory for March is predicted to be 600 units at a cost of $35 each.

d. The budgeted income statement for March shows net income of $48,000. Depreciation expense of $1,000 and $26,000 in income tax expense were used in computing net income for March. Accrued taxes will be paid in April.

e. The balance sheet for February shows equipment of $84,000 with accumulated depreciation of $46,000, common stock of $25,000, and ending retained earnings of $8,000. There are no changes budgeted in the equipment or common stock accounts.

Prepare a budgeted balance sheet for March.

Exercise 20-18

Merchandising: Budgeted income statement

P2

Fortune, Inc., is preparing its master budget for the first quarter. The company sells a single product at a price of $25 per unit. Sales (in units) are forecasted at 45,000 for January, 55,000 for February, and 50,000 for March. Cost of goods sold is $14 per unit. Other expense information for the first quarter follows. Prepare a budgeted income statement for this first quarter.

Commissions	8% of sales
Rent	$14,000 per month
Advertising	15% of sales
Office salaries	$75,000 per month
Depreciation	$40,000 per month
Interest	15% annually on a $250,000 note payable
Tax rate.	30%

Exercise 20-19^A

Manufacturing: Direct labor budget

P3

The production budget for Manner Company shows units to be produced as follows: July, 620; August, 680; September, 540. Each unit produced requires two hours of direct labor. The direct labor rate is currently $20 per hour but is predicted to be $21 per hour in September. Prepare a direct labor budget for the months July, August, and September.

Exercise 20-20^A

Manufacturing: Production budget

P3

Hospitable Co. provides the following sales forecast for the next four months:

	April	May	June	July
Sales (units)	500	580	540	620

The company wants to end each month with ending finished goods inventory equal to 25% of next month's sales. Finished goods inventory on April 1 is 190 units. Assume July's budgeted production is 540 units. Prepare a production budget for the months of April, May, and June.

Exercise 20-21^A

Manufacturing: Direct materials budget   P3

Refer to the information in Exercise 20-20. In addition, assume each finished unit requires five pounds of raw materials and the company wants to end each month with raw materials inventory equal to 30% of next month's production needs. Beginning raw materials inventory for April was 663 pounds.

Prepare a direct materials budget for April, May, and June.

Match the definitions 1 through 9 with the term or phrase a through i.

A. Budget

B. Merchandise purchases budget

C. Cash budget

D. Safety stock

E. Budgeted income statement

F. General and administrative expense budget

G. Sales budget

H. Master budget

I. Budgeted balance sheet

_____ **1.** A comprehensive business plan that includes specific plans for expected sales, the units of product to be produced, the merchandise or materials to be purchased, the expenses to be incurred, the long-term assets to be purchased, and the amounts of cash to be borrowed or loans to be repaid, as well as a budgeted income statement and balance sheet.

_____ **2.** A quantity of inventory or materials over the minimum to reduce the risk of running short.

_____ **3.** A plan showing the units of goods to be sold and the sales to be derived; the usual starting point in the budgeting process.

_____ **4.** An accounting report that presents predicted amounts of the company's revenues and expenses for the budgeting period.

_____ **5.** An accounting report that presents predicted amounts of the company's assets, liabilities, and equity balances at the end of the budget period.

_____ **6.** A plan that shows the units or costs of merchandise to be purchased by a merchandising company during the budget period.

_____ **7.** A formal statement of a company's future plans, usually expressed in monetary terms.

_____ **8.** A plan that shows predicted operating expenses not included in the selling expenses budget.

_____ **9.** A plan that shows the expected cash inflows and cash outflows during the budget period, including receipts from any loans needed to maintain a minimum cash balance and repayments of such loans.

Exercise 20-22
Master budget definitions
C2

Participatory budgeting can sometimes lead to negative consequences. Identify three potential negative outcomes that can arise from participatory budgeting.

Exercise 20-23
Budget consequences   C1

Render Co. CPA is preparing activity-based budgets for 2013. The partners expect the firm to generate billable hours for the year as follows:

Data entry	2,200 hours
Auditing	4,800 hours
Tax	4,300 hours
Consulting	750 hours

The company pays $10 per hour to data-entry clerks, $40 per hour to audit personnel, $50 per hour to tax personnel, and $50 per hour to consulting personnel. Prepare a schedule of budgeted labor costs for 2013 using activity-based budgeting.

Exercise 20-24
Activity-based budgeting
A1

Rida, Inc., a manufacturer in a seasonal industry, is preparing its direct materials budget for the second quarter. It forecasts sales of 225,000 units in the second quarter and 262,500 units in the third quarter. It also plans production of 52,500 units for the third quarter. Based on this information, the company plans to produce 240,000 units in the second quarter. Other information is as follows:

Direct materials	Each unit requires 0.60 pounds of a key raw material, priced at $175 per pound. The company plans to end each quarter with an ending inventory of materials equal to 50% of next quarter's budgeted materials requirements.
Direct labor	Each finished unit requires 4 direct labor hours, at a cost of $9 per hour.
Variable overhead	Applied at the rate of $11 per direct labor hour.
Fixed overhead	Budgeted at $450,000 per quarter

Prepare a direct materials budget for the second quarter.

Exercise 20-25
Manufacturing: Direct materials budget
P3

Exercise 20-26
Manufacturing: Direct labor and factory overhead budgets
P3

Refer to Exercise 20-25. For the second quarter, prepare (1) a direct labor budget and (2) a factory overhead budget.

Exercise 20-27
Manufacturing: Direct materials budget ·
P3

Rad Co. provides the following sales forecast and production budget for the next four months:

	April	May	June	July
Sales (units)	500	580	530	600
Budgeted production (units)	442	570	544	540

The company plans for finished goods inventory of 120 units at the end of June. In addition, each finished unit requires five pounds of raw materials and the company wants to end each month with raw materials inventory equal to 30% of next month's production needs. Beginning raw materials inventory for April was 663 pounds. Each finished unit requires 0.50 hours of direct labor at the rate of $16 per hour. The company budgets variable overhead at the rate of $20 per direct labor hour and budgets fixed overhead of $8,000 per month. Prepare a raw materials budget for April, May, and June.

Exercise 20-28
Manufacturing: Direct labor and factory overhead budgets
P3

Refer to Exercise 20-27. For April, May, and June, prepare (1) a direct labor budget and (2) a factory overhead budget.

PROBLEM SET A

Problem 20-1A
Merchandising: Preparation and analysis of purchases budgets

C2 P1

mhhe.com/wildFINMAN5e

Keggler's Supply is a merchandiser of three different products. The company's February 28 inventories are footwear, 20,000 units; sports equipment, 80,000 units; and apparel, 50,000 units. Management believes that excessive inventories have accumulated for all three products. As a result, a new policy dictates that ending inventory in any month should equal 30% of the expected unit sales for the following month. Expected sales in units for March, April, May, and June follow.

	Budgeted Sales in Units			
	March	April	May	June
Footwear	15,000	25,000	32,000	35,000
Sports equipment	70,000	90,000	95,000	90,000
Apparel	40,000	38,000	37,000	25,000

Check (l) March budgeted purchases Footwear, 2,500; Sports equip., 17,000; Apparel, 1,400

Required

1. Prepare a merchandise purchases budget (in units) for each product for each of the months of March, April, and May.

Analysis Component

2. The purchases budgets in part 1 should reflect fewer purchases of all three products in March compared to those in April and May. What factor caused fewer purchases to be planned? Suggest business conditions that would cause this factor to both occur and impact the company in this way.

Problem 20-2A
Merchandising: Preparation of cash budgets (for three periods)

C2 P2

mhhe.com/wildFINMAN5e

During the last week of August, Oneida Company's owner approaches the bank for an $100,000 loan to be made on September 2 and repaid on November 30 with annual interest of 12%, for an interest cost of $3,000. The owner plans to increase the store's inventory by $80,000 during September and needs the loan to pay for inventory acquisitions. The bank's loan officer needs more information about Oneida's ability to repay the loan and asks the owner to forecast the store's November 30 cash position. On September 1, Oneida is expected to have a $5,000 cash balance, $148,000 of accounts receivable, and $125,000 of accounts payable. Its budgeted sales, merchandise purchases, and various cash disbursements for the next three months follow.

Budgeted Figures*	September	October	November
1			
2 Sales	$250,000	$375,000	$400,000
3 Merchandise purchases	240,000	225,000	200,000
4 Cash disbursements			
5 Payroll	20,000	22,000	24,000
6 Rent	10,000	10,000	10,000
7 Other cash expenses	35,000	30,000	20,000
8 Repayment of bank loan			100,000
9 Interest on the bank loan			3,000

* Operations began in August; August sales were $215,000 and purchases were $125,000.

The budgeted September merchandise purchases include the inventory increase. All sales are on account. The company predicts that 25% of credit sales is collected in the month of the sale, 45% in the month following the sale, 20% in the second month, 9% in the third, and the remainder is uncollectible. Applying these percents to the August credit sales, for example, shows that $96,750 of the $215,000 will be collected in September, $43,000 in October, and $19,350 in November. All merchandise is purchased on credit; 80% of the balance is paid in the month following a purchase, and the remaining 20% is paid in the second month. For example, of the $125,000 August purchases, $100,000 will be paid in September and $25,000 in October.

Required

Prepare a cash budget for September, October, and November for Oneida Company. Show supporting calculations as needed.

Check Budgeted cash balance: September, $99,250; October, $69,500; November, $22,600

Aztec Company sells its product for $180 per unit. Its actual and projected sales follow.

	Units	Dollars
April (actual)	4,000	$ 720,000
May (actual)	2,000	360,000
June (budgeted)	6,000	1,080,000
July (budgeted)	5,000	900,000
August (budgeted)	3,800	684,000

Problem 20-3A

Merchandising: Preparation and analysis of cash budgets with supporting inventory and purchases budgets

C2 P2

All sales are on credit. Recent experience shows that 20% of credit sales is collected in the month of the sale, 50% in the month after the sale, 28% in the second month after the sale, and 2% proves to be uncollectible. The product's purchase price is $110 per unit. All purchases are payable within 12 days. Thus, 60% of purchases made in a month is paid in that month and the other 40% is paid in the next month. The company has a policy to maintain an ending monthly inventory of 20% of the next month's unit sales plus a safety stock of 100 units. The April 30 and May 31 actual inventory levels are consistent with this policy. Selling and administrative expenses for the year are $1,320,000 and are paid evenly throughout the year in cash. The company's minimum cash balance at month-end is $100,000. This minimum is maintained, if necessary, by borrowing cash from the bank. If the balance exceeds $100,000, the company repays as much of the loan as it can without going below the minimum. This type of loan carries an annual 12% interest rate. On May 31, the loan balance is $25,000, and the company's cash balance is $100,000. (Round amounts to the nearest dollar.)

Required

1. Prepare a table that shows the computation of cash collections of its credit sales (accounts receivable) in each of the months of June and July.
2. Prepare a table that shows the computation of budgeted ending inventories (in units) for April, May, June, and July.
3. Prepare the merchandise purchases budget for May, June, and July. Report calculations in units and then show the dollar amount of purchases for each month.
4. Prepare a table showing the computation of cash payments on product purchases for June and July.
5. Prepare a cash budget for June and July, including any loan activity and interest expense. Compute the loan balance at the end of each month.

Check (1) Cash collections: June, $597,600; July, $820,800

(3) Budgeted purchases: May, $308,000; June, $638,000

(5) Budgeted ending loan balance: June, $43,650; July, $0

Analysis Component

6. Refer to your answer to part 5. Aztec's cash budget indicates the company will need to borrow more than $18,000 in June. Suggest some reasons that knowing this information in May would be helpful to management.

Problem 20-4A

Merchandising: Preparation and analysis of budgeted income statements

C2 P2

Merline, a one-product mail-order firm, buys its product for $75 per unit and sells it for $150 per unit. The sales staff receives a 10% commission on the sale of each unit. Its December income statement follows.

MERLINE COMPANY	
Income Statement	
For Month Ended December 31, 2013	
Sales	$2,250,000
Cost of goods sold	1,125,000
Gross profit	1,125,000
Expenses	
Sales commissions (10%)	225,000
Advertising	250,000
Store rent	30,000
Administrative salaries	45,000
Depreciation	50,000
Other expenses	10,000
Total expenses	610,000
Net income	$ 515,000

Management expects December's results to be repeated in January, February, and March of 2014 without any changes in strategy. Management, however, has an alternative plan. It believes that unit sales will increase at a rate of 10% *each* month for the next three months (beginning with January) if the item's selling price is reduced to $125 per unit and advertising expenses are increased by 15% and remain at that level for all three months. The cost of its product will remain at $75 per unit, the sales staff will continue to earn a 10% commission, and the remaining expenses will stay the same.

Required

Check (1) Budgeted net income: January, $196,250; February, $258,125; March, $326,187

1. Prepare budgeted income statements for each of the months of January, February, and March that show the expected results from implementing the proposed changes. Use a three-column format, with one column for each month.

Analysis Component

2. Use the budgeted income statements from part 1 to recommend whether management should implement the proposed changes. Explain.

Problem 20-5A

Merchandising: Preparation of a complete master budget

C2 P1 P2

Near the end of 2013, the management of Dimsdale Sports Co., a merchandising company, prepared the following estimated balance sheet for December 31, 2013.

DIMSDALE SPORTS COMPANY					
Estimated Balance Sheet					
December 31, 2013					
Assets			**Liabilities and Equity**		
Cash	$ 36,000		Accounts payable	$360,000	
Accounts receivable	525,000		Bank loan payable	15,000	
Inventory	150,000		Taxes payable (due 3/15/2014)	90,000	
Total current assets		$ 711,000	Total liabilities		$465,000
Equipment	540,000		Common stock	472,500	
Less accumulated depreciation	67,500		Retained earnings	246,000	
Equipment, net		472,500	Total stockholders' equity		718,500
Total assets		$1,183,500	Total liabilities and equity		$1,183,500

To prepare a master budget for January, February, and March of 2014, management gathers the following information.

a. Dimsdale Sports' single product is purchased for $30 per unit and resold for $55 per unit. The expected inventory level of 5,000 units on December 31, 2013, is more than management's desired level for 2014, which is 20% of the next month's expected sales (in units). Expected sales are: January, 7,000 units; February, 9,000 units; March, 11,000 units; and April, 10,000 units.

b. Cash sales and credit sales represent 25% and 75%, respectively, of total sales. Of the credit sales, 60% is collected in the first month after the month of sale and 40% in the second month after the month of sale. For the December 31, 2013, accounts receivable balance, $125,000 is collected in January and the remaining $400,000 is collected in February.

c. Merchandise purchases are paid for as follows: 20% in the first month after the month of purchase and 80% in the second month after the month of purchase. For the December 31, 2013, accounts payable balance, $80,000 is paid in January and the remaining $280,000 is paid in February.

d. Sales commissions equal to 20% of sales are paid each month. Sales salaries (excluding commissions) are $60,000 per year.

e. General and administrative salaries are $144,000 per year. Maintenance expense equals $2,000 per month and is paid in cash.

f. Equipment reported in the December 31, 2013, balance sheet was purchased in January 2013. It is being depreciated over eight years under the straight-line method with no salvage value. The following amounts for new equipment purchases are planned in the coming quarter: January, $36,000; February, $96,000; and March, $28,800. This equipment will be depreciated under the straight-line method over eight years with no salvage value. A full month's depreciation is taken for the month in which equipment is purchased.

g. The company plans to acquire land at the end of March at a cost of $150,000, which will be paid with cash on the last day of the month.

h. Dimsdale Sports has a working arrangement with its bank to obtain additional loans as needed. The interest rate is 12% per year, and interest is paid at each month-end based on the beginning balance. Partial or full payments on these loans can be made on the last day of the month. The company has agreed to maintain a minimum ending cash balance of $25,000 in each month.

i. The income tax rate for the company is 40%. Income taxes on the first quarter's income will not be paid until April 15.

Required

Prepare a master budget for each of the first three months of 2014; include the following component budgets (show supporting calculations as needed, and round amounts to the nearest dollar):

1. Monthly sales budgets (showing both budgeted unit sales and dollar sales).

2. Monthly merchandise purchases budgets.

3. Monthly selling expense budgets.

4. Monthly general and administrative expense budgets.

5. Monthly capital expenditures budgets.

6. Monthly cash budgets.

7. Budgeted income statement for the entire first quarter (not for each month).

8. Budgeted balance sheet as of March 31, 2014.

Check (2) Budgeted purchases:
January, $114,000; February, $282,000
(3) Budgeted selling
expenses: January, $82,000;
February, $104,000
(6) Ending cash bal.:
January, $30,100; February, $210,300
(8) Budgeted total assets at
March 31, $1,568,650

Black Diamond Company produces snow skis. Each ski requires 2 pounds of carbon fiber. The company's management predicts that 5,000 skis and 6,000 pounds of carbon fiber will be in inventory on June 30 of the current year and that 150,000 skis will be sold during the next (third) quarter. A set of two skis sells for $300. Management wants to end the third quarter with 3,500 skis and 4,000 pounds of carbon fiber in inventory. Carbon fiber can be purchased for $15 per pound. Each ski requires 0.5 hours of direct labor at $20 per hour. Variable overhead is applied at the rate of $8 per direct labor hour. The company budgets fixed overhead of $1,782,000 for the quarter.

Problem 20-6A[A]
Manufacturing: Preparing production and manufacturing budgets
C2 P3

Required

1. Prepare the third-quarter production budget for skis.

2. Prepare the third-quarter direct materials (carbon fiber) budget; include the dollar cost of purchases.

[continued on next page]

Check (1) Units manuf., 148,500;
(2) Cost of carbon fiber
purchases, $4,425,000

3. Prepare the direct labor budget for the third quarter.

4. Prepare the factory overhead budget for the third quarter.

Problem 20-7A
Manufacturing: Preparation of a complete master budget
C2 P1 P2 P3

The management of Zigby Manufacturing prepared the following estimated balance sheet for March, 2013:

ZIGBY MANUFACTURING Estimated Balance Sheet March 31, 2013			
Assets		**Liabilities and Equity**	
Cash	$ 40,000	Accounts payable	$ 200,500
Accounts receivable	342,248	Short-term notes payable	12,000
Raw materials inventory...........	98,500	Total current liabilities	212,500
Finished goods inventory	325,540	Long-term note payable	500,000
Total current assets.............	806,288	Total liabilities	712,500
Equipment, gross.................	600,000	Common stock	335,000
Accumulated depreciation	(150,000)	Retained earnings	208,788
Equipment, net	450,000	Total stockholders' equity	543,788
Total assets	$1,256,288	Total liabilities and equity	$1,256,288

To prepare a master budget for April, May, and June of 2013, management gathers the following information:

a. Sales for March total 20,500 units. Forecasted sales in units are as follows: April, 20,500; May, 19,500; June, 20,000; July, 20,500. Sales of 240,000 units are forecasted for the entire year. The product's selling price is $23.85 per unit and its total product cost is $19.85 per unit.

b. Company policy calls for a given month's ending raw materials inventory to equal 50% of the next month's materials requirements. The March 31 raw materials inventory is 4,925 units, which complies with the policy. The expected June 30 ending raw materials inventory is 4,000 units. Raw materials cost $20 per unit. Each finished unit requires 0.50 units of raw materials.

c. Company policy calls for a given month's ending finished goods inventory to equal 80% of the next month's expected unit sales. The March 31 finished goods inventory is 16,400 units, which complies with the policy.

d. Each finished unit requires 0.50 hours of direct labor at a rate of $15 per hour.

e. Overhead is allocated based on direct labor hours. The predetermined variable overhead rate is $2.70 per direct labor hour. Depreciation of $20,000 per month is treated as fixed factory overhead.

f. Sales representatives' commissions are 8% of sales and are paid in the month of the sales. The sales manager's monthly salary is $3,000 per month.

g. Monthly general and administrative expenses include $12,000 administrative salaries and 0.9% monthly interest on the long-term note payable.

h. The company expects 30% of sales to be for cash and the remaining 70% on credit. Receivables are collected in full in the month following the sale (none is collected in the month of the sale).

i. All raw materials purchases are on credit, and no payables arise from any other transactions. One month's raw materials purchases are fully paid in the next month.

j. The minimum ending cash balance for all months is $40,000. If necessary, the company borrows enough cash using a short-term note to reach the minimum. Short-term notes require an interest payment of 1% at each month-end (before any repayment). If the ending cash balance exceeds the minimum, the excess will be applied to repaying the short-term notes payable balance.

k. Dividends of $10,000 are to be declared and paid in May.

l. No cash payments for income taxes are to be made during the second calendar quarter. Income tax will be assessed at 35% in the quarter and paid in the third calendar quarter.

m. Equipment purchases of $130,000 are budgeted for the last day of June.

Required

Prepare the following budgets and other financial information as required. All budgets and other financial information should be prepared for the second calendar quarter, except as otherwise noted below. Round calculations up to the nearest whole dollar, except for the amount of cash sales, which should be rounded down to the nearest whole dollar.:

   1. Sales budget.
   2. Production budget.
   3. Raw materials budget.
   4. Direct labor budget.
   5. Factory overhead budget.
   6. Selling expense budget.
   7. General and administrative expense budget.
   8. Cash budget.
   9. Budgeted income statement for the entire first quarter (not for each month separately).
   10. Budgeted statement of retained earnings.
   11. Budgeted balance sheet as of the end of the second calendar quarter.

Check   (2) Units to produce: April, 19,700; May, 19,900

(3) Cost of raw materials purchases, April, $198,000

(5) Total overhead cost, May, $46,865

(8) Ending cash balance: April, $83,346; May, $124,295

(10) Budgeted total assets, June 30: $1,299,440

H20 Sports Company is a merchandiser of three different products. The company's March 31 inventories are water skis, 40,000 units; tow ropes, 90,000 units; and life jackets, 150,000 units. Management believes that excessive inventories have accumulated for all three products. As a result, a new policy dictates that ending inventory in any month should equal 10% of the expected unit sales for the following month. Expected sales in units for April, May, June, and July follow.

PROBLEM SET B

Problem 20-1B
Merchandising: Preparation and analysis of purchases budgets

C2 P1

	Budgeted Sales in Units			
	April	**May**	**June**	**July**
Water skis	70,000	90,000	130,000	100,000
Tow ropes	100,000	90,000	110,000	100,000
Life jackets	160,000	190,000	200,000	120,000

Required

   1. Prepare a merchandise purchases budget (in units) for each product for each of the months of April, May, and June.

Check   (1) April budgeted purchases: Water skis, 39,000; Tow ropes, 19,000; Life jackets, 29,000

Analysis Component

   2. The purchases budgets in part 1 should reflect fewer purchases of all three products in April compared to those in May and June. What factor caused fewer purchases to be planned? Suggest business conditions that would cause this factor to both occur and affect the company as it has.

During the last week of March, Sony Stereo's owner approaches the bank for a $80,000 loan to be made on April 1 and repaid on June 30 with annual interest of 12%, for an interest cost of $2,400. The owner plans to increase the store's inventory by $60,000 in April and needs the loan to pay for inventory acquisitions. The bank's loan officer needs more information about Sony Stereo's ability to repay the loan and asks the owner to forecast the store's June 30 cash position. On April 1, Sony Stereo is expected to have a $3,000 cash balance, $135,000 of accounts receivable, and $100,000 of accounts

Problem 20-2B
Merchandising: Preparation of cash budgets (for three periods)

C2 P2

payable. Its budgeted sales, merchandise purchases, and various cash disbursements for the next three months follow.

	File Edit View Insert Format Tools Data Window Help			
	Budgeted Figures*	**April**	**May**	**June**
1				
2	Sales	$220,000	$300,000	$380,000
3	Merchandise purchases	210,000	180,000	220,000
4	Cash disbursements			
5	Payroll	16,000	17,000	18,000
6	Rent	6,000	6,000	6,000
7	Other cash expenses	64,000	8,000	7,000
8	Repayment of bank loan			80,000
9	Interest on the bank loan.........			2,400
10				

*Operations began in March; March sales were $180,000 and purchases were $100,000.

The budgeted April merchandise purchases include the inventory increase. All sales are on account. The company predicts that 25% of credit sales is collected in the month of the sale, 45% in the month following the sale, 20% in the second month, 9% in the third, and the remainder is uncollectible. Applying these percents to the March credit sales, for example, shows that $81,000 of the $180,000 will be collected in April, $36,000 in May, and $16,200 in June. All merchandise is purchased on credit; 80% of the balance is paid in the month following a purchase and the remaining 20% is paid in the second month. For example, of the $100,000 March purchases, $80,000 will be paid in April and $20,000 in May.

Check Budgeted cash balance: April, $53,000; May, $44,000; June, $34,800

Required

Prepare a cash budget for April, May, and June for Sony Stereo. Show supporting calculations as needed.

Problem 20-3B
Merchandising: Preparation and analysis of cash budgets with supporting inventory and purchases budgets

C2 P2

Connick Company sells its product for $22 per unit. Its actual and projected sales follow.

	Units	Dollars
January (actual)	18,000	$396,000
February (actual)	22,500	495,000
March (budgeted)	19,000	418,000
April (budgeted)	18,750	412,500
May (budgeted)	21,000	462,000

All sales are on credit. Recent experience shows that 40% of credit sales is collected in the month of the sale, 35% in the month after the sale, 23% in the second month after the sale, and 2% proves to be uncollectible. The product's purchase price is $12 per unit. All purchases are payable within 21 days. Thus, 30% of purchases made in a month is paid in that month and the other 70% is paid in the next month. The company has a policy to maintain an ending monthly inventory of 20% of the next month's unit sales plus a safety stock of 100 units. The January 31 and February 28 actual inventory levels are consistent with this policy. Selling and administrative expenses for the year are $1,920,000 and are paid evenly throughout the year in cash. The company's minimum cash balance for month-end is $50,000. This minimum is maintained, if necessary, by borrowing cash from the bank. If the balance exceeds $50,000, the company repays as much of the loan as it can without going below the minimum. This type of loan carries an annual 12% interest rate. At February 28, the loan balance is $12,000, and the company's cash balance is $50,000.

Required

Check (1) Cash collections: March, $431,530; April, $425,150

1. Prepare a table that shows the computation of cash collections of its credit sales (accounts receivable) in each of the months of March and April.
2. Prepare a table showing the computations of budgeted ending inventories (units) for January, February, March, and April.

Check (3) Budgeted purchases: February, $261,600; March, $227,400

3. Prepare the merchandise purchases budget for February, March, and April. Report calculations in units and then show the dollar amount of purchases for each month.
4. Prepare a table showing the computation of cash payments on product purchases for March and April.

Check (5) Ending cash balance: March, $58,070, April, $94,920

5. Prepare a cash budget for March and April, including any loan activity and interest expense. Compute the loan balance at the end of each month.

6. Refer to your answer to part 5. Connick's cash budget indicates whether the company must borrow additional funds at the end of March. Suggest some reasons that knowing the loan needs in advance would be helpful to management.

Comp-Media buys its product for $60 and sells it for $130 per unit. The sales staff receives a 10% commission on the sale of each unit. Its June income statement follows.

Problem 20-4B

Merchandising: Preparation and analysis of budgeted income statements

C2 P2

COMP-MEDIA COMPANY Income Statement For Month Ended June 30, 2013	
Sales	$1,300,000
Cost of goods sold	600,000
Gross profit	700,000
Expenses	
Sales commissions (10%)	130,000
Advertising	200,000
Store rent	24,000
Administrative salaries	40,000
Depreciation	50,000
Other expenses	12,000
Total expenses	456,000
Net income	$ 244,000

Management expects June's results to be repeated in July, August, and September without any changes in strategy. Management, however, has another plan. It believes that unit sales will increase at a rate of 10% *each* month for the next three months (beginning with July) if the item's selling price is reduced to $115 per unit and advertising expenses are increased by 25% and remain at that level for all three months. The cost of its product will remain at $60 per unit, the sales staff will continue to earn a 10% commission, and the remaining expenses will stay the same.

Required

1. Prepare budgeted income statements for each of the months of July, August, and September that show the expected results from implementing the proposed changes. Use a three-column format, with one column for each month.

Check Budgeted net income: July, $102,500; August, $150,350; September, $202,985

Analysis Component

2. Use the budgeted income statements from part 1 to recommend whether management should implement the proposed plan. Explain.

Near the end of 2013, the management of Isle Corp., a merchandising company, prepared the following estimated balance sheet for December 31, 2013.

Problem 20-5B

Merchandising: Preparation of a complete master budget

C2 P1 P2

ISLE CORPORATION Estimated Balance Sheet December 31, 2013				
Assets		**Liabilities and Equity**		
Cash	$ 36,000	Accounts payable	$360,000	
Accounts receivable	525,000	Bank loan payable	15,000	
Inventory	150,000	Taxes payable (due 3/15/2014) . . .	90,000	
Total current assets		$ 711,000	Total liabilities		$ 465,000
Equipment	540,000	Common stock	472,500	
Less accumulated depreciation . . .	67,500	Retained earnings	246,000	
Equipment, net		472,500	Total stockholders' equity		718,500
Total assets		$1,183,500	Total liabilities and equity		$1,183,500

888   Chapter 20   Master Budgets and Performance Planning

To prepare a master budget for January, February, and March of 2014, management gathers the following information.

a. Isle Corp.'s single product is purchased for $30 per unit and resold for $45 per unit. The expected inventory level of 5,000 units on December 31, 2013, is more than management's desired level for 2014, which is 25% of the next month's expected sales (in units). Expected sales are: January, 6,000 units; February, 8,000 units; March, 10,000 units; and April, 9,000 units.

b. Cash sales and credit sales represent 25% and 75%, respectively, of total sales. Of the credit sales, 60% is collected in the first month after the month of sale and 40% in the second month after the month of sale. For the $525,000 accounts receivable balance at December 31, 2013, $315,000 is collected in January 2014 and the remaining $210,000 is collected in February 2014.

c. Merchandise purchases are paid for as follows: 20% in the first month after the month of purchase and 80% in the second month after the month of purchase. For the $360,000 accounts payable balance at December 31, 2013, $72,000 is paid in January 2014 and the remaining $288,000 is paid in February 2014.

d. Sales commissions equal to 20% of sales are paid each month. Sales salaries (excluding commissions) are $90,000 per year.

e. General and administrative salaries are $144,000 per year. Maintenance expense equals $3,000 per month and is paid in cash.

f. Equipment reported in the December 31, 2013, balance sheet was purchased in January 2013. It is being depreciated over 8 years under the straight-line method with no salvage value. The following amounts for new equipment purchases are planned in the coming quarter: January, $72,000; February, $96,000; and March, $28,800. This equipment will be depreciated using the straight-line method over 8 years with no salvage value. A full month's depreciation is taken for the month in which equipment is purchased.

g. The company plans to acquire land at the end of March at a cost of $150,000, which will be paid with cash on the last day of the month.

h. Isle Corp. has a working arrangement with its bank to obtain additional loans as needed. The interest rate is 12% per year, and interest is paid at each month-end based on the beginning balance. Partial or full payments on these loans can be made on the last day of the month. Isle has agreed to maintain a minimum ending cash balance of $36,000 in each month.

i. The income tax rate for the company is 40%. Income taxes on the first quarter's income will not be paid until April 15.

Required

Prepare a master budget for each of the first three months of 2014; include the following component budgets (show supporting calculations as needed, and round amounts to the nearest dollar):

Check (2) Budgeted purchases: January, $90,000; February, $255,000;
(3) Budgeted selling expenses: January, $61,500; February, $79,500

(6) Ending cash bal.: January, $182,500; February, $107,850

(8) Budgeted total assets at March 31, $1,346,875

1. Monthly sales budgets (showing both budgeted unit sales and dollar sales).
2. Monthly merchandise purchases budgets.
3. Monthly selling expense budgets.
4. Monthly general and administrative expense budgets.
5. Monthly capital expenditures budgets.
6. Monthly cash budgets.
7. Budgeted income statement for the entire first quarter (not for each month).
8. Budgeted balance sheet as of March 31, 2014.

Problem 20-6B[A]
Manufacturing: Preparing production and manufacturing budgets

C2 P3

NSA Company produces baseball bats. Each bat requires 3 pounds of aluminum alloy. Management predicts that 8,000 bats and 15,000 pounds of aluminum alloy will be in inventory on March 31 of the current year and that 250,000 bats will be sold during this year's second quarter. Bats sell for $80 each. Management wants to end the second quarter with 6,000 finished bats and 12,000 pounds of aluminum alloy in inventory. Aluminum alloy can be purchased for $4 per pound. Each bat requires 0.5 hours of direct labor at $18 per hour. Variable overhead is applied at the rate of $12 per direct labor hour. The company budgets fixed overhead of $1,776,000 for the quarter.

Required

1. Prepare the second-quarter production budget for bats.

2. Prepare the second-quarter direct materials (aluminum alloy) budget; include the dollar cost of purchases.

3. Prepare the direct labor budget for the second quarter.

4. Prepare the factory overhead budget for the second quarter.

Check (1) Units manuf., 248,000;
(2) Cost of materials
purchases, $2,964,000

The management of Nabar Manufacturing prepared the following estimated balance sheet for June, 2013:

Problem 20-7B
Manufacturing: Preparation
of a complete master budget

C2 P1 P2 P3

NABAR MANUFACTURING				
Estimated Balance Sheet				
June 30, 2013				
Assets			**Liabilities and Equity**	
Cash	$ 40,000		Accounts payable	$ 51,400
Accounts receivable	249,900		Income taxes payable.............	10,000
Raw materials inventory...........	35,000		Short-term notes payable	24,000
Finished goods inventory	241,080		Total current liabilities	85,400
Total current assets.............	565,980		Long-term note payable	300,000
Equipment, gross.................	720,000		Total liabilities	385,400
Accumulated depreciation	(240,000)		Common stock	600,000
Equipment, net	480,000		Retained earnings	60,580
			Total stockholders' equity	660,580
Total assets	$1,045,980		Total liabilities and equity	$1,045,980

To prepare a master budget for July, August, and September of 2013, management gathers the following information:

a. Sales were 20,000 units in June. Forecasted sales in units are as follows: July, 21,000; August, 19,000; September, 20,000; October, 24,000. The product's selling price is $17 per unit and its total product cost is $14.35 per unit.

b. Company policy calls for a given month's ending finished goods inventory to equal 70% of the next month's expected unit sales. The June 30 finished goods inventory is 16,800 units, which does not comply with the policy.

c. Company policy calls for a given month's ending raw materials inventory to equal 20% of the next month's materials requirements. The June 30 raw materials inventory is 4,375 units (which also fails to meet the policy). The budgeted September 30 raw materials inventory is 1,980 units. Raw materials cost $8 per unit. Each finished unit requires 0.50 units of raw materials.

d. Each finished unit requires 0.50 hours of direct labor at a rate of $16 per hour.

e. Overhead is allocated based on direct labor hours. The predetermined variable overhead rate is $1.35 per direct labor hour. Depreciation of $20,000 per month is treated as fixed factory overhead.

f. Monthly general and administrative expenses include $9,000 administrative salaries and 0.9% monthly interest on the long-term note payable.

g. Sales representatives' commissions are 10% of sales and are paid in the month of the sales. The sales manager's monthly salary is $3,500 per month.

h. The company expects 30% of sales to be for cash and the remaining 70% on credit. Receivables are collected in full in the month following the sale (none is collected in the month of the sale).

i. All raw materials purchases are on credit, and no payables arise from any other transactions. One month's raw materials purchases are fully paid in the next month.

j. Dividends of $20,000 are to be declared and paid in August.

890   Chapter 20   Master Budgets and Performance Planning

k. Income taxes payable at June 30 will be paid in July. Income tax expense will be assessed at 35% in the quarter and paid in October.

l. Equipment purchases of $100,000 are budgeted for the last day of September.

m. The minimum ending cash balance for all months is $40,000. If necessary, the company borrows enough cash using a short-term note to reach the minimum. Short-term notes require an interest payment of 1% at each month-end (before any repayment). If the ending cash balance exceeds the minimum, the excess will be applied to repaying the short-term notes payable balance.

Required

Prepare the following budgets and other financial information as required. All budgets and other financial information should be prepared for the second calendar quarter, except as otherwise noted below. Round calculations to the nearest whole dollar:

Check (2) Units to produce: July, 17,500; August, 19,700

(3) Cost of raw materials purchases, July, $50,760

(5) Total overhead cost, August, $46,595

(8) Ending cash balance: July, $96,835; August, $141,180

(10) Budgeted total assets, Sept. 30: $1,054,920

1. Sales budget.
2. Production budget.
3. Raw materials budget.
4. Direct labor budget.
5. Factory overhead budget.
6. Selling expense budget.
7. General and administrative expense budget.
8. Cash budget.
9. Budgeted income statement for the entire quarter (not for each month separately).
10. Budgeted statement of retained earnings for the quarter.
11. Budgeted balance sheet as of September 30, 2013.

SERIAL PROBLEM
Success Systems

P2

(This serial problem began in Chapter 1 and continues through most of the book. If previous chapter segments were not completed, the serial problem can begin at this point. It is helpful, but not necessary, to use the Working Papers that accompany the book.)

SP 20   Adria Lopez expects second quarter 2014 sales of her new line of computer furniture to be the same as the first quarter's sales (reported below) without any changes in strategy. Monthly sales averaged 40 desk units (sales price of $1,250) and 20 chairs (sales price of $500).

SUCCESS SYSTEMS	
Segment Income Statement*	
For Quarter Ended March 31, 2014	
Sales[†]	$180,000
Cost of goods sold[‡]	115,000
Gross profit	65,000
Expenses	
Sales commissions (10%)	18,000
Advertising expenses	9,000
Other fixed expenses	18,000
Total expenses	45,000
Net income	$ 20,000

* Reflects revenue and expense activity only related to the computer furniture segment.

[†] Revenue: (120 desks × $1,250) + (60 chairs × $500) = $150,000 + $30,000 = $180,000

[‡] Cost of goods sold: (120 desks × $750) + (60 chairs × $250) + $10,000 = $115,000

Adria Lopez believes that sales will increase each month for the next three months (April, 48 desks, 32 chairs; May, 52 desks, 35 chairs; June, 56 desks, 38 chairs) *if* selling prices are reduced to $1,150 for desks and $450 for chairs, and advertising expenses are increased by 10% and remain at that level for all three months. The products' variable cost will remain at $750 for desks and $250 for chairs. The sales staff will continue to earn a 10% commission, the fixed manufacturing costs per month will remain at $10,000 and other fixed expenses will remain at $6,000 per month.

Required

1. Prepare budgeted income statements for each of the months of April, May, and June that show the expected results from implementing the proposed changes. Use a three-column format, with one column for each month.

2. Use the budgeted income statements from part 1 to recommend whether Adria Lopez should implement the proposed changes. Explain.

Check   (1) Budgeted income (loss): April, $(660); May, $945

Beyond the Numbers

BTN 20-1   Financial statements often serve as a starting point in formulating budgets. Review Polaris' financial statements to determine its cash paid for acquisitions of property and equipment in the current year and the budgeted cash needed for such acquisitions in the next year.

REPORTING IN ACTION

P2

Polaris

Required

1. Which financial statement reports the amount of cash paid for acquisitions of property and equipment? Explain where on the statement this information is reported.

2. Indicate the amount of cash (a) paid for acquisitions of property and equipment in the year ended December 31, 2011, and (b) to be paid (budgeted for) next year under the assumption that annual acquisitions of property and equipment equal 40% of the prior year's net income.

Fast Forward

3. Access Polaris' financial statements for a year ending after December 31, 2011, from either its Website [Polaris.com] or the SEC's EDGAR database [www.sec.gov]. Compare your answer for part 2 with actual cash paid for acquisitions of property and equipment for that fiscal year. Compute the error, if any, in your estimate. Speculate as to why cash paid for acquisitions of property and equipment was higher or lower than your estimate.

BTN 20-2   One source of cash savings for a company is improved management of inventory. To illustrate, assume that Polaris and Arctic Cat both have $1,000,000 per month in sales of one model of snowmobiles in Canada, and both forecast this level of sales per month for the next 24 months. Also assume that both Polaris and Arctic Cat have a 20% contribution margin, their fixed costs are equal, and that cost of goods sold is the only variable cost. Assume that the main difference between Polaris and Arctic Cat is the distribution system. Polaris uses a just-in-time system and requires ending inventory of only 10% of next month's sales in inventory at each month-end. However, Arctic Cat is building an improved distribution system and currently requires 30% of next month's sales in inventory at each month-end.

COMPARATIVE ANALYSIS

P2

Polaris
Arctic Cat

Required

1. Compute the amount by which Arctic Cat can reduce its inventory level if it can match Polaris' system of maintaining an inventory equal to 10% of next month's sales. (*Hint:* Focus on the facts given and only on the Canadian market.)

2. Explain how the analysis in part 1 that shows ending inventory levels for both the 30% and 10% required inventory policies can help justify a just-in-time inventory system. Assume a 15% interest cost for resources that are tied up in ending inventory.

892   Chapter 20   Master Budgets and Performance Planning

**ETHICS
CHALLENGE**

C1

BTN 20-3   Both the budget process and budgets themselves can impact management actions, both positively and negatively. For instance, a common practice among not-for-profit organizations and government agencies is for management to spend any amounts remaining in a budget at the end of the budget period, a practice often called "use it or lose it." The view is that if a department manager does not spend the budgeted amount, top management will reduce next year's budget by the amount not spent. To avoid losing budget dollars, department managers often spend all budgeted amounts regardless of the value added to products or services. All of us pay for the costs associated with this budget system.

Required

Write a one-half page report to a local not-for-profit organization or government agency offering a solution to the "use it or lose it" budgeting problem.

**COMMUNICATING
IN PRACTICE**

C2

BTN 20-4   The sales budget is usually the first and most crucial of the component budgets in a master budget because all other budgets usually rely on it for planning purposes.

Required

Assume that your company's sales staff provides information on expected sales and selling prices for items making up the sales budget. Prepare a one-page memorandum to your supervisor outlining concerns with the sales staff's input in the sales budget when its compensation is at least partly tied to these budgets. More generally, explain the importance of assessing any potential bias in information provided to the budget process.

**TAKING IT TO
THE NET**

C1

BTN 20-5   Access information on e-budgets through The Manage Mentor:
http://www.themanagementor.com/kuniverse/kmailers_universe/finance_kmailers/cfa/budgeting2.htm
Read the information provided.

Required

1. Assume the role of a senior manager in a large, multidivision company. What are the benefits of using e-budgets?
2. As a senior manager, what concerns do you have with the concept and application of e-budgets?

**TEAMWORK IN
ACTION**

A1

BTN 20-6   Your team is to prepare a budget report outlining the costs of attending college (full-time) for the next two semesters (30 hours) or three quarters (45 hours). This budget's focus is solely on attending college; do not include personal items in the team's budget. Your budget must include tuition, books, supplies, club fees, food, housing, and all costs associated with travel to and from college. This budgeting exercise is similar to the initial phase in activity-based budgeting. Include a list of any assumptions you use in completing the budget. Be prepared to present your budget in class.

**ENTREPRENEURIAL
DECISION**

C1

BTN 20-7   Freshii sells fresh foods with a focus on healthy fare. Company founder Matthew Corrin stresses the importance of planning and budgeting for business success.

Required

1. How can budgeting help Matthew Corrin efficiently develop and operate his business?
2. Why would sales forecasts and purchases budgets be particularly important for a business like Freshii?

BTN 20-8 To help understand the factors impacting a sales budget, you are to visit three businesses with the same ownership or franchise membership. Record the selling prices of two identical products at each location, such as regular and premium gas sold at Chevron stations. You are likely to find a difference in prices for at least one of the three locations you visit.

HITTING THE ROAD

C2 P1

Required

1. Identify at least three external factors that must be considered when setting the sales budget. (*Note:* There is a difference between internal and external factors that impact the sales budget.)
2. What factors might explain any differences identified in the prices of the businesses you visited?

BTN 20-9 Access KTM's income statement (in Appendix A) for the business year 2011.

GLOBAL DECISION

P1

KTM

Required

1. Is KTM's infrastructure and administration expense budget likely to be an important budget in its master budgeting process? Explain.
2. Identify three types of expenses that would be reported as infrastructure and administration expenses on KTM's income statement.
3. Who likely has the initial responsibility for KTM's infrastructure and administration expense budget? Explain.

ANSWERS TO MULTIPLE CHOICE QUIZ

1. c
2. e; Budgeted purchases = $36,000 + $7,000 − $6,000 = $37,000
3. b; Cash collected = 25% of September sales + 75% of August sales = $(0.25 \times \$240,000) + (0.75 \times \$220,000) = \$225,000$

4. d
5. a; 560 units + (0.30 × 600 units) − (0.30 × 560 units) = 572 units

Flexible Budgets and Standard Costs

Learning Objectives

Decision Insight

Whoosh!

"Skiing is not just a sport, it's a life-long choice."
—MIKE McCABE

BOULDER, CO—Self-described "ski bum" Jordan Grano wanted a pair of skis that could handle more than one ski season. Frustrated by the quality and performance of "off-the-rack" skis, Jordan began researching how to build better skis. The result is **Folsom Custom Skis (folsomskis.com)**, the company he founded in 2007. In addition to building custom skis to precise customer specifications, the company also builds "semi-custom" skis which allow customers fewer choices.

Master Builder and current company President Mike McCabe says customers can "take their favorite skis and alter them to suit their needs and wants. We come up with a finished ski built exactly to customer specifications." The company's manufacturing process demands precision. "Design elements like ski turn radius, camber, and taper interact in complex ways and require careful measurement," says Mike. The result is a better-quality and more durable ski as Mike, a professional skier, can attest to. "I was hired to break a set of skis. I failed."

Manufacturers like Folsom Custom Skis must control materials, labor, and overhead costs. Determining standard costs helps. For example, Mike estimates it takes 12 hours to go from design to a complete ski. "We make them as fast as we can but we don't cut corners; we make sure we put an equal amount of time into every one of our skis," explains Mike. Putting too much time into a ski could waste the company's productive capacity,

but putting too little time into a ski could result in an inferior product. Attention to variances from standards can keep the manufacturing process on track.

The company uses only the highest quality poplar and bamboo in their skis. Here too, Mike analyzes materials price and quantity variances to control costs. Mike stresses the importance of "having precise specifications and controls to detect problems; we don't use any material that does not meet our requirements." Unfavorable materials price variances could result from rising raw materials prices, which could cause the company to consider alternative suppliers or raising prices.

At an average price of about $1,300 per pair, the company reports revenue of about $300,000 per year. While currently operating at about a break-even level, Mike hopes to double the company's output and ultimately make profits. The use of flexible budgets, reflecting cost estimates at different production levels, can be useful in making business decisions. While attention to budgeting, standards, and variances is important, Mike encourages entrepreneurs to "build a business on something you feel passionate about."

[Sources: *Folsom Custom Skis website*, January 2013; *Boulder County Business Report*, November 13, 2009; *Skiing mag* (www.skinet.com), July 2009.]

Chapter Preview

Budgeting helps organize and formalize management's planning activities. This chapter extends the study of budgeting to look more closely at the use of budgets to evaluate performance. Evaluations are important for controlling and monitoring business activities. This chapter also describes and illustrates the use of standard costs and variance analyses. These managerial tools are useful for both evaluating and controlling organizations and for the planning of future activities.

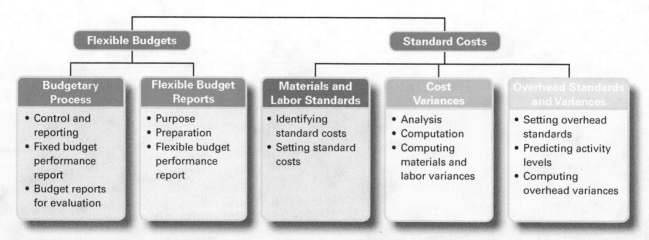

Flexible Budgets

Standard Costs

Budgetary Process	Flexible Budget Reports	Materials and Labor Standards	Cost Variances	Overhead Standards and Variances
• Control and reporting • Fixed budget performance report • Budget reports for evaluation	• Purpose • Preparation • Flexible budget performance report	• Identifying standard costs • Setting standard costs	• Analysis • Computation • Computing materials and labor variances	• Setting overhead standards • Predicting activity levels • Computing overhead variances

Section 1—Flexible Budgets

This section introduces fixed budgets and fixed budget performance reports. It then introduces flexible budgets and flexible budget performance reports and illustrates their advantages.

BUDGETARY PROCESS

A master budget reflects management's planned objectives for a future period. The preparation of a master budget is based on a predicted level of activity such as sales volume for the budget period. This section discusses the effects on the usefulness of budget reports when the actual level of activity differs from the predicted level.

Budgetary Control and Reporting

Budgetary control refers to management's use of budgets to monitor and control a company's operations. This includes using budgets to see that planned objectives are met. **Budget reports** contain relevant information that compares actual results to planned activities. This comparison is motivated by a need to both monitor performance and control activities. Budget reports are sometimes viewed as progress reports, or *report cards,* on management's performance in achieving planned objectives. These reports can be prepared at any time and for any period. Three common periods for a budget report are a month, quarter, and year.

Point: Budget reports are often used to determine bonuses of managers.

The budgetary control process involves at least four steps: (1) develop the budget from planned objectives, (2) compare actual results to budgeted amounts and analyze any differences, (3) take corrective and strategic actions, and (4) establish new planned objectives and prepare a new budget. Exhibit 21.1 shows this continual process of budgetary control. Budget reports and

EXHIBIT 21.1

Process of Budgetary Control

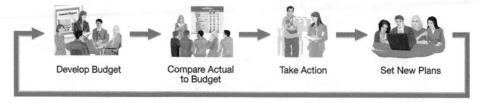

Develop Budget → Compare Actual to Budget → Take Action → Set New Plans

related documents are effective tools for managers to obtain the greatest benefits from this budgetary process.

Fixed Budget Performance Report

In a fixed budgetary control system, the master budget is based on a single prediction for sales volume or other activity level. The budgeted amount for each cost essentially assumes that a specific (or *fixed*) amount of sales will occur. A **fixed budget,** also called a *static budget,* is based on a single predicted amount of sales or other measure of activity.

One benefit of a budget is its usefulness in comparing actual results with planned activities. Information useful for analysis is often presented for comparison in a performance report. As shown in Exhibit 21.2, a **fixed budget performance report** for **Optel** compares actual results for January 2013 with the results expected under its fixed budget that predicted 10,000 (composite) units of sales. Optel manufactures inexpensive eyeglasses, frames, contact lens, and related supplies. For this report, its production volume equals sales volume (its inventory level did not change).

OPTEL Fixed Budget Performance Report For Month Ended January 31, 2013	Fixed Budget	Actual Results	Variances*
Sales (in units)	10,000	12,000	
Sales (in dollars)	$100,000	$125,000	$25,000 F
Cost of goods sold			
Direct materials	10,000	13,000	3,000 U
Direct labor	15,000	20,000	5,000 U
Overhead			
Factory supplies	2,000	2,100	100 U
Utilities	3,000	4,000	1,000 U
Depreciation—machinery	8,000	8,000	0
Supervisory salaries	11,000	11,000	0
Selling expenses			
Sales commissions	9,000	10,800	1,800 U
Shipping expenses	4,000	4,300	300 U
General and administrative expenses			
Office supplies	5,000	5,200	200 U
Insurance expenses	1,000	1,200	200 U
Depreciation—office equipment	7,000	7,000	0
Administrative salaries	13,000	13,000	0
Total expenses	88,000	99,600	11,600 U
Income from operations	$ 12,000	$ 25,400	$13,400 F

EXHIBIT 21.2

Fixed Budget Performance Report

* F = Favorable variance; U = Unfavorable variance.

This type of performance report designates differences between budgeted and actual results as variances. We see the letters *F* and *U* located beside the numbers in the third number column of this report. Their meanings are as follows:

F = **Favorable variance**   When compared to budget, the actual cost or revenue contributes to a *higher* income. That is, actual revenue is higher than budgeted revenue, or actual cost is lower than budgeted cost.

U = **Unfavorable variance**   When compared to budget, the actual cost or revenue contributes to a *lower* income; actual revenue is lower than budgeted revenue, or actual cost is higher than budgeted cost.

This convention is common in practice and is used throughout this chapter.

Example: How is it that the favorable sales variance in Exhibit 21.2 is linked with so many unfavorable cost and expense variances? *Answer:* Costs have increased with the increase in sales.

Budget Reports for Evaluation

A primary use of budget reports is as a tool for management to monitor and control operations. Evaluation by Optel management is likely to focus on a variety of questions that might include these:

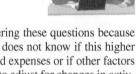

- Why is actual income from operations $13,400 higher than budgeted?
- Are amounts paid for each expense item too high?
- Is manufacturing using too much direct material?
- Is manufacturing using too much direct labor?

The performance report in Exhibit 21.2 provides little help in answering these questions because actual sales volume is 2,000 units higher than budgeted. A manager does not know if this higher level of sales activity is the cause of variations in total dollar sales and expenses or if other factors have influenced these amounts. This inability of fixed budget reports to adjust for changes in activity levels is a major limitation of a fixed budget performance report. That is, it fails to show whether actual costs are out of line due to a change in actual sales volume or some other factor.

 Decision Insight ════════════════════════════

Cruise Control Budget reporting and evaluation are used at service providers such as **Royal Carribbean Cruises Ltd.** It regularly prepares performance plans and budget requests for its fleet of cruise ships, which describe performance goals, measure outcomes, and analyze variances. ■

FLEXIBLE BUDGET REPORTS

Purpose of Flexible Budgets

To help address limitations with the fixed budget performance report, particularly from the effects of changes in sales volume, management can use a flexible budget. A **flexible budget,** also called a *variable budget,* is a report based on predicted amounts of revenues and expenses corresponding to the actual level of output. Flexible budgets are useful both before and after the period's activities are complete.

A flexible budget prepared before the period is often based on several levels of activity. Budgets for those different levels can provide a "what-if" look at operations. The different levels often include both a best case and worst case scenario. This allows management to make adjustments to avoid or lessen the effects of the worst case scenario.

A flexible budget prepared after the period helps management evaluate past performance. It is especially useful for such an evaluation because it reflects budgeted revenues and costs based on the actual level of activity. Thus, comparisons of actual results with budgeted performance are more likely to identify the causes of any differences. This can help managers focus attention on real problem areas and implement corrective actions. This is in contrast to a fixed budget, whose primary purpose is to assist managers in planning future activities and whose numbers are based on a single predicted amount of budgeted sales or production.

Point: A flexible budget yields an "apples to apples" comparison because budgeted activity levels are the same as the actual.

Preparation of Flexible Budgets

P1 Prepare a flexible budget and interpret a flexible budget performance report.

A flexible budget is designed to reveal the effects of volume of activity on revenues and costs. To prepare a flexible budget, management relies on the distinctions between fixed and variable costs. Recall that the cost per unit of activity remains constant for variable costs so that the total amount of a variable cost changes in direct proportion to a change in activity level. The total amount of fixed cost remains unchanged regardless of changes in the level of activity within a relevant (normal) operating range. (Assume that costs can be reasonably classified as variable or fixed within a relevant range.)

When we create the numbers constituting a flexible budget, we express each variable cost as either a constant amount per unit of sales or as a percent of a sales dollar. In the case of a fixed cost, we express its budgeted amount as the total amount expected to occur at any sales volume within the relevant range.

Exhibit 21.3 shows a set of flexible budgets for Optel for January 2013. Seven of its expenses are classified as variable costs. Its remaining five expenses are fixed costs. These classifications result from management's investigation of each expense. Variable and fixed expense categories are *not* the same for every company, and we must avoid drawing conclusions from specific cases. For example, depending on the nature of a company's operations, office supplies expense can be either fixed or variable with respect to sales.

Point: The usefulness of a flexible budget depends on valid classification of variable and fixed costs. Some costs are mixed and must be analyzed to determine their variable and fixed portions.

OPTEL Flexible Budgets For Month Ended January 31, 2013	Flexible Budget		Flexible Budget for Unit Sales of		
	Variable Amount per Unit	Total Fixed Cost	10,000	12,000	14,000
Sales	$10.00		$100,000	$120,000	$140,000
Variable costs					
Direct materials.......................	1.00		10,000	12,000	14,000
Direct labor...........................	1.50		15,000	18,000	21,000
Factory supplies.......................	0.20		2,000	2,400	2,800
Utilities	0.30		3,000	3,600	4,200
Sales commissions	0.90		9,000	10,800	12,600
Shipping expenses	0.40		4,000	4,800	5,600
Office supplies	0.50		5,000	6,000	7,000
Total variable costs	4.80		48,000	57,600	67,200
Contribution margin	$ 5.20		$ 52,000	$ 62,400	$ 72,800
Fixed costs					
Depreciation—machinery		$ 8,000	8,000	8,000	8,000
Supervisory salaries...................		11,000	11,000	11,000	11,000
Insurance expense....................		1,000	1,000	1,000	1,000
Depreciation—office equipment		7,000	7,000	7,000	7,000
Administrative salaries.................		13,000	13,000	13,000	13,000
Total fixed costs		$40,000	40,000	40,000	40,000
Income from operations			$ 12,000	$ 22,400	$ 32,800

EXHIBIT 21.3

Flexible Budgets

The layout for the flexible budgets in Exhibit 21.3 follows a *contribution margin format*—beginning with sales followed by variable costs and then fixed costs. Both the expected individual and total variable costs are reported and then subtracted from sales. The difference between sales and variable costs equals contribution margin. The expected amounts of fixed costs are listed next, followed by the expected income from operations before taxes.

The first and second number columns of Exhibit 21.3 show the flexible budget amounts for variable costs per unit and each fixed cost for any volume of sales in the relevant range. The third, fourth, and fifth columns show the flexible budget amounts computed for three different sales volumes. For instance, the third column's flexible budget is based on 10,000 units. These numbers are the same as those in the fixed budget of Exhibit 21.2 because the expected volumes are the same for these two budgets.

Recall that Optel's actual sales volume for January is 12,000 units. This sales volume is 2,000 units more than the 10,000 units originally predicted in the master budget. When differences between actual and predicted volume arise, the usefulness of a flexible budget is apparent. For instance, compare the flexible budget for 10,000 units in the third column (which is the same as the fixed budget in Exhibit 21.2) with the flexible budget for 12,000 units in the fourth

Example: Using Exhibit 21.3, what is the budgeted income from operations for unit sales of (a) 11,000 and (b) 13,000? *Answers:* $17,200 for unit sales of 11,000; $27,600 for unit sales of 13,000.

Point: Flexible budgeting allows a budget to be prepared at the *actual* output level. Performance reports are then prepared comparing the flexible budget to actual revenues and costs.

column. The higher levels for both sales and variable costs reflect nothing more than the increase in sales activity. Any budget analysis comparing actual with planned results that ignores this information is less useful to management.

To illustrate, when we evaluate Optel's performance, we need to prepare a flexible budget showing actual and budgeted values at 12,000 units. As part of a complete profitability analysis, managers could compare the actual income of $25,400 (from Exhibit 21.2) with the $22,400 income expected at the actual sales volume of 12,000 units (from Exhibit 21.3). This results in a total favorable income variance of $3,000 to be explained and interpreted. This variance is markedly lower from the $13,400 favorable variance identified in Exhibit 21.2 using a fixed budget, but still suggests good performance. After receiving the flexible budget based on January's actual volume, management must determine what caused this $3,000 difference. The next section describes a flexible budget performance report that provides guidance in this analysis.

Decision Maker

Entrepreneur The heads of both the strategic consulting and tax consulting divisions of your financial services firm complain to you about the unfavorable variances on their performance reports. "We worked on more consulting assignments than planned. It's not surprising our costs are higher than expected. To top it off, this report characterizes our work as *poor!*" How do you respond? ■ [Answer—p. 920]

Flexible Budget Performance Report

A **flexible budget performance report** lists differences between actual performance and budgeted performance based on actual sales volume or other activity level. This report helps direct management's attention to those costs or revenues that differ substantially from budgeted amounts. Exhibit 21.4 shows Optel's flexible budget performance report for January. We prepare this report after the actual volume is known to be 12,000 units. This report shows a $5,000 favorable variance in total dollar sales. Because actual and budgeted volumes are both 12,000 units, the $5,000 sales variance must have resulted from a higher than expected selling price.

EXHIBIT 21.4

Flexible Budget
Performance Report

OPTEL Flexible Budget Performance Report For Month Ended January 31, 2013	Flexible Budget	Actual Results	Variances*
Sales (12,000 units)......................	$120,000	$125,000	$5,000 F
Variable costs			
Direct materials	12,000	13,000	1,000 U
Direct labor	18,000	20,000	2,000 U
Factory supplies	2,400	2,100	300 F
Utilities	3,600	4,000	400 U
Sales commissions	10,800	10,800	0
Shipping expenses	4,800	4,300	500 F
Office supplies	6,000	5,200	800 F
Total variable costs	57,600	59,400	1,800 U
Contribution margin	62,400	65,600	3,200 F
Fixed costs			
Depreciation—machinery	8,000	8,000	0
Supervisory salaries	11,000	11,000	0
Insurance expense	1,000	1,200	200 U
Depreciation—office equipment	7,000	7,000	0
Administrative salaries	13,000	13,000	0
Total fixed costs	40,000	40,200	200 U
Income from operations	$ 22,400	$ 25,400	$3,000 F

* F = Favorable variance; U = Unfavorable variance.

Further analysis of the facts surrounding this $5,000 sales variance reveals a favorable sales variance per unit of nearly $0.42 as shown here:

Actual average price per unit (rounded to cents)	$125,000/12,000 = $10.42
Budgeted price per unit	$120,000/12,000 = 10.00
Favorable sales variance per unit	$5,000/12,000 = $ 0.42

The other variances in Exhibit 21.4 also direct management's attention to areas where corrective actions can help control Optel's operations. Each expense variance is analyzed as the sales variance was. We can think of each expense as the joint result of using a given number of units of input and paying a specific price per unit of input. Optel's expense variances total $2,000 unfavorable, suggesting poor control of some costs, particularly direct materials and direct labor.

Each variance in Exhibit 21.4 is due in part to a difference between *actual price* per unit of input and *budgeted price* per unit of input. This is a **price variance.** Each variance also can be due in part to a difference between *actual quantity* of input used and *budgeted quantity* of input. This is a **quantity variance.** We explain more about this breakdown, known as **variance analysis,** next in the standard costs section of this chapter.

Quick Check
Answers — p. 921

1. A flexible budget (*a*) shows fixed costs as constant amounts of cost per unit of activity, (*b*) shows variable costs as constant amounts of cost per unit of activity, or (*c*) is prepared based on one expected amount of budgeted sales or production.
2. What is the initial step in preparing a flexible budget?
3. What is the main difference between a fixed and a flexible budget?
4. What is the contribution margin?

Section 2—Standard Costs

Standard costs are preset costs for delivering a product or service under normal conditions. These costs are established by personnel, engineering, and accounting studies using past experiences and data. Management uses these costs to assess the reasonableness of actual costs incurred for producing the product or providing the service. When actual costs vary from standard costs, management follows up to identify potential problems and take corrective actions. **Management by exception** means that managers focus attention on the most significant differences between actual costs and standard costs and give less attention to areas where performance is reasonably close to standard. Management by exception is especially useful when directed at controllable items, enabling top management to affect the actions of lower-level managers responsible for the company's revenues and costs.

Standard costs are often used in preparing budgets because they are the anticipated costs incurred under normal conditions. Terms such as *standard materials cost, standard labor cost,* and *standard overhead cost* are often used to refer to amounts budgeted for direct materials, direct labor, and overhead.

While many managers use standard costs to investigate manufacturing costs, standard costs can also help control *nonmanufacturing* costs. Companies providing services instead of products can also benefit from the use of standard costs. For example, while quality medical service is paramount, efficiency in providing that service is also important to medical professionals. The use of budgeting and standard costing is touted as an effective means to control and monitor medical costs, especially overhead.

 C1 Define *standard costs* and explain how standard cost information is useful for management by exception.

Point: Business practice often uses the word *budget* when speaking of total amounts and *standard* when discussing per unit amounts.

◼ Decision Ethics

Internal Auditor   You discover a manager who always spends exactly what is budgeted. About 30% of her budget is spent just before the period-end. She admits to spending what is budgeted, whether or not it is needed. She offers three reasons: (1) she doesn't want her budget cut, (2) "management by exception" focuses on budget deviations; and (3) she believes the money is budgeted to be spent. What action do you take? ◼   [Answer—p. 920]

MATERIALS AND LABOR STANDARDS

This section explains how to set materials and labor standards and how to prepare a standard cost card.

Identifying Standard Costs

Managerial accountants, engineers, personnel administrators, and other managers combine their efforts to set standard costs. To identify standards for direct labor costs, we can conduct time and motion studies for each labor operation in the process of providing a product or service. From these studies, management can learn the best way to perform the operation and then set the standard labor time required for the operation under normal conditions. Similarly, standards for materials are set by studying the quantity, grade, and cost of each material used. Standards for overhead costs are explained later in the chapter.

Example: What factors might be considered when deciding whether to revise standard costs? *Answer:* Changes in the processes and/or resources needed to carry out the processes.

Regardless of the care used in setting standard costs and in revising them as conditions change, actual costs frequently differ from standard costs, often as a result of one or more factors. For instance, the actual quantity of material used can differ from the standard, or the price paid per unit of material can differ from the standard. Quantity and price differences from standard amounts can also occur for labor. That is, the actual labor time and actual labor rate can vary from what was expected. The same analysis applies to overhead costs.

◼ Decision Insight

Cruis'n Standards   The **Corvette** consists of hundreds of parts for which engineers set standards. Various types of labor are also involved in its production, including machining, assembly, painting, and welding, and standards are set for each. Actual results are periodically compared with standards to assess performance. ◼

Setting Standard Costs

To illustrate the setting of a standard cost, we consider a professional league baseball bat manufactured by **ProBat.** Its engineers have determined that manufacturing one bat requires 0.90 kg. of high-grade wood. They also expect some loss of material as part of the process because of inefficiencies and waste. This results in adding an *allowance* of 0.10 kg., making the standard requirement 1.0 kg. of wood for each bat.

The 0.90 kg. portion is called an *ideal standard;* it is the quantity of material required if the process is 100% efficient without any loss or waste. Reality suggests that some loss of material usually occurs with any process. The standard of 1.0 kg. is known as the *practical standard,* the quantity of material required under normal application of the process.

Point: Companies promoting continuous improvement strive to achieve ideal standards by eliminating inefficiencies and waste.

High-grade wood can be purchased at a standard price of $25 per kg. The purchasing department sets this price as the expected price for the budget period. To determine this price, the purchasing department considers factors such as the quality of materials, future economic conditions, supply factors (shortages and excesses), and any available discounts. The engineers also decide that two hours of labor time (after including allowances) are required to manufacture a bat. The wage rate is $20 per hour (better than average skilled labor is required). ProBat assigns all overhead at the rate of $10 per labor hour. The standard costs of direct materials, direct labor, and overhead for one bat are shown in Exhibit 21.5 in what is called a *standard cost card.* These cost amounts are then used to prepare manufacturing budgets for a budgeted level of production.

STANDARD COST CARD		
Production factor	**Cost factor**	**Total**
Direct materials (wood)	1 kg. @ $25 per kg.	$25
Direct labor	2 hours @ $20 per hour	40
Overhead	2 labor hours @ $10 per hour	20
	Total	**$85**

REMARKS:

Based on standard costs of direct materials, direct labor, and overhead for a single ProBat

SUMMARY:

Materials	$25
Labor	40
Overhead	20
Total cost	$85

COST VARIANCES

A **cost variance,** also simply called a *variance,* is the difference between actual and standard costs. A cost variance can be favorable or unfavorable. A variance from standard cost is considered favorable if actual cost is less than standard cost. It is considered unfavorable if actual cost is more than standard cost.[1] This section discusses variance analysis.

C2 Describe variances and what they reveal about performance.

Cost Variance Analysis

Variances are usually identified in performance reports. When a variance occurs, management wants to determine the factors causing it. This often involves analysis, evaluation, and explanation. The results of these efforts should enable management to assign responsibility for the variance and then to take actions to correct the situation.

To illustrate, ProBat's standard materials cost for producing 500 bats is $12,500. Assume that its actual materials cost for those 500 bats is $13,000. The $500 unfavorable variance raises questions that call for answers that, in turn, can lead to changes to correct the situation and eliminate this variance in the next period. A performance report often identifies the existence of a problem, but we must follow up with further investigation to see what can be done to improve future performance.

Exhibit 21.6 shows the flow of events in the effective management of variance analysis. It shows four steps: (1) preparing a standard cost performance report, (2) computing and analyzing variances, (3) identifying questions and their explanations, and (4) taking corrective and strategic actions. These variance analysis steps are interrelated and are frequently applied in good organizations.

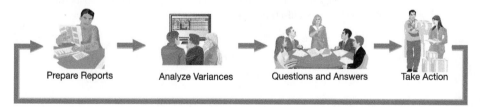

Prepare Reports   Analyze Variances   Questions and Answers   Take Action

EXHIBIT 21.6

Variance Analysis

Cost Variance Computation

Management needs information about the factors causing a cost variance, but first it must properly compute the variance. In its most simple form, a cost variance (CV) is computed as the difference between actual cost (AC) and standard cost (SC) as shown in Exhibit 21.7.

---

[1] Short-term favorable variances can sometimes lead to long-term unfavorable variances. For instance, if management spends less than the budgeted amount on maintenance or insurance, the performance report would show a favorable variance. Cutting these expenses can lead to major losses in the long run if machinery wears out prematurely or insurance coverage proves inadequate.

EXHIBIT 21.7

Cost Variance Formulas

Cost Variance (CV) = Actual Cost (AC) − Standard Cost (SC)

where:

Actual Cost (AC) = Actual Quantity (AQ) × Actual Price (AP)

Standard Cost (SC) = Standard Quantity (SQ) × Standard Price (SP)

A cost variance is further defined by its components. Actual quantity (AQ) is the input (material or labor) used to manufacture the quantity of output. Standard quantity (SQ) is the expected input for the quantity of output. Actual price (AP) is the amount paid to acquire the input (material or labor), and standard price (SP) is the expected price.

Point: Price and quantity variances for direct labor are nearly always referred to as *rate* and *efficiency variances,* respectively.

Two main factors cause a cost variance: (1) the difference between actual price and standard price results in a *price* (or rate) *variance* and (2) the difference between actual quantity and standard quantity results in a *quantity* (or usage or efficiency) *variance*. To assess the impacts of these two factors in a cost variance, we use the formulas in Exhibit 21.8.

EXHIBIT 21.8

Price Variance and Quantity Variance Formulas

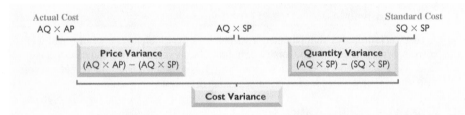

In computing a price variance, the quantity (actual) is held constant. In computing a quantity variance, the price (standard) is held constant. The cost variance, or total variance, is the sum of the price and quantity variances. These formulas identify the sources of the cost variance. Managers sometimes find it useful to apply an alternative (but equivalent) computation for the price and quantity variances as shown in Exhibit 21.9.

EXHIBIT 21.9

Alternative Price Variance and Quantity Variance Formulas

Price Variance (PV) = [Actual Price (AP) − Standard Price (SP)] × Actual Quantity (AQ)

Quantity Variance (QV) = [Actual Quantity (AQ) − Standard Quantity (SQ)] × Standard Price (SP)

The results from applying the formulas in Exhibits 21.8 and 21.9 are identical.

Computing Materials and Labor Variances

P2 Compute materials and labor variances.

We illustrate the computation of the materials and labor cost variances using data from **G-Max,** a company that makes specialty golf equipment and accessories for individual customers. This company has set the following standard quantities and costs for materials and labor per unit for one of its hand-crafted golf clubheads:

Direct materials (0.5 lb. per unit at $20 per lb.)	$10.00
Direct labor (1 hr. per unit at $8 per hr.)	8.00
Total standard direct cost per unit	$18.00

Materials Cost Variances   During May 2013, G-Max budgeted to produce 4,000 clubheads (units). It actually produced only 3,500 units. It used 1,800 pounds of direct materials (titanium) costing $21.00 per pound, meaning its total materials cost was $37,800. This information allows us to compute both actual and standard direct materials costs for G-Max's 3,500 units and its direct materials cost variance as follows:

Actual cost	1,800 lbs. @ $21.00 per lb.	= $37,800
Standard cost	1,750 lbs. @ $20.00 per lb.	= 35,000
Direct materials cost variance (unfavorable)		= $ 2,800

To better isolate the causes of this $2,800 unfavorable total direct materials cost variance, the materials price and quantity variances for these G-Max clubheads are computed and shown in Exhibit 21.10.

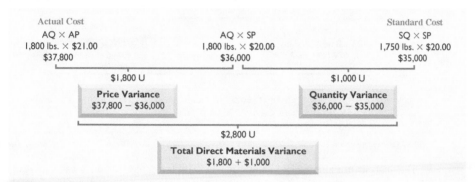

EXHIBIT 21.10

Materials Price and Quantity Variances*

*AQ is actual quantity; AP is actual price; SP is standard price; SQ is standard quantity allowed for actual output.

The $1,800 unfavorable price variance results from paying $1 more per unit than the standard price, computed as 1,800 lbs. × $1. The $1,000 unfavorable quantity variance is due to using 50 lbs. more materials than the standard quantity, computed as 50 lbs. × $20. The total direct materials variance is $2,800 and it is unfavorable. This information allows management to ask the responsible individuals for explanations and corrective actions.

Example: Identify at least two factors that might have caused the unfavorable quantity variance and the unfavorable price variance in Exhibit 21.10. *Answer:* Poor quality materials or untrained workers for the former; poor price negotiation or higher-quality materials for the latter.

The purchasing department is usually responsible for the price paid for materials. Responsibility for explaining the price variance in this case rests with the purchasing manager if a price higher than standard caused the variance. The production department is usually responsible for the amount of material used and in this case is responsible for explaining why the process used more than the standard amount of materials.

Variance analysis presents challenges. For instance, the production department could have used more than the standard amount of material because its quality did not meet specifications and led to excessive waste. In this case, the purchasing manager is responsible for explaining why inferior materials were acquired. However, the production manager is responsible for explaining what happened if analysis shows that waste was due to inefficiencies, not poor quality material.

In evaluating price variances, managers must recognize that a favorable price variance can indicate a problem with poor product quality. Redhook Ale, a micro brewery in the Pacific Northwest, can probably save 10% to 15% in material prices by buying six-row barley malt instead of the better two-row from Washington's Yakima valley. Attention to quality, however, has helped Redhook Ale increase its sales. Redhook's purchasing activities are judged on both the quality of the materials and the purchase price variance.

Labor Cost Variances   Labor cost for a specific product or service depends on the number of hours worked (quantity) and the wage rate paid to employees (price). When actual amounts for a task differ from standard, the labor cost variance can be divided into a rate (price) variance and an efficiency (quantity) variance.

To illustrate, G-Max's direct labor standard for 3,500 units of its hand-crafted clubheads is one hour per unit, or 3,500 hours at $8 per hour. Since only 3,400 hours at $8.30 per hour were actually used to complete the units, the actual and standard labor costs are

Actual cost	3,400 hrs. @ $8.30 per hr.	= $28,220
Standard cost	3,500 hrs. @ $8.00 per hr.	= 28,000
Direct labor cost variance (unfavorable)		= $ 220

This analysis shows that actual cost is merely $220 over the standard and suggests no immediate concern. Computing both the labor rate and efficiency variances reveals a different picture, however, as shown in Exhibit 21.11.

EXHIBIT 21.11

Labor Rate and
Efficiency Variances*

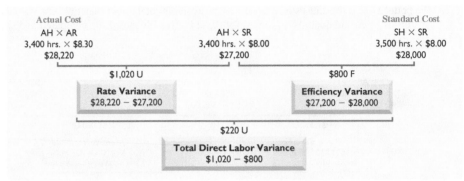

* AH is actual direct labor hours: AR is actual wage rate; SH is standard direct labor hours allowed for actual output; SR is standard wage rate.

Example: Compute the rate variance and the efficiency variance for Exhibit 21.11 if 3,700 actual hours are used at an actual price of $7.50 per hour. *Answer:* $1,850 favorable labor rate variance and $1,600 unfavorable labor efficiency variance.

The analysis in Exhibit 21.11 shows that an $800 favorable efficiency variance results from using 100 fewer direct labor hours than standard for the units produced, but this favorable variance is more than offset by a wage rate that is $0.30 per hour higher than standard. The personnel administrator or the production manager needs to explain why the wage rate is higher than expected. The production manager should also explain how the labor hours were reduced. If this experience can be repeated and transferred to other departments, more savings are possible.

One possible explanation of these labor rate and efficiency variances is the use of workers with different skill levels. If this is the reason, senior management must discuss the implications with the production manager who has the responsibility to assign workers to tasks with the appropriate skill level. In this case, an investigation might show that higher-skilled workers were used to produce 3,500 units of hand-crafted clubheads. As a result, fewer labor hours might be required for the work, but the wage rate paid these workers is higher than standard because of their greater skills. The effect of this strategy is a higher than standard total cost, which would require actions to remedy the situation or adjust the standard.

■ Decision Maker

Production Manager You receive the manufacturing variance report for June and discover a large unfavorable labor efficiency (quantity) variance. What factors do you investigate to identify its possible causes? ■ [Answer—p. 920]

Quick Check   Answers — p. 921

5. A standard cost (a) changes in direct proportion to changes in the level of activity, (b) is an amount incurred at the actual level of production for the period, or (c) is an amount incurred under normal conditions to provide a product or service.

6. What is a cost variance?

7. The following information is available for York Company.

Actual direct labor hours per unit	2.5 hours
Standard direct labor hours per unit	2.0 hours
Actual production (units)	2,500 units
Budgeted production (units)	3,000 units
Actual rate per hour	$3.10
Standard rate per hour	$3.00

The labor efficiency variance is (a) $3,750 U, (b) $3,750 F, or (c) $3,875 U.

8. Refer to Quick Check 7; the labor rate variance is (a) $625 F or (b) $625 U.

9. If a materials quantity variance is favorable and a materials price variance is unfavorable, can the total materials cost variance be favorable?

OVERHEAD STANDARDS AND VARIANCES

When standard costs are used, a predetermined overhead rate is used to assign standard overhead costs to products or services produced. This predetermined rate is often based on some overhead allocation base (such as standard labor cost, standard labor hours, or standard machine hours).

Setting Overhead Standards

Standard overhead costs are the amounts expected to occur at a certain activity level. Unlike direct materials and direct labor, overhead includes fixed costs and variable costs. This results in the average overhead cost per unit changing as the predicted volume changes. Since standard costs are also budgeted costs, they must be established before the reporting period begins. Standard overhead costs are therefore average per unit costs based on the predicted activity level.

To establish the standard overhead cost rate, management uses the same cost structure it used to construct a flexible budget at the end of a period. This cost structure identifies the different overhead cost components and classifies them as variable or fixed. To get the standard overhead rate, management selects a level of activity (volume) and predicts total overhead cost. It then divides this total by the allocation base to get the standard rate. Standard direct labor hours expected to be used to produce the predicted volume is a common allocation base and is used in this section.

Point: With increased automation, machine hours are frequently used in applying overhead instead of labor hours.

To illustrate, Exhibit 21.12 shows the overhead cost structure used to develop G-Max's flexible overhead budgets for May 2013. The predetermined standard overhead rate for May is set before the month begins. The first two number columns list the per unit amounts of variable costs and the monthly amounts of fixed costs. The four right-most columns show the costs expected to occur at four different levels of production activity. The predetermined overhead rate per labor hour is smaller as volume of activity increases because total fixed costs remain constant.

EXHIBIT 21.12

Flexible Overhead Budgets

G-MAX Flexible Overhead Budgets For Month Ended May 31, 2013 Flexible Budget	Variable Amount per Unit	Total Fixed Cost	Flexible Budget at Capacity Level of			
			70%	80%	90%	100%
Production (in units)	1 unit		3,500	4,000	4,500	5,000
Factory overhead						
Variable costs						
Indirect labor	$0.40/unit		$1,400	$1,600	$1,800	$2,000
Indirect materials	0.30/unit		1,050	1,200	1,350	1,500
Power and lights	0.20/unit		700	800	900	1,000
Maintenance	0.10/unit		350	400	450	500
Total variable overhead costs	$1.00/unit		3,500	4,000	4,500	5,000
Fixed costs (per month)						
Building rent		$1,000	1,000	1,000	1,000	1,000
Depreciation—machinery		1,200	1,200	1,200	1,200	1,200
Supervisory salaries		1,800	1,800	1,800	1,800	1,800
Total fixed overhead costs		$4,000	4,000	4,000	4,000	4,000
Total factory overhead			$7,500	$8,000	$8,500	$9,000
Standard direct labor hours 1 hr./unit . .			3,500 hrs.	4,000 hrs.	4,500 hrs.	5,000 hrs.
Predetermined overhead rate per standard direct labor hour			$ 2.14	$ 2.00	$ 1.89	$ 1.80

Predicting Activity Levels

When choosing the predicted activity level, management considers many factors. The level can be set as high as 100% of capacity, but this is rare. Factors causing the activity level to be less than full capacity include difficulties in scheduling work, equipment under repair or maintenance, and insufficient product demand. Good long-run management practices often call for some plant capacity in excess of current operating needs to allow for special opportunities and demand changes.

G-Max managers predicted an 80% activity level for May, or a production volume of 4,000 clubheads. At this volume, they budget $8,000 as the May total overhead. This choice implies a $2 per unit (labor hour) average overhead cost ($8,000/4,000 units). Since G-Max has a standard of one direct labor hour per unit, the predetermined standard overhead rate for May is $2 per standard direct labor hour. The variable overhead rate remains constant at $1 per direct labor hour regardless of the budgeted production level. The fixed overhead rate changes according to the budgeted production volume. For instance, for the predicted level of 4,000 units of production, the fixed rate is $1 per hour ($4,000 fixed costs/4,000 units). For a production level of 5,000 units, however, the fixed rate is $0.80 per hour ($4,000 fixed costs/5,000 units).

Point: Variable costs per unit remain constant, but fixed costs per unit decline with increases in volume. This means the average total overhead cost per unit declines with increases in volume.

 Decision Insight ━━━━━━━━━━━━━━━━━━━━━━━━━━━━━━━━━━

Measuring Up   In the spirit of continuous improvement, competitors compare their processes and performance standards against benchmarks established by industry leaders. Those that use **benchmarking** include Jiffy Lube, All Tune and Lube, and Speedee Oil Change and Tune-Up. ■

P3 Compute overhead variances.

Computing Overhead Cost Variances

When standard costs are used, the cost accounting system applies overhead to the good units produced using the predetermined standard overhead rate. At period-end, the difference between the total overhead cost applied to products and the total overhead cost actually incurred is called an **overhead cost variance** (total overhead variance), which is defined in Exhibit 21.13.

EXHIBIT 21.13

Overhead Cost Variance

> **Overhead cost variance (OCV) = Actual overhead incurred (AOI) − Standard overhead applied (SOA)**

The standard overhead applied is based on the predetermined overhead rate (at the predicted activity level) and the standard number of hours that should have been used, based on the actual production. To illustrate, G-Max produced 3,500 units during the month, which should have used 3,500 direct labor hours. From Exhibit 21.12, G-Max's predetermined overhead rate at the predicted capacity level of 4,000 units was $2.00 per direct labor hour, so the standard overhead applied is $7,000 (computed as 3,500 direct labor hours × $2.00). Additional data from cost reports show that the actual overhead cost incurred in the month is $7,650. G-Max's total overhead variance is thus $650, computed as:

Actual total overhead (given)	$7,650
Standard overhead applied (3,500 DLH × $2.00)	7,000
Total overhead variance (unfavorable).	$ 650

This variance is unfavorable, as G-Max's actual overhead was higher than it should have been based on budgeted amounts.

Controllable and Volume Variances   To help identify factors causing the overhead cost variance, managers analyze this variance separately for controllable and volume variances, as illustrated in Exhibit 21.14. The results provide information useful for taking strategic actions to improve company performance.

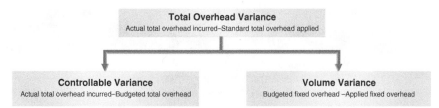

EXHIBIT 21.14

Framework for Understanding Total Overhead Variance

The **controllable variance** is the difference between actual overhead costs incurred and the budgeted overhead costs based on a flexible budget. The controllable variance is so named because it refers to activities usually under management control. A **volume variance** occurs when there is a difference between the actual volume of production and the standard volume of production. The volume variance is based solely on *fixed* overhead. The budgeted fixed overhead amount is the same regardless of the volume of production (within the relevant range). The applied fixed overhead is based, however, on the standard direct labor hours allowed for the actual volume of production, using the flexible budget. When a company operates at a capacity level different from what it expected, the volume variance will differ from zero. We next compute the controllable and volume variances for G-Max.

Returning to the G-Max data, the flexible budget in Exhibit 21.12 shows budgeted factory overhead of $7,500 at the production volume of 3,500 units during the month. The controllable variance is then computed as:

Controllable Variance	
Actual total overhead (given)	$7,650
Applied total overhead (from flexible budget)	7,500
Controllable variance (unfavorable)	$ 150

We then compute the volume variance. G-Max's budgeted fixed overhead at the predicted capacity level for the month was $4,000. Recall from Exhibit 21.12 that G-Max's predetermined fixed overhead at the predicted capacity level of 4,000 units was $1 per hour. Thus, G-Max's applied fixed overhead was $3,500, computed as 3,500 direct labor hours $\times$ $1.00 per unit. G-Max's volume variance is then computed as:

Volume Variance	
Budgeted fixed overhead (at predicted capacity)	$4,000
Applied fixed overhead (3,500 DLH $\times$ $1.00)	3,500
Volume variance (unfavorable)	$ 500

Analyzing Controllable and Volume Variances   How should the top management of G-Max interpret the unfavorable controllable and volume variances? An unfavorable volume variance means that the company did not reach its predicted operating level. In this case, 80% of manufacturing capacity was budgeted but only 70% was used. Management needs to know why the actual level of production differs from the expected level. The main purpose of the volume variance is to identify what portion of the total overhead variance is caused by failing to meet the expected production level. Often the reasons for failing to meet this expected production level are due to factors, for example customer demand, that are beyond employees' control. This information permits management to focus on explanations for the controllable variance, as we discuss next.

Overhead Variance Reports   To help management isolate the reasons for the $150 unfavorable controllable variance, an *overhead variance report* can be prepared. A complete overhead variance report provides managers information about specific overhead costs and how they differ from budgeted amounts. Exhibit 21.15 shows G-Max's overhead variance report for May. It reveals that (1) fixed costs and maintenance costs were incurred as expected, (2) costs for indirect labor and power and lights were higher than expected, and (3) indirect materials cost was less than expected.

910   Chapter 21   Flexible Budgets and Standard Costs

EXHIBIT 21.15

Overhead Variance Report

G-MAX			
Overhead Variance Report			
For Month Ended May 31, 2013			
Volume Variance			
Expected production level	80% of capacity		
Production level achieved	70% of capacity		
Volume variance	$500 (unfavorable)		
Controllable Variance	**Flexible Budget**	**Actual Results**	**Variances***
Variable overhead costs			
Indirect labor	$1,400	$1,525	$125 U
Indirect materials	1,050	1,025	25 F
Power and lights	700	750	50 U
Maintenance	350	350	0
Total variable overhead costs	3,500	3,650	150 U
Fixed overhead costs			
Building rent	1,000	1,000	0
Depreciation—machinery	1,200	1,200	0
Supervisory salaries	1,800	1,800	0
Total fixed overhead costs	4,000	4,000	0
Total overhead costs	$7,500	$7,650	$150 U

* F = Favorable variance; U = Unfavorable variance.

The total controllable variance amount ($150 unfavorable) is also readily available from Exhibit 21.15. The overhead variance report shows the total volume variance as $500 unfavorable (shown at the top) and the $150 unfavorable controllable variance (reported at the bottom right). The sum of the controllable variance and the volume variance equals the total overhead variance of $650 unfavorable.

Appendix 21A describes an expanded analysis of overhead variances.

Quick Check   Answers — p. 921

10. Under what conditions is an overhead volume variance considered favorable?

11. To use management by exception, a company (a) need not study fixed overhead variances, (b) should compute variances from flexible budget amounts to allow management to focus its attention on significant differences between actual and budgeted results, or (c) should analyze only variances for direct materials and direct labor.

GLOBAL VIEW

BMW, a German automobile manufacturer, uses concepts of standard costing and variance analysis. Production begins with huge rolls of steel and aluminum, which are then cut and pressed by large machines. Material must meet high quality standards, and the company sets standards for each of its machine operations. In the Assembly department, highly-trained employees complete the assembly of the painted car chassis, often to customer specifications. Again, BMW sets standards for how much labor should be used and monitors its employee performance. The company then computes and analyzes materials price and quantity variances and labor rate and efficiency variances and takes action as needed.

Sales Variances ⬜⬜⬜ **Decision Analysis**

This chapter explained the computation and analysis of cost variances. A similar variance analysis can be applied to sales. To illustrate, consider the following sales data from G-Max for two of its golf products, Excel golf balls and Big Bert® drivers.

A1 Analyze changes in sales from expected amounts.

	Budgeted	Actual
Sales of Excel golf balls (units)	1,000 units	1,100 units
Sales price per Excel golf ball	$10	$10.50
Sales of Big Bert® drivers (units)	150 units	140 units
Sales price per Big Bert® driver	$200	$190

Using this information, we compute both the *sales price variance* and the *sales volume variance* as shown in Exhibit 21.16. The total sales price variance is $850 unfavorable, and the total sales volume variance is $1,000 unfavorable. Neither total variance implies anything positive about these two products. However, further analysis of these total sales variances reveals that both the sales price and sales volume variances for Excel golf balls are favorable, meaning that both the unfavorable total sales price variance and the unfavorable total sales volume variance are due to the Big Bert driver.

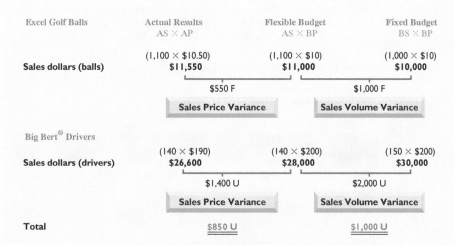

EXHIBIT 21.16

Computing Sales Variances*

* AS = actual sales units; AP = actual sales price; BP = budgeted sales price; BS = budgeted sales units (fixed budget).

Managers use sales variances for planning and control purposes. The sales variance information is used to plan future actions to avoid unfavorable variances. G-Max sold 90 total combined units (both balls and drivers) more than planned, but these 90 units were not sold in the proportion budgeted. G-Max sold fewer than the budgeted quantity of the higher-priced driver, which contributed to the unfavorable total sales variances. Managers use such detail to question what caused the company to sell more golf balls and fewer drivers. Managers also use this information to evaluate and even reward their salespeople. Extra compensation is paid to salespeople who contribute to a higher profit margin. Finally, with multiple products, the sales volume variance can be separated into a *sales mix variance* and a *sales quantity variance*. The sales mix variance is the difference between the actual and budgeted sales mix of the products. The sales quantity variance is the difference between the total actual and total budgeted quantity of units sold.

⬛ **Decision Maker** ━━━━━━━━━━━━━━━━━━━━━━━━━━

Sales Manager   The current performance report reveals a large favorable sales volume variance but an unfavorable sales price variance. You did not expect to see a large increase in sales volume. What steps do you take to analyze this situation? ■   [Answer—p. 920]

DEMONSTRATION PROBLEM

Pacific Company provides the following information about its budgeted and actual results for June 2013. Although the expected June volume was 25,000 units produced and sold, the company actually produced and sold 27,000 units as detailed here:

	Budget (25,000 units)	Actual (27,000 units)
Selling price	$5.00 per unit	$5.23 per unit
Variable costs (per unit)		
Direct materials	1.24 per unit	1.12 per unit
Direct labor	1.50 per unit	1.40 per unit
Factory supplies*	0.25 per unit	0.37 per unit
Utilities*	0.50 per unit	0.60 per unit
Selling costs	0.40 per unit	0.34 per unit
Fixed costs (per month)		
Depreciation—machinery*	$3,750	$3,710
Depreciation—building*	2,500	2,500
General liability insurance	1,200	1,250
Property taxes on office equipment	500	485
Other administrative expense	750	900

* Indicates factory overhead item; $0.75 per unit or $3 per direct labor hour for variable overhead, and $0.25 per unit or $1 per direct labor hour for fixed overhead.

Standard costs based on expected output of 25,000 units

	Per Unit of Output	Quantity to Be Used	Total Cost
Direct materials, 4 oz. @ $0.31/oz.	$1.24/unit	100,000 oz.	$31,000
Direct labor, 0.25 hrs. @ $6.00/hr.	1.50/unit	6,250 hrs.	37,500
Overhead	1.00/unit		25,000

Actual costs incurred to produce 27,000 units

	Per Unit of Output	Quantity Used	Total Cost
Direct materials, 4 oz. @ $0.28/oz.	$1.12/unit	108,000 oz.	$30,240
Direct labor, 0.20 hrs. @ $7.00/hr.	1.40/unit	5,400 hrs.	37,800
Overhead	1.20/unit		32,400

Standard costs based on expected output of 27,000 units

	Per Unit of Output	Quantity to Be Used	Total Cost
Direct materials, 4 oz. @ $0.31/oz.	$1.24/unit	108,000 oz.	$33,480
Direct labor, 0.25 hrs. @ $6.00/hr.	1.50/unit	6,750 hrs.	40,500
Overhead			26,500

Required

1. Prepare June flexible budgets showing expected sales, costs, and net income assuming 20,000, 25,000, and 30,000 units of output produced and sold.
2. Prepare a flexible budget performance report that compares actual results with the amounts budgeted if the actual volume had been expected.
3. Apply variance analysis for direct materials and direct labor.
4. Compute the total overhead variance, and the controllable and volume variances.
5. Compute spending and efficiency variances for overhead. (Refer to Appendix 21A.)
6. Prepare journal entries to record standard costs, and price and quantity variances, for direct materials, direct labor, and factory overhead. (Refer to Appendix 21A.)

PLANNING THE SOLUTION

- Prepare a table showing the expected results at the three specified levels of output. Compute the variable costs by multiplying the per unit variable costs by the expected volumes. Include fixed costs at the given amounts. Combine the amounts in the table to show total variable costs, contribution margin, total fixed costs, and income from operations.
- Prepare a table showing the actual results and the amounts that should be incurred at 27,000 units. Show any differences in the third column and label them with an *F* for favorable if they increase income or a *U* for unfavorable if they decrease income.
- Using the chapter's format, compute these total variances and the individual variances requested:
  - Total materials variance (including the direct materials quantity variance and the direct materials price variance).
  - Total direct labor variance (including the direct labor efficiency variance and rate variance).
  - Total overhead variance (including both controllable and volume overhead variances and their component variances).

SOLUTION TO DEMONSTRATION PROBLEM

1.

PACIFIC COMPANY Flexible Budgets For Month Ended June 30, 2013	Variable Amount per Unit	Total Fixed Cost	Flexible Budget for Unit Sales of 20,000	Flexible Budget for Unit Sales of 25,000	Flexible Budget for Unit Sales of 30,000
Sales	$5.00		$100,000	$125,000	$150,000
Variable costs					
Direct materials.....................	1.24		24,800	31,000	37,200
Direct labor........................	1.50		30,000	37,500	45,000
Factory supplies	0.25		5,000	6,250	7,500
Utilities	0.50		10,000	12,500	15,000
Selling costs	0.40		8,000	10,000	12,000
Total variable costs	3.89		77,800	97,250	116,700
Contribution margin	$1.11		22,200	27,750	33,300
Fixed costs					
Depreciation—machinery		$3,750	3,750	3,750	3,750
Depreciation—building		2,500	2,500	2,500	2,500
General liability insurance		1,200	1,200	1,200	1,200
Property taxes on office equipment		500	500	500	500
Other administrative expense		750	750	750	750
Total fixed costs		$8,700	8,700	8,700	8,700
Income from operations			$ 13,500	$ 19,050	$ 24,600

2.

PACIFIC COMPANY Flexible Budget Performance Report For Month Ended June 30, 2013	Flexible Budget	Actual Results	Variance*
Sales (27,000 units)	$135,000	$141,210	$6,210 F
Variable costs			
Direct materials	33,480	30,240	3,240 F
Direct labor	40,500	37,800	2,700 F
Factory supplies	6,750	9,990	3,240 U
Utilities	13,500	16,200	2,700 U
Selling costs	10,800	9,180	1,620 F
Total variable costs	105,030	103,410	1,620 F
Contribution margin	29,970	37,800	7,830 F
Fixed costs			
Depreciation—machinery	3,750	3,710	40 F
Depreciation—building	2,500	2,500	0
General liability insurance	1,200	1,250	50 U
Property taxes on office equipment	500	485	15 F
Other administrative expense	750	900	150 U
Total fixed costs	8,700	8,845	145 U
Income from operations	$ 21,270	$ 28,955	$7,685 F

* F = Favorable variance; U = Unfavorable variance.

3. Variance analysis of materials and labor costs.

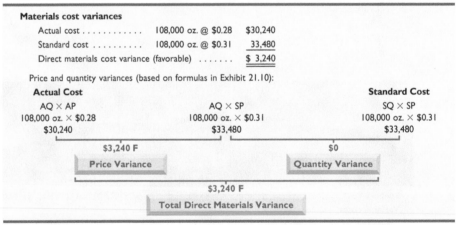

Materials cost variances

Actual cost	108,000 oz. @ $0.28	$30,240
Standard cost	108,000 oz. @ $0.31	33,480
Direct materials cost variance (favorable)		$ 3,240

Price and quantity variances (based on formulas in Exhibit 21.10):

Actual Cost		Standard Cost
AQ × AP	AQ × SP	SQ × SP
108,000 oz. × $0.28	108,000 oz. × $0.31	108,000 oz. × $0.31
$30,240	$33,480	$33,480

$3,240 F — Price Variance

$0 — Quantity Variance

$3,240 F

Total Direct Materials Variance

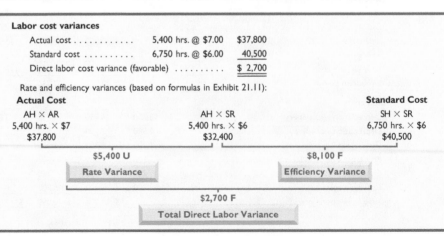

Labor cost variances

Actual cost	5,400 hrs. @ $7.00	$37,800
Standard cost	6,750 hrs. @ $6.00	40,500
Direct labor cost variance (favorable)		$ 2,700

Rate and efficiency variances (based on formulas in Exhibit 21.11):

Actual Cost		Standard Cost
AH × AR	AH × SR	SH × SR
5,400 hrs. × $7	5,400 hrs. × $6	6,750 hrs. × $6
$37,800	$32,400	$40,500

$5,400 U — Rate Variance

$8,100 F — Efficiency Variance

$2,700 F

Total Direct Labor Variance

4. Total, controllable, and volume variances for overhead.

Overhead cost variances

Total overhead cost incurred	27,000 units @ $1.20	$32,400
Total overhead applied	27,000 units @ $1.00	27,000
Overhead cost variance (unfavorable)		$ 5,400

Controllable variance

Actual overhead (given)	$32,400
Applied overhead (from flexible budget for 27,000 units)	26,500
Controllable variance (unfavorable)	$ 5,900

Volume variance

Budgeted fixed overhead (at predicted capacity)	$ 6,250
Applied fixed overhead (6,750 × $1.00)	6,750
Volume variance (favorable)	$ 500

5. Variable and fixed overhead spending and efficiency variances.

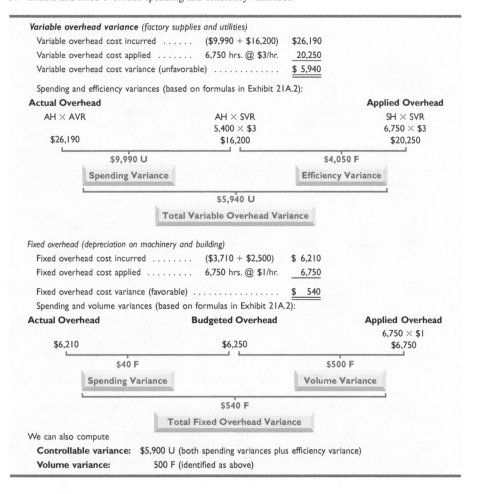

Variable overhead variance (factory supplies and utilities)

Variable overhead cost incurred	($9,990 + $16,200)	$26,190
Variable overhead cost applied	6,750 hrs. @ $3/hr.	20,250
Variable overhead cost variance (unfavorable)		$ 5,940

Spending and efficiency variances (based on formulas in Exhibit 21A.2):

Actual Overhead		**Applied Overhead**
AH × AVR	AH × SVR	SH × SVR
	5,400 × $3	6,750 × $3
$26,190	$16,200	$20,250
$9,990 U		$4,050 F
Spending Variance		Efficiency Variance
	$5,940 U	
	Total Variable Overhead Variance	

Fixed overhead (depreciation on machinery and building)

Fixed overhead cost incurred	($3,710 + $2,500)	$ 6,210
Fixed overhead cost applied	6,750 hrs. @ $1/hr.	6,750
Fixed overhead cost variance (favorable)		$ 540

Spending and volume variances (based on formulas in Exhibit 21A.2):

Actual Overhead	**Budgeted Overhead**	**Applied Overhead**
		6,750 × $1
$6,210	$6,250	$6,750
$40 F		$500 F
Spending Variance		Volume Variance
	$540 F	
	Total Fixed Overhead Variance	

We can also compute

Controllable variance:	$5,900 U (both spending variances plus efficiency variance)
Volume variance:	500 F (identified as above)

6.

Goods in Process Inventory	33,480	
Direct Materials Price Variance		3,240
Raw Materials Inventory		30,240
Goods in Process Inventory	40,500	
Direct Labor Rate Variance	5,400	
Direct Labor Efficiency Variance		8,100
Factory Payroll		37,800
Goods in Process Inventory*	27,000	
Variable Overhead Spending Variance	9,990	
Variable Overhead Efficiency Variance		4,050
Fixed Overhead Spending Variance		40
Fixed Overhead Volume Variance		500
Factory Overhead†		32,400

* $20,250 + $6,750   † $26,190 + $6,210

APPENDIX

21A

Expanded Overhead Variances and Standard Cost Accounting System

Expanded Overhead Variances   Similar to analysis of direct materials and direct labor, overhead variances can be more completely analyzed. Exhibit 21A.1 shows an expanded framework for understanding these component overhead variances. This framework uses classifications of overhead costs as either variable or fixed. A **spending variance** occurs when management pays an amount different than the standard price to acquire an item. For instance, the actual wage rate paid to indirect labor might be higher than the standard rate. Similarly, actual supervisory salaries might be different than expected. Spending variances such as these cause management to investigate the reasons that the amount paid differs from the standard. Both variable and fixed overhead costs can yield their own spending variances. Analyzing variable overhead includes computing an **efficiency variance,** which occurs when standard direct labor hours (the allocation base) expected for actual production differ from the actual direct labor hours used. This efficiency variance reflects on the cost-effectiveness in using the overhead allocation base (such as direct labor).

Exhibit 21A.1 shows that we can combine the variable overhead spending variance, the fixed overhead spending variance, and the variable overhead efficiency variance to get the controllable variance.

EXHIBIT 21A.1

Expanded Framework for Total Overhead Variance

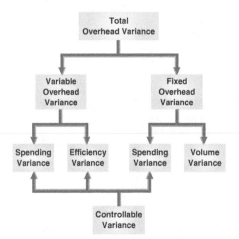

Computing Variable and Fixed Overhead Cost Variances   To illustrate the computation of more detailed overhead cost variances, we return to the G-Max data. We know that G-Max produced 3,500 units when 4,000 units were budgeted. Additional data from cost reports show that the actual overhead cost incurred is $7,650 (the variable portion of $3,650 and the fixed portion of $4,000). Recall from Exhibit 21.12 that each unit requires 1 hour of direct labor, that variable overhead is applied at a rate of $1.00 per direct labor hour, and that the predetermined fixed overhead rate is $1.00 per direct labor hour. Using this information, we can compute overhead variances for both variable and fixed overhead as follows:

Actual variable overhead (given)	$3,650
Applied variable overhead (3,500 × $1.00)	3,500
Variable overhead variance (unfavorable)	$ 150

Actual fixed overhead (given)	$4,000
Applied fixed overhead (3,500 × $1.00)	3,500
Fixed overhead variance (unfavorable)	$ 500

Management should seek to determine the causes of these unfavorable variances and take corrective action. To help better isolate the causes of these variances, more detailed overhead variances can be used, as shown in the next section.

Expanded Overhead Variance Formulas   Exhibit 21A.2 shows formulas to use in computing detailed overhead variances that can better identify reasons for variable and fixed overhead variances.

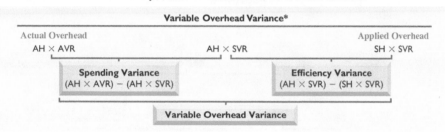

Variable Overhead Variance*

* AH = actual direct labor hours; AVR = actual variable overhead rate; SH = standard direct labor hours; SVR = standard variable overhead rate.

EXHIBIT 21A.2

Variable and Fixed Overhead Variances

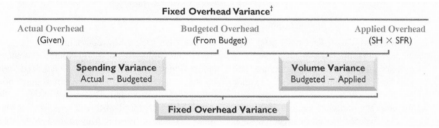

Fixed Overhead Variance†

†SH = standard direct labor hours; SFR = standard fixed overhead rate.

Variable Overhead Cost Variances   Using these formulas, Exhibit 21A.3 offers insight into the causes of G-Max's $150 unfavorable variable overhead cost variance. Recall that G-Max applies overhead based on direct labor hours as the allocation base. We know that it used 3,400 direct labor hours to produce 3,500 units. This compares favorably to the standard requirement of 3,500 direct labor hours at one labor hour per unit. At a standard variable overhead rate of $1.00 per direct labor hour, this should have resulted in variable overhead costs of $3,400 (middle column of Exhibit 21A.3).

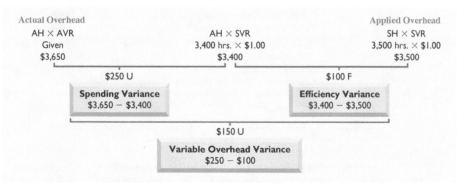

EXHIBIT 21A.3

Computing Variable Overhead Cost Variances

918   Chapter 21   Flexible Budgets and Standard Costs

G-Max's cost records, however, report actual variable overhead of $3,650, or $250 higher than expected. This means G-Max has an unfavorable variable overhead spending variance of $250 ($3,650 − $3,400). On the other hand, G-Max used 100 fewer labor hours than expected to make 3,500 units, and its actual variable overhead is lower than its applied variable overhead. Thus, G-Max has a favorable variable overhead efficiency variance of $100 ($3,400 − $3,500).

Fixed Overhead Cost Variances   Exhibit 21A.4 provides insight into the causes of G-Max's $500 unfavorable fixed overhead variance. G-Max reports that it incurred $4,000 in actual fixed overhead; this amount equals the budgeted fixed overhead for May at the expected production level of 4,000 units (see Exhibit 21.12). Thus, the fixed overhead spending variance is zero, suggesting good control of fixed overhead costs. G-Max's budgeted fixed overhead application rate is $1 per hour ($4,000/4,000 direct labor hours), but the actual production level is only 3,500 units. Using this information, we can compute the fixed overhead volume variance shown in Exhibit 21A.4. The applied fixed overhead is computed by multiplying 3,500 standard hours allowed for the actual production by the $1 fixed overhead allocation rate. The volume variance of $500 occurs because 500 fewer units are produced than budgeted; namely, 80% of the manufacturing capacity is budgeted but only 70% is used.

EXHIBIT 21A.4

Computing Fixed Overhead Cost Variances

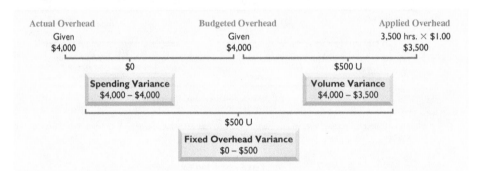

Standard Cost Accounting System   We have shown how companies use standard costs in management reports. Most standard cost systems also record these costs and variances in accounts. This practice simplifies recordkeeping and helps in preparing reports. Although we do not need knowledge of standard cost accounting practices to understand standard costs and their use, we must know how to interpret the accounts in which standard costs and variances are recorded. The entries in this section briefly illustrate the important aspects of this process for G-Max's standard costs and variances for May.

The first of these entries records standard materials cost incurred in May in the Goods in Process Inventory account. This part of the entry is similar to the usual accounting entry, but the amount of the debit equals the standard cost ($35,000) instead of the actual cost ($37,800). This entry credits Raw Materials Inventory for actual cost. The difference between standard and actual direct materials costs is recorded with debits to two separate materials variance accounts (recall Exhibit 21.10). Both the materials price and quantity variances are recorded as debits because they reflect additional costs higher than the standard cost (if actual costs were less than the standard, they are recorded as credits). This treatment (debit) reflects their unfavorable effect because they represent higher costs and lower income.

P4   Prepare journal entries for standard costs and account for price and quantity variances.

Assets = Liabilities + Equity
+35,000   −1,000
−37,800   −1,800

May 31	Goods in Process Inventory	35,000	
	Direct Materials Price Variance*	**1,800**	
	Direct Materials Quantity Variance	**1,000**	
	Raw Materials Inventory		37,800
	To charge production for standard quantity of materials used (1,750 lbs.) at the standard price ($20 per lb.), and to record material price and material quantity variances.		

* Many companies record the materials price variance when materials are purchased. For simplicity, we record both the materials price and quantity variances when materials are issued to production.

The second entry debits Goods in Process Inventory for the standard labor cost of the goods manufactured during May ($28,000). Actual labor cost ($28,220) is recorded with a credit to the Factory Payroll account. The difference between standard and actual labor costs is explained by two variances (see Exhibit 21.11). The direct labor rate variance is unfavorable and is debited to that account. The direct labor efficiency variance is favorable and that account is credited. The direct labor efficiency variance is favorable because it represents a lower cost and a higher net income.

May 31	Goods in Process Inventory	28,000	
	Direct Labor Rate Variance	1,020	
	Direct Labor Efficiency Variance		800
	Factory Payroll		28,220
	To charge production with 3,500 standard hours of direct labor at the standard $8 per hour rate, and to record the labor rate and efficiency variances.		

Assets = Liabilities + Equity
+28,000   +28,220
                                − 1,020
                                +   800

The entry to assign standard predetermined overhead to the cost of goods manufactured must debit the $7,000 predetermined amount to the Goods in Process Inventory account. Actual overhead costs of $7,650 were debited to Factory Overhead during the period (entries not shown here). Thus, when Factory Overhead is applied to Goods in Process Inventory, the actual amount is credited to the Factory Overhead account. To account for the difference between actual and standard overhead costs, the entry includes a $250 debit to the Variable Overhead Spending Variance, a $100 credit to the Variable Overhead Efficiency Variance, and a $500 debit to the Volume Variance (recall Exhibits 21A.3 and 21A.4). An alternative (simpler) approach is to record the difference with a $150 debit to the Controllable Variance account and a $500 debit to the Volume Variance account (recall from Exhibit 21A.1 that controllable variance is the sum of both variable overhead variances and the fixed overhead spending variance).

May 31	Goods in Process Inventory	7,000	
	Volume Variance	500	
	Variable Overhead Spending Variance	250	
	Variable Overhead Efficiency Variance		100
	Factory Overhead		7,650
	To apply overhead at the standard rate of $2 per standard direct labor hour (3,500 hours), and to record overhead variances.		

Assets = Liabilities + Equity
+7,000   +7,650
                                − 250
                                − 500
                                + 100

The balances of these different variance accounts accumulate until the end of the accounting period. As a result, the unfavorable variances of some months can offset the favorable variances of other months.

These ending variance account balances, which reflect results of the period's various transactions and events, are closed at period-end. If the amounts are *immaterial,* they are added to or subtracted from the balance of the Cost of Goods Sold account. This process is similar to that shown in the job order costing chapter for eliminating an underapplied or overapplied balance in the Factory Overhead account. (*Note:* These variance balances, which represent differences between actual and standard costs, must be added to or subtracted from the materials, labor, and overhead costs recorded. In this way, the recorded costs equal the actual costs incurred in the period; a company must use actual costs in external financial statements prepared in accordance with generally accepted accounting principles.)

Point: If variances are material they can be allocated between Goods in Process Inventory, Finished Goods Inventory, and Cost of Goods Sold. This closing process is explained in advanced courses.

Quick Check   Answers − p. 921

12. A company uses a standard cost accounting system. Prepare the journal entry to record these direct materials variances:

Direct materials cost actually incurred.	$73,200
Direct materials quantity variance (favorable)	3,800
Direct materials price variance (unfavorable)	1,300

13. If standard costs are recorded in the manufacturing accounts, how are recorded variances treated at the end of an accounting period?

Summary

C1 **Define *standard costs* and explain how standard cost information is useful for management by exception.** Standard costs are the normal costs that should be incurred to produce a product or perform a service. They should be based on a careful examination of the processes used to produce a product or perform a service as well as the quantities and prices that should be incurred in carrying out those processes. On a performance report, standard costs (which are flexible budget amounts) are compared to actual costs, and the differences are presented as variances. Standard cost accounting provides management information about costs that differ from budgeted (expected) amounts. Performance reports disclose the costs or areas of operations that have significant variances from budgeted amounts. This allows managers to focus attention on the exceptions and less attention on areas proceeding normally.

C2 **Describe variances and what they reveal about performance.** Management can use variances to monitor and control activities. Total cost variances can be broken into price and quantity variances to direct management's attention to those responsible for quantities used and prices paid.

A1 **Analyze changes in sales from expected amounts.** Actual sales can differ from budgeted sales, and managers can investigate this difference by computing both the sales price and sales volume variances. The *sales price variance* refers to that portion of total variance resulting from a difference between actual and budgeted selling prices. The *sales volume variance* refers to that portion of total variance resulting from a difference between actual and budgeted sales quantities.

P1 **Prepare a flexible budget and interpret a flexible budget performance report.** A flexible budget expresses variable costs in per unit terms so that it can be used to develop budgeted amounts for any volume level within the relevant range. Thus, managers compute budgeted amounts for evaluation after a period for the volume that actually occurred. To prepare a flexible budget, we express each variable cost as a constant amount per unit of sales (or as a percent of sales dollars). In contrast, the budgeted amount

of each fixed cost is expressed as a total amount expected to occur at any sales volume within the relevant range. The flexible budget is then determined using these computations and amounts for fixed and variable costs at the expected sales volume.

P2 **Compute materials and labor variances.** Materials and labor variances are due to differences between the actual costs incurred and the budgeted costs. The price (or rate) variance is computed by comparing the actual cost with the flexible budget amount that should have been incurred to acquire the actual quantity of resources. The quantity (or efficiency) variance is computed by comparing the flexible budget amount that should have been incurred to acquire the actual quantity of resources with the flexible budget amount that should have been incurred to acquire the standard quantity of resources.

P3 **Compute overhead variances.** Overhead variances are due to differences between the actual overhead costs incurred and the overhead applied to production. An overhead spending variance arises when the actual amount incurred differs from the budgeted amount of overhead. An overhead efficiency (or volume) variance arises when the flexible overhead budget amount differs from the overhead applied to production. It is important to realize that overhead is assigned using an overhead allocation base, meaning that an efficiency variance (in the case of variable overhead) is a result of the overhead application base being used more or less efficiently than planned.

P4^A **Prepare journal entries for standard costs and account for price and quantity variances.** When a company records standard costs in its accounts, the standard costs of materials, labor, and overhead are debited to the Goods in Process Inventory account. Based on an analysis of the material, labor, and overhead costs, each quantity variance, price variance, volume variance, and controllable variance is recorded in a separate account. At period-end, if the variances are material, they are allocated among the balances of the Goods in Process Inventory, Finished Goods Inventory, and Cost of Goods Sold accounts. If they are not material, they are simply debited or credited to the Cost of Goods Sold account.

Guidance Answers to Decision Maker and Decision Ethics

Entrepreneur From the complaints, this performance report appears to compare actual results with a fixed budget. This comparison is useful in determining whether the amount of work actually performed was more or less than planned, but it is not useful in determining whether the divisions were more or less efficient than planned. If the two consulting divisions worked on more assignments than expected, some costs will certainly increase. Therefore, you should prepare a flexible budget using the actual number of consulting assignments and then compare actual performance to the flexible budget.

Internal Auditor Although the manager's actions might not be unethical, this action is undesirable. The internal auditor should report this behavior, possibly recommending that for the purchase of such discretionary items, the manager must provide budgetary requests using an activity-based budgeting process. The internal auditor would then be given full authority to verify this budget request.

Production Manager As production manager, you should investigate the causes for any labor-related variances although you may not be responsible for them. An unfavorable labor efficiency variance occurs because more labor hours than standard were used during the period. There are at least three possible reasons for this: (1) materials quality could be poor, resulting in more labor consumption due to rework; (2) unplanned interruptions (strike, breakdowns, accidents) could have occurred during the period; and (3) a different labor mix might have occurred for a strategic reason such as to expedite orders. This new labor mix could have consisted of a larger proportion of untrained labor, which resulted in more labor hours.

Sales Manager The unfavorable sales price variance suggests that actual prices were lower than budgeted prices. As the sales manager, you want to know the reasons for a lower than expected price. Perhaps your salespeople lowered the price of certain products by offering quantity discounts. You then might want to know what prompted them to offer the quantity discounts (perhaps competitors were offering discounts). You want to break the sales volume variance into both the sales mix and sales quantity variances. You could find that although the sales quantity variance is favorable, the sales mix variance is not. Then you need to investigate why the actual sales mix differs from the budgeted sales mix.

Guidance Answers to Quick Checks

1. *b*

2. The first step is classifying each cost as variable or fixed.

3. A fixed budget is prepared using an expected volume of sales or production. A flexible budget is prepared using the actual volume of activity.

4. The contribution margin equals sales less variable costs.

5. *c*

6. It is the difference between actual cost and standard cost.

7. *a*; Total actual hours: 2,500 × 2.5 = 6,250
   Total standard hours: 2,500 × 2.0 = 5,000
   Efficiency variance = (6,250 − 5,000) × $3.00
                  = $3,750 U

8. *b*; Rate variance = ($3.10 − $3.00) × 6,250 = $625 U

9. Yes, this will occur when the materials quantity variance is more than the materials price variance.

10. The overhead volume variance is favorable when the actual operating level is higher than the expected level.

11. *b*

12.

Goods in Process Inventory	75,700	
Direct Materials Price Variance	1,300	
Direct Materials Quantity Variance		3,800
Raw Materials Inventory		73,200

13. If the variances are material, they should be prorated among the Goods in Process Inventory, Finished Goods Inventory, and Cost of Goods Sold accounts. If they are not material, they can be closed to Cost of Goods Sold.

Key Terms

Benchmarking (p. 908)

Budget report (p. 896)

Budgetary control (p. 896)

Controllable variance (p. 909)

Cost variance (p. 903)

Efficiency variance (p. 916)

Favorable variance (p. 897)

Fixed budget (p. 897)

Fixed budget performance report (p. 897)

Flexible budget (p. 898)

Flexible budget performance report (p. 900)

Management by exception (p. 901)

Overhead cost variance (p. 908)

Price variance (p. 901)

Quantity variance (p. 901)

Spending variance (p. 916)

Standard costs (p. 901)

Unfavorable variance (p. 897)

Variance analysis (p. 901)

Volume variance (p. 909)

Multiple Choice Quiz
Answers on p. 939   mhhe.com/wildFINMAN5e

Additional Quiz Questions are available at the book's Website.

1. A company predicts its production and sales will be 24,000 units. At that level of activity, its fixed costs are budgeted at $300,000, and its variable costs are budgeted at $246,000. If its activity level declines to 20,000 units, what will be its fixed costs and its variable costs?
  a. Fixed, $300,000; variable, $246,000
  b. Fixed, $250,000; variable, $205,000
  c. Fixed, $300,000; variable, $205,000
  d. Fixed, $250,000; variable, $246,000
  e. Fixed, $300,000; variable, $300,000

2. Using the following information about a single product company, compute its total actual cost of direct materials used.
  • Direct materials standard cost: 5 lbs. × $2 per lb. = $10.
  • Total direct materials cost variance: $15,000 unfavorable.
  • Actual direct materials used: 300,000 lbs.
  • Actual units produced: 60,000 units.

  a. $585,000
  b. $600,000
  c. $300,000
  d. $315,000
  e. $615,000

3. A company uses four hours of direct labor to produce a product unit. The standard direct labor cost is $20 per hour. This period the company produced 20,000 units and used 84,160 hours of direct labor at a total cost of $1,599,040. What is its labor rate variance for the period?
  a. $83,200 F
  b. $84,160 U
  c. $84,160 F
  d. $83,200 U
  e. $ 960 F

4. A company's standard for a unit of its single product is $6 per unit in variable overhead (4 hours × $1.50 per hour). Actual data for the period show variable overhead costs of $150,000 and production of 24,000 units. Its total variable overhead cost variance is
  a. $ 6,000 F.
  b. $ 6,000 U.
  c. $114,000 U.
  d. $114,000 F.
  e. $ 0.

5. A company's standard for a unit of its single product is $4 per unit in fixed overhead ($24,000 total/6,000 units budgeted). Actual data for the period show total actual fixed overhead of $24,100 and production of 4,800 units. Its volume variance is
  a. $4,800 U.
  b. $4,800 F.
  c. $ 100 U.
  d. $ 100 F.
  e. $4,900 U.

---

^A *Superscript letter A denotes assignments based on Appendix 21A.*
🄸 Icon denotes assignments that involve decision making.

Discussion Questions

1. 🄸 What limits the usefulness to managers of fixed budget performance reports?

2. 🄸 Identify the main purpose of a flexible budget for managers.

3. Prepare a flexible budget performance report title (in proper form) for Spalding Company for the calendar year 2013. Why is a proper title important for this or any report?

4. 🄸 What type of analysis does a flexible budget performance report help management perform?

5. In what sense can a variable cost be considered constant?

6. 🄸 What department is usually responsible for a direct labor rate variance? What department is usually responsible for a direct labor efficiency variance? Explain.

7. What is a price variance? What is a quantity variance?

8. 🄸 What is the purpose of using standard costs?

9. KTM monitors its fixed overhead. In an analysis of fixed overhead cost variances, what is the volume variance? *KTM*

10. What is the predetermined standard overhead rate? How is it computed?

11. In general, variance analysis is said to provide information about _____ and _____ variances.

12. 🄸 Polaris monitors its overhead. In an analysis of overhead cost variances, what is the controllable variance and what causes it? *Polaris*

13. What are the relations among standard costs, flexible budgets, variance analysis, and management by exception?

14. 🄸 How can the manager of snowmobile sales at Arctic Cat use flexible budgets to enhance performance? *Arctic Cat*

15. 🄸 Is it possible for a retail store such as Apple to use variances in analyzing its operating performance? Explain. *Apple*

16. 🄸 Assume that Piaggio is budgeted to operate at 80% of capacity but actually operates at 75% of capacity. What effect will the 5% deviation have on its controllable variance? Its volume variance? *PIAGGIO*

🄵 connect

QUICK STUDY

QS 21-1
Flexible budget performance report
P1

Beech Company sold 105,000 units of its product in May. For the level of production achieved in May, the budgeted amounts were: sales, $1,300,000; variable costs, $750,000; and fixed costs, $300,000. The following actual financial results are available for May. Prepare a flexible budget performance report for May.

Sales (105,000 units)	$1,275,000
Variable costs.	712,500
Fixed costs	300,000

QS 21-2
Standard cost card   C1

BatCo makes metal baseball bats. Each bat requires 1 kg. of aluminum at $18 per kg. and 0.25 direct labor hours at $20 per hour. Overhead is assigned at the rate of $40 per labor hour. What amounts would appear on a standard cost card for BatCo?

QS 21-3
Cost variances   C2

Refer to information in QS 21-2. Assume the actual cost to manufacture one metal bat was $40. Compute the cost variance and classify it as favorable or unfavorable.

QS 21-4
Management by exception
C1 🄸

Managers use *management by exception* for control purposes. (1) Describe the concept of management by exception. (2) Explain how standard costs help managers apply this concept to monitor and control costs.

Juan Company's output for the current period was assigned a $150,000 standard direct materials cost. The direct materials variances included a $12,000 favorable price variance and a $2,000 favorable quantity variance. What is the actual total direct materials cost for the current period?

QS 21-5
Materials cost variances P2

Frontera Company's output for the current period results in a $20,000 unfavorable direct labor rate variance and a $10,000 unfavorable direct labor efficiency variance. Production for the current period was assigned an $400,000 standard direct labor cost. What is the actual total direct labor cost for the current period?

QS 21-6
Labor cost variances P2

For the current period, Kayenta Company's manufacturing operations yield a $4,000 unfavorable price variance on its direct materials usage. The actual price per pound of material is $78; the standard price is $77.50. How many pounds of material are used in the current period?

QS 21-7
Materials cost variances P2

Alvarez Company's output for the current period yields a $20,000 favorable overhead volume variance and a $60,400 unfavorable overhead controllable variance. Standard overhead charged to production for the period is $225,000. What is the actual total overhead cost incurred for the period?

QS 21-8
Overhead cost variances P3

Refer to the information in QS 21-8. Alvarez records standard costs in its accounts. Prepare the journal entry to charge overhead costs to the Goods in Process Inventory account and to record any variances.

QS 21-9[A]
Preparing overhead entries P4

Mosaic Company applies overhead using machine hours and reports the following information. Compute the total variable overhead cost variance.

QS 21-10
Total overhead cost variance

P3

Actual machine hours used	4,700 hours
Standard machine hours	5,000 hours
Actual variable overhead rate per hour	$4.15
Standard variable overhead rate per hour	$4.00

Refer to the information from QS 21-10. Compute the variable overhead spending variance and the variable overhead efficiency variance.

QS 21-11[A]
Overhead spending and efficiency variances P3

Farad, Inc. specializes in selling used SUVs. During the first six months of 2013, the dealership sold 50 trucks at an average price of $9,000 each. The budget for the first six months of 2013 was to sell 45 trucks at an average price of $9,500 each. Compute the dealership's sales price variance and sales volume variance for the first six months of 2013.

QS 21-12
Computing sales price and volume variances A1

Based on predicted production of 24,000 units, a company anticipates $300,000 of fixed costs and $246,000 of variable costs. If the company actually produces 20,000 units, what are the flexible budget amounts of fixed and variable costs?

QS 21-13
Flexible budget P1

Brodrick Company expects to produce 20,000 units for the year ending December 31. A flexible budget for 20,000 units of production reflects sales of $400,000; variable costs of $80,000; and fixed costs of $150,000. If the company instead produces and sells 26,000 units for the year, calculate the expected level of income from operations.

QS 21-14
Flexible budget

P1

Refer to information in QS 21-14. Assume that actual sales are $480,000, actual variable costs for the year are $112,000, and actual fixed costs for the year are $145,000. Prepare a flexible budget performance report for the year.

QS 21-15
Flexible budget performance report P1

Tercer reports the following on one of its products. Compute the direct materials price and quantity variances.

QS 21-16
Materials variances

P2

Direct materials standard (4 lbs. @ $2/lb.)	$8 per finished unit
Actual direct materials used	300,000 lbs.
Actual finished units produced	60,000 units
Actual cost of direct materials used	$535,000

924   Chapter 21   Flexible Budgets and Standard Costs

QS 21-17
Direct labor variances
P2

The following information describes a company's usage of direct labor in a recent period. Compute the direct labor rate and efficiency variances for the period.

Actual direct labor hours used	65,000
Actual direct labor rate per hour	$15
Standard direct labor rate per hour	$14
Standard direct labor hours for units produced.........	67,000

QS 21-18
Controllable overhead variance
P3

Fogel Co. expects to produce 116,000 units for the year. The company's flexible budget for 116,000 units of production shows variable overhead costs of $162,400 and fixed overhead costs of $124,000. For the year, the company incurred actual overhead costs of $262,800 while producing 110,000 units. Compute the controllable overhead variance.

QS 21-19
Controllable overhead variance
P3

AirPro Corp. reports the following for November. Compute the controllable overhead variance for November.

Actual total factory overhead incurred	$28,175
Standard factory overhead:	
Variable overhead	$3.10 per unit produced
Fixed overhead	
($12,000/12,000 predicted units to be produced)	$1 per unit
Predicted units produced	12,000 units
Actual units produced	9,800 units

---

QS 21-20
Volume variance   P3

Refer to information in QS 21-19. Compute the overhead volume variance for November.

QS 21-21
Sales variances   A1

In a recent year, BMW sold 216,944 of its 1 Series cars. Assume the company expected to sell 225,944 of these cars during the year. Also assume the budgeted sales price for each car was $30,000, and the actual sales price for each car was $30,200. Compute the sales price variance and the sales volume variance.

🔲 connect

EXERCISES

Exercise 21-1
Classification of costs as fixed or variable
P1

JPAK Company manufactures and sells mountain bikes. It normally operates eight hours a day, five days a week. Using this information, classify each of the following costs as fixed or variable. If additional information would affect your decision, describe the information.

a. Bike frames   **e.** Bike tires   **i.** Office supplies
b. Screws for assembly   **f.** Gas used for heating   **j.** Depreciation on tools
c. Repair expense for tools   **g.** Incoming shipping expenses   **k.** Management salaries
d. Direct labor   **h.** Taxes on property

Exercise 21-2
Preparation of flexible budgets
P1

Tempo Company's fixed budget for the first quarter of calendar year 2013 reveals the following. Prepare flexible budgets following the format of Exhibit 21.3 that show variable costs per unit, fixed costs, and three different flexible budgets for sales volumes of 6,000, 7,000, and 8,000 units.

Sales (7,000 units)		$2,800,000
Cost of goods sold		
Direct materials	$280,000	
Direct labor	490,000	
Production supplies	175,000	
Plant manager salary	65,000	1,010,000
Gross profit		1,790,000
Selling expenses		
Sales commissions	140,000	
Packaging	154,000	
Advertising	125,000	419,000
Administrative expenses		
Administrative salaries	85,000	
Depreciation—office equip.	35,000	
Insurance	20,000	
Office rent........................	36,000	176,000
Income from operations		$1,195,000

Check Income (at 6,000 units), $972,000

Solitaire Company's fixed budget performance report for June follows. The $315,000 budgeted expenses include $294,000 variable expenses and $21,000 fixed expenses. Actual expenses include $27,000 fixed expenses. Prepare a flexible budget performance report showing any variances between budgeted and actual results. List fixed and variable expenses separately.

Exercise 21-3

Preparation of a flexible budget performance report

P1

	Fixed Budget	Actual Results	Variances
Sales (in units)	8,400	10,800	
Sales (in dollars)	$420,000	$540,000	$120,000 F
Total expenses	315,000	378,000	63,000 U
Income from operations	$105,000	$162,000	$ 57,000 F

Check Income variance, $21,000 F

Bay City Company's fixed budget performance report for July follows. The $647,500 budgeted expenses include $487,500 variable expenses and $160,000 fixed expenses. Actual expenses include $158,000 fixed expenses. Prepare a flexible budget performance report that shows any variances between budgeted results and actual results. List fixed and variable expenses separately.

Exercise 21-4

Preparation of a flexible budget performance report

P1

	Fixed Budget	Actual Results	Variances
Sales (in units)	7,500	7,200	
Sales (in dollars)	$750,000	$737,000	$13,000 U
Total expenses	647,500	641,000	6,500 F
Income from operations	$102,500	$ 96,000	$ 6,500 U

Check Income variance, $4,000 F

After evaluating Null Company's manufacturing process, management decides to establish standards of 3 hours of direct labor per unit of product and $15 per hour for the labor rate. During October, the company uses 16,250 hours of direct labor at a $247,000 total cost to produce 5,600 units of product. In November, the company uses 22,000 hours of direct labor at a $335,500 total cost to produce 6,000 units of product. (1) Compute the rate variance, the efficiency variance, and the total direct labor cost variance for each of these two months. (2) Interpret the October direct labor variances.

Exercise 21-5

Computation and interpretation of labor variances P2

Check (1) October rate variance, $3,250 U

Sedona Company set the following standard costs for one unit of its product for 2013.

Exercise 21-6

Computation of total variable and fixed overhead variances

P3

Direct material (20 lbs. @ $2.50 per lb.)	$ 50.00
Direct labor (10 hrs. @ $8.00 per hr.)	80.00
Factory variable overhead (10 hrs. @ $4.00 per hr.)	40.00
Factory fixed overhead (10 hrs. @ $1.60 per hr.)	16.00
Standard cost	$186.00

The $5.60 ($4.00 + $1.60) total overhead rate per direct labor hour is based on an expected operating level equal to 75% of the factory's capacity of 50,000 units per month. The following monthly flexible budget information is also available.

	Operating Levels (% of capacity)		
	70%	75%	80%
Budgeted output (units)	35,000	37,500	40,000
Budgeted labor (standard hours)	350,000	375,000	400,000
Budgeted overhead (dollars)			
Variable overhead	$1,400,000	$1,500,000	$1,600,000
Fixed overhead	600,000	600,000	600,000
Total overhead	$2,000,000	$2,100,000	$2,200,000

During the current month, the company operated at 70% of capacity, employees worked 340,000 hours, and the following actual overhead costs were incurred.

Variable overhead costs	$1,375,000
Fixed overhead costs	628,600
Total overhead costs	$2,003,600

(1) Show how the company computed its predetermined overhead application rate per hour for total overhead, variable overhead, and fixed overhead. (2) Compute the total variable and total fixed overhead variances.

Exercise 21-7^A

Computation and interpretation of overhead spending, efficiency, and volume variances   P3

Refer to the information from Exercise 21-6. Compute and interpret the following.
1. Variable overhead spending and efficiency variances.
2. Fixed overhead spending and volume variances.
3. Controllable variance.

Exercise 21-8

Computation and interpretation of materials variances   P2

Hart Company made 3,000 bookshelves using 22,000 board feet of wood costing $266,200. The company's direct materials standards for one bookshelf are 8 board feet of wood at $12 per board foot. (1) Compute the direct materials variances incurred in manufacturing these bookshelves. (2) Interpret the direct materials variances.

Exercise 21-9^A

Materials variances recorded and closed

P4

Refer to Exercise 21-8. Hart Company records standard costs in its accounts and its material variances in separate accounts when it assigns materials costs to the Goods in Process Inventory account. (1) Show the journal entry that both charges the direct materials costs to the Goods in Process Inventory account and records the materials variances in their proper accounts. (2) Assume that Hart's material variances are the only variances accumulated in the accounting period and that they are immaterial. Prepare the adjusting journal entry to close the variance accounts at period-end. (3) Identify the variance that should be investigated according to the management by exception concept. Explain.

Exercise 21-10

Computation of total overhead rate and total overhead variance

P3

World Company expects to operate at 80% of its productive capacity of 50,000 units per month. At this planned level, the company expects to use 25,000 standard hours of direct labor. Overhead is allocated to products using a predetermined standard rate based on direct labor hours. At the 80% capacity level, the total budgeted cost includes $50,000 fixed overhead cost and $275,000 variable overhead cost. In the current month, the company incurred $305,000 actual overhead and 22,000 actual labor hours while producing 35,000 units. (1) Compute the overhead application rate for total overhead. (2) Compute the total overhead variance.

Exercise 21-11

Computation of volume and controllable overhead variances

P3

Refer to the information from Exercise 21-10. Compute the (1) overhead volume variance and (2) overhead controllable variance.

Exercise 21-12

Computing and interpreting sales variances

A1

Comp Wiz sells computers. During May 2013, it sold 350 computers at a $1,200 average price each. The May 2013 fixed budget included sales of 365 computers at an average price of $1,100 each. (1) Compute the sales price variance and the sales volume variance for May 2013. (2) Interpret the findings.

Match the terms labeled a through e with their correct definition labeled 1 through 5.

a. Standard cost card

b. Management by exception

c. Standard cost

d. Ideal standard

e. Practical standard

1. Quantity of input required under normal conditions.

2. Quantity of input required if a production process is 100% efficient.

3. Managing by focusing on large differences from standard costs.

4. Record that accumulates standard cost information.

5. Preset cost for delivering a product or service under normal conditions.

Exercise 21-13
Standard costs
C1

Presented below are terms preceded by letters a through j and a list of definitions 1 through 10. Enter the letter of the term with the definition, using the space preceding the definition.

a. Fixed budget

b. Standard costs

c. Price variance

d. Quantity variance

e. Volume variance

f. Controllable variance

g. Cost variance

h. Flexible budget

i. Variance analysis

j. Management by exception

Exercise 21-14
Cost variances
C2

_____ **1.** The difference between actual and budgeted sales or cost caused by the difference between the actual price per unit and the budgeted price per unit.

_____ **2.** A planning budget based on a single predicted amount of sales or production volume; unsuitable for evaluations if the actual volume differs from the predicted volume.

_____ **3.** Preset costs for delivering a product, component, or service under normal conditions.

_____ **4.** A process of examining the differences between actual and budgeted sales or costs and describing them in terms of the amounts that resulted from price and quantity differences.

_____ **5.** The difference between the total budgeted overhead cost and the overhead cost that was allocated to products using the predetermined fixed overhead rate.

_____ **6.** A budget prepared based on predicted amounts of revenues and expenses corresponding to the actual level of output.

_____ **7.** The difference between actual and budgeted cost caused by the difference between the actual quantity and the budgeted quantity.

_____ **8.** The combination of both overhead spending variances (variable and fixed) and the variable overhead efficiency variance.

_____ **9.** A management process to focus on significant variances and give less attention to areas where performance is close to the standard.

_____ **10.** The difference between actual cost and standard cost, made up of a price variance and a quantity variance.

Resset Co. provides the following results of April's operations: F indicates favorable and U indicates unfavorable. Applying the management by exception approach, which of the variances are of greatest concern? Why?

Exercise 21-15
Analyzing variances
C1

Direct materials price variance	$ 300 F
Direct materials quantity variance	3,000 U
Direct labor rate variance	100 U
Direct labor efficiency variance	2,200 F
Controllable overhead variance	400 U
Fixed overhead volume variance	500 F

The following information describes production activities of Mercer Manufacturing for the year:

Exercise 21-16
Direct materials and direct labor variances
P2

Actual raw materials used	16,000 lbs. at $4.05 per lb.
Actual factory payroll	5,545 hours for a total of $105,355
Actual units produced	30,000

928   Chapter 21   Flexible Budgets and Standard Costs

Budgeted standards for each unit produced are 0.50 pounds of raw material at $4.00 per pound and 10 minutes of direct labor at $20 per hour. (1) Compute the direct materials price and quantity variances. (2) Compute the direct labor rate and efficiency variances. Indicate whether each variance is favorable or unfavorable.

≣ connect·

PROBLEM SET A

Problem 21-1A
Computation of materials, labor, and overhead variances

P2   P3

mhhe.com/wildFINMAN5e

Trico Company set the following standard unit costs for its single product.

Direct materials (30 lbs. @ $4 per lb.)	$120.00
Direct labor (5 hrs. @ $14 per hr.)	70.00
Factory overhead—variable (5 hrs. @ $8 per hr.)	40.00
Factory overhead—fixed (5 hrs. @ $10 per hr.)	50.00
Total standard cost	$280.00

The predetermined overhead rate is based on a planned operating volume of 80% of the productive capacity of 60,000 units per quarter. The following flexible budget information is available.

	Operating Levels		
	70%	80%	90%
Production in units	42,000	48,000	54,000
Standard direct labor hours	210,000	240,000	270,000
Budgeted overhead			
Fixed factory overhead	$2,400,000	$2,400,000	$2,400,000
Variable factory overhead	$1,680,000	$1,920,000	$2,160,000

During the current quarter, the company operated at 90% of capacity and produced 54,000 units of product; actual direct labor totaled 265,000 hours. Units produced were assigned the following standard costs:

Direct materials (1,620,000 lbs. @ $4 per lb.)	$ 6,480,000
Direct labor (270,000 hrs. @ $14 per hr.)	3,780,000
Factory overhead (270,000 hrs. @ $18 per hr.)........	4,860,000
Total standard cost................................	$15,120,000

Actual costs incurred during the current quarter follow:

Direct materials (1,615,000 lbs. @ $4.10)	$ 6,621,500
Direct labor (265,000 hrs. @ $13.75)	3,643,750
Fixed factory overhead costs	2,350,000
Variable factory overhead costs	2,200,000
Total actual costs	$14,815,250

Required

1. Compute the direct materials cost variance, including its price and quantity variances.
2. Compute the direct labor variance, including its rate and efficiency variances.
3. Compute the overhead controllable and volume variances.

Problem 21-2A[A]
Expanded overhead variances

P3

Refer to information in Problem 21-1A.

Required

Compute these variances: (a) variable overhead spending and efficiency, (b) fixed overhead spending and volume, and (c) total overhead controllable.

Phoenix Company's 2013 master budget included the following fixed budget report. It is based on an expected production and sales volume of 15,000 units.

Problem 21-3A

Preparation and analysis of a flexible budget   P1

PHOENIX COMPANY Fixed Budget Report For Year Ended December 31, 2013		
Sales		$3,000,000
Cost of goods sold		
Direct materials	$975,000	
Direct labor	225,000	
Machinery repairs (variable cost)	60,000	
Depreciation—plant equipment	300,000	
Utilities ($45,000 is variable)	195,000	
Plant management salaries	200,000	1,955,000
Gross profit		1,045,000
Selling expenses		
Packaging	75,000	
Shipping	105,000	
Sales salary (fixed annual amount)	250,000	430,000
General and administrative expenses		
Advertising expense	125,000	
Salaries	241,000	
Entertainment expense	90,000	456,000
Income from operations		$ 159,000

Required

1. Classify all items listed in the fixed budget as variable or fixed. Also determine their amounts per unit or their amounts for the year, as appropriate.

2. Prepare flexible budgets (see Exhibit 21.3) for the company at sales volumes of 14,000 and 16,000 units.

3. The company's business conditions are improving. One possible result is a sales volume of approximately 18,000 units. The company president is confident that this volume is within the relevant range of existing capacity. How much would operating income increase over the 2013 budgeted amount of $159,000 if this level is reached without increasing capacity?

4. An unfavorable change in business is remotely possible; in this case, production and sales volume for 2013 could fall to 12,000 units. How much income (or loss) from operations would occur if sales volume falls to this level?

Check   (2) Budgeted income at 16,000 units, $260,000

(4) Potential operating loss, $(144,000)

Refer to the information in Problem 21-3A. Phoenix Company's actual income statement for 2013 follows.

Problem 21-4A

Preparation and analysis of a flexible budget performance report

P1 P2 A1

mhhe.com/wildFINMAN5e

PHOENIX COMPANY Statement of Income from Operations For Year Ended December 31, 2013		
Sales (18,000 units)		$3,648,000
Cost of goods sold		
Direct materials	$1,185,000	
Direct labor	278,000	
Machinery repairs (variable cost)	63,000	
Depreciation—plant equipment	300,000	
Utilities (fixed cost is $147,500)	200,500	
Plant management salaries	210,000	2,236,500
Gross profit		1,411,500
Selling expenses		
Packaging	87,500	
Shipping	118,500	
Sales salary (annual)	268,000	474,000
General and administrative expenses		
Advertising expense	132,000	
Salaries	241,000	
Entertainment expense	93,500	466,500
Income from operations		$ 471,000

930   Chapter 21   Flexible Budgets and Standard Costs

Required

1. Prepare a flexible budget performance report for 2013.

Analysis Component

2. Analyze and interpret both the (a) sales variance and (b) direct materials variance.

Problem 21-5A
Flexible budget preparation; computation of materials, labor, and overhead variances; and overhead variance report

P1 P2 P3 C2

Antuan Company set the following standard costs for one unit of its product.

Direct materials (6 lbs. @ $5 per lb.)	$ 30
Direct labor (2 hrs. @ $17 per hr.)	34
Overhead (2 hrs. @ $18.50 per hr.)	37
Total standard cost	$101

The predetermined overhead rate ($18.50 per direct labor hour) is based on an expected volume of 75% of the factory's capacity of 20,000 units per month. Following are the company's budgeted overhead costs per month at the 75% level.

Overhead Budget (75% Capacity)		
Variable overhead costs		
Indirect materials	$ 45,000	
Indirect labor	180,000	
Power	45,000	
Repairs and maintenance	90,000	
Total variable overhead costs		$360,000
Fixed overhead costs		
Depreciation—building	24,000	
Depreciation—machinery	80,000	
Taxes and insurance	12,000	
Supervision	79,000	
Total fixed overhead costs		195,000
Total overhead costs		$555,000

The company incurred the following actual costs when it operated at 75% of capacity in October.

Direct materials (91,000 lbs. @ $5.10 per lb.)		$ 464,100
Direct labor (30,500 hrs. @ $17.25 per hr.)		526,125
Overhead costs		
Indirect materials	$ 44,250	
Indirect labor	177,750	
Power	43,000	
Repairs and maintenance	96,000	
Depreciation—building	24,000	
Depreciation—machinery	75,000	
Taxes and insurance	11,500	
Supervision	89,000	560,500
Total costs		$1,550,725

Required

1. Examine the monthly overhead budget to (a) determine the costs per unit for each variable overhead item and its total per unit costs, and (b) identify the total fixed costs per month.

2. Prepare flexible overhead budgets (as in Exhibit 21.12) for October showing the amounts of each variable and fixed cost at the 65%, 75%, and 85% capacity levels.

3. Compute the direct materials cost variance, including its price and quantity variances.

4. Compute the direct labor cost variance, including its rate and efficiency variances.

5. Prepare a detailed overhead variance report (as in Exhibit 21.15) that shows the variances for individual items of overhead.

(4) Labor variances: Rate, $7,625 U; Efficiency, $8,500 U

Kegler Company has set the following standard costs per unit for the product it manufactures.

Direct materials (15 lbs. @ $4 per lb.)	$ 60.00
Direct labor (3 hrs. @ $15 per hr.)	45.00
Overhead (3 hrs. @ $3.85 per hr.)	11.55
Total standard cost	$116.55

Problem 21-6A[A]

Materials, labor, and overhead variances; overhead variance report

C2   P2   P3

The predetermined overhead rate is based on a planned operating volume of 80% of the productive capacity of 10,000 units per month. The following flexible budget information is available.

	Operating Levels		
	70%	80%	90%
Production in units	7,000	8,000	9,000
Standard direct labor hours	21,000	24,000	27,000
Budgeted overhead			
Variable overhead costs			
Indirect materials	$13,125	$15,000	$16,875
Indirect labor	21,000	24,000	27,000
Power	5,250	6,000	6,750
Maintenance	2,625	3,000	3,375
Total variable costs	42,000	48,000	54,000
Fixed overhead costs			
Rent of factory building	15,000	15,000	15,000
Depreciation—machinery	10,000	10,000	10,000
Supervisory salaries	19,400	19,400	19,400
Total fixed costs	44,400	44,400	44,400
Total overhead costs	$86,400	$92,400	$98,400

During May, the company operated at 90% of capacity and produced 9,000 units, incurring the following actual costs.

Direct materials (138,000 lbs. @ $3.75 per lb.)		$ 517,500
Direct labor (31,000 hrs. @ $15.10 per hr.)		468,100
Overhead costs		
Indirect materials	$15,000	
Indirect labor	26,500	
Power	6,750	
Maintenance	4,000	
Rent of factory building	15,000	
Depreciation—machinery	10,000	
Supervisory salaries	22,000	99,250
Total costs		$1,084,850

Required

1. Compute the direct materials variance, including its price and quantity variances.

2. Compute the direct labor variance, including its rate and efficiency variances.

[continued on next page]

Check   (1) Materials variances: Price, $34,500 F; Quantity, $12,000 U
(2) Labor variances: Rate, $3,100 U; Efficiency, $60,000 U

932   Chapter 21   Flexible Budgets and Standard Costs

3. Compute these variances: (a) variable overhead spending and efficiency, (b) fixed overhead spending and volume, and (c) total overhead controllable.

4. Prepare a detailed overhead variance report (as in Exhibit 21.15) that shows the variances for individual items of overhead.

Problem 21-7A[A]
Materials, labor, and overhead variances recorded and analyzed

C1   P4

Boss Company's standard cost accounting system recorded this information from its December operations.

Standard direct materials cost	$100,000
Direct materials quantity variance (unfavorable)	3,000
Direct materials price variance (favorable)	500
Actual direct labor cost	90,000
Direct labor efficiency variance (favorable).............	7,000
Direct labor rate variance (unfavorable)	1,200
Actual overhead cost	375,000
Volume variance (unfavorable)........................	12,000
Controllable variance (unfavorable)..................	9,000

Required

Check (1) Dr. Goods in Process Inventory (for overhead), $354,000

1. Prepare December 31 journal entries to record the company's costs and variances for the month. (Do not prepare the journal entry to close the variances.)

Analysis Component

2. Identify the areas that would attract the attention of a manager who uses management by exception. Explain what action(s) the manager should consider.

PROBLEM SET B

Problem 21-1B
Computation of materials, labor, and overhead variances

P2   P3

Kryll Company set the following standard unit costs for its single product.

Direct materials (25 lbs. @ $4 per lb.)	$100.00
Direct labor (6 hrs. @ $8 per hr.)	48.00
Factory overhead—variable (6 hrs. @ $5 per hr.)	30.00
Factory overhead—fixed (6 hrs. @ $7 per hr.)	42.00
Total standard cost	$220.00

The predetermined overhead rate is based on a planned operating volume of 80% of the productive capacity of 60,000 units per quarter. The following flexible budget information is available.

	Operating Levels		
	70%	**80%**	**90%**
Production in units	42,000	48,000	54,000
Standard direct labor hours	252,000	288,000	324,000
Budgeted overhead			
Fixed factory overhead	$2,016,000	$2,016,000	$2,016,000
Variable factory overhead	1,260,000	1,440,000	1,620,000

During the current quarter, the company operated at 70% of capacity and produced 42,000 units of product; direct labor hours worked were 250,000. Units produced were assigned the following standard costs:

Direct materials (1,050,000 lbs. @ $4 per lb.)	$4,200,000
Direct labor (252,000 hrs. @ $8 per hr.)	2,016,000
Factory overhead (252,000 hrs. @ $12 per hr.)	3,024,000
Total standard cost	$9,240,000

Actual costs incurred during the current quarter follow:

Direct materials (1,000,000 lbs. @ $4.25).........	$4,250,000
Direct labor (250,000 hrs. @ $7.75).............	1,937,500
Fixed factory overhead costs	1,960,000
Variable factory overhead costs	1,200,000
Total actual costs............................	$9,347,500

Required

1. Compute the direct materials cost variance, including its price and quantity variances.
2. Compute the direct labor variance, including its rate and efficiency variances.
3. Compute the total overhead controllable and volume variances.

Check (1) Materials variances:
Price, $250,000 U; Quantity,
$200,000 F (2) Labor variances: Rate,
$62,500 F; Efficiency, $16,000 F

Refer to information in Problem 21-1B.

Required

Compute these variances: (a) variable overhead spending and efficiency, (b) fixed overhead spending and volume, and (c) total overhead controllable.

Problem 21-2B[A]
Expanded overhead variances

P3

Tohono Company's 2013 master budget included the following fixed budget report. It is based on an expected production and sales volume of 20,000 units.

Problem 21-3B
Preparation and analysis of a
flexible budget P1 A1

TOHONO COMPANY
Fixed Budget Report
For Year Ended December 31, 2013

Sales		$3,000,000
Cost of goods sold		
Direct materials	$1,200,000	
Direct labor	260,000	
Machinery repairs (variable cost)	57,000	
Depreciation—machinery	250,000	
Utilities (25% is variable cost)	200,000	
Plant manager salaries	140,000	2,107,000
Gross profit		893,000
Selling expenses		
Packaging	80,000	
Shipping	116,000	
Sales salary (fixed annual amount)	160,000	356,000
General and administrative expenses		
Advertising	81,000	
Salaries	241,000	
Entertainment expense	90,000	412,000
Income from operations		$ 125,000

Required

1. Classify all items listed in the fixed budget as variable or fixed. Also determine their amounts per unit or their amounts for the year, as appropriate.
2. Prepare flexible budgets (see Exhibit 21.3) for the company at sales volumes of 18,000 and 24,000 units.
3. The company's business conditions are improving. One possible result is a sales volume of approximately 28,000 units. The company president is confident that this volume is within the relevant range of existing capacity. How much would operating income increase over the 2013 budgeted amount of $125,000 if this level is reached without increasing capacity?
4. An unfavorable change in business is remotely possible; in this case, production and sales volume for 2013 could fall to 14,000 units. How much income (or loss) from operations would occur if sales volume falls to this level?

Check (2) Budgeted income at
24,000 units, $372,400

(4) Potential operating loss,
$(246,100)

Problem 21-4B
Preparation and analysis
of a flexible budget
performance report

P1   A1

Refer to the information in Problem 21-3B. Tohono Company's actual income statement for 2013 follows.

TOHONO COMPANY
Statement of Income from Operations
For Year Ended December 31, 2013

Sales (24,000 units)		$3,648,000
Cost of goods sold		
Direct materials	$1,400,000	
Direct labor	360,000	
Machinery repairs (variable cost)	60,000	
Depreciation—machinery	250,000	
Utilities (variable cost, $64,000)	218,000	
Plant manager salaries	155,000	2,443,000
Gross profit		1,205,000
Selling expenses		
Packaging	90,000	
Shipping	124,000	
Sales salary (annual)	162,000	376,000
General and administrative expenses		
Advertising expense	104,000	
Salaries	232,000	
Entertainment expense	100,000	436,000
Income from operations		$ 393,000

Required

1. Prepare a flexible budget performance report for 2013.

Analysis Component

2. Analyze and interpret both the (a) sales variance and (b) direct materials variance.

Problem 21-5B
Flexible budget preparation;
computation of materials, labor,
and overhead variances; and
overhead variance report

P1   P2   P3   C2

Suncoast Company set the following standard costs for one unit of its product.

Direct materials (4.5 lb. @ $6 per kg.)	$27
Direct labor (1.5 hrs. @ $12 per hr.)	18
Overhead (1.5 hrs. @ $16 per hr.)	24
Total standard cost........................	$69

The predetermined overhead rate ($16.00 per direct labor hour) is based on an expected volume of 75% of the factory's capacity of 20,000 units per month. Following are the company's budgeted overhead costs per month at the 75% level.

Overhead Budget (75% Capacity)

Variable overhead costs		
Indirect materials	$22,500	
Indirect labor	90,000	
Power	22,500	
Repairs and maintenance	45,000	
Total variable overhead costs		$180,000
Fixed overhead costs		
Depreciation—building	24,000	
Depreciation—machinery...........	72,000	
Taxes and insurance	18,000	
Supervision	66,000	
Total fixed overhead costs		180,000
Total overhead costs		$360,000

The company incurred the following actual costs when it operated at 75% of capacity in December.

Direct materials (69,000 lbs. @ $6.10)		$ 420,900
Direct labor (22,800 hrs. @ $12.30)		280,440
Overhead costs		
Indirect materials	$21,600	
Indirect labor	82,260	
Power	23,100	
Repairs and maintenance	46,800	
Depreciation—building	24,000	
Depreciation—machinery	75,000	
Taxes and insurance	16,500	
Supervision	66,000	355,260
Total costs		$1,056,600

Required

1. Examine the monthly overhead budget to (a) determine the costs per unit for each variable overhead item and its total per unit costs, and (b) identify the total fixed costs per month.
2. Prepare flexible overhead budgets (as in Exhibit 21.12) for December showing the amounts of each variable and fixed cost at the 65%, 75%, and 85% capacity levels.
3. Compute the direct materials cost variance, including its price and quantity variances.
4. Compute the direct labor cost variance, including its rate and efficiency variances.
5. Prepare a detailed overhead variance report (as in Exhibit 21.15) that shows the variances for individual items of overhead.

Check   (2) Budgeted total overhead at 17,000 units, $384,000

(3) Materials variances: Price, $6,900 U; Quantity, $9,000 U

(4) Labor variances: Rate, $6,840 U; Efficiency, $3,600 U

Guadelupe Company has set the following standard costs per unit for the product it manufactures.

Direct materials (10 lbs. @ $3.00 per lb.)	$30.00
Direct labor (4 hr. @ $6 per hr.)	24.00
Overhead (4 hr. @ $2.50 per hr.)	10.00
Total standard cost	$64.00

Problem 21-6B[A]

Materials, labor, and overhead variances; overhead variance report

C2   P2   P3

The predetermined overhead rate is based on a planned operating volume of 80% of the productive capacity of 10,000 units per month. The following flexible budget information is available.

	Operating Levels		
	70%	80%	90%
Production in units	7,000	8,000	9,000
Standard direct labor hours	28,000	32,000	36,000
Budgeted overhead			
Variable overhead costs			
Indirect materials	$ 8,750	$10,000	$11,250
Indirect labor	14,000	16,000	18,000
Power	3,500	4,000	4,500
Maintenance	1,750	2,000	2,250
Total variable costs	28,000	32,000	36,000
Fixed overhead costs			
Rent of factory building	12,000	12,000	12,000
Depreciation—machinery	20,000	20,000	20,000
Taxes and insurance.............	2,400	2,400	2,400
Supervisory salaries	13,600	13,600	13,600
Total fixed costs	48,000	48,000	48,000
Total overhead costs	$76,000	$80,000	$84,000

936 Chapter 21 Flexible Budgets and Standard Costs

During March, the company operated at 90% of capacity and produced 9,000 units, incurring the following actual costs.

Direct materials (92,000 lbs. @ 2.95 per lb.)		$271,400
Direct labor (37,600 hrs. @ $6.05 per hr.)		227,480
Overhead costs		
Indirect materials............................	$10,000	
Indirect labor.................................	16,000	
Power......................................	4,500	
Maintenance.................................	3,000	
Rent of factory building	12,000	
Depreciation—machinery	19,200	
Taxes and insurance..........................	3,000	
Supervisory salaries..........................	14,000	81,700
Total costs		$580,580

Required

1. Compute the direct materials cost variance, including its price and quantity variances.
2. Compute the direct labor variance, including its rate and efficiency variances.
3. Compute these variances: (a) variable overhead spending and efficiency, (b) fixed overhead spending and volume, and (c) total overhead controllable.
4. Prepare a detailed overhead variance report (as in Exhibit 21.15) that shows the variances for individual items of overhead.

Problem 21-7B[A]
Materials, labor, and overhead variances recorded and analyzed

C1 P4

Kenya Company's standard cost accounting system recorded this information from its June operations.

Standard direct materials cost	$130,000
Direct materials quantity variance (favorable)	5,000
Direct materials price variance (favorable)	1,500
Actual direct labor cost	65,000
Direct labor efficiency variance (favorable)	3,000
Direct labor rate variance (unfavorable)	500
Actual overhead cost	250,000
Volume variance (unfavorable)	12,000
Controllable variance (unfavorable).................	8,000

Required

1. Prepare journal entries dated June 30 to record the company's costs and variances for the month. (Do not prepare the journal entry to close the variances.)

Analysis Component

2. Identify the areas that would attract the attention of a manager who uses management by exception. Describe what action(s) the manager should consider.

SERIAL PROBLEM
Success Systems

P1

(This serial problem began in Chapter 1 and continues through most of the book. If previous chapter segments were not completed, the serial problem can begin at this point. It is helpful, but not necessary, to use the working papers that accompany the book.)

SP 21 Success Systems' second quarter 2014 fixed budget performance report for its computer furniture operations follows. The $156,000 budgeted expenses include $108,000 in variable expenses for desks and $18,000 in variable expenses for chairs, as well as $30,000 fixed expenses. The actual expenses include

$31,000 fixed expenses. Prepare a flexible budget performance report that shows any variances between budgeted results and actual results. List fixed and variable expenses separately.

	Fixed Budget	Actual Results	Variances
Desk sales (in units)............	144	150	
Chair sales (in units)	72	80	
Desk sales (in dollars)	$180,000	$186,000	$6,000 F
Chair sales (in dollars)..........	$ 36,000	$ 41,200	$5,200 F
Total expenses	$156,000	$163,880	$7,880 U
Income from operations	$ 60,000	$ 63,320	$3,320 F

Check Variances: Fixed expenses, $1,000 U

Beyond the Numbers

BTN 21-1   Analysis of flexible budgets and standard costs emphasizes the importance of a similar unit of measure for meaningful comparisons and evaluations. When Polaris compiles its financial reports in compliance with GAAP, it applies the same unit of measurement, U.S. dollars, for most measures of business operations. One issue for Polaris is how best to adjust account values for its subsidiaries that compile financial reports in currencies other than the U.S. dollar.

REPORTING IN ACTION

C1

Polaris

Required

1. Read Polaris's Note 1 in Appendix A and identify the financial statement where it reports the annual adjustment (remeasurement) for foreign currency translation.

2. Translating financial statements requires the use of a currency exchange rate. For each of the following three financial statement items, explain the exchange rate the company would apply to translate into U.S. dollars.

   a. Cash

   b. Sales revenue

   c. Property, plant and equipment

BTN 21-2   The usefulness of budgets, variances, and related analyses often depends on the accuracy of management's estimates of future sales activity.

COMPARATIVE ANALYSIS

A1

Polaris

Arctic Cat

Required

1. Identify and record the prior three years' sales (in dollars) for Polaris and for Arctic Cat using their financial statements in Appendix A.

2. Using the data in part *1*, predict both companies' sales activity for the next two to three years. (If possible, compare your predictions to actual sales figures for those years.)

BTN 21-3   Setting materials, labor, and overhead standards is challenging. If standards are set too low, companies might purchase inferior products and employees might not work to their full potential. If standards are set too high, companies could be unable to offer a quality product at a profitable rate and employees could be overworked. The ethical challenge is to set a high but reasonable standard. Assume that as a manager, you are asked to set the standard materials price and quantity for the new 1,000 CKB Mega-Max chip, a technically advanced product. To properly set the price and quantity standards, you assemble a team of specialists to provide input.

ETHICS CHALLENGE

C1

Required

Identify four types of specialists that you would assemble to provide information to help set the materials price and quantity standards. Briefly explain why you chose each individual.

COMMUNICATING IN PRACTICE

P4 C2

BTN 21-4   The reason we use the words *favorable* and *unfavorable* when evaluating variances is made clear when we look at the closing of accounts. To see this, consider that (1) all variance accounts are closed at the end of each period (temporary accounts), (2) a favorable variance is always a credit balance, and (3) an unfavorable variance is always a debit balance. Write a one-half page memorandum to your instructor with three parts that answer the three following requirements. (Assume that variance accounts are closed to Cost of Goods Sold.)

Required

1. Does Cost of Goods Sold increase or decrease when closing a favorable variance? Does gross margin increase or decrease when a favorable variance is closed to Cost of Goods Sold? Explain.
2. Does Cost of Goods Sold increase or decrease when closing an unfavorable variance? Does gross margin increase or decrease when an unfavorable variance is closed to Cost of Goods Sold? Explain.
3. Explain the meaning of a favorable variance and an unfavorable variance.

TAKING IT TO THE NET

C1

BTN 21-5   Access iSixSigma's Website (iSixSigma.com) to search for and read information about *benchmarking* to complete the following requirements. (*Hint:* Look in the "dictionary" link.)

Required

1. Write a one-paragraph explanation (in layperson's terms) of benchmarking.
2. How does standard costing relate to benchmarking?

TEAMWORK IN ACTION

C2

BTN 21-6   Many service industries link labor rate and time (quantity) standards with their processes. One example is the standard time to board an aircraft. The reason time plays such an important role in the service industry is that it is viewed as a competitive advantage: best service in the shortest amount of time. Although the labor rate component is difficult to observe, the time component of a service delivery standard is often readily apparent—for example, "Lunch will be served in less than five minutes, or it is free."

Required

Break into teams and select two service industries for your analysis. Identify and describe all the time elements each industry uses to create a competitive advantage.

ENTREPRENEURIAL DECISION

C1 C2

BTN 21-7   Folsom Custom Skis, as discussed in the chapter opener, uses a costing system with standard costs for direct materials, direct labor, and overhead costs. Two comments frequently are mentioned in relation to standard costing and variance analysis: "Variances are not explanations" and "Management's goal is not to minimize variances."

Required

Write a short memo to Mike McCabe, Folsom Custom Skis' President, (no more than 1 page) interpreting these two comments in the context of his business.

HITTING THE ROAD

C1

BTN 21-8   Training employees to use standard amounts of materials in production is common. Typically large companies invest in this training but small organizations do not. One can observe these different practices in a trip to two different pizza businesses. Visit both a local pizza business and a national pizza chain business and then complete the following.

Required

1. Observe and record the number of raw material items used to make a typical cheese pizza. Also observe how the person making the pizza applies each item when preparing the pizza.
2. Record any differences in how items are applied between the two businesses.
3. Estimate which business is more profitable from your observations. Explain.

BTN 21-9   Access the annual report of Piaggio (at www.piaggio.com) for the year ended December 31, 2011. The usefulness of its budgets, variances, and related analyses depends on the accuracy of management's estimates of future sales activity.

Required

1. Identify and record the prior two years' sales (in € thousands) for Piaggio from its income statement.
2. Using the data in part *1*, predict sales activity for Piaggio for the next two years. Explain your prediction process.

ANSWERS TO MULTIPLE CHOICE QUIZ

1. c; Fixed costs remain at $300,000; Variable costs = ($246,000/24,000 units) × 20,000 units = $205,000.

2. e; Budgeted direct materials + Unfavorable variance = Actual cost of direct materials used; or, 60,000 units × $10 per unit = $600,000 + $15,000 U = $615,000.

3. c; (AH × AR) − (AH × SR) = $1,599,040 − (84,160 hours × $20 per hour) = $84,160 F.

4. b; Actual variable overhead − Variable overhead applied to production = Variable overhead cost variance; or $150,000 − (96,000 hours × $1.50 per hour) = $6,000 U.

5. a; Budgeted fixed overhead − Fixed overhead applied to production = Volume variance; or $24,000 − (4,800 units × $4 per unit) = $4,800 U.

Performance Measurement and Responsibility Accounting

A Look Back

Chapter 21 discussed flexible budgets, variance analysis, and standard costs. It explained how management uses each to control and monitor business activities.

A Look at This Chapter

This chapter describes responsibility accounting, measuring departmental performance, allocating common costs across departments, and transfer pricing. It also explains financial and nonfinancial performance measures used to evaluate investment center performance.

A Look Ahead

Chapter 23 explains several tools and procedures used in making and evaluating short-term managerial decisions.

Learning Objectives

CONCEPTUAL

C1 Distinguish between direct and indirect expenses and identify bases for allocating indirect expenses to departments. (p. 945)

C2 *Appendix 22A*—Explain transfer pricing and methods to set transfer prices. (p. 961)

C3 *Appendix 22B*—Describe allocation of joint costs across products. (p. 962)

ANALYTICAL

A1 Analyze investment centers using return on assets and residual income. (p. 953)

A2 Analyze investment centers using profit margin and investment turnover. (p. 954)

A3 Analyze investment centers using the balanced scorecard. (p. 955)

A4 Compute cycle time and cycle efficiency, and explain their importance to production management. (p. 957)

PROCEDURAL

P1 Prepare a responsibility report for a cost center. (p. 944)

P2 Allocate indirect expenses to departments (p. 946)

P3 Prepare departmental income statements and contribution reports. (p. 947)

Decision Insight

Go Blue!

"Do the dirty work yourself."
—BRIAN LINTON

PHILADELPHIA, PA—Brian Linton has a passion for oceans. Growing up in Singapore, Brian spent time scuba diving and tending to his 30 fish tanks. Traveling the world enabled Brian to see the "good, the bad, and the ugly of oceans and waterways." Combining his love of the water with an entrepreneurial spirit, Brian started his company **United By Blue (UnitedByBlue.com)**, an apparel and jewelry company that removes one pound of trash in oceans and waterways for every product sold. As Brian notes, the company's unique business model was driven by "a quest for concrete ways to contribute to real and significant conservation efforts."

Building off Brian's college experiences selling jewelry he imported from Thailand, United By Blue sells men's and women's clothing, bags, and jewelry. The company uses organic cotton and creative designs to make products that elicit a fun vibe associated with oceans and harbor villages. Offering a diverse product line requires Brian to pay attention to cost management and departmental profits. The Sand Shack, a product in the company's jewelry department, "is a line of jewelry with chunky turquoise stones that generates much of the profits the company runs on," says Brian. His managers monitor direct, indirect, and controllable costs; allocate indirect costs to departments; and "measure return on investment (ROI)," explains Brian.

While focusing on controlling costs, United By Blue also strives to remove plastic from its packaging. "The number one material we collect during cleanups is plastic debris. We try to eliminate as much plastic as we can from our supply chain," says Brian. Apparel tags are made from biodegradable substances, infused with flower seeds. T-shirts are packaged in banana fiber paper. "We use things that go back to the earth in a very natural way and actually grow life." While these materials are more costly than plastic, they better fit the company's philosophy and, Brian believes, help generate new business. "We have customers that double their orders the next season because of the cleanups," Brian notes.

As United By Blue continues to grow, Brian focuses on financial *and* nonfinancial performance measures. Revenues were $330,000 in 2010, and were projected to exceed $800,000 in 2011. A focus on departmental contribution margins enables the company to operate efficiently to finance future growth. Likewise, more revenues mean the company collects more trash, over 80,000 pounds by the end of 2011 and a goal of over a million pounds by the end of 2012. As company founder and chief trash collector, this nonfinancial indicator measures progress toward Brian's vision of "doing the most good possible."

Brian encourages young entrepreneurs to "leave a positive impact on this world" by focusing on what you love. "My heart is in the ocean, so whatever I am doing is going to be in that realm. Whatever your passion is, leave that positive impact."

[Sources: *United By Blue* Website, January 2013; *Bloomberg Businessweek*, January 9, 2012; *MO.com* interview, http://www.mo.com/brian-linton-united-by-blue; *Philadelphia Magazine*, July 2011; *PRweb.com*, January 2012.]

Chapter Preview

This chapter describes how to measure performance when organizations are split into separate departments. It discusses responsibility accounting and how to allocate indirect costs of shared items such as utilities, advertising, and rent. This knowledge helps managers better measure and evaluate departmental performance. The chapter also introduces additional managerial accounting reports useful in managing a company's activities and explains how and why management divides companies into departments.

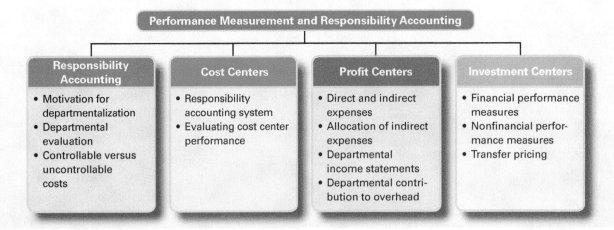

Performance Measurement and Responsibility Accounting

Responsibility Accounting	Cost Centers	Profit Centers	Investment Centers
• Motivation for departmentalization • Departmental evaluation • Controllable versus uncontrollable costs	• Responsibility accounting system • Evaluating cost center performance	• Direct and indirect expenses • Allocation of indirect expenses • Departmental income statements • Departmental contribution to overhead	• Financial performance measures • Nonfinancial performance measures • Transfer pricing

RESPONSIBILITY ACCOUNTING

Point: Responsibility accounting is sometimes referred to as *departmental accounting*.

Companies are divided into *departments,* also called *subunits,* when they are too large to be managed effectively as a single unit. The use of departments creates a need for performance measures to evaluate department performance. A **responsibility accounting system** can be set up to control costs and expenses and evaluate department managers' performance by assigning costs and expenses to the managers responsible for controlling them. This chapter introduces responsibility accounting and departmental performance measures.

Motivation for Departmentalization

Many companies are so large and complex that they are broken into separate divisions for efficiency and/or effectiveness purposes. Divisions then are usually organized into separate departments. When a company is departmentalized, each department is often placed under the direction of a manager. As a company grows, management often divides departments into new departments so that responsibilities for a department's activities do not overwhelm the manager's ability to oversee and control them. A company also creates departments to take advantage of the skills of individual managers. Departments are broadly classified as either operating or service departments.

Operating departments perform an organization's main functions. For example, an accounting firm's main functions usually include auditing, tax, and advisory services. Similarly, the production and selling departments of a manufacturing firm perform its main functions and serve as operating departments. *Service departments* provide support to an organization's operating departments. Examples of service departments are payroll, human resource management, accounting, and executive management. Service departments do not engage in activities that generate revenues, yet their support is crucial for the operating departments' success.

Departmental Evaluation

When a company is divided into departments, managers need to know how each department is performing. The accounting system must supply information about resources used and outputs achieved by each department. This requires a system to measure and accumulate revenue and expense information for each department whenever possible.

Departmental information is rarely distributed publicly because of its potential usefulness to competitors. Information about departments is prepared for internal managers to help control operations, appraise performance, allocate resources, and plan strategy. If a department is highly profitable, management may decide to expand its operations, or if a department is performing poorly, information about revenues or expenses can suggest useful changes.

More companies are emphasizing customer satisfaction as a main responsibility of many departments. This has led to changes in the measures reported. Increasingly, financial measurements are being supplemented with quality and customer satisfaction indexes. Motorola, for instance, uses two key measures: the number of defective parts per million parts produced and the percent of orders delivered on time to customers. (Note that some departments have only "internal customers.")

Financial information used to evaluate a department depends on whether it is evaluated as a profit center, cost center, or investment center. A **profit center** incurs costs and generates revenues; selling departments are often evaluated as profit centers. A **cost center** incurs costs without directly generating revenues. An **investment center** incurs costs and generates revenues, and is responsible for effectively using center assets. The manufacturing departments of a manufacturer and its service departments such as accounting, advertising, and purchasing, are all cost centers.

Evaluating managers' performance depends on whether they are responsible for profit centers, cost centers, or investment centers. Profit center managers are judged on their abilities to generate revenues in excess of the department's costs. They are assumed to influence both revenue generation and cost incurrence. Cost center managers are judged on their abilities to control costs by keeping them within a satisfactory range under an assumption that only they influence costs. Investment center managers are evaluated on their use of center assets to generate income.

Point: Selling departments are often treated as *revenue centers*; their managers are responsible for maximizing sales revenues.

Controllable versus Uncontrollable Costs

We often evaluate a manager's performance using responsibility accounting reports that describe a department's activities in terms of **controllable costs.**[1] A cost is controllable if a manager has the power to determine or at least significantly affect the amount incurred. **Uncontrollable costs** are not within the manager's control or influence. For example, department managers often have little or no control over depreciation expense because they cannot affect the amount of equipment assigned to their departments. Also, department managers rarely control their own salaries. However, they can control or influence items such as the cost of supplies used in their department. When evaluating managers' performances, we should use data reflecting their departments' outputs along with their controllable costs and expenses.

Distinguishing between controllable and uncontrollable costs depends on the particular manager and time period under analysis. For example, the cost of property insurance is usually not controllable at the department manager's level but by the executive responsible for obtaining the company's insurance coverage. Likewise, this executive might not control costs resulting from insurance policies already in force. However, when a policy expires, this executive can renegotiate a replacement policy and then controls these costs. Therefore, all costs are controllable at some management level if the time period is sufficiently long. We must use good judgment in identifying controllable costs.

Quick Check   Answers — p. 965

1. Service departments (*a*) manufacture products, (*b*) make sales directly to customers, (*c*) produce revenues, (*d*) assist operating departments.
2. Explain the difference between a cost center and a profit center. Cite an example of each.
3. Performance reports to evaluate managers should [select *a, b* or *c*] (*a*) include data about controllable expenses, (*b*) compare actual results with budgeted levels, or (*c*) both (*a*) and (*b*).

---

[1] The terms *cost* and *expense* are often used interchangeably in managerial accounting, but they are not necessarily the same. *Cost* often refers to the monetary outlay to acquire some resource that can have present and future benefit. *Expense* usually refers to an expired cost. That is, as the benefit of a resource expires, a portion of its cost is written off as an expense.

COST CENTERS

Responsibility Accounting System

| P1 | Prepare a responsibility accounting report for a cost center |

A *responsibility accounting system* uses the concept of controllable costs to assign managers the responsibility for costs and expenses under their control. Prior to each reporting period, a company prepares plans that identify costs and expenses under each manager's control. These **responsibility accounting budgets** are typically based on the flexible budgeting approach we showed in Chapter 21. To ensure the cooperation of managers and the reasonableness of budgets, managers should be involved in preparing their budgets.

EXHIBIT 22.1

Organizational Responsibility Chart

Board of Directors

President

Executive Vice President Marketing

Executive Vice President Operations

Executive Vice President Finance

Vice President Operational Consulting

Vice President Strategic Consulting

Manager Benchmarking Department

Manager Cost Management Department

Manager Outsourcing Department

Manager Service Department

A responsibility accounting system also involves performance reports. A **responsibility accounting performance report** accumulates and reports costs and expenses that a manager is responsible for and their budgeted amounts. Management's analysis of differences between budgeted amounts and actual costs and expenses often results in corrective or strategic managerial actions. Upper-level management uses performance reports to evaluate the effectiveness of lower-level managers in controlling costs and expenses and keeping them within budgeted amounts.

A responsibility accounting system recognizes that control over costs and expenses belongs to several levels of management. We illustrate this by considering the organization chart in Exhibit 22.1. The lines in this chart connecting the managerial positions reflect channels of authority. For example, the four department managers of this consulting firm (benchmarking, cost management, outsourcing, and service) are responsible for controllable costs and expenses incurred in their departments, but these same costs are subject to the overall control of the vice president (VP) for operational consulting. Similarly, this VP's costs are subject to the control of the executive vice president (EVP) for operations, the president, and, ultimately, the board of directors.

Point: Responsibility accounting does not place blame. Instead, responsibility accounting is used to identify opportunities for improving performance.

At lower levels, managers have limited responsibility and relatively little control over costs and expenses. Performance reports for low-level management typically cover few controllable costs. Responsibility and control broaden for higher-level managers; therefore, their reports span a wider range of costs. However, reports to higher-level managers seldom contain the details reported to their subordinates but are summarized for two reasons: (1) lower-level managers are often responsible for these detailed costs and (2) detailed reports can obscure broader, more important issues facing a company.

Evaluating Cost Center Performance

Exhibit 22.2 shows summarized performance reports for the three management levels identified in Exhibit 22.1. Exhibit 22.2 shows that costs under the control of the benchmarking department manager are totaled and included among controllable costs of the VP for operational consulting. Also, costs under the control of the VP are totaled and included among controllable costs of the EVP for operations. In this way, a responsibility accounting system provides relevant information for each management level.

Point: Responsibility accounting usually divides a company into subunits, or *responsibility centers*. A center manager is evaluated on how well the center performs, as reported in responsibility accounting reports.

Technological advances increase our ability to produce vast amounts of information that often exceed our ability to use it. Good managers select relevant data for planning and controlling the areas under their responsibility. A good responsibility accounting system makes every effort to provide relevant information to the right person (the one who controls the cost) at the right time (before a cost is out of control).

Executive Vice President, Operations	For July		
Controllable Costs	**Budgeted Amount**	**Actual Amount**	**Over (Under) Budget**
Salaries, VPs	$ 80,000	$ 80,000	$ 0
Quality control costs	21,000	22,400	1,400
Office costs	29,500	28,800	(700)
Operational consulting	276,700	279,500	2,800
Strategic consulting	390,000	380,600	(9,400)
Totals	$ 797,200	$ 791,300	$ (5,900)

Vice President, Operational Consulting	For July		
Controllable Costs	**Budgeted Amount**	**Actual Amount**	**Over (Under) Budget**
Salaries, department managers	$ 75,000	$ 78,000	$ 3,000
Depreciation	10,600	10,600	0
Insurance	6,800	6,300	(500)
Benchmarking department	79,600	79,900	300
Cost management department	61,500	60,200	(1,300)
Outsourcing department	24,300	24,700	400
Service department	18,900	19,800	900
Totals	$276,700	$279,500	$2,800

Manager, Benchmarking Department	For July		
Controllable Costs	**Budgeted Amount**	**Actual Amount**	**Over (Under) Budget**
Salaries	$ 51,600	$ 52,500	$ 900
Supplies	8,000	7,800	(200)
Other controllable costs	20,000	19,600	(400)
Totals	$ 79,600	$ 79,900	$ 300

EXHIBIT 22.2

Responsibility Accounting Performance Reports for Cost Centers

PROFIT CENTERS

When departments are organized as profit centers, responsibility accounting focuses on how well each department controlled costs and generated revenues. This leads to **departmental income statements** as a common way to report profit center performance. When a company computes departmental profits, it confronts some accounting challenges that involve allocating expenses across its operating departments. We next illustrate these allocations and departmental income statement reporting.

C1 Distinguish between direct and indirect expenses and identify bases for allocating indirect expenses to departments.

Direct and Indirect Expenses

Direct expenses are costs readily traced to a department because they are incurred for that department's sole benefit. They require no allocation across departments. For example, the salary of an employee who works in only one department is a direct expense of that one department. Direct expenses are often, but not always, controllable costs.

  Indirect expenses are costs that are incurred for the joint benefit of more than one department and cannot be readily traced to only one department. For example, if two or more departments share a single building, all enjoy the benefits of the expenses for rent, heat, and light. Indirect expenses are allocated across departments benefiting from them when we need information about departmental profits. Ideally, we allocate indirect expenses by using a cause-effect relation. When we cannot identify cause-effect relations, we allocate each indirect expense on a

Point: Utility expense has elements of both direct and indirect expenses.

basis approximating the relative benefit each department receives. Measuring the benefit for each department from an indirect expense can be difficult. Indirect expenses are typically considered uncontrollable costs when evaluating a department manager's performance.

Illustration of Indirect Expense Allocation   To illustrate how to allocate an indirect expense, we consider a retail store that purchases janitorial services from an outside company. Management allocates this cost across the store's three departments according to the floor space each occupies. Costs of janitorial services for a recent month are $300. Exhibit 22.3 shows the square feet of floor space each department occupies. The store computes the percent of total square feet allotted to each department and uses it to allocate the $300 cost.

EXHIBIT 22.3

Indirect Expense Allocation

Department	Square Feet	Percent of Total	Allocated Cost
Jewelry	2,400	60%	$180
Watch repair	600	15	45
China and silver	1,000	25	75
Totals	4,000	100%	$300

Specifically, because the jewelry department occupies 60% of the floor space, 60% of the total $300 cost is assigned to it. The same procedure is applied to the other departments. When the allocation process is complete, these and other allocated costs are deducted from the gross profit for each department to determine net income for each. One consideration in allocating costs is to motivate managers and employees to behave as desired. As a result, a cost incurred in one department might be best allocated to other departments when one of the other departments caused the cost.

Allocation of Indirect Expenses

P2 Allocate indirect expenses to departments.

This section describes how to identify the bases used to allocate indirect expenses across departments. No standard rule identifies the best basis because expense allocation involves several factors, and the relative importance of these factors varies across departments and organizations. Judgment is required, and people do not always agree. Employee morale suffers when allocations are perceived as unfair. Thus, it is important to carefully design and explain the allocation of service department costs. In our discussion, note the parallels between activity-based costing and the departmental expense allocation procedures described here.

Wages and Salaries   Employee wages and salaries can be either direct or indirect expenses. If their time is spent entirely in one department, their wages are direct expenses of that department. However, if employees work for the benefit of more than one department, their wages are indirect expenses and must be allocated across the departments benefited. An employee's contribution to a department usually depends on the number of hours worked in contributing to that department. Thus, a reasonable basis for allocating employee wages and salaries is the *relative amount of time spent in each department*. In the case of a supervisor who manages more than one department, recording the time spent in each department may not always be practical. Instead, a company can allocate the supervisor's salary to departments on the basis of the number of employees in each department—a reasonable basis if a supervisor's main task is managing people. Another basis of allocation is on sales across departments, also a reasonable basis if a supervisor's job reflects on departmental sales.

Point: Some companies ask supervisors to estimate time spent supervising specific departments for purposes of expense allocation.

Rent and Related Expenses   Rent expense for a building is reasonably allocated to a department on the basis of floor space it occupies. Location can often make some floor space more valuable than other space. Thus, the allocation method can charge departments that occupy more valuable space a higher expense per square foot. Ground floor retail space, for instance, is often more valuable than basement or upper-floor space because all customers pass departments near the entrance but fewer go beyond the first floor. When no precise measures of floor space values exist, basing allocations on data such as customer traffic and real estate assessments is helpful. When a company owns its building, its expenses for depreciation, taxes, insurance, and other related building expenses are allocated like rent expense.

Advertising Expenses   Effective advertising of a department's products increases its sales and customer traffic. Moreover, advertising products for some departments usually helps other departments' sales because customers also often buy unadvertised products. Thus, many stores treat advertising as an indirect expense allocated on the basis of each department's proportion of total sales. For example, a department with 10% of a store's total sales is assigned 10% of advertising expense. Another method is to analyze each advertisement to compute the Web/newspaper space or TV/radio time devoted to the products of a department and charge that department for the proportional costs of advertisements. Management must consider whether this more detailed and costly method is justified.

Equipment and Machinery Depreciation   Depreciation on equipment and machinery used only in one department is a direct expense of that department. Depreciation on equipment and machinery used by more than one department is an indirect expense to be allocated across departments. Accounting for each department's depreciation expense requires a company to keep records showing which departments use specific assets. The number of hours that a department uses equipment and machinery is a reasonable basis for allocating depreciation.

Utilities Expenses   Utilities expenses such as heating and lighting are usually allocated on the basis of floor space occupied by departments. This practice assumes their use is uniform across departments. When this is not so, a more involved allocation can be necessary, although there is often a trade-off between the usefulness of more precise allocations and the effort to compute them. Manufacturers often allocate electricity cost to departments on the basis of the horsepower of equipment located in each department.

Service Department Expenses   To generate revenues, operating departments require support services provided by departments such as personnel, payroll, advertising, and purchasing. Such service departments are typically evaluated as cost centers because they do not produce revenues. (Evaluating them as profit centers requires the use of a system that "charges" user departments a price that then serves as the "revenue" generated by service departments.) A departmental accounting system can accumulate and report costs incurred directly by each service department for this purpose. The system then allocates a service department's expenses to operating departments benefiting from them. Exhibit 22.4 shows some commonly used bases for allocating service department expenses to operating departments.

Point: When a service department "charges" its user departments within a company, a *transfer pricing system* must be set up to determine the "revenue" from its services provided.

Service Department	Common Allocation Bases
Office expenses	Number of employees or sales in each department
Personnel expenses	Number of employees in each department
Payroll expenses	Number of employees in each department
Advertising expenses	Sales or amount of advertising charged directly to each department
Purchasing costs	Dollar amounts of purchases or number of purchase orders processed
Cleaning expenses	Square feet of floor space occupied
Maintenance expenses	Square feet of floor space occupied

EXHIBIT 22.4

Bases for Allocating Service Department Expenses

Departmental Income Statements

An income statement can be prepared for each operating department once expenses have been assigned to it. Its expenses include both direct expenses and its share of indirect expenses. For this purpose, compiling all expenses incurred in service departments before assigning them to

P3   Prepare departmental income statements and contribution reports.

operating departments is useful. We illustrate the steps to prepare departmental income statements using **A-1 Hardware** and its five departments. Two of them (office and purchasing) are service departments and the other three (hardware, housewares, and appliances) are operating (selling) departments. Allocating costs to operating departments and preparing departmental income statements involves four steps.

Step 1: Accumulating revenues and direct expenses by department.

Step 2: Allocating indirect expenses across departments.

Step 3: Allocating service department expenses to operating departments.

Step 4: Preparing departmental income statements.

Exhibit 22.5 summarizes the steps in preparing departmental performance reports for cost centers and profit centers. A-1 Hardware's service departments (general office and purchasing) are cost centers, so their performance will be based on how well they controlled total service department expenses. The company's operating departments (hardware, housewares, and appliances) are profit centers, and their performance will be based on how well they generated departmental net income.

EXHIBIT 22.5

Departmental Performance Reporting

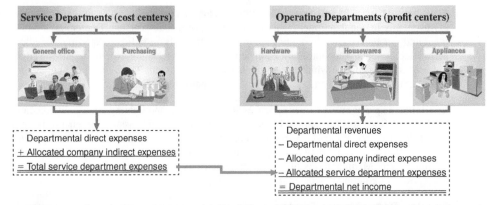

Step 1:   Step 1 accumulates revenues and direct expenses in departmental accounts for each department. As cost centers, the service departments do not generate revenues. Direct expenses include salaries, wages, and other expenses that each department incurs but does not share with any other department.

Step 2:   Step 2 allocates indirect company expenses across all service and operating departments. Indirect expenses can include items such as depreciation, rent, advertising, and any other expenses that cannot be directly assigned to a department. Indirect expenses are recorded in *company* accounts, an allocation base is identified for each expense, and costs are allocated using a *departmental expense allocation spreadsheet* described next.

Point: We sometimes allocate service department costs across other service departments before allocating them to operating departments. This "step-wise" process is in advanced courses.

Step 3:   Step 3 allocates service department expenses to operating departments. Service department expenses are not allocated to other service departments.[2] Exhibit 22.6 reflects the allocation of service department expenses using the allocation base(s). All of the direct and indirect expenses of service departments are allocated to operating departments.

Computations for both steps 2 and 3 are commonly made using a departmental expense allocation spreadsheet as shown in Exhibit 22.6. The first two sections of this spreadsheet list direct expenses and indirect expenses by department. The third section lists the service department expenses and their allocations to operating departments. The allocation bases are identified in the second column, and total expense amounts are reported in the third column.

---

[2] In some cases we allocate a service department's expenses to other service departments when they use its services. For example, expenses of a payroll office benefit all service and operating departments and can be assigned to all departments. Nearly all examples and assignment materials in this book allocate service expenses only to operating departments for simplicity.

EXHIBIT 22.6

Departmental Expense Allocation Spreadsheet

	File Edit View Insert Format Tools Data Window Help								

A-1 HARDWARE
Departmental Expense Allocations
For Year Ended December 31, 2013

	Allocation Base	Expense Account Balance	Allocation of Expenses to Departments				
			General Office Dept.	Purchasing Dept.	Hardware Dept.	Housewares Dept.	Appliances Dept.
Direct expenses							
Salaries expense..................	Payroll records.......................	$51,900	$13,300	$8,200	$15,600	$ 7,000	$ 7,800
Depreciation—Equipment......	Depreciation records.............	1,500	500	300	400	100	200
Supplies expense..................	Requisitions............................	900	200	100	300	200	100
Indirect expenses							
Rent expense	Amount and value of space..	12,000	600	600	4,860	3,240	2,700
Utilities expense.....................	Floor space............................	2,400	300	300	810	540	450
Advertising expense...............	Sales.....................................	1,000			500	300	200
Insurance expense..................	Value of insured assets	2,500	400	200	900	600	400
Total department expenses		72,200	15,300	9,700	23,370	11,980	11,850
Service department expenses							
General office department.......	Sales.....................................		(15,300)		→7,650	→4,590	→3,060
Purchasing department	Purchase orders....................			(9,700)	→3,880	→2,630	→3,190
Total expenses allocated to operating departments................................		$72,200	$ 0	$ 0	$34,900	$19,200	$18,100

Second (step 2), the four indirect expenses of rent, utilities, advertising, and insurance are allocated to all departments using the allocation bases identified. For example, consider rent allocation. Exhibit 22.7 lists the five departments' square footage of space occupied.

EXHIBIT 22.7

Departments' Allocation Bases

Department	Floor Space (Square Feet)	Value of Insured Assets ($)	Sales ($)	Number of Purchase Orders
General office	1,500	$ 38,000		—
Purchasing	1,500	19,000		*
Hardware	4,050	85,500	$119,500	394
Housewares	2,700	57,000	71,700	267
Appliances	2,250	38,000	47,800	324
Total	12,000	$237,500	$239,000	985

* Purchasing department tracks purchase orders by department.

The two service departments (office and purchasing) occupy 25% of the total space (3,000 sq. feet/ 12,000 sq. feet). However, they are located near the back of the building, which is of lower value than space near the front that is occupied by operating departments. Management estimates that space near the back accounts for $1,200 of the total rent expense of $12,000. Exhibit 22.8 shows how we allocate the $1,200 rent expense between these two service departments in proportion to their square footage. Exhibit 22.8 shows a simple rule for cost

EXHIBIT 22.8

Allocating Indirect (Rent) Expense to Service Departments

Department	Square Feet	Percent of Total	Allocated Cost
General office	1,500	50.0%	$ 600
Purchasing	1,500	50.0	600
Totals	3,000	100.0%	$1,200

allocations: Allocated cost = Percentage of allocation base × Total cost. We then allocate the remaining $10,800 of rent expense to the three operating departments as shown in Exhibit 22.9.

EXHIBIT 22.9

Allocating Indirect (Rent)
Expense to Operating Departments

Department	Square Feet	Percent of Total	Allocated Cost
Hardware	4,050	45.0%	$ 4,860
Housewares	2,700	30.0	3,240
Appliances	2,250	25.0	2,700
Totals	9,000	100.0%	$10,800

We continue step 2 by allocating the $2,400 of utilities expense to all departments based on the square footage occupied as shown in Exhibit 22.10.

EXHIBIT 22.10

Allocating Indirect (Utilities)
Expense to All Departments

Department	Square Feet	Percent of Total	Allocated Cost
General office	1,500	12.50%	$ 300
Purchasing	1,500	12.50	300
Hardware	4,050	33.75	810
Housewares	2,700	22.50	540
Appliances	2,250	18.75	450
Totals	12,000	100.00%	$2,400

Exhibit 22.11 shows the allocation of $1,000 of advertising expense to the three operating departments on the basis of sales dollars. We exclude service departments from this allocation because they do not generate sales.

EXHIBIT 22.11

Allocating Indirect (Advertising)
Expense to Operating Departments

Department	Sales	Percent of Total	Allocated Cost
Hardware	$119,500	50.0%	$ 500
Housewares	71,700	30.0	300
Appliances	47,800	20.0	200
Totals	$239,000	100.0%	$1,000

To complete step 2 we allocate insurance expense to each service and operating department as shown in Exhibit 22.12.

EXHIBIT 22.12

Allocating Indirect (Insurance)
Expense to All Departments

Department	Value of Insured Assets	Percent of Total	Allocated Cost
General office	$ 38,000	16.0%	$ 400
Purchasing	19,000	8.0	200
Hardware	85,500	36.0	900
Housewares	57,000	24.0	600
Appliances	38,000	16.0	400
Total	$237,500	100.0%	$2,500

Third (step 3), total expenses of the two service departments are allocated to the three operating departments as shown in Exhibits 22.13 and 22.14.

EXHIBIT 22.13

Allocating Service Department
(General Office) Expenses to
Operating Departments

Department	Sales	Percent of Total	Allocated Cost
Hardware	$119,500	50.0%	$ 7,650
Housewares	71,700	30.0	4,590
Appliances	47,800	20.0	3,060
Total	$239,000	100.0%	$15,300

Department	Number of Purchase Orders	Percent of Total	Allocated Cost
Hardware	394	40.00%	$3,880
Housewares	267	27.11	2,630
Appliances	324	32.89	3,190
Total	985	100.00%	$9,700

EXHIBIT 22.14

Allocating Service Department (Purchasing) Expenses to Operating Departments

Step 4:   The departmental expense allocation spreadsheet can now be used to prepare performance reports for the company's service and operating departments. The general office and purchasing departments are cost centers, and their managers will be evaluated on their control of costs. Actual amounts of service department expenses can be compared to budgeted amounts to help assess cost center manager performance.

Amounts in the operating department columns are used to prepare departmental income statements as shown in Exhibit 22.15. This exhibit uses the spreadsheet for its operating expenses; information on sales and cost of goods sold comes from departmental records.

Example: If the $15,300 general office expenses in Exhibit 22.6 are allocated equally across departments, what is net income for the hardware department and for the combined company? *Answer:* Hardware income, $13,350; combined income, $19,000.

A-1 HARDWARE
Departmental Income Statements
For Year Ended December 31, 2013

	Hardware Department	Housewares Department	Appliances Department	Combined	
Sales	$119,500	$71,700	$47,800	$239,000	
Cost of goods sold	73,800	43,800	30,200	147,800	
Gross profit	45,700	27,900	17,600	91,200	
Operating expenses					
Salaries expense	15,600	7,000	7,800	30,400	⎱ Direct expenses
Depreciation expense—Equipment	400	100	200	700	
Supplies expense	300	200	100	600	⎰
Rent expense.......................	4,860	3,240	2,700	10,800	⎱
Utilities expense	810	540	450	1,800	Allocated indirect expenses
Advertising expense	500	300	200	1,000	
Insurance expense...................	900	600	400	1,900	⎰
Share of general office expenses	7,650	4,590	3,060	15,300	⎱ Allocated service department expenses
Share of purchasing expenses	3,880	2,630	3,190	9,700	⎰
Total operating expenses	34,900	19,200	18,100	72,200	
Net income (loss)	$10,800	$ 8,700	$ (500)	$19,000	

EXHIBIT 22.15

Departmental Income Statements (Operating Departments)

Departmental Contribution to Overhead

Data from departmental income statements are not always best for evaluating each profit center's performance, especially when indirect expenses are a large portion of total expenses and when weaknesses in assumptions and decisions in allocating indirect expenses can markedly affect net income. Also, operating department managers might have no control over the level of service department services they use. In these and other cases, we might better evaluate profit center performance using the **departmental contribution to overhead,** which is a report of the amount of sales less *direct* expenses.[3] (We can also examine cost center performance by focusing on control of direct expenses.)

---

[3] A department's contribution is said to be "to overhead" because of the practice of considering all indirect expenses as overhead. Thus, the excess of a department's sales over direct expenses is a contribution toward at least a portion of its total overhead.

EXHIBIT 22.16

Departmental Contribution to Overhead

	Hardware Department	Housewares Department	Appliances Department	Combined
A-1 HARDWARE				
Income Statement Showing Departmental Contribution to Overhead				
For Year Ended December 31, 2013				
Sales	$119,500	$ 71,700	$47,800	$239,000
Cost of goods sold	73,800	43,800	30,200	147,800
Gross profit	45,700	27,900	17,600	91,200
Direct expenses				
Salaries expense	15,600	7,000	7,800	30,400
Depreciation expense—Equipment	400	100	200	700
Supplies expense	300	200	100	600
Total direct expenses	16,300	7,300	8,100	31,700
Departmental contributions				
to overhead.......................	$ 29,400	$20,600	$ 9,500	$59,500
Indirect expenses				
Rent expense........................				10,800
Utilities expense				1,800
Advertising expense..................				1,000
Insurance expense				1,900
General office department expense				15,300
Purchasing department expense				9,700
Total indirect expenses				40,500
Net income				$19,000
Contribution as percent of sales	24.6%	28.7%	19.9%	24.9%

Point: Net income is the same in Exhibits 22.15 and 22.16. The method of reporting indirect expenses in Exhibit 22.16 does not change total net income but does identify each operating department's contribution to overhead and net income.

The upper half of Exhibit 22.16 shows a departmental (profit center) contribution to overhead as part of an expanded income statement. This format is common when reporting departmental contributions to overhead. Using the information in Exhibits 22.15 and 22.16, we can evaluate the profitability of the three profit centers. For instance, let's compare the performance of the appliances department as described in these two exhibits. Exhibit 22.15 shows a $500 net loss resulting from this department's operations, but Exhibit 22.16 shows a $9,500 positive contribution to overhead, which is 19.9% of the appliance department's sales. The contribution of the appliances department is not as large as that of the other selling departments, but a $9,500 contribution to overhead is better than a $500 loss. This tells us that the appliances department is not a money loser. On the contrary, it is contributing $9,500 toward defraying total indirect expenses of $40,500.

Quick Check   Answers — p. 965

4. If a company has two operating (selling) departments (shoes and hats) and two service departments (payroll and advertising), which of the following statements is correct? (a) Wages incurred in the payroll department are direct expenses of the shoe department, (b) Wages incurred in the payroll department are indirect expenses of the operating departments, or (c) Advertising department expenses are allocated to the other three departments.

5. Which of the following bases can be used to allocate supervisors' salaries across operating departments? (a) Hours spent in each department, (b) number of employees in each department, (c) sales achieved in each department, or (d) any of the above, depending on which information is most relevant and accessible.

6. What three steps are used to allocate expenses to operating departments?

7. An income statement showing departmental contribution to overhead, (a) subtracts indirect expenses from each department's revenues, (b) subtracts only direct expenses from each department's revenues, or (c) shows net income for each department.

EVALUATING INVESTMENT CENTER PERFORMANCE

This section introduces both financial and nonfinancial measures of investment center performance.

Financial Performance Evaluation Measures

Investment center managers are typically evaluated using performance measures that combine income and assets. Consider the following data for ZTel, a company which operates two divisions: LCD and S-Phone. The LCD division manufactures liquid crystal display (LCD) touch-screen monitors and sells them for use in computers, cellular phones, and other products. The S-Phone division sells smartphones, mobile phones that also function as personal computers, MP3 players, cameras, and global positioning satellite (GPS) systems. Exhibit 22.17 shows current year income and assets for those divisions.

	LCD	S-Phone
Net income	$ 526,500	$ 417,600
Average invested assets	2,500,000	1,850,000

A1 Analyze investment centers using return on assets and residual income.

EXHIBIT 22.17

Investment Center Income and Assets

Investment Center Return on (Assets) Investment   One measure to evaluate division performance is the **investment center return on total assets,** commonly called *return on investment* (ROI) or *return on assets* (ROA). This measure is computed as follows:

$$\text{Return on investment} = \frac{\text{Investment center net income}}{\text{Investment center average invested assets}}$$

The return on investment for the LCD division is 21% (rounded), computed as $526,500/$2,500,000. The S-Phone division's return on investment is 23% (rounded), computed as $417,600/$1,850,000. Though the LCD division earned more dollars of net income, it was less efficient in using its assets to generate income compared to the S-Phone division.

Investment Center Residual Income   Another way to evaluate division performance is to compute **investment center residual income,** which is computed as follows:

$$\text{Residual income} = \frac{\text{Investment center}}{\text{net income}} - \frac{\text{Target investment center}}{\text{net income}}$$

Assume ZTel's top management sets target net income at 8% of divisional assets. For an investment center, this **hurdle rate** is typically the cost of obtaining financing. Applying this hurdle rate using the data from Exhibit 22.17 yields the residual income for ZTel's divisions in Exhibit 22.18.

	LCD	S-Phone
Net income	$526,500	$417,600
Less: Target net income		
$2,500,000 × 8%	200,000	
$1,850,000 × 8%		148,000
Investment center residual income	$326,500	$269,600

EXHIBIT 22.18

Investment Center Residual Income

Unlike return on assets, residual income is expressed in dollars. The LCD division outperformed the S-Phone division on the basis of residual income. However, this result is due in part to the LCD division having a larger asset base than the S-Phone division.

Using residual income to evaluate division performance encourages division managers to accept all opportunities that return more than the target net income, thus increasing company value. For example, the S-Phone division might not want to accept a new customer that will provide a 15% return on investment, since that will reduce the S-Phone division's overall return on investment (23% as shown above). However, the S-Phone division should accept this opportunity because the new customer would increase residual income by providing net income above the target net income.

Issues in Computing Return on (Assets) Investment and Residual Income

Evaluations of investment center performance using return on assets and residual income can be impacted by how a company answers the questions below:

1. How do you compute average invested assets? It is common to compute the average by adding the year's beginning amount of invested assets to the year's ending amount of invested assets, and dividing that sum by 2. Averages based on monthly or quarterly asset amounts are also acceptable.

2. How do you measure invested assets? It is common to measure invested assets using their *net* book values. For example, depreciable assets would be measured at their cost minus accumulated depreciation. As net book value declines over a depreciable asset's useful life, the result is that return on assets and residual income would increase over that asset's life. This might cause managers not to invest in new assets. In addition, in measuring invested assets, companies commonly exclude assets that are not used in generating investment center net income such as land held for resale.

3. How do you measure investment center income? It is common to exclude both interest expense and tax expense from investment center income. Interest expense reflects a company's financing decisions, and tax expense is typically considered outside the control of an investment center manager. Excluding interest and taxes in these calculations enables more meaningful comparisons of return on assets and residual income across investment centers and companies.

Point: *Economic Value Added* (EVA®), developed and trademarked by Stern, Stewart, and Co., is an approach to address issues in computing residual income. This method uses a variety of adjustments to compute income, assets, and the hurdle rate.

Decision Insight

In-the-Money   Executive pay is often linked to performance measures. Bonus payments are often based on exceeding a target return on investment or certain balanced scorecard indicators. Stock awards, such as stock options and restricted stock, reward executives when their company's stock price rises. The goal of bonus plans and stock awards is to encourage executives to make decisions that increase company performance and value. ▪

A2 Analyze investment centers using profit margin and investment turnover.

Investment Center Profit Margin and Investment Turnover   We can further examine investment center (division) performance by splitting return on investment into **profit margin** and **investment turnover** as follows

Return on investment	=	Profit margin	×	Investment turnover

$$\frac{\text{Investment center net income}}{\text{Investment center average assets}} = \frac{\text{Investment center net income}}{\text{Investment center sales}} \times \frac{\text{Investment center sales}}{\text{Investment center average assets}}$$

Profit margin measures the income earned per dollar of sales. **Investment turnover** measures how efficiently an investment center generates sales from its invested assets. Profit margin is expressed as a percent, while investment turnover is interpreted as the number of times assets were converted into sales. Higher profit margin and higher investment turnover indicate better performance. To illustrate, consider Best Buy which reports in Exhibit 22.19 results for two divisions (segments): Domestic and International.

($ millions)	Domestic	International
Sales......................	$37,186	$13,086
Net income	2,031	83
Average invested assets	10,021	8,055

EXHIBIT 22.19

Best Buy Division Sales, Income, and Assets

Profit margin and investment turnover for its Domestic and International divisions are computed and shown in Exhibit 22.20:

($ millions)	Domestic	International
Profit Margin		
$2,031/$37,186	5.55%	
$83/$13,086		0.6%
Investment Turnover		
$37,186/$10,021	3.71	
$13,086/$8,055		1.62
Return on Investment		
5.55% × 3.71	20.59%	
0.6% × 1.62		1.01%

EXHIBIT 22.20

Best Buy Division Profit Margin and Investment Turnover

Best Buy's Domestic division generates 5.55 cents of profit per $1 of sales, while its International division generates less than 1 cent of profit per dollar of sales. Its Domestic division also uses its assets more efficiently; its investment turnover of 3.71 is over twice that of its International division's 1.62. Alternatively, if Best Buy's Domestic division instead had sales of $40 billion, net income of $3 billion, and average invested assets of $4 billion, its profit margin, investment turnover, and return on assets would be 7.5%, 4%, and 30%, respectively. Top management can use profit margin and investment turnover to evaluate the performance of division managers. The measures can also aid management when considering further investment in its divisions. As a result of both a much higher profit margin and a more rapid investment turnover, the Domestic division's return on investment (20.59%) is much greater than that of the International division (0.97%).

Decision Maker

Division Manager   You manage a division in a highly competitive industry. You will receive a cash bonus if your division achieves an ROI above 12%. Your division's profit margin is 7%, equal to the industry average, and your division's investment turnover is 1.5. What actions can you take to increase your chance of receiving the bonus? ■   [Answer—p. 965]

Quick Check   Answers — p. 965

8. A division reports sales of $50,000, income of $2,000, and average invested assets of $10,000. Compute the division's (a) profit margin, (b) investment turnover, and (c) return on investment.

Nonfinancial Performance Evaluation Measures

Evaluating performance solely on financial measures such as return on investment or residual income has limitations. For example, some investment center managers might forgo profitable opportunities to keep their return on investment high. Also, residual income is less useful when comparing investment centers of different size. And, both return on investment and residual income can encourage managers to focus too heavily on short-term financial goals.

In response to these limitations, companies consider nonfinancial measures. For example, a delivery company such as FedEx might track the percentage of on-time deliveries. The percentage

A3 Analyze investment centers using the balanced scorecard.

of defective tennis balls manufactured can be used to assess performance of Penn's production managers. Walmart's credit card screens commonly ask customers at check-out whether the cashier was friendly or the store was clean. This kind of information can help division managers run their divisions and help top management evaluate division manager performance.

Balanced Scorecard   The **balanced scorecard** is a system of performance measures, including nonfinancial measures, used to assess company and division manager performance. The balanced scorecard requires managers to think of their company from four perspectives:

1. **Customer:** What do customers think of us?
2. **Internal processes:** Which of our operations are critical to meeting customer needs?
3. **Innovation and learning:** How can we improve?
4. **Financial:** What do our owners think of us?

Point: One survey indicates that nearly 60% of global companies use some form of a balanced scorecard.

The balanced scorecard collects information on several key performance indicators within each of the four perspectives. These key indicators vary across companies. Exhibit 22.21 lists common performance measures.

EXHIBIT 22.21

Balanced Scorecard Performance Indicators

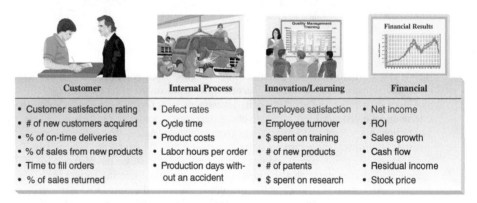

Customer	Internal Process	Innovation/Learning	Financial
• Customer satisfaction rating	• Defect rates	• Employee satisfaction	• Net income
• # of new customers acquired	• Cycle time	• Employee turnover	• ROI
• % of on-time deliveries	• Product costs	• $ spent on training	• Sales growth
• % of sales from new products	• Labor hours per order	• # of new products	• Cash flow
• Time to fill orders	• Production days without an accident	• # of patents	• Residual income
• % of sales returned		• $ spent on research	• Stock price

After selecting key performance indicators, companies collect data on each indicator and compare actual amounts to expected amounts to assess performance. For example, a company might have a goal of filling 98% of customer orders within two hours. Balanced scorecard reports are often presented in graphs or tables that can be updated frequently. Such timely information aids division managers in their decisions, and can be used by top management to evaluate division manager performance.

Exhibit 22.22 is an example of balanced scorecard reporting on the customer perspective for an Internet retailer. This scorecard reports for example that the retailer is getting 62% of its potential customers successfully through the checkout process, and that 2.2% of all orders are returned. The *color* of the arrows in the right-most column reveals whether the company is exceeding its goal (green), barely meeting the goal (yellow), or not meeting the goal (red). The *direction* of the arrows reveals any trend in performance: an upward arrow indicates improvement, a downward arrow indicates declining performance, and an arrow pointing sideways indicates no change. A

EXHIBIT 22.22

Balanced Scorecard Reporting: Internet Retailer

Customer Perspective	Actual	Goal
Checkout success	62%	⬆
Orders returned	2.2%	⬌
Customer satisfaction rating	9.5	⬆
Number of customer complaints	142	⬇

review of these arrows' color and direction suggests the retailer is meeting or exceeding its goals on checkout success, orders returned, and customer satisfaction. Further, checkout success and customer satisfaction are improving. The red arrow shows the company has received more customer complaints than was hoped for; however, the number of customer complaints is declining. A manager would combine this information with similar information on the internal process, innovation and learning, and financial perspectives to get an overall view of division performance.

Decision Maker

Center Manager   Your center's usual return on total assets is 19%. You are considering two new investments for your center. The first requires a $250,000 average investment and is expected to yield annual net income of $50,000. The second requires a $1 million average investment with an expected annual net income of $175,000. Do you pursue either? ■   [Answer—p. 965]

GLOBAL VIEW

L'Oreal is an international cosmetics company incorporated in France. With multiple brands and operations in over 100 countries, the company uses concepts of departmental accounting and controllable costs to evaluate performance. For example, its 2010 annual report shows the following for the major divisions in its Cosmetics branch:

Division	Operating Profit (€ millions)	
Consumer products	€1,765	
Professional products	552	
Luxury products	791	
Active cosmetics	277	€3,385 ◄— Similar to "Departmental contributions to overhead" in Exhibit 22.16
Nonallocated costs		(513)
Cosmetics branch total		€2,872 ◄— Similar to "Net income" in Exhibit 22.16

For L'Oreal, nonallocated costs include costs that are not controllable by division managers, including fundamental research and development and costs of service operations like insurance and banking. Excluding noncontrollable costs enables L'Oreal to prepare more meaningful division performance evaluations.

 Cycle Time and Cycle Efficiency   **Decision Analysis**

Manufacturing companies commonly use nonfinancial measures to evaluate the performance of their production processes. For example, as lean manufacturing practices help companies move toward just-in-time manufacturing, it is important for these companies to reduce the time to manufacture their products and to improve manufacturing efficiency. One metric that measures that time element is **cycle time (CT)**. A definition of cycle time is in Exhibit 22.23.

> A4   Compute cycle time and cycle efficiency, and explain their importance to production management.

Cycle time = Process time + Inspection time + Move time + Wait time

EXHIBIT 22.23

Cycle Time

Process time is the time spent producing the product. *Inspection time* is the time spent inspecting (1) raw materials when received, (2) goods in process while in production, and (3) finished goods prior to shipment. *Move time* is the time spent moving (1) raw materials from storage to production and (2) goods in process from one factory location to another factory location. *Wait time* is the time that an order or job sits with no production applied to it; this can be due to order delays, bottlenecks in production, and poor scheduling.

958   Chapter 22   Performance Measurement and Responsibility Accounting

Process time is considered **value-added time** because it is the only activity in cycle time that adds value to the product from the customer's perspective. The other three time activities are considered **non-value-added time** because they add no value to the customer.

Companies strive to reduce non-value-added time to improve **cycle efficiency (CE).** Cycle efficiency is the ratio of value-added time to total cycle time—see Exhibit 22.24.

EXHIBIT 22.24

Cycle Efficiency

$$\text{Cycle efficiency} = \frac{\text{Value-added time}}{\text{Cycle time}}$$

To illustrate, assume that Rocky Mountain Bikes receives and produces an order for 500 Tracker® mountain bikes. Assume that the following times were measured during production of this order.

Process time... 1.8 days **Inspection time... 0.5 days** **Move time... 0.7 days** **Wait time... 3.0 days**

In this case, cycle time is 6.0 days, computed as 1.8 days + 0.5 days + 0.7 days + 3.0 days. Also, cycle efficiency is 0.3, or 30%, computed as 1.8 days divided by 6.0 days. This means that Rocky Mountain Bikes spends 30% of its time working on the product (value-added time). The other 70% is spent on non-value-added activities.

If a company has a CE of 1, it means that its time is spent entirely on value-added activities. If the CE is low, the company should evaluate its production process to see if it can identify ways to reduce non-value-added activities. The 30% CE for Rocky Mountain Bikes is low and its management should look for ways to reduce non-value-added activities.

DEMONSTRATION PROBLEM

Management requests departmental income statements for Hacker's Haven, a computer store that has five departments. Three are operating departments (hardware, software, and repairs) and two are service departments (general office and purchasing).

	General Office	Purchasing	Hardware	Software	Repairs
Sales	—	—	$960,000	$600,000	$840,000
Cost of goods sold	—	—	500,000	300,000	200,000
Direct expenses					
Payroll	$60,000	$45,000	80,000	25,000	325,000
Depreciation	6,000	7,200	33,000	4,200	9,600
Supplies	15,000	10,000	10,000	2,000	25,000

The departments incur several indirect expenses. To prepare departmental income statements, the indirect expenses must be allocated across the five departments. Then the expenses of the two service departments must be allocated to the three operating departments. Total cost amounts and the allocation bases for each indirect expense follow.

Indirect Expense	Total Cost	Allocation Basis
Rent	$150,000	Square footage occupied
Utilities	50,000	Square footage occupied
Advertising	125,000	Dollars of sales
Insurance	30,000	Value of assets insured
Service departments		
General office	?	Number of employees
Purchasing	?	Dollars of cost of goods sold

The following additional information is needed for indirect expense allocations.

Department	Square Feet	Sales	Insured Assets	Employees	Cost of Goods Sold
General office	500		$ 60,000		
Purchasing	500		72,000		
Hardware............	4,000	$ 960,000	330,000	5	$ 500,000
Software.............	3,000	600,000	42,000	5	300,000
Repairs	2,000	840,000	96,000	10	200,000
Totals	10,000	$2,400,000	$600,000	20	$1,000,000

Required

1. Prepare a departmental expense allocation spreadsheet for Hacker's Haven.
2. Prepare a departmental income statement reporting net income for each operating department and for all operating departments combined.

PLANNING THE SOLUTION

- Set up and complete four tables to allocate the indirect expenses—one each for rent, utilities, advertising, and insurance.
- Allocate the departments' indirect expenses using a spreadsheet like the one in Exhibit 22.6. Enter the given amounts of the direct expenses for each department. Then enter the allocated amounts of the indirect expenses that you computed.
- Complete two tables for allocating the general office and purchasing department costs to the three operating departments. Enter these amounts on the spreadsheet and determine the total expenses allocated to the three operating departments.
- Prepare departmental income statements like the one in Exhibit 22.15. Show sales, cost of goods sold, gross profit, individual expenses, and net income for each of the three operating departments and for the combined company.

SOLUTION TO DEMONSTRATION PROBLEM

Allocations of the four indirect expenses across the five departments.

Rent	Square Feet	Percent of Total	Allocated Cost
General office	500	5.0%	$ 7,500
Purchasing	500	5.0	7,500
Hardware............	4,000	40.0	60,000
Software	3,000	30.0	45,000
Repairs	2,000	20.0	30,000
Totals	10,000	100.0%	$150,000

Utilities	Square Feet	Percent of Total	Allocated Cost
General office	500	5.0%	$ 2,500
Purchasing	500	5.0	2,500
Hardware............	4,000	40.0	20,000
Software	3,000	30.0	15,000
Repairs	2,000	20.0	10,000
Totals	10,000	100.0%	$50,000

Advertising	Sales Dollars	Percent of Total	Allocated Cost
Hardware...........	$ 960,000	40.0%	$ 50,000
Software............	600,000	25.0	31,250
Repairs	840,000	35.0	43,750
Totals	$2,400,000	100.0%	$125,000

Insurance	Assets Insured	Percent of Total	Allocated Cost
General office	$ 60,000	10.0%	$ 3,000
Purchasing	72,000	12.0	3,600
Hardware	330,000	55.0	16,500
Software	42,000	7.0	2,100
Repairs	96,000	16.0	4,800
Totals	$600,000	100.0%	$30,000

1. Allocations of service department expenses to the three operating departments.

General Office Allocations to	Employees	Percent of Total	Allocated Cost
Hardware..............	5	25.0%	$23,500
Software..............	5	25.0	23,500
Repairs...............	10	50.0	47,000
Totals	20	100.0%	$94,000

Purchasing Allocations to	Cost of Goods Sold	Percent of Total	Allocated Cost
Hardware..............	$ 500,000	50.0%	$37,900
Software..............	300,000	30.0	22,740
Repairs...............	200,000	20.0	15,160
Totals	$1,000,000	100.0%	$75,800

HACKER'S HAVEN
Departmental Expense Allocations
For Year Ended December 31, 2013

	Allocation Base	Expense Account Balance	General Office Dept.	Purchasing Dept.	Hardware Dept.	Software Dept.	Repairs Dept.
Direct Expenses							
Payroll.........................		$ 535,000	$ 60,000	$ 45,000	$ 80,000	$ 25,000	$ 325,000
Depreciation		60,000	6,000	7,200	33,000	4,200	9,600
Supplies		62,000	15,000	10,000	10,000	2,000	25,000
Indirect Expenses							
Rent	Square ft.	150,000	7,500	7,500	60,000	45,000	30,000
Utilities.........................	Square ft.	50,000	2,500	2,500	20,000	15,000	10,000
Advertising.......................	Sales	125,000	—	—	50,000	31,250	43,750
Insurance	Assets	30,000	3,000	3,600	16,500	2,100	4,800
Total expenses		1,012,000	94,000	75,800	269,500	124,550	448,150
Service Department Expenses							
General office	Employees		(94,000)		23,500	23,500	47,000
Purchasing	Goods sold			(75,800)	37,900	22,740	15,160
Total expenses allocated to operating departments		$1,012,000	$ 0	$ 0	$330,900	$170,790	$510,310

2. Departmental income statements for Hacker's Haven.

HACKER'S HAVEN
Departmental Income Statements
For Year Ended December 31, 2013

	Hardware	Software	Repairs	Combined
Sales	$ 960,000	$ 600,000	$ 840,000	$2,400,000
Cost of goods sold	500,000	300,000	200,000	1,000,000
Gross profit	460,000	300,000	640,000	1,400,000
Expenses				
Payroll	80,000	25,000	325,000	430,000
Depreciation	33,000	4,200	9,600	46,800
Supplies	10,000	2,000	25,000	37,000
Rent	60,000	45,000	30,000	135,000
Utilities	20,000	15,000	10,000	45,000
Advertising.................	50,000	31,250	43,750	125,000
Insurance	16,500	2,100	4,800	23,400
Share of general office	23,500	23,500	47,000	94,000
Share of purchasing	37,900	22,740	15,160	75,800
Total expenses	330,900	170,790	510,310	1,012,000
Net income	$129,100	$129,210	$129,690	$ 388,000

APPENDIX

Transfer Pricing 22A

C2 Explain transfer pricing and methods to set transfer prices.

Divisions in decentralized companies sometimes do business with one another. For example, a separate division of Harley-Davidson manufactures its plastic and fiberglass parts used in the company's motorcycles. Anheuser-Busch's metal container division makes cans and lids used in its brewing operations, and also sells cans and lids to soft-drink companies. A division of Prince produces strings used in tennis rackets made by Prince and other manufacturers.

Determining the price that should be used to record transfers between divisions in the same company is the focus of this appendix. Because these transactions are transfers within the same company, the price to record them is called the **transfer price.** In decentralized organizations, division managers have input on or decide those prices. Transfer prices can be used in cost, profit, and investment centers. Since these transfers are not with customers outside the company, the transfer price has no direct impact on the company's overall profits. However, transfer prices can impact performance evaluations and, if set incorrectly, lead to bad decisions.

Point: Transfer pricing can impact company profits when divisions are located in countries with different tax rates; this is covered in advanced courses.

Alternative Transfer Prices Exhibit 22A.1 reports data on the LCD division of ZTel. LCD manufactures liquid crystal display (LCD) touch-screen monitors for use in ZTel's S-Phone division's smartphones, which sell for $400 each. The monitors can also be used in other products. So, LCD can sell its monitors to buyers other than S-Phone. Likewise, the S-Phone division can purchase monitors from suppliers other than LCD.

EXHIBIT 22A.1

LCD Division Manufacturing Information—Monitors

Production capacity	100,000 units
Selling price per unit to outside customers	$80
Variable manufacturing costs per unit	$40
Fixed manufacturing costs	$2,000,000

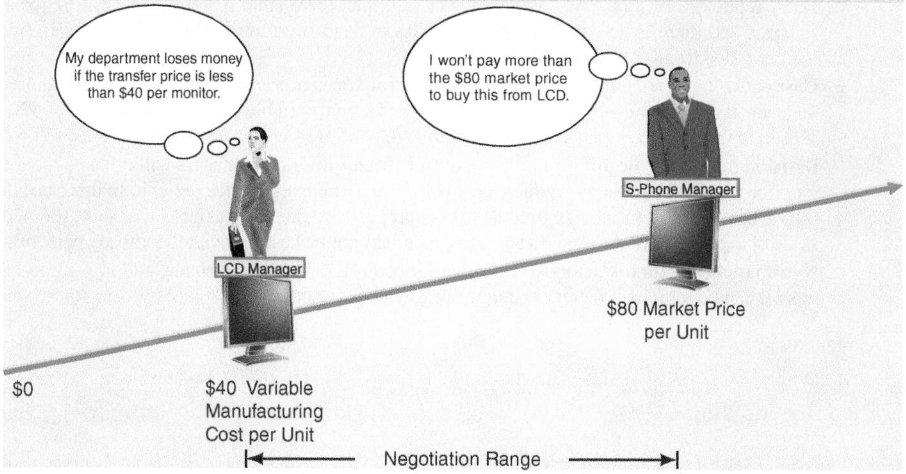

Exhibit 22A.1 reveals the range of transfer prices for transfers of monitors from LCD to S-Phone. The manager of LCD wants to report a division profit; thus, this manager will not accept a transfer price less than $40 (variable manufacturing cost per unit) because doing so would cause the division to lose money on each monitor transferred. The LCD manager will only consider transfer prices of $40 or more. On the other hand, the S-Phone division manager also wants to report a division profit. Thus, this manager will not pay more than $80 per monitor because similar monitors can be bought from outside suppliers at that price. The S-Phone manager will only consider transfer prices of $80 or less. As any transfer price between $40 and $80 per monitor is possible, how does ZTel determine the transfer price? The answer depends in part on whether the LCD division has excess capacity to manufacture monitors.

No Excess Capacity   Assume the LCD division can sell every monitor it produces, and thus is producing 100,000 units. In that case, a **market-based transfer price** of $80 per monitor is preferred. At that price, the LCD division manager is willing to either transfer monitors to S-Phone or sell to outside customers. The S-Phone manager cannot buy monitors for less than $80 from outside suppliers, so the $80 price is acceptable. Further, with a transfer price of $80 per monitor, top management of ZTel is indifferent to S-Phone buying from LCD or buying similar-quality monitors from outside suppliers.

With no excess capacity, the LCD manager will not accept a transfer price less than $80 per monitor. For example, suppose the S-Phone manager suggests a transfer price of $70 per monitor. At that price the LCD manager incurs an unnecessary *opportunity cost* of $10 per monitor (computed as $80 market price minus $70 transfer price). This would lower the LCD division's income and hurt its performance evaluation.

Excess Capacity   Assume that the LCD division has excess capacity. For example, the LCD division might currently be producing only 80,000 units. Because LCD has $2,000,000 of fixed manufacturing costs, both LCD and the top management of ZTel prefer that S-Phone purchases its monitors from LCD. For example, if S-Phone purchases its monitors from an outside supplier at the market price of $80 each, LCD manufactures no units. Then, LCD reports a division loss equal to its fixed costs, and ZTel overall reports a lower net income as its costs are higher. Consequently, with excess capacity, LCD should accept any transfer price of $40 per unit or greater and S-Phone should purchase monitors from LCD. This will allow LCD to recover some (or all) of its fixed costs and increase ZTel's overall profits. For example, if a transfer price of $50 per monitor is used, the S-Phone manager is pleased to buy from LCD, since that price is below the market price of $80. For each monitor transferred from LCD to S-Phone at $50, the LCD division receives a *contribution margin* of $10 (computed as $50 transfer price less $40 variable cost) to contribute towards recovering its fixed costs. This form of transfer pricing is called **cost-based transfer pricing.** Under this approach the transfer price might be based on variable costs, total costs, or variable costs plus a markup. Determining the transfer price under excess capacity is complex and is covered in advanced courses.

Transfer Pricing Approaches Used by Companies

Cost 46%

Market 37%

Negotiated 17%

Additional Issues in Transfer Pricing   Several additional issues arise in determining transfer prices which include the following:

- **No market price exists.** Sometimes there is no market price for the product being transferred. The product might be a key component that requires additional conversion costs at the next stage and is not easily replicated by an outside company. For example, there is no market for a console for a **Nissan** Maxima and there is no substitute console **Nissan** can use in assembling a Maxima. In this case a market-based transfer price cannot be used.
- **Cost control.** To provide incentives for cost control, transfer prices might be based on standard, rather than actual costs. For example, if a transfer price of actual variable costs plus a markup of $20 per unit is used in the case above, LCD has no incentive to control its costs.
- **Division managers' negotiation.** With excess capacity, division managers will often negotiate a transfer price that lies between the variable cost per unit and the market price per unit. In this case, the **negotiated transfer price** and resulting departmental performance reports reflect, in part, the negotiating skills of the respective division managers. This might not be best for overall company performance.
- **Nonfinancial factors.** Factors such as quality control, reduced lead times, and impact on employee morale can be important factors in determining transfer prices.

22B Joint Costs and Their Allocation

C3   Describe allocation of joint costs across products.

Most manufacturing processes involve **joint costs,** which refer to costs incurred to produce or purchase two or more products at the same time. A joint cost is like an indirect expense in the sense that more than one cost object share it. For example, a sawmill company incurs a joint cost when it buys logs that it cuts into lumber as shown in Exhibit 22B.1. The joint cost includes the logs (raw material) and its cutting (conversion) into boards classified as Clear, Select, No. 1 Common, No. 2 Common, No. 3 Common, and other types of lumber and by-products.

When a joint cost is incurred, a question arises as to whether to allocate it to different products resulting from it. The answer is that when management wishes to estimate the costs of individual products, joint costs are included and must be allocated to these joint products. However, when management needs information to help decide whether to sell a product at a certain point in the production process or to process it further, the joint costs are ignored.

Financial statements prepared according to GAAP must assign joint costs to products. To do this, management must decide how to allocate joint costs across products benefiting from these costs. If some products are sold and others remain in inventory, allocating joint costs involves assigning costs to both cost of goods sold and ending inventory.

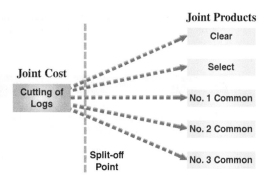

EXHIBIT 22B.1

Joint Products from Logs

The two usual methods to allocate joint costs are the (1) *physical basis* and (2) the *value basis*. The physical basis typically involves allocating joint cost using physical characteristics such as the ratio of pounds, cubic feet, or gallons of each joint product to the total pounds, cubic feet, or gallons of all joint products flowing from the cost. This method is not preferred because the resulting cost allocations do not reflect the relative market values the joint cost generates. The preferred approach is the value basis, which allocates joint cost in proportion to the sales value of the output produced by the process at the "split-off point"; see Exhibit 22B.1.

Physical Basis Allocation of Joint Cost   To illustrate the physical basis of allocating a joint cost, we consider a sawmill that bought logs for $30,000. When cut, these logs produce 100,000 board feet of lumber in the grades and amounts shown in Exhibit 22B.2. The logs produce 20,000 board feet of No. 3 Common lumber, which is 20% of the total. With physical allocation, the No. 3 Common lumber is assigned 20% of the $30,000 cost of the logs, or $6,000 ($30,000 × 20%). Because this low-grade lumber sells for $4,000, this allocation gives a $2,000 loss from its production and sale. The physical basis for allocating joint costs does not reflect the extra value flowing into some products or the inferior value flowing into others. That is, the portion of a log that produces Clear and Select grade lumber is worth more than the portion used to produce the three grades of common lumber, but the physical basis fails to reflect this.

Grade of Lumber	Board Feet Produced	Percent of Total	Allocated Cost	Sales Value	Gross Profit
Clear and Select............	10,000	10.0%	$ 3,000	$12,000	$ 9,000
No. 1 Common	30,000	30.0	9,000	18,000	9,000
No. 2 Common	40,000	40.0	12,000	16,000	4,000
No. 3 Common	20,000	20.0	6,000	4,000	(2,000)
Totals	100,000	100.0%	$30,000	$50,000	$20,000

EXHIBIT 22B.2

Allocating Joint Costs on a Physical Basis

Value Basis Allocation of Joint Cost   Exhibit 22B.3 illustrates the value basis method of allocation. It determines the percents of the total costs allocated to each grade by the ratio of each grade's sales value to the total sales value of $50,000 (sales value is the unit selling price multiplied by the number of units produced). The Clear and Select lumber grades receive 24% of the total cost ($12,000/$50,000) instead of the 10% portion using a physical basis. The No. 3 Common lumber receives only 8% of the total cost, or $2,400, which is much less than the $6,000 assigned to it using the physical basis.

Grade of Lumber	Sales Value	Percent of Total	Allocated Cost	Gross Profit
Clear and Select	$12,000	24.0%	$ 7,200	$ 4,800
No. 1 Common	18,000	36.0	10,800	7,200
No. 2 Common	16,000	32.0	9,600	6,400
No. 3 Common	4,000	8.0	2,400	1,600
Totals	$50,000	100.0%	$30,000	$20,000

EXHIBIT 22B.3

Allocating Joint Costs on a Value Basis

Example: Refer to Exhibit 22B.3. If the sales value of Clear and Select lumber is changed to $10,000, what is the revised ratio of the market value of No. I Common to the total? *Answer:* $18,000/$48,000 = 37.5%

An outcome of value basis allocation is that *each* grade produces exactly the same 40% gross profit at the split-off point. This 40% rate equals the gross profit rate from selling all the lumber made from the $30,000 logs for a combined price of $50,000.

Quick Check   Answers — p. 965

9. A company produces three products, B1, B2, and B3. The joint cost incurred for the current month for these products is $180,000. The following data relate to this month's production:

Product	Units Produced	Unit Sales Value
BI	96,000	$3.00
B2	64,000	6.00
B3	32,000	9.00

The amount of joint cost allocated to product B3 using the value basis allocation is (*a*) $30,000, (*b*) $54,000, or (*c*) $90,000.

Summary

C1 Distinguish between direct and indirect expenses and identify bases for allocating indirect expenses to departments. Direct expenses are traced to a specific department and are incurred for the sole benefit of that department. Indirect expenses benefit more than one department. Indirect expenses are allocated to departments when computing departmental net income. Ideally, we allocate indirect expenses by using a cause-effect relation for the allocation base. When a cause-effect relation is not identifiable, each indirect expense is allocated on a basis reflecting the relative benefit received by each department.

C2 Explain transfer pricing and methods to set transfer prices. Transfer prices are used to record transfers of items between divisions of the same company. Transfer prices can be based on costs or market prices, or can be negotiated by division managers.

C3 Describe allocation of joint costs across products. A joint cost refers to costs incurred to produce or purchase two or more products at the same time. When income statements are prepared, joint costs are usually allocated to the resulting joint products using either a physical or value basis.

A1 Analyze investment centers using return on assets and residual income. A financial measure often used to evaluate an investment center manager is the *investment center return on total assets,* also called *return on investment.* This measure is computed as the center's net income divided by the center's average total assets. Residual income, computed as investment center net income minus a target net income is an alternative financial measure of investment center performance.

A2 Analyze investment centers using profit margin and investment turnover. Return on investment can also be computed as profit margin times investment turnover. Profit margin (equal to net income/sales) measures the income earned per dollar of sales and investment turnover (equal to sales/assets) measures how efficiently a division uses its assets.

A3 A balanced scorecard uses a combination of financial and nonfinancial measures to evaluate performance. Customer, internal process, and innovation and learning are the three primary perspectives of nonfinancial measures used in balanced scorecards.

A4 Compute cycle time and cycle efficiency, and explain their importance to production management. It is important for companies to reduce the time to produce their products and to improve manufacturing efficiency. One measure of that time is cycle time (CT), defined as Process time + Inspection time + Move time + Wait time. Process time is value-added time; the others are non-value-added time. Cycle efficiency (CE) is the ratio of value-added time to total cycle time. If CE is low, management should evaluate its production process to see if it can reduce non-value-added activities.

P1 Prepare a responsibility report for a cost center. Responsibility accounting systems provide information for evaluating the performance of department managers. A responsibility accounting system's performance reports for evaluating department managers should include only the expenses (and revenues) that each manager controls.

P2 Allocate indirect expenses to departments. Indirect expenses include items like depreciation, rent, advertising, and other expenses that cannot be assigned directly to departments. Indirect expenses are recorded in company accounts, an allocation base is identified for each expense, and costs are allocated to departments. Departmental expense allocation spreadsheets are often used in allocating indirect expenses to departments.

P3 Prepare departmental income statements and contribution reports. Each profit center (department) is assigned its expenses to yield its own income statement. These costs include its direct expenses and its share of indirect expenses. The departmental income statement lists its revenues and costs of goods sold to determine gross profit. Its operating expenses (direct expenses and its indirect expenses allocated to the department) are deducted from gross profit to yield departmental net income. The departmental contribution report is similar to the departmental income statement in terms of computing the gross profit for each department. Then the direct operating expenses for each department are deducted from gross profit to determine the contribution generated by each department. Indirect operating expenses are deducted *in total* from the company's combined contribution.

Guidance Answers to Decision Maker and Decision Ethics

Division Manager   Your division's ROI without further action is 10.5% (equal to 7% × 1.5). In a highly competitive industry, it is difficult to increase profit margins by raising prices. Your division might be better able to control its costs to increase its profit margin. In addition, you might engage in a marketing program to increase sales without increasing your division's invested assets. Investment turnover and thus ROI will increase if the marketing campaign attracts customers.

Center Manager   We must first realize that the two investment opportunities are not comparable on the basis of absolute dollars of

income or on assets. For instance, the second investment provides a higher income in absolute dollars but requires a higher investment. Accordingly, we need to compute return on total assets for each alternative: (1) $50,000 ÷ $250,000 = 20%, and (2) $175,000 ÷ $1 million = 17.5%. Alternative 1 has the higher return and is preferred over alternative 2. Do you pursue one, both, or neither? Because alternative 1's return is higher than the center's usual return of 19%, it should be pursued, assuming its risks are acceptable. Also, since alternative 1 requires a small investment, top management is likely to be more agreeable to pursuing it. Alternative 2's return is lower than the usual 19% and is not likely to be acceptable.

Guidance Answers to Quick Checks

1. *d*

2. A cost center, such as a service department, incurs costs without directly generating revenues. A profit center, such as a product division, incurs costs but also generates revenues.

3. *c*

4. *b*

5. *d*

6. (1) Assign the direct expenses to each department. (2) Allocate indirect expenses to all departments. (3) Allocate the service department expenses to the operating departments.

7. *b*

8. a) $2,000/50,000 = 4%; b) $50,000/10,000 = 5; $2,000/10,000 = 20%.

9. *b*; $180,000 × ([32,000 × $9]/[96,000 × $3 + 64,000 × $6 + 32,000 × $9]) = $54,000.

Key Terms

Balanced scorecard (p. 956)	Indirect expenses (p. 945)	Profit center (p. 943)
Controllable costs (p. 943)	Investment center (p. 943)	Profit margin (p. 954)
Cost-based transfer pricing (p. 962)	Investment center residual income (p. 953)	Responsibility accounting budget (p. 944)
Cost center (p. 943)		Responsibility accounting performance report (p. 944)
Cycle efficiency (p. 958)	Investment center return on total assets (p. 953)	
Cycle Time (CT) (p. 957)	Investment turnover (p. 954)	Responsibility accounting system (p. 942)
Departmental contribution to overhead (p. 951)	Joint cost (p. 962)	Transfer price (p. 961)
Departmental income statements (p. 945)	Market-based transfer price (p. 962)	Uncontrollable costs (p. 943)
Direct expenses (p. 945)	Negotiated transfer price (p. 962)	Value-added time (p. 958)
Hurdle rate (p. 953)	Non-value-added time (p. 958)	

Multiple Choice Quiz   Answers on p. 983   mhhe.com/wildFINMAN5e

Additional Quiz Questions are available at the book's Website.

1. A retailer has three departments—housewares, appliances, and clothing—and buys advertising that benefits all departments. Advertising expense is $150,000 for the year, and departmental sales for the year follow: housewares, $356,250; appliances, $641,250; clothing, $427,500. How much advertising expense is allocated to appliances if allocation is based on departmental sales?

a. $37,500
b. $67,500
c. $45,000
d. $150,000
e. $641,250

2. Indirect expenses
  a. Cannot be readily traced to one department.
  b. Are allocated to departments based on the relative benefit each department receives.
  c. Are the same as uncontrollable expenses.
  d. a, b, and c above are all true.
  e. a and b above are true.

3. A division reports the information below. What is the division's investment (asset) turnover?

Sales	$500,000
Income	75,000
Average assets	200,000

  a. 37.5%
  b. 15.0
  c. 2.5
  d. 2.67
  e. 4.0

4. A company operates three retail departments as profit centers, and the following information is available for each. Which department has the largest dollar amount of departmental contribution to overhead and what is the dollar amount contributed?

Department	Sales	Cost of Goods Sold	Direct Expenses	Allocated Indirect Expenses
X	$500,000	$350,000	$50,000	$40,000
Y	200,000	75,000	20,000	50,000
Z	350,000	150,000	75,000	10,000

  a. Department Y, $ 55,000
  b. Department Z, $125,000
  c. Department X, $500,000
  d. Department Z, $200,000
  e. Department X, $ 60,000

5. Using the data in question 4, Department X's contribution to overhead as a percentage of sales is
  a. 20%
  b. 30%
  c. 12%
  d. 48%
  e. 32%

A(B) *Superscript letter A (B) denotes assignments based on Appendix 22A (22B).*
🔲 Icon denotes assignments that involve decision making.

Discussion Questions

1. Why are many companies divided into departments?
2. What is the difference between operating departments and service departments?
3. 🔲 What are controllable costs?
4. Controllable and uncontrollable costs must be identified with a particular _____ and a definite _____ period.
5. 🔲 Why should managers be closely involved in preparing their responsibility accounting budgets?
6. 🔲 What are two main goals in managerial accounting for reporting on and analyzing departments?
7. 🔲 Is it possible to evaluate a cost center's profitability? Explain.
8. What is the difference between direct and indirect expenses?
9. 🔲 Suggest a reasonable basis for allocating each of the following indirect expenses to departments: (a) salary of a supervisor who manages several departments, (b) rent, (c) heat, (d) electricity for lighting, (e) janitorial services, (f) advertising, (g) expired insurance on equipment, and (h) property taxes on equipment.
10. Piaggio has many departments. How is a department's contribution to overhead measured? **PIAGGIO**
11. 🔲 KTM aims to give its managers timely cost reports. In responsibility accounting, who receives timely cost reports and specific cost information? Explain. **KTM**

12.ᴬ What is a transfer price? Under what conditions is a market-based transfer price most likely to be used?
13.ᴮ What is a joint cost? How are joint costs usually allocated among the products produced from them?
14.ᴮ 🔲 Give two examples of products with joint costs.
15. 🔲 Each retail store of Apple has several departments. Why is it useful for its management to (a) collect accounting information about each department and (b) treat each department as a profit center? **Apple**
16. 🔲 Polaris delivers its products to locations around the world. List three controllable and three uncontrollable costs for its delivery department. **Polaris**
17. 🔲 Define and describe *cycle time* and identify the components of cycle time.
18. 🔲 Explain the difference between value-added time and non-value-added time.
19. Define and describe *cycle efficiency*.
20. 🔲 Can management of a company such as Arctic Cat use cycle time and cycle efficiency as useful measures of performance? Explain. **Arctic Cat**

Connect

In each blank next to the following terms, place the identifying letter of its best description.

1. _____ Cost center
2. _____ Investment center
3. _____ Departmental accounting system
4. _____ Operating department
5. _____ Profit center
6. _____ Responsibility accounting system
7. _____ Service department

A. Incurs costs without directly yielding revenues.

B. Provides information used to evaluate the performance of a department.

C. Holds manager responsible for revenues, costs, and investments.

D. Engages directly in manufacturing or in making sales directly to customers.

E. Does not directly manufacture products but contributes to profitability of the entire company.

F. Incurs costs and also generates revenues.

G. Provides information used to evaluate the performance of a department manager.

QUICK STUDY

QS 22-1
Allocation and measurement terms
C1

For each of the following types of indirect expenses and service department expenses, identify one allocation basis that could be used to distribute it to the departments indicated.

1. Computer service expenses of production scheduling for operating departments.
2. General office department expenses of the operating departments.
3. Maintenance department expenses of the operating departments.
4. Electric utility expenses of all departments.

QS 22-2
Basis for cost allocation

C1

In each blank next to the following terms, place the identifying letter of its best description.

1. _____ Indirect expenses
2. _____ Controllable costs
3. _____ Direct expenses
4. _____ Uncontrollable costs

A. Costs not within a manager's control or influence
B. Costs that can be readily traced to a department
C. Cost that a manager has the ability to affect
D. Costs incurred for the joint benefit of more than one department

QS 22-3
Responsibility accounting terms
C1

Use the information in the following table to compute each department's contribution to overhead (both in dollars and as a percent). Which department contributes the largest dollar amount to total overhead? Which contributes the highest percent (as a percent of sales)? Round percents to one decimal.

QS 22-4
Departmental contribution to overhead
P3

	Dept. A	Dept. B	Dept. C
Sales	$53,000	$180,000	$84,000
Cost of goods sold	34,185	103,700	49,560
Gross profit	18,815	76,300	34,440
Total direct expenses	3,660	37,060	7,386
Contribution to overhead	$_____	$_____	$_____
Contribution percent	_____%	_____%	_____%

Compute return on assets for each of the divisions below (each is an investment center). Comment on the relative performance of each investment center.

QS 22-5
Computing investment center return on assets
A1

Investment Center	Net Income	Average Assets	Return on Assets
Cameras and camcorders	$4,500,000	$20,000,000	_____
Phones and communications	1,500,000	12,500,000	_____
Computers and accessories	800,000	10,000,000	_____

Refer to information in QS 22-5. Assume a target income of 12% of average invested assets. Compute residual income for each division.

QS 22-6
Computing residual income A1

A company's shipping division (an investment center) has sales of $2,420,000, net income of $516,000, and average invested assets of $2,250,000. Compute the division's profit margin and investment turnover.

QS 22-7
Computing profit margin and investment turnover A2

QS 22-8
Performance measures
A1   A2

Fill in the blanks in the schedule below for two separate investment centers A and B. Round answers to the nearest whole percent.

	Investment Center	
	A	B
Sales	$_____	$10,400,000
Net income	$ 352,000	$_____
Average invested assets	$1,400,000	$_____
Profit margin	8%	_____%
Investment turnover	_____	1.5
Return on (assets) investment	_____%	12%

QS 22-9
Performance measures—
balanced scorecard
A3

Classify each of the performance measures below into the most likely balanced scorecard perspective it relates to. Label your answers using C (customer), P (internal process), I (innovation and growth), or F (financial).

1. Customer wait time   _____
2. Number of days of employee absences   _____
3. Profit margin   _____
4. Number of new products introduced   _____
5. Change in market share   _____
6. Employee training sessions attended   _____
7. Length of time raw materials are in inventory   _____
8. Customer satisfaction index   _____

QS 22-10
Performance measures—
balanced scorecard
A3

Walt Disney reports the following information for its two Parks and Resorts divisions.

	East Coast		West Coast	
	Current year	Prior year	Current year	Prior year
Hotel occupancy rates	89%	86%	92%	93%

Assume Walt Disney uses a balanced scorecard and sets a target of 90% occupancy in its resorts. Using Exhibit 22.22 as a guide, show how the company's performance on hotel occupancy would appear on a balanced scorecard report.

QS 22-11^A
Determining transfer prices without excess capacity
C2

The Windshield division of Fast Car Co. makes windshields for use in Fast Car's Assembly division. The Windshield division incurs variable costs of $200 per windshield and has capacity to make 500,000 windshields per year. The market price is $450 per windshield. The Windshield division incurs total fixed costs of $3,000,000 per year. If the Windshield division is operating at full capacity, what transfer price should be used on transfers between the Windshield and Assembly divisions? Explain.

QS 22-12^A
Determining transfer prices with excess capacity   C2

Refer to information in QS 22-11. If the Windshield division has excess capacity, what is the range of possible transfer prices that could be used on transfers between the Windshield and Assembly divisions? Explain.

QS 22-13^B
Joint cost allocation
C3

A company purchases a 10,020 square foot commercial building for $325,000 and spends an additional $50,000 to divide the space into two separate rental units and prepare it for rent. Unit A, which has the desirable location on the corner and contains 3,340 square feet, will be rented for $1.00 per square foot. Unit B contains 6,680 square feet and will be rented for $0.75 per square foot. How much of the joint cost should be assigned to Unit B using the value basis of allocation?

QS 22-14
Rent expense allocated to departments
P2

Car Mart pays $130,000 rent each year for its two-story building. The space in this building is occupied by five departments as specified here.

Paint department	1,440 square feet of first-floor space
Engine department	3,360 square feet of first-floor space
Window department	2,016 square feet of second-floor space
Electrical department	960 square feet of second-floor space
Accessory department	1,824 square feet of second-floor space

The company allocates 65% of total rent expense to the first floor and 35% to the second floor, and then allocates rent expense for each floor to the departments occupying that floor on the basis of space occupied. Determine the rent expense to be allocated to each department. (Round percents to the nearest one-tenth and dollar amounts to the nearest whole dollar.)

Check Allocated to Paint Dept., $25,350

For a recent year **L'Oreal** reported operating profit of €3,385 (in millions) for its Cosmetics division. Total assets were €12,888 at the beginning of the year and €13,099 (in millions) at the end of the year. Compute return on investment for the year. State your answer as a percent, rounded to one decimal.

QS 22-15

Return on investment A1

Compute and interpret (*a*) manufacturing cycle time and (*b*) manufacturing cycle efficiency using the following information from a manufacturing company.

Process time	15 minutes
Inspection time	2 minutes
Move time	6.4 minutes
Wait time	36.6 minutes

QS 22-16

Manufacturing cycle time and efficiency

A4

Macee Department Store has three departments, and it conducts advertising campaigns that benefit all departments. Advertising costs are $100,000 this year, and departmental sales for this year follows. How much advertising cost is allocated to each department if the allocation is based on departmental sales?

Department	Sales
Department 1	$220,000
Department 2	400,000
Department 3	180,000

QS 22-17

Allocating costs to departments

P1

Mervon Company has two operating departments: Mixing and Bottling. Mixing has 300 employees and occupies 22,000 square feet. Bottling has 200 employees and occupies 18,000 square feet. Indirect factory costs for the current period follow: Administrative, $160,000; and Maintenance, $200,000. Administrative costs are allocated to operating departments based on the number of workers. Determine the administrative cost allocated to each operating department.

QS 22-18

Allocating costs to departments

P1

Refer to the information in QS 22-18. If the maintenance costs are allocated to operating departments based on square footage, determine the amount of maintenance costs allocated to each operating department.

QS 22-19

Allocating costs to departments

P1

≡ connect

Woh Che Co. has four departments: materials, personnel, manufacturing, and packaging. In a recent month, the four departments incurred three shared indirect expenses. The amounts of these indirect expenses and the bases used to allocate them follow.

Indirect Expense	Cost	Allocation Base
Supervision	$ 82,500	Number of employees
Utilities	50,000	Square feet occupied
Insurance	22,500	Value of assets in use
Total	$155,000	

EXERCISES

Exercise 22-1

Departmental expense allocations

P2

Departmental data for the company's recent reporting period follow.

Department	Employees	Square Feet	Asset Values
Materials	27	25,000	$ 6,000
Personnel............	9	5,000	1,200
Manufacturing	63	55,000	37,800
Packaging	51	15,000	15,000
Total	150	100,000	$60,000

(1) Use this information to allocate each of the three indirect expenses across the four departments.
(2) Prepare a summary table that reports the indirect expenses assigned to each of the four departments.

Check (2) Total of $29,600 assigned to Materials Dept.

Exercise 22-2
Managerial performance
evaluation

P1

Maryanne Dinardo manages an auto dealership's service department. The recent month's income statement for his department follows. (1) Analyze the items on the income statement and identify those that definitely should be included on a performance report used to evaluate Dinardo's performance. List them and explain why you chose them. (2) List and explain the items that should definitely be excluded. (3) List the items that are not definitely included or excluded and explain why they fall into that category.

Revenues		
Sales of parts	$ 72,000	
Sales of services.........................	105,000	$177,000
Costs and expenses		
Cost of parts sold	30,000	
Building depreciation	9,300	
Income taxes allocated to department........	8,700	
Interest on long-term debt	7,500	
Manager's salary..........................	12,000	
Payroll taxes.............................	8,100	
Supplies	15,900	
Utilities..................................	4,400	
Wages (hourly)............................	16,000	
Total costs and expenses		111,900
Departmental net income		$ 65,100

Exercise 22-3
Departmental contribution report

P3

Below are departmental income statements for a guitar manufacturer. The manufacturer is considering dropping its electric guitar department since it has a net loss. The company classifies advertising, rent, and utilities expenses as indirect. (1) Prepare a departmental contribution report that shows each department's contribution to overhead. (2) Based on contribution to overhead, should the electric guitar department be eliminated?

WHOLESALE GUITARS		
Departmental Income Statements		
For Year Ended December 31, 2013		
	Acoustic	**Electric**
Sales	$111,500	$105,500
Cost of goods sold	55,675	66,750
Gross profit	56,825	38,750
Operating expenses		
Advertising expense...................	8,075	6,250
Depreciation expense-equipment	10,150	9,000
Salaries expense.....................	17,300	13,500
Supplies expense	2,030	1,700
Rent expense	6,105	5,950
Utilities expense....................	3,045	2,550
Total operating expenses..............	46,705	38,950
Net income (loss)	$ 10,120	($200)

Exercise 22-4
Departmental expense
allocation spreadsheet

P2

Marathon Running Shop has two service departments (advertising and administration) and two operating departments (shoes and clothing). During 2013, the departments had the following direct expenses and occupied the following amount of floor space.

Department	Direct Expenses	Square Feet
Advertising	$ 18,000	1,120
Administrative	25,000	1,400
Shoes	103,000	7,140
Clothing	15,000	4,340

The advertising department developed and distributed 120 advertisements during the year. Of these, 90 promoted shoes and 30 promoted clothing. The store sold $350,000 of merchandise during the year. Of this amount, $273,000 is from the shoes department, and $77,000 is from the clothing department. The utilities expense of $64,000 is an indirect expense to all departments. Prepare a departmental expense allocation spreadsheet for Marathon Running Shop. The spreadsheet should assign (1) direct expenses to each of the four departments, (2) the $64,000 of utilities expense to the four departments on the basis of floor space occupied, (3) the advertising department's expenses to the two operating departments on the basis of the number of ads placed that promoted a department's products, and (4) the administrative department's expenses to the two operating departments based on the amount of sales. Provide supporting computations for the expense allocations.

Check Total expenses allocated to Shoes Dept., $177,472

The following is a partially completed lower section of a departmental expense allocation spreadsheet for Cozy Bookstore. It reports the total amounts of direct and indirect expenses allocated to its five departments. Complete the spreadsheet by allocating the expenses of the two service departments (advertising and purchasing) to the three operating departments.

Exercise 22-5

Service department expenses allocated to operating departments P2

			Allocation of Expenses to Departments				
	Allocation Base	Expense Account Balance	Advertising Dept.	Purchasing Dept.	Books Dept.	Magazines Dept.	Newspapers Dept.
Total department expenses..........		$698,000	$24,000	$34,000	$425,000	$90,000	$125,000
Service department expenses							
Advertising department............ Sales			?		?	?	?
Purchasing department............ Purch. orders				?	?	?	?
Total expenses allocated to operating departments.............		?	$ 0	$ 0	?	?	?

Advertising and purchasing department expenses are allocated to operating departments on the basis of dollar sales and purchase orders, respectively. Information about the allocation bases for the three operating departments follows.

Department	Sales	Purchase Orders
Books...............	$495,000	516
Magazines...........	198,000	360
Newspapers.........	207,000	324
Total...............	$900,000	1,200

Check Total expenses allocated to Books Dept., $452,820

Jessica Porter works in both the jewelry department and the hosiery department of a retail store. Porter assists customers in both departments and arranges and stocks merchandise in both departments. The store allocates Porter's $30,000 annual wages between the two departments based on a sample of the time worked in the two departments. The sample is obtained from a diary of hours worked that Porter kept in a randomly chosen two-week period. The diary showed the following hours and activities spent in the two departments. Allocate Porter's annual wages between the two departments.

Exercise 22-6

Indirect payroll expense allocated to departments P2

Selling in jewelry department...	51 hours
Arranging and stocking merchandise in jewelry department........................	6 hours
Selling in hosiery department	12 hours
Arranging and stocking merchandise in hosiery department	7 hours
Idle time spent waiting for a customer to enter one of the selling departments	4 hours

Check Assign $7,500 to Hosiery

You must prepare a return on investment analysis for the regional manager of Fast & Great Burgers. This growing chain is trying to decide which outlet of two alternatives to open. The first location (A) requires a $1,000,000 investment and is expected to yield annual net income of $160,000. The second location (B) requires a $600,000 investment and is expected to yield annual net income of $108,000. Compute the return on investment for each Fast & Great Burgers alternative and then make your recommendation in a one-half page memorandum to the regional manager. (The chain currently generates an 18% return on total assets.)

Exercise 22-7

Investment center analysis

A1

Exercise 22-8

Computing return on assets and residual income; investing decision

A1

Megamart, a retailer of consumer goods, provides the following information on two of its departments (each considered an investment center).

Investment Center	Sales	Net Income	Average Invested Assets
Electronics..................	$40,000,000	$2,880,000	$16,000,000
Sporting goods..............	20,000,000	2,040,000	12,000,000

(1) Compute return on investment for each department. Using return on investment, which department is most efficient at using assets to generate returns for the company? (2) Assume a target income level of 12% of average invested assets. Compute residual income for each department. Which department generated the most residual income for the company? (3) Assume the Electronics department is presented with a new investment opportunity that will yield a 15% return on assets. Should the new investment opportunity be accepted? Explain.

Exercise 22-9

Computing margin and turnover; department efficiency   A2

Refer to information in Exercise 22-8. Compute profit margin and investment turnover for each department. Which department generates the most net income per dollar of sales? Which department is most efficient at generating sales from average invested assets?

Exercise 22-10

Performance measures— balanced scorecard

A3

USA Airlines uses the following performance measures. Classify each of the performance measures below into the most likely balanced scorecard perspective it relates to. Label your answers using C (customer), P (internal process), I (innovation and growth), or F (financial).

1. Cash flow from operations   _____
2. Number of reports of mishandled or lost baggage   _____
3. Percentage of on-time departures   _____
4. On-time flight percentage   _____
5. Percentage of ground crew trained   _____
6. Return on investment   _____
7. Market value   _____
8. Accidents or safety incidents per mile flown   _____
9. Customer complaints   _____
10. Flight attendant training sessions attended   _____
11. Time airplane is on ground between flights   _____
12. Airplane miles per gallon of fuel   _____
13. Revenue per seat   _____
14. Cost of leasing airplanes   _____

Exercise 22-11^A

Determining transfer prices

C2

The Trailer department of Baxter Bicycles makes bike trailers that attach to bicycles and can carry children or cargo. The trailers have a retail price of $200 each. Each trailer incurs $80 of variable manufacturing costs. The Trailer department has capacity for 40,000 trailers per year, and incurs fixed costs of $1,000,000 per year.

Required

1. Assume the Assembly division of Baxter Bicycles wants to buy 15,000 trailers per year from the Trailer division. If the Trailer division can sell all of the trailers it manufactures to outside customers, what price should be used on transfers between Baxter Bicycle's divisions? Explain.
2. Assume the Trailer division currently only sells 20,000 trailers to outside customers, and the Assembly division wants to buy 15,000 trailers per year from the Trailer division. What is the range of acceptable prices that could be used on transfers between Baxter Bicycle's divisions? Explain.
3. Assume transfer prices of either $80 per trailer or $140 per trailer are being considered. Comment on the preferred transfer prices from the perspectives of the Trailer division manager, the Assembly division manager, and the top management of Baxter Bicycles.

Heart & Home Properties is developing a subdivision that includes 600 home lots. The 450 lots in the Canyon section are below a ridge and do not have views of the neighboring canyons and hills; the 150 lots in the Hilltop section offer unobstructed views. The expected selling price for each Canyon lot is $55,000 and for each Hilltop lot is $110,000. The developer acquired the land for $4,000,000 and spent another $3,500,000 on street and utilities improvements. Assign the joint land and improvement costs to the lots using the value basis of allocation and determine the average cost per lot.

Exercise 22-12[B]
Joint real estate costs assigned
C3

Check Total Hilltop cost, $3,000,000

Pirate Seafood Company purchases lobsters and processes them into tails and flakes. It sells the lobster tails for $21 per pound and the flakes for $14 per pound. On average, 100 pounds of lobster are processed into 52 pounds of tails and 22 pounds of flakes, with 26 pounds of waste. Assume that the company purchased 2,400 pounds of lobster for $4.50 per pound and processed the lobsters with an additional labor cost of $1,800. No materials or labor costs are assigned to the waste. If 1,096 pounds of tails and 324 pounds of flakes are sold, what is (1) the allocated cost of the sold items and (2) the allocated cost of the ending inventory? The company allocates joint costs on a value basis. (Round the dollar cost per pound to the nearest thousandth.)

Exercise 22-13[B]
Joint product costs assigned
C3

Check (2) Inventory cost, $2,268

L'Oreal reports the following for a recent year for the major divisions in its Cosmetics branch.

Exercise 22-14
Profit margin and investment turnover

A2

(€ millions)	Sales	Income	Total Assets End of Year	Total Assets Beginning of Year
Professional products	€ 2,717	€ 552	€ 2,624	€ 2,516
Consumer products	9,530	1,765	5,994	5,496
Luxury products	4,507	791	3,651	4,059
Active cosmetics	1,386	278	830	817
Total	€18,140	€3,386	€13,099	€12,888

1. Compute profit margin for each division. State your answers as percents, rounded to two decimal places. Which L'Oreal division has the highest profit margin?

2. Compute investment turnover for each division. Round your answers to two decimal places. Which L'Oreal division has the best investment turnover?

connect

National Bank has several departments that occupy both floors of a two-story building. The departmental accounting system has a single account, Building Occupancy Cost, in its ledger. The types and amounts of occupancy costs recorded in this account for the current period follow.

PROBLEM SET A

Problem 22-1A
Allocation of building occupancy costs to departments

P2

mhhe.com/wildFINMAN5e

Depreciation—Building	$18,000
Interest—Building mortgage	27,000
Taxes—Building and land	9,000
Gas (heating) expense	3,000
Lighting expense	3,000
Maintenance expense	6,000
Total occupancy cost	$66,000

The building has 4,000 square feet on each floor. In prior periods, the accounting manager merely divided the $66,000 occupancy cost by 8,000 square feet to find an average cost of $8.25 per square foot and then charged each department a building occupancy cost equal to this rate times the number of square feet that it occupied.

Diane Linder manages a first-floor department that occupies 1,000 square feet, and Juan Chiro manages a second-floor department that occupies 1,800 square feet of floor space. In discussing the departmental reports, the second-floor manager questions whether using the same rate per square foot for all departments makes sense because the first-floor space is more valuable. This manager also references a recent real estate study of average local rental costs for similar space that shows first-floor space worth $30 per square foot and second-floor space worth $20 per square foot (excluding costs for heating, lighting, and maintenance).

Required

1. Allocate occupancy costs to the Linder and Chiro departments using the current allocation method.

2. Allocate the depreciation, interest, and taxes occupancy costs to the Linder and Chiro departments in proportion to the relative market values of the floor space. Allocate the heating, lighting, and maintenance costs to the Linder and Chiro departments in proportion to the square feet occupied (ignoring floor space market values).

Analysis Component

3. Which allocation method would you prefer if you were a manager of a second-floor department? Explain.

Problem 22-2A

Departmental income statements; forecasts

P3

mhhe.com/wildFINMAN5e

Williams Company began operations in January 2013 with two operating (selling) departments and one service (office) department. Its departmental income statements follow.

WILLIAMS COMPANY Departmental Income Statements For Year Ended December 31, 2013			
	Clock	Mirror	Combined
Sales	$130,000	$55,000	$185,000
Cost of goods sold	63,700	34,100	97,800
Gross profit	66,300	20,900	87,200
Direct expenses			
Sales salaries	20,000	7,000	27,000
Advertising	1,200	500	1,700
Store supplies used	900	400	1,300
Depreciation—Equipment	1,500	300	1,800
Total direct expenses	23,600	8,200	31,800
Allocated expenses			
Rent expense	7,020	3,780	10,800
Utilities expense	2,600	1,400	4,000
Share of office department expenses	10,500	4,500	15,000
Total allocated expenses	20,120	9,680	29,800
Total expenses	43,720	17,880	61,600
Net income	$ 22,580	$ 3,020	$ 25,600

Williams plans to open a third department in January 2014 that will sell paintings. Management predicts that the new department will generate $50,000 in sales with a 55% gross profit margin and will require the following direct expenses: sales salaries, $8,000; advertising, $800; store supplies, $500; and equipment depreciation, $200. It will fit the new department into the current rented space by taking some square footage from the other two departments. When opened the new painting department will fill one-fifth of the space presently used by the clock department and one-fourth used by the mirror department. Management does not predict any increase in utilities costs, which are allocated to the departments in proportion to occupied space (or rent expense). The company allocates office department expenses to the operating departments in proportion to their sales. It expects the painting department to increase total office department expenses by $7,000. Since the painting department will bring new customers into the store, management expects sales in both the clock and mirror departments to increase by 8%. No changes for those departments' gross profit percents or their direct expenses are expected except for store supplies used, which will increase in proportion to sales.

Required

Prepare departmental income statements that show the company's predicted results of operations for calendar year 2014 for the three operating (selling) departments and their combined totals. (Round percents to the nearest one-tenth and dollar amounts to the nearest whole dollar.)

Problem 22-3A

Responsibility accounting performance reports; controllable and budgeted costs P1

Billie Whitehorse, the plant manager of Travel Free's Indiana plant, is responsible for all of that plant's costs other than her own salary. The plant has two operating departments and one service department. The camper and trailer operating departments manufacture different products and have their own managers. The office department, which Whitehorse also manages, provides services equally to the two operating departments. A budget is prepared for each operating department and the office department. The company's responsibility accounting system must assemble information to present budgeted and actual costs in performance reports for each operating department manager and the plant manager. Each performance report includes only those costs that a particular operating department manager can control: raw materials, wages, supplies used, and equipment depreciation. The plant manager is responsible for the department managers' salaries, utilities, building rent, office salaries other than her own, and other office costs plus all costs controlled by the two operating department managers. The annual departmental budgets and actual costs for the two operating departments follow.

	Budget			Actual		
	Campers	Trailers	Combined	Campers	Trailers	Combined
Raw materials	$195,000	$275,000	$ 470,000	$194,200	$273,200	$ 467,400
Employee wages	104,000	205,000	309,000	106,600	206,400	313,000
Dept. manager salary	43,000	52,000	95,000	44,000	53,500	97,500
Supplies used	33,000	90,000	123,000	31,700	91,600	123,300
Depreciation—Equip.	60,000	125,000	185,000	60,000	125,000	185,000
Utilities..................	3,600	5,400	9,000	3,300	5,000	8,300
Building rent	5,700	9,300	15,000	5,300	8,700	14,000
Office department costs	68,750	68,750	137,500	67,550	67,550	135,100
Totals	$513,050	$830,450	$1,343,500	$512,650	$830,950	$1,343,600

The office department's annual budget and its actual costs follow.

	Budget	Actual
Plant manager salary	$ 80,000	$ 82,000
Other office salaries	32,500	30,100
Other office costs	25,000	23,000
Totals	$137,500	$135,100

Required

1. Prepare responsibility accounting performance reports like those in Exhibit 22.2 that list costs controlled by the following:

   a. Manager of the camper department.

   b. Manager of the trailer department.

   c. Manager of the Indiana plant.

In each report, include the budgeted and actual costs and show the amount that each actual cost is over or under the budgeted amount.

Analysis Component

2. Did the plant manager or the operating department managers better manage costs? Explain.

Check   (1a) $500 total over budget

(1c) Indiana plant controllable costs, $1,900 total under budget

Georgia Orchards produced a good crop of peaches this year. After preparing the following income statement, the company believes it should have given its No. 3 peaches to charity and saved its efforts.

Problem 22-4A[B]
Allocation of joint costs

C3

GEORGIA ORCHARDS Income Statement For Year Ended December 31, 2013				
	No. 1	No. 2	No. 3	Combined
Sales (by grade)				
No. 1: 300,000 lbs. @ $1.50/lb	$450,000			
No. 2: 300,000 lbs. @ $1.00/lb		$300,000		
No. 3: 750,000 lbs. @ $0.25/lb			$ 187,500	
Total sales				$937,500
Costs				
Tree pruning and care @ $0.30/lb	90,000	90,000	225,000	405,000
Picking, sorting, and grading @ $0.15/lb	45,000	45,000	112,500	202,500
Delivery costs	15,000	15,000	37,500	67,500
Total costs	150,000	150,000	375,000	675,000
Net income (loss)	$300,000	$150,000	$(187,500)	$262,500

In preparing this statement, the company allocated joint costs among the grades on a physical basis as an equal amount per pound. The company's delivery cost records show that $30,000 of the $67,500 relates to crating the No. 1 and No. 2 peaches and hauling them to the buyer. The remaining $37,500 of delivery costs is for crating the No. 3 peaches and hauling them to the cannery.

Check (1) $129,600 tree pruning and care costs allocated to No. 2

(2) Net income from No. 1 & No. 2 peaches, $140,400 & $93,600

Required

1. Prepare reports showing cost allocations on a sales value basis to the three grades of peaches. Separate the delivery costs into the amounts directly identifiable with each grade. Then allocate any shared delivery costs on the basis of the relative sales value of each grade.

2. Using your answers to part 1, prepare an income statement using the joint costs allocated on a sales value basis.

Analysis Component

3. Do you think delivery costs fit the definition of a joint cost? Explain.

Problem 22-5A
Manufacturing cycle time and efficiency

A4

Oakwood Company produces maple bookcases to customer order. It received an order from a customer to produce 5,000 bookcases. The following information is available for the production of the bookcases.

Process time	6.0 days
Inspection time	0.8 days
Move time	3.2 days
Wait time	5.0 days

Required

1. Compute the company's manufacturing cycle time.

Check (2) Manufacturing cycle efficiency, 0.40

2. Compute the company's manufacturing cycle efficiency. Interpret your answer.

Analysis Component

3. Assume that Oakwood wishes to increase its manufacturing cycle efficiency to 0.75. What are some ways that it can accomplish this?

Problem 22-6A
Departmental contribution to income

P1

Vortex Company operates a retail store with two departments. Information about those departments follows.

	Department A	Department B
Sales	$800,000	$450,000
Cost of goods sold	497,000	291,000
Direct expenses		
Salaries	125,000	88,000
Insurance	20,000	10,000
Utilities.................	24,000	14,000
Depreciation	21,000	12,000
Maintenance.............	7,000	5,000

The company also incurred the following indirect costs.

Salaries	$36,000
Insurance	6,000
Depreciation	15,000
Office expenses	50,000

Indirect costs are allocated as follows: salaries on the basis of sales; insurance and depreciation on the basis of square footage; and office expenses on the basis of number of employees. Additional information about the departments follows.

Department	Square footage	Number of employees
A	28,000	75
B	12,000	50

Chapter 22   Performance Measurement and Responsibility Accounting   **977**

Required

1. For each department, determine the departmental contribution to overhead and the departmental net income.

2. Should Department B be eliminated? Explain.

Check   (1) Dept. A net income, $38,260

Harmon's has several departments that occupy all floors of a two-story building that includes a basement floor. Harmon rented this building under a long-term lease negotiated when rental rates were low. The departmental accounting system has a single account, Building Occupancy Cost, in its ledger. The types and amounts of occupancy costs recorded in this account for the current period follow.

PROBLEM SET B

Problem 22-1B
Allocation of building occupancy costs to departments

P2

Building rent	$400,000
Lighting expense	25,000
Cleaning expense	40,000
Total occupancy cost	$465,000

The building has 7,500 square feet on each of the upper two floors but only 5,000 square feet in the basement. In prior periods, the accounting manager merely divided the $465,000 occupancy cost by 20,000 square feet to find an average cost of $23.25 per square foot and then charged each department a building occupancy cost equal to this rate times the number of square feet that it occupies.

Jordan Style manages a department that occupies 2,000 square feet of basement floor space. In discussing the departmental reports with other managers, she questions whether using the same rate per square foot for all departments makes sense because different floor space has different values. Style checked a recent real estate report of average local rental costs for similar space that shows first-floor space worth $40 per square foot, second-floor space worth $20 per square foot, and basement space worth $10 per square foot (excluding costs for lighting and cleaning).

Required

1. Allocate occupancy costs to Style's department using the current allocation method.

2. Allocate the building rent cost to Style's department in proportion to the relative market value of the floor space. Allocate to Style's department the lighting and cleaning costs in proportion to the square feet occupied (ignoring floor space market values). Then, compute the total occupancy cost allocated to Style's department.

Check   Total costs allocated to Style's Dept., (1) $46,500; (2) Total occupancy cost to Style $22,500

Analysis Component

3. Which allocation method would you prefer if you were a manager of a basement department?

Bonanza Entertainment began operations in January 2013 with two operating (selling) departments and one service (office) department. Its departmental income statements follow.

Problem 22-2B
Departmental income statements; forecasts P3

BONANZA ENTERTAINMENT			
Departmental Income Statements			
For Year Ended December 31, 2013			
	Movies	**Video Games**	**Combined**
Sales	$600,000	$200,000	$800,000
Cost of goods sold	420,000	154,000	574,000
Gross profit	180,000	46,000	226,000
Direct expenses			
Sales salaries	37,000	15,000	52,000
Advertising	12,500	6,000	18,500
Store supplies used	4,000	1,000	5,000
Depreciation—Equipment	4,500	3,000	7,500
Total direct expenses...................	58,000	25,000	83,000
Allocated expenses			
Rent expense...........................	41,000	9,000	50,000
Utilities expense	7,380	1,620	9,000
Share of office department expenses	56,250	18,750	75,000
Total allocated expenses	104,630	29,370	134,000
Total expenses	162,630	54,370	217,000
Net income (loss)	$ 17,370	$ (8,370)	$ 9,000

The company plans to open a third department in January 2014 that will sell compact discs. Management predicts that the new department will generate $300,000 in sales with a 35% gross profit margin and will require the following direct expenses: sales salaries, $18,000; advertising, $10,000; store supplies, $2,000; and equipment depreciation, $1,200. The company will fit the new department into the current rented space by taking some square footage from the other two departments. When opened, the new compact disc department will fill one-fourth of the space presently used by the movie department and one-third of the space used by the video game department. Management does not predict any increase in utilities costs, which are allocated to the departments in proportion to occupied space (or rent expense). The company allocates office department expenses to the operating departments in proportion to their sales. It expects the compact disc department to increase total office department expenses by $10,000. Since the compact disc department will bring new customers into the store, management expects sales in both the movie and video game departments to increase by 8%. No changes for those departments' gross profit percents or for their direct expenses are expected, except for store supplies used, which will increase in proportion to sales.

Required

Check   2014 forecasted movies net income (sales), $52,450 ($648,000)

Prepare departmental income statements that show the company's predicted results of operations for calendar year 2014 for the three operating (selling) departments and their combined totals. (Round percents to the nearest one-tenth and dollar amounts to the nearest whole dollar.)

Problem 22-3B
Responsibility accounting performance reports; controllable and budgeted costs
P1

Britney Brown, the plant manager of LMN Co.'s Chicago plant, is responsible for all of that plant's costs other than her own salary. The plant has two operating departments and one service department. The refrigerator and dishwasher operating departments manufacture different products and have their own managers. The office department, which Brown also manages, provides services equally to the two operating departments. A monthly budget is prepared for each operating department and the office department. The company's responsibility accounting system must assemble information to present budgeted and actual costs in performance reports for each operating department manager and the plant manager. Each performance report includes only those costs that a particular operating department manager can control: raw materials, wages, supplies used, and equipment depreciation. The plant manager is responsible for the department managers' salaries, utilities, building rent, office salaries other than her own, and other office costs plus all costs controlled by the two operating department managers. The April departmental budgets and actual costs for the two operating departments follow.

	Budget			Actual		
	Refrigerators	Dishwashers	Combined	Refrigerators	Dishwashers	Combined
Raw materials	$400,000	$200,000	$ 600,000	$385,000	$202,000	$ 587,000
Employee wages	170,000	80,000	250,000	174,700	81,500	256,200
Dept. manager salary	55,000	49,000	104,000	55,000	46,500	101,500
Supplies used	15,000	9,000	24,000	14,000	9,700	23,700
Depreciation—Equip.	53,000	37,000	90,000	53,000	37,000	90,000
Utilities.......................	30,000	18,000	48,000	34,500	20,700	55,200
Building rent	63,000	17,000	80,000	65,800	16,500	82,300
Office department costs	70,500	70,500	141,000	75,000	75,000	150,000
Totals	$856,500	$480,500	$1,337,000	$857,000	$488,900	$1,345,900

The office department's budget and its actual costs for April follow.

	Budget	Actual
Plant manager salary	$ 80,000	$ 85,000
Other office salaries	40,000	35,200
Other office costs	21,000	29,800
Totals	$141,000	$150,000

Required

1. Prepare responsibility accounting performance reports like those in Exhibit 22.2 that list costs controlled by the following:

   a. Manager of the refrigerator department.

   b. Manager of the dishwasher department.

   c. Manager of the Chicago plant.

   In each report, include the budgeted and actual costs for the month and show the amount by which each actual cost is over or under the budgeted amount.

Analysis Component

2. Did the plant manager or the operating department managers better manage costs? Explain.

Check (1a) $11,300 total under budget

(1c) Chicago plant controllable costs, $3,900 total over budget

Rita and Rick Redding own and operate a tomato grove. After preparing the following income statement, Rita believes they should have offered the No. 3 tomatoes to the public for free and saved themselves time and money.

Problem 22-4B[B]

Allocation of joint costs

C3

RITA AND RICK REDDING Income Statement For Year Ended December 31, 2013				
	No. 1	**No. 2**	**No. 3**	**Combined**
Sales (by grade)				
No. 1: 500,000 lbs. @ $1.80/lb	$900,000			
No. 2: 400,000 lbs. @ $1.25/lb		$500,000		
No. 3: 100,000 lbs. @ $0.40/lb			$ 40,000	
Total sales				$1,440,000
Costs				
Land preparation, seeding, and cultivating @ $0.70/lb	350,000	280,000	70,000	700,000
Harvesting, sorting, and grading @ $0.04/lb	20,000	16,000	4,000	40,000
Delivery costs	10,000	7,000	3,000	20,000
Total costs	380,000	303,000	77,000	760,000
Net income (loss)	$520,000	$197,000	$(37,000)	$ 680,000

In preparing this statement, Rita and Rick allocated joint costs among the grades on a physical basis as an equal amount per pound. Also, their delivery cost records show that $17,000 of the $20,000 relates to crating the No. 1 and No. 2 tomatoes and hauling them to the buyer. The remaining $3,000 of delivery costs is for crating the No. 3 tomatoes and hauling them to the cannery.

Required

1. Prepare reports showing cost allocations on a sales value basis to the three grades of tomatoes. Separate the delivery costs into the amounts directly identifiable with each grade. Then allocate any shared delivery costs on the basis of the relative sales value of each grade. (Round percents to the nearest one-tenth and dollar amounts to the nearest whole dollar.)

2. Using your answers to part 1, prepare an income statement using the joint costs allocated on a sales value basis.

Check (1) $1,120 harvesting, sorting and grading costs allocated to No. 3

(2) Net income from No. 1 & No. 2 tomatoes, $426,569 & $237,151

Analysis Component

3. Do you think delivery costs fit the definition of a joint cost? Explain.

Best Ink produces ink-jet printers for personal computers. It received an order for 500 printers from a customer. The following information is available for this order.

Problem 22-5B

Manufacturing cycle time and efficiency

A4

Process time	16.0 hours
Inspection time	3.5 hours
Move time	9.0 hours
Wait time	21.5 hours

Required

1. Compute the company's manufacturing cycle time.
2. Compute the company's manufacturing cycle efficiency. Interpret your answer.

Analysis Component

3. Assume that Best Ink wishes to increase its manufacturing cycle efficiency to 0.80. What are some ways that it can accomplish this?

Problem 22-6B

Departmental contribution to income

P1

Sadar Company operates a store with two departments: videos and music. Information about those departments follows.

	Videos Department	Music Department
Sales	$370,500	$279,500
Cost of goods sold	320,000	175,000
Direct expenses		
Salaries	35,000	25,000
Maintenance	12,000	10,000
Utilities	5,000	4,500
Insurance	4,200	3,700

The company also incurred the following indirect costs.

Advertising	$15,000
Salaries	27,000
Office expenses	3,200

Indirect costs are allocated as follows: advertising on the basis of sales; salaries on the basis of number of employees; and office expenses on the basis of square footage. Additional information about the departments follows.

Department	Square footage	Number of employees
Videos	5,000	3
Music	3,000	2

Required

Check   (1) Music dept. net income, $42,850

1. For each department, determine the departmental contribution to overhead and the departmental net income.
2. Should the video department be eliminated? Explain.

SERIAL PROBLEM

Success Systems

A3

(This serial problem began in Chapter 1 and continues through most of the book. If previous chapter segments were not completed, the serial problem can begin at this point. It is helpful, but not necessary, to use the Working Papers that accompany the book.)

SP 22   Adria Lopez's two departments, computer consulting services and computer workstation furniture manufacturing, have each been profitable. Adria has heard of the balanced scorecard and wants you to provide details on how it could be used to measure performance of her departments.

Required

1. Explain the four performance perspectives included in a balanced scorecard.
2. For each of the four performance perspectives included in a balanced scorecard, provide examples of measures Adria could use to measure performance of her departments.

Beyond the Numbers

BTN 22-1   Review Polaris's income statement in Appendix A and identify its revenues for the years ended December 31, 2011, December 31, 2010, and December 31, 2009. For the year ended December 31, 2011, Polaris reports the following product revenue mix. (Assume that its product revenue mix is the same for each of the three years reported when answering the requirements.)

Off-Road Vehicles	Snowmobiles	On-Road Vehicles	Parts, Garments, & Accessories
69%	11%	5%	15%

Required

1. Compute the amount of revenue from each of its product lines for the years ended December 31, 2011, December 31, 2010, and December 31, 2009.

2. If Polaris wishes to evaluate each of its product lines, how can it allocate its operating expenses to each of them to determine each product line's profitability?

Fast Forward

3. Access Polaris's annual report for a fiscal year ending after December 31, 2011, from its Website (Polaris.com) or the SEC's EDGAR database (sec.gov). Compute its revenues for its product lines for the most recent year(s). Compare those results to those from part 1. How has its product mix changed?

REPORTING IN ACTION

C1

Polaris

BTN 22-2   Polaris and Arctic Cat compete in several on-road and off-road motorized vehicle categories. Sales, income, and asset information is provided for each company below.

(in thousands)	Polaris	Arctic Cat
Sales...............................	$2,656,949	$464,651
Net income	227,575	13,007
Invested assets, beginning of year	1,061,647	246,084
Invested assets, end of year.............	1,228,024	272,906

Required

1. Compute profit margin for each company.

2. Compute investment turnover for each company.

Analysis Component

3. Using your answers to the questions above, compare the companies' performance during the most recent year.

COMPARATIVE ANALYSIS

A2

Polaris

Arctic Cat

BTN 22-3   Senior Security Co. offers a range of security services for senior citizens. Each type of service is considered within a separate department. Mary Pincus, the overall manager, is compensated partly on the basis of departmental performance by staying within the quarterly cost budget. She often revises operations to make sure departments stay within budget. Says Pincus, "I will not go over budget even if it means slightly compromising the level and quality of service. These are minor compromises that don't significantly affect my clients, at least in the short term."

Required

1. Is there an ethical concern in this situation? If so, which parties are affected? Explain.

2. Can Mary Pincus take action to eliminate or reduce any ethical concerns? Explain.

3. What is Senior Security's ethical responsibility in offering professional services?

ETHICS CHALLENGE

P3

COMMUNICATING IN PRACTICE

P2

BTN 22-4 Improvement Station is a national home improvement chain with more than 100 stores throughout the country. The manager of each store receives a salary plus a bonus equal to a percent of the store's net income for the reporting period. The following net income calculation is on the Denver store manager's performance report for the recent monthly period.

Sales	$2,500,000
Cost of goods sold	800,000
Wages expense	500,000
Utilities expense	200,000
Home office expense	75,000
Net income	$ 925,000
Manager's bonus (0.5%)	$ 4,625

In previous periods, the bonus had also been 0.5%, but the performance report had not included any charges for the home office expense, which is now assigned to each store as a percent of its sales.

Required

Assume that you are the national office manager. Write a one-half page memorandum to your store managers explaining why home office expense is in the new performance report.

TAKING IT TO THE NET

P2

BTN 22-5 This chapter described and used spreadsheets to prepare various managerial reports (see Exhibit 22-6). You can download from Websites various tutorials showing how spreadsheets are used in managerial accounting and other business applications.

Required

1. Link to the Website Lacher.com. Select "Excel Examples." Identify and list three tutorials for review.
2. Describe in a one-half page memorandum to your instructor how the applications described in each tutorial are helpful in business and managerial decision making.

TEAMWORK IN ACTION

P1

Polaris

Arctic Cat

BTN 22-6 Polaris, and Arctic Cat compete across the world in several markets.

Required

1. Design a three-tier responsibility accounting organizational chart assuming that you have available internal information for both companies. Use Exhibit 22.1 as an example. The goal of this assignment is to design a reporting framework for the companies; numbers are not required. Limit your reporting framework to sales activity only.
2. Explain why it is important to have similar performance reports when comparing performance within a company (and across different companies). Be specific in your response.

ENTREPRENEURIAL DECISION

P3

BTN 22-7 Brian Linton's company, United By Blue, sells jewelry and apparel. His company's plans call for continued expansion into other types of products.

Required

1. How can United By Blue use departmental income statements to assist in understanding and controlling operations?
2. Are departmental income statements always the best measure of a department's performance? Explain.
3. Provide examples of nonfinancial performace indicators United By Blue might use as part of a balanced scorecard system of performance evaluation.

BTN 22-8   Visit a local movie theater and check out both its concession area and its showing areas. The manager of a theater must confront questions such as:

HITTING THE ROAD
C1 P1

- How much return do we earn on concessions?
- What types of movies generate the greatest sales?
- What types of movies generate the greatest net income?

Required

Assume that you are the new accounting manager for a 16-screen movie theater. You are to set up a responsibility accounting reporting framework for the theater.

1. Recommend how to segment the different departments of a movie theater for responsibility reporting.
2. Propose an expense allocation system for heat, rent, insurance, and maintenance costs of the theater.

BTN 22-9   Selected product data from Piaggio (www.piaggio.com) follow.

GLOBAL DECISION
P3

PIAGGIO

Product Segment for Year Ended (millions)	Net Sales		Gross Margin	
	December 31, 2011	December 31, 2010	December 31, 2011	December 31, 2010
Two-wheeler vehicles............	€1,025.3	€988.1	€337.1	€330.7
Commercial vehicles	491.1	497.3	117.5	131.6

Required

1. Compute the percentage growth in net sales for each product line from fiscal year 2010 to 2011. Round percents to one decimal.
2. Which product line's net sales grew the fastest?
3. Which segment was the most profitable?
4. How can Piaggio's managers use this information?

ANSWERS TO MULTIPLE CHOICE QUIZ

1. b; [$641,250/($356,250 + $641,250 + $427,500)] × $150,000 = $67,500
2. d;
3. c; $500,000/200,000 = 2.5
4. b;

	Department X	Department Y	Department Z
Sales	$500,000	$200,000	$350,000
Cost of goods sold	350,000	75,000	150,000
Gross profit	150,000	125,000	200,000
Direct expenses...........	50,000	20,000	75,000
Departmental contribution...........	$100,000	$105,000	$125,000

5. a; $100,000/$500,000 = 20%

Relevant Costing for Managerial Decisions

A Look Back

Chapter 22 focused on responsibility accounting and performance measurement. We identified several reports useful in measuring and analyzing the activities of a company, its departments, and its managers.

A Look at This Chapter

This chapter explains several tools and procedures useful for making and evaluating short-term managerial decisions. It also describes how to assess the consequences of such decisions.

A Look Ahead

Chapter 24 focuses on capital budgeting decisions. It explains and illustrates several methods that help identify projects with the higher return on investment.

Learning Objectives

CONCEPTUAL

C1 Describe the importance of relevant costs for short-term decisions. (p. 986)

ANALYTICAL

A1 Evaluate short-term managerial decisions using relevant costs. (p. 987)

A2 Determine product selling price based on total costs. (p. 994)

PROCEDURAL

P1 Identify relevant costs and apply them to managerial decisions. (p. 988)

Decision Insight

Sweet Success

"Put all of your love into your product."
—CHARLIE FYFFE

LOS ANGELES—Noticing long lines and an inadequate supply of sweets to satisfy his high school friends' cravings, Charlie Fyffe began making brownies and selling them at school. His brownies were an instant hit, and as his clientele and passion for baking grew, so did his desire to start his own business. "I started **Charlie's Brownies (CharliesBrownies.com)** because sweets make people happy and baking is a fun industry," explains Charlie. "I developed a quality original recipe and started selling brownies in simple cake boxes. Staying simple and consistent opened the door to a viable business."

After six months of professional baking classes to sharpen his skills, Charlie turned to the business side. "I had a lot to learn," admits Charlie. "I read entrepreneurial books and did internships to learn how to run a business. Becoming an entrepreneur was hard work, but it allows me a life of freedom outside the cubicle and the opportunity to pursue my dreams and visions." Charlie had to learn how to use accounting information to make important business decisions. For example, attention to contribution margins enables Charlie to decide if adding new product lines, like vegan and gluten-free brownies, would increase profits. Focusing on contribution margins, his own and his competition's, also helps Charlie decide whether to eliminate certain products because they are not profitable.

Charlie applies high standards to his production process. Unlike some companies that can rework substandard materials into a viable product, Charlie explains that "raw materials that don't

meet our standards never enter the baking process." Further, although expensive, exotic ingredients like "Chardonnay-infused sea salts create a pop and that undeniable urge to eat another brownie. It isn't heavy, and you want another one." Charlie has also managed to control overhead costs by doing much of the baking, marketing, and delivery himself. "I do whatever it takes to get the job done" he says. "There is never a dull moment!"

Much of Charlie's Brownies business is done online. To meet Charlie's goal of developing the company into a "nationwide and global Brownie Experience," he must focus on relevant costs to help him make good decisions. Determining the optimal sales mix requires Charlie to understand product contribution margins. Charlie also explains that "we need to upgrade our space and add to our capacity." The decision to keep or replace equipment is common in growing businesses, and assessing relevant costs helps Charlie with this and other key managerial decisions.

Charlie advises young entrepreneurs to follow their passion. "Hang out with other overachievers and young entrepreneurs to stay one step ahead," he says. "Stay focused, work hard, and seek guidance from other successful business people." Sounds like a recipe for success.

[Sources: *Charlie's Brownies* Website, January 2013; *JaredSurnamer.com*, August 2011; *PopularFinesse.tumblr.com*, October 2011; *Twentity.com*, February 2011.]

Chapter Preview

Making business decisions involves choosing between alternative courses of action. Many factors affect business decisions, yet analysis typically focuses on finding the alternative that offers the highest return on investment or the greatest reduction in costs. In all situations, managers can reach a sounder decision if they identify the consequences of alternative choices in financial terms. This chapter explains several methods of analysis that can help managers make short-term business decisions.

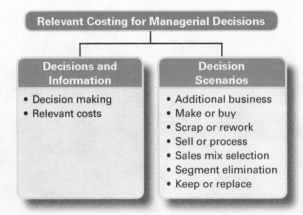

Relevant Costing for Managerial Decisions

Decisions and Information	Decision Scenarios
• Decision making • Relevant costs	• Additional business • Make or buy • Scrap or rework • Sell or process • Sales mix selection • Segment elimination • Keep or replace

This chapter focuses on methods that use accounting information to make important managerial decisions. Most of these cases involve short-term decisions. This differs from methods used for longer-term managerial decisions that are described in the next chapter.

DECISIONS AND INFORMATION

This section explains how managers make decisions and the information relevant to those decisions.

Decision Making

Managerial decision making involves five steps: (1) define the decision task, (2) identify alternative courses of action, (3) collect relevant information and evaluate each alternative, (4) select the preferred course of action, and (5) analyze and assess decisions made. These five steps are illustrated in Exhibit 23.1.

EXHIBIT 23.1

Managerial Decision Making

Define Task and Goal	Identify Alternative Actions	Collect Relevant Information	Select Course of Action	Analyze and Assess Decision

Both managerial and financial accounting information play an important role in most management decisions. The accounting system is expected to provide primarily *financial* information such as performance reports and budget analyses for decision making. *Nonfinancial* information is also relevant, however; it includes information on environmental effects, political sensitivities, and social responsibility.

Relevant Costs

C1 Describe the importance of relevant costs for short-term decisions.

Most financial measures of revenues and costs from accounting systems are based on historical costs. Although historical costs are important and useful for many tasks such as product pricing and the control and monitoring of business activities, we sometimes find that an analysis of *relevant costs,* or *avoidable costs,* is especially useful. Three types of costs are pertinent to our discussion of relevant costs: sunk costs, out-of-pocket costs, and opportunity costs.

A *sunk cost* arises from a past decision and cannot be avoided or changed; it is irrelevant to future decisions. An example is the cost of computer equipment previously purchased by a company. Most of a company's allocated costs, including fixed overhead items such as depreciation and administrative expenses, are sunk costs.

An *out-of-pocket cost* requires a future outlay of cash and is relevant for current and future decision making. These costs are usually the direct result of management's decisions. For instance, future purchases of computer equipment involve out-of-pocket costs. Depreciation and amortization are allocations of the original cost of plant and intangible assets. They are sunk costs, not out-of-pocket costs.

An *opportunity cost* is the potential benefit lost by taking a specific action when two or more alternative choices are available. An example is a student giving up wages from a job to attend summer school. Companies continually must choose from alternative courses of action. For instance, a company making standardized products might be approached by a customer to supply a special (nonstandard) product. A decision to accept or reject the special order must consider not only the profit to be made from the special order but also the profit given up by devoting time and resources to this order instead of pursuing an alternative project. The profit given up is an opportunity cost. Consideration of opportunity costs is important. The implications extend to internal resource allocation decisions. For instance, a computer manufacturer must decide between internally manufacturing a chip versus buying it externally. In another case, management of a multidivisional company must decide whether to continue operating or close a particular division.

Besides relevant costs, management must also consider the relevant benefits associated with a decision. **Relevant benefits** refer to the additional or *incremental* revenue generated by selecting a particular course of action over another. For instance, a student must decide the relevant benefits of taking one course over another. In sum, both relevant costs and relevant benefits are crucial to managerial decision making.

"Sunk costs are not relevant to my decision."

"I must consider out-of-pocket and opportunity costs."

Point: Opportunity costs are not entered in accounting records. This does not reduce their relevance for managerial decisions.

MANAGERIAL DECISION SCENARIOS

Managers experience many different scenarios that require analyzing alternative actions and making a decision. We describe several different types of decision scenarios in this section. We set these tasks in the context of FasTrac, an exercise supplies and equipment manufacturer introduced earlier. *We treat each of these decision tasks as separate from each other.*

A1 Evaluate short-term managerial decisions using relevant costs.

Additional Business

FasTrac is operating at its normal level of 80% of full capacity. At this level, it produces and sells approximately 100,000 units of product annually. Its per unit and annual total sales and costs are shown in Exhibit 23.2.

	Per Unit	Annual Total
Sales (100,000 units)	$10.00	$1,000,000
Direct materials	(3.50)	(350,000)
Direct labor	(2.20)	(220,000)
Overhead	(1.10)	(110,000)
Selling expenses	(1.40)	(140,000)
Administrative expenses	(0.80)	(80,000)
Total costs and expenses	(9.00)	(900,000)
Operating income	$ 1.00	$ 100,000

EXHIBIT 23.2

Selected Operating Income Data

A current buyer of FasTrac's products wants to purchase additional units of its product and export them to another country. This buyer offers to buy 10,000 units of the product at $8.50 per unit, or $1.50 less than the current price. The offer price is low, but FasTrac is considering the proposal because this sale would be several times larger than any single previous sale and it would use idle capacity. Also, the units will be exported, so this new business will not affect current sales.

To determine whether to accept or reject this order, management needs to know whether accepting the offer will increase net income. The analysis in Exhibit 23.3 shows that if management relies incorrectly on per unit historical costs, it would reject the sale because the selling price ($8.50) per unit is less than the total costs per unit ($9.00), and it thus yields a loss. However, historical costs are *not* relevant to this decision. Instead, the relevant costs are the additional costs, called **incremental costs.** These costs, also called *differential costs,* are the additional costs incurred if a company pursues a certain course of action. FasTrac's incremental costs are those related to the added volume that this new order would bring.

EXHIBIT 23.3

Analysis of Additional Business Using Historical Costs

	Per Unit	Total
Sales (10,000 additional units)	$ 8.50	$ 85,000
Total costs and expenses	(9.00)	(90,000)
Operating loss	$(0.50)	$ (5,000)

P1 Identify relevant costs and apply them to managerial decisions.

To correctly make its decision, FasTrac must analyze the costs of this new business in a different manner. The following information regarding the order is available:

- Manufacturing 10,000 additional units requires direct materials of $3.50 per unit and direct labor of $2.20 per unit (same as for all other units).
- Manufacturing 10,000 additional units adds $5,000 of incremental overhead costs for power, packaging, and indirect labor (all variable costs).
- Incremental commissions and selling expenses from this sale of 10,000 additional units would be $2,000 (all variable costs).
- Incremental administrative expenses of $1,000 for clerical efforts are needed (all fixed costs) with the sale of 10,000 additional units.

We use this information, as shown in Exhibit 23.4 to assess how accepting this new business will affect FasTrac's income.

EXHIBIT 23.4

Analysis of Additional Business Using Relevant Costs

	Additional Business	Current Business	Combined
Sales	$ 85,000	$1,000,000	$1,085,000
Direct materials	(35,000)	(350,000)	(385,000)
Direct labor	(22,000)	(220,000)	(242,000)
Overhead	(5,000)	(110,000)	(115,000)
Selling expenses	(2,000)	(140,000)	(142,000)
Administrative expense	(1,000)	(80,000)	(81,000)
Total costs and expenses	(65,000)	(900,000)	(965,000)
Operating income	$ 20,000	$ 100,000	$ 120,000

The analysis of relevant costs in Exhibit 23.4 suggests that the additional business be accepted. It would provide $85,000 of added revenue while incurring only $65,000 of added costs. This would yield $20,000 of additional pretax income, or a pretax profit margin of 23.5%. More generally, FasTrac would increase its income with any price that exceeded $6.50 per unit ($65,000 incremental cost/10,000 additional units). The key point is that *management must not blindly use historical costs, especially allocated overhead costs.* Instead, the accounting system needs to provide information about the incremental costs to be incurred if the additional business is accepted.

Other Factors   An analysis of the incremental costs pertaining to the additional volume is always relevant for this type of decision. We must proceed cautiously, however, when the additional volume approaches or exceeds the factory's existing available capacity. If the additional volume requires the company to expand its capacity by obtaining more equipment, more space, or more personnel, the incremental costs could quickly exceed the incremental revenue. Another cautionary note is the effect on existing sales. All new units of the extra business will be sold outside FasTrac's normal domestic sales channels. If accepting additional business would cause existing sales to decline, this information must be included in our analysis. The contribution margin lost from a decline in sales is an opportunity cost.

Decision Maker

Partner   You are a partner in a small accounting firm that specializes in keeping the books and preparing taxes for clients. A local restaurant is interested in obtaining these services from your firm. Identify factors that are relevant in deciding whether to accept the engagement. ■   [Answer—p. 998]

Make or Buy

The managerial decision to make or buy a component for one of its current products is common and depends on incremental costs. To illustrate, FasTrac has excess productive capacity it can use to manufacture Part 417, a component of the main product it sells. The part is currently purchased and delivered to the plant at a cost of $1.20 per unit. FasTrac estimates that making Part 417 would cost $0.45 for direct materials, $0.50 for direct labor, and an undetermined amount for overhead. The task is to determine how much overhead to add to these costs so we can decide whether to make or buy Part 417. If FasTrac's normal predetermined overhead application rate is 100% of direct labor cost, we might be tempted to conclude that overhead cost is $0.50 per unit, computed as 100% of the $0.50 direct labor cost. We would then mistakenly conclude that total cost is $1.45 per unit ($0.45 of materials + $0.50 of labor + $0.50 of overhead). A wrong decision in this case would be to conclude that the company is better off buying the part at $1.20 each than making it for $1.45 each.

Instead, as we explained earlier, only incremental overhead costs are relevant in this situation. Thus, we must compute an *incremental overhead rate.* Incremental overhead costs might include, for example, additional power for operating machines, extra supplies, added cleanup costs, materials handling, and quality control. We can prepare a per unit analysis in this case as shown in Exhibit 23.5.

	Make	Buy
Direct materials	$0.45	—
Direct labor	0.50	—
Overhead costs	[?]	—
Purchase price	—	$1.20
Total incremental costs	$0.95 + [?]	$1.20

EXHIBIT 23.5
Make or Buy Analysis

We can see that if incremental overhead costs are less than $0.25 per unit, ($1.20 − $0.95) the total cost of making the component is less than the purchase price of $1.20 and FasTrac should make the part. FasTrac's decision rule in this case is that any amount of overhead less than $0.25 per unit yields a total cost for Part 417 that is less than the $1.20 purchase price. FasTrac must consider several nonfinancial factors in the make or buy decision, including product quality, timeliness of delivery (especially in a just-in-time setting), reactions of customers and suppliers, and other intangibles such as employee morale and workload. It must also consider whether making the part requires incremental fixed costs to expand plant capacity. When these added factors are considered, small cost differences may not matter.

Decision Insight

Make or Buy IT   Companies apply make or buy decisions to their services. Many now outsource their information technology activities. Information technology companies provide infrastructure and services to enable businesses to focus on their key activities. It is argued that outsourcing saves money and streamlines operations, and without the headaches. ■

Scrap or Rework

Managers often must make a decision on whether to scrap or rework products in process. Remember that costs already incurred in manufacturing the units of a product that do not meet quality standards are sunk costs that have been incurred and cannot be changed. Sunk costs are irrelevant in any decision on whether to sell the substandard units as scrap or to rework them to meet quality standards.

To illustrate, assume that FasTrac has 10,000 defective units of a product that have already cost $1 per unit to manufacture. These units can be sold as is (as scrap) for $0.40 each, or they can be reworked for $0.80 per unit and then sold for their full price of $1.50 each. Should FasTrac sell the units as scrap or rework them?

To make this decision, management must recognize that the already incurred manufacturing costs of $1 per unit are sunk (unavoidable). These costs are *entirely irrelevant* to the decision. In addition, we must be certain that all costs of reworking defects, including interfering with normal operations, are accounted for in our analysis. For instance, reworking the defects means that FasTrac is unable to manufacture 10,000 *new* units with an incremental cost of $1 per unit and a selling price of $1.50 per unit, meaning it incurs an *opportunity cost* equal to the lost $5,000 net return from making and selling 10,000 new units. This opportunity cost is the difference between the $15,000 revenue (10,000 units × $1.50) from selling these new units and their $10,000 manufacturing costs (10,000 units × $1). Our analysis is reflected in Exhibit 23.6.

EXHIBIT 23.6

Scrap or Rework Analysis

	Scrap	Rework
Sale of scrapped/reworked units (10,000 units)	$ 4,000	$15,000
Less out-of-pocket costs to rework defects ($0.80 per unit)		(8,000)
Less opportunity cost of not making new units		**(5,000)**
Incremental net income	$4,000	$ 2,000

The analysis yields a $2,000 difference in favor of scrapping the defects, yielding a total incremental net income of $4,000. If we had failed to include the opportunity costs of $5,000, the rework option would have shown an income of $7,000 instead of $2,000, mistakenly making reworking appear more favorable than scrapping.

Quick Check   Answers — p. 998

1. A company receives a special order for 200 units that requires stamping the buyer's name on each unit, yielding an additional fixed cost of $400 to its normal costs. Without the order, the company is operating at 75% of capacity and produces 7,500 units of product at the following costs:

Direct materials	$37,500
Direct labor	60,000
Overhead (30% variable)	20,000
Selling expenses (60% variable)	25,000

   The special order will not affect normal unit sales and will not increase fixed overhead and selling expenses. Variable selling expenses on the special order are reduced to one-half the normal amount. The price per unit necessary to earn $1,000 on this order is (a) $14.80, (b) $15.80, (c) $19.80, (d) $20.80, or (e) $21.80.

2. What are the incremental costs of accepting additional business?

Sell or Process

The managerial decision to sell partially completed products as is or to process them further for sale depends significantly on relevant costs. To illustrate, suppose that FasTrac has 40,000 units of partially finished Product Q. It has already spent $0.75 per unit to manufacture these 40,000 units at a $30,000 total cost. FasTrac can sell the 40,000 units to another manufacturer as raw material for $50,000. Alternatively, it can process them further and produce finished products X, Y, and Z at an incremental cost of $2 per unit. The added processing yields the products and revenues shown in Exhibit 23.7. FasTrac must decide whether the added revenues from selling finished products X, Y, and Z exceed the costs of finishing them.

Product	Price	Units	Revenues
Product X	$4.00	10,000	$ 40,000
Product Y..........	6.00	22,000	132,000
Product Z	8.00	6,000	48,000
Spoilage	—	2,000	0
Totals		40,000	$220,000

EXHIBIT 23.7

Revenues from Processing Further

Exhibit 23.8 shows the two-step analysis for this decision. First, FasTrac computes its incremental revenue from further processing Q into products X, Y, and Z. This amount is the difference between the $220,000 revenue from the further processed products and the $50,000 FasTrac will give up by not selling Q as is (a $50,000 opportunity cost). Second, FasTrac computes its incremental costs from further processing Q into X, Y, and Z. This amount is $80,000 (40,000 units × $2 incremental cost). The analysis shows that FasTrac can earn incremental net income of $90,000 from a decision to further process Q. (Notice that the earlier incurred $30,000 manufacturing cost for the 40,000 units of Product Q does not appear in Exhibit 23.8 because it is a sunk cost and as such is irrelevant to the decision.)

Example: Does the decision change if incremental costs in Exhibit 23.8 increase to $4 per unit and the opportunity cost increases to $95,000? *Answer:* Yes. There is now an incremental net loss of $35,000.

Revenue if processed..............	$220,000
Revenue if sold as is...............	(50,000)
Incremental revenue	170,000
Incremental cost to process	(80,000)
Incremental net income	$90,000

EXHIBIT 23.8

Sell or Process Analysis

Quick Check   Answers — p. 998

3. A company has already incurred a $1,000 cost in partially producing its four products. Their selling prices when partially and fully processed follow with additional costs necessary to finish these partially processed units:

Product	Unfinished Selling Price	Finished Selling Price	Further Processing Costs
Alpha	$300	$600	$150
Beta	450	900	300
Gamma............	275	425	125
Delta	150	210	75

Which product(s) should *not* be processed further, (a) Alpha, (b) Beta, (c) Gamma, or (d) Delta?

4. Under what conditions is a sunk cost relevant to decision making?

Sales Mix Selection

When a company sells a mix of products, some are likely to be more profitable than others. Management is often wise to concentrate sales efforts on more profitable products. If production facilities or other factors are limited, an increase in the production and sale of one product usually requires reducing the production and sale of others. In this case, management must identify the most profitable combination, or *sales mix* of products. To identify the best sales mix, management must know the contribution margin of each product, the facilities required to produce each product, any constraints on these facilities, and its markets.

Point: A method called *linear programming* is useful for finding the optimal sales mix for several products subject to many market and production constraints. This method is described in advanced courses.

To illustrate, assume that FasTrac makes and sells two products, A and B. The same machines are used to produce both products. A and B have the following selling prices and variable costs per unit:

	Product A	Product B
Selling price per unit...............	$5.00	$7.50
Variable costs per unit	3.50	5.50
Contribution margin per unit.........	$1.50	$2.00

The variable costs are included in the analysis because they are the incremental costs of producing these products within the existing capacity of 100,000 machine hours per month. We consider three separate cases.

Demand Is Unlimited and Products Use Same Inputs   Assume that (1) each product requires 1 machine hour per unit for production and (2) the demand for these products is unlimited. Under these conditions, FasTrac should produce as much of Product B as it can because of its larger contribution margin of $2 per unit. At full capacity, FasTrac would produce $200,000 of total contribution margin per month, computed as $2 per unit times 100,000 machine hours.

Demand Is Unlimited and Products Use Different Inputs   Assume that (1) Product A requires 1 machine hour per unit, (2) Product B requires 2 machine hours per unit, and (3) the demand for these products is unlimited. Under these conditions, FasTrac should produce as much of Product A as it can because it has a contribution margin of $1.50 per machine hour compared with only $1 per machine hour for Product B. Exhibit 23.9 shows the relevant analysis.

EXHIBIT 23.9

Sales Mix Analysis

	Product A	Product B
Selling price per unit	$5.00	$7.50
Variable costs per unit	3.50	5.50
Contribution margin per unit	$1.50	$2.00
Machine hours per unit.........................	1.0	2.0
Contribution margin per machine hour.........	**$1.50**	**$1.00**

At its full capacity of 100,000 machine hours, FasTrac would produce 100,000 units of Product A, yielding $150,000 of total contribution margin per month. In contrast, if it uses all 100,000 hours to produce Product B, only 50,000 units would be produced yielding a contribution margin of $100,000. These results suggest that when a company faces unlimited demand and limited capacity, only the most profitable product per input should be manufactured.

Demand Is Limited and Products Use Different Inputs   The need for a mix of different products arises when market demand is not sufficient to allow a company to sell all that it produces. For instance, assume that (1) Product A requires 1 machine hour per unit, (2) Product B requires 2 machine hours per unit, and (3) the market for Product A is limited to 80,000 units. Under these conditions, FasTrac should produce no more than 80,000 units of Product A. This would leave another 20,000 machine hours of capacity for making Product B. FasTrac should use this spare capacity to produce 10,000 units of Product B. This sales mix would maximize FasTrac's total contribution margin per month at an amount of $140,000. In this case, the company first produces its most profitable product, up to the point of total demand (or its capacity constraint). It then uses remaining capacity to produce its next most profitable product.

Example: If Product B's variable costs per unit increase to $6, Product A's variable costs per unit decrease to $3, and the same machine hours per unit are used, which product should FasTrac produce? *Answer:* Product A. Its contribution margin of $2 per machine hour is higher than B's $.75 per machine hour.

Point: FasTrac might consider buying another machine to reduce the constraint on production. A strategy designed to reduce the impact of constraints or bottlenecks, on production, is called the *theory of constraints.*

Decision Insight

Companies such as Gap, Abercrombie & Fitch, and American Eagle must continuously monitor and manage the sales mix of their product lists. Selling their products in hundreds of countries and territories further complicates their decision process. The contribution margin of each product is crucial to their product mix strategies. ∎

Segment Elimination

When a segment such as a department or division is performing poorly, management must consider eliminating it. Segment information on either net income (loss) or its contribution to overhead is not sufficient for this decision. Instead, we must look at the segment's avoidable expenses and unavoidable expenses. **Avoidable expenses,** also called *escapable expenses,* are amounts the company would not incur if it eliminated the segment. **Unavoidable expenses,** also called *inescapable expenses,* are amounts that would continue even if the segment is eliminated.

To illustrate, FasTrac considers eliminating its treadmill division because its $48,300 total expenses are higher than its $47,800 sales. Classification of this division's operating expenses into avoidable or unavoidable expenses is shown in Exhibit 23.10.

	Total	Avoidable Expenses	Unavoidable Expenses
Cost of goods sold	$ 30,000	$ 30,000	—
Direct expenses			
Salaries expense	7,900	7,900	—
Depreciation expense—Equipment	200	—	$ 200
Indirect expenses			
Rent and utilities expense	3,150	—	3,150
Advertising expense	400	400	—
Insurance expense	400	300	100
Service department costs			
Share of office department expenses	3,060	2,200	860
Share of purchasing expenses	3,190	1,000	2,190
Total	$48,300	$41,800	$6,500

EXHIBIT 23.10

Classification of Segment Operating Expenses for Analysis

FasTrac's analysis shows that it can avoid $41,800 expenses if it eliminates the treadmill division. Because this division's sales are $47,800, eliminating it will cause FasTrac to lose $6,000 of income. *Our decision rule is that a segment is a candidate for elimination if its revenues are less than its avoidable expenses.* Avoidable expenses can be viewed as the costs to generate this segment's revenues.

When considering elimination of a segment, we must assess its impact on other segments. A segment could be unprofitable on its own, but it might still contribute to other segments' revenues and profits. It is possible then to continue a segment even when its revenues are less than its avoidable expenses. Similarly, a profitable segment might be discontinued if its space, assets, or staff can be more profitably used by expanding existing segments or by creating new ones. Our decision to keep or eliminate a segment requires a more complex analysis than simply looking at a segment's performance report. Such reports provide useful information, but they do not provide all the information necessary for this decision.

Example: How can insurance be classified as either avoidable or unavoidable? *Answer:* Depends on whether the assets insured can be removed and the premiums canceled.

Example: Give an example of a segment that a company might profitably use to attract customers even though it might incur a loss. *Answer:* Warranty and post-sales services.

Keep or Replace Equipment

Businesses periodically must decide whether to keep using equipment or replace it. Advances in technology typically mean newer equipment can operate more efficiently and at lower cost than older equipment. In making the decision to keep or replace equipment, managers must decide whether the reduction in *variable* manufacturing costs with the new equipment over its useful life is greater than the net purchase price of the equipment. In this setting, the net purchase price of the equipment is its total cost minus any trade-in allowance or cash receipt for the old equipment.

For example, FasTrac has a piece of manufacturing equipment with a book value (cost minus accumulated depreciation) of $20,000 and a remaining useful life of four years. At the end of four years the equipment will have a salvage value of zero. The market value of the equipment is currently $25,000.

FasTrac can purchase a new machine for $100,000 and receive $25,000 in return for trading in its old machine. The new machine will reduce FasTrac's variable manufacturing costs by $18,000 per year over the four-year life of the new machine. FasTrac's incremental analysis is shown in Exhibit 23.11.

EXHIBIT 23.11

Keep or Replace Analysis

	Increase or (Decrease) in Net Income
Cost to buy new machine	$(100,000)
Cash received to trade in old machine	25,000
Reduction in variable manufacturing costs*	72,000
Total increase (decrease) in net income	$ (3,000)

*18,000 × 4 years

The analysis in Exhibit 23.11 shows that FasTrac should not replace the old equipment with this newer version as it will decrease income by $3,000. Note, the book value of the old equipment ($20,000) is not relevant to this analysis. Book value is a sunk cost, and it cannot be changed regardless of whether FasTrac keeps or replaces this equipment.

Qualitative Decision Factors

Managers must consider qualitative factors in making managerial decisions. Consider a decision on whether to buy a component from an outside supplier or continue to make it. Several qualitative decision factors must be considered. For example, the quality, delivery, and reputation of the proposed supplier are important. The effects from deciding not to make the component can include potential layoffs and impaired worker morale. Consider another situation in which a company is considering a one-time sale to a new customer at a special low price. Qualitative factors to consider in this situation include the effects of a low price on the company's image and the threat that regular customers might demand a similar price. The company must also consider whether this customer is really a one-time customer. If not, can it continue to offer this low price in the long run? Clearly, management cannot rely solely on financial data to make such decisions.

Quick Check   Answers — p. 998

5. What is the difference between avoidable and unavoidable expenses?
6. A segment is a candidate for elimination if (a) its revenues are less than its avoidable expenses, (b) it has a net loss, (c) its unavoidable expenses are higher than its revenues.

Decision Analysis ▢▢▢   Setting Product Price

A2 Determine product selling price based on total costs.

Relevant costs are useful to management in determining prices for special short-term decisions. But longer run pricing decisions of management need to cover both variable and fixed costs, and yield a profit.

There are several methods to help management in setting prices. The *cost-plus* methods are probably the most common, where management adds a markup to cost to reach a target price. We will describe the **total cost method,** where management sets price equal to the product's total costs plus a desired profit on the product. This is a four-step process:

1. Determine total costs.

$$\text{Total costs} = \frac{\text{Production (direct materials,}}{\text{direct labor, and overhead)}} + \frac{\text{Nonproduction (selling and}}{\text{administrative) costs}}$$

2. Determine total cost per unit.

$$\text{Total cost per unit} = \text{Total costs} \div \text{Total units expected to be produced and sold}$$

3. Determine the dollar markup per unit.

> **Markup per unit = Total cost per unit × Markup percentage**

where Markup percentage = Desired profit/Total costs

4. Determine selling price per unit.

> **Selling price per unit = Total cost per unit + Markup per unit**

To illustrate, consider a company that produces MP3 players. The company desires a 20% return on its assets of $1,000,000, and it expects to produce and sell 10,000 players. The following additional company information is available:

Variable costs (per unit)	
Production costs.............	$44
Nonproduction costs	6
Fixed costs (in dollars)	
Overhead..................	$140,000
Nonproduction.............	60,000

We apply our four-step process to determine price.

1. Total costs = Production costs + Nonproduction costs
     = [($44 × 10,000 units) + $140,000] + [($6 × 10,000 units) + $60,000]
     = $700,000

2. Total cost per unit = Total costs/Total units expected to be produced and sold
        = $700,000/10,000
        = $70

3. Markup per unit = Total cost per unit × (Desired profit/Total costs)
        = $70 × [(20% × $1,000,000)/$700,000]
        = $20

4. Selling price per unit = Total cost per unit + Markup per unit
        = $70 + $20
        = $90

To verify that our price yields the $200,000 desired profit (20% × $1,000,000), we compute the following simplified income statement using the information above.

Sales ($90 × 10,000)	$900,000
Expenses	
Variable ($50 × 10,000)	500,000
Fixed ($140,000 + $60,000)	200,000
Income	$200,000

Companies use cost-plus pricing as a starting point for determining selling prices. Many factors determine price, including consumer preferences and competition.

DEMONSTRATION PROBLEM

Determine the appropriate action in each of the following managerial decision situations.

1. Packer Company is operating at 80% of its manufacturing capacity of 100,000 product units per year. A chain store has offered to buy an additional 10,000 units at $22 each and sell them to customers so as not to compete with Packer Company. The following data are available.

Costs at 80% Capacity	Per Unit	Total
Direct materials	$ 8.00	$ 640,000
Direct labor	7.00	560,000
Overhead (fixed and variable)	12.50	1,000,000
Totals	$27.50	$2,200,000

In producing 10,000 additional units, fixed overhead costs would remain at their current level but incremental variable overhead costs of $3 per unit would be incurred. Should the company accept or reject this order?

2. Green Company uses Part JR3 in manufacturing its products. It has always purchased this part from a supplier for $40 each. It recently upgraded its own manufacturing capabilities and has enough excess capacity (including trained workers) to begin manufacturing Part JR3 instead of buying it. The company prepares the following cost projections of making the part, assuming that overhead is allocated to the part at the normal predetermined rate of 200% of direct labor cost.

Direct materials	$11
Direct labor	15
Overhead (fixed and variable) (200% of direct labor)	30
Total	$56

The required volume of output to produce the part will not require any incremental fixed overhead. Incremental variable overhead cost will be $17 per unit. Should the company make or buy this part?

3. Gold Company's manufacturing process causes a relatively large number of defective parts to be produced. The defective parts can be (a) sold for scrap, (b) melted to recover the recycled metal for reuse, or (c) reworked to be good units. Reworking defective parts reduces the output of other good units because no excess capacity exists. Each unit reworked means that one new unit cannot be produced. The following information reflects 500 defective parts currently available.

Proceeds of selling as scrap	$2,500
Additional cost of melting down defective parts	400
Cost of purchases avoided by using recycled metal from defects	4,800
Cost to rework 500 defective parts	
Direct materials	0
Direct labor	1,500
Incremental overhead	1,750
Cost to produce 500 new parts	
Direct materials	6,000
Direct labor	5,000
Incremental overhead	3,200
Selling price per good unit	40

Should the company melt the parts, sell them as scrap, or rework them?

PLANNING THE SOLUTION

- Determine whether Packer Company should accept the additional business by finding the incremental costs of materials, labor, and overhead that will be incurred if the order is accepted. Omit fixed costs that the order will not increase. If the incremental revenue exceeds the incremental cost, accept the order.
- Determine whether Green Company should make or buy the component by finding the incremental cost of making each unit. If the incremental cost exceeds the purchase price, the component should be purchased. If the incremental cost is less than the purchase price, make the component.
- Determine whether Gold Company should sell the defective parts, melt them down and recycle the metal, or rework them. To compare the three choices, examine all costs incurred and benefits received

from the alternatives in working with the 500 defective units versus the production of 500 new units. For the scrapping alternative, include the costs of producing 500 new units and subtract the $2,500 proceeds from selling the old ones. For the melting alternative, include the costs of melting the defective units, add the net cost of new materials in excess over those obtained from recycling, and add the direct labor and overhead costs. For the reworking alternative, add the costs of direct labor and incremental overhead. Select the alternative that has the lowest cost. The cost assigned to the 500 defective units is sunk and not relevant in choosing among the three alternatives.

SOLUTION TO DEMONSTRATION PROBLEM

1. This decision involves accepting additional business. Since current unit costs are $27.50, it appears initially as if the offer to sell for $22 should be rejected, but the $27.50 cost includes fixed costs. When the analysis includes only *incremental* costs, the per unit cost is as shown in the following table. The offer should be accepted because it will produce $4 of additional profit per unit (computed as $22 price less $18 incremental cost), which yields a total profit of $40,000 for the 10,000 additional units.

Direct materials	$ 8.00
Direct labor	7.00
Variable overhead (given)	3.00
Total incremental cost	$18.00

2. For this make or buy decision, the analysis must not include the $13 nonincremental overhead per unit ($30 − $17). When only the $17 incremental overhead is included, the relevant unit cost of manufacturing the part is shown in the following table. It would be better to continue buying the part for $40 instead of making it for $43.

Direct materials	$11.00
Direct labor	15.00
Variable overhead	17.00
Total incremental cost	$43.00

3. The goal of this scrap or rework decision is to identify the alternative that produces the greatest net benefit to the company. To compare the alternatives, we determine the net cost of obtaining 500 marketable units as follows:

Incremental Cost to Produce 500 Marketable Units	Sell as Is	Melt and Recycle	Rework Units
Direct materials			
New materials	$ 6,000	$6,000	
Recycled metal materials		(4,800)	
Net materials cost		1,200	
Melting costs		400	
Total direct materials cost	6,000	1,600	
Direct labor	5,000	5,000	$1,500
Incremental overhead	3,200	3,200	1,750
Cost to produce 500 marketable units	14,200	9,800	3,250
Less proceeds of selling defects as scrap	(2,500)		
Opportunity costs*			5,800
Net cost	$11,700	$9,800	$9,050

* The $5,800 opportunity cost is the lost contribution margin from not being able to produce and sell 500 units because of reworking, computed as ($40 − [$14,200/500 units]) × 500 units.

The incremental cost of 500 marketable parts is smallest if the defects are reworked.

Summary

C1   Describe the importance of relevant costs for short-term decisions. A company must rely on relevant costs pertaining to alternative courses of action rather than historical costs. Out-of-pocket expenses and opportunity costs are relevant because these are avoidable; sunk costs are irrelevant because they result from past decisions and are therefore unavoidable. Managers must also consider the relevant benefits associated with alternative decisions.

A1   Evaluate short-term managerial decisions using relevant costs. Relevant costs are useful in making decisions such as to accept additional business, make or buy, and sell as is or process further. For example, the relevant factors in deciding whether to

produce and sell additional units of product are incremental costs and incremental revenues from the additional volume.

A2   Determine product selling price based on total costs. Product selling price is estimated using total production and nonproduction costs plus a markup. Price is set to yield management's desired profit for the company.

P1   Identify relevant costs and apply them to managerial decisions. Several illustrations apply relevant costs to managerial decisions, such as whether to accept additional business; make or buy; scrap or rework products; sell products or process them further; or eliminate a segment and how to select the best sales mix.

Guidance Answer to Decision Maker

Partner   You should identify the differences between existing clients and this potential client. A key difference is that the restaurant business has additional inventory components (groceries, vegetables, meats, etc.) and is likely to have a higher proportion of depreciable assets. These differences imply that the partner must spend more

hours auditing the records and understanding the business, regulations, and standards that pertain to the restaurant business. Such differences suggest that the partner must use a different "formula" for quoting a price to this potential client vis-à-vis current clients.

Guidance Answers to Quick Checks

1. *e*; Variable costs per unit for this order of 200 units follow:

Direct materials ($37,500/7,500)	$ 5.00
Direct labor ($60,000/7,500)	8.00
Variable overhead [(0.30 × $20,000)/7,500]	0.80
Variable selling expenses [(0.60 × $25,000 × 0.5)/7,500]	1.00
Total variable costs per unit	$14.80

Cost to produce special order: (200 × $14.80) + $400
= $3,360.

Price per unit to earn $1,000: ($3,360 + $1,000)/200 = $21.80.

2. They are the additional (new) costs of accepting new business.

3. *d*;

	Incremental benefits		Incremental costs
Alpha	$300 ($600 − $300)	>	$150 (given)
Beta	$450 ($900 − $450)	>	$300 (given)
Gamma	$150 ($425 − $275)	>	$125 (given)
Delta	$ 60 ($210 − $150)	<	$ 75 (given)

4. A sunk cost is *never* relevant because it results from a past decision and is already incurred.

5. Avoidable expenses are ones a company will not incur by eliminating a segment; unavoidable expenses will continue even after a segment is eliminated.

6. *a*

Key Terms

Avoidable expense (p. 993)

Incremental cost (p. 988)

Markup (p. 994)

Relevant benefits (p. 987)

Total cost method (p. 994)

Unavoidable expense (p. 993)

Multiple Choice Quiz Answers on p. 1013 mhhe.com/wildFINMAN5e

Additional Quiz Questions are available at the book's Website.

1. A company inadvertently produced 3,000 defective MP3 players. The players cost $12 each to produce. A recycler offers to purchase the defective players as they are for $8 each. The production manager reports that the defects can be corrected for $10 each, enabling them to be sold at their regular market price of $19 each. The company should:
   a. Correct the defect and sell them at the regular price.
   b. Sell the players to the recycler for $8 each.
   c. Sell 2,000 to the recycler and repair the rest.
   d. Sell 1,000 to the recycler and repair the rest.
   e. Throw the players away.

2. A company's productive capacity is limited to 480,000 machine hours. Product X requires 10 machine hours to produce; and Product Y requires 2 machine hours to produce. Product X sells for $32 per unit and has variable costs of $12 per unit; Product Y sells for $24 per unit and has variable costs of $10 per unit. Assuming that the company can sell as many of either product as it produces, it should:
   a. Produce X and Y in the ratio of 57% and 43%.
   b. Produce X and Y in the ratio of 83% X and 17% Y.
   c. Produce equal amounts of Product X and Product Y.
   d. Produce only Product X.
   e. Produce only Product Y.

3. A company receives a special one-time order for 3,000 units of its product at $15 per unit. The company has excess capacity and it currently produces and sells the units at $20 each to its regular customers. Production costs are $13.50 per unit, which includes $9 of variable costs. To produce the special order, the company must incur additional fixed costs of $5,000. Should the company accept the special order?
   a. Yes, because incremental revenue exceeds incremental costs.
   b. No, because incremental costs exceed incremental revenue.
   c. No, because the units are being sold for $5 less than the regular price.
   d. Yes, because incremental costs exceed incremental revenue.
   e. No, because incremental cost exceeds $15 per unit when total costs are considered.

4. A cost that cannot be changed because it arises from a past decision and is irrelevant to future decisions is
   a. An uncontrollable cost.
   b. An out-of-pocket cost.
   c. A sunk cost.
   d. An opportunity cost.
   e. An incremental cost.

5. The potential benefit of one alternative that is lost by choosing another is known as
   a. An alternative cost.
   b. A sunk cost.
   c. A differential cost.
   d. An opportunity cost.
   e. An out-of-pocket cost.

🚹 Icon denotes assignments that involve decision making.

Discussion Questions

1. 🚹 Identify the five steps involved in the managerial decision-making process.

2. Is nonfinancial information ever useful in managerial decision making?

3. What is a relevant cost? Identify the two types of relevant costs.

4. 🚹 Why are sunk costs irrelevant in deciding whether to sell a product in its present condition or to make it into a new product through additional processing?

5. Arctic Cat has many types of costs. What is an out-of-pocket cost? What is an opportunity cost? Are opportunity costs recorded in the accounting records? Arctic Cat

6. 🚹 Piaggio must confront sunk costs. Why are sunk costs irrelevant in deciding whether to sell a product in its present condition or to make it into a new product through additional processing? **PIAGGIO**

7. 🚹 Identify some qualitative factors that should be considered when making managerial decisions.

8. 🚹 Identify the incremental costs incurred by Apple for shipping one additional iPod from a warehouse to a retail store along with the store's normal order of 75 iPods. Apple

9. 🚹 KTM is considering eliminating one of its stores in a large U.S. city. What are some factors that it should consider in making this decision? **KTM**

10. 🚹 Assume that Polaris manufactures and sells 60,000 units of a product at $11,000 per unit in domestic markets. It costs $6,000 per unit to manufacture ($4,000 variable cost per unit, $2,000 fixed cost per unit). Can you describe a situation under which the company is willing to sell an additional 8,000 units of the product in an international market at $5,000 per unit? **Polaris**

QUICK STUDY

QS 23-1

Identification of relevant costs

P1

Helix Company has been approached by a new customer to provide 2,000 units of its regular product at a special price of $6 per unit. The regular selling price of the product is $8 per unit. Helix is operating at 75% of its capacity of 10,000 units. Identify whether the following costs are relevant to Helix's decision as to whether to accept the order at the special selling price. No additional fixed manufacturing overhead will be incurred because of this order. The only additional selling expense on this order will be a $0.50 per unit shipping cost. There will be no additional administrative expenses because of this order. Place an X in the appropriate column to identify whether the cost is relevant or irrelevant to accepting this order.

Item	Relevant	Not relevant
a. Selling price of $6.00 per unit	_____	_____
b. Direct materials cost of $1.00 per unit	_____	_____
c. Direct labor of $2.00 per unit	_____	_____
d. Variable manufacturing overhead of $1.50 per unit	_____	_____
e. Fixed manufacturing overhead of $0.75 per unit	_____	_____
f. Regular selling expenses of $1.25 per unit	_____	_____
g. Additional selling expenses of $0.50 per unit	_____	_____
h. Administrative expenses of $0.60 per unit	_____	_____

QS 23-2

Analysis of relevant costs   A1

Refer to the data in QS 23-1. Based on financial considerations alone, should Helix accept this order at the special price? Explain.

QS 23-3

Identification of relevant nonfinancial factors   P1

Refer to QS 23-1 and QS 23-2. What nonfinancial factors should Helix consider before accepting this order? Explain.

QS 23-4

Sell or process

P1 A1

Garcia Company has 10,000 units of its product that were produced last year at a total cost of $150,000. The units were damaged in a rain storm because the warehouse where they were stored developed a leak in the roof. Garcia can sell the units as is for $2 each or it can repair the units at a total cost of $18,000 and then sell them for $5 each. Should Garcia sell the units as is or repair them and then sell them? Explain.

QS 23-5

Relevant costs

C1

Label each of the following statements as either true ("T") or false ("F").

1. Relevant costs are also known as unavoidable costs.

2. Incremental costs are also known as differential costs.

3. An out-of-pocket cost requires a current and/or future outlay of cash.

4. An opportunity cost is the potential benefit that is lost by taking a specific action when two or more alternative choices are available.

5. A sunk cost will change with a future course of action.

QS 23-6

Analysis of incremental costs

A1 P1

Kando Company incurs a $9 per unit cost for Product A, which it currently manufactures and sells for $13.50 per unit. Instead of manufacturing and selling this product, the company can purchase Product B for $5 per unit and sell it for $12 per unit. If it does so, unit sales would remain unchanged and $5 of the $9 per unit costs assigned to Product A would be eliminated. Should the company continue to manufacture Product A or purchase Product B for resale?

QS 23-7

Selection of sales mix

A1

Excel Memory Company can sell all units of computer memory X and Y that it can produce, but it has limited production capacity. It can produce two units of X per hour *or* three units of Y per hour, and it has 4,000 production hours available. Contribution margin is $5 for product X and $4 for product Y. What is the most profitable sales mix for this company?

QS 23-8

Sell or process decision

A1 P1

Holmes Company produces a product that can either be sold as is or processed further. Holmes has already spent $50,000 to produce 1,250 units that can be sold now for $67,500 to another manufacturer. Alternatively, Holmes can process the units further at an incremental cost of $250 per unit. If Holmes processes further, the units can be sold for $375 each. Compute the incremental income if Holmes processes further.

Signal mistakenly produced 10,000 defective cell phones. The phones cost $60 each to produce. A salvage company will buy the defective phones as they are for $30 each. It would cost Signal $80 per phone to rework the phones. If the phones are reworked, Signal could sell them for $110 each. Compute the incremental net income from reworking the phones.

QS 23-9

Scrap or rework

A1 P1

Radar Company sells bikes for $300 each. The company currently sells 3,750 bikes per year and could make as many as 5,000 bikes per year. The bikes cost $225 each to make; $150 in variable costs per bike and $75 of fixed costs per bike. Radar received an offer from a potential customer who wants to buy 750 bikes for $250 each. Incremental fixed costs to make this order are $50,000. No other costs will change if this order is accepted. Compute Radar's additional income (ignore taxes) if it accepts this order.

QS 23-10

Decision to accept additional business

A1 P1

A guitar manufacturer is considering eliminating its electric guitar division because its $76,000 expenses are higher than its $72,000 sales. The company reports the following expenses for this division. Should the division be eliminated?

QS 23-11

Segment elimination

A1 P1

	Avoidable Expenses	Unavoidable Expenses
Cost of goods sold	$56,000	
Direct expenses	9,250	$1,250
Indirect expenses	470	1,600
Service department costs	6,000	1,430

Rory Company has a machine with a book value of $75,000 and a remaining five-year useful life. A new machine is available at a cost of $112,500, and Rory can also receive $60,000 for trading in its old machine. The new machine will reduce variable manufacturing costs by $12,000 per year over its five-year useful life. Should the machine be replaced?

QS 23-12

Keep or replace decision

A1 P1

connect

Fill in each of the blanks below with the correct term.

EXERCISES

1. A _____ arises from a past decision and cannot be avoided or changed; it is irrelevant to future decisions.

Exercise 23-1

Relevant costs

C1

2. _____ refer to the incremental revenue generated from taking one particular action over another.

3. Relevant costs are also known as _____.

4. An _____ requires a future outlay of cash and is relevant for current and future decision making.

5. An _____ is the potential benefit lost by taking a specific action when two or more alternative choices are available.

Xinhong Company is considering replacing one of its manufacturing machines. The machine has a book value of $45,000 and a remaining useful life of 5 years, at which time its salvage value will be zero. It has a current market value of $52,000. Variable manufacturing costs are $36,000 per year for this machine. Information on two alternative replacement machines follows. Should Xinhong keep or replace its manufacturing machine? If the machine should be replaced, which alternative new machine should Xinhong purchase?

Exercise 23-2

Keep or replace

A1 P1

	Alternative A	Alternative B
Cost	$115,000	$125,000
Variable manufacturing costs per year.........	19,000	15,000

A company must decide between scrapping or reworking units that do not pass inspection. The company has 22,000 defective units that cost $6 per unit to manufacture. The units can be sold as is for $2.50 each, or they can be reworked for $4.50 each and then sold for the full price of $8.50 each. If the units are sold as is, the company will have to build 22,000 replacement units at a cost of $6 each, and sell them at the full price of $8.50 each. (1) What is the incremental income from selling the units as scrap? (2) What is the incremental income from reworking and selling the units? (3) Should the company sell the units as scrap or rework them?

Exercise 23-3

Scrap or rework

A1 P1

Exercise 23-4

Decision to accept additional business or not

A1   P1

Farrow Co. expects to sell 150,000 units of its product in the next period with the following results.

Sales (150,000 units)	$2,250,000
Costs and expenses	
Direct materials	300,000
Direct labor	600,000
Overhead	150,000
Selling expenses	225,000
Administrative expenses	385,500
Total costs and expenses	1,660,500
Net income	$ 589,500

The company has an opportunity to sell 15,000 additional units at $12 per unit. The additional sales would not affect its current expected sales. Direct materials and labor costs per unit would be the same for the additional units as they are for the regular units. However, the additional volume would create the following incremental costs: (1) total overhead would increase by 15% and (2) administrative expenses would increase by $64,500. Prepare an analysis to determine whether the company should accept or reject the offer to sell additional units at the reduced price of $12 per unit.

Check   Income increase, $3,000

Exercise 23-5

Decision to accept new business or not

P1   A1

Goshford Company produces a single product and has capacity to produce 100,000 units per month. Costs to produce its current sales of 80,000 units follow. The regular selling price of the product is $100 per unit. Management is approached by a new customer who wants to purchase 20,000 units of the product for $75 per unit. If the order is accepted, there will be no additional fixed manufacturing overhead, and no additional fixed selling and administrative expenses. The customer is not in the company's regular selling territory, so there will be a $5 per unit shipping expense in addition to the regular variable selling and administrative expenses.

	Per Unit	Costs at 80,000 Units
Direct materials	$12.50	$1,000,000
Direct labor	15.00	1,200,000
Variable manufacturing overhead	10.00	800,000
Fixed manufacturing overhead	17.50	1,400,000
Variable selling and administrative expenses	14.00	1,120,000
Fixed selling and administrative expenses	13.00	1,040,000
Totals	$82.00	$6,560,000

Required

Check   (1) Additional volume effect on net income, $370,000

1. Determine whether management should accept or reject the new business.

2. What nonfinancial factors should management consider when deciding whether to take this order?

Exercise 23-6

Make or buy decision

A1

Gilberto Company currently manufactures one of its crucial parts at a cost of $4.45 per unit. This cost is based on a normal production rate of 65,000 units per year. Variable costs are $1.95 per unit, fixed costs related to making this part are $65,000 per year, and allocated fixed costs are $58,500 per year. Allocated fixed costs are unavoidable whether the company makes or buys the part. Gilberto is considering buying the part from a supplier for a quoted price of $3.50 per unit guaranteed for a three-year period. Should the company continue to manufacture the part, or should it buy the part from the outside supplier? Support your answer with analyses.

Check $35,750 increased costs to buy

Exercise 23-7

Make or buy decision   P1   A1

Gelb Company currently manufactures 40,000 units of a key component for its manufacturing process at a cost of $4.45 per unit. Variable costs are $1.95 per unit, fixed costs related to making this component are $65,000 per year, and allocated fixed costs are $58,500 per year. The allocated fixed costs are unavoidable whether the company makes or buys this component. The company is considering buying this component from a supplier for $3.50 per unit. Should it continue to manufacture the component, or should it buy this component from the outside supplier? Support your decision with analysis of the data provided.

Check   Increased cost to make, $3,000

Cobe Company has already manufactured 28,000 units of Product A at a cost of $28 per unit. The 28,000 units can be sold at this stage for $700,000. Alternatively, the units can be further processed at a $420,000 total additional cost and be converted into 5,600 units of Product B and 11,200 units of Product C. Per unit selling price for Product B is $105 and for Product C is $70. Prepare an analysis that shows whether the 28,000 units of Product A should be processed further or not.

Exercise 23-8
Sell or process decision

A1

Varto Company has 7,000 units of its sole product in inventory that it produced last year at a cost of $22 each. This year's model is superior to last year's and the 7,000 units cannot be sold at last year's regular selling price of $35 each. Varto has two alternatives for these items: (1) they can be sold to a wholesaler for $8 each, or (2) they can be reworked at a cost of $125,000 and then sold for $25 each. Prepare an analysis to determine whether Varto should sell the products as is or rework them and then sell them.

Exercise 23-9
Sell or rework decision
P1 A1
Check Incremental net income of reworking, $(6,000)

Suresh Co. expects its five departments to yield the following income for next year.

Exercise 23-10
Analysis of income effects from eliminating departments

A1

	Dept. M	Dept. N	Dept. O	Dept. P	Dept. T
Sales	$63,000	$35,000	$56,000	$42,000	$ 28,000
Expenses					
Avoidable	9,800	36,400	22,400	14,000	37,800
Unavoidable	51,800	12,600	4,200	29,400	9,800
Total expenses	61,600	49,000	26,600	43,400	47,600
Net income (loss)	$ 1,400	$(14,000)	$29,400	$(1,400)	$ (19,600)

Recompute and prepare the departmental income statements (including a combined total column) for the company under each of the following separate scenarios: Management (1) does not eliminate any department, (2) eliminates departments with expected net losses, and (3) eliminates departments with sales dollars that are less than avoidable expenses. Explain your answers to parts 2 and 3.

Check Total income (loss) (2) $(21,000), (3) $7,000

Marinette Company makes several products, including canoes. The company has been experiencing losses from its canoe segment and is considering dropping that product line. The following information is available regarding its canoe segment. Should management discontinue the manufacturing of canoes? Support your decision.

Exercise 23-11
Income analysis of eliminating departments
A1

MARINETTE COMPANY
Income Statement—Canoe Segment

Sales		$2,000,000
Variable costs		
Direct materials	$450,000	
Direct labor	500,000	
Variable overhead	300,000	
Variable selling and administrative	200,000	
Total variable costs		1,450,000
Contribution margin		550,000
Fixed costs		
Direct	375,000	
Indirect	300,000	
Total fixed costs		675,000
Net income		$ (125,000)

Check Income impact if canoe segment dropped, $(175,000)

Exercise 23-12

Sales mix determination
and analysis

A1

Colt Company owns a machine that can produce two specialized products. Production time for Product TLX is two units per hour and for Product MTV is five units per hour. The machine's capacity is 2,750 hours per year. Both products are sold to a single customer who has agreed to buy all of the company's output up to a maximum of 4,700 units of Product TLX and 2,500 units of Product MTV. Selling prices and variable costs per unit to produce the products follow. Determine (1) the company's most profitable sales mix and (2) the contribution margin that results from that sales mix.

	Product TLX	Product MTV
Selling price per unit	$15.00	$9.50
Variable costs per unit	4.80	5.50

Check   (2) $55,940

Exercise 23-13

Sales mix

A1

Childress Company produces three products, K1, S5, and G9. Each product uses the same type of direct material. K1 uses 4 pounds of the material, S5 uses 3 pounds of the material, and G9 uses 6 pounds of the material. Demand for all products is strong, but only 50,000 pounds of material are available. Information about the selling price per unit and variable cost per unit of each product follows. Orders for which product should be produced and filled first, then second, and then third? Support your answer.

	K1	S5	G9
Selling price	$160	$112	$210
Variable costs	96	85	144

Check   K1 contribution margin per
pound, $16

≒ connect

PROBLEM SET A

Problem 23-1A

Analysis of income effects of
additional business

A1   P1

mhhe.com/wildFINMAN5e

Jones Products manufactures and sells to wholesalers approximately 400,000 packages per year of underwater markers at $6 per package. Annual costs for the production and sale of this quantity are shown in the table.

Direct materials	$576,000
Direct labor	144,000
Overhead	320,000
Selling expenses	150,000
Administrative expenses	100,000
Total costs and expenses	$1,290,000

A new wholesaler has offered to buy 50,000 packages for $5.20 each. These markers would be marketed under the wholesaler's name and would not affect Jones Products' sales through its normal channels. A study of the costs of this additional business reveals the following:

● Direct materials costs are 100% variable.
● Per unit direct labor costs for the additional units would be 50% higher than normal because their production would require overtime pay at one-and-one-half times the usual labor rate.
● 25% of the normal annual overhead costs are fixed at any production level from 350,000 to 500,000 units. The remaining 75% of the annual overhead cost is variable with volume.
● Accepting the new business would involve no additional selling expenses.
● Accepting the new business would increase administrative expenses by a $5,000 fixed amount.

Required

Check   Operating income:
(1) $1,110,000

(2) $126,000

Prepare a three-column comparative income statement that shows the following:
1. Annual operating income without the special order (column 1).
2. Annual operating income received from the new business only (column 2).
3. Combined annual operating income from normal business and the new business (column 3).

Calla Company produces skateboards that sell for $50 per unit. The company currently has the capacity to produce 90,000 skateboards per year, but is selling 80,000 skateboards per year. Annual costs for 80,000 skateboards follow.

Problem 23-2A

Analysis of income effects of additional business

P1 A1

Direct materials...............	$ 800,000
Direct labor...................	640,000
Overhead.....................	960,000
Selling expenses..............	560,000
Administrative expenses........	480,000
Total costs and expenses........	$3,440,000

A new retail store has offered to buy 10,000 of its skateboards for $45 per unit. The store is in a different market from Calla's regular customers and it would not affect regular sales. A study of its costs in anticipation of this additional business reveals the following:

- Direct materials and direct labor are 100% variable.
- Thirty percent of overhead is fixed at any production level from 80,000 units to 90,000 units; the remaining 70% of annual overhead costs are variable with respect to volume.
- Selling expenses are 60% variable with respect to number of units sold, and the other 40% of selling expenses are fixed.
- There will be an additional $2 per unit selling expense for this order.
- Administrative expenses would increase by a $1,000 fixed amount.

Required

1. Prepare a three-column comparative income statement that reports the following:
   a. Annual income without the special order.
   b. Annual income from the special order.
   c. Combined annual income from normal business and the new business.
2. Should Calla accept this order? What nonfinancial factors should Calla consider? Explain.

Check   (1b) Added income from order, $123,000

Analysis Component

3. Assume that the new customer wants to buy 15,000 units instead of 10,000 units—it will only buy 15,000 units or none and will not take a partial order. Without any computations, how does this change your answer for part 2?

Haver Company currently produces component RX5 for its sole product. The current cost per unit to manufacture the required 50,000 units of RX5 follows.

Problem 23-3A

Make or buy

P1 A1

Direct materials...........	$ 5.00
Direct labor..............	8.00
Overhead................	9.00
Total cost per unit.........	$22.00

Direct materials and direct labor are 100% variable. Overhead is 80% fixed. An outside supplier has offered to supply the 50,000 units of RX5 for $18.00 per unit.

Required

1. Determine whether the company should make or buy the RX5.
2. What factors beside cost must management consider when deciding whether to make or buy RX5?

Check   (1) Incremental cost to make RX5, $740,000

Harold Manufacturing produces denim clothing. This year, it produced 5,000 denim jackets at a manufacturing cost of $45 each. These jackets were damaged in the warehouse during storage. Management investigated the matter and identified three alternatives for these jackets.

Problem 23-4A

Sell or process

P1 A1

1. Jackets can be sold to a second-hand clothing shop for $6 each.
2. Jackets can be disassembled at a cost of $32,000 and sold to a recycler for $12 each.

1006   Chapter 23   Relevant Costing for Managerial Decisions

3. Jackets can be reworked and turned into good jackets. However, with the damage, management estimates it will be able to assemble the good parts of the 5,000 jackets into only 3,000 jackets. The remaining pieces of fabric will be discarded. The cost of reworking the jackets will be $102,000, but the jackets can then be sold for their regular price of $45 each.

Check Incremental income for alternative 2, $28,000

Required

Which alternative should Harold choose? Show analysis for each alternative.

Problem 23-5A
Analysis of sales mix strategies

A1

Edgerron Company is able to produce two products, G and B, with the same machine in its factory. The following information is available.

	Product G	Product B
Selling price per unit	$120	$160
Variable costs per unit.	40	90
Contribution margin per unit	$ 80	$ 70
Machine hours to produce 1 unit	0.4 hours	1.0 hours
Maximum unit sales per month.	600 units	200 units

The company presently operates the machine for a single eight-hour shift for 22 working days each month. Management is thinking about operating the machine for two shifts, which will increase its productivity by another eight hours per day for 22 days per month. This change would require $15,000 additional fixed costs per month.

Required

1. Determine the contribution margin per machine hour that each product generates.

Check Units of Product G:
  (2) 440

2. How many units of Product G and Product B should the company produce if it continues to operate with only one shift? How much total contribution margin does this mix produce each month?

  (3) 600

3. If the company adds another shift, how many units of Product G and Product B should it produce? How much total contribution margin would this mix produce each month? Should the company add the new shift? Explain.

  (4) 700

4. Suppose that the company determines that it can increase Product G's maximum sales to 700 units per month by spending $12,000 per month in marketing efforts. Should the company pursue this strategy and the double shift? Explain.

Problem 23-6A
Analysis of possible elimination of a department

A1

Elegant Decor Company's management is trying to decide whether to eliminate Department 200, which has produced losses or low profits for several years. The company's 2013 departmental income statement shows the following.

ELEGANT DECOR COMPANY Departmental Income Statements For Year Ended December 31, 2013			
	Dept. 100	Dept. 200	Combined
Sales	$436,000	$290,000	$726,000
Cost of goods sold	262,000	207,000	469,000
Gross profit	174,000	83,000	257,000
Operating expenses			
Direct expenses			
Advertising	17,000	12,000	29,000
Store supplies used	4,000	3,800	7,800
Depreciation—Store equipment.	5,000	3,300	8,300
Total direct expenses	26,000	19,100	45,100

[continued on next page]

[continued from previous page]

Allocated expenses			
Sales salaries	65,000	39,000	104,000
Rent expense	9,440	4,720	14,160
Bad debts expense	9,900	8,100	18,000
Office salary	18,720	12,480	31,200
Insurance expense	2,000	1,100	3,100
Miscellaneous office expenses	2,400	1,600	4,000
Total allocated expenses	107,460	67,000	174,460
Total expenses	133,460	86,100	219,560
Net income (loss)	$ 40,540	$ (3,100)	$ 37,440

In analyzing whether to eliminate Department 200, management considers the following:

a. The company has one office worker who earns $600 per week, or $31,200 per year, and four sales-clerks who each earn $500 per week, or $26,000 per year for each salesclerk.

b. The full salaries of two salesclerks are charged to Department 100. The full salary of one salesclerk is charged to Department 200. The salary of the fourth clerk, who works half-time in both departments, is divided evenly between the two departments.

c. Eliminating Department 200 would avoid the sales salaries and the office salary currently allocated to it. However, management prefers another plan. Two salesclerks have indicated that they will be quit-ting soon. Management believes that their work can be done by the other two clerks if the one office worker works in sales half-time. Eliminating Department 200 will allow this shift of duties. If this change is implemented, half the office worker's salary would be reported as sales salaries and half would be reported as office salary.

d. The store building is rented under a long-term lease that cannot be changed. Therefore, Department 100 will use the space and equipment currently used by Department 200.

e. Closing Department 200 will eliminate its expenses for advertising, bad debts, and store supplies; 70% of the insurance expense allocated to it to cover its merchandise inventory; and 25% of the mis-cellaneous office expenses presently allocated to it.

Required

1. Prepare a three-column report that lists items and amounts for (a) the company's total expenses (including cost of goods sold)—in column 1, (b) the expenses that would be eliminated by closing Department 200—in column 2, and (c) the expenses that will continue—in column 3.

2. Prepare a forecasted annual income statement for the company reflecting the elimination of Depart-ment 200 assuming that it will not affect Department 100's sales and gross profit. The statement should reflect the reassignment of the office worker to one-half time as a salesclerk.

Check (1) Total expenses: (a) $688,560, (b) $284,070

(2) Forecasted net income without Department 200, $31,510

Analysis Component

3. Reconcile the company's combined net income with the forecasted net income assuming that Depart-ment 200 is eliminated (list both items and amounts). Analyze the reconciliation and explain why you think the department should or should not be eliminated.

Windmire Company manufactures and sells to local wholesalers approximately 300,000 units per month at a sales price of $4 per unit. Monthly costs for the production and sale of this quantity follow.

PROBLEM SET B

Problem 23-1B
Analysis of income effects of additional business

A1 P1

Direct materials	$384,000
Direct labor	96,000
Overhead	288,000
Selling expenses	120,000
Administrative expenses	80,000
Total costs and expenses	$968,000

A new out-of-state distributor has offered to buy 50,000 units next month for $3.44 each. These units would be marketed in other states and would not affect Windtrax's sales through its normal channels. A study of the costs of this new business reveals the following:

- Direct materials costs are 100% variable.
- Per unit direct labor costs for the additional units would be 50% higher than normal because their production would require overtime pay at one and one half times their normal rate to meet the distributor's deadline.
- Twenty-five percent of the normal annual overhead costs are fixed at any production level from 250,000 to 400,000 units. The remaining 75% is variable with volume.
- Accepting the new business would involve no additional selling expenses.
- Accepting the new business would increase administrative expenses by a $4,000 fixed amount.

Required

Prepare a three-column comparative income statement that shows the following:

Check Operating income: (1) $232,000, (2) $44,000

1. Monthly operating income without the special order (column 1).
2. Monthly operating income received from the new business only (column 2).
3. Combined monthly operating income from normal business and the new business (column 3).

Problem 23-2B
Analysis of income effects of additional business

P1 A1

Mervin Company produces circuit boards that sell for $8 per unit. It currently has capacity to produce 600,000 circuit boards per year, but is selling 550,000 boards per year. Annual costs for the 550,000 circuit boards follow.

Direct materials................	$ 825,000
Direct labor...................	1,100,000
Overhead.....................	1,375,000
Selling expenses...............	275,000
Administrative expenses	550,000
Total costs and expenses........	$4,125,000

An overseas customer has offered to buy 50,000 circuit boards for $6 per unit. The customer is in a different market from its regular customers and would not affect regular sales. A study of its costs in anticipation of this additional business reveals the following:

- Direct materials and direct labor are 100% variable.
- Twenty percent of overhead is fixed at any production level from 550,000 units to 600,000 units; the remaining 80% of annual overhead costs are variable with respect to volume.
- Selling expenses are 40% variable with respect to number of units sold, and the other 60% of selling expenses are fixed.
- There will be an additional $0.20 per unit selling expense for this order.
- Administrative expenses would increase by a $700 fixed amount.

Required

Check (1b) Additional income from order, $4,300

1. Prepare a three-column comparative income statement that reports the following:
   a. Annual income without the special order.
   b. Annual income from the special order.
   c. Combined annual income from normal business and the new business.
2. Should management accept the order? What nonfinancial factors should Mervin consider? Explain.

Analysis Component

3. Assume that the new customer wants to buy 100,000 units instead of 50,000 units—it will only buy 100,000 units or none and will not take a partial order. Without any computations, how does this change your answer in part 2?

Alto Company currently produces component TH1 for its sole product. The current cost per unit to manufacture its required 400,000 units of TH1 follows.

Direct materials	$1.20
Direct labor	1.50
Overhead	6.00
Total cost per unit	$8.70

Direct materials and direct labor are 100% variable. Overhead is 75% fixed. An outside supplier has offered to supply the 400,000 units of TH1 for $4 per unit.

Required

1. Determine whether management should make or buy the TH1.

2. What factors besides cost must management consider when deciding whether to make or buy TH1?

Micron Manufacturing produces electronic equipment. This year, it produced 7,500 oscilloscopes at a manufacturing cost of $300 each. These oscilloscopes were damaged in the warehouse during storage and, while usable, cannot be sold at their regular selling price of $500 each. Management has investigated the matter and has identified three alternatives for these oscilloscopes.

1. They can be sold to a wholesaler for $75 each.

2. They can be disassembled at a cost of $400,000 and the parts sold to a recycler for $130 each.

3. They can be reworked and turned into good units. The cost of reworking the units will be $3,200,000, after which the units can be sold at their regular price of $500 each.

Required

Which alternative should management pursue? Show analysis for each alternative.

Sung Company is able to produce two products, R and T, with the same machine in its factory. The following information is available.

	Product R	Product T
Selling price per unit	$60	$80
Variable costs per unit	20	45
Contribution margin per unit	$40	$35
Machine hours to produce 1 unit	0.4 hours	1.0 hours
Maximum unit sales per month	550 units	175 units

The company presently operates the machine for a single eight-hour shift for 22 working days each month. Management is thinking about operating the machine for two shifts, which will increase its productivity by another eight hours per day for 22 days per month. This change would require $3,250 additional fixed costs per month.

Required

1. Determine the contribution margin per machine hour that each product generates.

2. How many units of Product R and Product T should the company produce if it continues to operate with only one shift? How much total contribution margin does this mix produce each month?

3. If the company adds another shift, how many units of Product R and Product T should it produce? How much total contribution margin would this mix produce each month? Should the company add the new shift? Explain.

4. Suppose that the company determines that it can increase Product R's maximum sales to 675 units per month by spending $4,500 per month in marketing efforts. Should the company pursue this strategy and the double shift? Explain.

Problem 23-6B
Analysis of possible elimination
of a department

A1

Esme Company's management is trying to decide whether to eliminate Department Z, which has produced low profits or losses for several years. The company's 2013 departmental income statement shows the following.

ESME COMPANY Departmental Income Statements For Year Ended December 31, 2013	Dept. A	Dept. Z	Combined
Sales	$700,000	$175,000	$875,000
Cost of goods sold	461,300	125,100	586,400
Gross profit	238,700	49,900	288,600
Operating expenses			
Direct expenses			
Advertising	27,000	3,000	30,000
Store supplies used	5,600	1,400	7,000
Depreciation—Store equipment	14,000	7,000	21,000
Total direct expenses	46,600	11,400	58,000
Allocated expenses			
Sales salaries	70,200	23,400	93,600
Rent expense......................	22,080	5,520	27,600
Bad debts expense	21,000	4,000	25,000
Office salary	20,800	5,200	26,000
Insurance expense	4,200	1,400	5,600
Miscellaneous office expenses	1,700	2,500	4,200
Total allocated expenses	139,980	42,020	182,000
Total expenses.......................	186,580	53,420	240,000
Net income (loss)	$ 52,120	$ (3,520)	$ 48,600

In analyzing whether to eliminate Department Z, management considers the following items:

a. The company has one office worker who earns $500 per week or $26,000 per year and four salesclerks who each earn $450 per week or $23,400 per year for each salesclerk.

b. The full salaries of three salesclerks are charged to Department A. The full salary of one salesclerk is charged to Department Z.

c. Eliminating Department Z would avoid the sales salaries and the office salary currently allocated to it. However, management prefers another plan. Two salesclerks have indicated that they will be quitting soon. Management believes that their work can be done by the two remaining clerks if the one office worker works in sales half-time. Eliminating Department Z will allow this shift of duties. If this change is implemented, half the office worker's salary would be reported as sales salaries and half would be reported as office salary.

d. The store building is rented under a long-term lease that cannot be changed. Therefore, Department A will use the space and equipment currently used by Department Z.

e. Closing Department Z will eliminate its expenses for advertising, bad debts, and store supplies; 65% of the insurance expense allocated to it to cover its merchandise inventory; and 30% of the miscellaneous office expenses presently allocated to it.

Required

Check   (1) Total expenses:
(a) $826,400, (b) $181,960

1. Prepare a three-column report that lists items and amounts for (a) the company's total expenses (including cost of goods sold)—in column 1, (b) the expenses that would be eliminated by closing Department Z—in column 2, and (c) the expenses that will continue—in column 3.

   (2) Forecasted net income
without Department Z, $55,560

2. Prepare a forecasted annual income statement for the company reflecting the elimination of Department Z assuming that it will not affect Department A's sales and gross profit. The statement should reflect the reassignment of the office worker to one-half time as a salesclerk.

Analysis Component

3. Reconcile the company's combined net income with the forecasted net income assuming that Department Z is eliminated (list both items and amounts). Analyze the reconciliation and explain why you think the department should or should not be eliminated.

(This serial problem began in Chapter 1 and continues through most of the book. If previous chapter segments were not completed, the serial problem can begin at this point. It is helpful, but not necessary, to use the Working Papers that accompany the book.)

SP 23   Adria Lopez has found that her line of computer desks and chairs has become very popular and she is finding it hard to keep up with demand. She knows that she cannot fill all of her orders for both items, so she decides she must determine the optimal sales mix given the resources she has available. Information about the desks and chairs follows.

	Desks	Chairs
Selling price per unit	$1,125	$375
Variable costs per unit	500	200
Contribution margin per unit	$ 625	$175
Direct labor hours per unit	5 hours	4 hours
Expected demand for next quarter	175 desks	50 chairs

Adria has determined that she only has 1,015 direct labor hours available for the next quarter and wants to optimize her contribution margin given the limited number of direct labor hours available.

Required

Determine the optimal sales mix and the contribution margin the business will earn at that sales mix.

Beyond the Numbers

BTN 23-1   Revenues for three of Polaris' four segments for the year ending December 31, 2011 are reported below. Assume that Polaris reports operating expenses for each of its segments for that same year below.

$ millions	Off-road	Snow	On-road
Revenues	$1,823	$280	$146
Operating expenses	1,586	294	140

Required

1. Compute operating income for each segment.

2. If the results in part 1 are typical, what segments, if any, might Polaris decide to eliminate?

BTN 23-2   Polaris and Arctic Cat sell several different products; most are profitable but some are not. Teams of employees in each company make advertising, investment, and product mix decisions. A certain portion of advertising for both companies is on a local basis to a target audience.

Required

1. Contact the local newspaper and ask the approximate cost of ad space (for example, cost of one page or one-half page of advertising) for a company's product or group of products (such as Polaris ATVs).

2. Estimate how many products this advertisement must sell to justify its cost. Begin by taking the product's sales price advertised for each company and assume a 20% contribution margin.

3. Prepare a one-half page memorandum explaining the importance of effective advertising when making a product mix decision. Be prepared to present your ideas in class.

SERIAL PROBLEM
Success Systems

P1   A1

REPORTING IN ACTION

A1

Polaris

COMPARATIVE ANALYSIS

A1

Polaris

Arctic Cat

ETHICS CHALLENGE

P1 A1

BTN 23-3   Bert Asiago, a salesperson for Convertco, received an order from a potential new customer for 50,000 units of Convertco's single product at a price $25 below its regular selling price of $65. Asiago knows that Convertco has the capacity to produce this order without affecting regular sales. He has spoken to Convertco's controller, Bia Morgan, who has informed Asiago that at the $40 selling price, Convertco will not be covering its variable costs of $42 for the product, and she recommends the order not be accepted. Asiago knows that variable costs include his sales commission of $4 per unit. If he accepts a $2 per unit commission, the sale will produce a contribution margin of zero. Asiago is eager to get the new customer because he believes that this could lead to the new customer becoming a regular customer.

Required

1. Determine the contribution margin per unit on the order as determined by the controller.
2. Determine the contribution margin per unit on the order as determined by Asiago if he takes the lower commission.
3. Do you recommend Convertco accept the special order? What factors must management consider?

COMMUNICATING IN PRACTICE

P1

BTN 23-4   Assume that you work for Greeble's Department Store, and your manager requests that you outline the pros and cons of discontinuing its hardware department. That department appears to be generating losses, and your manager believes that discontinuing it will increase overall store profits.

Required

Prepare a memorandum to your manager outlining what Greeble's management should consider when trying to decide whether to discontinue its hardware department.

TAKING IT TO THE NET

A1

BTN 23-5   Many companies must determine whether to internally produce their component parts or to outsource them. Further, some companies now outsource key components or business processes to international providers. Access the Website BizBrim.com and review the available information on business process outsourcing.

Required

1. What types of processes are commonly outsourced, according to Bizbrim?
2. What are some of the benefits listed for business process outsourcing?

TEAMWORK IN ACTION

P1

BTN 23-6   Break into teams and identify costs that an airline such as Delta Airlines would incur on a flight from Green Bay to Minneapolis. (1) Identify the individual costs as variable or fixed. (2) Assume that Delta is trying to decide whether to drop this flight because it seems to be unprofitable. Determine which costs are likely to be saved if the flight is dropped. Set up your answer in the following format.

Cost	Variable or Fixed	Cost Saved if Flight Is Dropped	Rationale

ENTREPRENEURIAL DECISION

A1

BTN 23-7   Charlie Fyffe of Charlie's Brownies makes brownies and other sweets. Charlie must decide on the best sales mix for his products. Assume that his company has a capacity of 400 hours of processing time available each month and it makes two types of brownies, Deluxe and Premium. Information on these foods follows.

	Deluxe	Premium
Selling price per carton	$70	$90
Variable costs per carton	$40	$50
Processing minutes per carton	60 minutes	120 minutes

Required

1. Assume the markets for both cartons of brownies are unlimited. How many Deluxe cartons and how many Premium cartons should the company make each month? Explain. How much total contribution margin does this mix produce each month?

2. Assume the market for the Deluxe carton is limited to 60 cartons per month, with no market limit for the Premium cartons. How many Deluxe cartons and how many Premium cartons should the company make each month? Explain. How much total contribution margin does this mix produce each month?

BTN 23-8 Restaurants are often adding and removing menu items. Visit a restaurant and identify a new food item. Make a list of costs that the restaurant must consider when deciding whether to add that new item. Also, make a list of nonfinancial factors that the restaurant must consider when adding that item.

HITTING THE ROAD

P3

BTN 23-9 Access KTM's 2011 annual report dated December 31, 2011, from its Website www.KTM.com. Identify and read the section in the Group Status Report—2011, section 12, regarding Sustainability.

GLOBAL DECISION

C1

KTM

Required

KTM reports that they developed a special KTM motorcyle logistics system on reusable metal plates. This special system eliminates additional packaging materials. These sustainability efforts are costly. Why would a company like KTM pursue these costly efforts?

ANSWERS TO MULTIPLE CHOICE QUIZ

1. a; Reworking provides incremental revenue of $11 per unit ($19 − $8); and, it costs $10 to rework them. The company is better off by $1 per unit when it reworks these products and sells them at the regular price.

2. e; Product X has a $2 contribution margin per machine hour [($32 − $12)/ 10 MH]; Product Y has a $7 contribution margin per machine hour [($24 − $10)/2 MH]. It should produce as much of Product Y as possible.

3. a; Total revenue from the special order = 3,000 units × $15 per unit = $45,000; and, Total costs for the special order = (3,000 units × $9 per unit) + $5,000 = $32,000. Net income from the special order = $45,000 − $32,000 = $13,000. Thus, yes, it should accept the order.

4. c

5. d

Financial Statement Information

This appendix includes financial information for (1) Polaris, (2) Arctic Cat, (3) KTM, and (4) Piaggio. Polaris is a manufacturer of ATVs, snowmobiles, motorcycles and electric vehicles; it competes with Arctic Cat in the United States and globally. KTM and Piaggio also compete with Polaris and Arctic Cat, and are two of Europe's leading manufacturers of two-, three-, and four-wheel vehicles. The information in this Appendix is taken from their annual 10-K reports (or annual reports for KTM and Piaggio) filed with the SEC or other regulatory agency. An **annual report** is a summary of a company's financial results for the year along with its current financial condition and future plans. This report is directed to external users of financial information, but it also affects the actions and decisions of internal users.

A company often uses an annual report to showcase itself and its products. Many annual reports include photos, diagrams, and illustrations related to the company. The primary objective of annual reports, however, is the *financial section,* which communicates much information about a company, with most data drawn from the accounting information system. The layout of an annual report's financial section is fairly established and typically includes the following:

- Letter to Shareholders
- Financial History and Highlights
- Management Discussion and Analysis
- Management's Report on Financial Statements and on Internal Controls
- Report of Independent Accountants (Auditor's Report) and on Internal Controls
- Financial Statements
- Notes to Financial Statements
- List of Directors and Officers

This appendix provides the financial statements for Polaris (plus selected notes), Arctic Cat, KTM, and Piaggio. The appendix is organized as follows:

- Polaris **A-2** through **A-9**
- Arctic Cat **A-10** through **A-13**
- KTM **A-14** through **A-17**
- Piaggio **A-18** through **A-21**

Polaris
Arctic Cat
KTM
PIAGGIO

Many assignments at the end of each chapter refer to information in this appendix. We encourage readers to spend time with these assignments; they are especially useful in showing the relevance and diversity of financial accounting and reporting.

Special note: The SEC maintains the EDGAR (**E**lectronic **D**ata **G**athering, **A**nalysis, and **R**etrieval) database at www.sec.gov for U.S. filers. The **Form 10-K** is the annual report form for most companies. It provides electronically accessible information. The **Form 10-KSB** is the annual report form filed by small businesses. It requires slightly less information than the Form 10-K. One of these forms must be filed within 90 days after the company's fiscal year-end. (Forms 10-K405, 10-KT, 10-KT405, and 10-KSB405 are slight variations of the usual form due to certain regulations or rules.)

POLARIS

POLARIS INDUSTRIES INC.
CONSOLIDATED BALANCE SHEETS

December 31 (In thousands, except per share data)	2011	2010
ASSETS		
Current Assets		
Cash and cash equivalents	$ 325,336	$ 393,927
Trade receivables, net	115,302	89,294
Inventories, net	298,042	235,927
Prepaid expenses and other	37,608	21,628
Income taxes receivable	24,723	—
Deferred tax assets	77,665	67,369
Total current assets	878,676	808,145
Property and Equipment		
Land, buildings and improvements	123,771	118,831
Equipment and tooling	524,382	488,562
	648,153	607,393
Less accumulated depreciation	(434,375)	(423,382)
Property and equipment, net	213,778	184,011
Investments in finance affiliate	42,251	37,169
Investments in other affiliates	5,000	1,009
Deferred tax assets	10,601	—
Goodwill and other intangible assets, net	77,718	31,313
Total Assets	**$1,228,024**	**$1,061,647**
LIABILITIES AND SHAREHOLDERS' EQUITY		
Current Liabilities		
Current portion of long-term borrowings under credit agreement	—	$ 100,000
Current portion of capital lease obligations	$ 2,653	—
Accounts payable	146,743	113,248
Accrued expenses		
Compensation	187,671	126,781
Warranties	44,355	32,651
Sales promotions and incentives	81,228	75,494
Dealer holdback	76,512	79,688
Other	75,730	53,744
Income taxes payable	639	2,604
Total current liabilities	615,531	584,210
Long term income taxes payable	7,837	5,509
Deferred income taxes	—	937
Capital lease obligations	4,600	—
Long-term debt	100,000	100,000
Total liabilities	727,968	690,656
Shareholders' Equity		
Preferred stock $0.01 par value, 20,000 shares authorized, no shares issued and outstanding	—	—
Common stock $0.01 par value, 160,000 shares authorized, 68,430 and 68,468 shares issued and outstanding	684	685
Additional paid-in capital	165,518	79,239
Retained earnings	321,831	285,169
Accumulated other comprehensive income, net	12,023	5,898
Total shareholders' equity	500,056	370,991
Total Liabilities and Shareholders' Equity	**$1,228,024**	**$1,061,647**

Shares outstanding, common stock, additional paid-in-capital, retained earnings and per share data
have been adjusted to give effect to the two-for-one stock split declared on July 20, 2011, paid on
September 12, 2011 to shareholders of record on September 2, 2011.

POLARIS INDUSTRIES INC.
CONSOLIDATED STATEMENTS OF INCOME

For the Years Ended December 31 (In thousands, except per share data)	2011	2010	2009
Sales	$2,656,949	$1,991,139	$1,565,887
Cost of sales	1,916,366	1,460,926	1,172,668
Gross profit	740,583	530,213	393,219
Operating expenses			
Selling and marketing	178,725	142,353	111,137
Research and development	105,631	84,940	62,999
General and administrative	130,395	99,055	71,184
Total operating expenses	414,751	326,348	245,320
Income from financial services	24,092	16,856	17,071
Operating income	349,924	220,721	164,970
Non-operating expense (income)			
Interest expense	3,987	2,680	4,111
(Gain) loss on securities available for sale	—	(825)	8,952
Other expense (income), net	(689)	325	733
Income before income taxes	346,626	218,541	151,174
Provision for income taxes	119,051	71,403	50,157
Net income	$ 227,575	$ 147,138	$ 101,017
Basic net income per share	$ 3.31	$ 2.20	$ 1.56
Diluted net income per share	$ 3.20	$ 2.14	$ 1.53
Weighted average shares outstanding:			
Basic	68,792	66,900	64,798
Diluted	71,057	68,765	66,148

Shares outstanding and per share data have been adjusted to give effect to the two-for-one stock split declared on
July 20, 2011, paid on September 12, 2011 to shareholders of record on September 2, 2011.

POLARIS

POLARIS INDUSTRIES INC.
CONSOLIDATED STATEMENTS OF SHAREHOLDERS'
EQUITY AND COMPREHENSIVE INCOME

(In thousands, except per share data)	Number of Shares	Common Stock	Additional Paid-In Capital	Retained Earnings	Accumulated Other Comprehensive Income (Loss)	Total
Balance, December 31, 2008	64,984	$650	—	$ 140,234	$ (3,857)	$ 137,027
Employee stock compensation	62	1	10,225			10,226
Proceeds from stock issuances under employee plans	472	4	4,729			4,733
Tax effect of exercise of stock options			(410)			(410)
Cash dividends declared ($0.78 per share)				(50,177)		(50,177)
Repurchase and retirement of common shares	(222)	(2)	(4,554)			(4,556)
Comprehensive income:						
Net Income				101,017		
Foreign currency translation adjustments, net of tax of $69					115	
Reclassification of unrealized loss on available for sale securities to the income statement, net of tax of $2,277					6,675	
Unrealized loss on available for sale securities, net of tax benefit of $230					(382)	
Unrealized gain on derivative instruments, net of tax of $165					273	
Total comprehensive income						107,698
Balance, December 31, 2009	65,296	653	9,990	191,074	2,824	204,541
Employee stock compensation	308	3	18,049			18,052
Proceeds from stock issuances under employee plans	4,066	41	68,064			68,105
Tax effect of exercise of stock options			10,610			10,610
Cash dividends declared ($0.80 per share)				(53,043)		(53,043)
Repurchase and retirement of common shares	(1,202)	(12)	(27,474)			(27,486)
Comprehensive income:						
Net Income				147,138		
Foreign currency translation adjustments, net of tax of $222					3,131	
Unrealized gain on available for sale securities, net of tax benefit of $230					382	
Unrealized loss on derivative instruments, net of tax benefit of $256					(439)	
Total comprehensive income						150,212
Balance, December 31, 2010	68,468	685	79,239	285,169	5,898	370,991
Employee stock compensation	290	3	20,545			20,548
Proceeds from stock issuances under employee plans	2,280	22	45,632			45,654
Tax effect of exercise of stock options			23,120			23,120
Cash dividends declared ($0.90 per share)				(61,585)		(61,585)
Repurchase and retirement of common shares	(2,608)	(26)	(3,018)	(129,328)		(132,372)
Comprehensive income:						
Net Income				227,575		
Foreign currency translation adjustments, net of tax benefit of $6,782					2,554	
Unrealized gain/(loss) on derivative instruments, net of tax of $2,125					3,571	
Total comprehensive income						233,700
Balance, December 31, 2011	68,430	$684	$165,518	$ 321,831	$12,023	$ 500,056

Shares outstanding, common stock, additional paid-in-capital, retained earnings and per share data
have been adjusted to give effect to the two-for-one stock split declared on July 20, 2011, paid on
September 12, 2011 to shareholders of record on September 2, 2011.

POLARIS INDUSTRIES INC.
CONSOLIDATED STATEMENTS OF CASH FLOWS

For the Year Ended December 31 (In thousands)	2011	2010	2009
Operating Activities			
Net income	$ 227,575	$147,138	$ 101,017
Adjustments to reconcile net income to net cash provided by operating activities:			
(Gain) loss on securities available for sale	—	(825)	8,952
Depreciation and amortization	66,390	66,519	64,593
Noncash compensation	20,548	18,052	10,226
Noncash income from financial services	(4,444)	(4,574)	(4,021)
Noncash expense from other affiliates	133	1,376	382
Deferred income taxes	(16,946)	(16,888)	13,573
Tax effect of share-based compensation exercises	(23,120)	(10,610)	410
Changes in current operating items:			
Trade receivables	(23,115)	1,111	8,192
Inventories	(49,973)	(56,612)	42,997
Accounts payable	27,232	37,580	(40,329)
Accrued expenses	80,668	107,363	(24,759)
Income taxes payable/receivable	(1,343)	7,033	7,325
Prepaid expenses and others, net	(1,075)	956	4,643
Net cash provided by operating activities	302,530	297,619	193,201
Investing Activities			
Purchase of property and equipment	(84,484)	(55,718)	(43,932)
Investments in finance affiliate	(12,588)	(9,173)	(3,007)
Distributions from finance affiliate	11,950	17,910	17,261
Investment in other affiliates	(5,000)	—	—
Proceeds from sale of investments	876	9,061	—
Acquisition of businesses, net of cash acquired	(51,899)	(4,738)	—
Net cash used for investment activities	(141,145)	(42,118)	(29,678)
Financing Activities			
Borrowings under credit agreement / senior notes	100,000	—	364,000
Repayments under credit agreement	(202,333)	—	(364,000)
Repurchase and retirement of common shares	(132,372)	(27,486)	(4,556)
Cash dividends to shareholders	(61,585)	(53,043)	(50,177)
Tax effect of proceeds from share-based compensation exercises	23,120	10,610	(410)
Proceeds from stock issuances under employee plans	45,654	68,105	4,733
Net cash used for financing activities	(227,516)	(1,814)	(50,410)
Impact of currency exchange rates on cash balances	(2,460)	—	—
Net increase (decrease) in cash and cash equivalents	(68,591)	253,687	113,113
Cash and cash equivalents at beginning of period	393,927	140,240	27,127
Cash and cash equivalents at end of period	$ 325,336	$393,927	$ 140,240
Supplemental Cash Flow Information:			
Interest paid on debt borrowings	$ 3,350	$ 2,813	$ 3,966
Income taxes paid	$ 132,088	$ 81,142	$ 29,039

POLARIS

POLARIS INDUSTRIES INC.
<u>SELECTED</u> NOTES TO CONSOLIDATED FINANCIAL STATEMENTS

Note 1.   Organization and Significant Accounting Policies

Polaris Industries Inc. ("Polaris" or the "Company") a Minnesota corporation, and its subsidiaries, are engaged in the design, engineering, manufacturing and marketing of innovative, high-quality, high-performance Off-Road Vehicles ("ORV"), Snowmobiles, and On-Road Vehicles, including motorcycles and Small Electric Vehicles. Polaris products, together with related parts, garments and accessories are sold worldwide through a network of dealers, distributors and its subsidiaries located in the United States, Canada, France, the United Kingdom, Australia, Norway, Sweden, Germany, Spain, China, India and Brazil.

Basis of presentation: The accompanying consolidated financial statements include the accounts of Polaris and its wholly-owned subsidiaries. All inter-company transactions and balances have been eliminated in consolidation. Income from financial services is reported as a component of operating income to better reflect income from ongoing operations, of which financial services has a significant impact.

During the 2011 third quarter, the Board of Directors declared a two-for-one split of the Company's outstanding shares of Common Stock. On September 12, 2011, Polaris shareholders received one additional share of Common Stock for each share they held of record at the close of business on September 2, 2011. All amounts, including shares and per share information, have been adjusted to give effect to the two-for-one stock split.

Investment in finance affiliate: The caption Investment in finance affiliate in the consolidated balance sheets represents Polaris' 50 percent equity interest in Polaris Acceptance, a partnership agreement between GE Commercial Distribution Finance Corporation ("GECDF") and one of Polaris' wholly-owned subsidiaries. Polaris Acceptance provides floor plan financing to Polaris dealers in the United States. Polaris' investment in Polaris Acceptance is accounted for under the equity method, and is recorded as investments in finance affiliate in the consolidated balance sheets.

Investment in other affiliates: The caption Investments in other affiliates in the consolidated balance sheets for the period ended December 31, 2011 represents the Company's October 2011 investment in Brammo, Inc., a privately held manufacturer of electric motorcycles. This investment represents a minority interest in Brammo and is accounted for under the cost method.

(Gain) Loss on Securities Available for Sale: The net gain of $825,000 in 2010 on securities available for sale resulted from a $1,594,000 gain on the sale of our remaining investment in KTM during the 2010 third quarter offset by a related non-cash impairment charge of $769,000 during the 2010 second quarter. In the first quarter 2009, we recorded a non-cash impairment charge on securities held for sales of $8,952,000 from the decline in the fair value of the KTM shares owned by Polaris as of March 31, 2009, when it was determined that the decline in the fair value of the KTM shares owned by the Company was other than temporary.

Use of estimates: The preparation of financial statements in conformity with accounting principles generally accepted in the United States requires management to make estimates and assumptions that affect the reported amounts of assets and liabilities and disclosure of contingent assets and liabilities at the date of the financial statements and the reported amounts of revenues and expenses during the reporting period. Ultimate results could differ from those estimates.

Cash equivalents: Polaris considers all highly liquid investments purchased with an original maturity of 90 days or less to be cash equivalents. Cash equivalents are stated at cost, which approximates fair value. Such investments consist principally of money market mutual funds.

Allowance for doubtful accounts: Polaris' financial exposure to collection of accounts receivable is limited due to its agreements with certain finance companies. For receivables not serviced through these finance companies, the Company provides a reserve for doubtful accounts based on historical rates and trends. This reserve is adjusted periodically as information about specific accounts becomes available.

Inventories: Inventories are stated at the lower of cost (first-in, first-out method) or market. The major components of inventories are as follows (in thousands):

December 31	2011	2010
Raw materials and purchased components	$ 61,296	$ 35,580
Service parts, garments and accessories	77,437	60,813
Finished goods	175,252	155,744
Less: reserves	(15,943)	(16,210)
Inventories	$298,042	$235,927

Property and equipment: Property and equipment is stated at cost. Depreciation is provided using the straight-line method over the estimated useful life of the respective assets, ranging from 10–40 years for buildings and improvements and from 1–7 years for equipment and tooling. Fully depreciated tooling is eliminated from the accounting records annually.

Research and Development Expenses: Polaris records research and development expenses in the period in which they are incurred as a component of operating expenses. In the years ended December 31, 2011, 2010, and 2009, Polaris incurred $105,631,000, $84,940,000, and $62,999,000, respectively.

Advertising Expenses: Polaris records advertising expenses as a component of selling and marketing expenses in the period in which they are incurred. In the years ended December 31, 2011, 2010, and 2009, Polaris incurred $48,877,000, $40,833,000 and $37,433,000, respectively.

Shipping and Handling Costs: Polaris records shipping and handling costs as a component of cost of sales at the time the product is shipped.

Product warranties: Polaris provides a limited warranty for its ORVs for a period of six months and for a period of one year for its snowmobiles and motorcycles and a two year period for SEVs. Polaris provides longer warranties in certain geographical markets as determined by local regulations and market conditions and may provide longer warranties related to certain promotional programs.

Polaris' standard warranties require the Company or its dealers to repair or replace defective products during such warranty periods at no cost to the consumer. The warranty reserve is established at the time of sale to the dealer or distributor based on management's best estimate using historical rates and trends. Adjustments to the warranty reserve are made from time to time as actual claims become known in order to properly estimate the amounts necessary to settle future and existing claims on products sold as of the balance sheet date. Factors that could have an impact on the warranty accrual in any given year include the following: improved manufacturing quality, shifts in product mix, changes in warranty coverage periods, snowfall and its impact on snowmobile usage, product recalls and any significant changes in sales volume. The activity in the warranty reserve during the years presented is as follows (in thousands):

For the Year Ended December 31	2011	2010	2009
Balance at beginning of year	$ 32,651	$ 25,520	$ 28,631
Additions to warranty reserve through acquisitions	2,727	—	—
Additions charged to expense	46,217	43,721	40,977
Warranty claims paid	(37,240)	(36,590)	(44,088)
Balance at end of year	$ 44,355	$ 32,651	$ 25,520

Sales promotions and incentives: Polaris provides for estimated sales promotion and incentive expenses, which are recognized as a reduction to sales, at the time of sale to the dealer or distributor. Polaris recorded accrued liabilities of $81,228,000 and $75,494,000 related to various sales promotions and incentive programs as of December 31, 2011 and 2010, respectively.

Dealer holdback programs: Dealer holdback represents a portion of the invoiced sales price that is expected to be subsequently returned to the dealer or distributor as a sales incentive upon the ultimate retail sale of the product. Polaris recorded accrued liabilities of $76,512,000 and $79,688,000, for dealer holdback programs in the consolidated balance sheets as of December 31, 2011 and 2010, respectively.

Foreign currency translation: The functional currency for each of the Polaris foreign subsidiaries is their respective local currencies. The assets and liabilities in all Polaris foreign entities are translated at the foreign exchange rate in effect at the balance sheet date. Translation gains and losses are reflected as a component of Accumulated other comprehensive income in the shareholders' equity section of the accompanying consolidated balance sheets. Revenues and expenses in all of Polaris' foreign entities are translated at the average foreign exchange rate in effect for each month of the quarter. Transaction gains and losses including intercompany transactions denominated in a currency other than the functional currency of the entity involved are included in "Other income (expense), net" on our Consolidated statements of income. The net Accumulated other comprehensive income related to translation gains and losses was a net gain of $9,545,000 and $6,991,000 at December 31, 2011 and 2010, respectively.

Revenue recognition: Revenues are recognized at the time of shipment to the dealer or distributor or other customers. Product returns, whether in the normal course of business or resulting from repossession under its customer financing program, have not been material. Polaris sponsors certain sales incentive programs and accrues liabilities for estimated sales promotion expenses and estimated holdback amounts that are recognized as reductions to sales when products are sold to the dealer or distributor customer.

Comprehensive income: Components of comprehensive income include net income, foreign currency translation adjustments, unrealized gains or losses on derivative instruments, and unrealized gains or losses on securities held for sale, net of tax. The Company has chosen to disclose comprehensive income in the accompanying consolidated statements of shareholders' equity and comprehensive income.

Note 3. Financing

The following summarizes activity under Polaris' credit arrangements (dollars in thousands):

	2011	2010	2009
Total borrowings at December 31,	$100,000	$200,000	$200,000
Average outstanding borrowings during year	$133,800	$200,000	$268,100
Maximum outstanding borrowings during year	$200,000	$200,000	$345,000
Interest rate at December 31	4.40%	0.65%	0.79%

The carrying amounts of the Company's long-term debt approximates its fair vale as December 31, 2011 and 2010.

Note 4. Goodwill and Other Intangible Assets

Goodwill and other intangible assets: ASC Topic 350 prohibits the amortization of goodwill and intangible assets with indefinite useful lives. Topic 350 requires that these assets be reviewed for impairment at least annually. An impairment charge for goodwill is recognized only when the estimated fair value of a reporting unit, including goodwill, is less than its carrying amount. The results of the analyses indicated that no goodwill or intangible impairment existed. In accordance with Topic 350, the Company will continue to complete an impairment analysis on an annual basis. Goodwill and other intangible assets, net, consist of $44,668,000 and $28,354,000 of goodwill and $33,050,000 and $2,959,000 of intangible assets, net of accumulated amortization, for the periods ended December 31, 2011 and December 31, 2010, respectively. Amortization expense for intangible assets during 2011 and 2010 was $1,018,000 and $188,000, respectively.

Note 9. Commitments and Contingencies

Product liability: Polaris is subject to product liability claims in the normal course of business. Polaris is currently self-insured for all product liability claims. The estimated costs resulting from any losses are charged to operating expenses when it is probable a loss has been incurred and the amount of the loss is reasonably determinable. The Company utilizes historical trends and actuarial analysis tools, along with an analysis of current claims, to assist in determining the appropriate loss reserve levels. At December 31, 2011, the Company had an accrual of $16,861,000 for the probable payment of pending claims related to product liability litigation associated with Polaris products. This accrual is included as a component of Other Accrued expenses in the accompanying consolidated balance sheets.

Leases: Polaris leases buildings and equipment under non-cancelable operating leases. Total rent expense under all operating lease agreements was $9,184,000, $5,553,000 and $4,999,000 for 2011, 2010 and 2009, respectively. Future minimum annual lease payments under capital and operating leases with non-cancelable terms in excess of one year as of December 31, 2011, including payments for the Monterrey, Mexico facility operating lease were as follows (in thousands):

Lease Obligations	Capital Leases	Operating Leases
2012	$2,653	$ 7,184
2013	2,190	5,845
2014	1,444	4,857
2015	701	3,899
2016	222	3,460
Thereafter	43	11,644
Total future minimum lease obligation	$7,253	$36,889

Note 12. Segment Reporting

Polaris has reviewed ASC Topic 280 and determined that the Company meets the aggregation criteria outlined since the Company's segments have similar (1) economic characteristics, (2) product and services, (3) production processes, (4) customers, (5) distribution channels, and (6) regulatory environments. Therefore, the Company reports as a single reportable business segment. The following data relates to Polaris' foreign operations:

For the Year Ended December 31 (In thousands)	2011	2010	2009
Canadian subsidiary:			
Sales	$368,487	$279,309	$239,240
Identifiable assets	18,008	42,936	35,462
Other foreign countries:			
Sales	$424,363	$305,864	$252,419
Identifiable assets	252,519	145,528	97,771

POLARIS INDUSTRIES INC.
SCHEDULE II—VALUATION AND QUALIFYING ACCOUNTS

(In thousands) Allowance for Doubtful Accounts	Balance at Beginning of Period	Additions Charged to Costs and Expenses	Additions Through Acquisition	Other Changes Add (Deduct)	Balance at End of Period
2009: Deducted from asset accounts—Allowance for doubtful accounts receivable	$6,098	$5,741	—	$(2,246)[1]	$9,593
2010: Deducted from asset accounts—Allowance for doubtful accounts receivable	$9,593	$1,599	—	$(4,823)[1]	$6,369
2011: Deducted from asset accounts—Allowance for doubtful accounts receivable	$6,369	$ 25	$532	$(2,453)[1]	$4,473
Inventory Reserve					
2009: Deducted from asset accounts—Allowance for obsolete inventory	$17,216	$6,400	—	$(8,023)[2]	$15,593
2010: Deducted from asset accounts—Allowance for obsolete inventory	$15,593	$5,840	—	$(5,223)[2]	$16,210
2011: Deducted from asset accounts—Allowance for obsolete inventory	$16,210	$4,611	$725	$(5,603)[2]	$15,943

[1] Uncollectible accounts receivable written off, net of recoveries.

[2] Inventory disposals, net of recoveries

POLARIS INDUSTRIES INC.

Selected Financial Data

(Dollars in millions, except per-share data)	2011	2010	2009	2008	2007	2006
Statement of Operations Data						
Sales Data:						
Total sales	$2,656.9	$1,991.1	$1,565.9	$1,948.3	$1,780.0	$1,656.5
Percent change from prior year	33%	27%	-20%	9%	7%	-11%
Sales mix by product:						
Off-Road Vehicles	69%	69%	65%	67%	67%	67%
Snowmobiles	11%	10%	12%	10%	10%	10%
On-Road Vehicles	5%	4%	3%	5%	6%	7%
Parts, Garments and Accessories	15%	17%	20%	18%	17%	16%
Gross Profit Data:						
Total gross profit	$ 740.6	$ 530.2	$ 393.2	$ 445.7	$ 393.0	$ 359.4
Percent of sales	27.9%	26.6%	25.1%	22.9%	22.1%	21.7%
Operating Expense Data:						
Total operating expenses	$ 414.7	$ 326.3	$ 245.3	$ 284.1	$ 262.3	$ 238.4
Percent of sales	15.6%	16.4%	15.7%	14.6%	14.7%	14.4%
Operating Income Data:						
Total operating income	$ 349.9	$ 220.7	$ 165.0	$ 182.8	$ 176.0	$ 168.1
Percent of sales	13.2%	11.1%	10.5%	9.4%	9.9%	10.1%
Net Income Data:						
Net income from continuing operations	$ 227.6	$ 147.1	$ 101.0	$ 117.4	$ 112.6	$ 112.8
Percent of sales	8.6%	7.4%	6.5%	6.0%	6.3%	6.8%
Diluted net income per share from continuing operations	$ 3.20	$ 2.14	$ 1.53	$ 1.75	$ 1.55	$ 1.36
Net income	$ 227.6	$ 147.1	$ 101.0	$ 117.4	$ 111.7	$ 107.0
Diluted net income per share	$ 3.20	$ 2.14	$ 1.53	$ 1.75	$ 1.54	$ 1.29
Cash Flow Data:						
Cash flow provided by continuing operations	$ 302.5	$ 297.9	$ 193.2	$ 176.2	$ 213.2	$ 152.8
Purchase of property and equipment for continuing operations	84.5	55.7	43.9	76.6	63.7	52.6
Repurchase and retirement of common stock	132.4	27.5	4.6	107.2	103.1	307.6
Cash dividends to shareholders	61.6	53.0	50.2	49.6	47.7	50.2
Cash dividends per share	$ 0.90	$ 0.80	$ 0.78	$ 0.76	$ 0.68	$ 0.62
Balance Sheet Data (at end of year):						
Cash and cash equivalents	$ 325.3	$ 393.9	$ 140.2	$ 27.2	$ 63.3	$ 19.6
Current assets	878.7	808.1	491.5	443.6	447.6	393.0
Total assets	1,228.0	1,061.6	763.7	751.1	769.9	778.8
Current liabilities	615.5	584.2	343.1	404.8	388.2	361.4
Long-term debt	104.6	100.0	200.0	200.0	200.0	250.0
Shareholders' equity	500.1	371.0	204.5	137.0	173.0	167.4

For the Years Ended December 31

ARCTIC CAT INC.
CONSOLIDATED BALANCE SHEETS

March 31	2011	2010
ASSETS		
Current Assets		
Cash and cash equivalents	$ 14,700,000	$ 31,811,000
Short term investments	110,413,000	39,251,000
Accounts receivable, less allowances	23,732,000	29,227,000
Inventories	61,478,000	81,361,000
Prepaid expenses	4,048,000	4,384,000
Deferred income taxes	17,669,000	14,981,000
Total current assets	232,040,000	201,015,000
Property and Equipment		
Machinery, equipment and tooling	195,189,000	185,023,000
Land, building and improvements	28,924,000	28,937,000
	224,113,000	213,960,000
Less accumulated depreciation	184,883,000	170,644,000
	39,230,000	43,316,000
Other Assets	1,636,000	1,753,000
	$272,906,000	$246,084,000
LIABILITIES AND SHAREHOLDERS' EQUITY		
Current Liabilities		
Accounts payable	$ 41,666,000	$ 37,303,000
Accrued expenses	44,398,000	35,042,000
Income taxes payable	1,380,000	2,975,000
Total current liabilities	87,444,000	75,320,000
Deferred Income Taxes	2,426,000	3,425,000
Commitments and Contingencies	—	—
Shareholders' Equity		
Preferred stock, par value $1.00; 2,050,000 shares authorized; none issued	—	—
Preferred stock—Series A Junior Participating, par value $1.00; 450,000 shares authorized; none issued	—	—
Common stock, par value $.01; 37,440,000 shares authorized; shares issued and outstanding: 12,199,271 in 2011 and 12,125,985 in 2010	122,000	121,000
Class B common stock, par value $.01; 7,560,000 shares authorized; shares issued and outstanding: 6,102,000 in 2011 and 2010	61,000	61,000
Additional paid-in-capital	7,280,000	5,053,000
Accumulated other comprehensive loss	(1,920,000)	(2,382,000)
Retained earnings	177,493,000	164,486,000
Total shareholders' equity	183,036,000	167,339,000
	$272,906,000	$246,084,000

ARCTIC CAT INC.

CONSOLIDATED STATEMENTS OF OPERATIONS

Years ended March 31	2011	2010	2009
Net sales			
Snowmobile & ATV units	$363,015,000	$350,871,000	$454,589,000
Parts, garments, & accessories	101,636,000	99,857,000	109,024,000
Total net sales	464,651,000	450,728,000	563,613,000
Cost of goods sold			
Snowmobile & ATV units	302,783,000	309,217,000	411,776,000
Parts, garments, & accessories	60,359,000	58,275,000	68,665,000
Total cost of goods sold	363,142,000	367,492,000	480,441,000
Gross profit	101,509,000	83,236,000	83,172,000
Operating expenses			
Selling & marketing	33,540,000	33,929,000	43,971,000
Research & development	15,029,000	12,926,000	18,404,000
General & administrative	34,805,000	35,045,000	33,904,000
Goodwill impairment charge	—	—	1,750,000
Total operating expenses	83,374,000	81,900,000	98,029,000
Operating profit (loss)	18,135,000	1,336,000	(14,857,000)
Other income (expense)			
Interest income	107,000	12,000	117,000
Interest expense	(11,000)	(250,000)	(1,015,000)
Total other income (expense)	96,000	(238,000)	(898,000)
Earnings (loss) before incomes taxes	18,231,000	1,098,000	(15,755,000)
Income tax expense (benefit)	5,224,000	(777,000)	(6,247,000)
Net earnings (loss)	$ 13,007,000	$ 1,875,000	$ (9,508,000)
Net earnings (loss) per share			
Basic	$ 0.71	$ 0.10	$ (0.53)
Diluted	$ 0.70	$ 0.10	$ (0.53)
Weighted average share outstanding			
Basic	18,232,000	18,220,000	18,070,000
Diluted	18,539,000	18,291,000	18,070,000

ARCTIC CAT

ARCTIC CAT INC.

CONSOLIDATED STATEMENTS OF SHAREHOLDERS' EQUITY

Years ended March 31	Common Stock Shares	Amount	Class B Common Stock Shares	Amount	Additional Paid-in Capital	Accumulated Other Comprehensive Income (Loss)	Retained Earnings	Total
Balances at March 31, 2008 ...	11,833,485	$118,000	6,102,000	$61,000	$ —	$ 4,768,000	$175,915,000	$180,862,000
Restricted stock awards	163,500	2,000	—	—	(2,000)	—	—	—
Restricted stock forfeited	(9,500)	—	—	—	—	—	—	—
Stock based compensation expense	—	—	—	—	2,570,000	—	—	2,570,000
Comprehensive loss:								
Net loss	—	—	—	—	—	—	(9,508,000)	(9,508,000)
Unrealized loss on derivative instruments, net of tax	—	—	—	—	—	(133,000)	—	(133,000)
Foreign currency adjustment	—	—	—	—	—	(5,147,000)	—	(5,147,000)
Total comprehensive loss ...								(14,788,000)
Dividends ($.21 per share) ..	—	—	—	—	—	—	(3,796,000)	(3,796,000)
Balances at March 31, 2009 ...	11,987,485	120,000	6,102,000	61,000	2,568,000	(512,000)	162,611,000	164,848,000
Restricted stock awards	140,500	1,000	—	—	(1,000)	—	—	—
Restricted stock forfeited	(2,000)	—	—	—	—	—	—	—
Stock based compensation expense	—	—	—	—	2,486,000	—	—	2,486,000
Comprehensive income:								
Net earnings	—	—	—	—	—	—	1,875,000	1,875,000
Unrealized gain on derivative instruments, net of tax	—	—	—	—	—	244,000	—	244,000
Foreign currency adjustment	—	—	—	—	—	(2,114,000)	—	(2,114,000)
Total comprehensive income								5,000
Balances at March 31, 2010 ...	12,125,985	121,000	6,102,000	61,000	5,053,000	(2,382,000)	164,486,000	167,339,000
Exercise of stock options	184,869	2,000	—	—	726,000	—	—	728,000
Tax benefits from stock options exercised	—	—	—	—	745,000	—	—	745,000
Repurchase of common stock	(183,953)	(2,000)	—	—	(2,417,000)	—	—	(2,419,000)
Restricted stock awards	78,500	1,000	—	—	(1,000)	—	—	—
Restricted stock forfeited	(6,130)	—	—	—	—	—	—	—
Stock based compensation expense	—	—	—	—	3,174,000	—	—	3,174,000
Comprehensive income:								
Net earnings	—	—	—	—	—	—	13,007,000	13,007,000
Unrealized loss on derivative instruments, net of tax	—	—	—	—	—	(1,147,000)	—	(1,147,000)
Foreign currency adjustment	—	—	—	—	—	1,609,000	—	1,609,000
Total comprehensive income								13,469,000
Balances at March 31, 2011 ..	12,199,271	$122,000	6,102,000	$61,000	$ 7,280,000	$(1,920,000)	$177,493,000	$183,036,000

ARCTIC CAT INC.

CONSOLIDATED STATEMENTS OF CASH FLOWS

Years ended March 31	2011	2010	2009
Cash flows from operating activities			
Net earnings (loss)	$ 13,007,000	$ 1,875,000	$ (9,508,000)
Adjustments to reconcile net earnings to net cash provided by (used in) operating activities			
Depreciation and amortization	15,816,000	22,779,000	28,981,000
Loss on the disposal of assets	105,000	144,000	252,000
Impairment of goodwill	—	—	1,750,000
Deferred income taxes benefit	(3,194,000)	(3,577,000)	(6,379,000)
Stock based compensation expense	3,174,000	2,486,000	2,570,000
Changes in operating assets and liabilities			
Trading securities	(71,162,000)	(39,082,000)	24,837,000
Accounts receivable, less allowances	5,543,000	9,400,000	(437,000)
Inventories	20,587,000	40,003,000	2,798,000
Prepaid expenses	345,000	205,000	(1,246,000)
Accounts payable	2,879,000	(7,668,000)	(29,615,000)
Accrued expenses	9,238,000	(585,000)	(3,392,000)
Income taxes	(1,461,000)	3,335,000	8,980,000
Net cash provided by (used in) operating activities	(5,123,000)	29,315,000	19,591,000
Cash flows from investing activities			
Purchases of property and equipment	(11,761,000)	(6,540,000)	(14,226,000)
Proceeds from the sale of assets	87,000	—	—
Net cash used in investing activities	(11,674,000)	(6,540,000)	(14,226,000)
Cash flows from financing activities			
Checks written in excess of bank balance	—	221,000	—
Proceeds from short-term borrowings	1,012,000	73,429,000	227,230,000
Payments on short-term borrowings	(1,012,000)	(73,429,000)	(227,230,000)
Proceeds from issuance of common stock	728,000	—	—
Tax benefit from stock option exercises	745,000	—	—
Repurchase of common stock	(2,419,000)	—	—
Dividends paid	—	—	(3,796,000)
Net cash provided by (used in) financing activities	(946,000)	221,000	(3,796,000)
Effect of exchange rate changes on cash and cash equivalents	632,000	(2,429,000)	(382,000)
Net increase (decrease) in cash and cash equivalents	(17,111,000)	20,567,000	1,187,000
Cash and cash equivalents at beginning of year	31,811,000	11,244,000	10,057,000
Cash and cash equivalents at end of year	$ 14,700,000	$ 31,811,000	$ 11,244,000
Supplemental disclosure of cash payments for:			
Income taxes	$ 9,179,000	$ 1,935,000	$ 409,000
Interest	$ 11,000	$ 250,000	$ 987,000

Supplemental disclosure of non-cash investing and financing activities:

As of March 31, 2011 and 2010, the unrealized gain (loss) on derivative instruments, net of tax was ($1,147,000) and $244,000.

KTM POWER SPORTS AG
CONSOLIDATED INCOME STATEMENT
FOR BUSINESS YEAR 2011

(In thousands of Euro)	2011
Net sales	526,801
Cost of goods sold	(371,752)
Gross margin	155,049
Selling and sport-activity expenses	(71,952)
R&D expenses	(23,099)
Infrastructure and administration expenses	(20,870)
Other operating expenses	(9,206)
Other operating Income	1,088
Operating result	31,009
Interest income	768
Interest expenses	(9,693)
Other financial and participation result	(2,975)
Pre-tax result	19,109
Tax on income and earnings	1,709
NET RESULT	20,818
Thereof net result to owners	*20,719*
Thereof net result to non-controlling shareholders	*99*
EARNINGS PER SHARE (EUR)	
Basic	2.003
Diluted	1.968

KTM POWER SPORTS AG
CONSOLIDATED STATEMENT OF COMPREHENSIVE INCOME
FOR BUSINESS YEAR 2011

(In thousands of Euro)	2011
Net result of the business year	20,818
Currency conversion	107
Valuation of cash flow hedges	11,393
Deferred tax on the valuation of cash flow hedges	(2,848)
Other income	8,652
TOTAL INCOME	29,470
Thereof net result to owners	*29,371*
Thereof net result to non-controlling shareholders	*99*

KTM

KTM POWER SPORTS AG
CONSOLIDATED BALANCE SHEET
AS AT DECEMBER 31

ASSETS

(In thousands of Euro)	12/31/2011	12/31/2010
SHORT-TERM ASSETS		
Liquid assets	14,962	8,946
Accounts receivable – trade to third parties	49,924	53,087
Accounts receivable – trade to affiliated companies	1,443	1,040
Accounts receivable – trade to associated companies	2,227	3,130
Inventory	113,979	108,910
Prepayments	1,649	1,169
Other short-term assets	9,701	7,231
	193,885	**183,513**
LONG-TERM ASSETS		
Financial fixed assets	7,458	6,222
Tangible fixed assets	84,256	63,204
Goodwill	78,793	78,492
Intangible fixed assets	118,202	110,118
Deferred taxes	3,132	3,725
Other long-term assets	49	51
	291,890	**261,812**
ASSETS	**485,775**	**445,325**

EQUITY AND LIABILITIES

(In thousands of Euro)	12/31/2011	12/31/2010
SHORT-TERM LIABILITIES		
Bank loans	5,415	14,061
Accounts payable – trade to third parties	54,578	37,725
Accounts payable – trade to affiliated companies	11,062	7,979
Accounts payable – trade to associated companies	2,600	2,895
Provisions	4,238	3,993
Liabilities – corporate tax	1,470	33
Prepayments	735	1,614
Other short-term liabilities	29,256	33,926
	109,353	**102,226**
LONG-TERM LIABILITIES		
Interest-bearing loans	132,898	129,957
Liabilities for personnel	7,699	6,479
Liabilities from deferred taxes	14,560	15,851
Liabilities to affiliated companies	0	13,021
Other long-term liabilities	1,490	1,005
	156,648	**166,313**
SHAREHOLDER'S EQUITY		
Share capital	10,509	10,109
Reserves including retained earnings	208,987	166,593
Non-controlling shares	279	84
	219,775	**176,786**
EQUITY AND LIABILITIES	**485,775**	**445,325**

KTM

KTM POWER SPORTS AG
CONSOLIDATED CASH FLOW STATEMENT
FOR BUSINESS YEAR 2011

(In thousands of Euro)	2011
CONSOLIDATED CASH FLOW FROM OPERATING ACTIVITIES	
+(−) Profit (loss) of the business year	20,818
+(−) Profit (loss) of non-controlling shareholders	(99)
+(−) Depreciation (write-up) of fixed assets	33,368
+(−) Depreciation (write-up) to financial assets	118
+(−) Deferred taxes	(3,352)
− Results from consolidation not affecting income	(649)
− Results from companies validated at-equity not affecting income	(657)
+(−) Addition (disposal) of liabilities for personnel	1,432
−(+) Profit (loss) from the sale of fixed assets	(59)
Consolidated cash flow from earnings	**50,919**
−(+) Increase (decrease) in inventories including prepayments	(5,069)
−(+) Increase (decrease) in accounts receiveable − trade, prepayments, other short- and longterm assets	831
−(+) Increase (decrease) in accounts receivable − trade from affiliated companies	430
−(+) Increase (decrease) in accounts receivable − trade from associated companies	903
(+)− Increase (decrease) in accounts payable − trade, prepayments and other short-term and long-term liabilities	16,346
(+)− Increase (decrease) in accounts payable − trade from affiliated companies	3,083
(+)− Increase (decrease) in accounts payable − trade from associated companies	(295)
(+)− Increase (decrease) from corporate taxes, deferred taxes and other provisions	3,201
	19,429
Cash flow from operating activities	**70,348**
CONSOLIDATED CASH FLOW FROM INVESTMENT ACTIVITIES	
− Investments in fixed assets (outflow of funds for investments)	(37,705)
− Investments in financial assets	(697)
(+)− Changes from first/final consolidation	273
+ Disposal of fixed assets (inflow of funds from sales: book value + profit (− loss) from the disposal of fixed assets)	871
(+)− Currency rate differences from fixed assets	(13)
Consolidated cash flow from investment activities	**(37,271)**
CONSOLIDATED CASH FLOW FROM FINANCING ACTIVITIES	
(+)− Currency rate differences	33
+ Capital increase	1,095
(+)− Increase (decrease) of short-term bank loans	(8,646)
(+)− Change in liabilities to affiliated and associated companies	(259)
(+)− Increase (decrease) in long-term interest bearing loans	(19,479)
+(−) Changes in non-controlling interests	196
+(−) Change deconsolidation Cost Plus subsidiaries	0
Consolidated cash flow from financing activities	**(27,060)**
CONSOLIDATED CASH FLOW	
+(−) Consolidated cash flow from operating activities	70,348
+(−) Consolidated cash flow from investment activities	(37,271)
+(−) Consolidated cash flow from financing activities	(27,060)
Change in the liquidity of the group	**6,017**
+ Starting cash and cash equivalents of the group	8,946
CASH AND CASH EQUIVALENTS OF THE GROUP AS AT DECEMBER 31	**14,962**
Consisting of cash in hand. cheques, cash at bank and term deposits	*14,962*
Interest paid	10,052
Taxes paid	547

KTM POWER SPORTS AG
DEVELOPMENT OF THE GROUP'S EQUITY CAPITAL
FOR BUSINESS YEAR 2011

(In thousands of Euro)	Nominal capital	Reserves incl. net result for the business year	Revaluation reserve	Cash flow hedge reserve	Currency translation adjustments	Total	Shares of non-controlling Interests	Total share capital
As at December 31, 2010	10,109	163,106	17,235	(13,648)	(100)	176,702	84	176,786
Currency conversion	0	0	0	0	105	105	0	105
Financial instruments	0	0	0	8,545	0	8,545	0	8,545
Profit and loss directly recognized in equity	0	0	0	8,545	105	8,650	0	8,650
Result of the business year	0	20,719	0	0	0	20,719	99	20,819
Total profit and loss recognized in equity	0	20,719	0	8,545	105	29,369	99	29,469
Capital increase	400	13,600	0	0	0	14,000	0	14,000
Cost of capital increase	0	(480)	0	0	0	(480)	0	(480)
Change in non-controlling interests	0	(96)	0	0	0	(96)	96	0
AS AT DECEMBER 31, 2011	10,509	196,849	17,235	(5,103)	5	219,495	279	219,775

KTM

Piaggio Group
Consolidated Income Statement

For Year Ended December 31 (In thousands of Euro)	2011	2010
Net revenues	**1,516,463**	**1,485,351**
Cost for materials	904,060	881,075
Cost for services and leases and rentals	266,484	258,358
Employee costs	247,600	240,115
Depreciation of property, plant and equipment	35,219	35,879
Amortisation of intangible assets	59,794	50,127
Other operating income	122,562	121,128
Other operating costs	20,323	29,821
Operating income	**105,545**	**111,104**
Income/(loss) from investments	2,481	5,252
Financial income	4,087	2,891
Borrowing Costs	31,853	33,905
Net exchange gains/(losses)	(932)	(1,518)
Earnings before tax	**79,328**	**83,824**
Taxation for the period	32,305	40,983
Earnings from continuing activities	**47,023**	**42,841**
Assets held for disposal:		
Profits or losses arising from assets held for disposal		
Net Income (Loss) for the period	**47,023**	**42,841**
Attributable to:		
Shareholders of the Parent Company	**47,053**	**42,811**
Non-controlling interests	**(30)**	**30**
Earnings per share (figures in €)	**0.126**	**0.113**
Diluted earnings per share (figures in €)	**0.126**	**0.112**

Piaggio Group
Consolidated Statement of Comprehensive Income

For Year Ended December 31 (In thousands of Euro)	2011	2010
Profit (loss) for the period (A)	**47,023**	**42,841**
Effective portion of profits (losses) on cash flow hedges	(1,283)	(354)
Profit (loss) deriving from the translation of financial statements of foreign companies denominated in foreign currency	(11,262)	3,060
Total Other Profits (and losses) for the period (B)	**(12,545)**	**2,706**
Total Profit (loss) for the period (A + B)	**34,478**	**45,547**
Attributable to:		
Shareholders of the Parent Company	**34,533**	**45,531**
Non-controlling interests	**(55)**	**16**

PIAGGIO

Piaggio Group
Consolidated Statement of Financial Position

As of December 31 (In thousands of Euro)	2011	2010
Assets		
Non-current assets		
Intangible assets	649,420	652,622
Property, plant and equipment	274,871	256,759
Investment property		
Investments	2,482	194
Other financial assets	11,836	334
Long-term tax receivables	976	967
Deferred tax assets	55,726	46,294
Trade receivables		
Other receivables	15,165	12,655
Total non-current assets	**1,010,476**	**969,825**
Assets held for sale		
Current assets		
Trade receivables	65,560	90,421
Other receivables	28,028	23,300
Short-term tax receivables	27,245	44,200
Inventories	236,988	240,066
Other financial assets	0	23,051
Cash and cash equivalents	151,887	154,859
Total current assets	**509,708**	**575,897**
Total assets	**1,520,184**	**1,545,722**
Shareholders' equity and liabilities		
Shareholders' equity		
Share capital and reserves attributable to the shareholders of the Parent Company	445,036	441,277
Share capital and reserves attributable to non-controlling interests	1,182	1,613
Total shareholders' equity	**446,218**	**442,890**
Non-current liabilities		
Financial liabilities falling due after one year	329,200	371,048
Trade payables	235	88
Other long-term provisions	12,429	16,993
Deferred tax liabilities	32,735	32,338
Retirement funds and employee benefits	46,603	58,636
Tax payables	2,539	3,361
Other long-term payables	5,948	4,202
Total non-current liabilities	**429,689**	**486,666**
Current liabilities		
Financial liabilities falling due within one year	170,261	156,800
Trade payables	375,263	352,627
Tax payables	20,920	19,290
Other short-term payables	64,718	69,503
Current portion of other long-term provisions	13,115	17,946
Total current liabilities	**644,277**	**616,166**
Total shareholders' equity and liabilities	**1,520,184**	**1,545,722**

PIAGGIO

Piaggio Group
Consolidated Cash Flow Statement

For Year Ended December 31 (In thousands of Euro)	2011	2010
Operating activities		
Consolidated net income	47,053	42,811
Allocation of profit to non-controlling interests	(30)	30
Taxation for the period	32,305	40,983
Depreciation of property, plant and equipment	35,219	35,879
Amortisation of intangible assets	59,794	50,127
Non-monetary costs for stock options	771	2,650
Allocations for risks and retirement funds and employee benefits	21,134	29,243
Write-downs / (Reversals)	(1,192)	1,755
Losses / (Gains) on the disposal of property, plants and equipment	(6,012)	(2,240)
Losses / (Gains) on the disposal of intangible assets	0	0
Financial income	(3,910)	(2,891)
Dividend income	(193)	(12)
Borrowing Costs	25,558	29,744
Income from public grants	(3,492)	(4,164)
Portion of earnings of affiliated companies	0	45
Change in working capital:		
(Increase)/Decrease in trade receivables	24,861	12,743
(Increase)/Decrease in other receivables	(18,740)	(1,157)
(Increase)/Decrease in inventories	3,078	12,430
Increase/(Decrease) in trade payables	22,783	6,640
Increase/(Decrease) in other payables	8,636	(12,347)
Increase/(Decrease) in provisions for risks	(21,782)	(26,974)
Increase/(Decrease) in retirement funds and employee benefits	(20,795)	(13,028)
Other changes	5,265	(43,774)
Cash generated from operating activities	**210,311**	**158,493**
Interest paid	(22,825)	(23,178)
Taxes paid	(31,862)	(12,774)
Cash flow from operating activities (A)	**155,624**	**122,541**
Investment activities		
Investment in property, plant and equipment	(61,790)	(37,132)
Sale price, or repayment value, of property, plant and equipment	6,542	3,823
Investment in intangible assets	(64,300)	(59,063)
Sale price, or repayment value, of intangible assets	122	261
Purchase of financial assets	0	(23,051)
Sale price of financial assets	23,051	4,127
Collected interests	11,666	2,360
Cash flow from investment activities (B)	**(84,709)**	**(108,675)**
Financing activities		
Exercise of stock options	2,843	
Purchase of treasury shares	(9,080)	(3,344)
Outflow for dividends paid	(25,684)	(25,765)
Loans received	71,400	37,652
Outflow for repayment of loans	(112,727)	(65,174)
Financing received for leases	227	0
Repayment of finance leases	(850)	(758)
Cash flow from funding activities (C)	**(73,871)**	**(57,389)**
Increase / (Decrease) in cash and cash equivalents (A+B+C)	(2,956)	(43,523)
Opening balance	154,758	198,281
Exchange differences		
Closing balance	151,802	154,758

PIAGGIO

Piaggio Group
Changes in Consolidated Shareholders' Equity

Movements from 1 January 2011 / 31 December 2011

In thousands of Euro	Share capital	Share premium reserve	Legal reserve	Reserve for measurement of financial instruments	IAS transition reserve	Group consolidation reserve	Group conversion reserve	Stock option reserve	Performance reserve	Consolidated Group shareholders' equity	Non-controlling interests capital and reserves	Total shareholders' equity
As of 1 January 2011	**203,348**	**3,493**	**11,299**	**(227)**	**(5,859)**	**993**	**(1,850)**	**11,929**	**218,151**	**441,277**	**1,613**	**442,890**
Charges for the period for stock option plans								771		771		771
Allocation of profits			942						(942)	0		0
Distribution of dividends									(25,684)	(25,684)		(25,684)
Purchase of treasury shares	(2,382)								(6,698)	(9,080)		(9,080)
Exercise of stock options	1,243								1,600	2,843		2,843
Reacquisition of the Simest investment									376	376	(376)	0
Total overall profit (loss)				(1,283)			(11,237)		47,053	34,533	(55)	34,478
As of 31 December 2011	**202,209**	**3,493**	**12,241**	**(1,510)**	**(5,859)**	**993**	**(13,087)**	**12,700**	**233,856**	**445,036**	**1,182**	**446,218**

Movements from 1 January 2010 / 31 December 2010

In thousands of Euro	Share capital	Share premium reserve	Legal reserve	Reserve for measurement of financial instruments	IAS transition reserve	Group consolidation reserve	Group conversion reserve	Stock option reserve	Performance reserve	Consolidated Group shareholders' equity	Non-controlling interests capital and reserves	Total shareholders' equity
As of 1 January 2010	**191,616**	**3,493**	**8,996**	**127**	**(5,859)**	**993**	**(5,468)**	**9,279**	**218,484**	**421,661**	**2,141**	**423,802**
Charges for the period for stock option plans								2,650		2,650		2,650
Allocation of profits			2,303						(2,303)	0		0
Distribution of dividends									(25,765)	(25,765)		(25,765)
Cancellation of treasury shares	12,608								(12,608)	0		0
Purchase of treasury shares	(876)								(2,468)	(3,344)		(3,344)
Total overall profit (loss)				(354)			3,618		42,811	46,075	(528)	45,547
As of 31 December 2010	**203,348**	**3,493**	**11,299**	**(227)**	**(5,859)**	**993**	**(1,850)**	**11,929**	**218,151**	**441,277**	**1,613**	**442,890**

Glossary

Absorption costing Costing method that assigns both variable and fixed costs to products. *(pp. 786 & 816)*

Accelerated depreciation method Method that produces larger depreciation charges in the early years of an asset's life and smaller charges in its later years. *(p. 342)*

Account Record within an accounting system in which increases and decreases are entered and stored in a specific asset, liability, equity, revenue, or expense. *(p. 53)*

Account balance Difference between total debits and total credits (including the beginning balance) for an account. *(p. 60)*

Account form balance sheet Balance sheet that lists assets on the left side and liabilities and equity on the right. *(p. 68)*

Account payable Liability created by buying goods or services on credit; backed by the buyer's general credit standing.

Accounting Information and measurement system that identifies, records, and communicates relevant information about a company's business activities. *(p. 4)*

Accounting cycle Recurring steps performed each accounting period, starting with analyzing transactions and continuing through the post-closing trial balance (or reversing entries). *(p. 116)*

Accounting equation Equality involving a company's assets, liabilities, and equity; Assets = Liabilities + Equity; also called *balance sheet equation*. *(p. 15)*

Accounting information system People, records, and methods that collect and process data from transactions and events, organize them in useful forms, and communicate results to decision makers. *(p. E-2)*

Accounting period Length of time covered by financial statements; also called *reporting period*. *(p. 98)*

Accounting rate of return Rate used to evaluate the acceptability of an investment; equals the after-tax periodic income from a project divided by the average investment in the asset; also called *rate of return on average investment*. *(p. 1019)*

Accounts payable ledger Subsidiary ledger listing individual creditor (supplier) accounts.

Accounts receivable Amounts due from customers for credit sales; backed by the customer's general credit standing. *(p. 302)*

Accounts receivable ledger Subsidiary ledger listing individual customer accounts. *(p. E-7)*

Accounts receivable turnover Measure of both the quality and liquidity of accounts receivable; indicates how often receivables are received and collected during the period; computed by dividing net sales by average accounts receivable. *(p. 317)*

Accrual basis accounting Accounting system that recognizes revenues when earned and expenses when incurred; the basis for GAAP. *(p. 99)*

Accrued expenses Costs incurred in a period that are both unpaid and unrecorded; adjusting entries for recording accrued expenses involve increasing expenses and increasing liabilities. *(p. 105)*

Accrued revenues Revenues earned in a period that are both unrecorded and not yet received in cash (or other assets); adjusting entries for recording accrued revenues involve increasing assets and increasing revenues. *(p. 107)*

Accumulated depreciation Cumulative sum of all depreciation expense recorded for an asset. *(p. 100)*

Acid-test ratio Ratio used to assess a company's ability to settle its current debts with its most liquid assets; defined as quick assets (cash, short-term investments, and current receivables) divided by current liabilities. *(p. 178)*

Activity An event that causes the consumption of overhead resources in an entity. *(p. 743)*

Activity-based budgeting (ABB) Budget system based on expected activities. *(p. 862)*

Activity-based costing (ABC) Cost allocation method that focuses on activities performed; traces costs to activities and then assigns them to cost objects. *(pp. 9 & 743)*

Activity cost driver Variable that causes an activity's cost to go up or down; a causal factor. *(pp. 12 & 746)*

Activity cost pool Temporary account that accumulates costs a company incurs to support an activity. *(pp. 9 & 743)*

Adjusted trial balance List of accounts and balances prepared after period-end adjustments are recorded and posted. *(p. 110)*

Adjusting entry Journal entry at the end of an accounting period to bring an asset or liability account to its proper amount and update the related expense or revenue account. *(p. 101)*

Aging of accounts receivable Process of classifying accounts receivable by how long they are past due for purposes of estimating uncollectible accounts. *(p. 310)*

Allowance for Doubtful Accounts Contra asset account with a balance approximating uncollectible accounts receivable; also called *Allowance for Uncollectible Accounts*. *(p. 307)*

Allowance method Procedure that (a) estimates and matches bad debts expense with its sales for the period and/or (b) reports accounts receivable at estimated realizable value. *(p. 307)*

Amortization Process of allocating the cost of an intangible asset to expense over its estimated useful life. *(p. 351)*

Annual financial statements Financial statements covering a one-year period; often based on a calendar year, but any consecutive 12-month (or 52-week) period is acceptable. *(p. 98)*

G

Annual report Summary of a company's financial results for the year with its current financial condition and future plans; directed to external users of financial information. *(p. A-1)*

Annuity Series of equal payments at equal intervals. *(pp. 441 & 1021)*

Appropriated retained earnings Retained earnings separately reported to inform stockholders of funding needs. *(p. 482)*

Asset book value (See *book value*.)

Assets Resources a business owns or controls that are expected to provide current and future benefits to the business. *(p. 15)*

Audit Analysis and report of an organization's accounting system, its records, and its reports using various tests. *(p. 13)*

Auditors Individuals hired to review financial reports and information systems. *Internal auditors* of a company are employed to assess and evaluate its system of internal controls, including the resulting reports. *External auditors* are independent of a company and are hired to assess and evaluate the "fairness" of financial statements (or to perform other contracted financial services). *(p. 13)*

Authorized stock Total amount of stock that a corporation's charter authorizes it to issue. *(p. 469)*

Available-for-sale (AFS) securities Investments in debt and equity securities that are not classified as trading securities or held-to-maturity securities. *(p. C-6)*

Average cost See *weighted average*.

Avoidable expense Expense (or cost) that is relevant for decision making; expense that is not incurred if a department, product, or service is eliminated. *(p. 993)*

Bad debts Accounts of customers who do not pay what they have promised to pay; an expense of selling on credit; also called *uncollectible accounts*. *(p. 306)*

Balance column account Account with debit and credit columns for recording entries and another column for showing the balance of the account after each entry. *(p. 60)*

Balance sheet Financial statement that lists types and dollar amounts of assets, liabilities, and equity at a specific date. *(p. 20)*

Balance sheet equation (See *accounting equation*.)

Balanced scorecard A system of performance measurement that collects information on several key performance indicators within each of four perspectives: customer, internal processes, innovation and learning, and financial. *(p. 956)*

Bank reconciliation Report that explains the difference between the book (company) balance of cash and the cash balance reported on the bank statement. *(p. 273)*

Bank statement Bank report on the depositor's beginning and ending cash balances, and a listing of its changes, for a period. *(p. 272)*

Basic earnings per share Net income less any preferred dividends and then divided by weighted-average common shares outstanding. *(p. 485)*

Batch level activities Activities that are performed each time a batch of goods is handled or processed, regardless of how many units are in a batch; the amount of resources used depends on the number of batches run rather than on the number of units in the batch. *(p. 750)*

Batch processing Accumulating source documents for a period of time and then processing them all at once such as once a day, week, or month. *(p. E-16)*

Bearer bonds Bonds made payable to whoever holds them (the *bearer*); also called *unregistered bonds*. *(p. 436)*

Benchmarking Practice of comparing and analyzing company financial performance or position with other companies or standards. *(p. 908)*

Betterments Expenditures to make a plant asset more efficient or productive; also called *improvements*. *(p. 347)*

Bond Written promise to pay the bond's par (or face) value and interest at a stated contract rate; often issued in denominations of $1,000. *(p. 422)*

Bond certificate Document containing bond specifics such as issuer's name, bond par value, contract interest rate, and maturity date. *(p. 424)*

Bond indenture Contract between the bond issuer and the bondholders; identifies the parties' rights and obligations. *(p. 424)*

Book value Asset's acquisition costs less its accumulated depreciation (or depletion, or amortization); also sometimes used synonymously as the *carrying value* of an account. *(pp. 104 & 341)*

Book value per common share Recorded amount of equity applicable to common shares divided by the number of common shares outstanding. *(p. 486)*

Book value per preferred share Equity applicable to preferred shares (equals its call price [or par value if it is not callable] plus any cumulative dividends in arrears) divided by the number of preferred shares outstanding. *(p. 486)*

Bookkeeping (See *recordkeeping*.)

Break-even point Output level at which sales equals fixed plus variable costs; where income equals zero. *(p. 785)*

Break-even time (BET) Time-based measurement used to evaluate the acceptability of an investment; equals the time expected to pass before the present value of the net cash flows from an investment equals its initial cost. *(p. 1026)*

Budget Formal statement of future plans, usually expressed in monetary terms. *(p. 848)*

Budget report Report comparing actual results to planned objectives; sometimes used as a progress report. *(p. 896)*

Budgetary control Management use of budgets to monitor and control company operations. *(p. 896)*

Budgeted balance sheet Accounting report that presents predicted amounts of the company's assets, liabilities, and equity balances as of the end of the budget period. *(p. 860)*

Budgeted income statement Accounting report that presents predicted amounts of the company's revenues and expenses for the budget period. *(p. 860)*

Budgeting Process of planning future business actions and expressing them as formal plans. *(p. 848)*

Business An organization of one or more individuals selling products and/or services for profit.

Business entity assumption Principle that requires a business to be accounted for separately from its owner(s) and from any other entity. *(p. 12)*

Business segment Part of a company that can be separately identified by the products or services that it provides or by the geographic markets that it serves; also called *segment*. *(p. 588)*

C corporation Corporation that does not qualify for nor elect to be treated as a proprietorship or partnership for income tax purposes and therefore is subject to income taxes; also called *C corp.* (p. 12)

Call price Amount that must be paid to call and retire a callable preferred stock or a callable bond. (p. 479)

Callable bonds Bonds that give the issuer the option to retire them at a stated amount prior to maturity. (p. 436)

Callable preferred stock Preferred stock that the issuing corporation, at its option, may retire by paying the call price plus any dividends in arrears. (p. 479)

Canceled checks Checks that the bank has paid and deducted from the depositor's account. (p. 272)

Capital budgeting Process of analyzing alternative investments and deciding which assets to acquire or sell. (p. 1016)

Capital expenditures Additional costs of plant assets that provide material benefits extending beyond the current period; also called *balance sheet expenditures.* (p. 346)

Capital expenditures budget Plan that lists dollar amounts to be both received from disposal of plant assets and spent to purchase plant assets. (p. 858)

Capital leases Long-term leases in which the lessor transfers substantially all risk and rewards of ownership to the lessee. (p. 446)

Capital stock General term referring to a corporation's stock used in obtaining capital (owner financing). (p. 469)

Capitalize Record the cost as part of a permanent account and allocate it over later periods.

Carrying (book) value of bonds Net amount at which bonds are reported on the balance sheet; equals the par value of the bonds less any unamortized discount or plus any unamortized premium; also called *carrying amount or book value.* (p. 426)

Cash Includes currency, coins, and amounts on deposit in bank checking or savings accounts. (p. 263)

Cash basis accounting Accounting system that recognizes revenues when cash is received and records expenses when cash is paid. (p. 99)

Cash budget Plan that shows expected cash inflows and outflows during the budget period, including receipts from loans needed to maintain a minimum cash balance and repayments of such loans. (p. 266)

Cash disbursements journal Special journal normally used to record all payments of cash; also called *cash payments journal.* (p. E-14)

Cash discount Reduction in the price of merchandise granted by a seller to a buyer when payment is made within the discount period. (p. 165)

Cash equivalents Short-term, investment assets that are readily convertible to a known cash amount or sufficiently close to their maturity date (usually within 90 days) so that market value is not sensitive to interest rate changes. (p. 264)

Cash flow on total assets Ratio of operating cash flows to average total assets; not sensitive to income recognition and measurement; partly reflects earnings quality. (p. 528)

Cash Over and Short Income statement account used to record cash overages and cash shortages arising from errors in cash receipts or payments. (p. 265)

Cash receipts journal Special journal normally used to record all receipts of cash. (p. E-11)

Change in an accounting estimate Change in an accounting estimate that results from new information, subsequent developments, or improved judgment that impacts current and future periods. (pp. 345 & 483)

Chart of accounts List of accounts used by a company; includes an identification number for each account. (p. 54)

Check Document signed by a depositor instructing the bank to pay a specified amount to a designated recipient. (p. 271)

Check register Another name for a cash disbursements journal when the journal has a column for check numbers. (pp. 282 & E-14)

Classified balance sheet Balance sheet that presents assets and liabilities in relevant subgroups, including current and noncurrent classifications. (p. 117)

Clock card Source document used to record the number of hours an employee works and to determine the total labor cost for each pay period. (p. 660)

Closing entries Entries recorded at the end of each accounting period to transfer end-of-period balances in revenue, gain, expense, loss, and withdrawal (dividend for a corporation) accounts to the capital account (to retained earnings for a corporation). (p. 112)

Closing process Necessary end-of-period steps to prepare the accounts for recording the transactions of the next period. (p. 112)

Columnar journal Journal with more than one column. (p. E-8)

Committee of Sponsoring Organizations (COSO) Committee of Sponsoring Organizations of the Treadway Commission (or COSO) is a joint initiative of five private sector organizations and is dedicated to providing thought leadership through the development of frameworks and guidance on enterprise risk management, internal control, and fraud deterrence. (p. 259)

Common stock Corporation's basic ownership share; also generically called *capital stock.* (pp. 13 & 468)

Common-size financial statement Statement that expresses each amount as a percent of a base amount. In the balance sheet, total assets is usually the base and is expressed as 100%. In the income statement, net sales is usually the base. (p. 571)

Comparative financial statement Statement with data for two or more successive periods placed in side-by-side columns, often with changes shown in dollar amounts and percents. (p. 566)

Compatibility principle Information system principle that prescribes an accounting system to conform with a company's activities, personnel, and structure. (p. E-3)

Complex capital structure Capital structure that includes outstanding rights or options to purchase common stock, or securities that are convertible into common stock. (p. 485)

Components of accounting systems Five basic components of accounting systems are source documents, input devices, information processors, information storage, and output devices. (p. E-3)

Composite unit Generic unit consisting of a specific number of units of each product; unit comprised in proportion to the expected sales mix of its products. (p. 793)

Compound journal entry Journal entry that affects at least three accounts. (p. 63)

Comprehensive income Net change in equity for a period, excluding owner investments and distributions. (p. C-10)

Computer hardware Physical equipment in a computerized accounting information system.

Computer network Linkage giving different users and different computers access to common databases and programs. *(p. E-16)*

Computer software Programs that direct operations of computer hardware.

Conceptual framework The basic concepts that underlie the preparation and presentation of financial statements for external users; can serve as a guide in developing future standards and to resolve accounting issues that are not addressed directly in current standards using the definitions, recognition criteria, and measurement concepts for assets, liabilities, revenues, and expenses. *(p. 10)*

Conservatism constraint Principle that prescribes the less optimistic estimate when two estimates are about equally likely. *(p. 220)*

Consignee Receiver of goods owned by another who holds them for purposes of selling them for the owner. *(p. 210)*

Consignor Owner of goods who ships them to another party who will sell them for the owner. *(p. 210)*

Consistency concept Principle that prescribes use of the same accounting method(s) over time so that financial statements are comparable across periods. *(p. 219)*

Consolidated financial statements Financial statements that show all (combined) activities under the parent's control, including those of any subsidiaries. *(p. C-9)*

Contingent liability Obligation to make a future payment if, and only if, an uncertain future event occurs. *(p. 390)*

Continuous budgeting Practice of preparing budgets for a selected number of future periods and revising those budgets as each period is completed. *(p. 851)*

Continuous improvement Concept requiring every manager and employee continually to look to improve operations. *(p. 626)*

Contra account Account linked with another account and having an opposite normal balance; reported as a subtraction from the other account's balance. *(p. 103)*

Contract rate Interest rate specified in a bond indenture (or note); multiplied by the par value to determine the interest paid each period; also called *coupon rate, stated rate,* or *nominal rate.* *(p. 425)*

Contributed capital Total amount of cash and other assets received from stockholders in exchange for stock; also called *paid-in capital.* *(p. 15)*

Contributed capital in excess of par value Difference between the par value of stock and its issue price when issued at a price above par.

Contribution format An income statement format that is geared to cost behavior in that costs are separated into variable and fixed categories rather than being separated according to the functions of production, sales, and administration. *(p. 826)*

Contribution margin Sales revenue less total variable costs. *(p. 785)*

Contribution margin income statement Income statement that separates variable and fixed costs; highlights the contribution margin, which is sales less variable expenses. *(p. 818)*

Contribution margin per unit Amount that the sale of one unit contributes toward recovering fixed costs and earning profit; defined as sales price per unit minus variable expense per unit. *(p. 785)*

Contribution margin ratio Product's contribution margin divided by its sale price. *(p. 785)*

Contribution margin report Product's contribution margin divided by its sale price. *(p. 819)*

Control Process of monitoring planning decisions and evaluating the organization's activities and employees. *(p. 611)*

Control principle Information system principle that prescribes an accounting system to aid managers in controlling and monitoring business activities. *(p. E-2)*

Controllable costs Costs that a manager has the power to control or at least strongly influence. *(pp. 615, 826 & 943)*

Controllable variance Combination of both overhead spending variances (variable and fixed) and the variable overhead efficiency variance. *(p. 909)*

Controlling account General ledger account, the balance of which (after posting) equals the sum of the balances in its related subsidiary ledger. *(p. E-7)*

Conversion costs Expenditures incurred in converting raw materials to finished goods; includes direct labor costs and overhead costs. *(p. 619)*

Conversion costs per equivalent unit The combined costs of direct labor and factory overhead per equivalent unit. *(p. 707)*

Convertible bonds Bonds that bondholders can exchange for a set number of the issuer's shares. *(p. 436)*

Convertible preferred stock Preferred stock with an option to exchange it for common stock at a specified rate. *(p. 478)*

Copyright Right giving the owner the exclusive privilege to publish and sell musical, literary, or artistic work during the creator's life plus 70 years. *(p. 352)*

Corporation Business that is a separate legal entity under state or federal laws with owners called *shareholders* or *stockholders.* *(pp. 12 & 466)*

Cost All normal and reasonable expenditures necessary to get an asset in place and ready for its intended use. *(pp. 337 & 339)*

Cost accounting system Accounting system for manufacturing activities based on the perpetual inventory system. *(p. 654)*

Cost-based transfer pricing A transfer pricing system based on the cost of goods or services being transferred across divisions within the same company. *(p. 962)*

Cost-benefit constraint The notion that the benefit of a disclosure exceeds the cost of that disclosure. *(p. 13)*

Cost-benefit principle Information system principle that prescribes the benefits from an activity in an accounting system to outweigh the costs of that activity. *(pp. 262 & E-3)*

Cost center Department that incurs costs but generates no revenues; common example is the accounting or legal department. *(p. 943)*

Cost object Product, process, department, or customer to which costs are assigned. *(pp. 615 & 739)*

Cost of capital Rate the company must pay to its long-term creditors and shareholders. *(p. 1020)*

Cost of goods available for sale Consists of beginning inventory plus net purchases of a period.

Cost of goods manufactured Total manufacturing costs (direct materials, direct labor, and factory overhead) for the period plus beginning goods in process less ending goods in process; also called *net cost of goods manufactured* and *cost of goods completed.* *(p. 705)*

Cost of goods sold Cost of inventory sold to customers during a period; also called *cost of sales.* *(p. 162)*

Costs of quality Costs resulting from manufacturing defective products or providing services that do not meet customer expectations. *(p. 750)*

Cost principle Accounting principle that prescribes financial statement information to be based on actual costs incurred in business transactions. *(p. 11)*

Cost variance Difference between the actual incurred cost and the standard cost. *(p. 903)*

Cost-volume-profit (CVP) analysis Planning method that includes predicting the volume of activity, the costs incurred, sales earned, and profits received. *(p. 778)*

Cost-volume-profit (CVP) chart Graphic representation of cost-volume-profit relations. *(p. 787)*

Coupon bonds Bonds with interest coupons attached to their certificates; bondholders detach coupons when they mature and present them to a bank or broker for collection. *(p. 436)*

Credit Recorded on the right side; an entry that decreases asset and expense accounts, and increases liability, revenue, and most equity accounts; abbreviated Cr. *(p. 57)*

Credit memorandum Notification that the sender has credited the recipient's account in the sender's records. *(p. 171)*

Credit period Time period that can pass before a customer's payment is due. *(p. 165)*

Credit terms Description of the amounts and timing of payments that a buyer (debtor) agrees to make in the future. *(p. 165)*

Creditors Individuals or organizations entitled to receive payments. *(p. 54)*

Cumulative preferred stock Preferred stock on which undeclared dividends accumulate until paid; common stockholders cannot receive dividends until cumulative dividends are paid. *(p. 477)*

Current assets Cash and other assets expected to be sold, collected, or used within one year or the company's operating cycle, whichever is longer. *(p. 118)*

Current liabilities Obligations due to be paid or settled within one year or the company's operating cycle, whichever is longer. *(pp. 119 & 379)*

Current portion of long-term debt Portion of long-term debt due within one year or the operating cycle, whichever is longer; reported under current liabilities. *(p. 387)*

Current ratio Ratio used to evaluate a company's ability to pay its short-term obligations, calculated by dividing current assets by current liabilities. *(p. 121)*

Curvilinear cost Cost that changes with volume but not at a constant rate. *(p. 781)*

Customer orientation Company position that its managers and employees be in tune with the changing wants and needs of consumers. *(p. 626)*

Cycle efficiency (CE) A measure of production efficiency, which is defined as value-added (process) time divided by total cycle time. *(p. 958)*

Cycle time (CT) A measure of the time to produce a product or service, which is the sum of process time, inspection time, move time, and wait time; also called *throughput time*. *(p. 957)*

Date of declaration Date the directors vote to pay a dividend. *(p. 473)*

Date of payment Date the corporation makes the dividend payment. *(p. 473)*

Date of record Date directors specify for identifying stockholders to receive dividends. *(p. 473)*

Days' sales in inventory Estimate of number of days needed to convert inventory into receivables or cash; equals ending inventory divided by cost of goods sold and then multiplied by 365; also called *days' stock on hand.* *(p. 223)*

Days' sales in raw materials inventory Measure of how much raw materials inventory is available in terms of the number of days' sales; defined as Ending raw materials inventory divided by Raw materials used and that quotient multiplied by 365 days. *(p. 628)*

Days' sales uncollected Measure of the liquidity of receivables computed by dividing the current balance of receivables by the annual credit (or net) sales and then multiplying by 365; also called *days' sales in receivables.* *(p. 277)*

Debit Recorded on the left side; an entry that increases asset and expense accounts, and decreases liability, revenue, and most equity accounts; abbreviated Dr. *(p. 57)*

Debit memorandum Notification that the sender has debited the recipient's account in the sender's records. *(p. 166)*

Debt ratio Ratio of total liabilities to total assets; used to reflect risk associated with a company's debts. *(p. 71)*

Debt-to-equity ratio Defined as total liabilities divided by total equity; shows the proportion of a company financed by non-owners (creditors) in comparison with that financed by owners. *(p. 437)*

Debtors Individuals or organizations that owe money. *(p. 51)*

Declining-balance method Method that determines depreciation charge for the period by multiplying a depreciation rate (often twice the straight-line rate) by the asset's beginning-period book value. *(p. 342)*

Deferred income tax liability Corporation income taxes that are deferred until future years because of temporary differences between GAAP and tax rules. *(p. 402)*

Degree of operating leverage (DOL) Ratio of contribution margin divided by pretax income; used to assess the effect on income of changes in sales. *(p. 795)*

Departmental accounting system Accounting system that provides information useful in evaluating the profitability or cost effectiveness of a department.

Departmental contribution to overhead Amount by which a department's revenues exceed its direct expenses. *(p. 951)*

Depletion Process of allocating the cost of natural resources to periods when they are consumed and sold. *(p. 350)*

Departmental income statements Income statements prepared for each operating department within a decentralized organization. *(p. 945)*

Deposit ticket Lists items such as currency, coins, and checks deposited and their corresponding dollar amounts. *(p. 271)*

Deposits in transit Deposits recorded by the company but not yet recorded by its bank. *(p. 274)*

Depreciable cost Cost of a plant asset less its salvage value. *(p. 340)*

Depreciation Expense created by allocating the cost of plant and equipment to periods in which they are used; represents the expense of using the asset. *(pp. 103 & 339)*

Diluted earnings per share Earnings per share calculation that requires dilutive securities be added to the denominator of the basic EPS calculation. *(p. 485)*

Dilutive securities Securities having the potential to increase common shares outstanding; examples are options, rights, convertible bonds, and convertible preferred stock. *(p. 485)*

Direct costs Costs incurred for the benefit of one specific cost object. *(p. 615)*

Direct expenses Expenses traced to a specific department (object) that are incurred for the sole benefit of that department. *(p. 945)*

Direct labor Efforts of employees who physically convert materials to finished product. *(p. 618)*

Direct labor costs Wages and salaries for direct labor that are separately and readily traced through the production process to finished goods. *(p. 618)*

Direct material Raw material that physically becomes part of the product and is clearly identified with specific products or batches of product. *(p. 618)*

Direct material costs Expenditures for direct material that are separately and readily traced through the production process to finished goods. *(p. 618)*

Direct method Presentation of net cash from operating activities for the statement of cash flows that lists major operating cash receipts less major operating cash payments. *(p. 516)*

Direct write-off method Method that records the loss from an uncollectible account receivable at the time it is determined to be uncollectible; no attempt is made to estimate bad debts. *(p. 306)*

Discount on bonds payable Difference between a bond's par value and its lower issue price or carrying value; occurs when the contract rate is less than the market rate. *(p. 425)*

Discount on note payable Difference between the face value of a note payable and the (lesser) amount borrowed; reflects the added interest to be paid on the note over its life.

Discount on stock Difference between the par value of stock and its issue price when issued at a price below par value. *(p. 471)*

Discount period Time period in which a cash discount is available and the buyer can make a reduced payment. *(p. 165)*

Discount rate Expected rate of return on investments; also called *cost of capital, hurdle rate,* or *required rate of return.* *(p. B-2)*

Discounts lost Expenses resulting from not taking advantage of cash discounts on purchases. *(p. 283)*

Dividend in arrears Unpaid dividend on cumulative preferred stock; must be paid before any regular dividends on preferred stock and before any dividends on common stock. *(p. 477)*

Dividend yield Ratio of the annual amount of cash dividends distributed to common shareholders relative to the common stock's market value (price). *(p. 486)*

Dividends Corporation's distributions of assets to its owners. *(p. 15)*

Dodd-Frank Wall Street Reform and Consumer Protection Act *(p. 14)*

Double-declining-balance (DDB) depreciation Depreciation equals beginning book value multiplied by 2 times the straight-line rate. *(p. 342)*

Double-entry accounting Accounting system in which each transaction affects at least two accounts and has at least one debit and one credit. *(p. 57)*

Double taxation Corporate income is taxed and then its later distribution through dividends is normally taxed again for shareholders. *(p. 13)*

Earnings (See *net income.*)

Earnings per share (EPS) Amount of income earned by each share of a company's outstanding common stock; also called *net income per share.* *(p. 485)*

Effective interest method Allocates interest expense over the bond life to yield a constant rate of interest; interest expense for a period is found

by multiplying the balance of the liability at the beginning of the period by the bond market rate at issuance; also called *interest method.* *(p. 442)*

Efficiency Company's productivity in using its assets; usually measured relative to how much revenue a certain level of assets generates. *(p. 565)*

Efficiency variance Difference between the actual quantity of an input and the standard quantity of that input. *(p. 916)*

Electronic funds transfer (EFT) Use of electronic communication to transfer cash from one party to another. *(p. 271)*

Employee benefits Additional compensation paid to or on behalf of employees, such as premiums for medical, dental, life, and disability insurance, and contributions to pension plans. *(p. 387)*

Employee earnings report Record of an employee's net pay, gross pay, deductions, and year-to-date payroll information. *(p. 398)*

Enterprise resource planning (ERP) software Programs that manage a company's vital operations, which range from order taking to production to accounting. *(p. E-17)*

Entity Organization that, for accounting purposes, is separate from other organizations and individuals.

EOM Abbreviation for *end of month;* used to describe credit terms for credit transactions. *(p. 165)*

Equity Owner's claim on the assets of a business; equals the residual interest in an entity's assets after deducting liabilities; also called *net assets.* *(p. 15)*

Equity method Accounting method used for long-term investments when the investor has "significant influence" over the investee. *(p. C-8)*

Equity ratio Portion of total assets provided by equity, computed as total equity divided by total assets. *(p. 579)*

Equity securities with controlling influence Long-term investment when the investor is able to exert controlling influence over the investee; investors owning 50% or more of voting stock are presumed to exert controlling influence. *(p. C-9)*

Equity securities with significant influence Long-term investment when the investor is able to exert significant influence over the investee; investors owning 20 percent or more (but less than 50 percent) of voting stock are presumed to exert significant influence. *(p. C-8)*

Equivalent units of production (EUP) Number of units that would be completed if all effort during a period had been applied to units that were started and finished. *(p. 699)*

Estimated liability Obligation of an uncertain amount that can be reasonably estimated. *(p. 387)*

Estimated line of cost behavior Line drawn on a graph to visually fit the relation between cost and sales. *(p. 782)*

Ethics Codes of conduct by which actions are judged as right or wrong, fair or unfair, honest or dishonest. *(pp. 7 & 614)*

Events Happenings that both affect an organization's financial position and can be reliably measured. *(p. 16)*

Expanded accounting equation Assets = Liabilities + Equity; Equity equals [Owner capital − Owner withdrawals + Revenues − Expenses] for a noncorporation; Equity equals [Contributed capital + Retained earnings + Revenues − Expenses] for a corporation where dividends are subtracted from retained earnings. *(p. 15)*

Expense recognition (or **matching**) **principle** (See *matching principle.*)

Expenses Outflows or using up of assets as part of operations of a business to generate sales. *(p. 15)*

External transactions Exchanges of economic value between one entity and another entity. *(p. 16)*

External users Persons using accounting information who are not directly involved in running the organization. *(p. 5)*

Extraordinary gains or losses Gains or losses reported separately from continuing operations because they are both unusual and infrequent. *(p. 588)*

Extraordinary repairs Major repairs that extend the useful life of a plant asset beyond prior expectations; treated as a capital expenditure. *(p. 347)*

Facility level activities Activities that relate to overall production and cannot be traced to specific products; cost associated with these activities pertain to a plant's general manufacturing process. *(p. 750)*

Factory overhead Factory activities supporting the production process that are not direct material or direct labor; also called *overhead* and *manufacturing overhead*. *(p. 618)*

Factory overhead costs Expenditures for factory overhead that cannot be separately or readily traced to finished goods; also called *overhead costs*. *(p. 618)*

Fair value option Fair Value Option (FVO) refers to an option to measure eligible items at fair value; eligible items include *financial assets*, such as HTM, AFS, and equity method investments, and *financial liabilities*. FVO is applied "instrument by instrument" and is elected when the eligible item is "first recognized"; once FVO is elected the decision is "irrevocable." When FVO is elected, it is measured at "fair value" and unrealized gains and losses are recognized in earnings. *(p. 435)*

Favorable variance Difference in actual revenues or expenses from the budgeted amount that contributes to a higher income. *(p. 897)*

Federal depository bank Bank authorized to accept deposits of amounts payable to the federal government. *(p. 395)*

Federal Insurance Contributions Act (FICA) Taxes Taxes assessed on both employers and employees; for Social Security and Medicare programs. *(p. 384)*

Federal Unemployment Taxes (FUTA) Payroll taxes on employers assessed by the federal government to support its unemployment insurance program. *(p. 386)*

FIFO method (See *first-in, first-out*.)

Financial accounting Area of accounting aimed mainly at serving external users. *(p. 5)*

Financial Accounting Standards Board (FASB) Independent group of full-time members responsible for setting accounting rules. *(p. 9)*

Financial leverage Earning a higher return on equity by paying dividends on preferred stock or interest on debt at a rate lower than the return earned with the assets from issuing preferred stock or debt; also called *trading on the equity*. *(p. 479)*

Financial reporting Process of communicating information relevant to investors, creditors, and others in making investment, credit, and business decisions. *(p. 565)*

Financial statement analysis Application of analytical tools to general-purpose financial statements and related data for making business decisions. *(p. 564)*

Financial statements Includes the balance sheet, income statement, statement of owner's (or stockholders') equity, and statement of cash flows. *(p. 5)*

Financing activities Transactions with owners and creditors that include obtaining cash from issuing debt, repaying amounts borrowed, and obtaining cash from or distributing cash to owners. *(p. 512)*

Finished goods inventory Account that controls the finished goods files, which acts as a subsidiary ledger (of the Inventory account) in which the costs of finished goods that are ready for sale are recorded. *(pp. 620 & 657)*

First-in, first-out (FIFO) Method to assign cost to inventory that assumes items are sold in the order acquired; earliest items purchased are the first sold. *(pp. 215 & 711)*

Fiscal year Consecutive 12-month (or 52-week) period chosen as the organization's annual accounting period. *(p. 99)*

Fixed budget Planning budget based on a single predicted amount of volume; unsuitable for evaluations if the actual volume differs from predicted volume. *(p. 897)*

Fixed budget performance report Report that compares actual revenues and costs with fixed budgeted amounts and identifies the differences as favorable or unfavorable variances. *(p. 897)*

Fixed cost Cost that does not change with changes in the volume of activity. *(p. 614)*

Fixed overhead cost deferred in inventory The portion of the fixed manufacturing overhead cost of a period that goes into inventory under the absorption costing method as a result of production exceeding sales. *(p. 823)*

Fixed overhead cost recognized from inventory The portion of the fixed manufacturing overhead cost of a prior period that becomes an expense of the current period under the absorption costing method as a result of sales exceeding production. *(p. 823)*

Flexibility principle Information system principle that prescribes an accounting system be able to adapt to changes in the company, its operations, and needs of decision makers. *(p. E-3)*

Flexible budget Budget prepared (using actual volume) once a period is complete that helps managers evaluate past performance; uses fixed and variable costs in determining total costs. *(p. 898)*

Flexible budget performance report Report that compares actual revenues and costs with their variable budgeted amounts based on actual sales volume (or other level of activity) and identifies the differences as variances. *(p. 900)*

FOB Abbreviation for *free on board*; the point when ownership of goods passes to the buyer; *FOB shipping point* (or *factory*) means the buyer pays shipping costs and accepts ownership of goods when the seller transfers goods to carrier; *FOB destination* means the seller pays shipping costs and buyer accepts ownership of goods at the buyer's place of business. *(p. 167)*

Foreign exchange rate Price of one currency stated in terms of another currency. *(p. C-16)*

Form 940 IRS form used to report an employer's federal unemployment taxes (FUTA) on an annual filing basis. *(p. 395)*

Form 941 IRS form filed to report FICA taxes owed and remitted. *(p. 395)*

Form 10-K (or 10-KSB) Annual report form filed with SEC by businesses (small businesses) with publicly traded securities. *(p. A-1)*

Form W-2 Annual report by an employer to each employee showing the employee's wages subject to FICA and federal income taxes along with amounts withheld. *(p. 397)*

Form W-4 Withholding allowance certificate, filed with the employer, identifying the number of withholding allowances claimed. *(p. 400)*

Franchises Privileges granted by a company or government to sell a product or service under specified conditions. *(p. 353)*

Full disclosure principle Principle that prescribes financial statements (including notes) to report all relevant information about an entity's operations and financial condition. *(p. 11)*

GAAP (See *generally accepted accounting principles.*)

General accounting system Accounting system for manufacturing activities based on the *periodic* inventory system. *(p. 654)*

General and administrative expenses Expenses that support the operating activities of a business. *(p. 175)*

General and administrative expense budget Plan that shows predicted operating expenses not included in the selling expenses budget. *(p. 857)*

General journal All-purpose journal for recording the debits and credits of transactions and events. *(pp. 58 & E-6)*

General ledger (See *ledger.*) *(p. 53)*

General partner Partner who assumes unlimited liability for the debts of the partnership; responsible for partnership management.

General partnership Partnership in which all partners have mutual agency and unlimited liability for partnership debts.

Generally accepted accounting principles (GAAP) Rules that specify acceptable accounting practices. *(p. 9)*

Generally accepted auditing standards (GAAS) Rules that specify acceptable auditing practices.

General-purpose financial statements Statements published periodically for use by a variety of interested parties; includes the income statement, balance sheet, statement of owner's equity (or statement of retained earnings for a corporation), statement of cash flows, and notes to these statements. *(p. 565)*

Going-concern assumption Principle that prescribes financial statements to reflect the assumption that the business will continue operating. *(p. 12)*

Goods in process inventory Account in which costs are accumulated for products that are in the process of being produced but are not yet complete; also called *work in process inventory.* *(pp. 620 & 656)*

Goodwill Amount by which a company's (or a segment's) value exceeds the value of its individual assets less its liabilities. *(p. 353)*

Gross margin (See *gross profit.*)

Gross margin ratio Gross margin (net sales minus cost of goods sold) divided by net sales; also called *gross profit ratio.* *(p. 178)*

Gross method Method of recording purchases at the full invoice price without deducting any cash discounts. *(p. 283)*

Gross pay Total compensation earned by an employee. *(p. 383)*

Gross profit Net sales minus cost of goods sold; also called *gross margin.* *(pp. 162 & 163)*

Gross profit method Procedure to estimate inventory by using the past gross profit rate to estimate cost of goods sold, which is then subtracted from the cost of goods available for sale. *(p. 235)*

Held-to-maturity (HTM) securities Debt securities that a company has the intent and ability to hold until they mature. *(p. C-6)*

High-low method Procedure that yields an estimated line of cost behavior by graphically connecting costs associated with the highest and lowest sales volume. *(p. 782)*

Horizontal analysis Comparison of a company's financial condition and performance across time. *(p. 566)*

Hurdle rate Minimum acceptable rate of return (set by management) for an investment. *(pp. 953 & 1024)*

Impairment Diminishment of an asset value. *(pp. 346 & 352)*

Imprest system Method to account for petty cash; maintains a constant balance in the fund, which equals cash plus petty cash receipts. *(p. 268)*

Inadequacy Condition in which the capacity of plant assets is too small to meet the company's production demands. *(p. 339)*

Income (See *net income.*) *(p. 15)*

Income statement Financial statement that subtracts expenses from revenues to yield a net income or loss over a specified period of time; also includes any gains or losses. *(p. 20)*

Income summary Temporary account used only in the closing process to which the balances of revenue and expense accounts (including any gains or losses) are transferred; its balance is transferred to the capital account (or retained earnings for a corporation). *(p. 113)*

Incremental cost Additional cost incurred only if a company pursues a specific course of action. *(p. 988)*

Indefinite life Asset life that is not limited by legal, regulatory, contractual, competitive, economic, or other factors. *(p. 351)*

Indirect costs Costs incurred for the benefit of more than one cost object. *(p. 615)*

Indirect expenses Expenses incurred for the joint benefit of more than one department (or cost object). *(p. 945)*

Indirect labor Efforts of production employees who do not work specifically on converting direct materials into finished products and who are not clearly identified with specific units or batches of product. *(p. 618)*

Indirect labor costs Labor costs that cannot be physically traced to production of a product or service; included as part of overhead. *(p. 618)*

Indirect material Material used to support the production process but not clearly identified with products or batches of product. *(p. 620)*

Indirect method Presentation that reports net income and then adjusts it by adding and subtracting items to yield net cash from operating activities on the statement of cash flows. *(p. 516)*

Information processor Component of an accounting system that interprets, transforms, and summarizes information for use in analysis and reporting. *(p. E-4)*

Information storage Component of an accounting system that keeps data in a form accessible to information processors.

Infrequent gain or loss Gain or loss not expected to recur given the operating environment of the business. *(p. 588)*

Input device Means of capturing information from source documents that enables its transfer to information processors. *(p. E-4)*

Installment note Liability requiring a series of periodic payments to the lender. *(p. 433)*

Institute of Management Accountants (IMA) A professional association of management accountants. *(p. 614)*

Intangible assets Long-term assets (resources) used to produce or sell products or services; usually lack physical form and have uncertain benefits. *(pp. 119 & 351)*

Interest Charge for using money (or other assets) loaned from one entity to another. *(p. 312)*

Interim financial statements Financial statements covering periods of less than one year; usually based on one-, three-, or six-month periods. *(pp. 98 & 234)*

Interim statements (See *interim financial statements.*)

Internal controls or **Internal control system** All policies and procedures used to protect assets, ensure reliable accounting, promote efficient operations, and urge adherence to company policies. *(pp. 258, 614 & E-2)*

Internal rate of return (IRR) Rate used to evaluate the acceptability of an investment; equals the rate that yields a net present value of zero for an investment. *(p. 1023)*

Internal transactions Activities within an organization that can affect the accounting equation. *(p. 16)*

Internal users Persons using accounting information who are directly involved in managing the organization. *(p. 6)*

International Accounting Standards Board (IASB) Group that identifies preferred accounting practices and encourages global acceptance; issues International Financial Reporting Standards (IFRS). *(p. 9)*

International Financial Reporting Standards (IFRS) Set of international accounting standards explaining how types of transactions and events are reported in financial statements; IFRS are issued by the International Accounting Standards Board *(p. 9)*

Inventory Goods a company owns and expects to sell in its normal operations. *(p. 163)*

Inventory turnover Number of times a company's average inventory is sold during a period; computed by dividing cost of goods sold by average inventory; also called *merchandise turnover.* *(p. 223)*

Investing activities Transactions that involve purchasing and selling of long-term assets, includes making and collecting notes receivable and investments in other than cash equivalents. *(p. 512)*

Investment center Center of which a manager is responsible for revenues, costs, and asset investments. *(p. 943)*

Investment center residual income The net income an investment center earns above a target return on average invested assets. *(p. 953)*

Investment center return on total assets Center net income divided by average total assets for the center. *(p. 953)*

Investment turnover The efficiency with which a company generates sales from its available assets; computed as sales divided by average invested assets. *(p. 954)*

Invoice Itemized record of goods prepared by the vendor that lists the customer's name, items sold, sales prices, and terms of sale. *(p. 281)*

Invoice approval Document containing a checklist of steps necessary for approving the recording and payment of an invoice; also called *check authorization.* *(p. 281)*

Job Production of a customized product or service. *(p. 654)*

Job cost sheet Separate record maintained for each job. *(p. 656)*

Job lot Production of more than one unit of a customized product or service. *(p. 654)*

Job order cost accounting system Cost accounting system to determine the cost of producing each job or job lot. *(pp. 656 & 695)*

Job order production Production of special-order products; also called *customized production.* *(p. 654)*

Joint cost Cost incurred to produce or purchase two or more products at the same time. *(p. 962)*

Journal Record in which transactions are entered before they are posted to ledger accounts; also called *book of original entry.* *(p. 58)*

Journalizing Process of recording transactions in a journal. *(p. 58)*

Just-in-time (JIT) manufacturing Process of acquiring or producing inventory only when needed. *(p. 626)*

Known liabilities Obligations of a company with little uncertainty; set by agreements, contracts, or laws; also called *definitely determinable liabilities.* *(p. 380)*

Land improvements Assets that increase the benefits of land, have a limited useful life, and are depreciated. *(p. 338)*

Large stock dividend Stock dividend that is more than 25% of the previously outstanding shares. *(p. 474)*

Last-in, first-out (LIFO) Method for assigning cost to inventory that assumes costs for the most recent items purchased are sold first and charged to cost of goods sold. *(p. 215)*

Lean accounting System designed to eliminate waste in the accounting process and better reflect the benefits of lean manufacturing techniques. *(p. 752)*

Lean business model Practice of eliminating waste while meeting customer needs and yielding positive company returns. *(p. 626)*

Lease Contract specifying the rental of property. *(pp. 353 & 446)*

Leasehold Rights the lessor grants to the lessee under the terms of a lease. *(p. 353)*

Leasehold improvements Alterations or improvements to leased property such as partitions and storefronts. *(p. 354)*

Least-squares regression Statistical method for deriving an estimated line of cost behavior that is more precise than the high-low method and the scatter diagram. *(p. 783)*

Ledger Record containing all accounts (with amounts) for a business; also called *general ledger.* *(p. 51)*

Lessee Party to a lease who secures the right to possess and use the property from another party (the lessor). *(p. 353)*

Lessor Party to a lease who grants another party (the lessee) the right to possess and use its property. *(p. 353)*

Liabilities Creditors' claims on an organization's assets; involves a probable future payment of assets, products, or services that a company is obligated to make due to past transactions or events. *(p. 15)*

Licenses (See *franchises.*)

Limited liability Owner can lose no more than the amount invested. *(p. 12)*

Limited liability company Organization form that combines select features of a corporation and a limited partnership; provides limited liability to its members (owners), is free of business tax, and allows members to actively participate in management. *(p. D-4)*

Limited liability partnership Partnership in which a partner is not personally liable for malpractice or negligence unless that partner is responsible for providing the service that resulted in the claim. *(p. D-3)*

Limited life (See *useful life.*)

Limited partners Partners who have no personal liability for partnership debts beyond the amounts they invested in the partnership. *(p. 483)*

Limited partnership Partnership that has two classes of partners, limited partners and general partners. *(p. D-3)*

Liquid assets Resources such as cash that are easily converted into other assets or used to pay for goods, services, or liabilities. *(p. 263)*

Liquidating cash dividend Distribution of assets that returns part of the original investment to stockholders; deducted from contributed capital accounts. *(p. 474)*

Liquidation Process of going out of business; involves selling assets, paying liabilities, and distributing remainder to owners.

Liquidity Availability of resources to meet short-term cash requirements. *(pp. 263 & 565)*

List price Catalog (full) price of an item before any trade discount is deducted. *(p. 164)*

Long-term investments Long-term assets not used in operating activities such as notes receivable and investments in stocks and bonds. *(pp. 119, 379 & C-2)*

Long-term liabilities Obligations not due to be paid within one year or the operating cycle, whichever is longer. *(p. 119)*

Lower of cost or market (LCM) Required method to report inventory at market replacement cost when that market cost is lower than recorded cost. *(p. 219)*

Maker of the note Entity who signs a note and promises to pay it at maturity. *(p. 312)*

Management by exception Management process to focus on significant variances and give less attention to areas where performance is close to the standard. *(p. 901)*

Managerial accounting Area of accounting aimed mainly at serving the decision-making needs of internal users; also called *management accounting*. *(pp. 6 & 610)*

Manufacturer Company that uses labor and operating assets to convert raw materials to finished goods. *(p. 16)*

Manufacturing budget Plan that shows the predicted costs for direct materials, direct labor, and overhead to be incurred in manufacturing units in the production budget. *(p. 868)*

Manufacturing statement Report that summarizes the types and amounts of costs incurred in a company's production process for a period; also called *cost of goods manufacturing statement*. *(p. 623)*

Marginal costing *(p. 816)*

Margin of safety Excess of expected sales over the level of break-even sales. *(p. 786)*

Market-based transfer price A transfer pricing system based on the market price of the goods or services being transferred across divisions within the same company. *(p. 962)*

Market prospects Expectations (both good and bad) about a company's future performance as assessed by users and other interested parties. *(p. 565)*

Market rate Interest rate that borrowers are willing to pay and lenders are willing to accept for a specific lending agreement given the borrowers' risk level. *(p. 425)*

Market value per share Price at which stock is bought or sold. *(p. 469)*

Master budget Comprehensive business plan that includes specific plans for expected sales, product units to be produced, merchandise (or materials) to be purchased, expenses to be incurred, plant assets to be purchased, and amounts of cash to be borrowed or loans to be repaid, as well as a budgeted income statement and balance sheet. *(p. 852)*

Matching (or **expense recognition**) **principle** Prescribes expenses to be reported in the same period as the revenues that were earned as a result of the expenses. *(pp. 11, 100 & 306)*

Materiality constraint Prescribes that accounting for items that significantly impact financial statement and any inferences from them adhere strictly to GAAP. *(pp. 13 & 306)*

Materials consumption report Document that summarizes the materials a department uses during a reporting period; replaces materials requisitions. *(p. 696)*

Materials ledger card Perpetual record updated each time units are purchased or issued for production use. *(p. 658)*

Materials requisition Source document production managers use to request materials for production; used to assign materials costs to specific jobs or overhead. *(p. 659)*

Maturity date of a note Date when a note's principal and interest are due. *(p. 312)*

Measurement principle Principle that prescribes financial statement information, and its underlying transactions and events, be based on relevant measures of valuation; also called the *cost principle*. *(p. 11)*

Merchandise (See *merchandise inventory*.) *(p. 162)*

Merchandise inventory Goods that a company owns and expects to sell to customers; also called *merchandise* or *inventory*. *(p. 163)*

Merchandise purchases budget Plan that shows the units or costs of merchandise to be purchased by a merchandising company during the budget period. *(p. 855)*

Merchandiser Entity that earns net income by buying and selling merchandise. *(p. 162)*

Merit rating Rating assigned to an employer by a state based on the employer's record of employment. *(p. 386)*

Minimum legal capital Amount of assets defined by law that stockholders must (potentially) invest in a corporation; usually defined as par value of the stock; intended to protect creditors. *(p. 469)*

Mixed cost Cost that behaves like a combination of fixed and variable costs. *(p. 780)*

Modified Accelerated Cost Recovery System (MACRS) Depreciation system required by federal income tax law. *(p. 344)*

Monetary unit assumption Principle that assumes transactions and events can be expressed in money units. *(p. 12)*

Mortgage Legal loan agreement that protects a lender by giving the lender the right to be paid from the cash proceeds from the sale of a borrower's assets identified in the mortgage. *(p. 434)*

Multinational Company that operates in several countries. *(p. C-16)*

Multiple-step income statement Income statement format that shows subtotals between sales and net income, categorizes expenses, and often reports the details of net sales and expenses. *(p. 175)*

Mutual agency Legal relationship among partners whereby each partner is an agent of the partnership and is able to bind the partnership to contracts within the scope of the partnership's business. *(p. 466)*

Natural business year Twelve-month period that ends when a company's sales activities are at their lowest point. *(p. 99)*

Natural resources Assets physically consumed when used; examples are timber, mineral deposits, and oil and gas fields; also called *wasting assets*. *(p. 350)*

Negotiated transfer price A system where division managers negotiate to determine the price to use to record transfers of goods or services across divisions within the same company. *(p. 962)*

Net assets (See *equity*.)

Net income Amount earned after subtracting all expenses necessary for and matched with sales for a period; also called *income, profit*, or *earnings*. *(p. 15)*

Net loss Excess of expenses over revenues for a period. *(p. 15)*

Net method Method of recording purchases at the full invoice price less any cash discounts. *(p. 283)*

Net pay Gross pay less all deductions; also called *take-home pay*. *(p. 384)*

Net present value (NPV) Dollar estimate of an asset's value that is used to evaluate the acceptability of an investment; computed by discounting future cash flows from the investment at a satisfactory rate and then subtracting the initial cost of the investment. *(p. 1020)*

Net realizable value Expected selling price (value) of an item minus the cost of making the sale. *(p. 210)*

Noncumulative preferred stock Preferred stock on which the right to receive dividends is lost for any period when dividends are not declared. *(p. 477)*

Noninterest-bearing note Note with no stated (contract) rate of interest; interest is implicitly included in the note's face value.

Nonparticipating preferred stock Preferred stock on which dividends are limited to a maximum amount each year. *(p. 478)*

No-par value stock Stock class that has not been assigned a par (or stated) value by the corporate charter. *(p. 469)*

Nonsufficient funds (NSF) check Maker's bank account has insufficient money to pay the check; also called *hot check*. *(p. 274)*

Non-value-added time The portion of cycle time that is not directed at producing a product or service; equals the sum of inspection time, move time, and wait time. *(p. 958)*

Not controllable costs Costs that a manager does not have the power to control or strongly influence. *(p. 615)*

Note (See *promissory note*.)

Note payable Liability expressed by a written promise to pay a definite sum of money on demand or on a specific future date(s). *(p. 52)*

Note receivable Asset consisting of a written promise to receive a definite sum of money on demand or on a specific future date(s). *(p. 51)*

Objectivity Concept that prescribes independent, unbiased evidence to support financial statement information. *(p. 11)*

Obsolescence Condition in which, because of new inventions and improvements, a plant asset can no longer be used to produce goods or services with a competitive advantage. *(p. 339)*

Off-balance-sheet financing Acquisition of assets by agreeing to liabilities not reported on the balance sheet. *(p. 447)*

Online processing Approach to inputting data from source documents as soon as the information is available. *(p. E-16)*

Operating activities Activities that involve the production or purchase of merchandise and the sale of goods or services to customers, including expenditures related to administering the business. *(p. 511)*

Operating cycle Normal time between paying cash for merchandise or employee services and receiving cash from customers. *(p. 117)*

Operating leases Short-term (or cancelable) leases in which the lessor retains risks and rewards of ownership. *(p. 446)*

Operating leverage Extent, or relative size, of fixed costs in the total cost structure. *(p. 795)*

Opportunity cost Potential benefit lost by choosing a specific action from two or more alternatives. *(p. 616)*

Ordinary repairs Repairs to keep a plant asset in normal, good operating condition; treated as a revenue expenditure and immediately expensed. *(p. 347)*

Organization expenses (costs) Costs such as legal fees and promoter fees to bring an entity into existence. *(p. 467)*

Other comprehensive income (See *comprehensive income.*)

Out-of-pocket cost Cost incurred or avoided as a result of management's decisions. *(p. 616)*

Output devices Means by which information is taken out of the accounting system and made available for use. *(p. E-5)*

Outsourcing Manager decision to buy a product or service from another entity; part of a *make-or-buy* decision; also called *make or buy.*

Outstanding checks Checks written and recorded by the depositor but not yet paid by the bank at the bank statement date. *(p. 274)*

Outstanding stock Corporation's stock held by its shareholders. *(p. 469)*

Overapplied overhead Amount by which the overhead applied to production in a period using the predetermined overhead rate exceeds the actual overhead incurred in a period. *(p. 665)*

Overhead cost variance Difference between the total overhead cost applied to products and the total overhead cost actually incurred. *(p. 908)*

Owner, Capital Account showing the owner's claim on company assets; equals owner investments plus net income (or less net losses) minus owner withdrawals since the company's inception; also referred to as *equity*. *(p. 15)*

Owner investment Assets put into the business by the owner. *(p. 15)*

Owner's equity (See *equity*.)

Owner, Withdrawals Account used to record asset distributions to the owner. (See also *withdrawals*.) *(p. 15)*

Paid-in capital (See *contributed capital*.)

Paid-in capital in excess of par value Amount received from issuance of stock that is in excess of the stock's par value. *(p. 471)*

Par value Value assigned a share of stock by the corporate charter when the stock is authorized. *(p. 469)*

Par value of a bond Amount the bond issuer agrees to pay at maturity and the amount on which cash interest payments are based; also called *face amount* or *face value* of a bond. *(p. 422)*

Par value stock Class of stock assigned a par value by the corporate charter. *(p. 469)*

Parent Company that owns a controlling interest in a corporation (requires more than 50% of voting stock). *(p. C-9)*

Participating preferred stock Preferred stock that shares with common stockholders any dividends paid in excess of the percent stated on preferred stock. *(p. 478)*

Partner return on equity Partner net income divided by average partner equity for the period. *(p. D-4)*

Partnership Unincorporated association of two or more persons to pursue a business for profit as co-owners. *(pp. 12 & D-2)*

Partnership contract Agreement among partners that sets terms under which the affairs of the partnership are conducted; also called *articles of partnership.*

Partnership liquidation Dissolution of a partnership by (1) selling noncash assets and allocating any gain or loss according to partners' income-and-loss ratio, (2) paying liabilities, and (3) distributing any remaining cash according to partners' capital balances. *(p. D-11)*

Patent Exclusive right granted to its owner to produce and sell an item or to use a process for 17 years. *(p. 352)*

Payback period (PBP) Time-based measurement used to evaluate the acceptability of an investment; equals the time expected to pass before an investment's net cash flows equal its initial cost. *(p. 1016)*

Payee of the note Entity to whom a note is made payable. *(p. 312)*

Payroll bank account Bank account used solely for paying employees; each pay period an amount equal to the total employees' net pay is deposited in it and the payroll checks are drawn on it. *(p. 400)*

Payroll deductions Amounts withheld from an employee's gross pay; also called *withholdings*. *(p. 384)*

Payroll register Record for a pay period that shows the pay period dates, regular and overtime hours worked, gross pay, net pay, and deductions. *(p. 397)*

Pension plan Contractual agreement between an employer and its employees for the employer to provide benefits to employees after they retire; expensed when incurred. *(p. 448)*

Period costs Expenditures identified more with a time period than with finished products costs; includes selling and general administrative expenses. *(p. 616)*

Periodic inventory system Method that records the cost of inventory purchased but does not continuously track the quantity available or sold to customers; records are updated at the end of each period to reflect the physical count and costs of goods available. *(p. 164)*

Permanent accounts Accounts that reflect activities related to one or more future periods; balance sheet accounts whose balances are not closed; also called *real accounts*. *(p. 112)*

Perpetual inventory system Method that maintains continuous records of the cost of inventory available and the cost of goods sold. *(p. 164)*

Petty cash Small amount of cash in a fund to pay minor expenses; accounted for using an imprest system. *(p. 268)*

Planning Process of setting goals and preparing to achieve them. *(p. 610)*

Plant asset age Plant asset age is an approximation of the age of plant assets, which is estimated by dividing accumulated depreciation by depreciation expense. *(p. 355)*

Plant assets Tangible long-lived assets used to produce or sell products and services; also called *property, plant and equipment (PP&E)* or *fixed assets*. *(pp. 103 & 336)*

Pledged assets to secured liabilities Ratio of the book value of a company's pledged assets to the book value of its secured liabilities. *(p. 703)*

Post-closing trial balance List of permanent accounts and their balances from the ledger after all closing entries are journalized and posted. *(p. 114)*

Posting Process of transferring journal entry information to the ledger; computerized systems automate this process. *(p. 58)*

Posting reference (PR) column A column in journals in which individual ledger account numbers are entered when entries are posted to those ledger accounts. *(p. 60)*

Predetermined overhead rate Rate established prior to the beginning of a period that relates estimated overhead to another variable, such as estimated direct labor, and is used to assign overhead cost to production. *(p. 662)*

Preemptive right Stockholders' right to maintain their proportionate interest in a corporation with any additional shares issued. *(p. 468)*

Preferred stock Stock with a priority status over common stockholders in one or more ways, such as paying dividends or distributing assets. *(p. 476)*

Premium on bonds Difference between a bond's par value and its higher carrying value; occurs when the contract rate is higher than the market rate; also called *bond premium*. *(p. 428)*

Premium on stock (See *contributed capital in excess of par value*.) *(p. 471)*

Prepaid expenses Items paid for in advance of receiving their benefits; classified as assets. *(p. 101)*

Price-earnings (PE) ratio Ratio of a company's current market value per share to its earnings per share; also called *price-to-earnings*. *(p. 485)*

Price variance Difference between actual and budgeted revenue or cost caused by the difference between the actual price per unit and the budgeted price per unit. *(p. 901)*

Prime costs Expenditures directly identified with the production of finished goods; include direct materials costs and direct labor costs. *(p. 619)*

Principal of a note Amount that the signer of a note agrees to pay back when it matures, not including interest. *(p. 312)*

Principles of internal control Principles prescribing management to establish responsibility, maintain records, insure assets, separate record-keeping from custody of assets, divide responsibility for related transactions, apply technological controls, and perform reviews. *(p. 259)*

Prior period adjustment Correction of an error in a prior year that is reported in the statement of retained earnings (or statement of stockholders' equity) net of any income tax effects. *(p. 483)*

Pro forma financial statements Statements that show the effects of proposed transactions and events as if they had occurred. *(p. 128)*

Process cost accounting system System of assigning direct materials, direct labor, and overhead to specific processes; total costs associated with each process are then divided by the number of units passing through that process to determine the cost per equivalent unit. *(p. 695)*

Process cost summary Report of costs charged to a department, its equivalent units of production achieved, and the costs assigned to its output. *(p. 704)*

Process operations Processing of products in a continuous (sequential) flow of steps; also called *process manufacturing* or *process production*. *(p. 692)*

Product costs Costs that are capitalized as inventory because they produce benefits expected to have future value; include direct materials, direct labor, and overhead. *(p. 616)*

Product level activities Activities that relate to specific products that must be carried out regardless of how many units are produced and sold or batches run. *(p. 750)*

Production budget Plan that shows the units to be produced each period. *(p. 868)*

Profit (See *net income*.)

Profit center Business unit that incurs costs and generates revenues. *(p. 943)*

Profit margin Ratio of a company's net income to its net sales; the percent of income in each dollar of revenue; also called *net profit margin*. *(pp. 121 & 954)*

Profitability Company's ability to generate an adequate return on invested capital. *(p. 565)*

Profitability index A measure of the relation between the expected benefits of a project and its investment, computed as the present value of expected future cash flows from the investment divided by the cost of the investment; a higher value indicates a more desirable investment, and a value below 1 indicates an unacceptable project. *(p. 1023)*

Promissory note (or **note**) Written promise to pay a specified amount either on demand or at a definite future date; is a *note receivable* for the lender but a *note payable* for the lendee. *(p. 312)*

Proprietorship (See *sole proprietorship.*)

Proxy Legal document giving a stockholder's agent the power to exercise the stockholder's voting rights. *(p. 467)*

Purchase discount Term used by a purchaser to describe a cash discount granted to the purchaser for paying within the discount period. *(p. 165)*

Purchase order Document used by the purchasing department to place an order with a seller (vendor). *(p. 280)*

Purchase requisition Document listing merchandise needed by a department and requesting it be purchased. *(p. 280)*

Purchases journal Journal normally used to record all purchases on credit. *(p. E-13)*

Quantity variance Difference between actual and budgeted revenue or cost caused by the difference between the actual number of units and the budgeted number of units. *(p. 901)*

Ratio analysis Determination of key relations between financial statement items as reflected in numerical measures. *(p. 566)*

Raw materials inventory Goods a company acquires to use in making products. *(p. 620)*

Raw materials inventory turnover ratio Measure of how many times a company turns over (uses in production) its raw materials inventory during a period; defined as Raw materials used divided by Average raw materials inventory. *(p. 628)*

Realizable value Expected proceeds from converting an asset into cash. *(p. 307)*

Receiving report Form used to report that ordered goods are received and to describe their quantity and condition. *(p. 281)*

Recordkeeping Part of accounting that involves recording transactions and events, either manually or electronically; also called *bookkeeping. (p. 4)*

Registered bonds Bonds owned by investors whose names and addresses are recorded by the issuer; interest payments are made to the registered owners. *(p. 436)*

Relevance principle Information system principle prescribing that its reports be useful, understandable, timely, and pertinent for decision making. *(p. E-2)*

Relevant benefits Additional or incremental revenue generated by selecting a particular course of action over another. *(p. 987)*

Relevant range of operations Company's normal operating range; excludes extremely high and low volumes not likely to occur. *(p. 788)*

Report form balance sheet Balance sheet that lists accounts vertically in the order of assets, liabilities, and equity. *(p. 22)*

Responsibility accounting budget Report of expected costs and expenses under a manager's control. *(p. 944)*

Responsibility accounting performance report Responsibility report that compares actual costs and expenses for a department with budgeted amounts. *(p. 944)*

Responsibility accounting system System that provides information that management can use to evaluate the performance of a department's manager. *(p. 942)*

Restricted retained earnings Retained earnings not available for dividends because of legal or contractual limitations. *(p. 482)*

Retail inventory method Method for estimating ending inventory based on the ratio of the amount of goods for sale at cost to the amount of goods for sale at retail. *(p. 234)*

Retailer Intermediary that buys products from manufacturers or wholesalers and sells them to consumers. *(p. 162)*

Retained earnings Cumulative income less cumulative losses and dividends. *(pp. 15 & 470)*

Retained earnings deficit Debit (abnormal) balance in Retained Earnings; occurs when cumulative losses and dividends exceed cumulative income; also called *accumulated deficit. (p. 473)*

Return Monies received from an investment; often in percent form. *(p. 27)*

Return on assets (See *return on total assets.*)

Return on equity Ratio of net income to average equity for the period.

Return on total assets Ratio reflecting operating efficiency; defined as net income divided by average total assets for the period; also called *return on assets* or *return on investment. (pp. 24 & C-11)*

Revenue expenditures Expenditures reported on the current income statement as an expense because they do not provide benefits in future periods. *(p. 346)*

Revenue recognition principle The principle prescribing that revenue is recognized when earned. *(p. 11)*

Revenues Gross increase in equity from a company's business activities that earn income; also called *sales. (p. 15)*

Reverse stock split Occurs when a corporation calls in its stock and replaces each share with less than one new share; increases both market value per share and any par or stated value per share. *(p. 476)*

Reversing entries Optional entries recorded at the beginning of a period that prepare the accounts for the usual journal entries as if adjusting entries had not occurred in the prior period. *(p. 129)*

Risk Uncertainty about an expected return. *(p. 27)*

Rolling budget New set of budgets a firm adds for the next period (with revisions) to replace the ones that have lapsed. *(p. 851)*

S corporation Corporation that meets special tax qualifications so as to be treated like a partnership for income tax purposes. *(p. D-3)*

Safety stock Quantity of inventory or materials over the minimum needed to satisfy budgeted demand. *(p. 855)*

Sales (See *revenues.*)

Sales budget Plan showing the units of goods to be sold or services to be provided; the starting point in the budgeting process for most departments. *(p. 854)*

Sales discount Term used by a seller to describe a cash discount granted to buyers who pay within the discount period. *(p. 165)*

Sales journal Journal normally used to record sales of goods on credit.

Sales mix Ratio of sales volumes for the various products sold by a company. *(p. 793)*

Salvage value Estimate of amount to be recovered at the end of an asset's useful life; also called *residual value* or *scrap value*. *(p. 339)*

Sarbanes-Oxley Act (SOX) Created the *Public Company Accounting Oversight Board,* regulates analyst conflicts, imposes corporate governance requirements, enhances accounting and control disclosures, impacts insider transactions and executive loans, establishes new types of criminal conduct, and expands penalties for violations of federal securities laws. *(pp. 13 & 258)*

Scatter diagram Graph used to display data about past cost behavior and sales as points on a diagram. *(p. 782)*

Schedule of accounts payable List of the balances of all accounts in the accounts payable ledger and their totals. *(p. E-14)*

Schedule of accounts receivable List of the balances of all accounts in the accounts receivable ledger and their totals. *(p. E-9)*

Section 404 (of SOX) Section 404 of SOX requires management and the external auditor to report on the adequacy of the company's internal control on financial reporting, which is the most costly aspect of SOX for companies to implement as documenting and testing important financial manual and automated controls require enormous efforts. Section 404 also requires management to produce an "internal control report" as part of each annual SEC report that affirms "the responsibility of management for establishing and maintaining an adequate internal control structure and procedures for financial reporting." *(p. 259)*

Secured bonds Bonds that have specific assets of the issuer pledged as collateral. *(p. 436)*

Securities and Exchange Commission (SEC) Federal agency Congress has charged to set reporting rules for organizations that sell ownership shares to the public. *(p. 9)*

Segment return on assets Segment operating income divided by segment average (identifiable) assets for the period.

Selling expense budget Plan that lists the types and amounts of selling expenses expected in the budget period. *(p. 856)*

Selling expenses Expenses of promoting sales, such as displaying and advertising merchandise, making sales, and delivering goods to customers. *(p. 175)*

Serial bonds Bonds consisting of separate amounts that mature at different dates. *(p. 436)*

Service company Organization that provides services instead of tangible products.

Shareholders Owners of a corporation; also called *stockholders*. *(p. 13)*

Shares Equity of a corporation divided into ownership units; also called *stock*. *(p. 13)*

Short-term investments Debt and equity securities that management expects to convert to cash within the next 3 to 12 months (or the operating cycle if longer); also called *temporary investments* or *marketable securities*. *(p. C-2)*

Short-term note payable Current obligation in the form of a written promissory note. *(p. 381)*

Shrinkage Inventory losses that occur as a result of theft or deterioration. *(p. 172)*

Signature card Includes the signatures of each person authorized to sign checks on the bank account. *(p. 271)*

Simple capital structure Capital structure that consists of only common stock and nonconvertible preferred stock; consists of no dilutive securities. *(p. 485)*

Single-step income statement Income statement format that includes cost of goods sold as an expense and shows only one subtotal for total expenses. *(p. 176)*

Sinking fund bonds Bonds that require the issuer to make deposits to a separate account; bondholders are repaid at maturity from that account. *(p. 436)*

Small stock dividend Stock dividend that is 25% or less of a corporation's previously outstanding shares. *(p. 474)*

Social responsibility Being accountable for the impact that one's actions might have on society. *(p. 8)*

Sole proprietorship Business owned by one person that is not organized as a corporation; also called *proprietorship*. *(p. 12)*

Solvency Company's long-run financial viability and its ability to cover long-term obligations. *(p. 565)*

Source documents Source of information for accounting entries that can be in either paper or electronic form; also called *business papers*. *(p. 52)*

Special journal Any journal used for recording and posting transactions of a similar type. *(p. E-6)*

Specific identification Method for assigning cost to inventory when the purchase cost of each item in inventory is identified and used to compute cost of inventory. *(pp. 213 & 230)*

Spending variance Difference between the actual price of an item and its standard price. *(p. 916)*

Spreadsheet Computer program that organizes data by means of formulas and format; also called *electronic work sheet*. *(pp. 123 & 532)*

Standard costs Costs that should be incurred under normal conditions to produce a product or component or to perform a service. *(p. 901)*

State Unemployment Taxes (SUTA) State payroll taxes on employers to support its unemployment programs. *(p. 386)*

Stated value stock No-par stock assigned a stated value per share; this amount is recorded in the stock account when the stock is issued. *(p. 470)*

Statement of cash flows A financial statement that lists cash inflows (receipts) and cash outflows (payments) during a period; arranged by operating, investing, and financing. *(pp. 20 & 510)*

Statement of owner's equity Report of changes in equity over a period; adjusted for increases (owner investment and net income) and for decreases (withdrawals and net loss). *(p. 20)*

Statement of partners' equity Financial statement that shows total capital balances at the beginning of the period, any additional investment by partners, the income or loss of the period, the partners' withdrawals, and the partners' ending capital balances; also called *statement of partners' capital*. *(p. D-7)*

Statement of retained earnings Report of changes in retained earnings over a period; adjusted for increases (net income), for decreases (dividends and net loss), and for any prior period adjustment. *(p. 20)*

Statement of stockholders' equity Financial statement that lists the beginning and ending balances of each major equity account and describes all changes in those accounts. *(p. 483)*

Statements of Financial Accounting Standards (SFAS) FASB publications that establish U.S. GAAP.

Step-wise cost Cost that remains fixed over limited ranges of volumes but changes by a lump sum when volume changes occur outside these limited ranges. *(p. 780)*

Stock (See *shares*) *(p. 13)*

Stock dividend Corporation's distribution of its own stock to its stockholders without the receipt of any payment. *(p. 474)*

Stock options Rights to purchase common stock at a fixed price over a specified period of time. *(p. 483)*

Stock split Occurs when a corporation calls in its stock and replaces each share with more than one new share; decreases both the market value per share and any par or stated value per share. *(p. 476)*

Stock subscription Investor's contractual commitment to purchase unissued shares at future dates and prices.

Stockholders (See *shareholders.*) *(p. 13)*

Stockholders' equity A corporation's equity; also called *shareholders' equity* or *corporate capital*. *(p. 470)*

Straight-line depreciation Method that allocates an equal portion of the depreciable cost of plant asset (cost minus salvage) to each accounting period in its useful life. *(pp. 103 & 341)*

Straight-line bond amortization Method allocating an equal amount of bond interest expense to each period of the bond life. *(p. 426)*

Subsidiary Entity controlled by another entity (parent) in which the parent owns more than 50% of the subsidiary's voting stock. *(p. C-9)*

Subsidiary ledger List of individual subaccounts and amounts with a common characteristic; linked to a controlling account in the general ledger. *(p. E-6)*

Sunk cost Cost already incurred and cannot be avoided or changed. *(p. 616)*

Supplementary records Information outside the usual accounting records; also called *supplemental records*. *(p. 168)*

Supply chain Linkages of services or goods extending from suppliers, to the company itself, and on to customers.

T-account Tool used to show the effects of transactions and events on individual accounts. *(p. 57)*

Target cost Maximum allowable cost for a product or service; defined as expected selling price less the desired profit. *(p. 655)*

Temporary accounts Accounts used to record revenues, expenses, and withdrawals (dividends for a corporation); they are closed at the end of each period; also called *nominal accounts*. *(p. 112)*

Term bonds Bonds scheduled for payment (maturity) at a single specified date. *(p. 436)*

Throughput time (See *cycle time.*)

Time period assumption Assumption that an organization's activities can be divided into specific time periods such as months, quarters, or years. *(pp. 12 & 98)*

Time ticket Source document used to report the time an employee spent working on a job or on overhead activities and then to determine the amount of direct labor to charge to the job or the amount of indirect labor to charge to overhead. *(p. 660)*

Times interest earned Ratio of income before interest expense (and any income taxes) divided by interest expense; reflects risk of covering interest commitments when income varies. *(p. 392)*

Total asset turnover Measure of a company's ability to use its assets to generate sales; computed by dividing net sales by average total assets. *(p. 355)*

Total quality management (TQM) Concept calling for all managers and employees at all stages of operations to strive toward higher standards and reduce number of defects. *(p. 626)*

Trade discount Reduction from a list or catalog price that can vary for wholesalers, retailers, and consumers. *(p. 164)*

Trademark or **trade (brand) name** Symbol, name, phrase, or jingle identified with a company, product, or service. *(p. 353)*

Trading on the equity (See *financial leverage.*)

Trading securities Investments in debt and equity securities that the company intends to actively trade for profit. *(p. C-5)*

Transfer price The price used to record transfers of goods or services across divisions within the same company. *(p. 961)*

Transaction Exchange of economic consideration affecting an entity's financial position that can be reliably measured. *(p. 16)*

Treasury stock Corporation's own stock that it reacquired and still holds. *(p. 480)*

Trial balance List of accounts and their balances at a point in time; total debit balances equal total credit balances. *(p. 67)*

Unadjusted trial balance List of accounts and balances prepared before accounting adjustments are recorded and posted. *(p. 110)*

Unavoidable expense Expense (or cost) that is not relevant for business decisions; an expense that would continue even if a department, product, or service is eliminated. *(p. 993)*

Unclassified balance sheet Balance sheet that broadly groups assets, liabilities, and equity accounts. *(p. 117)*

Uncontrollable costs Costs that a manager does not have the power to determine or strongly influence. *(pp. 826 & 943)*

Underapplied overhead Amount by which overhead incurred in a period exceeds the overhead applied to that period's production using the predetermined overhead rate. *(p. 665)*

Unearned revenue Liability created when customers pay in advance for products or services; earned when the products or services are later delivered. *(pp. 55 & 104)*

Unfavorable variance Difference in revenues or costs, when the actual amount is compared to the budgeted amount, that contributes to a lower income. *(p. 897)*

Unit contribution margin Amount a product's unit selling price exceeds its total unit variable cost. *(p. 785)*

Unit level activities Activities that arise as a result of the total volume of goods and services that are produced, and that are performed each time a unit is produced *(p. 750)*

Units-of-production depreciation Method that charges a varying amount to depreciation expense for each period of an asset's useful life depending on its usage. *(p. 341)*

Unlimited liability Legal relationship among general partners that makes each of them responsible for partnership debts if the other partners are unable to pay their shares. *(p. D-3)*

Unrealized gain (loss) Gain (loss) not yet realized by an actual transaction or event such as a sale. *(p. C-5)*

Unsecured bonds Bonds backed only by the issuer's credit standing; almost always riskier than secured bonds; also called *debentures*. *(p. 436)*

Unusual gain or loss Gain or loss that is abnormal or unrelated to the company's ordinary activities and environment. *(p. 588)*

Useful life Length of time an asset will be productively used in the operations of a business; also called *service life* or *limited life*. *(pp. 339 & 351)*

Value-added activities Activities that add to the value of a product or service *(p. 749)*

Value-added time The portion of cycle time that is directed at producing a product or service; equals process time. *(p. 958)*

Value chain Sequential activities that add value to an entity's products or services; includes design, production, marketing, distribution, and service. *(p. 626)*

Variable cost Cost that changes in proportion to changes in the activity output volume. *(p. 614)*

Variable costing A costing method that includes only variable manufacturing costs—direct materials, direct labor, and variable manufacturing overhead—in unit product costs; also called *direct* or *marginal costing* *(p. 816)*

Variable costing income statement An income statement in which costs are classified as variable or fixed; also called *contribution margin income statement*. *(p. 786)*

Variance analysis Process of examining differences between actual and budgeted revenues or costs and describing them in terms of price and quantity differences. *(p. 901)*

Vendee Buyer of goods or services. *(p. 281)*

Vendor Seller of goods or services. *(p. 280)*

Vertical analysis Evaluation of each financial statement item or group of items in terms of a specific base amount. *(p. 566)*

Volume variance Difference between two dollar amounts of fixed overhead cost; one amount is the total budgeted overhead cost, and the other is the overhead cost allocated to products using the predetermined fixed overhead rate. *(p. 909)*

Voucher Internal file used to store documents and information to control cash disbursements and to ensure that a transaction is properly authorized and recorded. *(p. 267)*

Voucher register Journal (referred to as *book of original entry*) in which all vouchers are recorded after they have been approved. *(p. 282)*

Voucher system Procedures and approvals designed to control cash disbursements and acceptance of obligations. *(p. 266)*

Wage bracket withholding table Table of the amounts of income tax withheld from employees' wages. *(p. 400)*

Warranty Agreement that obligates the seller to correct or replace a product or service when it fails to perform properly within a specified period. *(p. 388)*

Weighted average Method for assigning inventory cost to sales; the cost of available-for-sale units is divided by the number of units available to determine per unit cost prior to each sale that is then multiplied by the units sold to yield the cost of that sale. *(pp. 216, 232 & 702)*

Weighted-average contribution margin The contribution margin per composite unit for a company that provides multiple goods or services; also called *contribution margin per composite unit*. *(p. 793)*

Weighted-average method (See *weighted average*.)

Wholesaler Intermediary that buys products from manufacturers or other wholesalers and sells them to retailers or other wholesalers. *(p. 162)*

Work sheet Spreadsheet used to draft an unadjusted trial balance, adjusting entries, adjusted trial balance, and financial statements. *(p. 123)*

Working capital Current assets minus current liabilities at a point in time. *(p. 575)*

Working papers Analyses and other informal reports prepared by accountants and managers when organizing information for formal reports and financial statements. *(p. 127)*

Index

Note: Page numbers followed by *n* indicate material in footnotes; defined terms and the page number on which the definition appears are shown in **boldface.**

Chart of Accounts

Following is a typical chart of accounts, which is used in several assignments. Every company has its own unique accounts and numbering system.

Assets

Current Assets

101 Cash
102 Petty cash
103 Cash equivalents
104 Short-term investments
105 Fair value adjustment, _____ securities (S-T)
106 Accounts receivable
107 Allowance for doubtful accounts
108 Legal fees receivable
109 Interest receivable
110 Rent receivable
111 Notes receivable
119 Merchandise inventory
120 _____ inventory
121 _____ inventory
124 Office supplies
125 Store supplies
126 _____ supplies
128 Prepaid insurance
129 Prepaid interest
131 Prepaid rent
132 Raw materials inventory
133 Goods in process inventory, _____
134 Goods in process inventory, _____
135 Finished goods inventory

Long-Term Investments

141 Long-term investments
142 Fair value adjustment, _____ securities (L-T)
144 Investment in _____
145 Bond sinking fund

Plant Assets

151 Automobiles
152 Accumulated depreciation—Automobiles
153 Trucks
154 Accumulated depreciation—Trucks
155 Boats
156 Accumulated depreciation—Boats
157 Professional library
158 Accumulated depreciation—Professional library
159 Law library
160 Accumulated depreciation—Law library
161 Furniture
162 Accumulated depreciation—Furniture
163 Office equipment
164 Accumulated depreciation—Office equipment
165 Store equipment

166 Accumulated depreciation—Store equipment
167 _____ equipment
168 Accumulated depreciation—_____ equipment
169 Machinery
170 Accumulated depreciation—Machinery
173 Building _____
174 Accumulated depreciation—Building _____
175 Building _____
176 Accumulated depreciation—Building _____
179 Land improvements _____
180 Accumulated depreciation—Land improvements _____
181 Land improvements _____
182 Accumulated depreciation—Land improvements _____
183 Land

Natural Resources

185 Mineral deposit
186 Accumulated depletion—Mineral deposit

Intangible Assets

191 Patents
192 Leasehold
193 Franchise
194 Copyrights
195 Leasehold improvements
196 Licenses
197 Accumulated amortization—_____

Liabilities

Current Liabilities

201 Accounts payable
202 Insurance payable
203 Interest payable
204 Legal fees payable
207 Office salaries payable
208 Rent payable
209 Salaries payable
210 Wages payable
211 Accrued payroll payable
214 Estimated warranty liability
215 Income taxes payable
216 Common dividend payable
217 Preferred dividend payable
218 State unemployment taxes payable
219 Employee federal income taxes payable
221 Employee medical insurance payable

222 Employee retirement program payable
223 Employee union dues payable
224 Federal unemployment taxes payable
225 FICA taxes payable
226 Estimated vacation pay liability

Unearned Revenues

230 Unearned consulting fees
231 Unearned legal fees
232 Unearned property management fees
233 Unearned _____ fees
234 Unearned _____ fees
235 Unearned janitorial revenue
236 Unearned _____ revenue
238 Unearned rent

Notes Payable

240 Short-term notes payable
241 Discount on short-term notes payable
245 Notes payable
251 Long-term notes payable
252 Discount on long-term notes payable

Long-Term Liabilities

253 Long-term lease liability
255 Bonds payable
256 Discount on bonds payable
257 Premium on bonds payable
258 Deferred income tax liability

Equity

Owner's Equity

301 _____, Capital
302 _____, Withdrawals
303 _____, Capital
304 _____, Withdrawals
305 _____, Capital
306 _____, Withdrawals

Paid-In Capital

307 Common stock, $_____ par value
308 Common stock, no-par value
309 Common stock, $_____ stated value
310 Common stock dividend distributable
311 Paid-in capital in excess of par value, Common stock

312 Paid-in capital in excess of stated value, No-par common stock
313 Paid-in capital from retirement of common stock
314 Paid-in capital, Treasury stock
315 Preferred stock
316 Paid-in capital in excess of par value, Preferred stock

Retained Earnings

318 Retained earnings
319 Cash dividends (or Dividends)
320 Stock dividends

Other Equity Accounts

321 Treasury stock, Common
322 Unrealized gain—Equity
323 Unrealized loss—Equity

Revenues

401 _____ fees earned
402 _____ fees earned
403 _____ services revenue
404 _____ services revenue
405 Commissions earned
406 Rent revenue (or Rent earned)
407 Dividends revenue (or Dividend earned)
408 Earnings from investment in _____
409 Interest revenue (or Interest earned)
410 Sinking fund earnings
413 Sales
414 Sales returns and allowances
415 Sales discounts

Cost of Sales

Cost of Goods Sold

502 Cost of goods sold
505 Purchases
506 Purchases returns and allowances
507 Purchases discounts
508 Transportation-in

Manufacturing

520 Raw materials purchases
521 Freight-in on raw materials
530 Factory payroll
531 Direct labor
540 Factory overhead
541 Indirect materials
542 Indirect labor
543 Factory insurance expired
544 Factory supervision
545 Factory supplies used
546 Factory utilities
547 Miscellaneous production costs
548 Property taxes on factory building
549 Property taxes on factory equipment
550 Rent on factory building
551 Repairs, factory equipment
552 Small tools written off
560 Depreciation of factory equipment
561 Depreciation of factory building

Standard Cost Variance

580 Direct material quantity variance
581 Direct material price variance
582 Direct labor quantity variance
583 Direct labor price variance
584 Factory overhead volume variance
585 Factory overhead controllable variance

Expenses

Amortization, Depletion, and Depreciation

601 Amortization expense—_____
602 Amortization expense—_____
603 Depletion expense—_____
604 Depreciation expense—Boats
605 Depreciation expense—Automobiles
606 Depreciation expense—Building _____
607 Depreciation expense—Building _____
608 Depreciation expense—Land improvements _____
609 Depreciation expense—Land improvements _____
610 Depreciation expense—Law library
611 Depreciation expense—Trucks
612 Depreciation expense—_____ equipment
613 Depreciation expense—_____ equipment
614 Depreciation expense—_____
615 Depreciation expense—_____

Employee-Related Expenses

620 Office salaries expense
621 Sales salaries expense
622 Salaries expense
623 _____ wages expense
624 Employees' benefits expense
625 Payroll taxes expense

Financial Expenses

630 Cash over and short
631 Discounts lost
632 Factoring fee expense
633 Interest expense

Insurance Expenses

635 Insurance expense—Delivery equipment
636 Insurance expense—Office equipment
637 Insurance expense—_____

Rental Expenses

640 Rent expense
641 Rent expense—Office space
642 Rent expense—Selling space
643 Press rental expense
644 Truck rental expense
645 _____ rental expense

Supplies Expenses

650 Office supplies expense
651 Store supplies expense
652 _____ supplies expense
653 _____ supplies expense

Miscellaneous Expenses

655 Advertising expense
656 Bad debts expense
657 Blueprinting expense
658 Boat expense
659 Collection expense
661 Concessions expense
662 Credit card expense
663 Delivery expense
664 Dumping expense
667 Equipment expense
668 Food and drinks expense
671 Gas and oil expense
672 General and administrative expense
673 Janitorial expense
674 Legal fees expense
676 Mileage expense
677 Miscellaneous expenses
678 Mower and tools expense
679 Operating expense
680 Organization expense
681 Permits expense
682 Postage expense
683 Property taxes expense
684 Repairs expense—_____
685 Repairs expense—_____
687 Selling expense
688 Telephone expense
689 Travel and entertainment expense
690 Utilities expense
691 Warranty expense
695 Income taxes expense

Gains and Losses

701 Gain on retirement of bonds
702 Gain on sale of machinery
703 Gain on sale of investments
704 Gain on sale of trucks
705 Gain on _____
706 Foreign exchange gain or loss
801 Loss on disposal of machinery
802 Loss on exchange of equipment
803 Loss on exchange of _____
804 Loss on sale of notes
805 Loss on retirement of bonds
806 Loss on sale of investments
807 Loss on sale of machinery
808 Loss on _____
809 Unrealized gain—Income
810 Unrealized loss—Income
811 Impairment gain
812 Impairment loss

Clearing Accounts

901 Income summary
902 Manufacturing summary

Online Supplements

ConnectPlus Accounting with LearnSmart Two-Semester Online Access for Financial and Managerial Accounting, Fifth Edition

McGraw-Hill Connect® is a web-based assignment and assessment platform that gives students the means to better connect with their coursework, with their instructors, and with the important concepts that they will need to know for success now and in the future. With Connect, instructors can deliver assignments, quizzes and tests easily online. Students can practice important skills at their own pace and on their own schedule.

GETTING STARTED:

To get started in Connect, you will need the following:

1. Your instructor's unique Connect URL

    Sample of Connect URL
    http://www.mcgrawhillconnect.com/class/instructorname_section_name

2. Connect Access Code

    Using a Print Book? Your access code will appear at the back of the book. Reference your Table of Contents for an exact page number.

    Using an eBook? Once you have purchased your Create eBook, you will automatically have access to Connect. Simply go to your instructor's unique URL and sign in using the username and password you established when accessing your Create eBook.

REGISTRATION AND SIGN IN:

- Go to the Connect Website address provided by your instructor.
- Click **Register Now**.
- Enter your email address.
     TIP: If you already have a McGraw-Hill account, you will be asked for your password and will not be required to create a new account.
- Enter your access code (This access code appears on the back cover of the Create book and is only redeemable once.)
- Follow the on-screen instructions.
     TIP: Please choose your Security Question carefully. We will ask you for this information if you forget your password.
- When registration is complete, click on **Go to Connect Now**.
- You are now ready to use **Connect.**

Need Help?
Contact us online: www.mcgrawhillconnect.com/support
Give us a call: 1-800-331-5094